THE AMERICAN SOLDIER:
COMBAT AND ITS AFTERMATH
VOLUME II

STUDIES IN SOCIAL PSYCHOLOGY
IN WORLD WAR II

Volume I.   The American Soldier: Adjustment During Army Life
Volume II.   The American Soldier: Combat and Its Aftermath
Volume III.   Experiments on Mass Communication
Volume IV.   Measurement and Prediction

The four volumes in this series were prepared and edited under the auspices of a Special Committee of the Social Science Research Council, comprising

Frederick Osborn, *Chairman*
Leonard S. Cottrell, Jr.
Leland C. DeVinney
Carl I. Hovland
John M. Russell
Samuel A. Stouffer
Donald Young, Ex Officio

The data on which these volumes are based were collected by the Research Branch, Information and Education Division, War Department, during World War II. In making the data available, the War Department assumes no responsibility for the analyses and interpretations contained in these volumes, which are the sole responsibility of the authors.

These volumes were prepared under a grant from the Carnegie Corporation of New York. That corporation is not, however, the author, owner, publisher, or proprietor of this publication, and is not to be understood as approving by virtue of its grant any of the statements made or views expressed therein.

THE
AMERICAN
SOLDIER:
COMBAT AND ITS
AFTERMATH

VOLUME II

BY

SAMUEL A. STOUFFER

ARTHUR A. LUMSDAINE

MARION HARPER LUMSDAINE

ROBIN M. WILLIAMS, Jr.

M. BREWSTER SMITH

IRVING L. JANIS

SHIRLEY A. STAR

LEONARD S. COTTRELL, Jr.

PRINCETON, NEW JERSEY

PRINCETON UNIVERSITY PRESS

1949

Printed in the United States of America by
The Colonial Press Inc., Clinton, Mass.

··

CONTENTS

··

CHAPTER 1. ATTITUDES BEFORE COMBAT AND BEHAVIOR IN COMBAT   3

CHAPTER 2. GENERAL CHARACTERISTICS OF GROUND COMBAT   59

CHAPTER 3. COMBAT MOTIVATIONS AMONG GROUND TROOPS   105

CHAPTER 4. PROBLEMS RELATED TO THE CONTROL OF FEAR IN COMBAT   192

CHAPTER 5. THE COMBAT REPLACEMENT   242

CHAPTER 6. ATTITUDES OF GROUND COMBAT TROOPS TOWARD REAR ECHELONS AND THE HOME FRONT   290

CHAPTER 7. MORALE ATTITUDES OF COMBAT FLYING PERSONNEL IN THE AIR CORPS   324

CHAPTER 8. OBJECTIVE FACTORS RELATED TO MORALE ATTITUDES IN THE AERIAL COMBAT SITUATION   362

CHAPTER 9. PSYCHONEUROTIC SYMPTOMS IN THE ARMY   411

CHAPTER 10. PROBLEMS OF ROTATION AND RECONVERSION   456

CHAPTER 11. THE POINT SYSTEM FOR REDEPLOYMENT AND DISCHARGE   520

CHAPTER 12. THE AFTERMATH OF HOSTILITIES   549

CHAPTER 13. THE SOLDIER BECOMES A VETERAN   596

APPENDIX   645

CONSOLIDATED INDEX FOR VOLUMES I AND II   653

THE AMERICAN SOLDIER:
COMBAT AND ITS AFTERMATH
VOLUME II

CHAPTER 1

ATTITUDES BEFORE COMBAT AND BEHAVIOR IN COMBAT[1]

T HE chapters in this volume contain a body of facts unique in the annals of war. Opinions of combat troops, both ground and air, have been ascertained and analyzed quantitatively. Thus it is possible to compare, with confidence in the representativeness of the responses, the feelings of men of varying degrees of experience or responsibility as they faced their combat jobs.

Before proceeding to a description of the attitudes of combat troops, it is desirable to discuss frankly, with such evidence as is at hand, the following question: "Suppose that many combat soldiers did have unfavorable attitudes. What of it? They fought, didn't they?" This chapter provides data which document the point that attitudes did mean something in terms of combat performance.

It was not until November 1943 that the Research Branch was enabled to make a detailed study of troops with combat experience, except for scattered interviews with wounded combat veterans in hospitals. At that time a survey was made of the combat veterans in ten rifle companies of the 1st Division, just arrived in England after successful campaigns in North Africa and Sicily. The study showed that these veterans, while exhibiting a rather fierce pride in their outfit, were more embittered than perhaps any other soldiers who had been studied by the Research Branch. The majority felt that they had done their share as compared with other soldiers—a

[1] By Samuel A. Stouffer, Arthur A. Lumsdaine, and Marion Harper Lumsdaine. Section I and part of Section III were written by Stouffer, based on his analysis of attitude data whose collection in Europe was initiated by Robert B. Wallace and of casualty data whose statistical treatment in Washington was organized by A. J. Jaffe, following a preliminary study made in Europe under the direction of Robin M. Williams, Jr. Section II is based on a research study carried out in Europe under the direction of Arthur A. Lumsdaine, who shared responsibility for the analysis and presentation with Marion Harper Lumsdaine, who also wrote par of Section III. The study in Section II made use of data on recruits collected under the direction of William W. McPeak in the United States, and in the European follow-up the technique for obtaining combat performance ratings was developed jointly by Arthur A. Lumsdaine and Irving L. Janis.

few of them repeating a mot current in the division, "The Army consists of the 1st Division and eight million replacements." Only a handful expressed any zeal for further combat, and a special tabulation showed that men who had been decorated for gallantry with the DSC or Silver Star were just as bitter as the rest.

The Research Branch report on the 1st Division was read by the Chief of Staff of the Army and sent by him to members of the General Staff for comment. A number of constructive suggestions for improving the situation for the combat soldier were brought forward, as well as admonitions from some quarters that the "gripes" of combat soldiers should not be taken too seriously.

The Chief of Staff felt that the value of the 1st Division study would be enhanced if comparable data were available for other combat divisions, and therefore he ordered such studies made. He personally selected three divisions in the Pacific for survey—the 7th, 25th, and 43rd. Thus began a series of surveys of combat troops which provides the basic data for the present volume. The first large-scale study of opinions of combat flying personnel was made in the spring of 1944 at the request of the commander of the 8th Air Force.

A persistent question mark remained. How do we know that the men's verbal reports have any relation to their subsequent performance in combat? It can be argued, forcefully, that griping is an outlet which helps make the hard life of a combat man a little more tolerable; therefore, griping is a healthy, positive sign. An alternative position would be that, while a certain amount of griping is healthy, too much is indicative of an unhealthy psychological atmosphere.

The present chapter is a contribution toward the elucidation of this problem, in that it shows that attitudes toward combat are related to subsequent behavior in combat. The chapter is in three sections. Section I compares attitudes prior to D Day of men in the 108 rifle companies and in 34 of the 36 heavy weapons companies in four divisions with the nonbattle casualty rates of these same companies in Normandy in June and July 1944. In this study 12,295 men participated. In Section II the attitudes of individual soldiers in a sample of infantrymen are compared with ratings of the battle performance of these same individuals in Europe made a year later. Section III serves as a methodological appendix to Sections I and II, giving the technical reader further details of how these studies were made.

SECTION I

COMPANY ATTITUDES AND NONBATTLE CASUALTY RATES IN COMBAT

Design of the Study

This report compares attitudes toward combat by companies before D Day with nonbattle casualty rates of the same companies after D Day, based on the 1st, 4th, 9th, and 29th Divisions.[2]

Three related attitudes are analyzed: Willingness for combat, confidence in combat stamina, confidence in combat skill.

The score on willingness for combat is based on answers to two questions with different check lists:

> Which of the following best tells how you feel about getting into an actual battle zone?

> Which of the following best describes your own feeling about getting into combat against the Germans?

The score on confidence in combat stamina is based on answers to three questions:

> Do you feel that you are in tough enough physical condition for going into combat?

> If and when you get into combat how well do you think you will stand up under battle conditions?

> Do you think you are in good physical condition?

The score on confidence in combat skill is based on answers to three questions:

> Do you feel that you are now trained and ready for combat or do you need more training?

> If you were given a group of men and told to take charge of them all by yourself on a mission under enemy fire, how well do you think you would do?

> Do you think that you have been given enough training and experience so that you could do a good job in taking charge of a group of men on your own in combat?

---

[2] Attitude data throughout Section I are from S-128, January 1944 (1st and 9th Divisions) and S-129, April 1944 (4th and 29th Divisions).

A detailed analysis of how the scores were derived from the check lists of answers to these items is presented in Section III of this chapter. Each individual analyzed in a given company received a score on these three attitudes, and a company average was then computed on each attitude. The average sample per company was 87, with considerable variation in sample size.

Statistics on nonbattle casualty rates by companies in Normandy in June and July 1944 are used as a criterion with which to compare the company averages on the pre D Day attitude variables. Nonbattle casualty rates indicate the number of combat men who became ineffective for reasons other than wounds or other battle injuries. They are by no means to be regarded as complete and infallible indexes of combat efficiency, let alone combat performance. But no other reliable measure was available. In one division which saw heavy and continuous fighting in Normandy, an intensive effort was made by the ETO staff of the Research Branch to find the best possible criteria. Opinions of staff officers and field commanders on individual company performance were sought but were not serviceable as criteria because of wide disagreement. How does one compare a company with a brilliant performance in one action and a later undistinguished record with a company which did its job day after day faithfully amid heavy casualties but never was conspicuous? Decorations for gallantry were studied and discarded as criteria because of command variation in the awards. AWOL's were simply too few in the Normandy campaign to provide useful indexes at the company level. Psychiatric casualties varied with the command, possibly not so much in relation to incidence of psychiatric breakdowns as to the degree of indulgence on the part of the command and the local medical personnel. In one division the division psychiatrist informed the research team that, although the psychiatric rate was twice as high in one regiment as in another, the difference was in his opinion entirely attributable to differences in policy in the two regiments with respect to labeling or not labeling nonbattle casualties as "exhaustion" cases. After a laborious study, the research team arrived at the conclusion that the only index, at the company level, which could be defended as both reliable and meaningful would be the nonbattle casualty rate.[3] Certainly, if A Company loses a *third* of its men during a campaign as

---

[3] This index, like one based explicitly on psychiatric casualties, is subject to some differences in command practice—but very much less so than would be an index based solely on "exhaustion" cases.

nonbattle casualties while B Company loses only a *tenth* of its men in this way, the latter company is the more effective company—everything else equal. Moreover, an unknown but possibly large percentage of the nonbattle casualties in Normandy may have been psychiatric or psychosomatic cases. This was summer, there were no serious epidemics, trench foot was not yet a problem, there was no malaria. Some units may have had much more serious exposure to risk of illness than others, but if we concentrate our analysis on *a comparison of companies within the same regiment,* variability in physical environment should tend to even out over a two months' period.

One factor responsible for variability in nonbattle casualty rates of companies can be partly controlled, namely, the incidence of battle casualties. If a company loses half of its original strength in the first week, there will be fewer survivors exposed to risk of nonbattle casualties than if it has only a few battle casualties initially.

Compensating, however, is the possibility that the shock of a heavy initial loss may be more productive of psychosomatic disorders among the survivors than would a smaller initial toll. Correlations, exhibited later in this report, indicate that the nonbattle casualty rate tended to be higher in those companies with the greater number of man-days of exposure to risk. Consequently, the index used expresses the nonbattle casualties in a company during the eight weeks beginning June 6, 1944 as a *ratio* ($\times$ 100) of the average number of men available for duty per day throughout the period, thus: nonbattle casualty rate

$$= 100 \times \frac{\text{number of nonbattle casualties}}{\text{average number of men available per day}}.$$

Since we are interested in relating the attitudes of men in companies studied prior to D Day to nonbattle casualty rates of the same companies after D Day, it is desirable to base the nonbattle casualty rates on only those men who *originally landed in Normandy with a given company.* Battle and nonbattle casualties in eight weeks among the original personnel were very high, as is shown in Table 1.

In order to compute casualty rates by companies based on the original men who landed in Normandy, it was necessary to go back to the original morning reports of the companies. This analysis was carried out by the Research Branch in Washington, working from photostats of all the morning reports of the letter companies in the Infantry regiments of four divisions. It was a detailed and laborious accounting operation. The steps in the process are outlined later in this report. Suffice it to say here that the morning reports proved quite adequate for the task. The accounting procedures set up enabled errors made in filling out the reports under field conditions to be largely detected and reconciled, and the rates here used may be taken as accurate with an average error of not over 1 or 2 per cent.

TABLE 1

CASUALTIES AMONG SOLDIERS ORIGINALLY ENTERING NORMANDY WITH
THEIR UNITS DURING EIGHT WEEKS BEGINNING JUNE 6, 1944*

	RIFLE COMPANIES		HEAVY WEAPONS COMPANIES	
	Officers	*Enlisted men*	*Officers*	*Enlisted men*
Strength on June 6	779	21,557	308	6,156
Strength on July 31	204	8,708	138	3,786
Percentage July 31 strength of original strength	26.2%	40.4%	44.8%	61.5%
Battle casualties	535	12,846	160	2,277
Battle casualties as a percentage of original strength	68.7%	59.6%	51.9%	37.0%
Nonbattle casualties	82	2,928	27	746
Nonbattle casualties as a percentage of original strength	10.5%	13.6%	8.8%	12.1%

* 1st, 4th, 9th, and 29th Divisions. Replacements received after D Day are excluded from this table. Nonbattle casualties here represent the category "sick, nonbattle casualty" only. Nonbattle injuries, AWOL's, and transfers to other units also were causes of separation. Successive casualties to the same individual are counted as separate casualties. The strength on July 31 is the original strength minus all separations plus all returns to duty. Hence the percentages in a given column do not add to 100.

We have, then, two sets of indexes: on the one hand, average attitude scores by company on willingness for combat, confidence in combat stamina, and confidence in combat skill, based on surveys made before D Day; and, on the other hand, nonbattle casualty rates in the eight weeks beginning June 6, 1944, among the men who landed in Normandy with these same companies.

Company Attitudes and Company Nonbattle Casualty Rates

The units surveyed included two veteran divisions, the 1st and the 9th, and two nonveteran divisions, the 4th and the 29th—all of whom were destined to play a conspicuous role in Normandy. Unfortunately for the purposes of the present analysis, a long time elapsed between the time of the attitude surveys and the Normandy landing. This was especially the case in the veteran divisions, which were surveyed late in January 1944—over five months before D Day. The nonveteran divisions were surveyed in April 1944— a little less than two months before D Day. After the time of the survey, the veteran divisions received substantial replacements who were trained with their units and who made the invasion with them. A small sample study, not large enough for basing company comparisons, was made in the 9th Division in April, and this serves as something of a bridge for interpreting changes between January and April.

Between the periods of the attitude surveys and D Day there were, then, substantial changes in the personnel of companies, especially in the veteran divisions, and some changes in officer leadership. After D Day there were very great changes in leadership. As Table 1 has shown, battle casualties among company officers were high and hence the turnover in leadership was high. The 108 rifle companies in the study retained, at the end of the eight weeks following June 6, only 26.2 per cent of their original company officers, while the heavy weapons companies retained 44.8 per cent. In addition to casualties, the rifle companies lost 10.5 per cent of their officers by transfer and the heavy weapons companies 14.9 per cent. Many of the casualties had returned to duty before the eight weeks' period was up.

Because of the changes between the time of the attitude surveys and D Day and because of the variability of conditions in Normandy and the turnover in officer leadership, one would not expect a high correlation between company attitudes at the time of the survey and nonbattle casualty rates in Normandy. Under these conditions a significant association, even if not high, between initial attitudes and subsequent combat behavior should be all the more convincing a demonstration of (a) the fact that attitudes as here studied are not mere casual and idle verbal expressions, (b) that attitudes persist through time, and (c) that they relate to other behavior which is important. The reader must remember that the present comparison is of *units*, not of individuals. The individuals in the attitude studies were queried anonymously and an equating of individual responses with subsequent individual combat behavior was not possible in this study. The problem can be stated as follows:

If the average score in A Company on willingness for combat was higher (that is, better) than the average score in B Company, did

A Company tend to have a *lower* nonbattle casualty rate in the eight weeks beginning June 6, 1944 than B Company? Similarly with average scores on confidence in combat stamina and confidence in combat skill. If the attitude scores reflect merely "healthy" negative attitudes toward combat, there should be no significant correlation. If better attitude scores tend to be predictive of lower nonbattle casualty rates and if worse attitude scores tend to be predictive of higher nonbattle casualty rates, then the correlations should tend to be negative. Here, of course, a correlation coefficient with a negative sign means a *positive* predictive relationship between "good" attitudes and the index of efficiency furnished by the nonbattle casualty rate. Thus a negative correlation means that the better the attitudes, the "better" (i.e., lower) the nonbattle casualty rate.

Let us look first at the rifle companies, which should be studied separately from the heavy weapons companies because the combat conditions and battle casualties of rifle companies are much more severe than those of other Infantry units.

Table 2 shows, among rifle companies, that the correlation coefficients of attitude scores and nonbattle casualty rates, though low, *tend to be negative*.

In 10 out of 12 regiments, the scores by companies within the regiments on willingness for combat tend to be negatively correlated with the nonbattle casualty rates. This means that in 10 out of the 12 regiments, those companies with the *worst* attitudes *tended* to have the *highest* nonbattle casualty rates, and vice versa. If positive or negative correlations were equally probable, the likelihood of getting by chance as many as 10 negative correlations in a sample of 12 would be 79 in 4,096, or less than 2 per cent. The average correlation coefficient for the 12 regiments was −.33. This does not mean, of course, that bad attitudes necessarily "caused" bad performance. Both might be reflections of other variables, such as actual physical condition. We are here focusing on the fact that attitudes tended to *predict* subsequent performance.

In all 12 regiments negative correlations indicate that the lower the average scores on confidence in combat stamina, the more likely the company would be to have a high nonbattle casualty rate. The average correlation is −.37.

In 11 of the 12 regiments the correlations are also negative between scores on confidence in combat skill and nonbattle casualty rates, with the average correlation being −.27.

Table 2 is based on rifle companies.   When we study separately the heavy weapons companies in the same regiments, we find that the correlations among heavy weapons companies are also negative (Table 3).   Since there are only three heavy weapons companies per regiment, the correlation coefficients are based on the division

TABLE 2

RIFLE COMPANIES—CORRELATION COEFFICIENTS OF PRE D DAY ATTITUDE
SCORES AND NONBATTLE CASUALTY RATES IN NORMANDY

	NONBATTLE CASUALTY RATES CORRELATED WITH SCORES ON:		
	Willingness for combat	*Confidence in combat stamina*	*Confidence in combat skill*
VETERAN DIVISIONS:			
1st Division			
16th Regiment	+.01	−.56	−.01
18th Regiment	.70	−.14	−.12
26th Regiment	−.25	−.41	−.32
Average	−.31	−.37	−.15
9th Division			
39th Regiment	−.25	−.45	−.26
47th Regiment	−.72	−.28	−.05
60th Regiment	−.60	−.66	−.13
Average	−.52	−.46	−.15
NONVETERAN DIVISIONS:			
4th Division			
8th Regiment	−.30	−.19	+.04
12th Regiment	−.32	−.34	−.40
22nd Regiment	−.25	−.46	−.32
Average	−.29	−.33	−.23
29th Division			
115th Regiment	+.16	−.19	−.72
116th Regiment	−.32	−.54	−.35
175th Regiment	−.43	−.16	−.51
Average	−.20	−.30	−.53
Average veteran regiments	−.42	−.42	−.15
Average nonveteran regiments	−.24	−.31	−.38
Average all regiments	−.33	−.37	−.27

Each correlation is based on 9 companies.

rather than the regiment, after expressing each company's attitude score and casualty rate as a deviation from its regimental mean. Two weapons companies, one in the 9th Division and one in the 29th Division, were unavailable for the attitude survey; hence the total number of weapons companies involved is only 34 instead of 36. The average correlation of nonbattle casualty rates with scores on willingness for combat was —.41, with scores on confidence in combat stamina —.34, and with scores on confidence in combat skill —.48.

While the correlations among either rifle or heavy weapons companies are not high, their consistency in sign establishes beyond reasonable doubt the fact of a tendency for companies with the worse attitudes to have the higher nonbattle casualty rates, and vice versa.

The basic data from which Tables 2 and 3 are drawn are shown in Tables 10 and 11 in Section III of this chapter.

In view of the fact that combat conditions and command practices affecting nonbattle casualty rates differed widely from one regiment

TABLE 3

HEAVY WEAPONS COMPANIES—CORRELATION COEFFICIENTS OF PRE D DAY ATTITUDE SCORES AND NONBATTLE CASUALTY RATES IN NORMANDY

| | NONBATTLE CASUALTY RATES CORRELATED WITH SCORES ON: | | |
	Willingness for combat	*Confidence in combat stamina*	*Confidence in combat skill*
Division			
1st	—.82	—.53	—.55
9th	—.11	—.21	—.74
4th	—.07	—.55	—.81
29th	—.64	—.07	+.18
Average	—.41	—.34	—.48

Within each division the attitude scores and casualty rates of the three heavy weapons companies in each regiment are recorded as deviations from the regimental average for the three companies. Each correlation in the 1st and 4th Divisions is based on 9 companies; in the 9th and 29th on 8, since data were not available for two companies.

to another even within a given division, it seemed unlikely a priori that a relationship between attitude averages for entire regiments and nonbattle casualty rates would be particularly meaningful. Actually, when a regimental attitude score is expressed as a deviation from the division mean and such deviations for the 12 regiments are correlated with corresponding deviations in nonbattle casualty rates, the correlation, just as in the case of companies within regiments, turns out to be negative. All the correlations are low, except possibly that between willingness for combat and nonbattle casualty rate, which is —.59, when each regimental score is the average of rifle companies only. The corresponding correlation when confidence in combat stamina is used as the sorting variable is —.28, and when confidence in combat skill is used, —.13. For regimental averages using heavy weapons companies only, the correlations are

−.03 with willingness for combat, −.19 with confidence in combat stamina, and −.20 with confidence in combat skill. In view of the fact that no further replication was possible and in view of the numerous a priori uncertainties about the meaning of the nonbattle casualty index for regimental comparisons, these data should not be cited as providing evidence either for or against the validity of attitude scores for regimental comparisons. A comparative test for whole divisions is even more hazardous—not only because of the conditions affecting the nonbattle casualty rates but also because two of the divisions in the present study were surveyed three months before the other two divisions.[4]

A further question is now in order. Granted that the consistency of the correlations between precombat attitudes and nonbattle casualty rates by companies indicates the tendency toward an association, how much difference does it make? There is a distinction between what may be called statistical significance and what may be called practical significance. Let us now look at the data from the latter point of view.[5]

---

[4] Because the 1st and 9th Divisions were surveyed in January and the 4th and 29th in April (the latter with somewhat different forms of questions) no direct comparison of the mean attitude scores of the veteran and nonveteran divisions is possible. Somewhat more defensible would be a comparison, on the one hand, of the mean attitude scores of the 1st Division with those of the 9th, and a comparison, on the other hand, of the mean attitude scores of the 4th Division with those of the 29th. We see at once that the picture is mixed. The mean scores of the 1st Division were somewhat higher than the 9th on willingness for combat and confidence in combat stamina, but somewhat lower than the 9th on confidence in combat skill. The mean scores of the 4th Division were somewhat lower than the 29th on willingness for combat and confidence in combat stamina, but somewhat higher on confidence in combat skill. What about comparative nonbattle casualty rates? The average rate in the 9th Division, 30, was higher than in the 1st, 21. The average rate in the 29th Division, 24, was higher than in the 4th, 19. But the conditions faced by the various divisions were so different that the nonbattle casualty rate, while very meaningful for comparing companies within the same regiment, may no longer have much significance. For example, two regiments of the 1st Division, the 16th and 18th, took severe punishment at Omaha Beach, but the division as a whole was largely engaged in a holding operation until the final break-through in late July, and sustained relatively light casualties after the landing attack. The battle casualties in the 9th Division were much higher than in the 1st Division, and were sustained throughout June and July, although the division did not disembark in Normandy until a week after D Day. Both the 4th and 29th Divisions had very heavy battle casualties throughout the Normandy campaign. Both participated in the landings, during which the 115th Regiment of the 29th Division took more severe punishment than other regiments in these two divisions.

For official accounts of action see "Omaha Beachhead" (1946) and "St.-Lo" (1947), two monographs in the *American Forces in Action* series published by the Historical Section of the War Department.

[5] In any analysis of relationships one can focus on the measure of correlation or on some measure of regression. The latter can be practically unimportant even if a correlation is rather high or can be practically important even if the correlation is rather low.

Suppose that a regimental commander before D Day had known the score of his nine rifle companies on willingness for combat. How much actual difference would he have had a right to expect between the average nonbattle casualty rates of his three rifle companies with the best attitude scores as compared with the three companies with the worst scores? Let us illustrate by the 8th Regiment of the 4th Division, where the correlation between nonbattle casualty rates and scores on willingness for combat was shown in Table 2 to be −.30. From Table 10 in Section III of this chapter we can see that the three companies with highest scores on willingness for combat are A, B, and I, with nonbattle casualty rates of 18, 8, and 20 respectively. The medium three companies are C, G, and L with nonbattle casualty rates of 16, 24, and 31. The lowest three are E, F, and K with rates of 17, 34, and 33. Averaging the nonbattle casualty rates for each group of three companies we have:

	Average nonbattle casualty rate
A, B, I	15.3
C, G, L	23.7
E, F, K	28.0

In this regiment, the companies with the highest scores on willingness for combat had a substantially lower average nonbattle casualty rate than companies with medium or low scores.

If we repeat this process for all twelve regiments and pool the results, we have the picture shown in Chart I, which also exhibits the results of comparable tabulations based on grouping companies within a regiment according to scores on confidence in combat stamina and, finally, on confidence in combat skill. Among the three rifle companies in each of the twelve regiments with worst pre D Day scores on willingness for combat the average nonbattle casualty rate in Normandy was 28.2, which is 1.62 times the average nonbattle casualty rate of the three companies in each regiment with best scores on this attitude. Corresponding ratios are 1.47 when confidence in combat stamina is the sorting variable and 1.35 when confidence in combat skill is the sorting variable.

From the standpoint, then, of practical as well as merely statistical significance, the relationship would seem to be important. In advance of D Day, attitudes could have been known which would have sorted out companies destined to have an average nonbattle

CHART I

RIFLE COMPANIES IN FOUR DIVISIONS—AVERAGE NONBATTLE CASUALTY RATES IN
NORMANDY AS RELATED TO PRE D DAY ATTITUDE SCORES

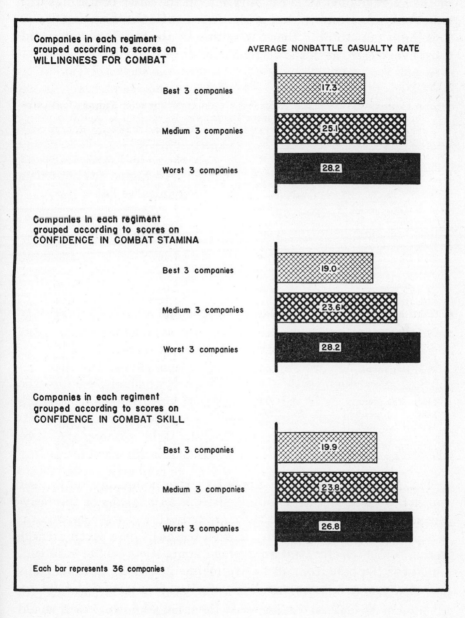

Each bar represents 36 companies

casualty rate *35 to 62 per cent* greater than that of another group of companies.[6]

While there was variation from regiment to regiment in the ratio of the average nonbattle casualty rate in the three companies with worst attitude scores to that of the three companies with best scores, it is important to note that the ratio was greater than unity in almost every case, as is shown by Table 4.

TABLE 4

RIFLE COMPANIES—AVERAGE NONBATTLE CASUALTY RATE OF THREE COMPANIES WITH WORST ATTITUDES IN THEIR REGIMENTS EXPRESSED AS A RATIO OF AVERAGE RATE OF THREE COMPANIES WITH BEST ATTITUDES, BY REGIMENTS

	Companies grouped by scores on willingness for combat	Companies grouped by scores on confidence in combat stamina	Companies grouped by scores on confidence in combat skill
1st Division			
16th Regiment	1.09	1.59	1.00
18th Regiment	1.65	1.04	.95
26th Regiment	1.19	1.48	1.43
9th Division			
39th Regiment	1.39	2.00	1.25
47th Regiment	1.54	1.13	1.45
60th Regiment	2.00	1.58	1.52
4th Division			
8th Regiment	1.82	1.17	1.12
12th Regiment	1.24	1.09	1.53
22nd Regiment	1.46	2.06	1.46
29th Division			
115th Regiment	.92	1.28	1.55
116th Regiment	2.09	2.17	2.08
175th Regiment	2.32	1.59	1.73
All regiments	1.62	1.47	1.35

The foregoing discussion applies to rifle companies only. But much the same picture is obtained from an analysis of the heavy weapons companies. Since there are only three such companies to a regiment, the best company in each regiment on a given attitude variable was selected and an average nonbattle casualty rate computed for the best from all twelve regiments. The same was done with the worst company on a given attitude variable and for the

[6] Of course, a regimental or higher commander should know enough about his companies so that he too should be able to sort them out on a basis better than chance alone, without this statistical information. How well in these divisions the command could have done this is not known.

CHART II

HEAVY WEAPONS COMPANIES IN FOUR DIVISIONS—AVERAGE NONBATTLE CASUALTY RATES IN NORMANDY AS RELATED TO PRE D DAY ATTITUDE SCORES

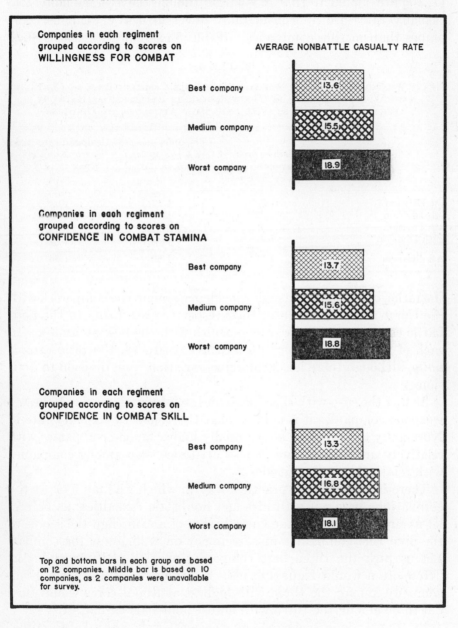

Companies in each regiment grouped according to scores on **WILLINGNESS FOR COMBAT**

AVERAGE NONBATTLE CASUALTY RATE

Best company — 13.6
Medium company — 15.5
Worst company — 18.9

Companies in each regiment grouped according to scores on **CONFIDENCE IN COMBAT STAMINA**

Best company — 13.7
Medium company — 15.6
Worst company — 18.8

Companies in each regiment grouped according to scores on **CONFIDENCE IN COMBAT SKILL**

Best company — 13.3
Medium company — 16.8
Worst company — 18.1

Top and bottom bars in each group are based on 12 companies. Middle bar is based on 10 companies, as 2 companies were unavailable for survey.

"middle" company, except that no "middle" companies are available for two regiments, in each of which one of the heavy weapons companies was unavailable for study. The pattern, shown in Chart II, is quite similar to that in Chart I, though the average nonbattle casualty rates are all considerably lower in heavy weapons companies than in rifle companies. Table 5 examines for consistency

TABLE 5

HEAVY WEAPONS COMPANIES—AVERAGE NONBATTLE CASUALTY RATE OF COMPANIES WITH WORST ATTITUDES IN THEIR REGIMENTS EXPRESSED AS RATIO OF AVERAGE RATE OF COMPANIES WITH BEST ATTITUDES, BY DIVISIONS

	Companies grouped by scores on willingness for combat	Companies grouped by scores on confidence in combat stamina	Companies grouped by scores on confidence in combat skill
1st Division	1.50	1.12	1.02
9th Division	1.32	1.55	1.65
4th Division	1.48	1.75	2.10
29th Division	1.22	1.22	1.14
All divisions	1.39	1.36	1.36

the ratios of nonbattle casualty incidence among the companies with the worst attitude scores in their respective regiments to the nonbattle casualty incidence of companies with the best attitudes. In each of the four divisions, on all three attitudes, the ratio *exceeds unity*, although there is considerable variation from division to division.

As was the case with rifle companies, so also with respect to heavy weapons companies it is evident that the nonbattle casualty rate in Normandy tended to be substantially higher among companies with relatively unfavorable pre D Day attitudes than among companies with relatively good attitudes.

There is still another practical way in which we may look at the correlations between attitudes and nonbattle casualties: as before, let us suppose that we knew in advance of a campaign the scores of the nine rifle companies in a regiment on willingness for combat. Let us pick the three best companies on this attitude and ask: "How often would I guess exactly right in predicting that a given company among the three with highest attitude scores would turn out to be among the three with lowest nonbattle casualties?"

By chance alone, one would guess exactly right a third of the time. Actually, as Chart III shows, one would have guessed exactly right,

CHART III

RELATIONSHIP BETWEEN RANK OF RIFLE COMPANIES WITHIN A REGIMENT IN
ATTITUDES AND IN NONBATTLE CASUALTY RATES
(Four Divisions)

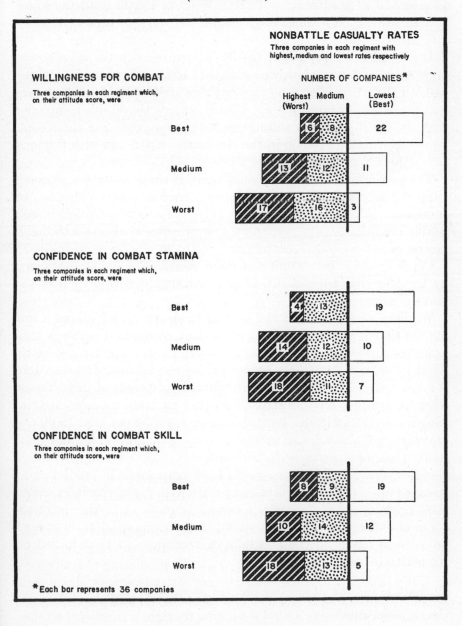

in the present study, 22 out of 36 times.   That is, among the 3 rifle companies with best attitudes in each of 12 regiments, 22 out of 36 turned out to be among the bottom three—and therefore best—in their regiments in nonbattle casualty rates in Normandy.   Of the 14 errors, 6 were extreme.   That is, 6 out of the 36 companies best in attitudes actually turned up among the worst in nonbattle casualty rates.

If we look in Chart III at the 36 companies with the *worst* scores on willingness for combat, we see that 17 of the 36 were among those making the worst record on nonbattle casualties and that there are only 3 extreme discrepancies.   That is, among the 36 rifle companies with the worst scores on willingness for combat, only 3 of these companies were among the 36 in the Normandy campaign with the lowest nonbattle casualty rates.

The picture is about the same, though perhaps not quite so good, when we use as sorting variables confidence in combat stamina or confidence in combat skill (Chart III).[7]   The same tendency seen in rifle companies is present also, though somewhat less strikingly, among heavy weapons companies.

Confidence in the stability of these relationships is strengthened by the fact that the pattern is quite consistent within each of the four divisions.

We have now reviewed the general evidence, which shows a low but consistent and statistically significant correlation between attitudes toward combat of companies before D Day and the nonbattle casualty rates in these companies during the Normandy campaign. We have seen also that the correlation is of practical importance, since, depending on the attitude sorting variable used, companies with the worst attitudes tended to have from 30 per cent to 60 per cent higher nonbattle casualty rates (basing figures on all four divisions) than companies with the best attitudes.   Finally, we have seen how few *extreme* errors would have been made in predicting in advance of the campaign how companies with given attitudes would show up relatively in nonbattle casualty rates.   A further interesting problem merits some attention, namely, comparisons between predictions based on the attitudes of veterans and those based on the attitudes of nonveterans.

---

[7] The three variables are intercorrelated and the results of taking all three into account simultaneously would be only a little better than the results in treating each variable individually.

Attitudes of Veterans and Nonveterans

It will be remembered that two of the four divisions, the 1st and the 9th, were veteran divisions. Before coming to England to prepare for the Normandy invasion both divisions had seen action in North Africa and Sicily. The 4th and 29th Divisions were to have their baptism of fire in France.

Unfortunately, a direct comparison of the average attitude scores of the two veteran divisions and two nonveteran divisions is complicated by the fact that the 1st and 9th were surveyed in late January 1944, while the 4th and 29th were not surveyed until April. There may have been changes in the average level of attitudes between January and April. Moreover, the form of the check list used on the questions on willingness for combat was different in April.

It happened, however, that a small sample resurvey of the 9th Division was made in April 1944. The sample was not large enough for company-by-company comparisons, since the average number of cases per company was only 33 and many companies were represented in the sample by only a handful of men. The same questionnaire was used as in the 4th and 29th Divisions. The 1st Division was not resurveyed in April.

If we combine the rifle companies in each regiment of the 9th Division in three groups of three companies each, according to nonbattle casualty rates in the eight weeks beginning June 6, we can compare the average attitude scores in January and April and also can break these scores down for veterans and nonveterans separately. It must be remembered that the 9th Division (and the 1st Division as well), while veteran outfits, received a substantial number of replacements without combat experience who were integrated into the units during the months prior to the Normandy landing. Since these nonveterans were part of the cohort who made the invasion, they have been included in all of the nonbattle casualty rate computations along with veterans in the same outfits. They need, however, to be distinguished sharply from replacements received *after* the Normandy landing. It will be remembered that replacements of the latter type were carefully excluded from the computation of nonbattle casualty rates and of course were not represented in the attitude surveys.

Chart IV, comparing attitudes of veterans and nonveterans in rifle companies in the 9th Division in January and April, brings out

CHART IV

COMPARISON OF VETERANS AND NONVETERANS IN NINTH DIVISION RIFLE COMPANIES GROUPED ACCORDING TO NONBATTLE CASUALTY RATES IN NORMANDY
(January and April 1944)

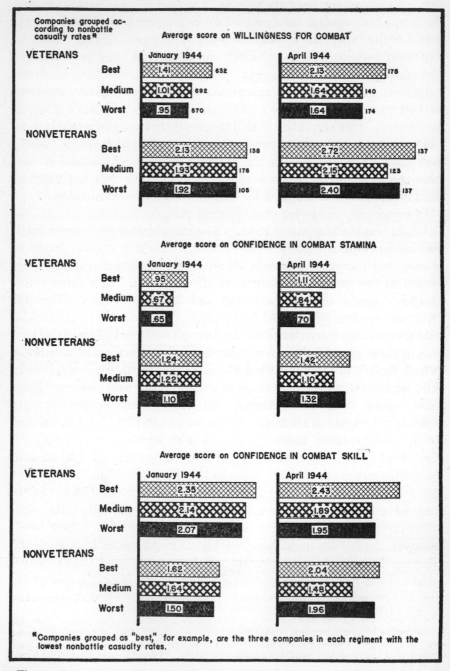

Companies grouped according to nonbattle casualty rates *

Average score on WILLINGNESS FOR COMBAT

VETERANS

	January 1944		April 1944	
Best	1.41	632	2.13	175
Medium	1.01	692	1.64	140
Worst	.95	570	1.64	174

NONVETERANS

Best	2.13	138	2.72	137
Medium	1.93	176	2.15	123
Worst	1.92	105	2.40	137

Average score on CONFIDENCE IN COMBAT STAMINA

VETERANS

	January 1944	April 1944
Best	.95	1.11
Medium	.67	.84
Worst	.65	.70

NONVETERANS

Best	1.24	1.42
Medium	1.22	1.10
Worst	1.10	1.32

Average score on CONFIDENCE IN COMBAT SKILL

VETERANS

	January 1944	April 1944
Best	2.35	2.43
Medium	2.14	1.89
Worst	2.07	1.95

NONVETERANS

Best	1.62	2.04
Medium	1.64	1.48
Worst	1.50	1.96

*Companies grouped as "best," for example, are the three companies in each regiment with the lowest nonbattle casualty rates.

The numbers following the bars are the numbers of cases on which the scores are based.

some quite interesting facts.   In *both* surveys, the companies with the best record on nonbattle casualty rates (that is, the lowest rates) tended to have the best attitude scores (that is, the highest scores). This was true among nonveterans as well as veterans, although the relationship may have been somewhat sharper among veterans. Between January and April many replacements were received and the attitudes of the replacements in April do not seem to be as closely related to subsequent unit nonbattle casualty rates as the attitudes of veterans in both January and April.[8]   What is most interesting to observe, however, is the fact *that nonveterans had consistently better attitude scores on willingness for combat and confidence in combat stamina than veterans.*   On the other hand, *veterans tended to have better attitude scores on confidence in combat skill than nonveterans.* This same relationship is seen in the 1st Division in January, although no replication for April is available.

Chart V provides a further interesting summary of attitudes in the rifle companies of the 9th Division in April 1944.   Here we compare the average attitude scores (the higher scores being more favorable) of veteran noncoms and veteran and nonveteran privates.[9]   Clearly, the relative favorableness of the various subgroups depends on the attitude studied.   On willingness for combat and confidence in combat stamina, the nonveteran privates make showings as good as or better than the veteran noncoms and definitely better than the veteran privates.   But on confidence in combat skill, as almost surely would be expected if the measures used are valid indexes, the highest scores are made by the veteran noncoms and the lowest scores are made by the nonveteran privates, although the veteran privates make scores almost as low.

Further light is thrown on the differences in attitude patterns if

---

[8] It is possible that, as Chart IV suggests, the average attitude scores of veterans improved between January and April.   For all three groups of companies there was a slight improvement in scores on confidence in combat stamina, but in two of the three groups of companies there was a deterioration in scores on confidence in combat skill. On the other hand, there was a large and, at first glance, impressive improvement among veterans in scores on willingness for combat.   However, as has been mentioned in the text, there was a change in the check list in the April survey from the check list used in January on the two questions involved in the willingness for combat score.   The change would not seem to be important enough to account for so large a shift, but question wording is tricky business, and it is well not to make too much of the data in Chart IV as representing a real improvement in veterans' attitudes.

[9] The fact that all the bars for, say, confidence in combat skill, are longer than all the corresponding bars for, say, confidence in combat stamina, has, of course, no necessary significance.   The absolute length of bars is an artifact of the way the scores were derived and only *relative* comparisons can be made.   This caution applies to both Chart IV and Chart V.

we go back to the original scores and examine cross tabulations. Table 6 shows, as would be expected both from the nature of the variables and as an artifact of the check lists used in deriving the scales, that there is quite a high correlation between the scales on

CHART V

NINTH DIVISION RIFLE COMPANIES—COMPARISON OF ATTITUDES OF VETERAN NONCOMS AND OF VETERAN AND NONVETERAN PRIVATES, APRIL 1944

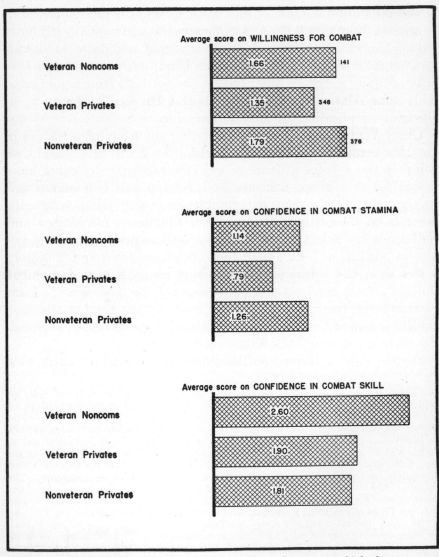

The numbers following the bars are the numbers of cases on which the scores are based.

confidence in combat stamina and confidence in combat skill.   The correlations between each of these scores and willingness for combat are equally high.   But let us focus our attention, not on the size of the correlations, but rather on the *difference in pattern* of relationship as between veteran noncoms at one extreme and nonveteran privates at the other.   (The categories in the original 5 x 5 tables are arbitrarily grouped in Table 6 so that, for all groups combined, the number of cases falling above and below the principal diagonal are about equal.)

Among veteran noncoms, in Table 6, the cases on the principal

TABLE 6

Ninth Division—Correlations Between Scores on Confidence in Combat Skill and Confidence in Combat Stamina, April 1944

| | | SCORE ON CONFIDENCE IN COMBAT SKILL | | | |
		0, 1	2	3, 4	Total
Veteran noncoms					
Score on confidence in	2, 3, 4	2	7	35	44
combat stamina	1	5	15	36	56
	0	19	11	11	41
	Total	26	33	82	141
Veteran privates					
Score on confidence in	2, 3, 4	9	12	48	69
combat stamina	1	34	29	43	106
	0	109	37	27	173
	Total	152	78	118	348
Nonveteran privates					
Score on confidence in	2, 3, 4	19	41	71	131
combat stamina	1	61	51	24	136
	0	82	14	13	109
	Total	162	106	108	376

diagonal are 19, 15, 35.   Fourteen cases lie above the diagonal—noncoms who may be thought of as having *relatively* higher (that is, better) scores on confidence in stamina than on confidence in skill. A total of 58 cases lie below the diagonal—noncoms who may be thought of as having *relatively* higher scores on confidence in skill than in stamina.   Thus, of the 72 cases lying off the diagonal, only 14, or 19 per cent, are of the former type.   Making corresponding computations for veteran privates and nonveteran privates, we can summarize the cases which lie off the diagonal for the three groups as follows:

	Above the diagonal (stamina scores relatively higher than skill scores)	Below the diagonal (skill scores relatively higher than stamina scores)	Total	Percentage with stamina scores relatively higher than skill scores
Veteran noncoms	14	58	72	19
Veteran privates	55	107	162	34
Nonveteran privates	121	51	172	70

These significant differences are, of course, just what would be expected *if the attitude variables have some specific meaning in addition to representing, as they doubtless also do, a general attitude toward combat.*

In summary, then, we have seen from Chart V that on two of the variables—willingness for combat and confidence in combat stamina—the nonveteran privates had better attitudes than the veteran privates, and as good or better attitudes than the veteran noncoms. On the third variable, confidence in combat skill, the veterans had better attitudes than the nonveterans. In other words, the complaint pattern is different for veterans and nonveterans. But does this difference in complaint patterns imply a difference between veterans and nonveterans in eventual nonbattle casualties? Since all three attitudes have been shown earlier to have a correlation, on a company basis, with nonbattle casualty rates, there is no necessary basis for inference, on an a priori basis, that veterans would differ widely from nonveterans in nonbattle casualty rates. Empirical data are required.

It would be ideal if we were in a position to compute separate nonbattle casualty rates for these three groups, all of whom were represented in the initial quota of troops landing in Normandy. The labor cost in obtaining and processing the necessary data was prohibitive at the time. However, at least a clue is obtained from a careful study of just one regiment—the 39th Regiment of the 9th Division. Pay-roll rosters of rifle companies of this Regiment were obtained for sample months throughout the year prior to the Normandy invasion. Separate cards were made out for each individual, on the basis of each pay roll, recording name, serial number, and rank. By collating these cards it was possible to classify all of the men in the companies as of the invasion date as to whether or not they had belonged to the Regiment during either the North African or Sicilian compaigns or both. Then the cards were checked against the morning reports for the eight weeks beginning June 6, and if an individual was recorded in a morning report as a battle or nonbattle casualty, the fact was entered on his card.   From this clerical operation it was possible to construct Table 7, which shows that there was only a small difference—not statistically significant—between the nonbattle casualty rates of the three subgroups, as measured by the ratio of nonbattle casualties to initial strength.   A better measure would have been the ratio of nonbattle casualties to the average daily strength—the measure used in the larger study—but this was

TABLE 7

NINTH DIVISION, 39TH REGIMENT—CASUALTIES IN RIFLE COMPANIES IN EIGHT WEEKS BEGINNING JUNE 6, 1944

	Initial strength	Battle casualties as a percentage of initial strength	Nonbattle casualties as a percentage of initial strength
Veteran noncoms	361	46.5	14.1
Veteran privates	704	45.6	17.4
Nonveteran privates	532	48.1	16.7

not computed because of the large additional amount of labor which it would have required.   It is not likely, however, that the more appropriate ratio would have changed the general picture presented by Table 7.   Under the circumstances, while the nonbattle casualty rate of veteran noncoms is lower than that of veteran or nonveteran privates for the Regiment, the data cannot be regarded as definitively indicating what to expect in other regiments with similar experiences.   It would be desirable if further tabulations of other regiments could eventually be made.

The data from the special tabulation for the 39th Regiment throw some further light on company differences.   Chart VI shows that in rifle companies in which veterans tended to have relatively low nonbattle casualty rates, the rates for nonveterans in the company tended to be low also.   In companies in which veterans had high nonbattle casualty rates, the rates for nonveterans tended to be high also.   The correlation coefficient is +.80.   These data suggest that factors—either in the combat situation or in the initial psychological atmosphere or in both—which differentiate companies from one another are more significantly related to nonbattle casualty rates than factors which differentiate veterans from nonveterans.

The foregoing analysis may have a bearing on the interpretation which must be placed on soldiers' complaints as analyzed in later chapters of the present volume. When "old beat up Joe" complained and said he was in no shape for further fighting, this did not necessarily mean that he was more likely to become a nonbattle casualty than a nonveteran in the same outfit. Very striking data shown in Chapter 5 of this volume, Chart III and Table 12, tend to show that the old veteran was not by any means considered by platoon leaders to be the most efficient soldier in the platoon, after several months' exposure to combat. On the other hand, when a nonveteran complained that he needed a lot more training before

CHART VI

NINTH DIVISION, 39TH REGIMENT RIFLE COMPANIES—CORRELATION BETWEEN
NONBATTLE CASUALTY RATES OF VETERANS AND NONVETERANS WHO
CONSTITUTED INITIAL STRENGTH AT BEGINNING OF INVASION,
BY COMPANIES

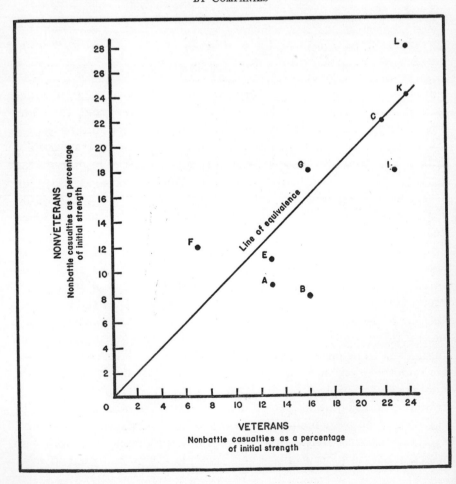

he would be up to fighting, this did not necessarily mean that he would acquire escape from battle by the sick route when he got there.   Both responses without doubt often served as rationalizations for not wanting to do a dirty job—and it is quite understandable that the veteran should tend to use the "physical condition" excuse while the nonveteran, as we have seen, tended more to use the "need more training" rationalization. With respect to the direct questions on willingness for combat, it is quite probable that neither veterans nor nonveterans were enthusiastic about combat. All the evidence studied in later chapters of this volume points to lack of enthusiasm.   But the fact that the veteran had been through battle may have given him a feeling of earned permission to say more frankly what he thought than the nonveteran felt he could admit, even anonymously.   This may account, in some degree, for the difference in scores on expressed willingness for combat as between veterans and nonveterans.

At the same time, the evidence reviewed in this section shows, with little room for doubt, that *companies* in which *more than the average* number of men had low scores on willingness for combat, confidence in combat stamina, or confidence in combat skill, were conspicuous among those units with high nonbattle casualty rates. The correlations are consistent and, taken as a whole, statistically significant, and the difference in nonbattle casualty rates between companies with the best and worst attitudes are certainly large enough to be considered important.   Furthermore, the relationships hold up in the companies of both experienced and inexperienced divisions.

Therefore, we have one answer to the question with which this chapter opened, "Suppose that many combat soldiers did have unfavorable attitudes.   What of it?   They fought, didn't they?" The answer is "Yes, they fought," but companies with more than their share of such men tended to have higher nonbattle casualty rates in Normandy than other companies—in other words, had fewer combat effectives on the battle line than companies with better initial attitudes.

In Section III we shall review the derivation of the attitude scores used and the procedure for computing the nonbattle casualty rates.

The foregoing analysis has represented a comparison of average attitude scores, *by companies*, before D Day with nonbattle casualty rates in those companies after D Day.   This was a study of unit behavior, not of individual behavior, because the questionnaires were administered anonymously and did not contain enough identifying data about the individual to permit a comparison of the individual's attitude and his subsequent combat record. We turn now to Section II of this chapter, which deals with a somewhat smaller study—as compared with that in Section I—relating the attitudes of a sample of Infantry recruits to their *individual* combat performance in Europe over a year later. The study represents the only available data directly relating attitudes to the combat performance of individual men.[10]

SECTION II

ATTITUDES OF INDIVIDUALS IN TRAINING AS RELATED
TO PERFORMANCE IN COMBAT

The previous section of this chapter has shown that companies in which attitudes toward combat were relatively unfavorable before combat made a relatively unfavorable showing in combat, in so far as combat behavior was measured by the nonbattle casualty rate.

The present section reports a study in which the focus of interest is the individual rather than the unit, and in which combat performance is measured by ratings made for the specific purposes of the study rather than being derived from casualty statistics.

Design of the Study

In the fall and winter of 1943 it was possible to ascertain attitudes of a sample of a newly activated division, then in training at Camp Adair,[11] Oregon, and to identify the questionnaires by comparing

---

[10] A more elaborately designed study to accomplish this same purpose was undertaken near the close of the war, in cooperation with the commanding general of a B-29 wing in the late stages of training in the United States. Detailed attitude questionnaires were filled out on an anonymous basis by all personnel, officer and enlisted. From the background information on the questionnaire it was possible, by checking against official records, to identify every questionnaire. Faith was kept with the respondents, in that this information was in the sole custody of the Research Branch in Washington and not accessible to anyone in Army Air Forces. At the same time, in cooperation with the office of the Air Surgeon, a special record form was designed and printed to enter all needed data on missions performed, washouts, casualties, illness, etc., for each crew member. A special research officer was assigned to wing headquarters to keep these records. Plans were approved for periodic resurveys of the attitudes in the wing after each fifteen missions or so. However, the wing arrived in the Pacific only a few days before the capitulation of Japan, and the projected study became a casualty of the peace. No study was made in Air Forces comparable to the investigation in Infantry described in the present chapter. However, the chapters in this volume on attitudes in the Air Forces have an advantage for purposes of interpretation over chapters on Ground Forces, since attitudes of crew members usually can be studied in relation to the specific number of missions flown.

[11] S-60. All attitude data in Section II are from this source.

background information like induction date, age, and state of birth with information on the Form 20 personnel cards. The questionnaires were filled out anonymously and faith was kept with the men, since by agreement with the commanding general the identifying information was known only to the Research Branch and never revealed to the local command.

One of the purposes of obtaining these individual identifications was eventually to compare the attitudes of individuals with their performance in combat. The division transferred more than half of its infantrymen as overseas replacements early in 1944, thus reducing greatly the number who could be followed up in their original units. However, the questionnaire responses of those transferred and those remaining were almost identical on all items, so that those remaining proved to be representative of the division with respect to attitudes.

The 274th Infantry Regiment, to which were assigned the greater part of the men for whom precombat data were available, arrived in France in December 1944, as part of a task force along with two other regiments. Until the artillery and the rest of the divisional troops arrived, they were attached to other divisions to plug the lines, here and there, wherever needed. Then, in February, they operated as part of the 70th Division. Their battle history includes heavy fighting at Philippsbourg, France, and in cracking the Siegfried Line outside of Saarbrucken. In their main actions they suffered quite severe casualties. The 275th and 276th Infantry Regiments and the 270th Engineer Battalion had much the same history. The four field artillery battalions, however, did not come into the line until mid February and had had only a little over a month of combat and few casualties when the entire division was withdrawn from combat on March 25, 1945.

Shortly after VE Day, a team of psychologists from the Research Branch, ETO, was sent to the 70th Division to obtain data on the combat performance of as many as possible of the individuals who had participated in the attitude surveys in Oregon.[12] The division command was fully cooperative. A carefully planned interviewing procedure was employed, and out of the interviewing were obtained reliable evaluations of the combat performance of individuals. The conditions were perhaps optimal for obtaining the kind of evaluation sought. Most of the men had been in the line for about three months—long enough to provide a thorough test under fire, yet

[12] S-60 follow-up. All combat ratings in Section II are from this source.

short enough so that there were still some men left to tell about it. And memories were still fresh. These conditions, and the manner in which the ratings were obtained, are critical factors in assessing the validity of the combat performance data. The rating interviews were conducted by specially trained interviewers, and in almost all cases the raters were the officers or noncoms who had worked most closely in combat with the man being rated.

At least two independent ratings were obtained on each man relative to *other men in the same outfits*, and men were regarded as "above average" or "below average" in the analysis only if the judgments of the raters showed substantial agreement as to the way in which a man had performed relative to the performance of other men in comparable jobs in the same outfit. The carefully worked out and standardized rating procedures used are described in more detail in Section III of this chapter. Usable combat ratings were obtained for 393 men for whom personnel and questionnaire data also were available. These men fell into three categories, as follows:

Above average in combat performance	33%
Average or indeterminate in combat performance	39
Below average in combat performance	28
	100%

Because it was particularly desired to control the influence of education, AGCT score, age, and marital condition on performance, and to evaluate the relationship between attitudes and combat ratings with these background factors held constant, the sample was reduced to 279 cases in the process of matching the three performance groups on these background factors.

Attitudes Relating to Combat as Correlated with Combat Performance

In the initial attitude surveys in Oregon, four questions were asked which had a direct reference to combat. These were:

If you were sent into actual fighting after finishing one year of training, how do you think you would do?

Do you ever worry about whether you will be injured in combat before the war is over?

How do you think you would feel about killing a Japanese soldier?

How do you think you would feel about killing a German soldier?

CHART VII

ATTITUDES OF INDIVIDUALS WHILE IN TRAINING AS RELATED TO RATINGS OF
THEIR COMBAT PERFORMANCE OVER A YEAR LATER

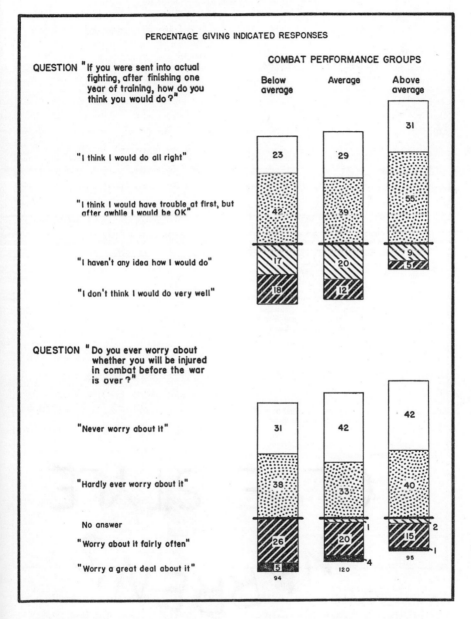

The numbers at the bottom of the bars are the numbers of cases on which the percentages are based.

CHART VII (Continued)

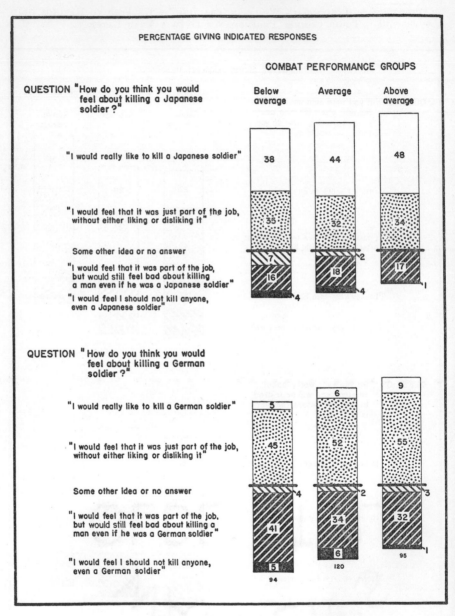

PERCENTAGE GIVING INDICATED RESPONSES

COMBAT PERFORMANCE GROUPS

QUESTION "How do you think you would feel about killing a Japanese soldier?"

Below average | Average | Above average

"I would really like to kill a Japanese soldier"
38 | 44 | 48

"I would feel that it was just part of the job, without either liking or disliking it"
35 | 32 | 34

Some other idea or no answer
| 2 |

"I would feel that it was part of the job, but would still feel bad about killing a man even if he was a Japanese soldier"
7 / 16 | 18 | 17

"I would feel I should not kill anyone, even a Japanese soldier"
4 | 4 | 1

QUESTION "How do you think you would feel about killing a German soldier?"

"I would really like to kill a German soldier"
5 | 6 | 9

"I would feel that it was just part of the job, without either liking or disliking it"
45 | 52 | 55

Some other idea or no answer
4 | 2 | 3

"I would feel that it was part of the job, but would still feel bad about killing a man even if he was a German soldier"
41 | 34 | 32

"I would feel I should not kill anyone, even a German soldier"
5 | 6 | 1

94 | 120 | 95

Chart VII shows that the men rated above average in combat performance tended to show, during their training period—over a year before combat—attitudes with respect to combat which were superior from the Army point of view, as compared with the other men.   That is, they were more likely to manifest confidence that they would perform satisfactorily in combat, they were more likely not to express anxiety about future injury in combat, and they were somewhat more likely to accept killing as their business.   The attitude differences between the above average and below average performance groups are consistent on all four items and are statistically significant on all items except that on killing Japanese.[13]

Actually, this is a conservative way of portraying the relationship between attitudes toward combat while in training and performance ratings in combat which took place over a year later.   It is conservative because background factors, such as age, marital condition, education, AGCT score, and mechanical aptitude scores, have been held constant in matching the three performance groups.   Attitude scores, as has been shown in Volume I, are related to some of these factors, and these factors are in turn related to ratings of combat performance.   For example, the more intelligent tend to have the "better" attitudes toward combat, and the more intelligent also get the better ratings on combat performance.   If the background factors, therefore, are not held constant, the differences in attitudes between the above average and below average performance groups are somewhat greater even than the differences portrayed in Chart VII.

It is also of interest to note that corresponding attitude differences between above average and below average combat performance groups, analyzed separately for the smaller sample of men who fought in line Infantry companies, tended to be even more marked than the differences charted.   For example, in line companies of the 274th Infantry Regiment the proportion who said during training that they "never" worried about combat injuries was 48 per cent for men later rated as above average in combat performance as against 24 per cent for the below average group.   The numbers of cases are too small to make comparisons between line companies and other units very stable, but the direction of the differences suggests that, if anything, attitudes concerning combat were most

---

[13] The comparisons made here are in terms of percentage differences in response to attitude questions, as between "above average" and "below average" combat performance groups.   If the combat performance data are expressed in terms of a five-point rating scale instead of an "above average," "average," and "below average" trichotomy, mean rating scores for those giving favorable and unfavorable responses to attitude questions may be computed.   These mean differences are, for almost all questions, more reliable than the converse percentage differences which have been used in this presentation for the sake of simplicity.

TABLE 8

BACKGROUND CHARACTERISTICS, AS OF TRAINING PERIOD, OF MEN GROUPED BY
RATINGS OF COMBAT PERFORMANCE

	COMBAT PERFORMANCE GROUPS		
	Below average	*Average*	*Above average*
Education			
College	15%	18%	24%
H.S. graduate	32	33	40
Some H.S.	28	32	20
Finished 8th grade	17	12	12
Less than 8th grade	8	5	4
Total	100%	100%	100%
Number of cases	*111*	*152*	*130*
AGCT Class			
I	4%	9%	8%
II	37	40	39
III	37	35	42
IV	19	14	9
V	3	2	2
Total	100%	100%	100%
Number of cases	*111*	*152*	*130*
Mechanical Aptitude Score			
130 or more	1%	9%	7%
120–129	6	11	26
110–119	29	21	19
100–109	23	22	23
90–99	17	24	13
80–89	6	9	8
Under 80	18	4	4
Total	100%	100%	100%
*Number of cases**	*101*	*139*	*118*
Marital Status			
Married	52%	58%	65%
Unmarried	48	42	35
Total	100%	100%	100%
*Number of cases**	*111*	*151*	*130*
Age			
35 and over	4%	5%	5%
30–34	19	22	24
25–29	28	28	34
22–24	18	15	14
21 and under	31	30	23
Total	100%	100%	100%
*Number of cases**	*110*	*151*	*128*

* Information lacking on one or more cases.

closely related to performance in units that saw the heaviest fighting.

Background Factors and Combat Performance

The relationship between background factors and combat performance ratings is shown in Table 8. The better educated, the men with the highest AGCT scores and highest mechanical aptitude scores, the older men, and the married men tend to get the better performance ratings.

Education and test scores are highly intercorrelated, as are age and marital condition. When combat performance groups are matched on educational level, difference in performance by AGCT score tends to disappear. When they are matched on educational level and AGCT score, however, significant differences by mechanical aptitude score, age, and marital condition remain. These results are shown in Table 9.

If we consider only men with high school education, relatively high AGCT score (Class I, II, or III), relatively high mechanical aptitude (score of 120 or over), and over 24 years of age at the time of the attitude survey (33 cases in all), we find that 58 per cent are in the above average group on combat performance and 6 per cent are in the below average group. At the other extreme, if we take men with grade school education only, mechanical aptitude scores below 120, and under 24 years of age (58 cases in all), we find only 22 per cent rated above average in combat performance but 40 per cent rated below average.

Attitudes Not Specifically Involving Combat

In reviewing the relationships of attitudes and combat performance, we have considered those attitudes in training which relate specifically to combat. In addition, there were other items in the questionnaires referring to the individual's sense of well-being at the time of the survey and to attitudes toward various aspects of Army life. When these responses are related to ratings of combat performance for our three groups matched on background factors, further interesting associations are found, but, with one exception, all of the relationships tended to be lower than in the case of the items directly applying to combat, and the sample is not large enough to insure their statistical significance.

The exception is a question on AWOL, where soldiers who in training said that AWOL was a "very serious" offense were considerably more likely to be found in the above average group on combat performance than other men.   In the above average group, 53 per cent answered "very serious" to the question, "In general how serious an offense do you think it is for a soldier to go AWOL (absent without leave)?" as compared with 36 per cent in the average group and 31

TABLE 9

BACKGROUND CHARACTERISTICS, AS OF TRAINING PERIOD, OF MEN GROUPED BY RATINGS OF COMBAT PERFORMANCE, HOLDING SPECIFIED FACTORS CONSTANT

	COMBAT PERFORMANCE GROUPS		
	Below average	*Average*	*Above average*
AGCT Score, when performance groups are matched by educational level			
I	4%	10%	8%
II	43	36	39
III	34	37	40
IV	16	15	10
V	3	2	3
Total	100%	100%	100%
Number of cases	*94*	*120*	*96*
Mechanical Aptitude Score, when performance groups are matched by educational level and AGCT score			
130 or over	1%	8%	7%
120–129	7	10	25
110–119	33	20	18
100–109	23	24	22
90–99	17	29	12
80–89	7	6	10
Less than 80	12	3	6
Total	100%	100%	100%
Number of cases	*86*	*108*	*85*
Marital Status, when performance groups are matched by educational level and AGCT score			
Married	53%	56%	70%
Unmarried	47	44	30
Total	100%	100%	100%
Number of cases	*94*	*120*	*95*
Age, when performance scores are matched by educational level and AGCT score			
35 and over	3%	4%	6%
30–34	16	23	27
25–29	32	28	32
22–24	18	16	13
21 and under	31	29	22
Total	100%	100%	100%
Number of cases	*93*	*119*	*93*

per cent in the below average group.   The difference of 22 per cent between above average and below average groups is highly reliable. Here again an even larger difference (about 40 per cent) is found when data for line Infantry companies are analyzed separately.

A group of questions relating to acceptance of the soldier role consistently showed some relationship, with differences not large enough, however, to be considered reliable.   An example is the question, "If it were up to you to choose, do you think that you could do more for your country as a soldier or as a worker in a war job?" In the above average group on combat performance, 46 per cent answered "soldier" when queried in training; in both the average and below average groups, 38 per cent gave this response.

Similarly, relatively little relationship was found with questions on personal adjustment in the Army at the time of the survey.   For example, in answering the question, "What sort of a time do you have in the Army?" 30 per cent of the above average group answered "I have a pretty good time," as compared with 29 per cent of the average group and 22 per cent in the below average group.

A similar pattern was found with respect to items on confidence in general ability to handle new jobs or situations, and confidence in equipment.

Finally, the items relating to attitudes toward the war all showed a consistent, but statistically not reliable, relationship, to combat performance ratings.   For example, in answer to the question, "Before the Japanese attacked Pearl Harbor, a lot of people thought we should not run the risk of getting into war by sending supplies to England and Russia—now what was your opinion before Pearl Harbor?" 79 per cent in the above average performance group answered, "Thought we should send supplies even at the risk of war," as compared with 69 per cent in the average group and 68 per cent in the below average group.

In other sets of items grouped by areas of content, the relationships were not consistent, although a number of the items tended to show a slight correlation with performance ratings.   The areas where either no relationship or no consistent relationship was found included attitudes toward officers and noncoms in the training situation, pride in company, attitudes toward allies, attitudes toward the home front, anxieties about family, job prospects and the postwar period, and a miscellany of attitudes toward details of Army life during training, such as job placement, promotions, training, recreation, food, and medical attention.   The array of subjects, and the number of questions, which did not consistently differentiate men as rated more than a year later by their combat performance, are rather formidable. It is, therefore, particularly unfortunate that it was not possible to replicate in a second study the relation of performance to questions on attitudes toward combat. It should also be noted, however, that many of the questionnaire items were *not* designed as ones which it was anticipated would probably be predictive of subsequent performance, but were instead included in the attitude surveys as useful items for the commanding general for appraising the overall attitude picture of his division (not of individuals) during the training period. On certain types of questions (such as those getting at faith in leadership ability of officers and noncoms) one might also reasonably have anticipated a larger number of predictive items had questionnaires been administered overseas prior to the men's entering into combat. Attitudes on such questions would be expected to change markedly as the situation and personnel changed from training to combat. In view of the preponderantly different leadership in training and combat, it is not so surprising that attitudes toward *training* officers were not predictive of combat performance.

As a final comment, it should be noted that some attitudes—particularly those related to unit esprit—might well be important differential predictors of performance as between different units, while at the same time differences in expression of these attitudes by various men *within* a unit might have little or no relation to differences in individual performance. The design of the present study, which involves comparative ratings within companies, precludes investigation of possible predictive relationships in terms of unit-to-unit variations. This limitation of the method used in the present study obviously restricts the generality of the finding that the reliably predictive attitude items were attitudes of personal confidence or personal conviction with respect to future combat performance and that no significant relationships were obtained for attitudes relating primarily to company or group morale.

In conclusion, it should be emphasized that the fact that a long interval elapsed between training and combat makes all the more significant the findings here reported as to the relation of attitudes toward combat and performance ratings.

Concluding Comments

While the two analyses which constitute the subject matter of this chapter are not ideal for the purpose, representing the only studies of their kind which the Research Branch was enabled to carry through amid pressures of war, they complement and reinforce one another.   In Section I we saw that *companies* with attitudes worse than the average in their regiment before combat tended to have a worse than average combat record in the Normandy campaign, in so far as the index used is the nonbattle casualty rate.   In Section II we have seen that *individuals* who, in early training in the United States, had the least satisfactory attitudes relating to combat, tended, more than other men, to be among those rated below average in combat performance more than a year after they were surveyed.

For a more detailed description of the methods used in securing the data portrayed in the foregoing pages, we turn now to Section III.   The nontechnical reader may wish to skip these pages and go directly to the chapters which follow—first with respect to ground combat and later with respect to combat in the air.

S E C T I O N   I I I

BASIC DATA AND TECHNICAL NOTES ON RELATION OF ATTITUDES TO BEHAVIOR IN COMBAT

This section is in two parts.

In Part 1 are presented the basic data lying behind the results presented in the first section of this chapter, together with a description of (a) how the attitude data were processed and (b) how the casualty data were computed.

In Part 2 the methods used in obtaining the data presented in the second section of this chapter are briefly summarized.

PART 1.   Company Attitudes and Nonbattle Casualty Rates

In Tables 10 and 11 are shown the basic data, by individual companies, on which Tables 2 to 5 and Charts I to III in the foregoing text are based.

Derivation of the Attitude Scores

Willingness for combat.   The score on willingness for combat is derived from a cross tabulation of two questions.   After cross tabulation the categories were combined objectively—so as to provide five final score categories with maximum reproducibility—in other words, to obtain total scores of such a nature that the answers to the individual questions could be inferred from the total scores with

TABLE 10

RIFLE COMPANIES—ATTITUDE SCORES PRIOR TO D DAY AND NONBATTLE
CASUALTY RATES IN EIGHT WEEKS BEGINNING JUNE 6, 1944

	1ST DIVISION						9TH DIVISION				
	Willingness for combat	Confidence in combat stamina	Confidence in combat skill	Nonbattle casualty rate	Size of sample in attitude survey		Willingness for combat	Confidence in combat stamina	Confidence in combat skill	Nonbattle casualty rate	Size of sample in attitude survey
16th Reg.						*39th Reg.*					
A Co.	1.70	1.02	2.07	10	*123*	A Co.	1.83	1.36	2.44	18	*70*
B Co.	1.36	.85	1.61	17	*102*	B Co.	1.71	1.36	2.39	17	*72*
C Co.	1.77	.91	2.03	41	*75*	C Co.	1.20	.52	2.07	34	*60*
E Co.	1.58	1.04	1.82	14	*84*	E Co.	1.23	.65	1.92	18	*97*
F Co.	1.80	1.06	1.81	12	*104*	F Co.	1.47	1.22	2.47	11	*73*
G Co.	1.95	1.08	2.14	17	*101*	G Co.	.41	.29	1.37	21	*70*
I Co.	1.67	.98	2.39	14	*57*	I Co.	1.27	.87	2.06	24	*109*
K Co.	1.75	.89	2.01	13	*100*	K Co.	.96	.60	1.67	36	*78*
L Co.	1.96	1.06	2.13	12	*107*	L Co.	1.68	1.20	2.60	31	*25*
Average	1.73	.99	2.00	16		Average	1.31	.90	2.11	23	
18th Reg.						*47th Reg.*					
A Co.	1.86	1.04	2.16	13	*91*	A Co.	.98	.56	2.14	32	*98*
B Co.	1.49	1.11	2.17	15	*95*	B Co.	.71	.46	1.80	50	*70*
C Co.	1.82	.86	2.20	13	*51*	C Co.	1.29	.68	1.81	26	*84*
E Co.	1.38	.98	2.40	23	*45*	E Co.	1.30	1.12	2.23	33	*84*
F Co.	1.34	.66	1.56	30	*73*	F Co.	1.67	1.26	2.64	26	*108*
G Co.	1.46	.83	1.77	14	*65*	G Co.	1.55	.80	2.38	19	*102*
I Co.	1.84	1.05	1.91	14	*101*	I Co.	1.53	.97	2.39	37	*66*
K Co.	1.74	.76	1.93	12	*97*	K Co.	1.46	.93	2.39	22	*85*
L Co.	1.62	1.15	2.28	24	*95*	L Co.	1.90	.82	2.28	25	*79*
Average	1.62	.94	2.04	17		Average	1.38	.84	2.23	30	
26th Reg.						*60th Reg.*					
A Co.	1.87	1.18	2.55	31	*98*	A Co.	1.03	.58	1.77	47	*97*
B Co.	1.46	.67	1.71	47	*112*	B Co.	.84	.58	1.81	49	*94*
C Co.	1.99	1.08	2.26	21	*86*	C Co.	1.17	.74	2.03	51	*101*
E Co.	1.85	1.04	2.23	22	*66*	E Co.	1.25	.82	2.05	15	*100*
F Co.	1.35	.80	1.94	26	*141*	F Co.	1.22	.79	2.04	42	*92*
G Co.	1.56	.95	2.00	28	*102*	G Co.	1.44	.87	2.14	35	*99*
I Co.	1.01	.68	1.41	25	*69*	I Co.	1.14	.76	1.87	21	*99*
K Co.	1.04	.45	1.77	29	*69*	K Co.	1.01	.83	1.93	40	*111*
L Co.	1.13	.51	1.53	34	*88*	L Co.	1.64	1.04	1.87	18	*90*
Average	1.47	.82	1.93	29		Average	1.19	.78	1.95	35	

TABLE 10 (Continued)

	4TH DIVISION						29TH DIVISION				
	Willingness for combat	*Confidence in combat stamina*	*Confidence in combat skill*	*Nonbattle casualty rate*	*Size of sample in attitude survey*		*Willingness for combat*	*Confidence in combat stamina*	*Confidence in combat skill*	*Nonbattle casualty rate*	*Size of sample in attitude survey*
8th Reg.						*115th Reg.*					
A Co.	3.04	1.70	2.50	18	*103*	A Co.	3.13	1.63	2.22	19	*83*
B Co.	2.84	1.53	2.21	8	*101*	B Co.	3.23	1.74	2.30	15	*64*
C Co.	2.82	1.64	2.52	16	*95*	C Co.	2.99	1.47	1.91	41	*98*
E Co.	2.35	1.55	2.33	17	*88*	E Co.	2.91	1.53	2.30	17	*44*
F Co.	2.65	1.57	2.31	34	*86*	F Co.	2.56	1.42	2.03	17	*34*
G Co.	2.69	1.50	2.32	24	*100*	G Co.	2.74	1.59	2.24	19	*109*
I Co.	3.26	1.84	2.81	20	*103*	I Co.	2.92	1.49	2.03	21	*108*
K Co.	2.54	1.63	2.24	33	*59*	K Co.	3.03	1.67	2.19	25	*108*
L Co.	2.73	1.43	2.69	31	*95*	L Co.	2.64	1.39	2.21	18	*87*
Average	2.77	1.60	2.44	22		Average	2.91	1.55	2.16	21	
12th Reg.						*116th Reg.*					
A Co.	2.94	1.55	2.25	19	*105*	A Co.	3.05	1.61	2.12	10	*89*
B Co.	2.50	1.09	1.96	19	*107*	B Co.	3.08	1.61	2.34	42	*59*
C Co.	2.78	1.39	2.10	11	*94*	C Co.	2.65	1.36	2.07	17	*81*
E Co.	3.01	1.68	2.43	8	*87*	E Co.	2.79	1.35	1.90	42	*78*
F Co.	2.56	1.42	2.33	18	*82*	F Co.	2.84	1.53	1.85	14	*89*
G Co.	2.71	1.40	1.96	28	*97*	G Co.	3.37	2.17	2.54	11	*70*
I Co.	3.24	1.75	2.78	17	*78*	I Co.	3.08	1.64	2.22	24	*88*
K Co.	2.87	1.38	1.94	19	*85*	K Co.	3.18	2.14	2.77	10	*82*
L Co.	2.64	1.28	2.06	18	*102*	L Co.	3.22	1.95	2.65	14	*95*
Average	2.81	1.44	2.20	17		Average	3.03	1.71	2.27	20	
22nd Reg.						*175th Reg.*					
A Co.	3.09	1.84	2.51	8	*93*	A Co.	3.22	2.10	2.75	18	*102*
B Co.	3.25	1.77	2.87	25	*100*	B Co.	3.04	1.77	2.40	16	*73*
C Co.	3.22	1.98	2.94	13	*85*	C Co.	2.96	1.80	2.62	18	*77*
E Co.	2.76	1.41	1.93	20	*76*	E Co.	2.94	1.69	2.15	50	*95*
F Co.	2.64	1.25	1.96	15	*113*	F Co.	2.80	1.50	2.10	22	*70*
G Co.	2.94	1.41	2.14	34	*113*	G Co.	3.06	1.78	2.45	22	*66*
I Co.	2.94	1.74	2.72	20	*104*	I Co.	3.00	1.53	2.03	20	*99*
K Co.	3.33	1.87	2.93	10	*97*	K Co.	2.90	1.70	2.18	50	*80*
L Co.	2.97	1.64	2.70	19	*103*	L Co.	2.92	1.73	2.14	58	*87*
Average	3.02	1.66	2.52	18		Average	2.98	1.73	2.31	30	

TABLE 11

HEAVY WEAPONS COMPANIES—ATTITUDE SCORES PRIOR TO D DAY AND
NONBATTLE CASUALTY RATES IN EIGHT WEEKS BEGINNING JUNE 6, 1944

	1ST DIVISION						9TH DIVISION				
	Willingness for combat	Confidence in combat stamina	Confidence in combat skill	Nonbattle casualty rate	Size of sample in attitude survey		Willingness for combat	Confidence in combat stamina	Confidence in combat skill	Nonbattle casualty rate	Size of sample in attitude survey
16th Reg.						*39th Reg.*					
D Co.	1.24	.80	2.32	17	103	D Co.	1.11	.70	2.37	18	63
H Co.	1.21	.65	2.04	13	101	H Co.	1.07	.80	2.38	17	45
M Co.	1.30	.67	2.01	8	90	M Co.	*	*	*	*	*
Average	1.25	.71	2.12	13		Average	1.09	.75	2.38	18	
18th Reg.						*47th Reg.*					
D Co.	1.76	1.08	2.30	13	110	D Co.	2.15	1.68	2.61	19	75
H Co.	1.64	1.05	2.23	15	83	H Co.	1.14	.83	2.23	13	65
M Co.	1.68	.90	2.15	10	80	M Co.	1.56	1.05	2.27	27	86
Average	1.69	1.01	2.23	13		Average	1.62	1.19	2.37	20	
26th Reg.						*60th Reg.*					
D Co.	1.42	.90	1.91	26	92	D Co.	1.11	.70	1.87	45	105
H Co.	1.94	1.16	2.49	19	98	H Co.	1.30	.95	2.39	13	88
M Co.	.99	.58	1.79	32	72	M Co.	1.45	.93	2.35	20	105
Average	1.45	.88	2.06	26		Average	1.29	.86	2.20	26	
	4TH DIVISION						29TH DIVISION				
8th Reg.						*115th Reg.*					
D Co.	3.12	1.85	2.56	2	87	D Co.	2.94	1.68	2.33	13	69
H Co.	2.97	1.58	2.24	17	94	H Co.	2.93	1.53	2.26	20	93
M Co.	3.06	1.65	2.38	10	90	M Co.	2.97	1.78	2.62	21	123
Average	3.05	1.69	2.39	10		Average	2.95	1.66	2.40	18	
12th Reg.						*116th Reg.*					
D Co.	3.15	1.82	2.38	10	96	D Co.	3.36	2.00	2.44	5	86
H Co.	2.83	1.49	2.22	8	96	H Co.	3.06	1.78	2.29	12	87
M Co.	2.80	1.51	2.53	6	98	M Co.	2.82	1.95	2.43	15	82
Average	2.93	1.61	2.38	8		Average	3.08	1.91	2.39	11	
22nd Reg.						*175th Reg.*					
D Co.	3.04	1.52	2.38	19	80	D Co.	3.04	1.64	2.10	15	77
H Co.	2.90	1.35	2.31	19	72	H Co.	2.84	1.56	1.92	15	88
M Co.	3.07	1.75	2.54	13	96	M Co.	*	*	*	*	*
Average	3.00	1.54	2.41	17		Average	2.94	1.60	2.01	15	

* Not available for survey.

minimum error.   (It is not, of course, claimed that the scores used in this chapter constitute scales in the sense defined in Volume IV. The reproducibility is quite satisfactory, but many more items would be needed before scalability could be established.)   To illustrate the procedure, actual data representing the total sample of 6,280 men in the 4th and 29th Divisions will be carried through each step.

The questions used in the April survey, together with assigned weights and illustrative frequencies, are as follows:

A. Which of the following best tells the way you feel about getting into an actual battle zone?

2	I want very much to get into it just as soon as possible	496
2	I'm ready to go any time	1,930
1	I'd like to go before it's over but I don't think I'm ready yet	544
1	I hope I won't have to go but if I do I think I'll do all right	2,013
0	I hope I won't have to go because I don't think I would do very well	611
0	No opinion	485
0	No answer	201
		6,280

B. Which of the following best describes your own feeling about getting into combat against the Germans?[14]

2	I'd like to get into the fight as soon as I can	848
1	I'm ready to go when my turn comes	3,554
1	I'd just as soon stay out of combat if possible	1,327
0	I don't want to get into combat at all	416
0	No answer	135
		6,280

Categories are combined according to their weights and yield the following table:

		Question A			
		0	1	2	Total
	2	74	1,644	708	2,426
Question	1	181	2,308	68	2,557
B	0	296	929	72	1,297
	Total	551	4,881	848	6,280

[14] The two questions were, of course, in different parts of the questionnaire.

The score distribution, adding the scores on A and B, becomes

Scale score	0	1	2	3	4	Total
Frequency	296	1,110	2,454	1,712	708	6,280

The check lists used in the January survey differed somewhat. On Question A there was no difference in the wording, but free comments of those who wrote in remarks were edited and where apparently contradictory with the check list were entered and punched with a separate code number. Since these were almost all extremely unfavorable comments they were given a score of 0 in the present analysis. On Question B in the January study the question asked was identical, but the check list was set up as follows, with weights used in the present analysis indicated:

> Which of the following best describes your own feeling about getting into combat against the Germans?
>
> 2   I want very much to get in and fight.
> 2   When my turn comes I want to go.
> 1   I don't care about combat, but I'd like it better than the way things are now.
> 0   I don't want to get into combat at all.
>   None of these fit me. I feel this way . . .

Categories were set up to code the free answers in the following groups:

> 0   Deserve to stay out of combat
> 0   Deserve temporary respite
> 0   Can't stand it
> 0   Not in good shape
> 1   Qualified acceptance of combat
> 1   No answer

Confidence in combat stamina.   This score was derived from three questions, for which the assigned weights and frequency of responses by 4th and 29th Division veteran privates in April are indicated:

> A. If and when you get into combat how well do you think you will stand up under battle conditions?
>
> 2   Very well   1,106
> 1   Fairly well   3,480
> 0   Not very well   917
> 0   Not well at all   475
> 1   No answer   302
>   _____
>   6,280

B. Do you think you are in good physical condition?

1	Yes, very good	1,446
0	Yes, fairly good	2,573
0	No	1,703
0	Undecided	472
0	No answer	86
		6,280

C. Do you think that you are in tough enough physical condition for going into combat?

1	Yes	2,741
0	No	1,938
0	Undecided	1,456
0	No answer	145
		6,280

The cross tabulation and score distribution are as follows:

			Question A			
			0	1	2	Total
Question C	Qu.	1	26	652	543	1,221
1	B	0	86	1,129	305	1,520
Question C	Qu.	1	35	140	50	225
0	B	0	1,245	1,861	208	3,314
			1,392	3,782	1,106	6,280

Scale score	0	1	2	3	4	Total
Frequency	1,245	1,982	1,503	1,007	543	6,280

The check lists for Questions A, B, and C were the same in January as in April, but there was more detailed editing in January of free answers, which were given separate codes when they seemed to contradict the check list, and which receive a weight of 0 in the present analysis.

Confidence in combat skill. Three questions were used to obtain this score:

A. Do you feel that you are now trained and ready for combat or do you need more training?

2	I'm ready for combat now	2,537
1	I need a little more of some kinds of training	2,267
0	I need a lot more of some kinds of training	1,226
1	No answer	250
		6,280

B. If you were given a group of men and told to take charge of them all by yourself on a mission under enemy fire, how well do you think you would do?

1	Very well	720
1	Fairly well	3,498
0	Not very well	1,292
0	Not well at all	480
0	No answer	290
		6,280

C. Do you think that you have been given enough training and experience so that you could do a good job of taking charge of a group of men of your own in combat?

1	Have been given enough training and experience	2,818
0	Have not been given quite enough training and experience	1,977
0	Have not been given nearly enough training and experience	1,177
0	No answer	308
		6,280

Following are the cross tabulation and score distribution:

			Question A			
			0	1	2	Total
Question C	Qu.	1	127	637	1,646	2,410
1	B	0	48	131	229	408
Question C	Qu.	1	387	974	447	1,808
0	B	0	664	775	215	1,654
			1,226	2,517	2,537	6,280

Scale score	0	1	2	3	4	Total
Frequency	664	1,210	1,447	1,313	1,646	6,280

In the January survey the question wording and the check lists were the same as in April. The only difference was in the editing of free answers and the provision of occasional separate codes in the January study. With minor exceptions, these special codes were scored 0 for the present analysis.

Nonbattle Casualty Rates and Their Computation

The major problem in obtaining the nonbattle casualty rate for a company was to separate the casualties among the men arriving in

Normandy with their units from the casualties among replacements who were sent to the company after June 6.

This task was made possible by use of photostats of the morning reports of the company, which record the strength as of the given day and report accessions or separations by name and serial number. The separation of each man is listed by cause—whether killed, wounded, injured, or missing in action (these are grouped in the present analysis as battle casualties), whether injured, nonbattle casualty (these were tabulated but are not counted for the purpose of the present analysis as either battle or nonbattle casualties), and whether "sick, nonbattle casualty." In some companies "exhaustion cases" were separately reported, but the practice was by no means uniform. Therefore, for purposes of the present analysis, all "exhaustion" cases have been included in the general category, "sick, nonbattle casualty." In addition, cases of AWOL or of transfers out of the company were listed.

Theoretically, the company's records were balanced each day and differences between the strength reported on two days should be accounted for exactly by the accessions and separations reported by name. The records, kept under field conditions, were not always accurate, and there was sometimes a lag of several days in reporting casualties, although late reports indicated the date on which the casualty occurred. On the whole, however, the records proved quite satisfactory, as measured by the fact that a company's strength on July 31, after two months of combat, usually was within two or three of the reported strength on June 6, plus the accessions reported by name in the preceding eight weeks, minus the separations reported by name in the same period.

The steps in assembling the needed data for a company were as follows:

1. For each accession or separation reported on a given day, a separate card was made out on which was recorded date, name, serial number, and all relevant information.

2. When the company records for eight weeks (56 morning reports) had been copied, the accession and separation cards were matched, where possible, by name or serial number. Names were sometimes spelled slightly differently on two cards and occasionally there would be a transposition of a digit in the serial number. But in general there was little difficulty in matching cards.

3. If a casualty card referred to a member of the company who had been received after June 6 from a replacement depot, the sym-

TABLE 12

RIFLE COMPANIES—SUMMARY OF DATA ON NONBATTLE CASUALTY RATES

	1ST DIVISION						9TH DIVISION				
	Initial strength	*Battle casualties*	*Nonbattle casualties*	*Average daily strength*	*Nonbattle casualty rate*		*Initial strength*	*Battle casualties*	*Nonbattle casualties*	*Average daily strength*	*Nonbattle casualty rate*
16th Reg.						*39th Reg.*					
A Co.	218	85	15	157	10	A Co.	160	111	19	108	18
B Co.	220	36	32	191	17	B Co.	172	88	21	126	17
C Co.	217	37	69	170	41	C Co.	173	93	41	119	34
E Co.	218	122	15	109	14	E Co.	177	105	22	124	18
F Co.	220	106	14	119	12	F Co.	180	94	15	136	11
G Co.	218	72	26	155	17	G Co.	173	65	29	135	21
I Co.	221	55	23	163	14	I Co.	170	70	34	140	24
K Co.	220	97	21	162	13	K Co.	172	84	41	115	36
L Co.	221	93	19	162	12	L Co.	178	74	42	136	31
Total	1,973	703	234	1,388		Total	1,555	784	264	1,139	
18th Reg.						*47th Reg.*					
A Co.	210	63	21	163	13	A Co.	166	85	36	113	32
B Co.	213	72	26	170	15	B Co.	141	63	59	118	50
C Co.	207	78	20	155	13	C Co.	183	109	32	125	26
E Co.	212	51	38	168	23	E Co.	171	124	34	102	33
F Co.	203	41	50	169	30	F Co.	164	97	30	115	26
G Co.	209	60	22	156	14	G Co.	169	109	22	113	19
I Co.	214	81	24	168	14	I Co.	167	94	38	102	37
K Co.	211	71	19	163	12	K Co.	170	119	21	96	22
L Co.	211	67	36	148	24	L Co.	151	109	22	88	25
Total	1,890	584	256	1,460		Total	1,482	909	294	972	
26th Reg.						*60th Reg.*					
A Co.	199	65	45	145	31	A Co.	164	124	41	88	47
B Co.	197	56	74	157	47	B Co.	176	123	45	92	49
C Co.	191	65	32	151	21	C Co.	173	109	56	110	51
E Co.	193	57	34	156	22	E Co.	164	127	16	106	15
F Co.	196	40	45	175	26	F Co.	168	120	45	107	42
G Co.	197	72	46	163	28	G Co.	166	107	39	112	35
I Co.	201	62	41	166	25	I Co.	174	126	24	112	21
K Co.	201	62	42	146	29	K Co.	175	123	44	110	40
L Co.	195	79	48	141	34	L Co.	163	121	20	110	18
Total	1,770	558	407	1,400		Total	1,523	1,080	330	947	

TABLE 12 (Continued)

	4TH DIVISION						29TH DIVISION				
	Initial strength	*Battle casualties*	*Nonbattle casualties*	*Average daily strength*	*Nonbattle casualty rate*		*Initial strength*	*Battle casualties*	*Nonbattle casualties*	*Average daily strength*	*Nonbattle casualty rate*
8th Reg.						*115th Reg.*					
A Co.	212	163	16	87	18	A Co.	202	177	20	103	19
B Co.	216	163	8	96	8	B Co.	199	173	14	93	15
C Co.	216	179	13	82	16	C Co.	192	155	38	93	41
E Co.	213	172	13	78	17	E Co.	204	139	17	103	17
F Co.	213	145	39	115	34	F Co.	208	119	21	125	17
G Co.	214	154	23	96	24	G Co.	198	161	19	98	19
I Co.	212	158	21	103	20	I Co.	206	158	20	96	21
K Co.	213	135	39	118	33	K Co.	203	138	25	102	25
L Co.	214	160	31	99	31	L Co.	213	140	21	118	18
Total	1,923	1,429	203	874		Total	8,125	1,360	195	931	
12th Reg.						*116th Reg.*					
A Co.	217	131	20	103	19	A Co.	206	198	4	39	10
B Co.	212	103	24	126	19	B Co.	197	178	18	43	42
C Co.	215	127	12	108	11	C Co.	198	154	14	82	17
E Co.	221	189	6	75	8	E Co.	200	159	38	91	42
F Co.	218	167	17	92	18	F Co.	202	171	11	79	14
G Co.	223	146	26	92	28	G Co.	207	168	11	100	11
I Co.	216	154	16	96	17	I Co.	216	193	24	98	24
K Co.	220	147	19	100	19	K Co.	206	140	10	101	10
L Co.	213	147	16	91	18	L Co.	212	166	16	112	14
Total	1,955	1,311	156	883		Total	1,853	1,527	146	745	
22nd Reg.						*175th Reg.*					
A Co.	214	161	8	95	8	A Co.	210	159	15	84	18
B Co.	216	133	28	113	25	B Co.	213	140	15	92	16
C Co.	220	149	15	119	13	C Co.	207	135	19	107	18
E Co.	215	149	20	99	20	E Co.	200	153	39	78	50
F Co.	213	170	12	82	15	F Co.	204	133	27	125	22
G Co.	214	171	29	86	34	G Co.	197	145	16	73	22
I Co.	230	137	24	121	20	I Co.	206	120	26	128	20
K Co.	217	122	11	115	10	K Co.	210	139	54	107	50
L Co.	215	153	18	95	19	L Co.	207	132	67	115	58
Total	1,954	1,345	165	925		Total	1,854	1,256	278	909	

TABLE 13

HEAVY WEAPONS COMPANIES—SUMMARY OF DATA ON NONBATTLE CASUALTY RATES

	Initial strength	Battle casualties	Nonbattle casualties	Average daily strength	Nonbattle casualty rate		Initial strength	Battle casualties	Nonbattle casualties	Average daily strength	Nonbattle casualty rate
1ST DIVISION						**9TH DIVISION**					
16th Reg.						*39th Reg.*					
D Co.	179	41	26	153	17	D Co.	151	51	26	141	18
H Co.	181	27	20	155	13	H Co.	143	36	20	121	17
M Co.	177	39	12	156	8	M Co.	148	47	18	130	14
Total	537	107	58	464		Total	442	134	64	392	
18th Reg.						*47th Reg.*					
D Co.	166	32	19	144	13	D Co.	147	30	23	124	19
H Co.	168	32	21	139	15	H Co.	150	57	16	119	13
M Co.	167	25	15	147	10	M Co.	147	57	31	114	27
Total	501	89	55	430		Total	444	144	70	357	
26th Reg.						*60th Reg.*					
D Co.	161	27	37	141	26	D Co.	137	45	49	110	45
H Co.	172	27	30	159	19	H Co.	151	79	15	115	13
M Co.	151	25	40	126	32	M Co.	150	58	25	127	20
Total	484	79	107	426		Total	438	182	89	352	
4TH DIVISION						**29TH DIVISION**					
8th Reg.						*115th Reg.*					
D Co.	192	97	3	126	2	D Co.	168	78	16	127	13
H Co.	197	105	21	124	17	H Co.	176	54	27	137	20
M Co.	193	79	15	143	10	M Co.	194	63	28	133	21
Total	582	281	39	393		Total	538	195	71	397	
12th Reg.						*116th Reg.*					
D Co.	183	72	13	124	10	D Co.	182	124	4	88	5
H Co.	183	94	8	104	8	H Co.	188	117	14	115	12
M Co.	188	95	7	111	6	M Co.	188	108	18	119	15
Total	554	261	28	339		Total	558	349	36	322	
22nd Reg.						*175th Reg.*					
D Co.	189	87	23	121	19	D Co.	174	81	18	119	15
H Co.	186	80	22	114	19	H Co.	169	73	18	120	15
M Co.	185	75	17	132	13	M Co.	175	60	31	140	22
Total	560	242	62	367		Total	518	214	67	379	

bol R was marked on the casualty card.   Otherwise, it could be assumed that the casualty occurred to a man who was a member of the company as of June 6.   This assumption was checked for one entire regiment by comparing the names of the supposed old men of a company who had become casualties with the names on the last company pay roll before D Day.   The errors were never more than one or two per company.[15]

4. A ledger sheet for the eight weeks was now prepared for the enlisted men of each company.   For example, the line for July 11 for the original men of A Company, 115th Regiment, 29th Division, shows the following:

Strength at beginning of day	99
Battle casualties	28
Sick, nonbattle casualties	3
Other separations	0
Returned to duty	0
Strength at end of day	68
Average strength	84

Corresponding entries were made in separate spaces for men who had joined the company after June 6.   Their strength was determined by counting the cards for all accessions and subtracting all cards for separations bearing corresponding names and serial numbers.   Thus for a given day the cumulated strength of old men plus the cumulated strength of replacements should exactly equal the total strength on the morning report and check the clerical operation.   No further use is made in the present analysis of the data on replacements, but it might be noted parenthetically that here exists a mine of data permitting an exact comparison on a day-to-day basis of casualty rates among men who were trained with their units and among replacements in the same units.

5. The daily figures entered on the ledger for the men who constituted the original cohort as of June 6 were now totaled for the eight-week period.   These data, in part, are summarized for the 108 rifle companies in Table 12 and for the 36 heavy weapons companies in Table 13.   The figure on average daily strength in Tables 12 and 13 is obtained by summing the daily figures for average strength (which are simply the average of strength at the beginning of the

---

[15] In a few instances, a small number of men were transferred from one company to another.   For bookkeeping purposes of the present analysis, they were recorded as "transferred out" of their present company and as "replacements" in their new company.   Such instances, fortunately, were rare and the analysis could not be materially affected, no matter how they were recorded.

day and strength at the end of the day) and dividing by the 56 days.

6. The nonbattle casualty rate for a company was computed by dividing the total nonbattle casualties by the average daily strength and multiplying by 100.

A final word may be said with respect to the relationship of battle and nonbattle casualties. In all regiments the correlation between the absolute number of battle and nonbattle casualties tended to be negative among rifle companies. If a company—as many did— lost the majority of its men through battle casualties, there would not be many left who would be exposed to the risk of nonbattle casualties. Of course, the converse could also be true—if the company lost a great many men through nonbattle casualties, there would be fewer left exposed to the risk of battle casualties. The former statement is somewhat more realistic for most regiments, however, due to the heavy initial casualties in storming the beaches.

All in all, the fairest way to compare the nonbattle casualties of the various companies seemed to be by taking account of the average number of men exposed to risk. This is measured by the average daily strength throughout the eight weeks. In all regiments the correlation between average daily strength and absolute number of nonbattle casualties tends to be positive. There were at least two alternative ways of proceeding. One was to express the nonbattle casualties as a function of the average daily strength and use the positive and negative deviations from this function as the measure with which to compare our pre D Day attitude data. The other alternative, which was adopted in the interest of simplicity, was to express the nonbattle casualties in a given company as a simple ratio of the average daily strength among men in the original cohort.

PART 2.   How Ratings of Individual Combat Performance
           Were Obtained

For the study of the relationship of *individual* background characteristics and precombat attitudes to combat performance, described in Section II of this chapter, a criterion of the latter was essential.

The criterion employed was in terms of rating procedures designed expressly for the purposes of the study, rather than in terms of routinely recorded statistics on casualties, awards, and the like, and provided an index of the combat performance of individual soldiers, rather than of entire organizations considered as units. Carefully standardized rating interviews were developed through pretesting and successive revisions of the procedure in several companies of one regiment. The combat performance of each available soldier for whom there were precombat data was rated in standardized fashion in comparison with the performance of other specific individuals doing the same kind of job, by the men who had had the best opportunity to observe his behavior in combat.

After learning with which platoons and squads the men for whom precombat data were available had seen action, a carefully trained Research Branch interviewer selected the men to do the rating. Most often the rater was a noncom in the same platoon (often in the same squad or section) as the subject who was to be rated. In general, the platoon leader, platoon sergeant, or platoon guide, plus the first sergeant and occasionally the company commander or executive officer, were interviewed to secure ratings on squad leaders and assistant squad leaders. To get ratings on men in squads, the interviewer started with the squad leader. For men in company headquarters,[16] the first sergeant, executive officer, etc., were interviewed. After obtaining one rating interview on a man, it was usually possible to obtain the names of other competent raters from the first interviewee. In all cases, the main criterion for selecting raters was the extent to which the rater was in a position to observe and evaluate the subject's performance in combat.

The interviews were, of course, conducted in privacy. The rater was given a brief introduction to explain the purpose of the interview, with special emphasis on the fact that the men would not be affected by what he said about them.[17] The interviewee was then

---

[16] Except company clerks, who were omitted from the study.

[17] The introduction was as follows (in the interviewer's own words):

"I am from the Research Branch of the War Department. The Research Branch does various kinds of scientific studies for the Army, which are used in planning Army policies, improving training, etc. [Show typical report, or explain that the data are reported only in percentages, etc., with no names or organizations.]

"At present we are collecting information on *factors related to men's performance in combat.* In preparation for one part of this important study, a number of men were selected at random in this regiment and some others *when they were in training back in the States. Now we are following up* some of the men in this Division for whom we have good records—especially of how they did in training—from the time when the outfit was back at Camp Adair. While we're here, we're *interviewing a lot* of platoon leaders and other personnel in infantry regiments, field artillery batteries, and other kinds of outfits.

"The men we use in this study, as in all Research Branch studies, *are kept anonymous.* To collect the information from many different sources, it is necessary to have names of some of the men but, actually, *names will not be used* at all once all of the information is collected.

"The only purpose of this interview is to help in making a scientific study of combat

asked to give the names of men who had certain specific jobs similar to the job of the subject or subjects for whom ratings were desired. For instance, if the man to be rated was a squad leader, and the interviewee a platoon sergeant during combat, he would be asked to give the names of all the men who were his squad leaders in combat, being prompted indirectly if necessary to include the subject on whom precombat data were available.   He would then be asked to name his combat assistant squad leaders.   The interviewer listed separately men who had been killed in action or given battlefield commissions.   These men were not rated along with the others, but were given ratings subsequently, as indicated below.   In this way about ten names were obtained on the main list—not less than nine if possible and sometimes as many as fifteen.[18]   Once the list was completed, the rater was given standardized instructions and asked specific questions to get *relative* ratings on the combat effectiveness of all the men on the list.   The verbatim instructions will give the clearest picture of the rating process:

Now I'd like to ask some questions to get your judgment on certain things about (some of) these men.

I want you to imagine that the war against Germany is still going on and you have it all to do over again; but suppose that you know everything you now actually know about what each of these men would be like in combat.   Imagine that your outfit was being prepared to go into combat, and assume that the type of combat you'd be up against would be just like what the outfit actually went through.

Suppose you had been told to weed out a certain number of men that would not be as good as some of the others in combat, in such a way that it would enable your outfit to do the best possible job in combat over a three or four month period.

Assume there would have been a chance to replace all the men weeded out with trained reinforcements and that any job for which you weeded out a man would be filled by a better man trained for that job.   [This point was elaborated if necessary.]

Now, which two (three)[19] of the men (on the list) would you *most hate to have*

men in general.   The information we get about individual men will *not affect* the man in any way.   This interview has *nothing to do with future assignments* or with redeployment of men in the Division.   As a matter of fact, a number of the men we want to find out about are not *even* in this Division any longer—*some of them were wounded in action, some killed in action*.   But as long as we are able to get information from their records, the information on them will be as valuable as information on men who are still in the Division.   None of the information you give us will be entered in any *man's record.*"

[18] For rating an ordinary member of a squad, other squad members comprised the list.   For men in company headquarters, names of other headquarters men in job roughly comparable in amount of exposure to fire were solicited.

[19] If there were 9, 10, 11, or 12 men on the main list, "two men" was used each time. If 13, or 14, "three" was used the first two times and "two" for the next two steps. If 15 or more, "three" was used throughout.   If less than 9, "two" was used the first time and 1 on later times, as required.

pulled out of your outfit—that is, which two (three) men would you *most want to keep in the outfit* in order to be sure of doing the *best possible job in combat* against the Germans?

In picking out the men, I want you to just consider the effect on how well the outfit would do in combat—please don't consider anything else such as how well you like the various men personally, and things like that. In the case of men wounded in action, just consider what they were like in combat up until the time they were wounded. [This was elaborated, if necessary, to make sure that the interviewee did not rate a man low because of his poor physical condition due to combat injury.] (This is all just for purposes of a study, and what men you pick here will have nothing at all to do with what happens to these particular men in the future.)

Now . . . which are the two (three)[19] men you would *most want to keep if the outfit were going into combat against the Germans?* [Interviewer writes a "1" after each of these two (or three) names.]

Now, in order to be sure the outfit would do the best possible job in combat, which two (three)[19] of the men would you feel it would be *most important* to *pull out* of the outfit to be replaced by *better men in their jobs.* [Interviewer writes a "5" after each of these.]

Now, after these two (three), [points to the No. 1 men] which two (three)[19] of the other men *would you name* next, as men you'd want to be sure to *keep* in the outfit if it were going into combat against the Germans? [Interviewer writes a "2" after each of these.]

Now which two (three)[19] of the other men would you name *next* as men that should be *pulled out* and replaced by better men (in order to do the best possible job in combat)? [Interviewer writes a "4" after each of these.]

[Interviewer writes a "3" after each of the remaining men.]

After the interviewee had finished rating the main list, it was pointed out to him that the numbers form a rating scale. He was then asked to rate any men who had been killed in action and any who had received battlefield commissions in similar terms by assigning a number.

In general, at least two rating interviews were obtained on each man in the sample, so that cases on which different raters disagreed in their judgments about the men could be eliminated from the analysis.[20]

---

[20] If the first two ratings on a given subject were "consistent," no more were deliberately obtained, though additional ratings might turn up incidentally to the rating of other men. The rating combinations regarded as "consistent" were: 1, 1; 1, 2; 2, 2; 3, 3; 4, 4; 4, 5; 5, 5. It will be remembered that a rating of 1 meant that an interviewee regarded the man as one of those he would most like to keep if the outfit were going into combat; 5 as one of the men he would most like to have replaced; 2 as one of those included in a second skimming of the most desirable men; 4 as one of those included in a second skimming of the least desirable men; and 3 indicates those remaining after this skimming process. If the first two ratings obtained were wholly inconsistent, no further rating was sought, unless the interviewer had previously felt real doubt about the intelligence or competence of one of the raters or about the degree of rapport attained in the interview. The rating combinations regarded as "wholly inconsistent" were: 1, 5; 1, 4; 2, 5; 2, 4.

If "partially inconsistent" ratings were obtained in the first two interviews (3, 4; 3, 5; 1, 3; 2, 3), at least one additional rating interview was obtained on the subject.

On the basis of the interview ratings, each subject was placed in one of three groups—above average, below average, and average (including indeterminate). Since some subjects were rated by two raters, some by three, and some by more than three, a rather complicated scheme was necessary for arriving at the final classification.[21]

The comparative rating procedure was adopted to avoid the pitfalls of absolute judgments—halo effect, and the lack of comparability of judgments from one outfit or kind of job or rater to another. To remove as far as possible another potential source of distortion, the respondents were kept from knowing which of the particular men on the list the interviewer was interested in.

We turn now to more detailed and interpretative analyses of attitudes of combat troops, on the ground and in the air, as related to a variety of characteristics of the individual soldiers and of the combat situations.

---

[21] The pattern of ratings characterizing each of the three groups varied according to the number of raters for a given subject. The groups were composed of men who received the following combinations of ratings:

	Ratings with two raters	SUM OF RATINGS WITH: Three raters	Four raters	Five raters	Mean rating for six or more raters
Above average	1, 1; 1, 2; 2, 2	3–6	4–8	5–10	1.00–2.19
Below average	3, 5; 4, 4; 4, 5; 5, 5	11–15	14–19	18–25	3.51–5.00
Average or indeterminate	(all other patterns)	7–10	9–13	11–17	2.20–3.50

CHAPTER 2

GENERAL CHARACTERISTICS OF GROUND COMBAT [1]

Introduction

COMBAT is the end toward which all the manifold activities of the Army are oriented, however indirectly. Organized combat is also the activity by which an Army is most differentiated from other social organizations. The role of the combat soldier may well be considered the most important single role for the understanding of the Army, not so much because of the number of men involved as because of its determining socio-psychological significance for combat and noncombat soldier alike. It was seen in Volume I that the very fact of whether a soldier was or was not assigned to combat duty defined one of the characteristics of his position which was most significant to him.

In studying the attitudes of American soldiers in combat, ground combat is probably the best place to start. Ground combat in the Second World War had more in common with traditional warfare than did the war in the air, and more American soldiers saw combat on the ground than in any other form. In a war in which the trend was clearly toward the development of intricate weapons requiring highly specialized skills for their management, ground warfare still required the maximum of physical and emotional endurance. This was particularly true in the Infantry, the most numerous branch involved in fighting on the ground, where the mechanical skills were subsidiary to personal skills of observation and maneuver, and these in turn were often subordinate to sheer endurance. In ground combat the stresses and countermotives involved in warfare can be seen in their simplest terms. The group of chapters to follow will provide a background against which the special features of aerial combat can be highlighted.

Few qualitatively new observations regarding the behavior of

---

[1] By Robin M. Williams, Jr., and M. Brewster Smith.

men in battle should be anticipated here. Insightful observers from a long series of recorded wars have reported, in essential agreement, upon a great many of the conceivable types of combat behavior. The recorded observations and insights are, however, fragmentary, relatively unsystematic, and nonquantitative. What can therefore be added is further systematization, based upon quantitative treatment of many soldiers' responses.

The following chapters deal with the soldier in combat on the ground. They will attempt to describe the social situation in which he fought, the attitudes he had, how he reacted to long-continued combat. They will pay some attention to the problem of fear in combat and the measures adopted for its control. They will focus briefly on the orphan of the Army—the individual combat replacement—and on the more fortunate men who joined their combat units away from the front. They will also describe some of the attitudes of combat soldiers toward their compatriots in the supply services and on the home front.

The present chapter is intended to provide a descriptive background of the general characteristics of combat as a social situation. Before proceeding to this, however, it will be profitable to pause for a brief survey of the place of combat in the context of the total activities of an active theater of operations, and for a glance at some of the various ways in which combat situations differ from one another. Seeing the combat situation in its military context will serve as a safeguard against misleading oversimplifications.

The Place of Combat in an Active Theater

The area of an active theater was normally divided into geographical subareas which corresponded roughly to the functions carried out in them. The general picture was as follows, from rear to front:

1. *Service and supply administrative areas:* This category usually included the largest part of the theater which was not in contact with the enemy. The main supply depots, repair installations, rear administrative headquarters, fixed medical installations, and the port-to-front transportation services were located here. The typical form of organization divided the area into subareas or "base sections," which were often combined administratively under one headquarters for the entire "communications zone." In a continental theater, one or more of the base sections was normally contiguous with army areas.

2. *Army areas:* Beginning a considerable distance behind the front and including the zone of actual combat were the areas under control of army groups and armies.   In the greater part of an army area, the principal activities differed little from those going on in the base sections to the rear.   Truck-driving companies from a base section, for example, moved supplies from a base section depot to another depot in an army area, whence other truck companies, this time assigned or attached to an army, moved the supplies to a point where some more forward element of the army picked them up.

3. *Corps areas:* An army area, or the more forward part of it, was usually subdivided into corps areas, each corps normally containing three or more divisions—in addition to service troops belonging to the corps and still performing the multiform functions of supply, maintenance, and evacuation.

4. *Division sectors:* The forward part of each corps area was divided into areas under the control of the different divisions.   A division is the smallest military unit which has all the kinds of troops necessary for maintaining itself in the field.   This means that, in addition to fighting troops, it too had its quartermaster truck drivers, its engineers, its military police, its ordnance to maintain its arms and vehicles, its signal troops to tend to communications, etc.

5. *Sectors held by smaller tactical units within a division:* These units, even at battalion level, had to allocate a considerable fraction of their personnel to the inescapable functions of housekeeping and supply.

The actual geographical arrangements of these areas varied with the military situation, the differences being greatest between continental and island theaters of operation.   The allocation of the smaller sectors at the front was constantly changing as units were shifted according to tactical plans, or relieved for rest and training.

This was the framework within which men were organized and sent into battle.   Even a simple sketch of the deployment of troops within a theater is enough to suggest a fact that is always surprising to the uninitiated: how small a part of a modern army ever comes into close combat with the enemy.   At peak strength the European theater contained over three million American troops.[2]   Yet there

[2] Cf. General Marshall's report, *The Winning of the War in Europe and the Pacific,* biennial report of the Chief of Staff of the United States Army, July 1, 1943, to June 30, 1945, to the Secretary of War.   Published for the War Department in cooperation with the Council on Books in Wartime by Simon and Schuster (no publication date), p. 42.

were probably no more than 50 divisions actually at the front, even in periods of maximum effort.[3]   Assuming for convenience that each division contained 15,000 men (actually they probably averaged nearer to 10,000), and assuming that all were in combat, this would give 750,000 men in action at any one time.   It certainly is an over-estimate to assume that all men in divisions were in actual combat. In an Infantry division, for example, the 36 rifle and heavy weapons companies account at most for only about one half of the division's strength.   Even if we assume that all divisional troops were in close combat, and add another 200,000 men for combat flyers in Air Forces, less than half of the men in Europe could reasonably have been called in combat at any one time.   The average figure for all theaters during the 1943–1945 period was certainly much lower.

What Is a Combat Outfit?

Within this context, just what soldiers are we to consider in combat for the purposes of our investigation?   In distinguishing a combat group, objective differences in the type of situation to which troops were subjected must of course be borne in mind.   But since we are primarily concerned with factors in which the men's own perceptions and evaluations are of paramount importance, the distinctions which the men themselves made are peculiarly relevant.

There was a tendency for those groups farthest removed from the battle zone, especially the civilian population at home, to generalize their impression of combat to include soldiers who would not themselves have considered what they were doing as combat.   The closer one went toward the areas of most intensive combat, the finer were the distinctions which were drawn.   In fact, most soldiers in a forward combat zone considered any duty to the rear of battalion headquarters as practically noncombat.

The typical soldier's conception of what constituted combat changed rather markedly during the course of the war.   In the beginning, when few troops were in direct contact with the enemy, the tendency was to consider that anyone who had been under enemy fire, including long-range shelling and bombing, had been in combat. Before the end of the war, the many men who had themselves experienced front-line fighting or had had close contact with Infantry troops were likely to deride this definition.   Front-line soldiers were

---

[3] As of May 7, 1945, there were sixty American divisions in the European theater, *ibid.*, pp. 52–53.   Presumably not all of these were committed at any one time.

decidedly not a good audience for tales of the dangers experienced by those who were subject to bombing in rear areas.

By the end of the European war, a definite pattern had emerged in regard to the kinds of units which the men at large thought had been in combat. Relevant data come from a survey of overseas soldiers which was conducted to gather evidence for appraising the point system for redeployment and demobilization prior to VJ Day. The men were asked how much combat credit should be given men in various kinds of outfits. As Chart I shows, there was a high degree of agreement among men in widely differing kinds of organizations about the types of troops which they thought should be given full combat credit. As one might expect, front-line infantrymen and tankmen would restrict combat credit more narrowly than would their fellow soldiers less exposed to intense combat. But the agreement among all four groups, including the men from rear communications zone units who were not themselves rated on the question, was great. On the one hand, more than 70 per cent of all the men, regardless of their own type of duty, agreed upon full combat credit for men in infantry rifle and heavy weapons companies, tank and tank destroyer companies, combat engineers, medical aid men and other front-line troops. At the other extreme, less than a fourth of the men, on the average, would allow full combat credit to the kinds of troops which can be grouped as forward headquarters and service troops—medical personnel in field hospitals; division, army and corps headquarters troops; and divisional supply troops. Intermediate combat troops—men in reconnaissance platoons, infantry cannon companies, chemical mortar outfits, and field artillery batteries, who if they engaged in close-range fighting did so less frequently than the first group—were accorded full combat credit by about half the men. There was more room for argument here: men in units of this sort were considerably more likely than others to think they should get full credit.

Table 1 shows the same data in greater detail. It will be seen that the grouping of types of troops in Chart I corresponds on the whole to marked differences in the proportion of men who would allot full combat credit to the specific units involved. The group of units classed as front-line troops is the most homogeneous in terms of the proportions of men voting full credit to the various kinds of units included in it.

These data agree in general with the judgment to which observation had already led research teams in the field. They furnish a useful basis for deciding which groups of men should be considered in analysis of the sociological and psychological aspects of combat. For practical purposes, it will be assumed here that when combat troops are mentioned the reference will be to line infantry, tank and tank destroyer units, and to medical and engineer troops serving along with these units. For the most part, consideration will be

CHART I

How GROUND AND SERVICE FORCE MEN WOULD ASSIGN COMBAT CREDIT TO DIFFERENT TYPES OF FORWARD GROUND TROOPS
(White Enlisted Men, European Theater, July 1945)

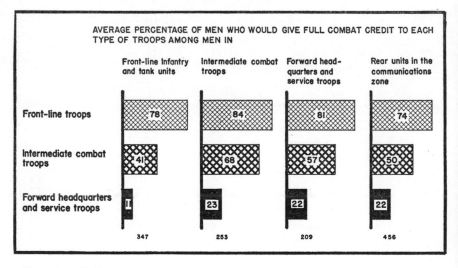

Data from S-220.

See Table 1 for the kinds of troops listed in each of these groupings. The present chart summarizes results given in greater detail in Table 1.

The numbers at the bottom of the bars are the numbers of cases on which percentages are based.

limited to men in infantry rifle and heavy weapons companies (the "lettered" companies), since for these the most adequate data are available.

Variables in the Combat Situation

Taken in their details, combat situations are almost infinitely varied. There are literally thousands of perceptible combinations of factors among the important variables. The list of "variables" itself is lengthy, including for example (cont. on page 66):

TABLE 1

RANKING OF TYPES OF UNITS ACCORDING TO AMOUNT OF COMBAT CREDIT THEY
SHOULD RECEIVE, AS JUDGED BY MEN IN VARIOUS TYPES OF OUTFITS*

TYPE OF TROOPS	PERCENTAGE WHO WOULD GIVE "FULL COMBAT CREDIT" TO EACH TYPE OF TROOPS AMONG MEN WHO WERE THEMSELVES IN:				
	Lettered Infantry and Tank Units ("front-line" units)	Field Artillery, Tank Destroyer, Chemical Mortar and Anti-aircraft Units	Divisional Troops Other Than Lettered Infantry and Field Artillery	Other Army and Corps Troops	Communications Zone Troops (rear area units)
Front-line Troops					
Rifle and heavy weapons companies	87	84	92	75	74
Aid men and other combat medics	79	84	84	76	72
Combat engineer units	76	85	85	81	73
Tank and tank destroyer companies	72	82	78	82	77
Average	79	84	85	79	74
Intermediate Combat Troops					
Reconnaissance platoons	60	73	76	76	61
Cannon companies (Infantry)	40	69	66	54	50
Chemical mortar outfits	33	53	43	43	38
Field artillery batteries	31	75	44	54	52
Average	41	68	57	57	50
Forward Headquarters and Service Troops					
Medics in field hospitals	23	43	32	42	39
Regimental headquarters troops	14	25	39	17	20
Division headquarters troops	6	20	16	15	18
Division quartermaster troops	6	13	15	24	20
Army and corps headquarters troops	4	13	7	12	15
Average	11	23	22	22	22
Number of cases	*347*	*253*	*82*	*127*	*456*
Percentage of men reporting "actual combat" experience	81	76	67	27	13

* Survey of a cross section of white enlisted men in the European theater during July 1945 (S-220).
The question was:
  "After VJ Day, if points were to be given for time in combat, which groups of men do you think
  should be given combat credit? Check how much combat credit you think should be given to
  men in *each* of these kinds of units. (Check *one* answer opposite *each* type of outfit.)"

_____ Should give them full combat credit
_____ Should give them part combat credit
_____ Should not give them any combat credit

1. Terrain (jungle, plain, forest, open areas or cities and towns, fortified positions, level or hilly or mountainous, etc.)
2. Climate and weather (all degrees of temperature, moisture, variability or monotony, etc.)
3. Adequacy of supply (ammunition, food, water, clothing, shelter, equipment of all kinds).
4. Adequacy of replacement system.
5. Competence of leadership.
6. Adequacy of troops' training.
7. Adequacy of medical attention.
8. Type and intensity of enemy resistance, including:
    a. Weapons used (tanks, artillery, planes, Infantry weapons).
    b. Intensity and duration of fire.
    c. Tactics (flanking attacks, frontal assaults, infiltration, night vs. day actions, etc.)
    d. Morale of enemy force (easy surrender or fanatical resistance).
9. Types and numbers of supporting or cooperating arms (planes, artillery, tanks, heavy weapons, reconnaissance units, rifle companies, etc.)
10. Adequacy of communication within the unit and with other units.
11. Goal of the unit's mission, including:
    a. Defense against local counterattack.
    b. Defense against large-scale attack.
    c. Raid or reconnaissance in force to gain information and/or take enemy position and/or do specified damage to the enemy.
    d. Patrolling to explore enemy deployment or to take prisoners.
    e. Local attack with specified objectives.
    f. General attack, aimed at large-scale maneuvers.
12. Success of antecedent action and prospects for success in ensuing mission.
13. Duration and severity of combat without a rest.
14. Casualties incurred.
15. Anticipated duration of action; anticipated length of the war.

Many other relevant variables could be outlined, but these are perhaps enough to indicate the great range of possible combinations. Within this range of variation, certain broad types of situations recurred often enough to make them rather generally relevant to understanding the context of combat behavior. A few of the more important, accordingly, should be outlined.

First of all, there was the classic picture of an advancing army fighting along an organized but flexible front. Where this was the framework of battle, there was a fairly clear demarcation between front and rear. In the extreme forward zone, the troops would be closing with the enemy. In this area, although hand-to-hand fighting may have been less conspicuous in this war than in World War I, there was always much close-range fighting. In the forward zone, the typical weapons were the grenade, the rifle, the pistol, the machine gun, the rocket missile (bazooka, *Panzerfaust*, etc.), and the mortar. During a rapid advance, the attacking troops were likely to be relatively free from artillery fire: they were moving rapidly and might be intermingled with enemy troops and the attack might be threatening enemy artillery positions.[4]   Since the enemy would typically be suffering considerable disorganization, the advancing troops would take many prisoners and suffer relatively light casualties.   The situation was favorable to high morale and to a sense of group cohesion in carrying out a great achievement.

In opposition to the relatively distinct fighting lines of the organized but fluid front was the confusion of infiltration warfare.   This is best exemplified in the jungle fighting of the campaigns in the Pacific.   Here the opposing forces were often so intermingled that a front could hardly be said to exist.   Combat units were continually under the necessity of maintaining organized perimeter defenses around their entire position.   Night infiltration attacks were common, and snipers often presented a continual harassing menace. Actual fighting was done in very small groups or individually.   Contact between friendly units was often tenuous and difficult to maintain.   The combination of relative isolation, confusion, and incessant danger—even far behind the most advanced positions —imposed a peculiarly insidious strain upon morale.

A third major type of battle was the assault on fortified positions. This was a type of action which put a premium upon technical knowledge and skill.   Such assaults always carried the threat of especially heavy casualties, which could be avoided only by superior weapons and tactics.   Careful planning was essential to success, and the action might be precisely rehearsed in detail long beforehand.   The task was made possible by all the devices specifically designed for the purpose, such as armor-piercing shells, flame throwers, specialized demolition charges.   American troops usually had these tools of war, and their leaders stressed ingenuity in tactics rather than the bloody frontal attack.   Nevertheless, when it was deemed necessary to take fortifications quickly in the face of an alert and resolute defending force, the battle called primarily for a morale which would enable men to press on in an organized team even when casualties seemed terribly great.

Fourth was the operation probably most dreaded by experienced combat soldiers: the assault on defended beaches or across defended water barriers.   As one veteran of three such landings said when

[4] As many combat soldiers will agree, this relative immunity from artillery was by no means perfect.   In fact, the situation of rapid advance required careful coordination to prevent troops from being fired upon by their own artillery, or attacked by their own aircraft.

his unit was being alerted for its fourth ordeal: "Amphibious—that is the only word that gets morale down around here." Landings on hostile beaches were subject to particular hazards of coordination, and unexpected events were normal.[5] The initial assault was always dogged by the unavoidable lack of heavy equipment and weapons, the probability of seasickness, and the expectation of heavy losses. To press an aggressive attack across open beaches raked by fire made extreme demands on the psychological preparation of the soldier. Cool and aggressive leadership was especially important. The quality needed is illustrated by the story of the officer who shouted to his troops huddled in the sand, "We are getting killed on the beaches—let's go inland and get killed."

War was not, of course, always a matter of attacking and advancing. Defending a position against heavy enemy attack could involve some of the most intensive combat. When the defending force had its back to the wall and could be subjected to round-the-clock harassment by the enemy, as on the Anzio beachhead in the spring of 1944, the corrosive effects of battle pressed the limits of human endurance for combat and service troops alike. In such situations there might be no hope of respite for indefinite periods.

The confusion and disorganization of retreat following an enemy break-through was certainly among the most difficult situations a soldier could face. The Ardennes bulge of December 1944 comes to mind. The uncertainty which screens almost any form of battle reaches a maximum here at a time when the resources of the men are hardest pressed. More frequent, happily, than the sudden collapse was the withdrawal—on larger or smaller scale—under pressure of enemy superiority. Aside from the psychological loss of abandoning hard-earned ground, such withdrawing action did not necessarily present special difficulty.

In contrast to these kinds of battles was the holding action. During intervals between more vigorous types of action, the mission might be merely to hold a stable front, as was the case during considerable periods toward the end of the Italian campaign. Small-arms fire was largely confined to patrol activity, but there was a certain amount of exchange of artillery fire. During the daytime, the men could lie low in cellars or dugouts; at night outposts were carefully manned against infiltration. Such a stable front, though

---

[5] See "Omaha Beachhead," War Department Historical Branch, Government Printing Office, Washington, D. C., 1946, for a circumstantial picture of this in the Normandy landings.

more clearly defined than in any other battle situation, was still an area of strong points and outposts rather than a visible line. Living conditions could vary during a holding action from poor to the best that were ever found in combat, when men had time to fix up relatively comfortable dugouts, and luxuries such as hot food could sometimes be brought up from the rear. Nevertheless, tedium, the anticipation and fact of frequent night patrol duty, the effects of harassing artillery and mortar fire, and the cumulative effects of poor living and sleeping conditions made this easiest of all combat conditions no real respite for the combat soldier.

The Combat Situation in Europe and the Pacific

There were important differences between the European and Pacific campaigns which the reader should keep in mind in evaluating the discussions and data to follow. Some of these differences may appropriately be summarized here.

In Italy and on the mainland of Europe after the landings in Normandy, the main bodies of combat troops were almost continually committed to action up to the closing weeks before the capitulation of Germany. Although men were given short rest periods, there were divisions in which a majority of the troops were in the line for months on end. Furthermore, the Germans made extensive and effective use of artillery. Partly for this reason, casualties were very heavy during many of the periods in which the front was relatively stable. Long periods of such heavy losses occurred, for example, in Normandy, in the Hurtgen Forest, in the fortified areas centering on the Siegfried Line, and at Anzio and Cassino. On the other hand, the troops were fighting in urbanized countries among people with a culture broadly similar to their own. Therefore, when they were out of the line, there were relatively favorable opportunities for familiar types of relaxation among relatively friendly populations. The troops were also favored by climatic conditions which, although at many times difficult, were not enervating and were reasonably similar to those encountered in their past experience. Furthermore, even with the winter menaces of trench foot and respiratory illness, they did not have to contend with such a persistent physical hazard as malaria proved to be in the Pacific.[6]

In the Pacific, for the first two years of the war, battle casualties were relatively light. Only small bodies of troops were committed

---

[6] However, malaria did constitute a problem in North Africa, Sicily, and Italy.

to action, and these only intermittently. The strategy of island-hopping typically meant that combat troops experienced short periods of intense fighting followed by long intervals out of combat. The sporadic character of any given organization's fighting was in sharp contrast to the situation in Europe. Japanese resistance was determined, and the fighting was often incredibly grueling, but the actual incidence of battle casualties suffered by the average division was considerably less than in the war against Germany. It must be remembered that the Pacific campaigns in which the Japanese made much use of artillery and heavy weapons generally came very late in the war. The heavy casualties in such actions as those on Saipan, Iwo Jima, and Okinawa were certainly not typical of what had happened in the preceding three years. Thus, with respect to *duration of continuous combat* and *incidence of battle casualties*, the Pacific fighting during the greater part of the war may be said to have been less severe than the combat in Europe.

In nearly every other respect, however, the men in the Pacific faced conditions which severely tested morale and combat efficiency. Infiltration warfare rather than a well-defined front was the rule. As compared with the forces in Europe, a high proportion of the combat troops had spent a long time overseas. Opportunities for relaxation when out of combat were typically poor. Many soldiers had the experience of going through a campaign only to camp for long months under trying physical circumstances on an isolated island. The incidence of malaria and other diseases was high, especially in the earlier phases of the war. For example, among two divisions surveyed by the Research Branch in the South Pacific in March and April 1944, 66 per cent of the enlisted Infantry veterans in one division, which had been overseas for more than two years, said they had been hospitalized or sent to a rest camp for malaria, as did 41 per cent in the other division, which had been overseas for a year and a half.[7]

The impact on the men of these differences between the two campaigns can be seen in Charts II and III. On the one hand, as Chart II shows, both officers and enlisted infantrymen in divisions which fought in the Mediterranean were more likely than their compatriots in the Pacific to say that combat became more frightening the more they saw of it. The officer samples in the two theaters are comparable, having been obtained at the same time in 1944. Al-

---

[7] Based on a survey of a cross section of veteran infantrymen in the divisions. Number of cases was 1,428 and 1,364, respectively (S-100).

though the officers in both theaters were markedly less likely than the enlisted men to admit fear in battle, there is a striking difference between the responses of officers in the two theaters.   The enlisted sample from the Mediterranean theater was surveyed a year later, and includes troops who saw more prolonged combat than any

CHART II

FEAR OF BATTLE IN THE MEDITERRANEAN AND PACIFIC CAMPAIGNS
(Infantry Enlisted Men and Company Grade Officers in
Veteran Infantry Divisions)

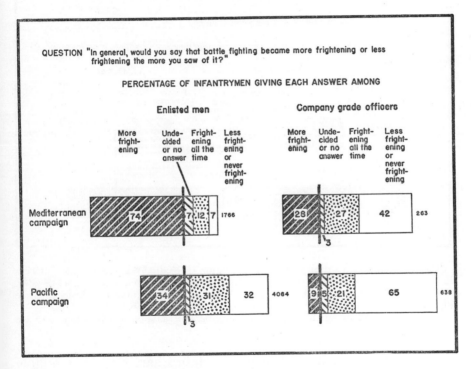

QUESTION "In general, would you say that battle fighting became more frightening or less frightening the more you saw of it?"

PERCENTAGE OF INFANTRYMEN GIVING EACH ANSWER AMONG

For source of data see footnote 8.
The numbers following the bars are the numbers of cases on which percentages are based.

others in the war.   Probably the average of combat troops who fought in France and Germany would not have differed so greatly in their responses from the men who fought in the Pacific.   But the difference does illustrate a real contrast between the two major campaigns of the war.[8]

[8] In the Mediterranean, enlisted men were from a cross section of line infantrymen in four Infantry divisions surveyed in Italy in April 1945 (S-177).   The wording of the question was slightly different for them: "In general, would you say that combat

On the other hand, officers of divisions which fought in the Mediterranean were somewhat more likely to report that they themselves and their men were in good physical condition than were officers of

CHART III

(Company Grade Infantry Officers in Three Pacific and
Two Mediterranean Divisions, April 1944)

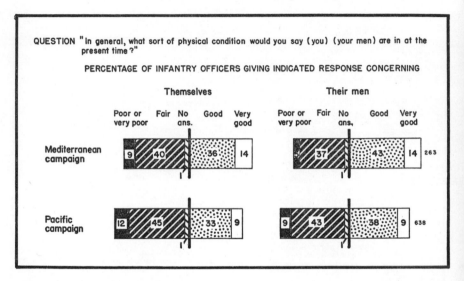

The Mediterranean sample was a cross section of company grade Infantry officers in two divisions which fought in North Africa and Sicily, surveyed in April 1944 (S-101).

The Pacific sample was a cross section of company grade Infantry officers in three divisions which fought in the Pacific, surveyed in April 1944 (S-101).

The numbers following the bars are the numbers of cases on which percentages are based.

divisions in the Pacific,[9] as may be seen in Chart III. The sample of officers is the same as in Chart II. Since the difference in regard

becomes more frightening or less frightening the more you see of it?" The category "never frightening" which was checked by no more than 2 per cent of the enlisted men and 5 per cent of the officers in the Pacific was omitted. The officers were from a cross section of company grade officers in two divisions which fought in both Africa and Sicily (S-101), surveyed in April 1944 at the same time that the enlisted men and officers in the Pacific were surveyed.

In the Pacific, enlisted men were from a cross section of veteran infantrymen in three Infantry divisions surveyed in the South and Central Pacific in March–April 1944 (S-100). Officers were from the same divisions and surveyed concurrently (S-101).

[9] In general, officers reported their men to be in better physical condition than the men themselves reported. The question was asked of enlisted men in only one division in Europe at that time, and not asked in the Mediterranean theater, so the results for enlisted men are not shown. They agree in direction of difference.

to fearfulness of combat as they reported it was in the opposite direction, the present difference between the theaters must be primarily the result of the several respects mentioned above in which the Pacific war was more arduous.

While there were differences as noted between combat in the Pacific and in Europe, there were also many similarities.   In the spring of 1944 veteran officers of Infantry rifle companies were presented with a check list of twenty factors which might be expected to have an effect on battle performance.   The instructions read as follows: "Even after the most successful fighting, it is useful to look back and see ways in which battle performance might have been still better.   In those instances where our battle performance as you saw it was not quite as good as it might have been, how much do you think each of the factors below contributed?   Put *one* check mark after each item."

Then followed a series of items, such as, for example, "Lack of necessary weapons or tools."   The check-list categories for each item were:

        _____ I never observed this
        _____ This had little effect on our battle performance
        _____ This had a rather bad effect on our battle performance
        _____ This had a very bad effect on our battle performance

In Chart IV a comparison is presented of the responses of officers in two divisions which saw heavy jungle fighting against the Japanese in the Solomons with the responses of officers in two divisions which played a large part in the North African and Sicilian campaigns. Since, as has been pointed out, the campaigns were quite different in these two parts of the world, differences in testimony of officers should appear where relevant to actual differences.

Actually, there is quite high agreement, as between the two parts of the world, as to what factors were most frequently observed as having a "very bad" or "rather bad" effect on combat performance. Much the most frequently cited in both areas was "Fatigue of troops from being in combat too long" (by 72 per cent of officers in the Pacific, 71 per cent in Europe).   Next in both areas was the problem of inadequate reconnaissance of enemy positions (cited by 52 per cent in the Pacific, 60 per cent in Europe).   "Lack of food, clothing, or personal equipment" was relatively high on the list in both areas (Pacific, 43 per cent; Europe, 36 per cent), as was "Underestimation of the fighting ability of the enemy" (Pacific, 38 per cent; Europe, 32 per cent).

CHART IV

Testimony of Infantry Company Officers as to Factors in Battle Performance—Pacific and Europe, Spring 1944

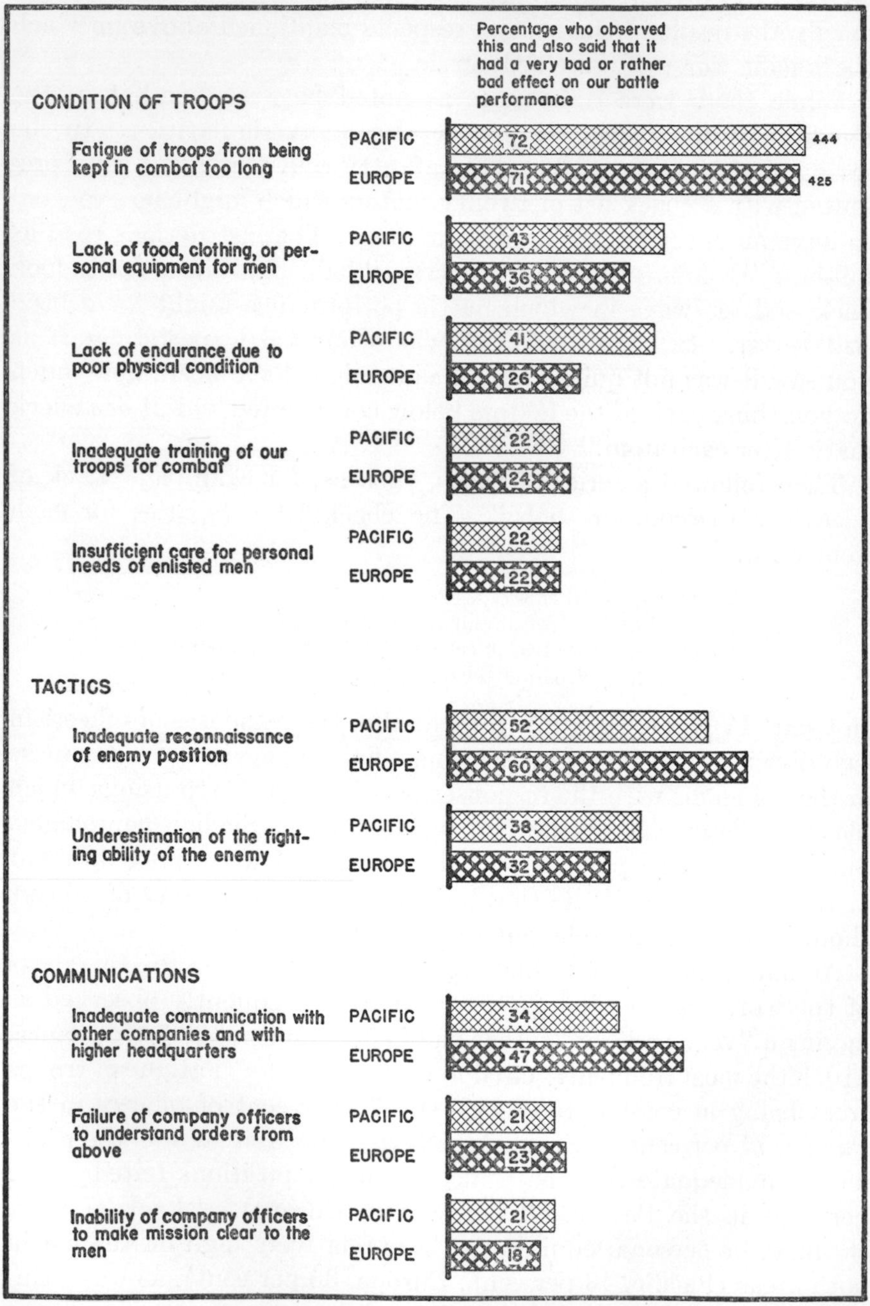

Percentage who observed this and also said that it had a very bad or rather bad effect on our battle performance

CONDITION OF TROOPS

Fatigue of troops from being kept in combat too long
- PACIFIC: 72 — 444
- EUROPE: 71 — 425

Lack of food, clothing, or personal equipment for men
- PACIFIC: 43
- EUROPE: 36

Lack of endurance due to poor physical condition
- PACIFIC: 41
- EUROPE: 26

Inadequate training of our troops for combat
- PACIFIC: 22
- EUROPE: 24

Insufficient care for personal needs of enlisted men
- PACIFIC: 22
- EUROPE: 22

TACTICS

Inadequate reconnaissance of enemy position
- PACIFIC: 52
- EUROPE: 60

Underestimation of the fighting ability of the enemy
- PACIFIC: 38
- EUROPE: 32

COMMUNICATIONS

Inadequate communication with other companies and with higher headquarters
- PACIFIC: 34
- EUROPE: 47

Failure of company officers to understand orders from above
- PACIFIC: 21
- EUROPE: 23

Inability of company officers to make mission clear to the men
- PACIFIC: 21
- EUROPE: 18

Data from S-101 representing 444 veteran officers from two Infantry divisions in the South Pacific and 425 veteran officers from two Infantry divisions in the Mediterranean.

The numbers following the bars are the numbers of cases on which percentages are based.

CHART IV (Continued)

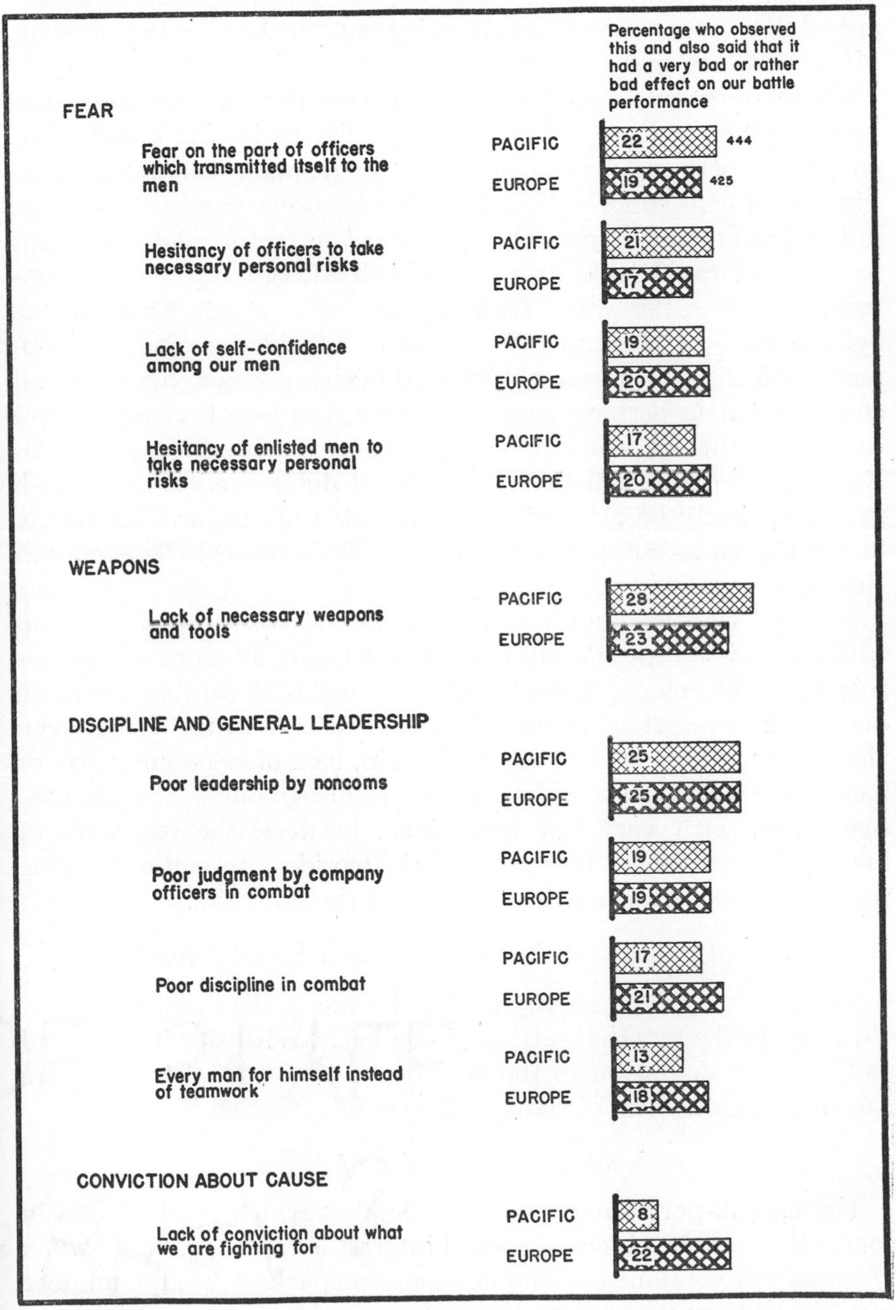

Percentage who observed this and also said that it had a very bad or rather bad effect on our battle performance

FEAR

Fear on the part of officers which transmitted itself to the men
PACIFIC 22 444
EUROPE 19 425

Hesitancy of officers to take necessary personal risks
PACIFIC 21
EUROPE 17

Lack of self-confidence among our men
PACIFIC 19
EUROPE 20

Hesitancy of enlisted men to take necessary personal risks
PACIFIC 17
EUROPE 20

WEAPONS

Lack of necessary weapons and tools
PACIFIC 28
EUROPE 23

DISCIPLINE AND GENERAL LEADERSHIP

Poor leadership by noncoms
PACIFIC 25
EUROPE 25

Poor judgment by company officers in combat
PACIFIC 19
EUROPE 19

Poor discipline in combat
PACIFIC 17
EUROPE 21

Every man for himself instead of teamwork
PACIFIC 13
EUROPE 18

CONVICTION ABOUT CAUSE

Lack of conviction about what we are fighting for
PACIFIC 8
EUROPE 22

As would be expected from the previous discussion, the officers in the Pacific considerably more frequently cited "Lack of endurance due to poor physical condition" than did the officers in Europe (41 per cent as against 26 per cent).

There were only two items which were significantly more frequently cited in Europe than in the Pacific as having a bad effect on battle performance. One was "Inadequate communications with other companies and with higher headquarters" (34 per cent in the Pacific and 47 per cent in Europe), a factor related perhaps to the more rapid mobility of the North African and Sicilian campaigns. The other was "Lack of conviction about what we are fighting for"—a phenomenon obviously difficult for officers to observe, and one which was seldom cited in either area as having a bad effect on battle performance. However, the fact that only 8 per cent cited this in the Pacific, as compared with 22 per cent in Europe, reflects a statistically significant difference and one which may very likely be attributable to the attitude toward the enemy in the Pacific as compared with the attitude toward the enemy in Europe.

The rest of this chapter and the chapters which follow will deal with some of the specific subjects cited in Chart IV along with other subjects. The chart, in detail, must be read with caution, for there may have been reticence on the part of officers in testifying, even though anonymously, to poor leadership, lack of self-confidence, or fear. The main point which this chart brings out is the close resemblance, with very few exceptions, between the responses of battle-tried officers in two parts of the world as to factors making for bad battle performance as *they* rated these factors.

General Characteristics of Combat as a Social Situation

The preceding brief survey explored some of the more important variables in the external setting of combat. With this background to give some definition to the subject we can proceed to the more salient characteristics of combat as a *social* situation.

Combat as a Situation of Stress

The one all-pervading quality of combat which most obviously marks it off as the object of special interest is that it was a *situation of stress*. It combined in one not-too-neat package a large number of major factors which men everywhere tend to regard as things to be avoided: "Adjustment to combat . . . means not only adjustment to killing, but also adjustment to danger, to frustration, to uncertainty, to noise and confusion and particularly to the wavering faith in the efficiency or success of one's comrades and command." [10]

The main types of stress in combat are reasonably clear. Not necessarily in order of their importance, they are:

1. Threats to life and limb and health.
2. Physical discomfort—from lack of shelter, excessive heat or cold, excessive moisture or dryness, inadequacy of food or water or clothing; from insects and disease; from filth; from injuries or wounds; from long-continued fatigue and lack of sleep.
3. Deprivation of sexual and concomitant social satisfactions.
4. Isolation from accustomed sources of affectional assurance.
5. Loss of comrades, and sight and sound of wounded and dying men.
6. Restriction of personal movement—ranging from the restrictions of military law to the immobility of the soldier pinned down under enemy fire.
7. Continual uncertainty and lack of adequate cognitive orientation.
8. Conflicts of values
   a. between the requirements of duty and the individual's impulses toward safety and comfort
   b. between military duty and obligations to family and dependents at home, to whose well-being the soldier's survival is important
   c. between informal group codes, as of loyalty to comrades, and the formal requirements of the military situation which may sometimes not permit mutual aid
   d. between previously accepted moral codes and combat imperatives.
9. Being treated as a means rather than an end in oneself; seemingly arbitrary and impersonal demands of coercive authority; sense of not counting as an individual.
10. Lack of "privacy"; the incessant demands and petty irritations of close living within the group.
11. Long periods of enforced boredom, mingled with anxiety, between actions.
12. Lack of terminal *individual* goals; poverty and uncertainty of individual rewards.

All of these broad categories of stress were found in combat situations. Not all of them were always operative for a given group or individual; some combat soldiers never experienced some of them *as stress* at all. Depending upon circumstances, also, the intensity of any particular sort of stress varied greatly. Each type of stress deserves preliminary comment. Although much that will be said is obvious, an explicit consideration has the advantage of giving at the outset a fairly full picture of what the combat men had to withstand.

Fear of death or injury is potentially present among persons gen-

---

[10] Report of Special Commission of Civilian Psychiatrists Covering Psychiatric Policy and Practice in the United States Army Medical Corps, European Theater, 20 April to 8 July, 1945. Mimeographed report, p. 12.

erally.   Combat as the prime occasion of deliberate risks to life and limb imposed severe stress, involving the deepest anxieties and the most primitive threats to personal integrity.   Chapter IV will discuss some of the measures the Army adopted for the control of fear. The data there presented indicate beyond any doubt the broad extent to which the men themselves admitted the fear they felt in battle.

Whereas any newspaper reader or movie-goer has a definite, sometimes exaggerated, notion of the dangers of combat, the degree of stress imposed by sheer physical discomfort is perhaps less widely

TABLE 2

AVERAGE AMOUNT OF SLEEP REPORTED BY INFANTRYMEN DURING A QUIET PERIOD

QUESTION: "When you were last on active duty, how many hours of sleep did you average each 24 hours?"

	Percentage of infantrymen giving each answer
Less than 2 hours	3
2 to 4 hours	28
5 to 6 hours	54
7 or more hours	13
No answer	2
Total	100

Survey of 1,766 veterans in rifle and heavy weapons companies of four Infantry divisions, Italy, early April 1945 (S-177).

appreciated.   Many a soldier will remember the mud and the K-rations after the memory of danger has grown dim.   Rarely, furthermore, was the combat soldier subject merely to one kind of physical discomfort; his ills came in flocks.[11]   It is thus not merely that he was cold and wet, but that he was also deadly tired, dirty, and without prospect of shelter.   Or, it is not only that his stomach staged a minor revolt against still another can of pork loaf, but that he was simultaneously lying in a filthy foxhole under steaming heat and incessantly irritated by swarms of malaria-bearing mosquitoes. The effects of long-continued, multiple physical discomforts of this sort were intensely distressing; and if no relief was in prospect for an indeterminable future, they could come to seem well nigh insupportable.   It is believed that most ground troops who saw frontline duty in this war will agree with this general appraisal.

Two illustrations to bring home the omnipresence of this kind of

---

[11] Cf. Bill Mauldin, *Up Front* (Henry Holt & Co., New York, 1945), pp. 144–51.

combat stress may be drawn from a survey made in Italy shortly before the end of the campaign in that theater. Although the front had been quiet for several months of holding action at the time the survey was made—and conditions were therefore probably as favorable as ever exist in combat—nearly one third of the men said that they averaged 4 hours or less of sleep out of each 24 hours the last time they were in the line, while only 13 per cent said they averaged 7 or more hours of sleep a day (Table 2).

Over half the men said they did not get as much to eat as they needed. Those who said they did not, gave the reason for the most

TABLE 3

EATING FRUSTRATIONS REPORTED BY COMBAT INFANTRYMEN DURING A
QUIET PERIOD

QUESTIONS: "When you were last on active combat duty, did you get as much to eat as you needed?"

"If you did not get as much to eat as you needed, what was the reason?"

	Percentage of infantrymen giving each answer
We couldn't get food	22
I didn't like the kind of food we had	30
I didn't feel like eating	10
Some other reason	*
I got as much as I needed	36
No answer	2
Total	100

Survey of 1,766 veterans in rifle and heavy weapons companies of four Infantry divisions, Italy, early April 1945 (S-177).
* Less than 0.5 per cent.

part that they did not like the food available, or that they couldn't get the food. (Table 3.) Again it should be remembered that conditions in the months prior to administration of the questionnaire had been exceptionally favorable. Hot food at the front at this time was by no means unheard of.

Opportunities for regularized sex relations are a necessary part of the institutions of every large social system. The average young man in our culture does not make a virtue out of sexual deprivation.[12] Furthermore, there are few psychiatric generalizations which are more widely documented than that sexual relations typically in-

[12] Ample evidence to this effect is presented in A. C. Kinsey, W. B. Pomeroy, and C. F. Martin, *Sexual Behavior in the Human Male* (W. B. Saunders Co., Philadelphia, 1948).

volve much more than physical gratification as such. They are bound up with needs for security, for feeling oneself a valued person, for reassurance that one is considered worth affection. The ostensibly sexual is often the bearer of many personal needs which have little to do with physical gratification as usually viewed. For men in combat there was a particular significance in all this. Under great anxiety and insecurity, men tended to lose many of their usual long-term perspectives. At the same time, their need for emotional reassurance was especially great; faced with the immediate possibility of personal annihilation amid the vast impersonal destruction of war, hedonistic drives and socially derived needs combined to make sexual deprivation a major stress.[13] A closely allied fact is the strain imposed upon most normal individuals by having to live under conditions of great difficulty without the taken-for-granted affectional support which is typically supplied by one's family, close friends, and local community.

Grief, rage, and horror are emotions which occurred among masses of men in every day of battle. Because the combat soldier was trained to anticipate and meet the shocks which occasion those emotions, he was better able to bear them than his civilian counterparts. Still, the recurring evidences of death, destruction, and mutilation imposed a sapping emotional drain upon the typical American soldier. And because men in combat were closely bound together by mutual dependence and affectional ties they were correspondingly shaken by the loss of comrades. Grief was added to fear, fatigue, and discouragement.[14]

The extent to which the front-line infantryman was exposed to the sight of death and suffering during a combat career may be underlined by data from the survey of combat infantrymen in Italy, only 10 per cent of whom had seen less than 3 months of combat and 54 per cent of whom had seen 6 months of combat or more. Of these men, 87 per cent said they had seen a close friend killed or wounded in action, while 83 per cent said they had seen "a man's nerves crack up" at the front.[15] Data from a division which saw

---

[13] Cf. Mauldin, *op. cit.*, p. 158; Jack Belden, *Still Time to Die* (Harper and Bros., New York, 1943), pp. 29–30.

[14] Report of Special Commission of Civilian Psychiatrists, *op. cit.*, p. 23.

[15] Survey of a cross section of 1,766 members of Infantry rifle and heavy weapons companies of four divisions, Italy, early April 1945 (S-177). The questions were:

"Have you ever had the experience of seeing a close friend killed or wounded in action?"

———— Yes

———— No

combat in the South Pacific indicate that, as might be expected, the effect of these stresses was cumulative. The men were asked how often they had various physical reactions to the dangers of battle when they were under fire. On the assumption that men who were successfully resisting the effects of combat stress should show relatively fewer of these physical symptoms when under fire, one

CHART V

DEGREE OF REPORTED BODILY EXPRESSION OF FEAR IN BATTLE, IN
RELATION TO VARIOUS SOURCES OF STRESS, IN COMBINATION

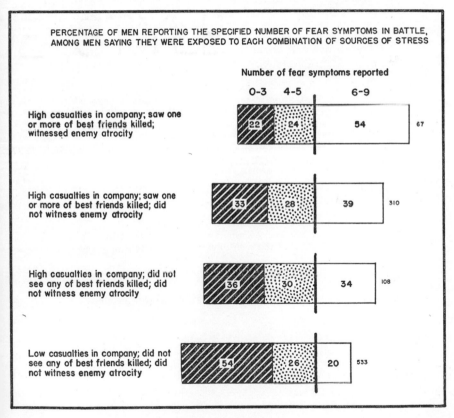

PERCENTAGE OF MEN REPORTING THE SPECIFIED NUMBER OF FEAR SYMPTOMS IN BATTLE, AMONG MEN SAYING THEY WERE EXPOSED TO EACH COMBINATION OF SOURCES OF STRESS

Number of fear symptoms reported

	0-3	4-5	6-9	
High casualties in company; saw one or more of best friends killed; witnessed enemy atrocity	22	24	54	67
High casualties in company; saw one or more of best friends killed; did not witness enemy atrocity	33	28	39	310
High casualties in company; did not see any of best friends killed; did not witness enemy atrocity	36	30	34	108
Low casualties in company; did not see any of best friends killed; did not witness enemy atrocity	54	26	20	533

Data from a survey of a cross section of combat veterans in an Infantry division in the South Pacific, March 1944 (S-100).

For the wording of questions and check-list categories see footnote 17.

The numbers following the bars are the numbers of cases on which percentages are based.

"Have you ever seen a man's nerves crack up at the front?"
_____ Yes
_____ No

Time in combat included all duty within range of enemy artillery.

would expect men who have been exposed to more severe stresses to admit to a greater number of symptoms.[16]   As Chart V indicates, such is indeed the case.   Men who said that their companies had suffered heavy casualties, that they had seen one of their best friends killed in action, and that they had witnessed enemy atrocities, reported many more fear symptoms than those who had not been subjected to any of these stresses;[17] groups intermediate in amount of stress were also intermediate in respect to fear symptoms.   The reservation must be made that, to the extent that more fearful men were more likely to overestimate casualties and more likely to interpret a given enemy action as an atrocity, the relationship may be spuriously high.

Loss of freedom of movement within accustomed limits is commonly felt as a deprivation.   The universality of confinement as

---

[16] It may have been that some men were hesitant to admit physical symptoms of fear.   In the context in which the question was asked, it seems unlikely that this happened to any great extent.   Even if the differential effects noted should be the result of greater frankness in admitting fear rather than less control of fear at a somatic level, this would represent only another way in which exposure to stimuli of this kind corroded the individual's ability to resist the stressful situation.

[17] The questions on sources of stress were:

"About how many battle casualties (killed and wounded) has your present company had since you first went into combat with it?"

_____ More than $\frac{1}{2}$ of the men have been casualties
_____ Between $\frac{1}{4}$ and $\frac{1}{2}$ of the men have been casualties
_____ Less than $\frac{1}{4}$ of the men have been casualties
_____ Don't know

(Comparison is between men checking the first or second category and all others.)

"Did you ever see any of your best friends get killed in combat?"

_____ Yes
_____ No

"How about atrocities?   Did you personally ever see with your own eyes a case of a Japanese using methods of fighting or treating prisoners which you would call dirty or inhuman?"

_____ No
_____ Yes

The question on fear symptoms stated, "Soldiers who have been under fire report different *physical reactions* to the *dangers of battle*.   Some of these reactions are given in the following list.   How often have you had these reactions when you were under fire?   *Check one answer after each of the reactions listed to show how often you had the reaction.*   Please do it carefully."

Following was a list of 10 physical symptoms of fear, in regard to each of which the men were to check "often," "sometimes," "once," or "never."   Men were counted as having had a fear symptom if they checked "often" or "sometimes" for it.   Men who failed to answer the questions are omitted.   The list of symptoms is presented in Chapter 4 on "Problems Related to the Control of Fear in Combat."

punishment is itself testimony to this human trait. The combat soldier was restricted by orders, under military law, to a narrow range of freedom of movement. Even when his unit was not committed to action, he might, for example, be forbidden to move outside his platoon area except under strict and limited orders. Enemy action, and the threat of enemy action, still further restricted his freedom of mobility. Under enemy fire, mobility may literally be reduced to zero, as when a soldier was pinned in his foxhole for hours or days. Many men have testified that the severest fear-producing situation they encountered in combat was just such immobilization under artillery or mortar fire.

War is a special province of chance, and the gods of luck rise to full stature on the field of battle. Uncertainty and confusion are inseparable from combat: "Every action . . . only produces a counteraction on the enemy's part, and the thousands of interlocking actions throw up millions of little frictions, accidents and chances, from which there emanates an all-embracing fog of uncertainty . . . the unknown is the first-born son of combat and uncertainty is its other self." [18]

In combat, the individual soldier was rarely sure of what had just happened, what was going on at the moment, or what was likely to occur next. He was subject to continual distraction by violent stimuli, and lived always under the tension of expecting the unexpected. This kind of unceasing confusion—the lack of firm constants to which behavior could be oriented—exposed the individual to insidious anxieties. All people need some stability in their environment; it has been repeatedly shown that personality integration and the development of regularized patterns of behavior are strongly conditioned upon the existence of stable referents for activity.[19] One of the prime functions of any sort of social organization is to provide the individual with a dependable set of expectations. Unless one knows, at least within broad limits, what behavior to expect from others, the very concept of adjustment becomes meaningless. So it is that the uncertainties and confusions of combat were themselves identifiable sources of stress. The frictions of battle, the mistiness of knowledge that goes under the name of "the fog of war," could be minimized by good provisions for trans-

---

[18] Belden, *op. cit.*, pp. 10 and 13.

[19] There is a large amount of evidence for this, ranging from experiments in animal psychology to clinical observation and culture history. Representative sources include Pavlov, Luria, M. Sherif, W. Kohler, Freud, K. Horney, many studies of crime, neuroses, panic, revolution, unemployment, etc.

portation and communication, and by good discipline and administrative organization; but uncertainty always remained. Enemy movements would not always be known; supplies would sometimes fail to arrive when and where most needed; reinforcements would be delayed; radios would refuse to work and telephone lines would be broken. The necessities of secrecy, among other things, would sometimes prevent the mass of soldiers from knowing the "big picture." Men would become lost from their units, enemy surprise attacks would be launched, units would be cut off from other units. The fact of never knowing what to expect was thus a sharply distinguishing mark of the situation of men in combat.

In some respects a group in conflict with another group represents a maximum of value integration: all are united in a common task with a definite and agreed-upon goal. Yet in other respects the combat situation was permeated with conflicts of values and obligations. Most clearly evident was the struggle between the individual's impulses toward personal safety and comfort and the social compulsions which drove him into danger and discomfort: "Sometimes a guy would say, 'How do I keep going?' You have to fight with yourself. You didn't want to be a quitter. You know you're all right." [20] In the case of the combat soldier, this internal fight was one of the factors which sometimes lay at the root of neuropsychiatric breakdowns involving gross disorganization of behavior.

Closely related to this struggle is the problem of the tension between the requirements of military duty and the individual's felt obligations to a social circle at home. Many men felt a deep obligation to a wife and children, or to a dependent mother and father. The society at large indicated that their highest obligation was to fight for their country. But it would be surprising if such men did not feel a strain between these obligations. Should they take risks which they might avoid but which seemed necessary for most effective accomplishment of their military mission?

Evidence that this conflict was felt can be drawn from an analysis of the special problems of married men. Married men presumably had closer home ties than most single men. This supposition is supported by Chart VI, which shows a tendency for married pri-

---

[20] From a personal interview with a wounded veteran of North Africa, Sicily, and Italy. A series of personal interviews with wounded combat veterans was conducted in a hospital in the United States over a two-week period in the spring of 1944, in the course of planning a questionnaire to be used with front-line troops. In this and the following chapter, the interview transcripts will be drawn on frequently for illustrative material.

vates, more frequently than single privates,[21] to say they worried about their families back home.[22] The tendency is independent of educational level. With noncoms, the tendency was weaker, presumably because other factors tended to mitigate the importance of home ties for them. At least for privates, then, one would expect the conflict between duty to outfit and to one's family to be more acute among married men. The conflict should be manifested by greater worry and fear in the battle situation. The data in Chart VI show that such was the case for combat men in Italy. The married men were more likely to say that when they were in combat they worried a lot[23] about their chances of becoming a casualty. They were also, among privates, somewhat more likely to say that combat became more frightening the more they saw of it and less likely to say that it became less frightening.[24] These differences remain when educational level is held constant. Corresponding differences among married and single noncoms, where they exist, are small and not statistically significant, but never in the reverse direction. Among veteran infantrymen in two Pacific divisions, much the same picture was obtained on the latter question, which was also asked in the Pacific theater. Except for the older noncoms, the tendency was for the single men to be more likely to say that battle becomes less frightening.

Similarly, the informal group codes which a man held might come into conflict with the exactions of the Army institution and the military situation. Personal loyalties and formal codes might not jibe. The orders might be to press the attack, not stopping to help the wounded, and a man might be torn between giving aid to a comrade and proceeding with his orders. A good soldier might give way to momentary cowardice, technically punishable, which might have endangered the lives of others. What was the right action for his leader to take? Literally thousands of such examples could and did occur.

Finally, combat required a sharp break with many moral prescriptions of peacetime society. As easy as it seems to be for men to kill when their immediate group sanctions it, and as ambivalent as

---

[21] Single men included those widowed, divorced, or separated.

[22] The answer categories were: "Very often," "sometimes," and "almost never."

[23] The answer categories were: "Worried about it a lot," "worried about it some but not a lot," "didn't worry so much about it," "hardly worried about it at all," and "never worried about it."

[24] The answer categories were: "More frightening," "less frightening," "frightening all the time," and "undecided."

normal people often are about killing, it is still true that to kill other human beings requires of most men from our culture an effort to overcome an initial moral repugnance. Under the requirements of the situation, men in combat were careful to hide this feeling, and it was not a subject of much discussion among soldiers. Killing is

CHART VI

RELATION OF MARITAL STATUS TO FAMILY AND BATTLE WORRIES, ACCORDING TO RANK AND AGE, AMONG COMBAT INFANTRYMEN

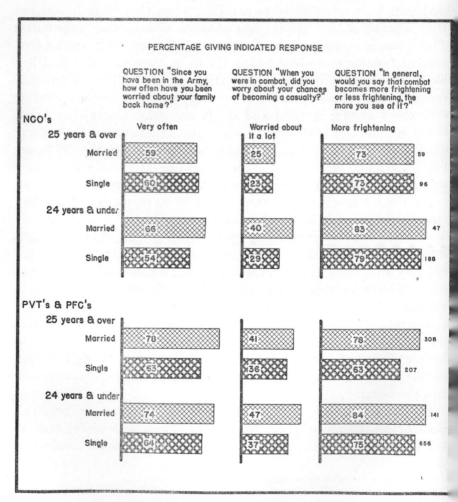

Data from a survey of a cross section of enlisted men in Infantry rifle and heavy weapons companies of four Infantry divisions, Italy, early April 1945 (S-177).

The numbers following the bars are the numbers of cases on which percentages are based.

the business of a combat soldier, and if he is to function at all he must accept its necessity. Yet the acceptance of killing did not prevent men from feeling the ambivalence revealed by such comments as that of a veteran rifleman who said, "I'll tell you a man sure feels funny inside the first time he squeezes down on a Kraut."

Not so often recognized as a fundamental source of strain was the sheer impersonality of combat. Over all else hung the thought that "we are expendable" and a sense of the enormous impersonal forces upon which one's personal fate might depend.[25] In the nature of the case, the combat soldier was to a large extent used as a means rather than an end. He was an instrument of war. It is usual for people in our culture to feel an aversion to being treated as numbers, to react negatively to being impersonally used. Although it could be increased or decreased, the feeling that "nobody gives a damn about us" was always ready to spring to the surface among the men who repeatedly were sent into situations resulting in high casualties. The stress was worsened by any seemingly capricious, arbitrary, and impersonal acts of higher authority. Acts interpreted by the men in these terms were not necessarily so regarded by the command, nor would they necessarily be so viewed by an impartial outside observer. But men's beliefs could represent the orders of higher command as further assaults on their already vulnerable sense of counting for something as individuals; and it must be remembered that commanders were themselves under stress and did not always see a necessity for keeping the men informed, for minimizing nonfunctional demands upon them, or for doing other things to bolster men's sense of personal worth.

Another source of stress came from the very thing which gave a combat soldier his strongest support: his social group.[26] From the beginning of their Army experience, soldiers learned that they had no privacy, and they learned not to mind this too much. Nevertheless, this sort of close in-group living had its disadvantages in the incessant demands and petty irritations it entailed. When in combat everybody was tense anyway, as a result of multiple stresses, the small frictions of intercourse with one's fellows sometimes came to take on an exaggerated importance.

Combat as actually experienced consisted of periods of intense

---

[25] Cf. Richard Tregaskis, *Guadalcanal Diary* (Random House, Inc., New York, 1943), . 43.

[26] For a discussion of the role of his social group in supporting the combat soldier ee the next chapter on "Combat Motivations Among Ground Troops."

activity and excitement punctuating the periods of routine and boredom. When men were not actually in the line of battle or even when they were in the line during quiet periods, they often spent long periods of enforced idleness in which the intense boredom of having no goals for activity was intermingled with the anticipatory anxiety of waiting for further combat. Monotony and boredom may appear to have been trivial compared with the shocks of the attack, but they did take a psychological toll of more than negligible importance.[27]

Finally, for American ground troops there was the particular burden of the apparent endlessness of combat—the lack of any terminal individual goal short of the end of the war. Under our system of replacing personnel losses by individuals rather than by units and of keeping divisions in action for extended periods, men easily concluded that there would be no end to the strain until they "broke" or were hit. In the words of an Infantry scout who was wounded at Salerno after fighting through the Sicilian campaign: "Men in our division gave up all hope of be'ng relieved. They thought the Army intended to keep them in action until everybody was killed . . . that they would simply replace casualties. . . . All the men have hope of getting back, but most of the hope is that you'll get hit someplace that won't kill you. That's all they talk about." [28] Or, later in the same interview: "You give up. You feel that you'll never get back anyway. You just try to postpone it as long as possible."

Infantrymen who had seen very extensive action were asked, near the end of the Italian campaign, "While you were in combat, did you have the feeling that it was just a matter of time until you would get hit?"

	The percentage of infantrymen giving each answer was:[29]
I almost always felt that way	26
I usually felt that way	13
I sometimes felt that way	23
I felt that way once in a while	21
I practically never felt that way	15
No answer	2
Total	100

[27] Cf. Mauldin, *op. cit.*, pp. 46–47.

[28] Personal interview in hospital in the United States, spring 1944.

[29] From a survey of a cross section of 1,766 enlisted men in Infantry rifle and heavy weapons companies of four Infantry divisions, Italy, early April 1945 (S-177). The men with longer combat experience did not differ in their answers markedly from men with briefer combat experience. This is not surprising in view of the likely development with extended combat time of compensating factors, such as a fatalistic attitude

While too much weight cannot be attached to answers to a single question, these answers suggest that many of the men conceived of combat dangers in a cumulative way, so that the lack of a time limit to combat duty must have had drastic implications for them.   As another veteran of the early fighting in Sicily and Italy put it, "You think you're living on borrowed time after a while."   At no stage of his career could the ground combat soldier look forward to a defi-

CHART VII

PROPORTION OF UNSOLICITED COMMENTS ON ROTATION IN RELATION TO
TIME OVERSEAS

(Veteran Infantrymen in Three Pacific Divisions, March–April 1944)

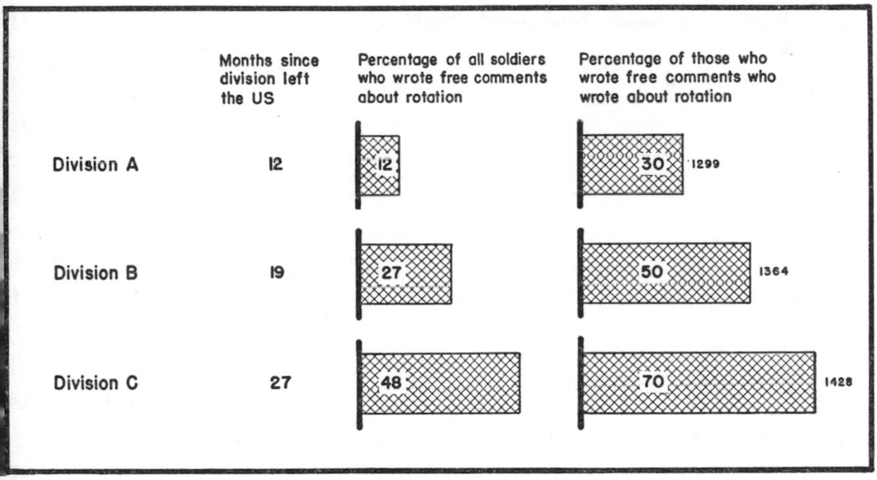

	Months since division left the US	Percentage of all soldiers who wrote free comments about rotation	Percentage of those who wrote free comments who wrote about rotation
Division A	12	12	30 1299
Division B	19	27	50 1364
Division C	27	48	70 1428

Data from S-100.
The numbers following the bars are the numbers of cases on which percentages are based.

nite time when he would be through with fighting, while the example of the tour of duty for combat flyers was ever present.

Rotation was introduced in an attempt to provide a partial solution to this problem.   It will be indicated elsewhere[30] that the number of men rotated was relatively small.   Consequently, rotation did not offer a realistic goal for the average soldier.   In a survey made in the spring of 1944 of combat veterans in three Infantry divisions which fought in the Pacific, by far the largest proportion of comments volunteered on the final blank page of the questionnaire referred to real or imagined injustice in respect to rotation, although no question asked for the men's views on the subject.   As

[30] Chapter 10, "Problems of Rotation and Reconversion."

Chart VII shows, in the division which had been overseas the longest, almost half the men wrote in unsolicited comments on rotation practice and policy; the frequency of comment on the subject was directly related to length of time overseas. These comments and similar ones from other theaters were often vitriolic in their bitterness. A few examples will serve better than anything else to convey the significance to many men of the apparent endlessness of combat and overseas duty:

New officers who come here to take over can't understand a man's feelings after living the way he does over here. A man feels he is downed at times. He feels as long as he is able to keep going he will be kept over here, until he is a physical wreck or his body is buried with 4 or 5 more in some dark jungle or scattered over the ground by artillery shells or bombs. No one back home can really understand our feelings.

I believe through experience that a man who has seen two campaigns shouldn't see any more action. The horrors of war will get any man down. I myself don't believe I could stand the shelling I received in both campaigns. If one shell dropped near me I believe I'd blow my top. Take it from me, a voice of experience, if my company makes one more invasion you had better tell the medical corps to be sure and have 42 straight jackets for there are only 42 of us left.

We feel that the only opportunity we will have to go home is to get wounded. There isn't an old man in the company who has any hope or confidence of being able to enjoy life again. I will go AWOL before I will make another invasion. I am willing to do my part, but I don't want to be the sucker while thousands of soldiers will never see action.

When men lost any hope of rotation, letters from home could simply make matters worse:

As far as I am concerned, I've lost all hope of ever getting back home. My own parents are tearing down my morale, because the radio and newspaper tell them that the men who have 2 years overseas are coming home and I know it will take a long time to rotate the entire division on the basis that they have it now. Why build up false hopes?

In Italy as well as in the Pacific, ground combat men showed the urgency of their concern about some limit to the requirements of combat duty by writing in comments which were not specifically called for by a question. They were asked[31] "If you had a chance to change one thing in the Army, what would you change?" Among the kinds of suggestions the men volunteered, "a fairer distribution of combat duty with troops not then in combat" and "a time limit

[31] Survey of a cross section of 1,766 enlisted men in Infantry rifle and heavy weapon companies of four Infantry divisions, Italy, early April 1945 (S-177).

on combat" were the first and third in frequency, respectively.   On the whole, probably nothing was a matter of greater concern to the veteran ground troops than the ramifications of the endlessness of their combat assignments.

CHART VIII

ATTITUDES TOWARD PHYSICAL CONDITION
(Veteran Infantrymen in Three Pacific Divisions,
March–April 1944)

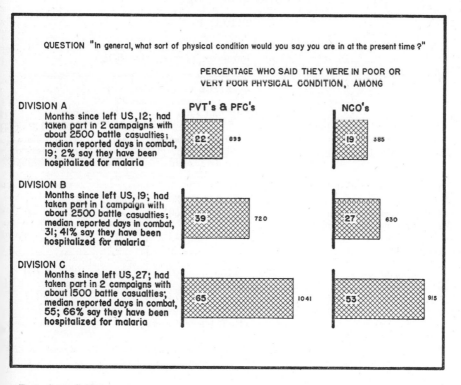

Data from S-100.
The answer categories were "very good physical condition," "good physical condition," "fair physical condition," "poor physical condition," and "very poor physical condition."
The numbers following the bars are the numbers of cases on which percentages are based.

All of these multiform stresses of combat—some of them experienced only in actual battle and others inseparable from life in primitive forward conditions—added up to take their toll from the fighting potential of the combat soldier.   The next chapter will show evidence that there was a deterioration in several motivational factors as men were kept on combat duty for extended periods.   In Chapter 9 on "Psychoneurotic Symptoms in the Army" it is indicated that there was an increase in the proportions of men who reported symptoms of anxiety and psychosomatic disturbance among groups with increasingly prolonged combat or life under combat conditions.   This increase was presumably a direct effect of the summation of these stresses.   Combat men's attitudes toward their physical condition also reflected the inroads of combat conditions on their physical and mental well-being.

TABLE 4

RELATION OF COMBAT TIME TO ATTITUDE TOWARD PHYSICAL CONDITION
(Infantry Veterans, European Theater, May 1945)

| QUESTION: "In general, what sort of physical condition would you say you are in at the present time?" | PERCENTAGE OF INFANTRY VETERANS GIVING EACH ANSWER AMONG | | | | | |
| | *Privates and Pfc's* | | | *Noncoms* | | |
	Less than 28 days combat	28 to 111 days combat	112 or more days of combat	Less than 28 days combat	28 to 111 days combat	112 or more days of combat
Very good or good physical condition	40	30	30	55	47	41
Fair physical condition	47	53	50	39	42	50
Poor or very poor physical condition	10	14	14	4	11	9
No answer	3	3	6	2	—	—
Total	100	100	100	100	100	100
Number of cases	*187*	*195*	*174*	*54*	*47*	*111*

Data from a cross section of enlisted men in the European theater (S-223).   The question on combat time was:

"About how many days have you been in combat since coming overseas?   (Do *not* count any time you were in rest camp or in the hospital or on furlough.)"

About _____ days in combat
_____ I have not been in combat

The most dramatic picture of deteriorating attitudes toward physical condition comes from the study of veteran infantrymen in three divisions which fought in the Pacific.   In a comparison of these divisions, the effects of the various separate sources of stress cannot be distinguished, as most of the men in any single division had been overseas about the same length of time, and individual estimates of length of combat time proved unreliable.[32]   Chart

[32] Conditions of warfare in the Pacific made it particularly hard to say when a man was in combat and when he was not.   However, in a given division, men who said they had been in combat for a longer time were somewhat more likely than those who claimed less combat experience to say they were in poor physical condition.

VIII does, however, show vividly how a number of these stresses could summate to result in a sharp deterioration of the men's feelings of physical well-being.

These data lend force to what has been said of the peculiarly trying conditions experienced in the Pacific war.   Table 4, on the other

CHART IX

RELATION BETWEEN ATTITUDE TOWARD PHYSICAL CONDITION AND
EXPRESSED READINESS FOR FURTHER COMBAT
(Veteran Infantrymen in Three Pacific Divisions,
March–April 1944)

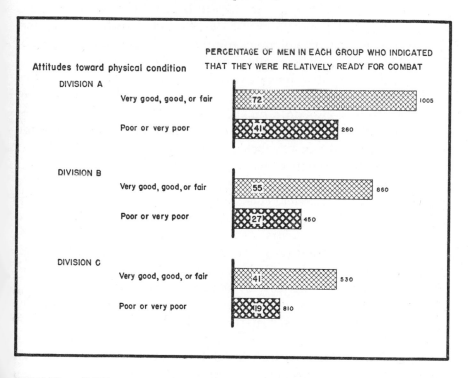

Data from S-100.
For the questions asked, see Chart VIII and footnote 33.
The numbers following the bars are the numbers of cases on which percentages are based.

hand, shows the relation of combat time to attitude toward physical condition among infantrymen in the European theater.   It will be noted that even among men with 112 days or more of combat, the proportion who said they were in poor or very poor physical condition was smaller than in any of the three Pacific divisions.   The range of amount of combat experience is too small in the European data for gross effects to be expected, and the data were gathered near the end of the war, when combat was less arduous than previously. Nevertheless, there was a tendency for men with more time in combat to be less likely to say their physical condition was good.

While there can be little question of the deterioration of men's attitudes toward their physical condition as a result of prolonged stress, one cannot of course take the men's self-evaluations as the equivalent of objective indices of health. The men's own estimates of their physical condition were certainly responsive to motivational pressures on at least two levels: emotional disturbance may have led to psychosomatic symptoms which made the effective physical condition of the soldier in fact worse; or, desire to be withdrawn from combat duty may have led the combat man to tend to put greater stress on relatively minor complaints in hope that they might justify his removal from combat, or at least excuse his own desires to leave it. In the divisions surveyed in the Pacific, attitude toward physical condition was strongly correlated both with an index of psychoneurotic complaints on the one hand and with whether or not a man had had malaria on the other, so there is a presumption that both physical and psychological factors were involved.

As one of the ways in which the men's fighting potential was reduced through the cumulation of combat stresses, the deterioration in self-estimate of physical condition is significant even though it is not possible to untangle the web of the physical and the psychogenetic. Chart IX indicates that in each of the three Pacific divisions, the men who said they were in poorer physical condition indicated a lower degree of readiness for combat,[33] as might be expected. The differences between the divisions in respect to the proportion of men in them who showed relatively high readiness for further combat cannot be entirely attributed to differences in the men's feelings about their physical condition, however, since the men in Division C who said they were in relatively good physical condition were no more likely to show readiness for combat than were the

---

[33] Readiness for combat was determined from the men's answers to the question:

"Which of the following statements best tells the way you feel about going back into actual battle?"

Want to get into it as soon as possible
Ready to go at any time
Hope I won't have to go, but if I go I think I will do all right
Hope I won't have to go because I don't think I will do very well
None of the above fits me. My feeling is this: _____

Men whose answers fell in the first three categories were considered relatively ready for combat; the remainder, relatively unready.

men in Division A who said they were in relatively poor physical condition.

The question which was used to differentiate men relatively more and less ready for further combat deserves some comment at this point, since it will frequently be employed to show the relationship between various factors and combat motivation. The men who are considered relatively ready for further combat are those who said: "want to get into it as soon as possible," "ready to go at any time," or "hope I won't have to go, but if I go I think I will do all right." Clearly the question does not measure a single dimension —both self-confidence and something equivalent to zeal appear to be involved. Also, those who are classed as relatively ready for further combat, as can be seen, were not necessarily showing any real eagerness. Perhaps because the question touches more than one factor, it turned out to be one of the most differentiating attitude questions for the prediction of combat performance in studies following up the records of divisional units surveyed just before the Normandy invasion.[34]

Although one cannot say unambiguously that poor attitude toward physical condition was a cause of poor combat motivation, it is evident that a feeling of being in poor condition was part of a complex of factors unfavorable to combat motivation. Deterioration in general well-being was one of the ways in which chronic exposure to combat stresses gradually undermined the bases of combat motivation.

General Social Characteristics of the Combat Situation Which Resist Stress

From what has now been said one might well wonder how soldiers ever managed to fight at all, if so many destructive and disorganizing forces were at work upon them. This wonder is justified and it is an indication of the strength of opposing factors that soldiers did fight—fight well, for long periods, and often without gross personality disorganization. Evidently the combat situation included factors other than those of stress which warrant attention. In this section, some of these important social features of the combat situation will be indicated. The following chapter, taking the individual combat soldier as the reference point, will examine in greater detail the part these social features played in combat motivation,

---

[34] The question used in this instance was different in certain minor respects. See Chapter 1 for a discussion of the predictive value of this and other attitude questions.

as well as introducing other elements that go into determining why soldiers fought.

Features Which Are Part of the Definition of the Combat Situation

From the mere fact that combat always consists in one group fighting an enemy, there follow certain features which make for social cohesion.   In the first place, combat involves *a major threat from outside to the group as a whole*.   Alone, the threat does not automatically result in group solidarity.   In conjunction, however, with other factors to be discussed later which keep the group in the situation, it results in a dramatic increase in mutually supportive action among members of the group.   In the face of great external danger common to the entire group, there is strong pressure to resolve or repress internal antagonisms and discordant behavior patterns.

Also inherent in the combat situation is the existence of a *socially approved outlet for aggressions* which are ordinarily tabooed within our society.   Many an intragroup quarrel has been checked by the curt advice from fellow soldiers: "Save that for the Germans." The enemy is a suitable target for many of the hostilities arising from the individual's personal history and his experience within the group.

A third characteristic of organized combat without which there would be no combat is that the activities of the men are *directed toward definite and tangible goals*.   Regardless of the extent to which the individual soldier accepts it as his own, there is always an unambiguous goal inherent in the situation: to overcome the enemy. Any unit is almost always under orders to take or hold a specific objective, and each man in action has a definite set of duties to perform.   The men have weapons which, ideally, they know how to use.   Their task, although difficult, is in a sense simple and straightforward.   But over and above the fact that the task is set by orders —a characteristic, after all, of most other military situations— is the immediacy and manifest importance of the combat goal. Whether the particular task was to capture an enemy observation post, or to hold a position, or even to engage in an action the strategic usefulness of which was not at all apparent, it directly involved overcoming or resisting the enemy, and this goal was a primary feature of the structure of the situation.   The goals set for the combat soldier were much less indirect than those of a soldier in the chain of supply.

There are, of course, many other concrete personal and group goals in combat, which may support or conflict with this goal in different degrees.   Also, men may vary in the extent to which they accept the goal of combat as important; that it is there to make simple sense of their behavior, however, raises it to a position of peculiar potency.   It is in part this immediacy of the goal which lends meaning to the phrase, "the battle is the pay-off."

Institutional Features Which Are Primarily Brought to the Combat Situation

Both informal and formal institutional factors entered into the control of behavior in combat.   While certain aspects of the informal controls grew out of attitudes common to our culture or were developed during the training period, the strong intragroup ties which lent so much potency to the informal controls in combat arose for the most part within the combat situation.   These controls will be the subject of extensive later consideration.   No understanding of combat behavior would, however, be possible if the obvious fact were ignored that the fighting is done by armies, which bring with them to the field a complex social organization and a set of prescribed ways of doing, interpreting, and evaluating things. Some of these institutional characteristics were discussed in Volume I.   Here the special relevance in combat of certain of these features will be considered.

The rigid and complexly hierarchical Army organization, with its accompanying set of formal rules, was the Army's main answer to the stress and confusion of battle.   The soldier was not an individual atom in the tide of warfare; he was an integral part of a vast system of discipline and coordination.   The chain of command was implemented by stringent sanctions for failures to conform.   Men faced combat in tightly organized formal groups, and were held in those groups by the ultimate sanctions their society wielded, including the power, almost never used, of punishment by death.   Thus, the individual in combat was simultaneously guided, supported, and coerced by a framework of organization.

A prime characteristic of the Army is the extent to which it relies on these impersonal controls.   Army organization is devised to work even when personal ties cannot be depended on—as in the last analysis they cannot be when any individual may have to be replaced as a combat casualty.   So great is the need for coordinated behavior in the battle situation, and so obdurate are the difficulties in the way of securing it, that the Army tries to aim for a margin of safety in establishing an organizational structure with supporting habits and sentiments to ensure prompt and exact carrying out of orders. This is the rationale for much that was resented by the men in their precombat training. Whether or not close-order drill and garrison discipline actually do aid in knitting together this automatically functioning organization and, if they do, whether or not they are more efficient than alternative types of training are moot questions which it is not possible to settle here. There can be little doubt, however, of the crucial importance of the mechanical, quasi-automatic aspects of Army operation in combat which such training is intended to promote. "You get a habit of taking orders when you're in training so that when they tell you to do something, you do so without hardly thinking," a wounded veteran of the Sicilian and early Italian campaign put it. During the confusion of combat, in which any course is problematical and dangerous and individual judgment must operate under a tremendous handicap, the fact that one knew to whom to look for direction and orders, that such orders were forthcoming, and that the range of possible behavior was closely limited by established rule, was one of the most important single determinants of behavior.

Social Features Which Arise Primarily Within the Combat Situation

Within the framework of formal organization on the one hand and of the inherent features of organized combat on the other, characteristic informal social features developed which, it will be seen in the following chapter, supported a potent system of informal controls.

The combat situation was one of mutual dependence. A man's life depended literally and immediately upon the actions of others; he in turn was responsible in his own actions for the safety of others. This vital interdependence was closer and more crucial in combat than in the average run of human affairs. Any individual's action which had conceivable bearing on the safety of others in the group became a matter of proper concern for the group as a whole. Mutual dependence, however, was more than a matter of mere survival. Isolated as he was from contact with the rest of the world, the combat man was thrown back on his outfit to meet the various affectional needs for response, recognition, approval, and in general for appreciation as a significant person rather than a means—needs which he would normally satisfy in his relations with his family and with friends of his own choosing.   Most aspects of combat as a stress situation served only to make these needs the more urgent. The group was thus in a favored position to enforce its standards on the individual.

Some illustrations of the close affectional ties which develop in combat may be drawn from an interview with an Infantry private first class who fought through seven months of the North African campaign before being returned to the United States as a casualty:

The men in my squad were my special friends.   My best friend was the sergeant of the squad.   We bunked together, slept together, fought together, told each other where our money was pinned in our shirts.   We write to each other now. Expect to get together when the war is over. . . .   If one man gets a letter from home over there, the whole company reads it.   Whatever belongs to me belongs to the whole outfit.[35]

An armored Infantry veteran says,

Practically all of the boys in your company are your friends.   One of the things a fellow learns in the Army is to make friends with anybody, and hold that friendship.[35]

The isolation of the front-line unit was such as to make the combat man feel completely set apart.   Even in the midst of his fellows, each man had the inner loneliness that comes from having to face death at each moment.   This psychological isolation was mitigated by the presence, example, and support of other soldiers in the unit. But the unit itself lived and died apart from that other great world of the rear—and that meant, for the rifleman, everyone out of range of small arms and mortars.   The "taken-for-grantedness" of personal survival vanished in the realization that death might come at any time and that often it was more likely to come than not.   In a thousand ways, great and small, the soldier coming into the line had defined for him a world that felt itself to be and was, in fact, removed physically and psychologically from all that lay behind it. Behind the front the great military machine inexorably continued to send forward supplies and men—and the orders that sent men into attack.   But the rifleman's world shrank to the tremendous immediacies of staying alive and destroying the enemy.

In this setting developed the feeling of fraternity of combat soldiers.   Those who had shot at the enemy and had themselves been

---

[35] Personal interviews in hospital in the United States, spring 1944.

fired upon in that thin forward zone, had a consciousness of shared experience under great emotional stress which they felt others could never understand. This consciousness became clear mostly after action, when in the rear or in reminiscence. But even during battle, soldiers at the front felt strongly their mutual dependence, their common loneliness, their separate destiny apart from all who were not at the front. The significant experience they had shared was a further bond between individual and group.

Formal Versus Informal Control of Combat Behavior

It is important to avoid any one-sided interpretation of the social forces that kept men in combat. The various factors in the situation worked in interaction. For instance, exposure to a common external threat became a unifying force only when escape from the situation was ruled out as by formal Army rules and sanctions and by informal codes of behavior enforced by the group. Affective ties binding the group together were important in keeping men in combat because, among other reasons, the group through its formal organization was inextricably committed to the fight: anything that tied the individual to the group therefore kept him in combat. The informal codes of the group drew on ideals of manliness common to our culture, but in a more immediate sense derived their force and urgency from the necessity for survival in the face of a common threat. In considering any single aspect of the social situation of combat separately, the fact that it has been abstracted from a most complicated context must be remembered.

Nevertheless, it may be profitable to weigh some considerations which may lead one to lay more stress on one or another aspect of the situation. The fact that most of the decorum in command relationships so evident in garrison was dropped on the battlefield, for instance, may be advanced in support of an explanation that would account for combat behavior primarily in terms of informal controls. True enough, salutes practically disappeared, insignia of rank were often not worn, and social distance between officers and men decreased (e.g., the use of "sir," tones of deference, formality of speech and behavior). It is also true that the situation itself, and informal group standards arising within it, exerted a controlling force over behavior to supplement and support the formal controls. But the extent to which formal controls were reduced in combat could easily be exaggerated. Many symbolic acts of obeisance and status were inappropriate and were dropped, but orders still came down the chain of command; that they should do so was accepted as right and natural; and behind the orders still rested the full weight of Army authority. And the standardized formal cultural pattern according to which the Army operates was in its essentials unchanged.

The significance of the standardized cultural pattern can be seen by imagining a company composed entirely of individual replacements, none of whom were acquainted prior to the day the unit entered combat. With the cultural framework available (i.e., known to the men) and with leaders motivated to carry out its prescriptions, an assemblage of strangers can quickly become a fairly effective fighting organization.[36] It can do this without calling upon any motives attributable directly to personal relations among its members. On the other hand, imagine a group in which the only basis of organization is that of affective ties and common social values among individuals, none of whom are invested with definite formal roles carrying explicit functions and behavior prescriptions. If such a group were sent into combat, presumably leaders would arise and the group take on a determinate structure—eventually— as a result of personal interactions and generalized social techniques of organization which could be carried over from nonmilitary situations. But it is difficult to see how this hypothetical collectivity could avoid initial chaos upon meeting the enemy.

Thus we are forced to the conclusion that personal motives and relationships are not uniquely determinate for organization in combat. By abstracting from actual organizations the theoretical pure type which would contain only these elements, one can see clearly their insufficiency. They do not furnish sufficient conditions, and only in a statistical sense are they necessary conditions: officers and men must be motivated to make the organization work, but not *all* of them have to be so motivated, nor must they all agree on details of social philosophy or be bound by ties of personal friendship in order for a functioning organization to exist. To put it another way, the best single predictor of combat behavior is the simple fact of institutionalized role: knowing that a man is a soldier rather than a civilian. The soldier role is a vehicle for getting a man into the position in which he has to fight or take the institutionally sanctioned consequences.

The facts of casualty and replacement rates also support the

---

[36] Not so effective, in all probability, as it would be if it had the in-group ties, but still an organized functioning group.

critical importance of formal organization. In Infantry outfits the tremendous turnover of both men and their officers during combat minimized the possible importance of strong personal attachments at the level of company or smaller units. Casualties among second lieutenants were in some cases as high or higher than among riflemen in the line. It was not unusual to find a rifle company which after two or three months in combat had none of its original officers remaining in the unit. When one remembers that some Infantry divisions considered in total (including all the rear echelon troops) had over 100 per cent cumulative casualties in six months of combat in Europe, the great attrition in line units becomes clearer.

A study of casualty rates of four Infantry divisions fighting in Italy[37] showed that the Infantry troops suffered 92 per cent of the battle casualties, although they constituted but 67 per cent of the authorized strength of an Infantry division. (Field Artillery troops made up 17 per cent of the divisional strength, but they incurred only 4 per cent of the battle casualties.) Within the Infantry itself there were great variations in casualty rates among the various specific types of jobs. Riflemen headed the list. As of the time of the study, they were only 11 per cent of an Infantry division's Table of Organization strength, yet accounted for 38 per cent of the battle casualties and 26 per cent of the nonbattle casualties.

Among the Infantry, second lieutenants constituted 0.9 per cent of the total strength—and were 2.7 per cent of all battle casualties. The average daily battle casualty rate per 1,000 Table of Organization strength for second lieutenants in Infantry was 11.4 in the divisions studied.[38] Assuming, for the sake of demonstration, that the full complement of 132 Infantry second lieutenants was present in a division on each day of combat, that there were no nonbattle casualties, and no duplication of battle casualties, the division would lose a full complement of its Infantry second lieutenants in 88 combat days. On the same assumptions, the divisional complement of 99 Infantry captains would require 294 days of battle for 100 per cent casualties. Of course, many of these casualties would be replacements, not original officers. Moreover, many of the casualties returned to the same unit after hospitalization or other treatment. On the other hand, nonbattle casualties were equal to or slightly

---

[37] The study was based on the experience of the 3rd, 34th, 36th, and 45th Infantry divisions from the beginning of the Italian campaign on September 9, 1943, until April 4, 1944.

[38] Rate based on authorized Table of Organization strength for periods when the division was officially committed in combat.

greater than battle casualties even during combat; and the shifting of officer personnel by transfers among units introduced further instability into the leader-follower relations in individual units. For example, in the divisions studied, the Infantry had a daily loss of 21 lieutenants per 1,000 T/O strength from *all* types of casualties. This represents a loss of slightly over 1 in every 50 per day, to be made up by returns-to-unit or by replacement in order to maintain T/O strength. Certainly the data just presented emphasize the fluidity of the group of officers in any given Infantry company.[39]

The situation in divisional Field Artillery was less dramatic; the average daily battle casualty rate for all commissioned officers was 2.1 as over against the Infantry rate of 6.1. Divisional Artillery batteries thus had relatively greater stability of leadership. The turnover of enlisted personnel was likewise relatively lower than in the Infantry—an average daily battle casualty rate per 1,000 Table of Organization strength of 0.8 as over against 5.1 in the Infantry. Thus, the Field Artillery units constituted relatively more stable social groups in which there was greater opportunity for the development of continuing interpersonal relationships.

Total casualties were, of course, much greater than the net turnover of personnel. In the divisions studied, returns of men to their units after hospitalization amounted on the average to 45 per 100 battle and nonbattle casualties. Thus, to maintain a constant number of men in a division there would have to be about 55 new replacements for every 100 battle and nonbattle casualties. In the Infantry 60 replacements would be required for every 100 battle and nonbattle casualties; for the Field Artillery, about 27 replacements; for all other divisional troops, about 30 replacements for every 100 battle and nonbattle casualties. Men evacuated as nonbattle casualties were more often eventually returned to their units than men who became battle casualties. And in the Infantry the proportion of all casualties which were nonbattle casualties was smaller than in other branches. For this reason the net turnover of personnel in the Infantry, in comparison with turnover in Artillery and other units, was greater than their respective total (battle and nonbattle) casualty rates would lead one to expect. Even

[39] The figures utilized here are necessarily rough, because of the difficulty of securing an accurate base of *actual* daily strength. Since divisions in combat usually operate with less than their authorized strengths, especially in the Infantry, the rates based on T/O strength understate the real incidence of casualties. It must be remembered also that the data are localized in time and space, and that the average experience of other divisions at other times and places may have been considerably different.

though Infantry units almost "normally" operated in combat with less than their authorized strengths, they were continually forced to assimilate disproportionately large numbers of new replacements as compared with other units.

Thus, among Infantry troops in combat under the individual replacement system, informal controls based on close personal ties and identifications developed in spite of the influence of the replacement system in the opposite direction. That such ties did develop to the extent observed indicates the strong pressure toward their formation; on the other hand, the fact that such a replacement system could work, with whatever defects, indicates the force of purely institutional controls. The emphasis in succeeding chapters on personal motivation and informal controls is not intended to create the impression that these factors, important and interesting to the social scientist as they may be, outweighed the all-pervading institutional factors.

CHAPTER 3

COMBAT MOTIVATIONS AMONG GROUND TROOPS[1]

Introduction

THE preceding chapter attempted a description of the general characteristics of ground combat as a social situation—in the forms that American troops experienced it in World War II. Notice has already been taken of certain general aspects of the situation which made it possible for the combat soldier to sustain the extraordinary stresses to which he was subjected. In the present section this problem will be given closer attention.

It must be noted that this is a very different question from "why men fight," or why the population at large may want a war or acquiesce in it. As a man changes from civilian to front-line soldier, the factors conditioning his behavior change and so do the motives to which he refers to account for his actions. It is also a more restricted problem than "why soldiers fight." A career army, a guerrilla army, or an army fighting in its own homeland may be expected to fight for a quite different cluster of "reasons" than the American combat man in the recent war.

Furthermore, it is necessary to be specific as to the meaning of "why." It would be possible to raise the question "why" in such a form as to require a complete knowledge of the individual life histories of every person in our culture. On the other hand, it would be possible to pose the problem solely in terms of institutional factors without reference to individual motives. The meaning of "why" depends on the frame of reference in terms of which the analysis is carried out.

In the following account, the central concern will be the more important ways in which social and situational factors impinge on the

---

[1] By M. Brewster Smith. In the preparation of this chapter extensive use was made of notes and suggestions by Robin M. Williams, Jr., who, as a member of the Research Branch in the European theater, accompanied one division in the drive from Normandy to Germany as a participant observer.

behavior of the ground soldier to keep him in combat. The focus will be on the individual, but no systematic attempt will be made to trace out the intricacies of combat motivation in intrapersonal terms. Indeed, the nature of the data available virtually imposes such a limitation, since without extensive psychiatric interviewing any attempt at a thorough account of intrapersonal factors would be merely speculative. The analysis therefore in general will not be concerned with personal traits, needs, or drives at the level of aggressiveness, wish for recognition, or need for affection. It will, on the other hand, touch upon such factors as hatred of the enemy, the prestige of the combat man, and loyalty to one's buddies—factors at a level of abstraction fairly close to the immediate combat situation.

While such a procedure is called for by the nature of the data, has other reasons to recommend it. In terms of any scheme of general personal motives, the same motives can operate in many different institutional structures, and, conversely, many different motives can lead to participation in the same group activity. Nevertheless, an institutional situation such as an army in combat does tend to elicit and encourage certain motivational patterns, which recur with a certain degree of uniformity. Our intent is to describe some of these patterns, without assuming, however, that they held for all combat soldiers, or that the same behavior might not result from quite different motivational patterns at various times or in different circumstances.

The various topics which it seemed important to discuss in this chapter will receive somewhat uneven treatment because on some subjects much more information was available than on others. Certain matters concerning which data were negligible or lacking will still be treated at least summarily, to avoid as much as possible distortion of the total picture. Nevertheless, the following treatment makes no pretense of completeness at its chosen level of description. The motivation of combat behavior was so complex that at most it can be hoped that few major factors have been entirely neglected.

This treatment has often drawn heavily on the men's own statements concerning factors in their motivation. Questionnaire data regarding combat were necessarily obtained after the fact, when a man's answer might reflect what he would then like to believe was the reason for his action rather than what he might have said at the time, or what an outside observer would have inferred. Since there is no simple way of separating valid reporting from wishful thinking, the reader can only be cautioned to bear this difficulty in mind.

The major interest in the present discussion is, then, to analyze the typical and general determinants of behavior in the immediate combat situation. A tired, cold, muddy rifleman goes forward with the bitter dryness of fear in his mouth into the mortar bursts and machine-gun fire of a determined enemy. A tremendous psychological mobilization is necessary to make an individual do this, not just once but many times. In combat surely, if anywhere, we should be able to observe behavioral determinants of great significance, since we already know that most soldiers did fight in the face of all the cumulative stresses tending to drive them out of combat.

The first topic to be discussed will be the role of coercive institutional authority in molding behavior in combat. The amount of space that will be devoted to it is undoubtedly not in proportion to the importance of a group of factors without which relatively few soldiers would have been in combat at all. Next, the role of combat leaders and the men's attitudes toward them will be treated. The company officer, and to a lesser extent the noncom, stood in a focal position between the formal coercive authority, which they represented, and the informal social group, of which they were participating members. The role of the informal social group will then be taken up, in regard to the codes of behavior it imposed and the ways in which it provided the otherwise vulnerable individual with sources of power and security. There will then be something to be said concerning the role of the men's convictions about the war and the enemy—convictions which were subject to pressure from the standards of the informal group but which had roots in prior attitudes and in combat experiences. A fifth section will touch on the role of certain residual goals not elsewhere discussed, such as the desire to get home again and the hope of victory. Finally, a section on prayer and personal philosophies in combat will be concerned with a group of psychological adjustments to which the men turned for support in situations of intense stress beyond their power to predict or control.

As an overview of this investigation of combat motivation, an analysis of the unguided statements of combat men and officers on the subject is instructive. Chart I presents a summary classification of the responses of enlisted infantrymen in a veteran division which saw action in two Mediterranean campaigns and of company grade officers in divisions in both European and Pacific theaters to questions in regard to the incentives which kept the men fighting. A more detailed presentation of the same data may be found in Tables 1 and 2. Both the question asked of the enlisted men and that asked of the officers invited answers of a somewhat more re-

CHART I

COMBAT INCENTIVES NAMED BY OFFICER AND ENLISTED VETERANS
(Summary of Tables 1 and 2)

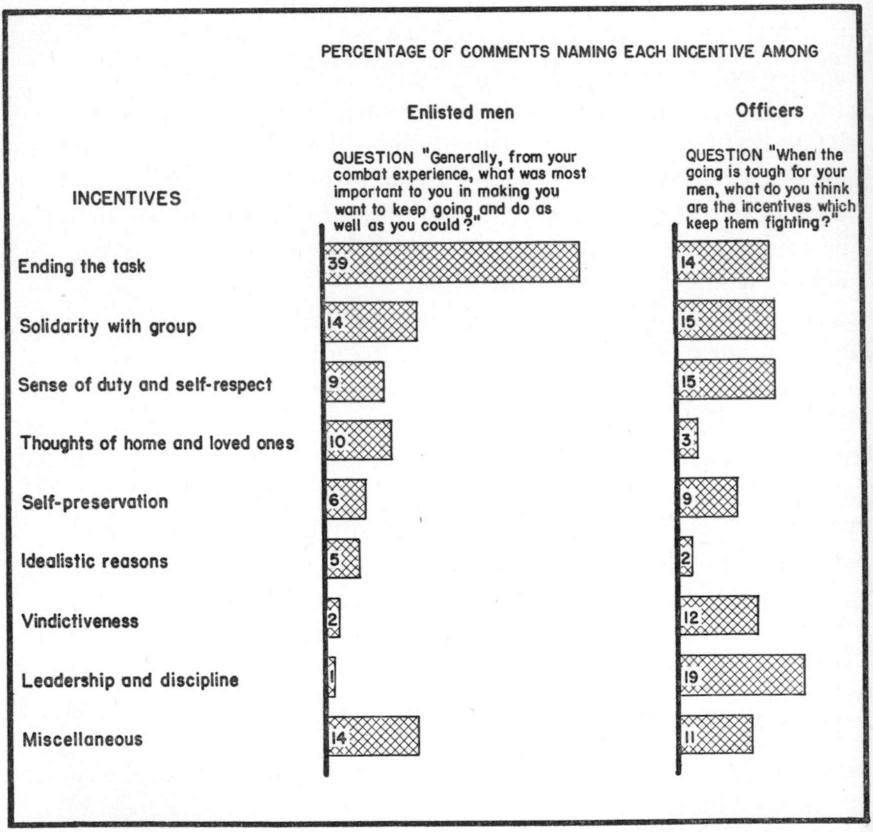

PERCENTAGE OF COMMENTS NAMING EACH INCENTIVE AMONG

INCENTIVES	Enlisted men QUESTION "Generally, from your combat experience, what was most important to you in making you want to keep going and do as well as you could?"	Officers QUESTION "When the going is tough for your men, what do you think are the incentives which keep them fighting?"
Ending the task	39	14
Solidarity with group	14	15
Sense of duty and self-respect	9	15
Thoughts of home and loved ones	10	3
Self-preservation	6	9
Idealistic reasons	5	2
Vindictiveness	2	12
Leadership and discipline	1	19
Miscellaneous	14	11

For breakdown on enlisted men see Table 1.
For breakdown on officers see Table 2. The figures shown here are an unweighted average of the figures for the three divisions presented in that table.

stricted scope than that of this chapter. The enlisted men were asked what was most important to them in making them *want* to keep going and do as well as they could, while the officers were asked what *incentives* kept their men fighting. One would not expect these questions to elicit reference to the several factors which appear to have been important in giving the men support without, however, providing a spur to further fighting, for instance prayer or fatalism. Neither would one expect the men's answers to make much of coercive institutional authority, since only indirectly can it be said to have been an incentive or to have made the men want

TABLE 1

COMBAT INCENTIVES NAMED BY ENLISTED INFANTRYMEN
(Enlisted Infantry Combat Veterans, European Theater, April 1944)

QUESTION: "Generally, in your combat experience, what was most important to you in making you want to keep going and do as well as you could?"

	Percentage of comments naming each incentive
Ending the task	39
Thoughts of getting the war over	*34*
Thoughts of getting relief or a rest	*5*
Solidarity with group	14
Cannot let the other fellows or the outfit down; sticking together; "buddies depending on me"; "my friends around me"	
Sense of duty and self-respect	9
Personal pride, self-respect	*7*
"Doing my part, my duty"	*2*
Thoughts of home and loved ones	10
Self-preservation; "kill or be killed"	6
A job to be done; "somebody has to do the fighting"	5
Idealistic reasons	5
Making a better world; crushing aggressor; "belief in what I'm fighting for"	*3*
Patriotism, protecting our people and their freedom	*2*
Vindictiveness	2
Anger, revenge, "fighting spirit"	
Lack of any alternative action	2
"There was nothing else to do"; "easier to keep going"	
Leadership and discipline	1
Indifference	1
"Too tired or mad to care"; "don't give a damn any more"	
Miscellaneous	6
Total	100
Number of comments	*568*

Survey of Infantry veterans of a division which had fought in North Africa and Sicily, April 1944 (S-100).

to keep going.   In other respects, the men's answers touch in one way or another on most of the principal sources of motivation with which we will be concerned.

Most frequently mentioned by the enlisted men was the prosaic goal of ending the task—getting the war over with to get home again, or hope of more immediate relief at the end of a particular mission. Presumably "thoughts of home and loved ones" had somewhat similar import, as something to look forward to when the job was over. Various aspects of solidarity with the group

TABLE 2

COMBAT INCENTIVES NAMED BY COMPANY OFFICERS
(Veteran Company Grade Infantry and Field Artillery Officers,
European and Pacific Theaters, April 1944*)

QUESTION: "When the going is tough for your men, what do you think are the incentives which keep them fighting?"

| | PERCENTAGE OF COMMENTS NAMING EACH INCENTIVE | | |
	Division A	*Division B*	*Division C*
Ending the task	15	11	15
Thoughts of getting the war over	*9*	*9*	*12*
Thoughts of getting relief or a rest	*6*	*2*	*3*
Solidarity with group	17	17	11
Pride in outfit and esprit de corps; loyalty to comrades; opinions of other men; seeing others doing their job			
Sense of duty and self-respect	14	16	14
Personal pride, self-respect	*12*	*12*	*9*
Sense of duty	*2*	*4*	*5*
Thoughts of home and loved ones	3	3	2
Self-preservation; "kill or be killed"	10	9	9
A job to be done; "somebody has to do the fighting"	4	5	†
Idealistic reasons	2	1	2
Ideals, patriotism, "what we're fighting for"			
Vindictiveness	9	8	18
Anger, revenge, "fighting spirit"			
Lack of any alternative action	5	3	†
"Nothing else for them to do"; "easier to keep going"			
Leadership and discipline	18	19	20
Indifference; "don't give a damn"	1	1	†
Miscellaneous	2	7	9
Total	100	100	100
Number of comments	*304*	*256*	*556*

* Divisions A and B fought in North Africa and Sicily while Division C fought in the Central Pacific. Data are from S-101.
† These categories were not used in the analysis, and such comments were classed as miscellaneous.

were mentioned second in frequency: sticking together, loyalty to comrades, pride in outfit, etc. The importance of the strong group ties that developed in combat will be the subject of considerable later discussion. A sense of duty and self-respect was mentioned by a number of the men. Rather than considering this as a separate motivational category, it will be treated as evidence of the internalization of both institutional and informal group requirements.

All of the incentives listed thus far (excepting "thoughts of home and loved ones," if this is considered separately from "ending the task") were also mentioned by substantial numbers of officers. The most striking discrepancy between the responses of officers and enlisted men was in regard to the role of leadership and discipline, cited more frequently than any other incentive by the officers, but by hardly any of the enlisted men. It is, of course, fairly clear that there were influences to divert both groups from a fully equitable appraisal of the importance of leadership. On the one hand, it was the prime occupational concern of the officers, their main function in the Army. From the point of view of the enlisted men, on the other hand, one would not expect mention here of the coercive aspects of leadership and discipline for reasons already stated, while one may suppose that the feelings many of them had toward officers as a group may have kept them from talking more about such of the other aspects of leadership as they had experienced.

Officers and enlisted men alike attached little importance to idealistic motives—patriotism and concern about war aims. Their evaluation appears to be in fundamental accord with other sources of evidence, though attributable in part to a socially prescribed avoidance of idealistic references that will be noted later. An intermediate proportion of both officers and enlisted men mentioned self-preservation as a motive; that combat was, as they put it, a matter of kill or be killed. In regard to vindictiveness—anger, revenge, etc.—the fact that the chart shows it to have been cited by more officers than enlisted men may be somewhat misleading. Reference to Table 2 will reveal that, in agreement with findings to be presented later, officers in combat against the Japanese were more likely than officers in Europe to say that vindictiveness was an important incentive. Since the present questions were not asked of enlisted men in the Pacific, the difference may be ascribable principally to the lack of comparability of the samples in this respect.

Several infrequently mentioned motives listed in Tables 1 and 2 are not shown in Chart I since it was not possible to present data for all groups surveyed. Among them was viewing the war as a job to be done—"somebody has to do the fighting." This has a certain similarity to the incentive of ending the task. A few men mentioned the lack of any alternative to going on fighting, thus recognizing indirectly the role of coercive institutional authority in restricting the range of choice. A few others, though asked to name incentives, pleaded mere indifference—that they "didn't give a damn" any more. This kind of adjustment will receive further notice in the section on personal philosophies in combat.

The broad picture given by the men's free comments is one which we will have little need to modify or correct, aside from including factors other than positive incentives. It is one of a matter-of-fact adjustment to combat, with a minimum of idealism or heroics, in which the elements which come closest to the conventional stereotype of soldier heroism enter through the close solidarity of the immediate combat group.

Role of Coercive Institutional Authority

The sheer coercive power of Army authority was a factor in combat motivation which must not be forgotten simply because it is easy to take for granted. It was omnipresent, and its existence had been impressed on the soldier from his first days in the Army when he was read the many punitive articles from the Articles of War, each ending with the ominous phrase, "punishable in time of war by death or such other penalty as a court-martial may direct." The Articles of War themselves specify that the punitive articles are to be read to all enlisted men at least every six months. This is only one of the minor ways already examined in earlier chapters in which every enlisted man long before he reached the scene of combat became fully aware of the coercive sanctions which stood back of official commands.

Nevertheless, one not familiar with military justice as exercised in combat commands is likely to take an oversimplified view of the role of naked coercion. Those combat offenses for which the extreme penalty was authorized—desertion, AWOL from the lines (legally equivalent to desertion), and misbehavior in the face of the enemy—were, of course, the ones which involved escape from the combat situation. But practically never was the death penalty actually enforced for purely military offenses. To quote a statement by former Under Secretary of War Robert P. Patterson, after the end of the European fighting: "During the entire length of this war, the Army has executed 102 of its soldiers. All executions but one were for murder or rape. One was for desertion, the first execution for a purely military crime since the Civil War. This man, serving in the European Theater, deserted twice under fire." [2]   Generally speaking, then, the death penalty was not used.

Severity of punishment varied greatly from one division to another and in respect to similar offenses within the same division. Sometimes charges were dropped entirely if the soldier would return to combat.   In other cases offenders were given six-month terms of hard labor, frequently on roads within range of artillery fire but under no greater danger than many forward service outfits.   In still other cases, heavy terms of imprisonment were sentenced, with the offender removed to a stockade or disciplinary training center. Dishonorable discharge was sometimes made mandatory at the end of the term.   But the death penalty was not normally considered for the purely military offense.[3]   In regard to the heavy prison terms, many men may have thought it likely that the more drastic sentences would be revised in response to public pressure at the end of the war.[4]

So the combat man did not in fact face a choice of possible death from the enemy versus certain death if he refused combat.   The role of the coercive system must have been of a more complex sort. Aside from the physical unpleasantness of life in a stockade, which was subject to wide variation, the ways in which the coercive formal sanctions could be effective appear to have involved informal factors in addition:

1. Some men expressed in interview the fear of losing pay, family allotments, etc., if they should be convicted by court-martial.   Thus family affectional ties became involved.

2. Both family ties and the reactions of a man's buddies were involved in the feeling that being convicted and confined was a disgrace.

3. A man's own established reactions to punishment imposed by established authority might be called up in varying degrees as a sense of shame or guilt.

---

[2] War Department, Bureau of Public Relations, press release, July 8, 1945.

[3] Although it is impossible to gather conclusive evidence concerning the *informal* use of death threats by combat leaders during actual battle, it was the impression of Research Branch interviewers that instances in which leaders compelled men to continue fighting at gun point were rare.   Rumors of such occurrences were rarely encountered whereas one would expect knowledge of any actual cases of this sort to spread widely and rapidly by rumor.

[4] No specific question was asked in regard to this, but the belief turned up frequently in a series of informal interviews with combat troops and men in division stockades, conducted in Italy during the winter of 1944–1945.

One important general function of the existence of formal sanctions was, therefore, that when imposed they called into automatic operation informal sanctions, both social and internalized. The existence of these informal sanctions gave the formal sanction much of its force.

To the extent that the force of formal sanctions was dependent on informal support, their effectiveness could decrease if informal group codes of behavior failed to back them up. Among men who had seen very extensive combat, such as members of some of the divisions which took part in the Italian campaign, the punishments which the Army could threaten appear to have lost much of their impressiveness in the face of the growing bitterness of the men at the daily punishment of life and death in the line. AWOL rates from combat units increased to such an extent that local commanders asked Research Branch personnel for whatever light they could throw on the problem.

This deterioration in the effective force of formal sanctions may be illustrated by comparing the responses of men in these divisions who had seen relatively little combat with those of the old-timers.[5] As Table 3 shows, men who had seen the most combat, among both privates and noncoms, were less likely than newer men to say that a dishonorable discharge is one of the worst things that can happen to a man. The difference remains when educational level is controlled. Such a static comparison does not in itself establish that there was a progressive change in attitude as the men remained in combat over a period of time. But since there is no reason to assume that selective processes could have been responsible for the result, it would seem likely that a progressive change occurred.

While the preceding data suggest that old-timers may have grown to take military punishments somewhat less seriously, the data in Table 4 suggest a parallel growth in toleration of military offenders when such offenders were also "old" combat men. As the table shows, there appears to have been a minor tendency for privates with two or more months of combat experience to be less likely than the newest privates to say that they "don't have any use for a fellow who lets his men down" by going AWOL from the front after

---

[5] The question by which length of time was determined asked for the length of time in which a man's job had kept him within range of enemy artillery. (See footnote to Table 3.) It is a quite broad definition of combat duty, but, when applied to a relatively homogeneous group such as infantrymen in rifle and heavy weapons companies provides a basis for distinguishing groups of different relative amounts of combat duty with probably greater reliability than alternative questions.

being in the line a long time.   This difference is of doubtful reliability.   Among the noncoms, however, there seems to have been a sharp decline in the proportion who would condemn the combat AWOL.   Initially, the noncoms appear to have agreed in endorsing the official sanctions against AWOL, although the sample of rela-

TABLE 3

EVALUATION OF DISHONORABLE DISCHARGE AS A PENALTY IN RELATION TO TIME IN COMBAT

(Enlisted Infantrymen in Line Companies, Italy, April 1945)

QUESTION: "When a court-martial gives a man a dishonorable discharge along with a prison term, do you think the dishonorable discharge makes the punishment much worse?"

| | PERCENTAGE OF MEN GIVING EACH ANSWER AMONG: | | | | | |
| | Privates and Pfc's who have been in combat* for | | | Noncoms who have been in combat* for | | |
ANSWER CATEGORIES	Less than 4 months	4 through 6 months	7 months or more	Less than 4 months	4 through 6 months	7 months or more
Not much worse—it doesn't mean much	19	20	22	16	14	16
Somewhat worse	19	22	22	7	18	26
A lot worse	20	20	22	12	25	22
A great deal worse—it is one of the worst things that can happen to a man	39	36	31	63	41	34
No answer	3	2	3	2	2	2
Total	100	100	100	100	100	100
Number of cases	*277*	*584*	*440*	*43*	*150*	*199*

S-177.

* The question from which the men's time in combat was determined was:

"Since you have been overseas, what is the *total* amount of time you have been on active combat duty?   We mean by active combat duty, doing whatever your job is, *within range of the enemy's artillery*.   Do *not* count time spent in rest periods or in hospitals or any time you were not on active duty for some other reasons."

. Less than 2 weeks
2 weeks up to 1 month
1 month up to 2 months
. . . .
9 months and over

tively new noncoms is small.   Even among those who had been in combat for four through six months, about half of them still said that they had no use for a man who goes AWOL.   But among those who had been in combat for at least nine months, only a quarter took this condemnatory view, approximately the same proportion as among privates of the same length of combat experience.   One

TABLE 4

ATTITUDE TOWARD MEN WHO GO AWOL FROM THE FRONT, IN RELATION TO TIME IN COMBAT

(Enlisted Infantrymen in Line Companies, Italy, April 1945)

QUESTION: "How do you feel about a soldier who goes AWOL from the front after being in the line a long time?"

PERCENTAGE OF MEN GIVING EACH ANSWER AMONG

ANSWER CATEGORIES	Privates and Pfc's who have been in combat* for:					Noncoms who have been in combat* for:			
	Less than 2 months	2 through 3 months	4 through 6 months	7 through 8 months	9 months or more	Less than 4 months	4 through 6 months	7 through 8 months	9 months or more
"I don't have any use for a fellow who lets the other fellows down like that"	31	25	22	25	24	93	48	37	26
"He shouldn't let the other fellows down like that, but probably couldn't help it"	42	44	49	46	45	5	32	42	48
"He probably did his share and they should go easy on him"	17	19	18	17	22	—	6	16	21
"It doesn't make any difference to me one way or the other"	2	6	5	8	4	—	3	4	2
Something else†	3	4	4	3	3	—	8	1	2
No answer	5	2	2	1	2	2	3	—	1
Total	100	100	100	100	100	100	100	100	100
Number of cases	101	181	585	253	196	43	152	89	111

S-177.

* See footnote to Table 3 for wording of question on time in combat.

† A space was provided for those who wished to write in their feeling in their own words.

would expect from this finding that these "old" noncoms had ceased to serve an important function in deterring their men from going AWOL. The widening gap between the official standard and the code of evaluation informally adhered to by the men was doubtless reflected in decreased effectiveness of the formal sanctions with old-timers.

Aside from its punitive aspects, coercive authority played the key role of prescribing concrete actions to be taken in a situation which might be so confused and uncertain that none of the possible actions seemed desirable. Such a situation provokes feelings of helplessness; any authoritative direction of a course of behavior is likely to be welcomed. The men expected this from their officers. If it was not forthcoming, they either sought elsewhere or suffered from disorganization. Some quotations from interviews with wounded veterans of the North African campaign illustrate the point:[6]

Regardless of the situation, men turn to the officer for leadership, and if he doesn't give it to them then they look to the strongest personality who steps forward and becomes a leader—maybe a staff sergeant if the platoon leader is a weak leader.

One time we begged our lieutenants to give orders. They were afraid to act because they didn't have the rank. We took a beating while they were waiting for orders—how did they know the commander hadn't been knocked off?

Previously ingrained reactions to established authority were of course important in making formal authority effective in combat. To the extent that internalized patterns of conformity had been built up, the men would feel guilty to disobey. It is relevant therefore at this point to give brief attention to the problem of the internalization of values and behavioral rules, a matter which will arise again in connection with informal group codes. A person may act in a given way because some outside agency requires it or because he himself wants to—that is, he thinks it is right, his duty, etc. Of course these alternative bases of motivation are not mutually exclusive, and, furthermore, reasons of the second kind may often be given as rationalizations for behavior which in fact is instigated primarily by the first sort of consideration. In the first type, the individual behaves in a given way because he is rewarded, or would be punished if he did not do so. These rewards and punishments, moreover, are changes in the external situation which advance or frustrate some other motivation which *is* internalized. In the case

---

[6] Made in a hospital in the United States, spring 1944.

of an internalized behavioral rule, a violation is in itself punishing to the individual while conformity may be rewarding, apart from changes in the external situation.

Internalization may be inferred when a person reports a *sense of duty*, or, in case he fails to conform, when he gives evidence of *feelings of guilt*.

To a large extent both types of motivation may produce similar effects. This is particularly true when informal group codes largely reinforce the requirements of institutional authority. A person would have to be beyond range of reward and punishment by either his group or formal authority before purely external motivation would cease to push him in the direction of conformity. However, internalization has the advantage of making motivation independent of external surveillance or reward.

In the concrete cases with which we are concerned, it is impossible to distinguish conclusively the degree to which the determining elements were internalized, and a further consideration of the dynamics of internalization would lead to the sort of maze of intrapersonal factors which we intend to avoid. The present section will therefore not attempt to make the dichotomy a primary analytic distinction. However, notice will occasionally be taken of cases in which the various group values and behavioral rules were stated differently as internalized motives.

Attitudes Toward Combat Leaders and Combat Motivation

The leadership relation between officer (and, secondarily, noncom) and enlisted man was crucial to the determination of combat behavior. On the one hand, the officer was the representative of impersonal, coercive institutional authority, discussed above. On the other, he too was a soldier, a person who was fitted into the informal group structure. Because of his salient institutional role, the officer could not be ignored in the informal pattern of attitudes which grew up in a combat unit. These attitudes invariably polarized around him in one way or another. The officer who commanded the personal respect and loyalty of his men could mobilize the full support of a willing followership; he therefore had at his disposal the resources of both the formal coercive system and the system of informal group controls. If, however, the officer had alienated his men and had to rely primarily on coercion, the informal sanctions of the group might cease to bear primarily on the combat mission. Furthermore, since the officer was a natural focus of group unity and a major factor in the everyday lives of the men in his command, the relationship he built up with his men would have an important effect on the solidarity and cohesiveness of the group.

Chapter 8 in Volume I has already discussed the Army leadership relation in detail. Here the configuration of attitudes toward officers in ground combat units and their relation to combat motivation will be considered more briefly.

The combat situation itself fostered a closer solidarity between officers and enlisted men than was usual in the rest of the Army. The makeshift character of front-line living arrangements meant that the contrast between provisions for officers and enlisted men was at a minimum. Formalities were largely abandoned in combat. Also, combat exigencies undoubtedly led a larger proportion of officers to try to exercise leadership rather than mere command, which might do well enough in less critical rear assignments. To be sure, when combat units were out of the line, the garrison situation was received by the men in unwelcome contrast to the greater democracy of the front. It still can be said, nevertheless, that officer-enlisted solidarity was greater on the whole in combat units.

This is supported by men's responses to a wide variety of questions on their attitudes towards their officers, of which the question reported in Chart II is representative.[7] Men in line Infantry companies in the European theater were considerably more likely to indicate favorable attitudes toward their officers than were men in organizations to the rear; there was likewise a tendency, less pronounced, for members of other relatively forward units to be more favorable toward their officers than men in the rear bases of the communications zone. These differences persist when educational level is controlled. Since practical exigencies prevented systematic study of combat troops while they were actually in the line, the relatively more favorable attitude toward their officers shown by combat men in Chart II must be interpreted as one which persisted

---

[7] As Chapter 8 in Volume I showed, questions asking men to evaluate their officers in specific respects tended to form a scale, such that if it is known what a man has to say about his officers in one respect, one can predict with a high degree of accuracy what he has to say about them in other respects. This means that in interpreting the men's answers to specific questions about their officers one must remember that they reflect a general rather than a specific attitude. The specific content of the question in Chart II concerns whether or not the men say their officers are the sort who expose themselves to anything they ask of their men. This appears to be an aspect of officer-enlisted solidarity, but a similar pattern of differences occurs with other questions, the manifest content of which bears on other aspects of the men's attitudes toward their officers.

CHART II

SOLIDARITY WITH OFFICERS IN DIFFERENT TYPES OF GROUND UNITS
(Ground and Service Force Troops from a Cross Section of White
Enlisted Men in the European Theater, April–May 1945)

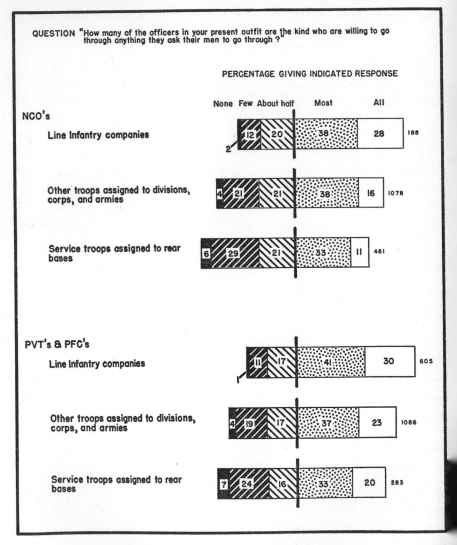

QUESTION "How many of the officers in your present outfit are the kind who are willing to go through anything they ask their men to go through ?"

PERCENTAGE GIVING INDICATED RESPONSE

None Few About half Most All

NCO's

Line Infantry companies — 2 / 12 / 20 / 38 / 28 — 188

Other troops assigned to divisions, corps, and armies — 4 / 21 / 21 / 38 / 16 — 1078

Service troops assigned to rear bases — 6 / 29 / 21 / 33 / 11 — 481

PVT's & PFC's

Line Infantry companies — 1 / 11 / 17 / 41 / 30 — 605

Other troops assigned to divisions, corps, and armies — 4 / 19 / 17 / 37 / 23 — 1086

Service troops assigned to rear bases — 7 / 24 / 16 / 33 / 20 — 283

S-223. Men who failed to answer the question (approximately 3 per cent) are omitted.

The numbers following the bars are the numbers of cases on which percentages are based.

even during periods of rest, training, and reserve, when informal observation indicated that enlisted men nursed some grievances against their officers which would not apply during combat.

While the evidence is that officer-enlisted solidarity was greater in combat units than in units to the rear, this does not mean that *within* combat units men with more combat experience were likely

TABLE 5

ATTITUDES TOWARD OFFICERS BY LENGTH OF TIME IN COMBAT
(Infantry Combat Veterans from a Cross Section of Enlisted Men
in the European Theater, April–May 1945*)

QUESTION: "How many of the officers in your present outfit are the kind who are willing to go through anything they ask their men to go through?"

PERCENTAGE OF INFANTRY VETERANS GIVING EACH
ANSWER AMONG

	Privates and Pfc's who had been in combat† for:			Noncoms who had been in combat† for:	
	Less than 28 days	28 to 111 days	112 days or more	Less than 112 days	112 days or more
All of them are	32 }68	27 }65	18 }65	23 }60	23 }61
Most of them are	36	38	47	37	38
About half of them are	18	20	18	22	23
Few of them are	10 }11	13 }14	16 }17	16 }17	13 }15
None of them are	1	1	1	1	2
No answer	3	1	—	1	1
	—	—	—	—	—
Total	100	100	100	100	100
Number of cases	*203*	*182*	*174*	*97*	*101*

* S-223. The total number of cases differs from that of men in line Infantry companies in Chart II because some men not at that time in line companies are included, while infantrymen who did not say they had been in actual combat with the enemy as opposed to having been subjected to enemy fire are omitted.

† The question on combat time was:

"About how many days have you been in combat since coming overseas?   (Do *not* count any time you were in rest camp or in the hospital or on furlough.)"

About _____ days in combat
_____ I have not been in combat

to have more favorable attitudes toward their officers. If any trend with combat experience existed, it was in the opposite direction. For example, Table 5 shows separately, according to the length of time they said they had been in combat, the responses of the veteran infantrymen included in Chart II, in answer to the same question. If the most favorable answer category is considered, it will be seen that privates with longer combat time were less likely than those with shorter combat time to give the favorable response. For the two most favorable categories taken together, there is no appreciable difference with time in combat for either privates or noncoms.

On two other questions concerning attitudes toward officers, also asked of the men in this sample, the men with longer combat service were if anything more critical than others of their officers. Asked "How many of the officers in your present outfit take a personal interest in the welfare of the men?" 63 per cent of the privates with less than 28 days in combat, as compared with 51 per cent of those with 112 days or more in combat, said "all" or "most of them do." Among noncoms the corresponding figures for those with less than 112 days and those with 112 days or more in combat are 60 per cent and 53 per cent. In response to the question, "How many of the officers in your present outfit do you think really know their job?" 72 per cent of the privates in the group with the least time in combat and 62 per cent of those with the longest combat time replied "all" or "most." Among noncoms, however, those with less combat time gave this response slightly less often (57 per cent) than those with longer combat service (61 per cent). On both questions the percentage of favorable responses among privates with intermediate time in combat is intermediate between the figures presented for the groups with shortest and longest time in combat.

Data from the survey of combat infantrymen in Italy,[8] among whom the range of combat experience was much broader than in the European theater, are in agreement with those just cited. O: privates with less than 4 months in combat, 64 per cent said they had confidence in "all" or "most" of the officers in their company or battery "as leaders under combat conditions." The same response was given by only 52 per cent of the privates with 7 month or more in combat. Corresponding figures for noncoms are 59 per cent and 54 per cent. And 57 per cent of the privates with least time in combat as compared with 47 per cent of those with most combat time said that "in most ways" the enlisted men in their present company or battery got "a square deal from their officers. Among noncoms the percentages giving this response were 63 per cent and 57 per cent. Among privates with intermediate time in combat (4 through 6 months), intermediate percentages were fe

---

[8] S-177.

vorable on both questions and the same was true of noncoms on the first question.[9]

The weight of the evidence is, then, that although men in forward units were more likely than men in rear areas to be favorable to their officers, they did not become more favorable with longer combat experience, and they may have become less favorable. This is not surprising in view of the changing composition of a unit in combat. The ranks of junior officers and enlisted men alike were constantly being thinned by casualties and replenished with replacements. An enlisted man who had survived extensive combat experience and remained in his front-line job would more often than not be senior in combat experience to many of his officers. Such men would not be expected to view their officers with the respect which a man would have for officers senior to him in combat experience. It is possible also that the more bitter attitudes of the "old" men may have been reflected in their feelings toward even those of their officers with whom they had served throughout combat, although there is no evidence available to show this. In any case, such a deterioration in attitude towards officers cannot have been very pronounced, in view of the relatively minor overall differences with time in combat.

The nature of the men's attitudes toward their officers was probably important in determining the kind of influence beyond mere coercion that the officers could have on their men's combat motivation. There were at least two related ways in which the men might regard an officer which would give him informal power to influence their behavior. He might be regarded as a figure of authority, and reacted to in terms of behavior patterns built up in

---

[9] See Table 3 for numbers of cases. The questions were:

"How many of the officers in your company or battery do you have confidence in as leaders under combat conditions?"

All of them
Most of them
About half of them
Few of them
None of them

"In general, do you think that the enlisted men in your present company or battery get a square deal from their officers?"

Yes, in most ways they do
In some ways, yes, in other ways, no
No, on the whole they do *not* get a square deal
I haven't been in this outfit long enough to know

their past experience from their relations with the father and subsequent authoritative persons. In this role, the officer might be a source of guidance and strength. As a wounded veteran of the North African campaign said, "About officers—everybody wants somebody to look up to when he's scared. It makes a lot of difference." For an officer to be readily available to be cast in this role by enlisted men, he must have their confidence that he is actually a source of strength. Sometimes it was difficult for the newly commissioned OCS graduate—the so-called ninety-day wonder—to play this role to hardened combat veterans, as some of Mauldin's cartoons attest.

Secondly, the officer's behavior might be taken as a model by the enlisted men, who might identify with him and try to be like him. This identification may have been most likely to occur when the officer had their respect and admiration; in any case, when the soldier modeled his behavior on the officer's, the role the officer chose for himself became important for its effect on the enlisted men. If the officer shared the dangers and hardships of the men successfully, they would then be the more likely to do their part, whereas the officer who held back from taking personal risks invited similar behavior from his men.

Many officers insisted for this reason that effective combat leadership at the level of the smaller units had to be from in front. To quote a platoon lieutenant who served in the North African campaign,

In combat you have to be out in front leading them, not directing them from the rear. The men say, "If the officer's going to stay back a hundred yards, then I'm going to stay back with him." You can't direct them—you have to lead them.

Enlisted men also made it explicit that they considered leadership from in front to be important. When veteran infantrymen were asked to characterize "one of the best combat soldiers" they had known, those of them who said they were referring to an officer frequently mentioned that he was always with his men in combat and led by personal example. (See Table 8.) The only attributes mentioned more frequently were having a personal interest in the men and courage, the latter of which was also important as a source of good example. Table 6 also is indicative of the importance the men attached to leadership by personal example. As this table shows, veteran infantrymen in a division which fought in the earlier phases of the Mediterranean campaign mentioned personal leadership in the face of danger as among the ways in which officers were particularly helpful in making their men more confident in a tough and frightening situation. While the number of men making comments is too small to attach significance to the fact that this category of comment was most frequent, it is important that the number of comments mentioning things officers *said* was less than half the number commenting on things that they *did*.

TABLE 6

OFFICERS' LEADERSHIP PRACTICES WHICH MEN REPORTED AS
GIVING THEM CONFIDENCE
(Veteran Infantrymen in a Division Which Fought in the
Mediterranean, April 1944)

QUESTION: "Can you recall a case in your experience in which an officer did a particularly good job of helping his men to feel more confident in a tough or frightening situation?"

	Percentage of comments falling into each category
Led by example; did dangerous things himself, displayed personal courage and coolness	31
Encouraged men; gave pep talks, joked, passed on information	26
Showed active concern for welfare and safety of men	23
Showed informal, friendly attitude; worked along with men	5
Miscellaneous or unclassifiable	15
Total	100
Number of men making comments	*144*
Number of men making no comment	*449*

S-100.

If, as has been suggested, the officer-enlisted man relationship had an important effect on the combat motivation of the enlisted men, one would expect men with relatively more favorable attitudes toward their unit officers to have been better motivated than men with less favorable attitudes. In terms of the question on readiness for further combat which was introduced in the previous chapter[10] such appears to have been the case, as Table 7 indicates. The question is one which, as mentioned before, was shown in Chapter 1 to be particularly differentiating between groups of men whose

---

[10] Chapter 2, Chart IX.

later combat performance was relatively better or worse.   In three different combat divisions which fought in the Pacific under quite different conditions, the men who gave consistently favorable answers to three questions concerning their feelings about their officers[11] were more likely to show themselves to be relatively ready for further combat than were those who gave consistently unfavorable

TABLE 7

ATTITUDE TOWARD COMPANY OFFICERS IN RELATION TO READINESS FOR COMBAT
(Veteran Enlisted Infantrymen in Three Pacific Divisions,
March–April 1944)

ATTITUDE TOWARD COMPANY OFFICERS†	PERCENTAGE RELATIVELY READY FOR FURTHER COMBAT* IN EACH SUBGROUP		
	Division A	*Division B*	*Division C*
	Men who say they are in very good, good, or fair physical condition		
Favorable	78 *(580)*	65 *(411)*	53 *(231)*
Intermediate	68 *(298)*	51 *(257)*	33 *(187)*
Unfavorable	58 *(130)*	42 *(196)*	29 *(135)*
	Men who say they are in poor or very poor physical condition		
Favorable	62 *(99)*	37 *(147)*	26 *(253)*
Intermediate	35 *(89)*	28 *(160)*	19 *(283)*
Unfavorable	26 *(92)*	17 *(154)*	13 *(317)*

S-100.
Numbers in parentheses are the numbers of cases on which percentages are based.
* See footnote 33 in Chapter 2 for question by which men were grouped according to readiness for combat.
† Men were grouped according to their answers to three questions:

"How many officers in your company are the kind you would want to serve under in combat?"

"How many of your company officers are the kind who are willing to go through anything they ask their men to go through?"

"How many of your officers take a personal interest in their men?"

Men who answered "about half" or more of their officers, on each of the three questions, were classified as having a favorable attitude toward their officers; men who said "few" or "none" on each of the questions were classified as having an unfavorable attitude; and the remainder were classified as intermediate.

answers, while men who expressed intermediate attitudes toward their officers were also intermediate in expressed readiness for combat.   Although there were pronounced differences in the proportion of men classed as relatively ready for combat between the divisions and between men who said they were in good or in poor physical condition, the table shows that, even when these differences are controlled, attitude toward officers remains strongly related to

---

[11] See footnote to Table 7 for these questions.

readiness for combat. An analysis of the data for one of the divisions showed that the relationship also held up when rank and education were controlled.

Confidence in company officers was also associated with a number of other attitudes favorable to combat motivation. For example, in one of the Pacific divisions surveyed which had seen combat under the most arduous conditions, 26 per cent of the men who said that about half or more of their officers were the kind they would want to serve under in combat, as compared with 37 per cent of those who said few or none were, indicated that they had less confidence in themselves the more times they went into combat. Sixty per cent of the former group but only 42 per cent of the latter said they were very proud of their company. Thirty-eight per cent of the men with a favorable attitude toward their officers as compared with 26 per cent of the others said they never got the feeling that this war was not worth fighting.[12]

There is thus no question that attitudes toward company officers were intimately associated with a group of attitudes which together were undoubtedly important to motivation in combat. The kinds of data available give no clue as to the causal pattern of these interrelated attitudes. One may be fairly sure that were the true picture known, it would turn out to involve a fairly complicated interplay. Attitudes toward officers, for one thing, were undoubtedly shaped by a number of factors in addition to the objective characteristics of the officers themselves. Some of these additional factors were doubtless in turn causally related to the men's willingness for combat. Matters of personality probably entered into the picture. The data merely establish that "good" attitudes toward officers were part of a favorable motivational complex. Apart from the data, it seems likely that the men's attitudes toward their officers had a real importance in determining whether men fought aggressively and stayed in the fight. When unfavorable attitudes toward the unit officers developed—whether or not the leadership practices of the officers concerned were the main cause of this deterioration—the formal, authoritative system of controls and the pattern of informal sanctions and values rooted in the men's attitudes would no longer merge in the person of the unit commander. One source of the ties of individual to group would be impaired, and the soldier would be less likely to take extra risks or withstand extra

---

[12] 713 and 670 cases, respectively (S-100). The differences are consistent in all rank and education groups.

stresses for the sake of his admired leader or in response to his support.

Attitudes toward unit noncoms are highly correlated with attitudes toward company officers (Chart III).   With this high correlation, one would expect that confidence in noncoms would be associated with essentially the same pattern of motivation as confidence in officers.   This is the case.   The men who were relatively confi-

CHART III

RELATION OF CONFIDENCE IN COMPANY NONCOMS TO CONFIDENCE IN
COMPANY OFFICERS
(Veteran Infantrymen in Two Pacific Divisions, March–April 1944)

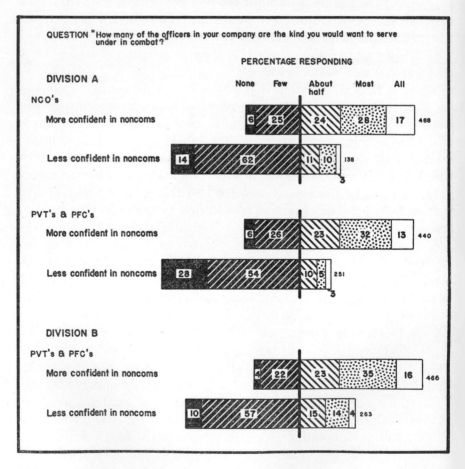

Data from S-100.
For grouping according to confidence in noncoms see text.
The numbers following the bars are the numbers of cases on which percentages are based.

dent in their noncoms[13] were more likely to indicate that they were ready for further combat, less likely to say they became less self-confident as they saw more combat, and more likely to show pride in their company.   As in the case of attitudes toward officers, there

CHART IV

RELATION OF CONFIDENCE IN OFFICERS AND IN NONCOMS TO READINESS FOR COMBAT
(Veteran Infantry Privates in Three Pacific Divisions, March–April 1944)

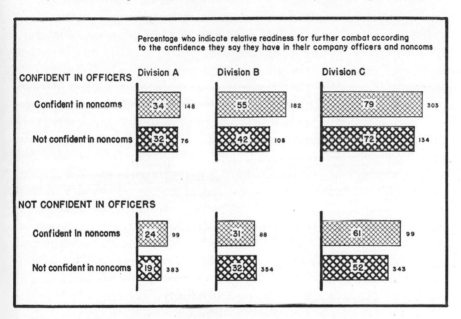

Data from S-100.
For grouping according to confidence in officers and noncoms see text.
The numbers following the bars are the numbers of cases on which percentages are based.

was no tendency for men of longer combat experience to be more favorable toward their noncoms.

In regard to the relative importance of confidence in unit officers and in noncoms for combat motivation, the kind of data available does not of course permit any conclusive answer.   Data from three

---

[13] Men were grouped according to their answers to the question, "How many of the noncoms in your outfit are the kind you would want to serve under in combat?"

| Relatively more confident in noncoms | { All of them are
Most of them are
About half of them are |
| Relatively less confident in noncoms | { Few of them are
None of them are |

divisions suggest that among combat veterans below noncommis-
sioned grade, confidence in officers may have been more closely related to willingness for combat than confidence in noncoms.   Chart
IV shows the result when the veteran privates and privates first
class in each of these divisions were sorted into four groups, according to whether they were relatively confident in their noncoms but
not in their officers, or vice versa, or relatively confident in both sets
or neither set of leaders.[14]   If one compares on the chart the proportion ready for combat[15] among men with a given attitude toward
their officers but more or less confident in their noncoms, relatively
little difference in the percentages is apparent.   If, on the other
hand, one compares the men with a given attitude toward their
noncoms, it appears that those who were more confident in their
officers were consistently and considerably more likely than those
who were less favorable toward their officers to indicate a relatively
high degree of willingness for combat.   These relationships remain
when educational level is controlled.   While on the face of it the
picture would lead one to attribute greater importance to attitudes
toward officers, it is merely suggestive, since the complexity of conceivable interrelationships which could enter into the findings is
almost unlimited.   If the question of the relative importance of
attitudes toward the two kinds of leaders is left aside, the empirical
fact remains that the men's attitudes toward their unit leadership
tended toward consistency, and that positive attitudes toward noncoms, like positive attitudes toward officers, were part of the empirical picture of good combat motivation.

The Informal Group and Combat Motivation

The group in its informal character, with its close interpersonal
ties, served two principal functions in combat motivation: it *set and
enforced group standards* of behavior, and it *supported and sustained
the individual* in stresses he would otherwise not have been able to

---

[14] Men were grouped according to confidence in officers and noncoms as follows:

Question: "How many of the officers in your company (how many of the noncoms
in your outfit) are the kind you would want to serve under in combat?"

Confident   { All of them are
            { Most of them are
            { About half of them are

Not confident { Few of them are
              { None of them are

[15] See footnote 33 in Chapter 2 for basis of grouping according to readiness for further
combat.

withstand. These are related functions: the group enforced its standards principally by offering or withholding recognition, respect, and approval, which were among the supports it had to offer, while the subjective reward of following an internalized group code enhanced an individual's resources for dealing with the situation.

Masculinity and the Role of the Combat Soldier

The codes according to which a combat unit judged the behavior of its members, and in terms of which conformity was enforced, differed in their generality. Perhaps the most general was one drawn largely from civilian culture but given its special interpretation in the combat situation: Be a man. Conceptions of masculinity vary among different American groups, but there is a core which is common to most: courage, endurance and toughness, lack of squeamishness when confronted with shocking or distasteful stimuli, avoidance of display of weakness in general, reticence about emotional or idealistic matters, and sexual competency. The conditions in which the code is applied also vary. For example, it seems not to have been invoked in the same way in the recent war as in World War I. In World War II there was much less community pressure on the young men to get into the Army. There were few real counterparts to the white feather, painting homes yellow, use of the epithet "slacker." The general attitude was that everyone should do what he was assigned as well as he could, but it was *not* considered essential that the individual "stick his neck out." To oversimplify, it might be said that in World War I the test of social manhood began much farther from actual fighting than in World War II. In the First World War, a man was more severely censured for failing to enter the armed services; this time, the test was more nearly whether he adequately filled his role once placed in the combat situation.

Combat posed a challenge for a man to prove himself to himself and others. Combat was a dare. One never knew for sure that he could take it until he had demonstrated that he could. Most soldiers facing the prospect of combat service had to deal with a heavy charge of anticipatory anxiety. The more they heard about how tough the fighting was, the greater the anxiety and the insecurity that came from doubt as to whether they could handle the anxiety. Thus, combat might actually come almost as a relief—it joined the issue and broke the strain of doubt and waiting.

A code as universal as "being a man" is very likely to have been deeply internalized. So the fear of failure in the role, as by showing cowardice in battle, could bring not only fear of social censure on this point as such, but also more central and strongly established fears related to sex-typing. To fail to measure up as a soldier in courage and endurance was to risk the charge of not being a man. ("Whatsa matter, bud—got lace on your drawers?" "Christ, he's acting like an old maid.") If one were not socially defined as a man, there was a strong likelihood of being branded a "woman," a dangerous threat to the contemporary male personality. The generally permissive attitude toward expression of fear that will be described in a later chapter mitigated the fear of failure in manliness, but by no means obviated it. A man could show and admit fear without necessarily being branded a "weak sister," but only so long as it was clear that he had done his utmost.

The generalized code of masculinity serves as a context for various more specific codes that may be isolated more or less arbitrarily. The prescribed avoidance to claims of idealistic motivation will be considered later. The most direct application of the masculinity code was to the social role of the combat soldier. In fact, the code of the combat soldier can be summarized by saying that behavior in combat was recognized as a test of being a man. When this code was internalized, or enforced by playing on an internalized code of manliness, a man once in combat had to fight in order to keep his own self-respect: "Hell, I'm a soldier."

The ingredients of the veterans' conception of the good combat soldier appear vividly in Chart V, which summarizes data presented in more detail in Table 8. Veteran infantrymen of a division which had fought in North Africa and Sicily were asked to think of one of the best combat soldiers they had known, and then to give his rank, and name some of the things they admired in him. As the chart shows, attributes characteristically ascribed to a good officer differed from those ascribed to a good private, while the pattern of attributes of the good noncom was intermediate between those of officer and private. Leadership ability and practices were most often mentioned in the case of officers, while courage and aggressiveness were most often mentioned for privates. "Knowledge and adequate performance of job"—a classification which did not include characteristics that could be grouped with leadership, and therefore tended to be descriptive of the good follower—was more often mentioned in regard to privates. Courage and aggressiveness ("guts"), which are central to the masculine ideal, thus were a prime ingredient of the combat man's notion of the good soldier. For privates and noncoms, characteristics in this category were mentioned more often than any others, while the category was second only to leadership qualities for officers. As may be seen in Table 8, the leadership practices attributed to the officers selected as good combat soldiers included sharing combat dangers and leading by personal example, which also involve courage and masculinity.

CHART V

How Veteran Enlisted Infantrymen Characterized One of the Best Combat Soldiers They Had Known

(Summary of Table 8)

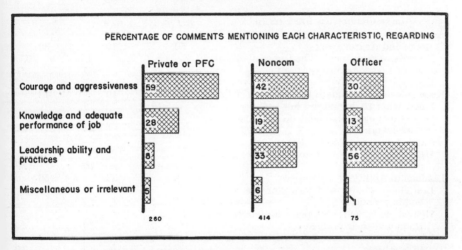

PERCENTAGE OF COMMENTS MENTIONING EACH CHARACTERISTIC, REGARDING

The numbers at the bottom of the bars are the numbers of cases on which percentages are based.

A more concrete impression of some of the elements of masculinity involved in being a combat soldier may be seen in the following fragment of an interview with a wounded Infantry veteran of the North African campaign:

One time me and another guy were in a hole. The guy says "Let's get out of here." I talked to him (tried to calm him down) but he never was a soldier—did typewriting, ran errands for officers. He was a suck-ass for a colonel, not a real soldier. A real soldier is a guy—he'll drink and swear—but he relies on himself; a guy that can take care of himself.[16]

Here the combat soldier, the real soldier, is defined partly by contrast with someone who does not qualify as a man.

[16] Made in a United States hospital in spring of 1944.

The man who lived up to the code of the combat soldier had proved his manhood; he could take pride in being a combat man and draw support in his role from this pride. Of this sort was the grim pride in being an "old beat-up Joe," who had suffered and endured

TABLE 8

How Veteran Enlisted Infantrymen Characterized One of the
Best Combat Soldiers They Had Known
(Division Which Had Fought in North Africa and Sicily, April 1944*)

	PERCENTAGE OF COMMENTS MENTIONING EACH CHARACTERISTIC, AMONG THOSE WHICH REFERRED TO		
CHARACTERISTICS MENTIONED	*A private or Pfc*	*A noncom*	*An officer*
Courage and Aggressiveness	59	42	30
Fearless, brave, cool, "had guts," disregarded personal safety	*46*	*35*	*21*
Displayed aggressiveness and initiative	*13*	*7*	*9*
Knowledge and Adequate Performance of Job	28	19	13
Knew what to do and did job well	*19*	*9*	*3*
Observant; alert; excellent on scouting and patrol work	*6*	—	—
Carried out orders to the letter	*3*	—	—
Used good judgment, common sense; good planner	—	*10*	*10*
Leadership Ability and Practices	8	33	56
Leadership ability and miscellaneous leadership practices	*2*	*13*	*14*
Helped other men; took personal interest in them and their problems	*3*	*10*	*24*
Led by personal example; always with men in combat	—	*9*	*18*
Cheered men by humorous remarks	*3*	*1*	—
Miscellaneous or Irrelevant	5	6	1
Total	100	100	100
Number of comments	*260*	*414*	*75*

* S-100. The question was: "Think over your combat experience and pick out some man who you would say was one of the best combat soldiers you have known. We won't want to know who he was but we would like to know something about him. What was his grade or rank? What were some of the things about him that made you think he was a good combat soldier?" Seventy-five per cent of the men (445 cases) made some answer to the question.

and took a perverse satisfaction that things were working out for the worst, just as he had expected they would. A second aspect of this pride of the combat man appears in his typical resentment of the rear echelon, a phenomenon which will merit closer attention in a later chapter. It will be suggested there that this resentment, springing in part from envy of the favored circumstances at the rear, served one function of devaluing what was inaccessible and placing a higher moral value on what had to be put up with. The fact that rear-echelon soldiers accepted the lower status made the right to feel this invidious pride a real support to the combat man.

The pride in being a combat man may be illustrated by an account told to an interviewer at the front in Europe by a sergeant in a veteran Infantry battalion. He had been wounded and later returned to his outfit through the chain of replacement depots. His account of this revealed that he was indifferent to the physical conditions encountered, but like many combat men of similar experience he was very bitter about the treatment of combat veterans by the permanent personnel of the replacement depots. He complained that the cadre were indifferent to the welfare of replacements, "showed no respect for what the combat men had been through," tried to "shove people around," and so on through a long list. When asked for an example, he told of a corporal who was in charge of a group of veteran combat replacements:

He kept ordering us around and putting combat men on kitchen details. Finally I got fed up. I told him: "Look here, damn you—you stay out of here. There are *men* in here, and I don't want them contaminated."

This was recounted with intensely explosive bitterness and contempt. Aside from its other complex aspects, the interview illustrates some of the strongest factors in the motivation of combat soldiers. The code of being a man is here explicit. The rear-echelon soldier is resented and despised because of his misuse of Army authority and his failure to share a community of experience and sentiment. And the final crushing comment which the combat soldier makes is to imply that the corporal is not a man—because he is not one of the fraternity of front-line fighters. The informant did not even feel it necessary to describe the corporal's reaction: the comment was conclusive, and no further argument had been deemed necessary. It is not difficult to imagine the tremendous sense of superiority which could be given by a social position which thus permitted having the last word.

Loyalty to Outfit and Pride in It

Loyalty to one's buddies and more generally to one's outfit was another stringent group code. It is allied to the code of masculinity, but independent in the sense that someone who let his buddies down through irresponsibility, not through cowardice, might not have his social manhood called into question. Loyalty to one's buddies was founded on the fact of vital mutual dependence and supported by the cluster of sentiments grouped under the term "pride in outfit." In the words of a former Infantry scout who was wounded at Salerno after fighting through Sicily,

You know the men in your outfit. You have to be loyal to them. The men get close-knit together. They like each other—quit their petty bickering and having enemies. They depend on each other—wouldn't do anything to let the rest of them down. They'd rather be killed than do that. They begin to think the world of each other. It's the main thing that keeps a guy from going haywire.[17]

The converse picture appears in a remark by another wounded veteran, who also touches aptly on the interrelations of group solidarity and command:

The worst thing a soldier can have is to see other guys dropping out. Sticking together is the important thing—with someone in command to push them along—everybody's afraid.[18]

Combat veterans in both Pacific and Mediterranean theaters agreed in rating highly the supporting value of this motive in keeping them fighting when the going was tough.[19] Asked about five possible sources of support in combat, the proportion who replied that thinking "that you couldn't let the other men down" helped them a lot, constituted a majority of the Infantry veterans in each theater and was second only to the proportion who said they were helped a lot by prayer. The data presented in Chart I at the beginning of this chapter also support the importance of the loyalty code. It will be remembered that among the combat incentives named by enlisted men, those classified as solidarity with the group were second in frequency of mention.

This code of loyalty seems sometimes to have been deeply internalized. Presumptive evidence of this lies in the indications of guilt feelings among men who were out of combat while their comrades were still fighting. Psychiatrists and other observers have noted these reactions among combat-exhaustion patients, wounded men, repatriated prisoners of war, limited assignment men reclassified from combat to rear-area duties, and among flyers completing a

---

[17] Personal interview made in hospital in the United States, spring 1944.
[18] Personal interview made in hospital in the United States, spring 1944.
[19] An identical set of questions was given to each group of men. For the questions asked and the responses, see Chart XII.

tour of duty.[20]   Stories were current in both the Mediterranean and the European theaters about how combat men awaiting return to their units at a replacement depot after hospitalization would go AWOL from the depot to rejoin their units in combat.   Evidence on the exact incidence of such reactions is lacking; but the fact that a certain number of men in these situations manifested guilt feelings can be taken as established.

Such guilt feelings appear to have been a highly specific reaction to leaving one's immediate social group, rather than an expression of a sense of not having done one's share.   This is clear in the case of the pilot completing a tour of combat missions, who had done his share by official and informal standards alike.   Furthermore, combat troops seem always to have been glad enough to permit some other regiment to have the privilege of making an attack, and no general sense of obligation prevented it from being quite acceptable for them to scrounge equipment and rations from other units.   The morality lying behind the guilt reactions of men who were removed from combat was much more concretely tied to the closely knit group in which the soldier fought.   The formulation tended to be: "I'm letting my buddies down—some of them are dead, and the others are still in there taking it, while I'm safe.   True, I've done my part, but I have no right to be out of it so long as they are still involved."

Closely related to the code of group loyalty is the sentiment of pride in outfit.   It is involved in the loyalty code, for if a combat soldier were to have disparaged his outfit and its record, it would have been taken as disloyalty by his fellows.   Also, the pride that a soldier, as a member of his outfit, could take in its accomplishments was one of the recompenses which supported him in his loyalty.   Pride in outfit was thus both an indication that the soldier had identified with his fighting unit and one of the forms in which this identification supported him in his combat role.

It is therefore not surprising that the members of a veteran organization were typically more likely to be proud of their outfit than members of untried divisions.   The only questions in this area asked alike of veterans and of troops in training referred to the men's pride in their company.   As Chart VI shows, men in divisions which had not yet seen combat—whether they were still in the States or await-

---

[20] Cf. R. R. Grinker and J. P. Spiegel, *Men Under Stress* (Blakiston, Philadelphia, 1945), pp. 183–84; Bill Mauldin, *Up Front* (Henry Holt and Co., New York, 1945), pp. 58–60, 126.

ing action overseas—were considerably less likely than combat veterans to say they were proud of their companies. Very few of the men in the veteran divisions said they were not proud.

From one veteran division to another there was of course marked variation in the proportion of men expressing a high degree of pride. Among the five veteran divisions combined in Chart VI, the pro-

CHART VI

PRIDE IN OUTFIT AMONG INFANTRYMEN

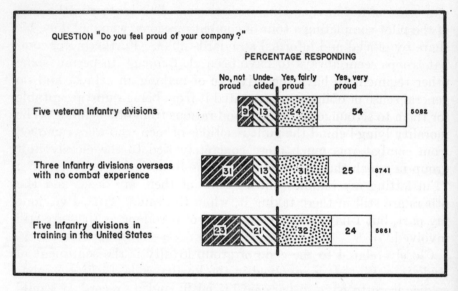

QUESTION "Do you feel proud of your company?"

PERCENTAGE RESPONDING

	No, not proud	Unde-cided	Yes, fairly proud	Yes, very proud	
Five veteran Infantry divisions	9	13	24	54	5082
Three Infantry divisions overseas with no combat experience	31	13	31	25	8741
Five Infantry divisions in training in the United States	23	21	32	24	5861

Veteran divisions were made up of three divisions in the Pacific and two in Europe (Mediterranean campaign), surveyed in November 1943 (S-91) and March–April 1944 (S-100).

Overseas divisions were surveyed in England, April–May 1944 (S-129). In this survey the negative answer category was worded "No, not very proud."

Divisions in training were surveyed in May 1944 (S-121).

The numbers following the bars are the numbers of cases on which percentages are based.

portion in each division who said they were "very proud" of their company ranged from 40 to 62 per cent. The division standing highest in unit pride was one of the first involved in fighting the Germans—a history which allowed the men to say jokingly but not without bitterness that the American Army consisted of their division and eight million replacements.

While the men's closest personal ties were within their companies, major tactical goals were the achievement of larger units, and the companies in a regiment or division on the whole shared essentially the same experiences. There are no data from combat troops as to the relative degree of pride the men felt in the successively larger groupings of which they were members. Such unit symbols as the shoulder patch, however, fostered identification and pride on a broader basis than the unit of immediate contact. Among ground and service troops, members of a given combat division shared the same shoulder patch. Rarely were there distinctive regimental insignia. Forward troops not assigned to a division—mostly service troops, except for some artillery and armored units—would wear the shoulder patch of the corps or army to which their unit was attached. For members of divisions, identification with the division undoubtedly eclipsed their identifications with these larger groupings, which were sometimes unstable as divisions were transferred from one corps or army to another. It was probably a different matter for the forward service troops, since identification with an army or corps assimilated them to the status of combat men, while the symbols of belonging to the larger unit served to distinguish them in the eyes of troops at large from men assigned to rear-area base sections.

Pride in outfit for the combat man included something over and above personal identification with the "other guys" and the leaders in the outfit. He took pride in its history as well as its present, and identified with the men who had died in the outfit as well as with the living. As it has been suggested, he owed it to them—they hadn't got off easy. The intrapersonal ways in which this operated are probably complex, but there is little doubt that the process occurred.

Since the soldier's outfit was the vehicle that conveyed him into danger and kept him there, one might expect feelings of antagonism toward it to have developed. But most of the men seemed to view the outfit in the personal terms of the men and leaders who had been in it, who could not be blamed for keeping them in combat, and managed to divert their hostility to the war, the Army, or higher headquarters, who kept them in combat, or to more fortunate persons to the rear. There was probably little ambivalence in expressions of pride in the smaller combat unit. The real ambivalence centered in the conflict between loyalty to one's outfit and buddies and the desire to escape from combat.

If hostility did gradually build up toward the outfit, it appears to have been at least balanced by satisfaction in what the group had endured and achieved. Among combat troops with a broad range of combat experience, men with widely differing lengths of time in combat behind them did not differ appreciably in the degree of pride they expressed in their outfit's record.   This lack of difference is in contrast to the more general tendency for men who had been long in combat to have poorer attitudes than others.   The question is different from the one previously quoted:[21]

QUESTION: "How well do you think your company or battery has shown up under combat conditions?"

ANSWER CATEGORIES	PERCENTAGE OF INFANTRYMEN GIVING EACH ANSWER AMONG THOSE WHO SAID THEY HAD BEEN IN COMBAT FOR		
	Less than 4 months	4 months through 6 months	7 months or more
Very well	63	68	64
Fairly well	26	27	28
Not so well	2	1	4
Poorly	1	1	1
Undecided or no answer	8	3	3
Total	100	100	100
Number of cases	*320*	*735*	*639*

No appreciable differences with combat time appeared within the subgroups when rank and education were simultaneously controlled.

Additional evidence that the men's ties to their group were not weakened by prolonged combat experience may be found in Table 18, which shows that men who had been in combat for a long time were little if at all less likely than newer men to say they were helped a lot "when the going was tough" by thinking that they could not let the other men down.

Pride in outfit and other aspects of intragroup bonds could be maintained at a high level without any corresponding tendency for the men to acquiesce with enthusiasm to the demands that the Army made on them.   Pride was often a bitter pride, and some divisions which had seen particularly long and heavy combat duty were characterized equally by a high degree of pride and a general agreement that they had done more than their full share and there was no point in "sticking one's neck out."   Loyalty to one's buddies could take the form of supporting them against the Army's demands as well as backing them up in combat.   Sometimes this could present a conflict situation.   For instance, men who tried to evade

[21] Survey of line infantrymen in Italy, April 1945 (S-177).

combat were subject to resentment for letting their buddies down and throwing a greater burden on their shoulders, but embittered "old" men might at the same time sympathize with their enterprise in resisting the system. Table 9 shows a tendency for men with longer combat experience to be more likely to excuse soldiers who tried to get out of combat by going on sick call unnecessarily, and less likely to say "I don't have any use for a fellow who would do that."

TABLE 9

ATTITUDE TOWARD MEN WHO EVADE COMBAT BY GOING ON SICK CALL IN
RELATION TO TIME IN COMBAT
(Enlisted Infantrymen in Line Companies, Italy, April 1945)

QUESTION: "How do you feel about a soldier who tries to get out of combat by going on sick call when he doesn't really need to?"

| | PERCENTAGE OF MEN GIVING EACH ANSWER AMONG | | | | | |
| | Privates and Pfc's who have been in combat for | | | Noncoms who have been in combat for | | |
ANSWER CATEGORIES	Less than 4 months	4 through 6 months	7 months or more	Less than 4 months	4 through 6 months	7 months or more
"I don't have any use for a fellow who would do that"	58	46	45	75	58	58
"It doesn't make any difference to me one way or the other"	9	14	16	7	14	5
"It's O.K. with me, if he can get away with it"	27	34	35	16	23	32
Something else, or no answer	6	6	4	2	5	5
Total	100	100	100	100	100	100
Number of cases	*277*	*584*	*440*	*43*	*150*	*198*

S-177.

For the reasons just indicated, one would not expect pride in outfit to be strongly related to our measure of readiness for further combat. Table 10 shows, nevertheless, that there was a tendency for men who said they were very proud of their company to be somewhat more likely than others to indicate that they were ready for more combat. It should be remembered that men who checked as reluctant a statement as "Hope I won't have to go, but if I go I think I will do all right" were classed as relatively ready for combat, in addition to the smaller number of men who checked more positive statements. The differences between men who checked "very proud" and other men in readiness for combat were in the same direction in all of six pairs of subgroups when rank and education were controlled. The men who said they were very proud of their company were also somewhat more likely to say that they became more confident in themselves the more times they went into combat. Thirty-four per cent of the very proud versus 21 per cent of the less proud said they became more self-confident.[22]

TABLE 10

RELATION OF PRIDE IN OUTFIT TO READINESS FOR COMBAT
(Veteran Infantrymen in a Pacific Division, March–April 1944)

| | PERCENTAGE OF MEN WHO INDICATE THAT THEY ARE RELATIVELY READY FOR FURTHER COMBAT* AMONG THOSE WHO | |
	Say they are "very proud" of their company	Do not say they are "very proud" of their company
Privates and Pfc's	27 *(331)*	21 *(403)*
Noncoms	37 *(382)*	27 *(267)*
All men	33 *(713)*	23 *(670)*

S-100.
Numbers in parentheses are the numbers of cases on which percentages are based.
* See footnote 33 in Chapter 2 for question on readiness for combat.

Pride in outfit, then, belongs in the cluster of attitudes associated with favorable combat motivation. But in line with what has been said before, pride in outfit was probably less important as an incentive to aggressive action than as a consolation prize for having put up with the unavoidable. It further reflected strong identification with the unit, which meant that the men would be more likely to hold together when orders called for combat action.

Sources of Power and Security from the Group

As we have seen in the foregoing discussion, the pride that the combat man felt in his outfit gave him a certain amount of support in his combat role. There were other ways in which group membership afforded him resources of power and security. The recognition, respect, and approval received by a member in good standing both reinforced the approved patterns of behavior and gave the

---

[22] Based on 713 and 670 cases, respectively (S-100). The differences hold up for the various subgroups when education and rank are controlled.

individual the security of belonging. On a very practical level, the soldier could count on being looked out for by his buddies if he were in a tough situation. If he were wounded, he could count on both his buddies and the medics to take care of him. While the important security of belonging to a powerful and trusted group is most dramatically seen in the soldier's reciprocal ties to his buddies in his immediate unit, on a different level it extended to his feeling of being on a powerful, winning team. The knowledge that one was part of a mighty war machine helped to ward off feelings of impotence and vulnerability. Anything that served to build up any of the components of which this perceived group power was constituted bolstered the soldier's hope of personal survival and ultimate victory and made the daily stresses of combat more endurable for him.

At the level of the soldier's immediate combat unit, he was bound to his company for reasons of self-interest, in addition to loyalty and pride. The men in the unit were his buddies, whom he had fought beside and learned to trust and depend upon, so he felt safer with them. Actually, this is merely another aspect of the strong group identifications that were built up in the combat unit. The soldier himself felt strong ties of pride and loyalty to his buddies, and by the same token knew he could depend on them to act according to similar ties. In a strange outfit to which he himself had not as yet built up a strong identification, he would not feel a secure trust in the dependability of the other men.

In explaining why he would not want to leave his outfit, a soldier might express either thought: that he didn't want to let his buddies down, or that he felt safer with his own outfit. A wounded veteran of combat in North Africa stressed the aspect of security when he said:

The fellows don't want to leave when they're sick. They're afraid to leave their own men—the men they know. They don't want to get put in a different outfit. Your own outfit—they're the men you have confidence in. It gives you more guts to be with them.[23]

A remark by a second veteran of the same campaign suggests that this feeling of safety in one's own outfit acted not merely as a deterrent against evading combat through medical channels but sometimes made straggling a dubious escape:

[23] Comments obtained in personal interview with wounded veteran of the North African campaign, made in a United States hospital in the spring of 1944.

I was scared if I fell behind, but never dropped out. Always felt safer when I was up with the company.[24]

One element in the men's reluctance to be transferred from the unit they knew intimately was probably the minimum security they felt in the knowledge that they would be cared for if they were wounded. Where strong mutual ties had developed, a man could feel sure that the other men would take the extra trouble and risk to care for him if he were hit. On patrol behind enemy lines, the trouble and risk involved in bringing a wounded man back was often considerable. The usual policy among divisions visited in Italy was that unless the mission of the patrol or the lives of the other men would be very seriously jeopardized, every attempt would be made by a patrol to bring back all its wounded personnel. This made patrol duty less threatening to the men than would have been the case if they could normally expect to be abandoned when seriously wounded. However, the fear undoubtedly remained, and was one reason why men wanted to face danger in the company of men with whom they shared deep mutual trust.

The presence of medical aid men with each combat company was a universal source of reassurance, and these medics were highly respected and admired. The men could and did expect that if they were wounded everything possible would be done for them, even at the cost of personal hazard to medical personnel, although they were not so sure of getting what they considered to be adequate medical care for other ills. The policy always was to keep a man in combat as long as he could fight, whereas the men naturally tended to feel that ailments which the surgeon did not regard as incapacitating were reason enough to leave combat. As a result, many felt as one soldier wrote: "The only comment I have to make is when a man is wounded he gets swell treatment, but when he goes on sick call at any time, the treatment is poor." The strictness of medical evacuation policy varied considerably from unit to unit. Where it was particularly rigorous, one source of security for the men was diminished; on the other hand, one avenue of possible escape from combat was made the more difficult.

The distinction between attitudes toward treatment of wounds and of other ailments, which emerged in informal interviews, somewhat obscures the meaning of men's answers to questions asking

[24] Comments obtained in personal interview with wounded veteran of the North African campaign, made in a United States hospital in the spring of 1944.

them to evaluate front-line medical care in general.   Nevertheless, 87 per cent of the front-line infantrymen surveyed in Italy said they received "very good" or "pretty good" medical care (38 per cent said "very good").[25]   The men's attitude toward care of the wounded is probably more accurately reflected in the answers of a sample of 200 wounded enlisted men in hospitals in the European theater.   Fully 85 per cent of these men rated the job being done by the front-line medics as "very good."   An additional 9 per cent rated it as "good," and only 3 per cent said it was "fair," "poor," or "very poor."   The men's expectations of succor when wounded were thus a source of security.   Against this must be balanced the uncertainty of what they would consider adequate attention for their day-to-day ailments.

The support and reassurance coming from confidence in company leadership has already been discussed.   Also not to be neglected is the bearing of confidence in the leadership, strategy, and tactics of the higher commands.   It can perhaps be generalized that usually this was of relatively minor consequence.   Unless the larger command was personalized by a highly popular individual commander, on the one hand, or unless things were going very badly, on the other, men did not give much concern to what went on above.   Their confidence in their own immediate leadership was probably a more important factor in combat motivation.

One element which could contribute to a feeling of participation in group power was the degree of confidence the men felt in the supply system and in their arms and equipment.   As will be shown in Chapter 6, where the attitudes of combat troops toward rear echelon elements are discussed, combat men tended to speak quite highly of the job the supply troops were doing, even though they felt considerable antagonism toward the men holding down rear area jobs.   In regard to equipment, American troops universally regarded themselves as better off than the enemy.   Particularly in the Pacific campaign, there was virtual unanimity about the superiority of American arms.   Ninety-seven per cent of the enlisted men and nearly all of the officers said, early in 1944, that most or all of our equipment was better than that of the Japanese, while a majority of the enlisted men said all of it was better (Table 11).   In the campaign against Germany at the same time (before V weapons were

---

[25] S-177, April 1945 (1,766 cases).   The question was: "What sort of medical care do you think a soldier usually gets at the front, considering what the medics are up against?"   Other answer categories were: "Rather poor medical care" and "Very poor medical care."

introduced), a considerable majority of both officers and men said that all or most of our equipment was better than that of the Germans, though, doubtless reflecting the actual situation, the majority was smaller than in the case of the Japanese. However, in spite of complaints about such weapons as the German "88," as many as 33 per cent of the enlisted veterans of fighting in the early Mediterranean campaigns said that all our equipment was better. Only 7 per cent of the officers made this extreme answer, a difference which

TABLE 11

ATTITUDES TOWARD EQUIPMENT

(Veteran Infantry Enlisted Men and Company Grade Officers)

QUESTION: "Do you think that the equipment of the American Army is better or worse than the equipment of the (German) (Japanese) Army?"

| | PERCENTAGE GIVING EACH ANSWER AMONG | | | |
| | Enlisted men* | | Officers† | |
ANSWER CATEGORIES	Europe	Pacific	Europe	Pacific
All our equipment is better	33	56	7	42
Most of our equipment is better	49	41	69	57
Our equipment is about the same as that of the (German) (Japanese) Army	10	1	19	‡
Most of our equipment is worse	3	‡	3	—
All of our equipment is worse	—	‡	‡	—
Don't know or no answer	5	2	2	1
Total	100	100	100	100
Number of cases	*431*	*4,064*	*263*	*638*

* Cross section of veteran infantrymen from 1 division which fought in North Africa and Sicily, surveyed in November 1943 (S-91), and from 3 divisions which fought in the Pacific, surveyed in March–April 1944 (S-100).

† Company grade Infantry officers from 2 divisions which fought in North Africa and Sicily and 3 which fought in the Pacific (S-101), surveyed in March–April 1944.

‡ Less than 0.5 per cent.

suggests a somewhat unrealistic appraisal on the part of the enlisted men.

Confidence in the superiority of our equipment was, as one would expect, related to confidence in the ease of our ultimate victory. In one division which fought against the Japanese, 63 per cent of the men who said that all of our equipment was better thought that to beat the Japanese would involve a tough job with heavy losses of men and equipment, while 76 per cent of the men who did not say that all of our equipment was better thought this.[26]

---

[26] S-100 (705 and 678 cases, respectively). See Chart VII for the wording of the question. The differences remain when rank and education are controlled.

As members of a powerful, well-equipped, and well-supplied Army —and of a nation which had never experienced military defeat— American soldiers rarely if ever entertained serious doubts about ultimate victory.[27] This sanguine view, not always based on real-

CHART VII

EXPECTATIONS IN REGARD TO EASE OF VICTORY
(Veteran Infantry Enlisted Men and Company Grade Officers,
and Infantry Enlisted Men in Training)

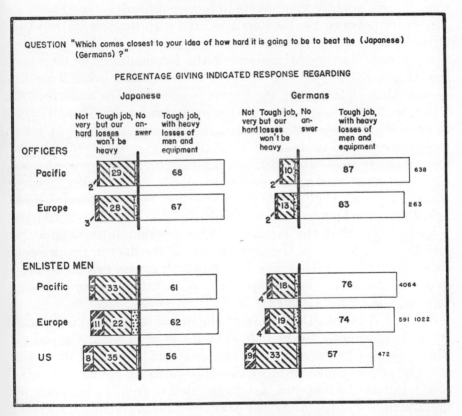

Pacific: Enlisted men were a cross section of veteran infantrymen in three divisions (S-100). Officers were of company grade only, from the same divisions (S-101), surveyed in March–April 1944.

Europe: Enlisted men were a cross section of veteran infantrymen in two divisions which fought in North Africa and Sicily, surveyed in November 1943 (S-91) and April 1944 (S-100). The question in regard to the Japanese was asked only of the second of these divisions. Officers were of company grade only, from both of these divisions, surveyed in April 1944 (S-101).

United States: Cross section of infantrymen in three divisions in training in the United States, February 1944 (S-95).

The numbers following the bars are the numbers of cases on which percentages are based.

----

[27] Cf. Volume I, Chapter 9.

istic considerations, undoubtedly made a difference in the frame of mind with which they faced their job. Men who fought against the Japanese in general regarded their job as an easier one than did the men who fought against the Germans, as Chart VII shows. While very few officers or men in either theater went so far as to say that it would not be very hard to beat their particular enemy, 61 per cent of the men surveyed in the Pacific as compared with 74 per cent of those in Europe said it would be a tough job with heavy losses. Officers were slightly more likely to foresee difficulty, but the same differences between the theaters appeared with them as in the case of the enlisted men. As the chart shows, men in the two theaters were in close agreement concerning the formidability of their respective enemies—the men in the Pacific agreeing with those in Europe that victory over the Germans would be the more costly. The data do not suggest any ready explanation for this, since it may be seen on the chart that enlisted infantrymen surveyed at that time in the United States considered the two enemies about equally formidable.[28] Combat experience against each enemy seems to have been associated with a decline in confidence in an easy victory over that enemy, but it remains a question by what process men fighting in the Pacific came to think that the Germans would be harder to beat than the Japanese. This question, interesting as it may be, is irrelevant to the main burden of the data in the present connection, which is that men fighting the Japanese had greater resources of confidence in the superiority of their forces than had men fighting against the Germans.

Belief in the strength of one's group and of one's side in the war certainly gave heart to the individual involved in a war the end of which was not yet in sight. In the short run, it is difficult to see how the effects could be other than favorable for combat motivation. But in the long run, an exaggerated degree of confidence in the superiority of the American Army could lead to unrealistic estimates of the probable length of the war and the difficulty of achieving ultimate victory, which in turn could result in disappointments and discouragement. With this possible boomerang effect in view, the orientation materials emanating from the War Department consistently played on the theme that our enemies were formidable, and that victory would only be at the cost of great effort and sacri-

---

[28] Preceding cross-section surveys of troops in the United States from the summer and fall of 1943 showed that even a greater proportion expected a tough job with the Japanese than expected a tough job with the Germans.

fice. So far as questionnaire data are concerned, the question as to when confidence becomes overconfidence must be left unanswered. At any given time, high confidence tended to be associated with other favorable attitudes. The proof of its worth, however, is in how it withstood further developments. If panel surveys had followed the same men over an extended time period, it would have been possible to see what happened to those men who had extreme confidence in an easy American victory.

The data in Chart VII would suggest that extreme overconfidence may have been fairly rare during the intermediate years of the war. Chart VII showed that even in the Pacific—where confidence in our relative superiority was greatest and a majority of veteran infantrymen, it will be remembered, thought that *all* of our equipment was better than the enemy's—a majority of the soldiers still believed that victory would be achieved only at the cost of heavy losses of men and equipment. And in view of the unexpectedly rapid denouement of the Pacific war, reactions which might previously have been considered overconfident had minimum opportunity to boomerang.

The sense of power and security which the combat soldier derived from being among buddies on whom he could depend and from being part of a strong and winning team should not be regarded as a combat *incentive*. But as one way in which the resources of the individual were maintained at a level at which he remained capable of coping with the stresses of combat, it was surely as important as more positive factors in combat motivation.

Role of Convictions About the War and the Enemy

Chapter 9 in Volume I on "The Orientation of Soldiers Toward the War" has already portrayed the American soldier as typically without deep personal commitment to a war which he nevertheless accepted as unavoidable. It has been seen there that in general he gave little concern to the conflicting values underlying the military struggle, and when asked for his conception of the reasons for American participation he could rarely give a consistent account. Although he showed a strong but tacit patriotism, this usually did not lead him in his thinking to subordinate his personal interests to the furtherance of ideal aims and values. In the present section we will be concerned more specifically with the role in combat motivation of these attitudes and convictions. First we will consider briefly the combat man's general convictions about the worth-whileness of the war. His attitudes toward the enemy, which were more directly related to his combat experience, will be the subject of more extensive treatment.

These attitudes and convictions had their main roots outside the immediate group which played such an important part in prescribing and supporting the combat soldier's adaptive attitudes and roles. His convictions about the purposes of the war depended in part on the point of view which prevailed in the social milieu prior to his Army experience,[29] while his feelings about the enemy stemmed partly from such sources and partly from concrete experiences in the combat situation. Nevertheless, the informal group imposed stringent norms on the expression of attitudes in this sphere. Undoubtedly group pressures tended to standardize the attitudes to which the men could give free expression.

Probably the strongest group code, except for condemnation of expressions of flagrant disloyalty, was the taboo against any talk of a flag-waving variety. Accounts of many informal observers indicate that this code was universal among American combat troops, and widespread throughout the Army. The core of the attitude among combat men seemed to be that any talk that did not subordinate idealistic values and patriotism to the harsher realities of the combat situation was hypocritical, and a person who expressed such ideas a hypocrite. The usual term by which disapproval of idealistic exhortation was invoked was "bullshit," which conveyed a scornful expression of the superiority of the combat man's hard-earned, tough-minded point of view.

Combat men were particularly intolerant of idealistic talk by persons not of their own fraternity, who had not in any way earned the right to treat the tough realities of combat cavalierly. For a civilian or someone from the rear to insist that the idealistic purposes of the war justified their sacrifices seemed to them an insult. No such person, they thought, could have any real conception of what they had been through. Although the taboo against idealistic or flag-waving talk or heroics was strongest against the outsider, it seems to have applied also within the combat group. One may conjecture that tender-minded expressions of idealism seemed incompatible with the role of the proud and tough combat man who drew his pride from what he had been through, and that the latter adjustment was of more crucial importance to most men. Unlike the civilian, whose situation neither demanded nor permitted drastic

---

[29] Cf. Volume I, Chapter 9.

self-sacrifice, the combat soldier lived in a world in which actions spoke louder than words. The nature of the situation as well as the code of masculine tough-mindedness may thus have combined to reduce expressions of idealistic motivation to a minimum.

The group pressures were probably directed more against verbalizations of idealistic attitudes that could be challenged as sentimental than against such attitudes in themselves. But the sanctions against their full expression probably further limited the role they could play in combat motivation.

Rather than a positive concern with war aims, the more typical frame of mind involved a tacit and fairly deep conviction that we were on the right side and that the war, once we were in it, was necessary. Leaving ultimate considerations aside, the soldier concerned himself with his job and with staying alive. At this level, he rarely doubted the importance of his function. When asked "How do you feel about the importance of the rifleman's job in modern battle?" between 40 and 50 per cent of the infantrymen in the veteran divisions surveyed[30] (not all riflemen themselves) said it was "more important than any other soldier's job," and nearly all the rest said that it was "important, but no more so than many others." Only 2 to 5 per cent thought it was "not very important compared with many others." Soldiers at large supported this almost unanimous verdict; only 4 per cent of a cross section of enlisted men in the United States thought that the rifleman's job was "not very important."[31] While one may deplore the combat soldier's lack of concern with the larger issues of the war, the fact remains that with the framework of the war as a "given," he knew that what he was doing was very important.

While relatively few combat men admitted that they very often felt that the war was not worth fighting, more of them than of soldiers in training said they sometimes felt doubts about the war. Chart VIII compares infantrymen in divisions in training, in divisions overseas before combat, and in veteran divisions in respect to how often they said they felt that the war was not worth fighting. The difference between combat veterans and trainees is considerable. While nearly half of the latter claimed never to have felt doubts, less than one third of the combat veterans said they had escaped them completely. This difference between veterans and trainees is not unexpected; more surprising is the fact that men in

---

[30] S-100, March–April 1944.
[31] S-95, February 1944 (3,594 cases).

untried divisions awaiting D Day in England responded almost exactly like the combat veterans. Evidently the added realism of being overseas with the certain expectation of combat had as much effect in this respect as actual combat.

If this implication is true, it suggests that the difference between

CHART VIII

CONVICTION ABOUT THE WAR AMONG INFANTRYMEN
(Enlisted Infantrymen in Veteran and New Divisions
Overseas and in Training)

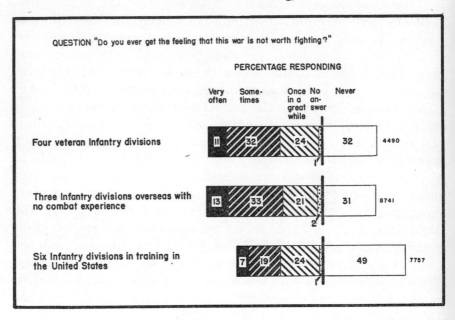

QUESTION "Do you ever get the feeling that this war is not worth fighting?"

PERCENTAGE RESPONDING

Very often — Some-times — Once in a great while — No answer — Never

Four veteran Infantry divisions   11   32   24   32   4490

Three Infantry divisions overseas with no combat experience   13   33   21   2   31   8741

Six Infantry divisions in training in the United States   7   19   24   49   7757

Veteran divisions were made up of three divisions in the Pacific surveyed in March–April 1944 (S-100) and one in Europe surveyed in November 1943 (S-91).

Overseas divisions were surveyed in England, April–May 1944 (S-129).

Divisions in training were surveyed in May 1944 (S-121).

The numbers following the bars are the numbers of cases on which percentages are based.

combat veterans and trainees does not so much reflect a difference in basic ideological convictions as relatively superficial differences in the extent to which the men had weighed for themselves the costs of war. In support of this is the finding among line infantrymen in Italy, where the range of time in combat was great, that men who had been in combat a very long time were no more likely than newer men to say they felt the war not worth fighting:

QUESTION: "Do you ever have the feeling that this war is not worth fighting?" [32]

	PERCENTAGE GIVING EACH ANSWER, AMONG MEN WHO SAID THEY HAD BEEN IN COMBAT FOR		
ANSWER CATEGORIES	*Less than 4 months*	*4 through 6 months*	*7 months or more*
Very often	15	17	15
Sometimes	33	34	33
Only once in a great while	25	27	26
Never	23	19	23
No answer	4	3	3
	—	—	—
Total	100	100	100
Number of cases	*320*	*735*	*639*

When finer gradations of combat time are examined, or when rank and education are controlled, no consistent differences between newer men and old-timers emerge. Thus, it appears that prolonged exposure to combat had little if any effect on the men's most generalized convictions about the war. One may conjecture that this somewhat unexpected result may have been related to the modest character of the men's convictions. If the main reason they believed we were fighting the war was, as Chapter 9 in Volume I suggested, that we had to because we were attacked, combat experience would hardly be expected to have suggested alternative courses of national policy.

On a question bearing more directly on the men's concrete experiences on the other hand, the combat men were more likely to waver. The question was: "When you were fighting a particular battle, did you ever have the feeling that it wasn't worth the cost?" While on the former question 43 per cent of the Infantry veterans surveyed in two theaters in 1944 said they at least sometimes felt the war was not worth fighting (see Chart VIII), 64 per cent of the same sample said that at least sometimes they had the feeling that a battle was not worth the cost. Data from Italy shown in Table 12 indicate that in this case the men who had seen longer combat were more likely to give unfavorable answers. One plausible interpretation of these findings is simply that the longer a man was in combat, the more likely it was that he would have taken part in some seemingly futile action against disheartening odds. Again the data do not

[32] S-177, April 1945.

TABLE 12

FEELING THAT A BATTLE WAS NOT WORTH THE COST, IN RELATION TO TIME IN COMBAT
(Enlisted Infantrymen in Line Companies, Italy, April 1945)

QUESTION: "When you were fighting a particular battle, did you ever have the feeling that it wasn't worth the cost?"

PERCENTAGE OF MEN GIVING EACH ANSWER AMONG

	Privates and Pfc's who have been in combat for					Noncoms who have been in combat for			
	Less than 2 months	2 through 3 months	4 through 6 months	7 through 8 months	9 months or more	Less than 4 months	4 through 6 months	7 through 8 months	9 months or more
Yes, almost always	17 ⎫58	22 ⎫63	22 ⎫77	17 ⎫72	24 ⎫77	12 ⎫49	12 ⎫69	16 ⎫74	14 ⎫89
Yes, sometimes	41 ⎭	41 ⎭	55 ⎭	55 ⎭	53 ⎭	37 ⎭	57 ⎭	58 ⎭	75 ⎭
No, never	13	10	11	14	12	7	14	15	3
Undecided	23	24	11	14	10	39	14	10	8
No answer	6	3	1	*	1	5	3	1	—
Total	100	100	100	100	100	100	100	100	100
Number of cases	101	180	587	252	195	143	151	89	110

S-177.
* Less than 0.5 per cent.

point unambiguously to a deterioration in fundamental convictions, though they are not inconsistent with such a process.   There is at any event little doubt that the men's conceptions of the cost of war, against which their convictions as to its value had to be weighed, became more somber the more they saw of it.

Correlational analysis cannot decide the relative importance in combat motivation of the men's convictions about the war since this is a causal problem.   It can establish, however, that conviction belongs to the complex of attitudes favorable to motivation in combat.   For infantrymen in three Pacific divisions, an index of conviction was derived from the men's answers to three questions: whether or not they ever felt the war was not worth fighting, and

TABLE 13

CONVICTION ABOUT THE WAR IN RELATION TO READINESS FOR COMBAT
(Veteran Infantrymen in Three Pacific Divisions, March–April 1944)

DEGREE OF CONVICTION†	PERCENTAGE RELATIVELY READY FOR FURTHER COMBAT* IN EACH SUBGROUP		
	Division A	*Division B*	*Division C*
	Men who say they are in very good, good, or fair physical condition		
High	82 *(252)*	66 *(250)*	50 *(160)*
Mixed	72 *(600)*	54 *(489)*	37 *(322)*
Low	60 *(156)*	44 *(130)*	38 *(772)*
	Men who say they are in poor or very poor physical condition		
High	47 *(36)*	40 *(85)*	30 *(194)*
Mixed	50 *(167)*	27 *(281)*	16 *(519)*
Low	26 *(77)*	17 *(90)*	14 *(139)*

S-100.
Numbers in parentheses are the numbers of cases on which percentages are based.
* See footnote 33 in Chapter 2 for question by which men were grouped according to readiness for combat.
† Men were grouped according to their answers to three questions:

1. "Do you ever get the feeling that this war is not worth fighting?"

    _Y_ Very often
    _Y_ Sometimes
    _X_ Only once in a great while
    _X_ Never

2–3. "If the *Germans (Japanese)* were to offer to stop fighting *now* and to give up all the countries and territory they have taken over, what do you think we should do?"

    _Y_ We should accept the offer and stop fighting now
    _Y_ We should consider the offer and try to work out some peace terms with them
    _X_ We should turn down the offer and keep on fighting until they give up completely
    _____ Undecided

Men who gave the answers marked "X" on all three questions were classed as having a high degree of conviction about the war; men who gave the answers marked "Y" on all three questions were classed as having low convictions; all other men were classed as mixed.

whether or not they would insist on unconditional surrender from the Germans and the Japanese if either enemy should make a compromise peace offer.   The men who gave favorable answers to all three questions can be said to be high in conviction in terms of the official war aims of that period.   As Table 13 shows, in each division, the higher the men's degree of conviction was, the more likely they were to indicate that they were relatively ready for further combat, even when such a major factor in their combat motivation as their attitude toward their physical condition was controlled. The single question on feeling that the war was not worth fighting showed a moderate but consistent relationship to readiness for combat when rank and education were controlled, in the single division for which this analysis was made.[33]

There are other interrelationships which indicate that conviction was associated with attitudes favorable to combat motivation. Among the men who said they had doubts about the war only once in a great while or never,[34] 32 per cent said they had more confidence in themselves the more times they went into combat, and 26 per cent said that combat became less frightening the more they saw of it.   These percentages drop to 23 per cent and 15 per cent, respectively, among the remaining men who indicated less conviction.[35] The differences are consistent in both cases when rank and education are simultaneously controlled.

These data of course do not prove that conviction about the war helped the men to fight their fear and gain self-confidence and therefore made them feel more ready for combat.   It is equally likely so far as the data go that for the men who found combat progressively more terrifying, the cost of fighting, against which they weighed their convictions, was a higher one.   There is much plausibility to the latter view, and to the extent that a causal relationship operated in this direction, the correlations obtained cannot be taken as an index of the effective role of conviction in combat motivation.   All that can be concluded is that conviction about the war was associated with a favorable motivational picture.

In attempting to estimate the importance to the American combat soldier of hatred and vindictiveness toward the enemy, we should remember that, compared with soldiers in some other armies, his general level of hatred was probably not very high.   He had

---

[33] S-100.
[34] S-100, 788 cases.
[35] 595 cases.

not, like the Russians, seen his country devastated and his family perhaps wiped out in cold blood. Neither had he, like the British, seen his home cities bombed and his country's national existence hanging by a thread. Nor did he have the ideological basis for a "sustained, steady anger . . . of the enemy system . . . which lasts until the final battle is won," like the members of the International Brigade in Spain studied by Dollard.[36] For this reason the range of degrees of hatred among the American soldiers surveyed was probably smaller than the same men might have displayed in a different sort of war. When little evidence is found that hatred played a very important role in combat motivation, then it must be remembered that the findings are limited in application to the American soldier in the recent conflict.

After the bombing of Pearl Harbor, the reasons for Americans to hate the Japanese were more nearly the kind which motivated most of our European allies against the Germans. If one adds to the effects of Pearl Harbor endemic American attitudes toward the Japanese as a race, one would certainly expect that American soldiers would have more hatred to draw on in fighting the Japanese than against the Germans. As Chart IX shows, such was the case. But the chart also shows several other relationships that are less obviously to be expected.

In terms of the fate which American infantrymen surveyed during the intermediate phase of the war would like to see visited upon the enemy after victory, Chart IX shows the following relationships:

1. As stated above, veteran enlisted men and officers in the Pacific were more vindictive toward the Japanese than their counterparts in Europe were toward the Germans.

2. But the men fighting the Japanese were strikingly less vindictive toward the Japanese than were either soldiers in training in the United States or soldiers fighting the Germans in Europe.

3. The men fighting the Germans did not differ greatly in hatred of the Germans from men in the United States or in the Pacific.

4. Men in the Pacific appear to have been less vindictive than men in Europe toward either enemy, while men in the United States appear to have been most vindictive.

Taken in conjunction, these findings present an interesting picture. Evidently combat did not increase the hatred of the enemy people which the men felt initially. The high degree of hatred of

[36] John Dollard, *Fear in Battle* (The Institute of Human Relations, Yale University, New Haven, 1943), p. 62.

the Japanese expressed by soldiers in training seems to have been particularly unstable. Perhaps this is simply the result of the fact that the Japanese were initially more hated; perhaps on the other hand, the initial grounds for hatred were somewhat shaky. It will be seen later that the available evidence suggests that men in the Pacific were no more likely to have seen enemy atrocities than men

CHART IX

VINDICTIVENESS TOWARD ENEMY PEOPLES
(Veteran Infantry Enlisted Men and Company Grade Officers,
and Infantry Enlisted Men in Training)

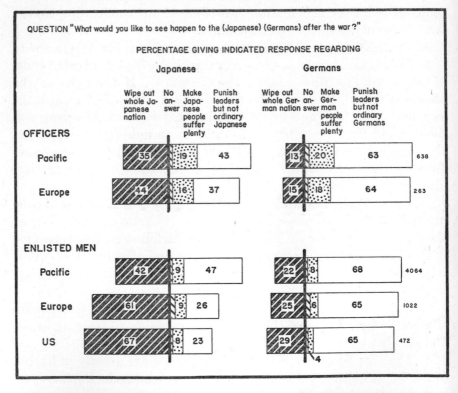

Pacific: Enlisted men were a cross section of veteran infantrymen in three divisions (S-100). Officers were of company grade only, from the same divisions (S-101). Surveyed in March–April 1944.

Europe: Enlisted men were a cross section of veteran infantrymen in two divisions which fought in North Africa and Sicily, surveyed in November 1943 (S-91) and April 1944 (S-100). Officers were of company grade only, from same divisions surveyed in April 1944 (S-101).

United States: Cross section of infantrymen in three divisions in training in the United States, February 1944 (S-95).

The numbers following the bars are the numbers of cases on which percentages are based.

in Europe.   The fact that infantrymen in the Pacific were also reliably less likely than infantrymen in training to say they would want to wipe out the whole German nation—though the difference was not large—suggests that their combat experiences may have led to a certain amount of generalization in regard to hatred of other enemies.   The relatively low degree of hatred toward the Germans expressed by trainees seems to have been fairly stable, though the small effects of combat experience in Europe seem to have been in the same direction as in the Pacific.

Perhaps one reason that combat veterans were less likely than trainees to be vindictive lay in their discovery that much dirty fighting which to the civilian and the inexperienced soldier seemed a special property of the enemy's viciousness was actually a general characteristic of war.   As Mauldin put it, "You don't fight a Kraut by Marquis of Queensbury rules: You shoot him in the back, you blow him apart with mines, you kill or maim him the quickest and most effective way you can with the least danger to yourself.   He does the same to you.   He tricks you and cheats you, and if you don't beat him at his own game you don't live to appreciate your own nobleness." [37]   When, as sometimes in the Pacific, it was exceptional to take prisoners, the men might well have been less inclined to place the blame for all the horrors of war on the shoulders of the enemy.

Vindictiveness against the enemy could be at any of several levels. On the one hand was the relatively temporary burst of anger at seeing one's buddies killed:

After the first battle, the fellows were real mad, seeing all their buddies killed. But the reaction of being mad wore off after a time.[38]

Then there might be relatively durable hatred of enemy soldiers. In the case of the Germans, with whom it will be seen that identification was relatively easy for the men, anger felt against an unseen enemy across the lines often did not withstand personal confrontation with its object when the latter appeared in the guise of a helpless prisoner:

The prisoners (that we took) were pitiful and bedraggled.   We felt sorry for them. But the (artillery) observers—those sons of bitches—they direct the fire and everybody hates them and wants to get a shot at them.[39]

[37] Mauldin, *op. cit.*, pp. 13–14.
[38] Interview with wounded veteran of Mediterranean fighting, 1944.
[39] Interview with another wounded Mediterranean veteran, 1944.

A third level was presumably tapped by the question which has been discussed: hatred of the enemy people as a whole. Still another kind was the hatred of the enemy system and ideology. There is no reason to suppose that these various levels of vindictiveness cohered in a unitary fashion. On the other hand, Chart X shows a

CHART X

RELATION BETWEEN TWO ASPECTS OF VINDICTIVENESS
(Veteran Infantrymen in Two Pacific Divisions, March–April 1944)

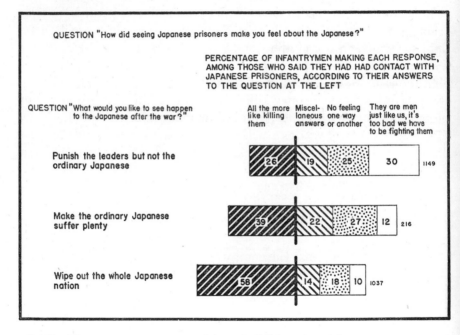

S-100. The same pattern appeared in each division separately.
The numbers following the bars are the numbers of cases on which percentages are based.

fairly strong relationship among veterans of fighting the Japanese between the way the men reported they reacted to seeing Japanese prisoners and their feelings toward the Japanese people as a whole.

Veterans of fighting against the Japanese in the Pacific were much more likely than their counterparts in the campaigns against Germany to express vindictive attitudes in the personalized context of reactions to enemy prisoners, as Chart XI shows. This would be expected from the data in Chart IX. Since we know that troops in the United States were considerably more vindictive toward the Japanese people than toward the Germans, this difference is probably not to be taken as a result of combat experience but rather as a condition of combat experience which may be expected to have affected the motivational picture. If hatred of the enemy was a help in fighting the Japanese, Chart XI raises the question as to whether identification with the enemy may not have been, on the other hand, a liability requiring counteraction in fighting the Germans.

CHART XI

REACTION TO SEEING ENEMY PRISONERS
(Veteran Enlisted Infantrymen in Three Pacific and One European Divisions)

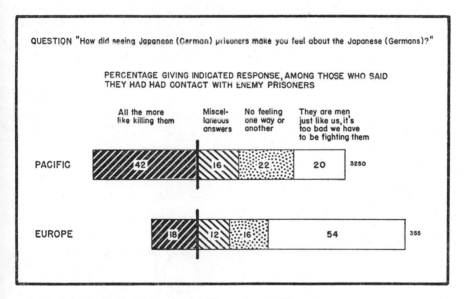

S-100, March–April 1944 and S-91, November 1943.
The numbers following the bars are the numbers of cases on which percentages are based.

In spite of the wide currency of atrocity stories about the Japanese, particularly among the American civilian population, there is yet additional evidence that the differences in hatred felt toward Japanese and Germans seem not to have been the result of actual combat experience. The proportion of front-line infantrymen who said they had personally witnessed enemy atrocities was the same in three divisions which fought in the Pacific as in the single available division which fought against the Germans, 13 per cent (Table 14). And although a considerably larger proportion in the Pacific said they had heard from others about true cases of atrocities, the majority of front-line infantrymen even there had not. If, as the data appear to indicate, the reason for the greater hatred of the Japanese lay outside of and prior to personal battle experience, the larger proportion in the Pacific who said they had heard true stories of an enemy atrocity can be partially ascribed to the persisting though perhaps waning predisposition to believe evil of the initially more hated enemy.

TABLE 14

ATROCITIES AND ATROCITY STORIES
(Veteran Enlisted Infantrymen in Three Pacific and One European Divisions)

QUESTIONS	PERCENTAGE WHO SAID THEY SAW OR HEARD OF ENEMY ATROCITIES AMONG	
	Infantrymen in the Pacific*	*Infantrymen in Europe*†
"How about atrocities? Did you personally ever see with your own eyes cases of Japanese (Germans) using methods of fighting or treating prisoners which you would call dirty or inhuman?"	13	13
"How about the stories you have heard from others? Did you hear any true cases of Japanese (Germans) using methods of fighting or treating prisoners which you would call dirty or inhuman?"	45	24
Number of cases	*4,064*	*431*

* S-100, March–April 1944.
† S-91, November 1943.

There can, however, be little question that vindictiveness was related to witnessing enemy atrocities. Sufficient cases for investigating this relationship are available only for divisions which fought in the Pacific. When the men are divided into groups according to the degree to which they expressed consistently vindictive attitudes,[40] the proportion of less vindictive men is lower among those who said they had seen enemy atrocities than among men who did not report seeing atrocities (Table 15). The relationship between witnessing atrocities and vindictiveness holds at all educational

---

[40] See footnote to Table 15 for the basis of grouping men according to vindictiveness. This grouping selects as a most vindictive type the men who consistently gave the most vindictive answer on the two questions so far discussed and in addition said they were helped a lot by hatred of the enemy; men who gave none of these answers are grouped as a least vindictive type.   This does not assume that vindictiveness is a unitary attitude, but picks out the men who are consistently more vindictive or less vindictive on several aspects of vindictiveness.

levels and also for both privates and noncoms. One possible source of spurious correlation may be involved: the men who were initially more vindictive may have been more likely to interpret a given enemy action as an atrocity. But unless we are to assume that a markedly smaller proportion of the troops in the Pacific than of soldiers in Europe actually witnessed enemy atrocities, the data in

TABLE 15

RELATION OF REPORTED WITNESSING OF ATROCITIES TO VINDICTIVENESS
(Veteran Enlisted Infantrymen in Two Pacific Divisions, March–April 1944)

| | PERCENTAGE OF MEN WHO INDICATE VARIOUS DEGREES OF VINDICTIVENESS, ACCORDING TO WHETHER OR NOT THEY REPORT HAVING WITNESSED JAPANESE ATROCITIES* | | | |
| | Division A | | Division B | |
DEGREE OF VINDICTIVENESS†	Witnessed atrocity	Did not witness atrocity	Witnessed atrocity	Did not witness atrocity
Relatively high	21	14	18	13
Intermediate	63	56	58	51
Relatively low	16	30	24	36
Total	100	100	100	100
Number of cases	*230*	*1,153*	*140*	*1,133*

S-100.
* The question was: "How about atrocities? Did you personally ever see with your own eyes cases of Japanese using methods of fighting or treating prisoners which you would call dirty or inhuman?"
_____ No _____ Yes
† Men were divided into three groups in respect to their answers to the following three questions:

1. "What would you like to see happen to the Japanese *after the war?*"

_____ Punish the leaders, but not the ordinary Japanese
_____ Make the ordinary Japanese suffer plenty
___X___ Wipe out the whole Japanese nation

2. "Did you ever have any contact with Japanese prisoners?"

_____ Yes
_____ No

"How did seeing Japanese prisoners make you feel about the Japanese?"

___X___ I felt all the more like killing them
_____ I felt that they are men just like us and it is too bad that we have to be fighting them
_____ I didn't have any feeling one way or another
_____ Some other feeling

3. "When the going was tough, how much were you helped by thoughts of *hatred for the enemy?*"

___X___ They helped a lot
_____ They helped some
_____ They helped a little
_____ They did not help at all
_____ I didn't have such thoughts

Men who gave the answer marked with an "X" to all three questions were classed as having relatively high vindictiveness; men who did not give the marked answer to any of the three questions were classed as having relatively low vindictiveness; and the remaining men were classed as intermediate in vindictiveness.

Table 14—together with the higher level of vindictiveness in the Pacific—mean that the effect cannot have been large or the proportion in the Pacific reporting having witnessed atrocities would have exceeded that in Europe.

While the witnessing of enemy atrocities was related to vindictiveness, there is no indication that experiencing heavy casualties was associated with consistently vindictive attitudes. No relationship could be discerned in the two divisions between the men's answers to the question, "About how many battle casualties (killed and wounded) has your present company had since you first went into combat with it?" and their consistent expression of vindictive attitudes. Since within each of the divisions most of the men had been overseas for about the same length of time, it is not likely that a possible decline in vindictiveness over time can have obscured real differences in the data.

The different patterns of vindictive attitudes toward the two major enemies and some of the factors in their genesis have been examined. The question remains, what role did vindictiveness play in the combat motivation of American soldiers? Here two kinds of evidence are available. There are the men's answers to the direct question, "When the going was tough, how much were you helped by thoughts of *hatred for the enemy?*" In addition, it is possible to compare more and less vindictive men in respect to other attitudes.

The men's answers to the direct question point to two conclusions. Men in the Pacific were more likely to say that thoughts of hatred for the enemy helped a lot than were men who fought against the Germans. On the other hand, neither in the Pacific nor in Europe did the men credit this attitude with helping them as much as some other attitudes about which they were also asked. In the three combat divisions surveyed in the Pacific, 38 per cent of the enlisted infantrymen said that thoughts of hatred of the enemy helped a lot.[41] In contrast, only 27 per cent of the enlisted infantrymen in a division which fought in the Mediterranean[42] and 28 per cent of the enlisted infantrymen in four combat divisions surveyed a year later in Italy[43] said that they were helped a lot by thoughts of hatred. This difference is consistent with the general pattern of greater vindictiveness toward the Japanese. However, hatred of the enemy was ascribed a position of lesser importance by the men than prayer

[41] Based on 4,064 cases.
[42] S-100, April 1944. Based on 591 cases.
[43] S-177, April 1945. Based on 1,766 cases.

and than thinking that "you couldn't let the other men down." [44] Even among the veterans of Pacific fighting, for example, 85 per cent of the Infantry officers and 61 per cent of the enlisted men said that when the going was tough they were helped a lot by thinking that "you couldn't let the other men down"—in contrast to 46 per cent of the officers and 38 per cent of the enlisted men who said they were helped a lot by thoughts of hatred of the enemy.

Among the Pacific veterans, who were the more likely to say that hatred of the enemy helped them in battle, there appears to have been very little relationship between vindictiveness and readiness for further combat as indicated by the same question employed in previous sections of this chapter. Divisions A and B (see Table 16)

TABLE 16

RELATION TO VINDICTIVENESS TO READINESS FOR COMBAT
(Veteran Enlisted Infantrymen in Two Pacific Divisions, March–April 1944)

| | PERCENTAGE IN EACH GROUP RELATIVELY READY FOR FURTHER COMBAT,* ACCORDING TO THE DEGREE OF VINDICTIVENESS WHICH THEY SHOW | | | |
| | *Division A* | | *Division B* | |
DEGREE OF VINDICTIVENESS†	Privates and Pfc's	Noncoms	Privates and Pfc's	Noncoms
Relatively high	26 *(110)*	33 *(96)*	67 *(125)*	75 *(44)*
Intermediate	25 *(403)*	32 *(386)*	67 *(445)*	71 *(214)*
Relatively low	21 *(221)*	34 *(167)*	59 *(321)*	64 *(124)*

S-100.
Numbers in parentheses are the numbers of cases on which percentages are based.
* See footnote 33 in Chapter 2 for question on readiness for further combat.
† See footnote to Table 15 for basis of grouping men according to vindictiveness.

differ markedly in the proportion of men indicating relative readiness for combat, but in neither of them is there any large relationship between vindictiveness and readiness for combat. In Division B, the difference between men consistently expressing extreme vindictive attitudes and those never expressing such attitudes approaches statistical significance; a slightly larger proportion of more vindictive men fall into the group who are relatively ready for more combat. In Division A, the difference is very small and unreliable. This is in marked contrast to other attitudes which were found to be strongly related to expressed mental readiness for combat. By itself this finding does not mean that vindictiveness played no part

---

[44] See Chart XII for a comparison of the men's answers to several parallel questions including these.

in readiness for combat. So many other attitudes and personality variables are related to mental readiness that a possible intrinsic relationship may easily have been obscured. But taken in connection with the preceding data, this lack of observed relationship adds to the presumption that hatred of the enemy, personal and impersonal, was not a major element in combat motivation.

TABLE 17

RELATION OF VINDICTIVENESS TO COMMITMENT TO THE WAR
(Veteran Enlisted Infantrymen in Two Pacific Divisions, March–April 1944)

QUESTION: "Do you ever get the feeling that this war is not worth fighting?"

	PERCENTAGE ANSWERING "NEVER" AMONG INFANTRYMEN WHO SHOW		
	Relatively low vindictiveness*	Intermediate vindictiveness	Relatively high vindictiveness
Division A			
Noncoms	27 *(167)*	38 *(386)*	37 *(96)*
Privates and Pfc's	22 *(221)*	31 *(403)*	40 *(110)*
Division B			
Noncoms	26 *(124)*	34 *(214)*	41 *(44)*
Privates and Pfc's	28 *(321)*	34 *(445)*	38 *(125)*

QUESTION: "If the Japanese were to offer to stop fighting now and to give up all the countries and territory they have taken over, what do you think we should do?"

	PERCENTAGE ANSWERING "WE SHOULD TURN DOWN THE OFFER AND KEEP ON FIGHTING UNTIL THEY GIVE UP COMPLETELY" AMONG MEN WHO SHOW		
	Relatively low vindictiveness	Intermediate vindictiveness	Relatively high vindictiveness
Division A			
Noncoms	43 *(167)*	65 *(386)*	78 *(96)*
Privates and Pfc's	39 *(221)*	57 *(403)*	75 *(110)*
Division B			
Noncoms	40 *(124)*	61 *(214)*	86 *(44)*
Privates and Pfc's	34 *(321)*	54 *(445)*	66 *(125)*

S-100.
Numbers in parentheses are the numbers of cases on which percentages are based.
* See footnote to Table 15 for basis of grouping men according to vindictiveness.

In other aspects of the favorable motivational complex, the relatively vindictive men did not differ notably from the relatively nonvindictive men. The two groups were essentially similar in the proportion who said that battle fighting became more frightening the more they saw of it, and in the proportion who said they had less self-confidence the more times they went into combat.

In one respect, however, vindictiveness among the soldiers fighting in the Pacific was associated with attitudes that have already been seen to be favorable components of combat motivation. On two questions bearing on the men's convictions about the war, the more vindictive men showed a markedly higher degree of commitment than did those who were less vindictive toward the enemy, as may be seen in Table 17. They were very much more likely to say they would favor an unconditional surrender policy in spite of any Japanese peace offer, and they were also more likely to say they never got the feeling that the war was not worth fighting. The demand for unconditional surrender is of course to be expected from those who had a high degree of hatred for the Japanese. It was one of the stated war aims, so that to the extent the men subscribed to it, they were in tune with the expressed goals of the war. It is perhaps less of a foregone conclusion that the more vindictive men should also have been more likely to say that they never had the feeling that the war was not worth fighting. This relationship suggests that their greater hatred of the enemy may have favored a more adequate adjustment to their own tasks in fighting the war.

The general picture that emerges, then, is that hatred of the enemy does not seem to have had much to do with encouraging the men to say that they felt ready for more fighting, but that it may have contributed to their mental adjustment to combat by giving them a definite goal to which they subscribed. As a result of the different initial attitudes with which Americans approached the two major enemies, this resource was more available to men fighting in the Pacific than it was in Europe, where additional adjustments may have been required of the men to counteract a major tendency to identify with enemy soldiers when they were seen as persons.

The combat soldier thus was likely to feel that the war was worth fighting, though this does not mean that ideological considerations were often in the forefront of his mind. While he might express feelings of hatred toward the enemy, depending partly on which enemy he was fighting, his hatred was not particularly stable or consistent and does not appear to have been central to his motivation. In his everyday concerns, the combat man mostly took the existence of the war and the general task of fighting the enemy for granted. His position in the Army gave him no real choice. The issues behind the war were singularly unreal to him in contrast to the issues and exigencies of his day-to-day existence.

Some Miscellaneous Goals

In the course of our discussion of combat motivation, we have touched in one way or another on several incentives which could be considered as goals of combat behavior—such objectives as to show one's masculinity, to stick up for one's buddies and win their approval, to preserve our way of life, to wreak vengeance on the enemy. Certain other goals, not considered thus far, deserve mention. Some of them raise problems on which direct evidence is not available but which appear to warrant at least passing mention to avoid serious gaps in the total picture.

First is a goal which should certainly not be neglected—the desire to get the job over with, to go home and get out of the Army. It will be remembered from Table 1 that more enlisted men in the Infantry divisions studied named this goal than named any other as the most important incentive in making them want to keep going and do as well as they could in combat. While this is presumptive evidence that the goal of getting home and out of the Army was in fact very important to the men, the very high frequency with which it was spontaneously mentioned may well have been more nearly a reflection of the way in which the desire to go home was constantly uppermost in the men's minds than an accurate indication of its relative importance in combat motivation. This interpretation is supported by the pattern of the men's answers to the series of questions concerning things it helped them to think about when the going was tough. It will be seen in Chart XII that in both the Pacific and Mediterranean theaters, considerably less than half of the men said that it helped a lot to "think that you had to finish the job in order to get home again." This proportion was smaller in each case than the proportion who said they were helped a lot by prayer and by thinking that they couldn't let the other men down. Data to be presented in Table 18 indicate that men with the longest combat experience were, if anything, less likely than newer men to say that thinking about getting the job finished in order to get home helped them a lot.

It cannot be denied that getting home again was among the most cherished wishes of all soldiers overseas, and of combat men in particular. What is more questionable is the extent to which this desire supported the men in doing their combat job. The very intensity of the desire is indicative of a corresponding weakness of alternative incentives which might find in the war itself sufficiently important values to override personal considerations.   Unlike such alternative bases of combat motivation, the desire to get home was double-edged.   For the battle-weary soldier, every dead enemy or captured position meant he was that much nearer home.   But every new mission, every additional day in the line, also meant postponing the happy day by so much and diminishing the chances that he would ever live to see it.   While the desire to go home could become a source of hatred for the enemy—"the sonovabitch who is keeping me from going home"—it could also be turned against our own side and its leaders.   When all but a few believed firmly in an inevitable Allied victory, the desire to see the job done and to get out of the Army did not at all imply the positive desire to do the job oneself.

More fundamental than the desire to go home, and involved in it, was the desire to survive.   The goal of survival, also mentioned by many of the men in Table 1, was an all-important one which intertwined with most other motivational factors in the combat situation.   It is easily neglected in consideration of why soldiers fight, since it is too easy to assume that it operated wholly to draw the individual out of the combat situation.   Like the desire to go home again, it was two-edged.   Certainly it made a soldier reluctant to go into combat, but, once in the lines, the situation might become one of kill or be killed.   By killing the enemy the soldier removed one more threat to his own life.   The goal of survival also enforced close teamwork with others in the outfit.   The life of each depended as much on the others' actions as on his own, so from this goal sprang much of the feeling of close mutual dependence which has been seen to be so important as a basis for other aspects of combat motivation.   The desire to survive was so intense that it might overshadow other and previous motivations.   As one combat veteran in Europe said when asked "what we are fighting for,"

Ask any dogface on the line.   You're fighting for your skin on the line.   When I enlisted I was patriotic as all hell.   There's no patriotism on the line.   A boy up there 60 days in the line is in danger every minute.   He ain't fighting for patriotism.

By itself the motive of desire to survive was certainly not one that made for dash and aggressiveness in combat, nor was it a sufficient motive.   But in combination with other factors it becomes a major element in combat motivation.

Victory was surely a goal of combat, and in the broadest sense it undoubtedly did lend a rationale to the soldier's activity.   But if one considers victory more concretely, in terms of specific victories and defeats, its relation to combat motivation is much more complex. In the first place, from the standpoint of the combat soldier it was not at all obvious what would be perceived as a victory and what as a defeat. Secondly, the specific rewards of actions perceived as victories were most various.

A victory for a soldier in combat had a meaning very different from that enjoyed by his countrymen at home. For most situations, Waller is quite right when he says, "For the soldiers victory or defeat meant just another battle with an enemy who was still full of fight." [45] When the end of the war was still not in view, one more victory may simply have meant the necessity to attack again tomorrow, and again the next day and so on into the seemingly endless bleak future with no hope of escape other than a good clean wound. That river was our objective last week, this hill here is our objective today, and beyond it lie other hills and other rivers, each with its toll of sacrifice in the taking. More than that, what the newspapers and radio heralded as a victory contained within itself many little victories and many local defeats. To the shattered remnants of a rifle company withdrawing from a slope raked by enemy fire, it might seem ironical that the nation knew the total battle as a great victory. The news that we had broken out of the Normandy Peninsula may have been scant comfort to the scattered survivors of a tank unit who had just seen most of their comrades lost. Victories were not won without casualties, and the sense of elation that often moved the homeland population was at best a bitter-sweet emotion at the front. And a particular victory might mark no pause in the fight; the next day often brought the same duties, hardships, dangers, as the day before.

With all this, there did still remain rewards in local victories. "Every hill taken means that we are that much nearer home": captured positions and enemies out of action carried a promise of ultimate victory and a quicker end to the war. In periods of very rapid advance, combat troops sometimes exhibited an almost "civilian" degree of high spirits. The period of late August and early September in 1944 when the American armies were pursuing the retreating Wehrmacht through France and Belgium is a large-scale example. Even here, however, victory was not a cause for unmixed feelings. Combat soldiers had a pessimism, a caution ingrained from bitter

---

[45] Willard Waller, *Veteran Comes Back* (The Dryden Press, Inc., New York, 1944), p. 103.

experience, which checked the exuberance of wish projection.   And when, as happened in that instance, infantrymen walked until completely exhausted—in one case observed by Research Branch interviewers, a regiment advanced forty miles in twenty-four hours—the factor of sheer fatigue temporarily overshadowed the psychological rewards of victory.   And always, there were comrades being killed and wounded.

So far as more immediate and tangible rewards are concerned, victory in the immediate tactical situation might carry any one of hundreds of specific rewards.   To men who have been in winter combat, for example, it will not appear at all fanciful to state that men sometimes were moved to attack for the simple purpose of taking a town which promised shelter and warmth.   It was no small matter to win a height which deprived the enemy of an artillery observation post, or permitted observation of enemy movements. Anything which gave even temporary and relative safety or comfort, in other words, could become a major motivating condition.   Under certain conditions, looting or souvenir hunting might come to be an important reward.   It is known that in the last weeks of the European war, after it had become evident that hostilities would soon be over, some units actually raced to be the first at an objective which promised valued booty—a jewelry store, camera shop, weapons cache, liquor warehouse, etc.—or which promised gratifying contacts with women.   The extent to which this occurred is not known, probably could not be ascertained with any high degree of accuracy, and is not important for present purposes.   In order to show that immediate rewards, even illegal ones, to be gained as the fruit of victory could provide incentives in combat, it is sufficient to know that there were a number of instances in which it happened.

To the incentives of securing temporary relative safety or comfort, of shortening the war, and of securing material gain must be added, in some situations, certain more exclusively social factors. A good case in point is the situation of attacking to relieve a unit which had been cut off by enemy forces or attacking to recover wounded men.   The relief of the garrison at Bastogne during the Battle of the Bulge in December 1944 is an example from the European war.   Uncounted smaller actions of the same pattern took place during World War II, and the historical record of past wars is studded with examples.   The special motivational feature of such situations for the relieving force is the reinforcement which was thereby provided to the individual's sense of obligation to, and social solidarity with, his comrades. It was easy for him to take the role of the other—to sense the desperate situation and the emotion it evoked—and to anticipate the gratitude which those who were threatened would feel toward supporting and relieving forces.

Prayer and Personal Philosophies in Combat

In attempting to answer the question, "Why did American combat soldiers fight?" we have so far examined the role of the requirements and values of the soldier's formal and informal groups, as well as of certain more general values and goals. These have in common the characteristic that they can be thought of as pushing or pulling the soldier away from channels of escape and holding him in combat with the enemy. In discussing the role of the informal group, we also considered certain sources of support the soldier derived from group membership, which did not impel him to take any action but increased his resources for action otherwise instigated. There was another class of relevant motivational factors similar to the latter in that they did not impel the individual toward active combat but did serve the important function of increasing his resources for enduring the conflict-ridden situation of combat stress. In comparison with the former category, they derived less immediately from group membership or group-sponsored values, although they were promulgated by social example and met with general approval. These are such psychological adjustments to the stress situation as prayer, fatalism, and restricting time perspective to the present moment—the various personal philosophies that made staying in combat more bearable.

Among these, a body of questionnaire data is available only for prayer, concerning the extent to which combat men said that it helped them. For the larger area of fatalism, living in the short run, and other combat philosophies, data are lacking, so the present section will in these cases merely touch on psychological adjustments which informal observation by Research Branch personnel, war correspondents, and others indicated were of considerable importance. The treatment of prayer will first show its general importance to combat men and then, by a description of the kind of men who said they were helped by it, attempt to throw some light on its special function.

The importance of prayer to the combat man has become a matter for popular bromides. Our questionnaire data, while they are not too informative in regard to what the men meant by prayer, do add evidence for the prevalent view that the men regarded it as a very important source of support. The importance of prayer is best high-lighted by considering it in comparison with various other possible mental adjustments to tough situations, concerning which combat troops in two theaters were questioned. Chart XII shows what the men had to say of five such adjustments, four of which involve factors which have already been discussed earlier in this chapter. In both the Pacific and Italy, at different stages of the war, a larger proportion of enlisted infantrymen said they were "helped a lot" by prayer than said this of any of the other adjustments cited. In four divisions surveyed in the Pacific in 1944, 70 per cent said it helped a lot, while 83 per cent of the line infantrymen surveyed a year later in four divisions in Italy gave this answer. The only other item approaching prayer in the proportion of men who said it helped them a lot was thinking that "you couldn't let the other men down"—touching on potent forces of group solidarity and loyalty —but in both theaters more of the men, regardless of educational level or of whether they were privates or noncoms, said that prayer was helpful.

Among officers the testimony was likewise that prayer was very important. Approximately 60 per cent of the company grade Infantry officers questioned in the European and Pacific theaters in the spring of 1944 said that prayer helped them a lot when the going was tough. As Chart XIII shows, however, thinking that one couldn't let the other men down was more frequently mentioned by officers as a very helpful source of support. This difference from enlisted men, and even from noncoms, cannot be attributed to the higher educational level of officers, since even the most highly educated enlisted men were more likely to say they were helped a lot by prayer. It should probably be ascribed rather to the special responsibilities of the officer role or possibly to the officer's having been subjected to less intensive stress in other respects.[46] Nevertheless, among officers prayer was still said to help a lot by larger proportions than found it helpful to think of "what we were fighting for," "hatred for the enemy," or of "having to finish the job in order to get home again."

A possible reservation which should be kept in mind in interpreting these data on the importance of prayer to officers and enlisted men lies in the fact that the men's answers were elicited by a check-

---

[46] As will be seen, enlisted combat men who were not subjected to so much stress as the line infantrymen were less likely to assign prior position to prayer.

CHART XII

THOUGHTS WHICH ENLISTED MEN SAID WERE HELPFUL WHEN THE GOING WAS TOUGH

(Veteran Enlisted Infantrymen in the Pacific and Mediterranean Theaters)

PERCENTAGE ANSWERING

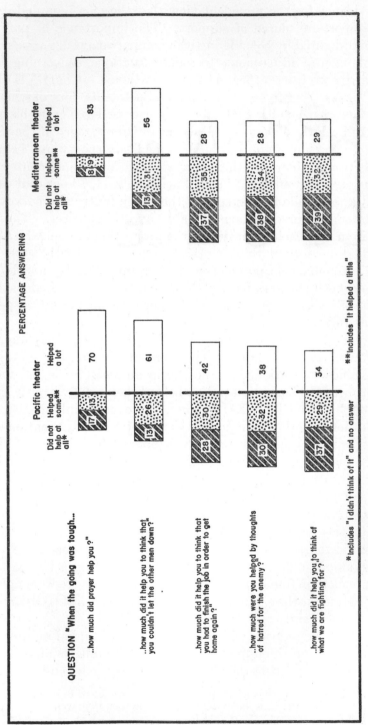

QUESTION "When the going was tough..."

..how much did prayer help you?"

..how much did it help you to think that you couldn't let the other men down?"

..how much did it help you to think that you had to finish the job in order to get home again?"

..how much were you helped by thoughts of hatred for the enemy?"

..how much did it help you to think of what we are fighting for?"

Pacific theater

Did not help at all* Helped some** Helped a lot

Mediterranean theater

Did not help at all* Helped some** Helped a lot

*Includes "I didn't think of it" and no answer

**Includes "It helped a little"

Pacific: Four divisions surveyed, March–April 1944, S-100.   Unweighted average of four divisions.   Numbers of cases in the four divisions were 1,428, 1,299, 1,364, and 643, respectively.
Mediterranean: Four divisions surveyed in Italy, April 1945, S-177.   1,766 cases.   In Italy the wording of the last question was: "...

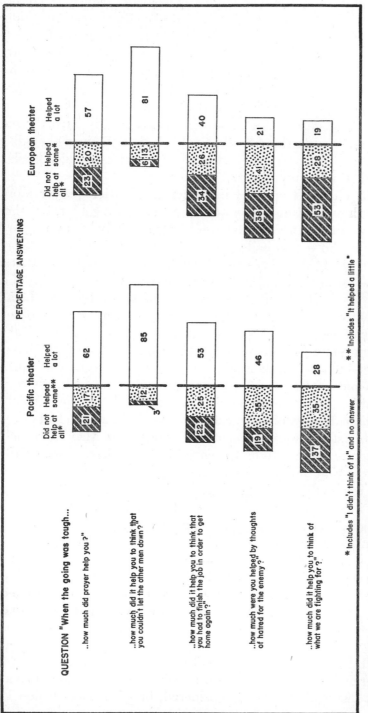

THOUGHTS WHICH OFFICERS SAID WERE HELPFUL WHEN THE GOING WAS TOUGH
(Veteran Company Grade Infantry Officers, Pacific and European Theaters)

PERCENTAGE ANSWERING

Pacific theater

European theater

QUESTION "When the going was tough...

...how much did prayer help you?"

...how much did it help you to think that you couldn't let the other men down?"

...how much did it help you to think that you had to finish the job in order to get home again?"

...how much were you helped by thoughts of hatred for the enemy?"

...how much did it help you to think of what we are fighting for?"

* Includes "I didn't think of it" and no answer   ** Includes "It helped a little"

Pacific:: Company grade Infantry officers in two Pacific divisions surveyed April 1944. 319 cases (S-101).
Europe: Company grade Infantry officers in two divisions which fought in North Africa and Sicily, surveyed in England, April 1944. 255 cases (S-101).

list question rather than volunteered spontaneously.   To the extent that prayer was a socially approved activity, the possibility of a kind of halo effect in the direction of saying that it helped a lot cannot be ruled out.   It should also be considered that checking "it helped a lot" may have reflected frequency of recourse to prayer more than it reflected the degree of comfort it afforded.   As will be pointed out in a later context, the present data do not provide a basis for deciding how much help prayer really gave the men who used it, though the data do establish that the men thought prayer important to them and, further, enable us to see which kinds of men found it most important.

Not only did enlisted infantrymen mention prayer more often than they mentioned any other item as helping a lot, but those who had seen the most combat were fully as likely to say prayer helped a lot as those who had been in combat for shorter lengths of time. Table 18 shows this for infantrymen in four divisions in Italy.   If there was any difference between men of different lengths of combat experience, it was in the direction of the old-timers' being more likely to say they were helped a lot by prayer.   On the other hand, fewer of the old-timers said they were helped by ideological considerations, and possibly fewer by thoughts of finishing the job in order to get home.   These findings are supported by less adequate data from one of the divisions in the Pacific, in which less confidence could be placed in the men's estimates of their time in combat.

These data would suggest that combat men who had experienced greater stress were at least as likely to say they were helped by prayer as those who had been subjected to less stress.   Other data suggest that prayer was particularly important to just those men who were subjected to the greatest stress.   Table 19 compares veteran infantrymen with combat veterans in other branches of service in regard to the things which they said it helped them to think about when the going was tough.   It will be seen that for all the items *except* prayer, infantrymen were in each case *less* likely to say they were helpful than were men in the other less arduous and dangerous branches.   All of the differences are in this direction, some of them reliably so when considered individually.   In the case of prayer however, infantrymen in two of the divisions were reliably *more* likely than noninfantrymen to say it helped them a lot, while in the third division the difference, although in the other direction, was of low reliability.   The picture remains the same when privates and noncoms are separately considered, or when men in non Infantry

TABLE 18

RELATION OF TIME IN COMBAT TO THOUGHTS WHICH VETERANS SAID WERE HELPFUL "WHEN THE GOING WAS TOUGH"
(Veteran Enlisted Infantrymen, Mediterranean Theater, April 1945)

PERCENTAGE IN EACH GROUP WHO SAID "IT HELPED A LOT" TO HAVE EACH SORT OF THOUGHT "WHEN THE GOING WAS TOUGH" AMONG

	Privates and Pfc's who had been in combat* for					*Noncoms who had been in combat* for*			
	Less than 2 months	2 through 3 months	4 through 6 months	7 through 8 months	9 months or more	Less than 4 months	4 through 6 months	7 through 8 months	9 months or more
Prayer	76	83	85	82	84	86	77	90	88
Thinking that you couldn't let the other men down	51	55	57	52	51	70	60	67	60
Thinking that you had to finish the job in order to get home again	33	28	26	32	22	32	29	30	21
Thoughts of hatred for the enemy	27	28	31	30	25	32	25	25	25
Thinking of the meaning of what we are fighting for	39	23	30	30	28	46	28	24	23
Number of cases	*101*	*180*	*587*	*252*	*195*	*43*	*151*	*89*	*110*

S-177.
* See footnote to Table 3 for criterion of length of time in combat.

branches are further divided to consider Field Artillery and other branches separately.

A similar pattern emerges if, among the infantrymen, those who indicated that they experienced greater fear in battle are compared with those who indicated that they experienced less fear.   Table 20

TABLE 19

COMPARISON OF INFANTRYMEN AND MEN IN OTHER BRANCHES, IN REGARD TO THE THOUGHTS WHICH THEY SAID HELPED THEM "WHEN THE GOING WAS TOUGH"
(Veteran Enlisted Men in Infantry Divisions, European and Pacific Theaters, March–April 1944)

| | PERCENTAGE WHO SAID "IT HELPED A LOT" TO HAVE EACH SORT OF THOUGHT "WHEN THE GOING WAS TOUGH"* AMONG | |
	Infantrymen	*Men in other branches†*
Prayer		
Division A	84	71
Division B	64	55
Division C‡	73	77
Thinking that you couldn't let the other men down		
Division A	62	65
Division B	56	59
Division C	57	63
Thinking that you had to finish the job in order to get home again		
Division A	40	47
Division B	35	41
Division C	35	43
Thoughts of hatred for the enemy		
Division A	38	43
Division B	37	46
Division C	27	41
Thinking of what we are fighting for		
Division A	38	42
Division B	33	44
Division C	25	36
Number of cases		
Division A (*South Pacific*)	*1,364*	*602*
Division B (*South Pacific*)	*1,428*	*648*
Division C (*Europe*)	*591*	*267*

* See Chart XII for wording of questions.
† For Divisions A and B, this constituted a cross section of all enlisted men except Infantry.   For Division C, data are available only for artillerymen.
‡ The wording of the questions was slightly different in Division C. A previous question had asked the men what one sort of situation they found the toughest.   The present series of questions was prefaced by the statement, "Many men report that thinking about certain things helps them to get through when the going gets tough. Soldiers with different types of experience have different views. Think of the one situation you just selected as being the one you found toughest. When you were in that situation how much did it help you..."

shows, for one of the divisions in the Pacific, that the "more frightened" men (those who said that battle became more frightening the more they saw of it or stayed frightening all the time, or who reported having had more bodily symptoms of fear in battle) were more likely to say that prayer helped a lot than were the "less frightened" men (those who said that battle never was frightening or became less frightening the more they saw of it, or who reported having had fewer bodily symptoms of fear in battle).   On the other hand, there was a consistent tendency for the relatively more frightened groups to be *less* likely to say they were helped by the other

TABLE 20

THOUGHTS WHICH VETERANS SAID HELPED THEM "WHEN THE GOING WAS TOUGH"
IN RELATION TO DEGREE OF FEAR IN BATTLE THAT THEY REPORT
(Veteran Enlisted Infantrymen in One Pacific Division, March–April 1944)

	PERCENTAGE SAYING THAT HAVING EACH TYPE OF THOUGHT HELPED A LOT* AMONG MEN WHO SAID			
	Battle became less frightening or never was frightening;†had low fear-symptom score‡	*Battle became less frightening or never was frightening; had high fear-symptom score*	*Battle became more frightening or was frightening all the time; had low fear-symptom score*	*Battle became more frightening or was frightening all the time; had high fear-symptom score*
Prayer	42	58	61	72
Thinking that you couldn't let the other men down	61	62	60	52
Thinking that you had to finish the job in order to get home again	41	37	35	28
Thoughts of hatred for the enemy	43	39	38	34
Thinking of what we are fighting for	34	40	32	29
Number of cases	*177*	*52*	*317*	*403*

S-100.
* See Chart XII for wording of questions on thoughts that helped "when the going was tough."
† The question was: "In general, would you say that battle fighting became more frightening or less frightening the more you saw of it?"

_____ It was more frightening the more I saw of it
_____ It was less frightening the more I saw of it
_____ It was never frightening
_____ It stayed frightening all the time

‡ See Chapter 4 on "Problems Related to the Control of Fear in Combat" for questions on fear symptoms in battle.   In regard to each symptom, each man was scored 1 or 0.   A score of 1 was given if "often" or "sometimes" was checked; otherwise, a score of 0 was given, except in the case of vomiting or losing control of bowels, in which cases a score of 1 was also given if "once" was checked.   Total scores ranged from 0 to 9.   Scores of 0–4 were considered *low*; scores of 5–9, *high*.   Men who failed to answer the entire series of fear-symptom questions are omitted from the tabulations.   When the latter men are divided according to whether they say battle fighting becomes more or less frightening, the same relationships obtain between those two subgroups as between corresponding subgroups in the table.

items.   These relationships hold when rank and education are controlled.   The data are, of course, two-edged.   To be sure, the more frightened men were "standing in the need of prayer," and the data could be said to indicate, in line with what has been said before, that those men actually found prayer most helpful who needed it most.   On the other hand, prayer, it might be said, could not in fact have been too helpful to them, as they remained the more frightened men.   Actually one cannot use the data to estimate how much prayer did help the men, as one has no basis for knowing that without recourse to it the more frightened men would not have been even more badly off.   The previous data comparing men in different branches are fortunately not subject to the same ambiguity of interpretation, and indicate that men who for objective reasons suffered more greatly from combat stress were more likely to think prayer helped them.   On purely statistical grounds, one could not rule out the possibility that in the present case the men who found combat more frightening did so partly because of their reliance on prayer.   But in conjunction with the branch comparisons, the more reasonable view is that both subjective and objective reasons for suffering more acutely from the stresses of combat inclined the men to rely more heavily on prayer.

Table 21 shows that similar relationships held for infantrymen in the Italian campaign.   Men who said they worried a lot about becoming a casualty were somewhat more likely to say they were helped a lot by prayer than were men who did not say they worried a lot about it, while they were somewhat less likely to say that they were helped by the other items.   The differences are small, but in agreement with those found in the Pacific.   Also, as the table shows, they hold up for both higher and lower educational levels in spite of the fact that there are considerable differences by education for the items other than prayer.   When rank is also controlled, the differences still hold.

Prayer then appears to enter into a different set of relationships from any other of the items in the series about when the going was tough.   To throw the differences into stronger relief, it will be fruitful to consider the differences in combat experiences and in reactions to battle of men who said they were helped a lot by prayer and those who said they were not.   First, however, it should be noted that in neither theater did these two groups differ in educational level.   The education level of the enlisted infantrymen in the two theaters according to whether or not they said they were helped a lot by prayer was as follows:

	PACIFIC		ITALY	
	Prayer helped a lot	Prayer did not help a lot	Prayer helped a lot	Prayer did not help a lot
At least some high school	64%	64%	67%	69%
Grade school education or less	36	36	33	31
	100%	100%	100%	100%

In the Pacific, men who said they were helped a lot by prayer were likely to have a somewhat higher score on a scale of psychoneurotic

TABLE 21

THOUGHTS WHICH VETERANS SAID HELPED THEM "WHEN THE GOING WAS TOUGH" IN RELATION TO HOW MUCH THEY SAID THEY WORRIED ABOUT THEIR CHANCES OF BECOMING A CASUALTY

(Veteran Enlisted Infantrymen in Italy, April 1945 *)

	PERCENTAGE SAYING THAT HAVING EACH TYPE OF THOUGHT HELPED A LOT† AMONG			
	Men with grade school education or less who		Men with at least some high school education who	
	Said they worried a lot about becoming a casualty ‡	Did not say they worried a lot about becoming a casualty	Said they worried a lot about becoming a casualty	Did not say they worried a lot about becoming a casualty
Prayer	87	81	87	82
Thinking that you couldn't let the other men down	52	65	50	59
Thinking that you had to finish the job in order to get home again	30	37	23	25
Thoughts of hatred for the enemy	27	35	24	28
Thinking of the meaning of what we are fighting for	39	42	22	24
Number of cases	*250*	*319*	*395*	*734*

* Cross section of enlisted men in rifle and heavy weapons companies of four Infantry divisions, Italy, early April 1945 (S-177).
† See Chart XII for wording of questions on thoughts that helped "when the going was tough."
‡ The question was: "When you were in combat did you worry about your chances of becoming a casualty?"

_____ Worried about it a lot
_____ Worried about it some but not a lot
_____ Didn't worry so much about it
_____ Hardly worried about it at all
_____ Never worried about it

symptoms, though there was practically no difference in this respect in the groups surveyed in Italy.   Privates were somewhat more likely to say they were helped a lot than were noncoms.

Table 22 shows for infantrymen in a Pacific division a consistent

TABLE 22

COMPARISON OF RELATIONSHIPS TO REACTIONS TO COMBAT, OF BEING HELPED A LOT BY PRAYER AND OF BEING HELPED A LOT BY THINKING THAT ONE CANNOT LET THE OTHER MEN DOWN

(Veteran Enlisted Infantrymen in One Pacific Division, March–April 1944 *)

| | PERCENTAGE WHO REPORTED A GIVEN REACTION TO COMBAT, ACCORDING TO WHETHER OR NOT THEY SAID THEY WERE HELPED A LOT BY | | | |
| | *Prayer* | | *Thinking that they couldn't let the other men down* | |
REPORTED REACTION	Helped a lot	Did not help a lot	Helped a lot	Did not help a lot
Battle became less frightening the more they saw of it	18	30	24	20
Low number of fear symptoms in combat†	45	63	56	47
Relatively ready for more combat‡	25	30	31	24
More scared during combat than before or after§	39	30	34	40
Had less confidence in self, the more times they went into combat**	34	27	28	36
Number of cases	*915*	*513*	*791*	*632*

* Cross section of Infantry combat veterans in a division which fought in the South Pacific, surveyed March–April 1944 (S-100).
† See footnote to Table 20.   Men who did not answer any of the items in the fear-symptom scale are omitted.
‡ See footnote 33 in Chapter 2.
§ The question was: "In general, did you feel more scared *before* going into combat, *during* combat or *after* combat?"

    _____ Before going into combat
    _____ During combat
    _____ After combat
    _____ Undecided

** The question was: "Did you have more confidence or less confidence in yourself, the more times you went into combat?"

    _____ Had more confidence, the more times I went into combat
    _____ Had less confidence, the more times I went into combat
    _____ Had about the same amount of confidence, the more times I went into combat
    _____ Undecided

pattern of differences between those who said they were helped a lot by prayer and those who said they were not.   The first two items show relationships already considered from a different vantage point in Table 20; the others are new.   The men who said they were helped a lot by prayer were less likely than other men to say that battle became less frightening the more they saw of it, less likely to report having had a low number of fear symptoms in combat, more likely to say that they were especially scared during combat rather than before or afterward, less likely to be relatively willing for more combat, and more likely to say that the more they saw of combat the less confidence they felt in themselves.

In the same table, parallel comparisons are shown for the men who did and who did not say that it helped them a lot to think that they "couldn't let the other men down." This provides an interesting contrast, since the differences throughout are in the opposite direction. The differences are for the most part small. But they consistently indicate that (1) saying that one is helped a lot by thinking that one cannot let the other men down was associated with lower fear and higher self-confidence and willingness for combat, whereas (2) saying that prayer helped a lot was associated with the opposite characteristics. When score on a scale of psychoneurotic symptoms and rank are simultaneously controlled, it turns out that saying that prayer helped a lot, and saying that it helped a lot to think that one could not let the other men down, were thus related to the men's reported battle reactions in 19 out of the 20 subcomparisons. The difference in pattern is thus stable, and remains when the influences of rank and personality differences are ruled out as much as possible.

Table 23 gives similar comparative data for the infantrymen in Italy, who had been asked a wider variety of questions about their combat experiences. As in the Pacific, the men who said they were helped by prayer were more likely to find battle increasingly frightening. On two related questions, they were more likely to say that when they first went into combat it was tougher than they expected, and less likely to say they hardly ever became so worried and discouraged that they wondered if anything was worth while. On the other hand, the comparison of men who said that they were or were not helped a lot by thinking that they couldn't let the other men down, shows either no differences on answers to these questions or differences in the opposite direction.

Unlike the case of thinking that one could not let the other men down, those who said they were helped a lot by prayer were reliably more likely than other men to have been replacements. They were reliably more likely to say they had been bombed or strafed by our own planes or fired on by our own artillery several times, and to say they had seen a close friend killed or wounded in action. There were no differences on these items in respect to thinking that one could not let the other men down. All the differences reported here with respect to being helped by prayer are still present when age, education, and score on a scale of psychoneurotic symptoms are simultaneously controlled. On the other hand, as between men who said they were helped a lot by thinking that they couldn't let

TABLE 23

COMPARISON OF RELATIONSHIPS TO COMBAT EXPERIENCES AND REACTIONS OF
BEING HELPED A LOT BY PRAYER AND OF BEING HELPED A LOT BY
THINKING THAT ONE CANNOT LET THE OTHER MEN DOWN
(Veteran Enlisted Infantrymen, Mediterranean Theater, April 1945)

| | PERCENTAGE WHO REPORTED A GIVEN EXPERIENCE OR REACTION, ACCORDING TO WHETHER OR NOT THEY SAID THEY WERE HELPED A LOT BY | | | |
| | *Prayer* | | *Thinking that they couldn't let the other men down* | |
REPORTED EXPERIENCE OR REACTION	Helped a lot	Did not help a lot	Helped a lot	Did not help a lot
Came overseas with outfit	33	41	38	30
Have been bombed or strafed by own planes or fired on by own artillery several times	62	50	61	59
Saw close friend killed or wounded in action	89	79	88	86
When first went into combat it was tougher than expected	47	37	46	46
Combat became more frightening the more they saw of it	77	65	75	74
Hardly ever became so worried and discouraged that they wondered whether anything is worth while	13	19	16	10
Number of cases	*1,433*	*297*	*974*	*757*

S-177.

the other men down and those who did not say this, either there were no differences on these items or the differences were in the opposite direction. The observed differences in respect to prayer were therefore not merely the result of differences in the extent to which the men said they were helped by any kind of thoughts.

Out of these data from two theaters and two widely differing campaigns, a fairly coherent picture emerges in regard to the sort of person who said prayer helped a lot when the going was tough. Such persons, first, appear on the average to have been subjected to a relatively stronger degree of stress than the minority who did not report finding prayer very helpful. Thus, men in the Infantry were more likely to say they found prayer helpful than were men in other branches, and, among infantrymen, men who said they were helped a lot by prayer were more likely than others to say that they had seen close friends become casualties and that they had taken air or artillery attack from their own side several times—situations that would be particularly hard to endure. Secondly, those who say they were helped a lot by prayer appear to have had somewhat less resources for coping with the stresses which they underwent. The replacement, as compared with the original members of a unit, could draw on less support from his ties to other members of the group, and, as we have seen, men who said they were helped a lot by prayer were more likely to have been replacements. The evidence that the more fearful, less self-confident men were more likely to say they were helped a lot by prayer and vice versa can probably be cited here too, although so far as the data go it is equally likely that these men may have suffered severer stress. At one psychological level, the two statements become equivalent, since those men who had less adequate personal resources would have experienced the same objective situation as one of severer stress. Reliance on prayer obviously had other roots in addition to extreme stress—for instance, the beliefs to which the men had been educated. And recourse to prayer was not an invariable reaction to extreme stress, since, for example, a majority even of those in Italy who did not say prayer helped a lot had seen friends killed or wounded. But the data establish a definite relationship between stress and reliance on prayer.

From the statistical evidence it is just as correct to say that men who claimed to be helped by prayer tended to be fearful and unwilling for combat as to say the converse. Nevertheless, the fact that such an overwhelming majority of combat men said that prayer helped them a lot certainly means that they almost universally had recourse to prayer and probably found relief, distraction, or consolation in the process.

What the act of prayer implied probably varied greatly from one man to another, depending among other things on his previous religious beliefs. On the one hand, there were men, previously religious, for whom prayer was a very direct and personal experience. The relatively uneducated wounded combat veteran who gave the following account had gone to church several times a week before entering the Army:

I sure prayed when I was in a tight spot. I just asked the old man above to lead the way and take care of me. When I was hit in the leg I asked the old man above to heal my leg. We had prayers sometimes before going into action. It helps a lot.[47]

Perhaps more typically, prayer was less a matter of conversation with a familiar figure than an expressive quasi-magical act. The following quotation suggests this:

I used to pray a lot. You just automatically pray to yourself when you're going in and when you're in. (Said things like "God help me" and "Why are they doing this?") You know the saying that there are no atheists in a fox hole.

There are practically no data available to throw light on the interesting question of the relationship between prayer in battle and formal religion. There is, however, some evidence of a lasting effect of the battlefield experience upon religious attitudes. After the end of the war, a cross section of enlisted men in the United States were given a questionnaire which included several agree-disagree items concerning the effects of Army experience on the men's religious beliefs. As Chart XIV shows, men with combat experience were reliably more likely than men who did not see combat to agree that their Army experiences had increased their faith in God, the difference between the two groups being 25 per cent. Little weight should be attached to the differences between the proportion who agreed with the statement that their Army experience increased their faith in God and the proportion who agreed with the statement that their experiences had decreased their faith. Those who did not think their faith had changed, for instance, might have been expected to check "agree" to the first statement, lest they give the possibly dangerous impression that they had lost their faith. The same persons would be expected to disagree with the second statement. This means that the difference among noncombat men between 54 per cent agreeing that their faith increased versus 17 per cent agreeing that it decreased does not establish the probability of any corresponding real increase in faith on their part. However the difference on each statement in the proportion of combat versus noncombat men who agreed with it is based on a valid comparison since the tendencies which would distort the men's answers were presumably equivalent for the two groups. Thus there seems to have been a real increase with combat experience in the proportion of men who said that Army experiences increased their faith in God

[47] Interview in hospital in the United States, spring 1944.

At the opposite end of the scale, on the other hand, combat experience does not seem to have made a difference: the combat and noncombat men did not differ in the proportions who thought that their experiences had decreased their faith.

CHART XIV

Reported Changes in Religious Beliefs as a Result of Army Experience
(Cross Section of Enlisted Men in Continental United States, December 1945)

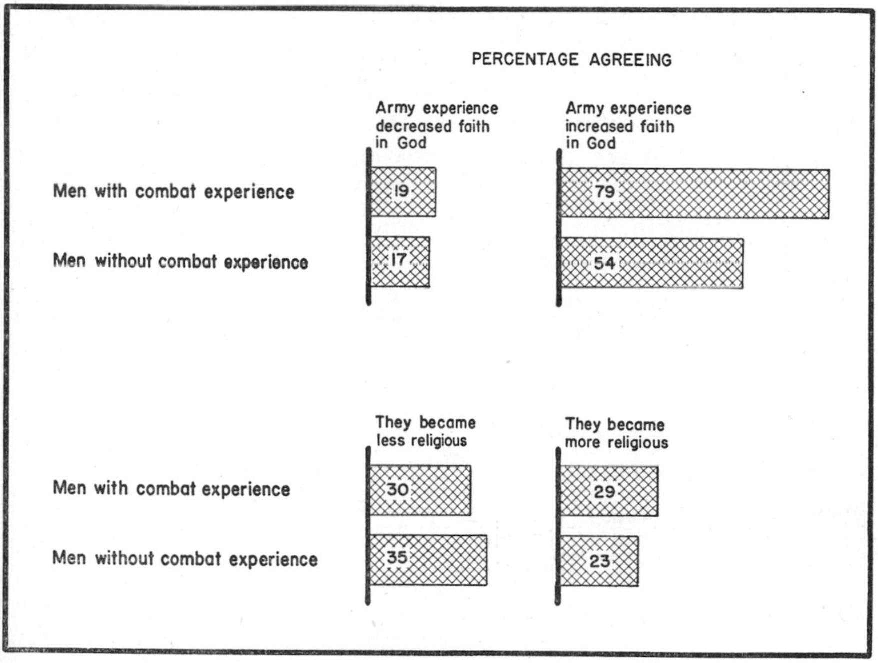

PERCENTAGE AGREEING

	Army experience decreased faith in God	Army experience increased faith in God
Men with combat experience	19	79
Men without combat experience	17	54

	They became less religious	They became more religious
Men with combat experience	30	29
Men without combat experience	35	23

The statements were:
"My experiences in the Army have decreased my faith in God."   (S-234B, 243 men with combat experience, 790 without.)
"My experiences in the Army have increased my faith in God."   (S-234A, administered at the same time as S-234B, on alternate questionnaires.   212 men with combat experience, 823 without.)
"I am less religious than when I first entered the Army."   (S-234A)
"I am more religious than when I first entered the Army."   (S-234B)

In contrast to the difference which appeared in regard to "faith in God," the combat and noncombat groups did not differ significantly in saying that they were more or less religious than when they first entered the Army, as can be seen on the chart.   One possible interpretation is that recourse to prayer during the stress of battle did increase the men's personal faith, perhaps because beliefs previously of little significance in their lives acquired an important function, but that this process did not markedly alter their feelings about formal religion.

The data in regard to the kind of men who were most likely to say that they found prayer helpful are in accord with a view which would regard prayer, magic (e.g., the rabbit's foot) and fatalism (e.g., the shell with a man's number on it) as, in part, alternative modes of adjustment to situations in which there is a high degree of stress and frustration from unpredictable circumstances which are beyond the control of the individual. Combat certainly maximized both the frustration and the uncertainty, and we have seen that those who felt the stress most keenly were those who were most likely to have recourse to prayer. Of these modes of adjustment, prayer and magic would alleviate anxiety by the use of suprarational techniques to bolster confidence and perhaps alter the course of events. Fatalism, on the other hand, allays anxiety by holding that there is in fact a single inevitable future course of events so worry is pointless. The threat of the unexpected and unpredictable is brought into acceptable bounds when the unexpected is redefined as the inevitable. There is no point in anxiety if you are only going to be hit when the shell has your number on it. Although there are no quantitative data on the incidence of magic and fatalistic points of view among combat troops or in regard to the relation of these adjustments to prayer, informal reports make it seem likely that possible logical inconsistencies did not prevent men from using all three techniques concurrently, or from "keeping their powder dry" at the same time, so far as possible.

Many magical or semimagical practices have been reported among combat men. Men might carry protective amulets or good-luck charms, some of which had religious symbolism and some of which did not: a cross, a Bible, a rabbit's foot, a medal. They might carry out prebattle preparations in a fixed, "ritual" order. They might jealously keep articles of clothing or equipment which were associated with some past experience of escape from danger. They might scrupulously avoid actions regarded as unlucky (some with implicit rational grounds): "three on a match," or saying "My number is about up." Among fatalistic beliefs expressed in the talk of combat men were such things as: you will not be killed until "your time has come"; "it's all a matter of luck"; and a man is "using up his chances."

A fatalistic phenomenon which has been reported from previous wars is the occurrence among fighting troops of a belief in persona invulnerability.   At a relatively superficial level, "green" troops in World War II were sometimes said to evade recognition of the fact that the dangers of battle intimately concerned them until their first direct experiences brought grim proof to the contrary.   Among seasoned troops, informal reports suggest that belief in invulnerability must have been quite rare.   One of the wounded combat veterans of fighting in the Mediterranean theater interviewed in 1944 mentioned such a reaction:

Toward the end some men get over-confident. It gets so that after each fight that the fellows pull through, they get the feeling they're bullet-proof.   Only thing that'll put them back in their place is some close shaves.

But the data to be presented in the next chapter showing how American soldiers generally admitted being afraid in battle at least rules out the possibility that belief in invulnerability was a widespread or broadly effective mode of adjustment.

A somewhat equivalent response which was occasionally observed among old combat troops might be called a "strategic abandonment of hope."   If one ceases to hope to get through, one can to some degree protect oneself against disintegrative extreme anxiety, though sometimes at the cost of objective appropriateness of response. Men who settled on this mode of reaction were characterized by apathy and minimal level of reaction to events.   A wounded Infantry veteran of European fighting who said "We stood in one damn fox hole for forty-seven days" described such men as follows:

Sometimes they pushed a fellow so long, they are too tired before they even start fighting.   They don't give a damn whether they get killed or not.   They lose courage.   They don't aim, can't hit the ground fast.   They're scared all right but they don't care.   When they're running they run about fifteen yards and then start walking—don't give a damn.

Sometimes the prospect of an end to combat reawakened intense anxiety in such men, when hope again seemed objectively justified. The best example of this was among Air Corps flyers on their final missions.   A rise in anxiety at this point has been described by psychiatric observers and is supported by data which are presented in Chapter 8 on a rise in the sick-call rate.[48]   Similar reactions no doubt occurred among combat infantrymen who knew that their names were high on the unit's rotation list.

Another passive adjustment allied to a fatalistic point of view in-

---

[48] See Chart XIII in Chapter 8.

volved a shortening of time perspective, living in the short run and focusing attention on means rather than ends. The hedonism of combat troops on leave is traditional. By banishing the long run to a status of limited reality, the combat man could to some extent escape facing the unpleasant probabilities and avoid a disorganizing level of anxiety.

While humor is perhaps not on the same level as the personal philosophies which we have been discussing, the bitter humor of the front deserves mention as yet another way in which the soldier could achieve a frame of mind in which it was possible for him to endure and accept what could not be avoided. Humor allowed a safe discharge of dangerous tensions; and by playing upon incongruities between normal values and the transmuted values of the combat situation, or between combat actualities and rearward conceptions of combat, or by exaggeration, understatement, or the singling out of the irrelevant, humor helped the men to achieve a kind of distance from their threatening experiences. Mauldin's combat cartoons illustrate all these roles of soldier humor, and his immense popularity with front-line men attests to the acuity with which he caught the combat man's point of view.[49]

Many of these adjustments which we have been describing appear frequently to have been adopted almost deliberately as an instrument of psychological self-defense. The men sometimes gave the impression of trying to believe what they were saying. Observers of men in combat have also reported a tendency for individuals to utilize simultaneously a wide range of devices, almost as if they were insuring that no possibility of safeguard had been overlooked. The formulation appears often to have been, "This may be silly, but what harm can it do? No use passing up a chance—there might be something to it." Even for men who did not really believe in the objective efficacy of magical practices, they could actually contribute to better-integrated behavior and thus to combat efficiency by bolstering confidence and lowering anxiety.

This discussion of some of the private adjustments the combat man arrived at in attempting to cope with a fundamentally unsatisfactory situation will close this chapter on the combat motivation

---

[49] In the Mediterranean edition of *Stars and Stripes*, Mauldin's cartoon was the most popular feature among Fifth Army troops, after United States news and news of the Italian and Western front, 83 per cent of the men saying they usually read it. Thirty-two per cent of the Army men said that *Stars and Stripes* gave too little space to Mauldin, making Mauldin second only to United States news on this measure of popularity. (Survey of cross section of 1,880 enlisted men in Italy, December 1944.)

of the ground soldier. It is an appropriate stopping point, since it brings us to a recognition of the final insufficiency of all the various compulsions, incentives, and supports in the face of extreme stress beyond individual powers of prediction and control. When all is said and done, no motivational structure was adequate to sustain the average soldier in stress of combat indefinitely. It became a psychiatric axiom that "every man has his breaking point." To win a war, however, it was not necessary that every man fight indefinitely. It was sufficient that men hold out long enough and fight well enough to keep organized and effective armies in the field. We have been considering some of the factors which made this possible—the guidance and support of the formal Army system and the informal combat group, convictions about the war and the enemy, various specific hopes and goals, and a few of the personal philosophies which made combat more endurable.

CHAPTER 4

PROBLEMS RELATED TO THE CONTROL OF FEAR IN COMBAT[1]

Introduction

IN THE preceding chapters, the overall combat situation has been described and the variety of intense psychological stresses engendered in combat have been discussed. In this chapter the focus will be narrowed down to concentrate on a number of problems arising from reactions to one primary source of stress in combat—physical danger.

From the standpoint of the individual soldier, it is primarily the danger of death or injury which makes the combat situation so harassing an experience. The intense emotional strains of actual battle are to a large extent rooted in the inescapable fear and anxiety reactions continually aroused by ever-present stimuli which signify objective threats of danger. The threats of being maimed, of undergoing unbearable pain, and of being completely annihilated elicit intense fear reactions which may severely interfere with successful performances. If soldiers are given no preparation for dealing with danger situations and if special techniques for controlling fear reactions are not utilized, many men are likely to react to combat in a way which would be catastrophic to themselves and to their military organization.

There is always the possibility, when men are exposed to the objective dangers of combat, that they will react by fleeing in panic or that they will be immobilized by uncontrollable terror. Even if these extreme reactions are averted, there is still the danger that many men will become so disorganized by fear that they will fail to carry out their military mission adequately. The preceding chapters describe some of the general institutional patterns of the Army which serve to impel soldiers to withstand the harassing conditions

---

[1] By Irving L. Janis. This chapter draws upon several Research Branch studies in which John Dollard, Donald Horton, John L. Finan, and Paul Wallin had especially important roles.

of combat so that they carry out the complex integrated activities of engaging the enemy. In this chapter we shall discuss some of the major practices of the Army during World War II which were designed either entirely or partially to minimize the potential damage of disruptive fear reactions in soldiers exposed to the objective dangers of combat:

1. The policy of encouraging soldiers to adopt a permissive attitude toward their own fear symptoms when confronted with objective danger.

2. The systematic elimination of men who were psychologically unfit for combat by the use of screening devices.

3. The training of men for combat by instruction and drill in specific, appropriate reactions to be made to various combat conditions and by exposing them to battle stimuli.

In discussing the data relevant to each of these three types of fear control practices, we shall devote especial attention to their suggestive implications for the general problems of fear control. It must be recognized, however, that only fragmentary data are available and they cannot be expected to lead to precise and unequivocal conclusions. It was not part of the general mission of the Research Branch to make studies of fear control; most of the data which we shall present were obtained as incidental results in the course of making a study of some other type of problem. But although the findings are fragmentary, they have suggestive value with respect to some of the general problems of fear control which are likely to be of importance for social science research. Such research aims at establishing general hypotheses on the conditions under which fear reactions are elicited, augmented, and diminished—hypotheses which would provide the framework for a systematic theory of the social psychology of fear.

If such a systematic scientific framework had been developed before the war, it would undoubtedly have permitted important practical applications throughout the Army by facilitating research on major military problems of fear control such as the following:

1. Under what conditions should troops receive their "baptism of fire"? Gradually, in order to habituate men to make appropriate responses in the presence of relatively familiar danger cues, or rapidly, in order to prevent men's anxieties from mounting over a period of increasing dosage?

2. Within the restricted conditions of actual combat operations, what leadership practices are most likely to be effective in reducing

the men's anxieties in situations of impending danger? What types of activity are effective in reducing fear reactions in the actual presence of danger?

3. Once maladaptive fear reactions are acquired, what reconditioning procedures are most effective? For various types of combat conditions, what are the optimal time periods with respect to exposure to danger alternating with rest periods in a nondanger environment? Under what conditions are the psychologically harmful effects of exposure to a traumatic danger situation reduced by immediate re-exposure to a similar situation (e.g., requiring a pilot to fly immediately after a plane crash)?

In spite of the critical need for answers to these and numerous other problems involved in the control of fear, very little fundamental research has been carried out. In large part, the absence of basic research in this field both before and during the war is attributable to a key methodological problem which remains to be solved before it will be possible to carry out well-controlled studies of variables related to disruptive fear reactions—the problem of developing valid criteria of maladaptive fear responses in the form of indices which can be practically applied in social science research.

Research is needed to delineate behavioral and physiological syndromes of fear and anxiety reactions to danger situations so that they may be differentiated according to pragmatic categories such as the following: (1) emotional reactions which, in general, are adaptive in danger situations in that there is a general increase of physiological readiness for carrying out rapid or strenuous motor action together with heightened cautiousness but without serious impairment of intelligent planning functions; (2) intense emotional reactions which are potentially adaptive as in *1* but also potentially maladaptive as in *3* depending upon the specific conditions of the danger situation in which they occur; (3) intense disruptive fear and anxiety reactions which, in general, are maladaptive in danger situations in that there is a generalized loss of discriminating ability, impairment of ability to plan appropriate actions, lack of integration in motor performances, and involuntary behavior which may augment the objective danger. From the point of view of military control of fear, it is the maladaptive type of reaction which is of primary interest—preventing the occurrence of involuntary stupid acts (or failures to act) which increase the degree of danger to the military unit.

Criteria need to be developed not only for identifying the occurrence of maladaptive emotional reactions to danger situations but also for evaluating the aftereffects of a given exposure to danger. In the military context, one of the major types of problems in fear control is to determine whether exposure to sample danger situations during the training period would have a beneficial effect with respect to preparing the men to face future danger situations in combat. To deal with this type of practical problem requires an evaluation of the aftereffects of a given type of fear experience. On the one hand, the elicitation of fear in a training situation may have beneficial effects upon the men's motivation, as was pointed out by Dollard in his study of American volunteers who had fought in the Civil War in Spain:

"Fear may be aroused in training so as to serve a useful purpose. It can motivate men to learn those habits which will reduce danger in battle. . . . In order to understand the value of training, the men should visualize the situation in which the training is to be used. For this reason, apparently, our informants stress the value of giving the trainees a real picture of the danger of battle." [2]

On the other hand, a phobic type of reaction toward combat may develop which might interfere with training and motivate the men to attempt to avoid combat duty. In addition to effects upon motivation, it is necessary to take account of the direct effect of experiences in training in terms of: adaptation to fear-eliciting stimuli, which would tend to reduce the intensity of fear reactions to future exposures; and sensitization, which would tend to increase the intensity of fear reactions to future exposures.

If sound criteria of maladaptive fear reactions had been available, military psychologists would have been in a position to carry out extensive experiments on the effectiveness of various training activities and personnel policies devised to reduce fear in danger situations. [3]

[2] John Dollard, *Fear in Battle* (Institute for Human Relations, Yale University, 1943), p. 14.

[3] The Research Branch was once requested to make a study to determine whether or not a given training technique aided or hindered the control of fear in battle. The study was abandoned because the possible criteria—such as the subsequent neuropsychiatric rate of the unit or the proportion of men who exhibited directly observable maladaptive reactions in the training danger-test situation—were recognized to be inadequate for obtaining a definite answer to the problem. For example, when criteria of this sort are used, only a few cases determine the rating of an entire unit and hence no account is taken of fear tendencies among the majority of the men. To develop adequate criteria would have required extensive methodological research to determine whether or not they successfully predict maladaptive fear reactions in combat. But validation studies of this kind are extremely difficult to carry out under combat con-

The Permissive Attitude Toward Fear and Anxiety

Early in World War II, the United States Army adopted the explicit policy of building up a permissive attitude toward fear and anxiety symptoms among the troops. Men were taught, from basic training on, that they need not be ashamed of feeling afraid in danger situations, that fear reactions are normal and are shared by everyone exposed to combat conditions. Emphasis was placed on the idea that even though a man feels afraid, he can keep going and do a good job, and that after a time his fear will die down.

This Army doctrine was communicated to the men by formal training lectures, by training movies, and by other official Army media employed in the indoctrination of troops. The following passage from *Army Life*,[4] the official handbook issued to all trainees in the Army, illustrates the typical way in which fear in combat was presented to the men in their training courses:

YOU'LL BE SCARED. Sure you'll be scared. Before you go into battle, you'll be frightened at the uncertainty, at the thought of being killed. Will it hurt? Will you know what to do?

If you say you're not scared, you'll be a cocky fool. Don't let anyone tell you you're a coward if you admit being scared. Fear before you're actually in the battle is a normal emotional reaction. It's the last step of preparation, the not-knowing, in spite of all that you've learned.

After you've become used to the picture and the sensations of the battlefield, you will change. All the things you were taught in training will come back to you. This is the answer. This is where you will prove that you are a good soldier. That first fight—that fight with yourself—will have gone. Then you will be ready to fight the enemy.

Another aspect of this Army policy of encouraging a lenient attitude toward fear in combat was the official procedure for handling men who showed abnormal fear or anxiety symptoms. Men who developed incapacitating fear reactions in combat were labeled as medical cases, and the prescribed procedure was to send them through medical channels for immediate treatment by a physician, with the intention of returning as many as possible to their combat units. Those neuropsychiatric cases who showed persistent incapacitating symptoms were evacuated to hospitals in the rear. From

---

ditions and, moreover, there are no simple measures of behavior in combat to use as validating criteria. In the absence of such studies, we are forced to rely upon correlational data, interview material, and clinical and other observations which furnish suggestive leads but do not provide incisive answers to the problems of military fear control.

[4] War Department Pamphlet 21–13, 1944, p. 159.

Army psychiatric reports it appears that the majority of men who developed extreme fear reactions were relieved of their symptoms after a few days of rest and medical care in the battalion aid station and were then returned to their company.

This method of dealing with cases of extreme fear reactions in combat became generally known to men throughout the Army, even though the Army made no effort to publicize it among the troops. In so far as the actual practice in an Army command fostered the realization that inability to control one's fear was not likely to elicit punishment from Army authorities, it undoubtedly reinforced the notion that one would not be blamed for extreme loss of control in the face of danger: If one couldn't take it and cracked up in combat he would simply be sent to the medics as a legitimate casualty rather than be treated as a coward or a weakling.

This conception of severe fear reactions may have been directly communicated to the men, informally, by their leaders in so far as the leaders' personal attitudes incorporated the official Army policy on neuropsychiatric casualties.[5]

The data from attitude surveys in several theaters indicate that the majority of combat officers adopted a tolerant attitude toward men who developed extreme fear reactions in combat (Table 1).

The data shown in Table 1 suggest that most combat officers accepted the Army's practice of treating extreme fear reactions as an objective medical problem rather than as a disciplinary problem requiring punitive action.   (A fuller elaboration of this attitude will be presented below in the section on attitudes of enlisted men.)

It would not be surprising if most enlisted men also developed a permissive attitude toward fear reactions.   Resistance toward adopting such an attitude was probably not very strong and acceptance of the attitude tended to be psychologically rewarding.[6]   Many soldiers might have felt insecure about whether or not they would be able to control themselves adequately when they were faced with the realities of combat danger.   But if it were taken for granted that everyone would be emotionally upset, and if one did not have to worry about being regarded as a culprit if he found himself unable to master his fear completely, then anticipatory anxieties about fail-

---

[5] As will be discussed later in this chapter, the official Army policy of permissiveness towards fear often tended in practice to be only permissiveness towards admitting fear prior to action.   In combat many officers and men were relatively intolerant of signs of fear in others.

[6] Though some rewards of pride, sadistic gratification, etc., would have followed from maintaining a nonpermissive attitude.

ing to maintain full emotional control in combat would tend to be reduced.

There is evidence from many attitude surveys that enlisted men did, in fact, adopt a permissive attitude toward fear and anxiety reactions.

The results for enlisted combat veterans in Infantry divisions, shown in Table 2, closely parallel those for their officers shown in

TABLE 1

ATTITUDES OF COMBAT OFFICERS TOWARD EXTREME FEAR REACTIONS

QUESTION: "In your opinion what should be done with men who crack up in action, that is, men who get shell-shocked, blow their tops, go haywire?"

Cross-section samples of company grade officers in Infantry divisions (April 1944)	Number of cases	Should be treated as sick men	PER CENT ANSWERING: MOST OF THEM Should be treated as cowards and punished	Should be treated some other way*	No answer	Total
Division A (European Theater)	228	77	6	15	2	100
Division B (European Theater)	196	70	3	17	10	100
Division C (South Pacific)	177	67	3	28	2	100
Division D (South Pacific)	267	67	3	29	1	100
Division E (Central Pacific)	311	70	1	27	2	100
Division F (Central Pacific)	92	77	1	20	2	100

Data from S-101.
* The third choice, "Most of them should be treated some other way," was followed by the question, "How should they be treated?" The majority of officers who responded to this question wrote in answers which indicated a tolerant attitude toward men who showed extreme emotional reactions.

Table 1.   A very sizable majority reported their own personal opinion to be that men who develop incapacitating fear and anxiety reactions in combat should be treated as medical casualties rather than as offenders.

Additional data are provided by a survey of 1,766 enlisted men in Italy, representing a cross section of rifle and heavy weapons companies in four combat divisions (April 1945).[7]   The majority of men in this sample (70 per cent) reported that they had been on active combat duty (i.e., at least within range of enemy artillery) for a period of five months or more.   A question similar to the one shown in Table 2 was included in the questionnaire: "What do you think should be done to a man who 'cracks up' mentally at the front?"   Eighty-six per cent answered "He should be given medical

---

[7] S-177.

treatment"; whereas only 3 per cent asserted "He should be court-martialed" or "He should be made to go right back into combat." The remainder of the sample gave "Don't know" as their response.

While these results, together with those in Table 2, indicate that combat troops tended to accept the Army's practice of withdrawing men who showed incapacitating symptoms, they should not be regarded as implying that the men were tolerant toward those who, because of their fear, attempted to avoid hazardous missions or to escape from combat altogether. From additional questions in-

TABLE 2

Attitudes of Combat Enlisted Men Toward Extreme Fear Reactions

Question: "In your opinion what should be done with men who crack up in action, that is, men who get shell-shocked, blow their tops, go haywire?"

		PER CENT ANSWERING: MOST OF THEM				
Cross-section samples of enlisted men in Infantry divisions (April 1944)	Number of cases	Should be treated as sick men	Should be treated as cowards and punished	Should be treated some other way*	No answer	Total
Division B (European Theater)	858	67	4	18	11	100
Division C (South Pacific)	1,983	72	6	18	4	100
Division D (South Pacific)	2,095	72	2	24	2	100
Division E (Central Pacific)	1,299	77	3	18	2	100
Division F (Central Pacific)	643	73	3	22	2	100

Data from S-100.
* The majority of men who wrote in an answer after checking this category expressed a tolerant attitude toward those who showed extreme emotional reactions.

cluded in the survey of combat troops in Italy we find that the majority conceived psychiatric casualties as men who were not deliberately attempting to evade combat duty:

Do you think that most of the men who "crack up" mentally at the front try as hard as they can to stay in the line?

Most of them *do* try as hard as they can	64%
About half of them try as hard as they can	8
Most of them *do not* try as hard as they can	7
Don't know and No answer	21
Total	100%

Do you think that most of the men who "crack up" mentally at the front could help it if they really wanted to?

Most of them *could* help it	7%
About half of them could help it and half can't	12
Most of them *can't* help it	58
Don't know and No answer	23
Total	100%

Interviews with officers and enlisted men who had had extensive combat experience reveal that a distinction was made between men who were yellow and those who were genuine psychiatric casualties. One important factor in making a judgment about another man's fear reaction was the extent to which he was physically incapacitated by his symptoms. A soldier whose symptoms persisted long after the objective danger subsided was generally regarded by his fellows as a sick man. But often distinctions were made between men who were cowards and men who were ill even though both might show the same fear symptoms. The key factor which was stressed by the interviewees was *effort to overcome the withdrawal tendencies engendered by intense fear.* The man who was visibly shaken by exposure to danger, who trembled violently and who burst out weeping like a baby, was not regarded as a coward unless he made no apparent effort to stick out his job. If, despite trying hard, the man could not perform his combat job adequately, he was regarded as a legitimate casualty and was not blamed for being unable to take it. But if a man showed exactly the same fear symptoms except that he made the claim that he was unable to go on and asked to be sent to the battalion aid station without having shown any previous attempt to disregard his symptoms in trying to do his share of the job at hand, he was labeled a coward and subject to the scorn of the other men in his unit. Thus men were not blamed for being afraid or for being emotionally upset by the threat of danger, but they were expected to try to put up a struggle to carry on despite their fear.

A number of surveys provide evidence of another aspect of the permissive attitude toward fear in combat. It appears that there was little tendency among combat troops to deny their own fear reactions. So far as the survey results go, they indicate that the majority of men were willing to admit readily that they experienced fear and anxiety in combat.

From a survey of combat divisions in Pacific areas we find that a high percentage of the men reported that they had experienced various physiological reactions which are popularly recognized as expressions of intense fear and which, in the questionnaire, were presented in the context of fear reactions.   (See Table 3.)

There is additional evidence from other surveys which supports the conclusion that enlisted men adopted a permissive attitude toward fear.

In a survey of 277 wounded combat veterans in the European Theater of Operations (August 1944), 65 per cent of the men admitted having had at least one experience in combat in which they

TABLE 3

FEAR SYMPTOMS REPORTED BY TROOPS IN COMBAT DIVISIONS
(Based on Surveys of Combat Veterans in Four Infantry Divisions, April 1944)

SYMPTOMS	PER CENT REPORTING OCCURRENCE OF THE SYMPTOM*			
	Division A (South Pacific, 2,095 men)	Division B (South Pacific, 1,983 men)	Division C (Central Pacific, 1,299 men)	Division D (Central Pacific, 643 men)
1. Violent pounding of the heart	84	78	74	68
2. Sinking feeling in the stomach	69	66	60	57
3. Shaking or trembling all over	61	54	53	39
4. Feeling sick at the stomach	55	50	46	39
5. Cold sweat	56	45	43	39
6. Feeling of weakness or feeling faint	49	46	36	34
7. Feeling of stiffness	45	44	43	31
8. Vomiting	27	21	18	8
9. Losing control of bowels	21	12	9	4
10. Urinating in pants	10	9	6	3

Data from S-100.
* Data presented in this table are based on answers to the following question:

"Soldiers who have been under fire report different *physical reactions* to the dangers of battle. Some of these physical reactions are given in the following list.   How often have you had these reactions when you were under fire?   *Check one answer after each of the reactions listed to show how often you had the reaction.*   Please do it carefully."

Check-list items for each reaction (symptoms) listed in the table were: Often, Sometimes, Once, Never.
The figures reported represent the percentage of men who reported the occurrence of the symptom one or more times, i.e. they represent the combined percentage for the categories "often," "sometimes," and "once."   A small proportion of the men (rarely over 10 per cent) answered "once."   Hence, except in cases of the most extreme symptoms, the majority of men who reported the occurrence of a symptom answered "often" or "sometimes."
The samples for Divisions A, B, and C represent a cross section of all troops in the division, including Service Force troops who rarely were subject to front-line combat conditions.   When the sample is restricted to infantrymen only, the percentage of men reporting the occurrence of each symptom is higher. Division D, unlike the other three divisions which had been in combat for a long period, had been exposed to combat for less than a week at the time it was surveyed—but during that one week of combat it had suffered extreme casualties.   The sample from Division D is a cross section of Infantry regiments only.
Some of the men, in answering these questions, may have been referring to symptoms of organic illness rather than to fear reactions.   It is unlikely, however, that the question was misinterpreted by a large percentage of men because whenever it was used it always occurred immediately after the following question: "In general, did you usually feel more scared *before* going into combat, *during* combat, or *after* combat?"

were unable to perform adequately because of intense fear.[8] Less than one third of the men said they "never had this experience," whereas 42 per cent said they had had such an experience "once or twice" or "a few times" and 23 per cent reported "several times" or "many times." While these questionnaire responses provide a fairly direct indication of willingness to admit disturbing fear reactions to combat, it should be noted that the sample was not a cross section but rather a random selection of wounded combat veterans in Army hospitals.[9]

From the survey of 1,766 combat veterans in Italy (April 1945),[10] the responses to a number of questions dealing with reactions to combat indicate that the majority of men were willing to admit having experienced fear and anxiety. The following are the replies to the question:

When you were in combat did you worry about your chances of becoming a casualty?

Worried about it a lot	36%
Worried about it some but not a lot	31
Didn't worry so much about it	15
Hardly worried about it at all	7
Never worried about it	7
No answer	4
Total	100%

Similarly, in response to another question, very few men made the claim that they got frightened or worried less often than others in their outfit. The percentage who stated that they experienced *less* than the average amount of fright or worry is somewhat lower than the percentage who admitted that they experienced *more* than the average amount, as is seen in the following replies to the question:

In general, do you get frightened or worried more often than most of the other men in your company or battery?

More often than most of the other men	15%
About the same as most of the other men	69
Less often than most of the other men	9
Undecided and No answer	7
Total	100%

[8] S-126. The question asked was: "How many times in your combat experience have you been so frightened that you couldn't do what you knew you should?"

[9] The fact that all of the men in the sample had been wounded in combat may have introduced a selective factor, and there is the possibility that some of the men may have been referring to emotional reactions they experienced immediately after they were wounded.

[10] S-177.

The absence of a defensive attitude toward fear and anxiety reactions in combat is further indicated by responses to questions dealing with two specific anxiety symptoms: hand tremors and anxiety dreams. The men were first asked if they had experienced these symptoms prior to going on active combat duty, and then a second question was asked on the occurrence of the symptoms since going on active combat duty.[11] As is seen in Chart I, there is a marked increase in the proportion giving an affirmative response to the latter question as compared with the former. This differential as well as the fact that a high proportion reported experiencing the symptoms "sometimes" or "often" may be interpreted as implying a relative absence of a need to minimize, in retrospect, the extent to which they were emotionally disturbed in combat.

The results which we have presented in this section tend to support the general conclusion that enlisted men with combat experience adopted a permissive attitude toward fear in combat, since a number of surveys carried out in various overseas theaters indicate: (1) that the majority of combat troops regarded men who crack up mentally in combat as genuine medical casualties rather than as cowards, and (2) that the majority of combat troops showed little tendency to deny having experienced emotional reactions to combat

---

[11] The data on hand tremors and anxiety dreams are based on answers to the following questions:

During your civilian and military life, but before you first went on active combat duty, did your hands ever tremble enough to bother you?   (Check one)

_____ Yes, often
_____ Yes, sometimes
_____ No, never

Since you have been on active combat duty, do your hands ever tremble enough to bother you?   (Check one)

_____ Yes, often
_____ Yes, sometimes
_____ No, never

During your civilian and military life, but before you first went on active combat duty, were you ever bothered by having nightmares (dreams that frightened or upset you very much)?   (Check one)

_____ Yes, many times
_____ Yes, a few times
_____ No, never

Since you have been on active combat duty, have you ever been bothered by having nightmares (dreams that frighten you or upset you very much)?   (Check one)

_____ Yes, many times
_____ Yes, a few times
_____ No, never

but rather appear to have been willing to admit readily that they experienced fear and anxiety.

While the prevalence of such attitudes may well have been in part a reflection of the spontaneous reactions of the men, these results suggest that the Army's policy of encouraging a permissive attitude

CHART I

ANXIETY SYMPTOMS REPORTED BY COMBAT TROOPS
(Based on a Survey of 1,766 Combat Veterans in Italy, April 1944)

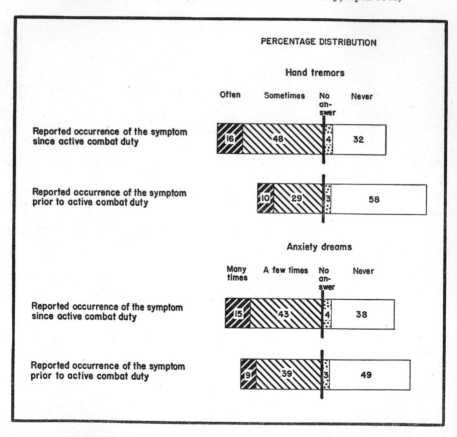

Data from S-177.
For wording of the questions, see footnote 11.

toward fear symptoms was effectively communicated to the men, presumably during the precombat training period. No data are available, however, for estimating the consequences of this policy.

On the basis of clinical findings, it might be expected that, on the whole, the policy would have had beneficial effects from the standpoint of mental hygiene. When a person regards fear reactions as a normal response to a dangerous situation, he is less likely to be disturbed, once the danger has subsided, by self-reproaches of cowardice, unmanliness, or other accusations which lower self-esteem. Moreover, in the face of danger, a source of conflict is eliminated if one accepts the notion that he need not fear the loss of status and esteem in the eyes of his fellows if he trembles, gasps, and exhibits other marked fear symptoms while carrying out his job.

Grinker and Spiegel suggest that sustained anxiety is less damaging to the personality if it is freely admitted:

"The men as a rule feel that they have not too much to lose if they admit their anxiety since it will be understood and accepted, as long as they continue to make a firm effort to control it. The teachings of psychiatrists and the enlightened attitude of the Army leadership are responsible for permeation of this tolerance throughout the services. . . . The ego is actually in a stronger position if it can freely admit its anxiety and deal with it as a reality than if it is forced to misrepresent the situation out of the need to feel itself like others. A repressive and hostile attitude toward free anxiety on the part of commanding officers does not cure anxiety, but only leads to less efficient techniques in dealing with it." [12]

It is possible that the overall neuropsychiatric casualty rate was considerably lower than it would have been if a less permissive attitude had been encouraged. On the other hand, as a consequence of the expectations fostered by this permissive attitude, neurotic symptoms may have been more readily seized upon as a means for escaping from combat dangers and, as a consequence, the NP rate may have been unduly increased both directly, as a means of escape, and indirectly, through the disturbing influence on other men of seeing frequent free expression of fear symptoms by their fellows.[13] So far as we know, no systematic study has been carried out to determine the effects upon the NP rate of encouraging a permissive attitude toward fear symptoms.[14]

[12] R. R. Grinker and J. P. Spiegel, *Men Under Stress* (Blakiston, Philadelphia, 1945), p. 135.

[13] See Table 4 for evidence of this disturbing influence.

[14] It would have been extremely difficult to carry out such a study because, in order to obtain incisive findings, it would have been necessary to compare NP rates among three types of military organizations: (1) units in which a suppressive attitude was deliberately fostered by indoctrinating the men with the notion that to experience fear in combat was *not* a normal reaction but rather a sign of cowardice, and by treating psychiatric casualties as disciplinary cases; (2) control units in which no indoctrination on the topic was given and in which psychiatric casualties were treated in the usual

There is a related set of problems on which future case studies of war neurosis may shed some light, namely the relationships between a permissive attitude toward fear and anxiety and the structure of neurosis. It is well known that certain types of neurotic reactions, such as the effort syndrome and conversion hysteria, were reported to have occurred frequently among combat troops in the First World War, whereas they were seldom observed in World War II. To some extent this type of change in symptomatology may be tied up with the different attitudes toward fear and anxiety reactions. Grinker and Spiegel suggest that an intolerant attitude toward fear and anxiety may result in more severe anxiety symptoms and, although they do not state the number of cases observed, they report some observations which are suggestive on this point:

"In only one class of flying personnel have we seen an approximation of the 'belle indifference' so characteristic of the classic conversion hysteria. This was in paratroops, who are not actually members of the Air Forces. These men, who face the highest casualty rates and the most difficult situations in combat, have a group attitude which does not permit free expressions of anxiety and fear. In an atmosphere where everyone is tough, rough and ready for the worst, anxiety cannot be verbalized or socially accepted. As a result, neurotic reactions among the paratroopers are apt to take the form of conversion symptoms involving the lower extremities. Weakness or paralysis of one or both legs is frequently seen and is accompanied by a total black-out of insight. The men lie comfortably in bed and show little or no distress concerning the severe disability." [15]

Further studies of war neurosis cases may provide valuable information about the changes in psychoneurotic symptoms and in the structure of underlying neurotic conflicts which are attributable to a change from (1) a severe attitude toward fear and anxiety which entails high demands upon the self to suppress (and possibly to repress) anxiety symptoms to (2) a tolerant attitude which tends to reduce anxieties about the consequences of emotional expression of

Army way; and (3) units in which the general Army policy was exceptionally well applied both with respect to indoctrination and the handling of psychiatric casualties. Even if the practical and administrative problems involved in setting up experimental units had been surmounted, there would still have been innumerable problems to solve in connection with insuring comparable amounts of exposure to combat among the various types of units and identical diagnostic criteria for determining the NP rates. The drastic interference with usual Army practices required by an experiment of this kind could hardly be expected to be undertaken in wartime.

[15] R. R. Grinker and J. P. Spiegel, *op. cit.*, p. 104.

fear and anxiety. If future investigations of the relationships between attitude toward anxiety and the characteristics of neurotic
behavior which develop under the stress of combat danger are centered upon the psychological mechanisms by means of which the
relationships are mediated, much valuable information may be
gained on the role of insight and verbalization in undergoing intense
environmental stress.

The Screening of Men Who Are Psychologically Unfit for Combat

Throughout the war, the Army maintained a continual screening
process designed to eliminate men who were psychologically inca-
pable of withstanding the stresses of combat duty. Beginning with
the preinduction psychiatric examination to determine whether or
not potential draftees were psychologically fit for military service in
general, screening was continued throughout the various stages of
precombat training and was extended into the period when men had
already been committed to combat.

It was primarily the psychiatrists who carried out the screening.
Their usual procedure was to examine the men in a clinical interview
in order to detect behavioral disturbances. This type of psychiatric screening was primarily directed toward eliminating men who
showed marked behavioral disorders: psychotics, prepsychotics,
psychoneurotics, psychopaths, and in general—irrespective of the
diagnostic label—men who showed signs of inability to tolerate
anxiety.

The general purpose of psychiatric screening was to eliminate
those who were likely to be a liability to the Army. During the
early stages of the men's military career, screening was primarily
intended to avoid the waste of attempting to train men who would
prove to be useless because their emotional disturbances seriously
interfered with adjustment to the Army. At staging areas for overseas shipment and in the overseas theaters of operation, psychiatric
screening was more directly oriented toward eliminating those who
were psychologically unfit for combat duty.

Both the early and late stages of psychiatric screening had important implications for the control of fear in combat and, to a large
extent, the screening procedures were based upon considerations of
the type listed below. The various working hypotheses which we
shall describe as the apparent rationale of Army psychiatric screening have rarely been stated explicitly. They pose a number of research problems on the relationship between pre-Army personality

structure and subsequent adjustment to military life, but, in the absence of large-scale follow-up studies, little can be said about their validity.   Perhaps it will be possible to make some empirical evaluations after there have been accumulated a number of intensive case studies of veterans in which explicit attempts are made to check on hypotheses such as the following:

1. If men who are predisposed to behavioral disorders are confronted with the objective dangers of combat, it is probable that they will develop incapacitating symptoms which would not only render them useless for military duty but would also require considerable medical attention.   Since these men are likely to be a drain on much-needed Army medical facilities both overseas and in the United States, they would be a poor risk from the standpoint of military economy.

2. Among those who are predisposed to neurotic behavioral disorders is a high percentage of men who are unable to tolerate anxiety. Even if they do not develop some form of incapacitating war neurosis, many of them are likely to react to objective danger situations by exhibiting the most extreme forms of overt fear reactions.   The presence of men who show marked terror or panic reactions is not only likely to increase the objective danger (e.g., drawing enemy fire) but may also be extremely demoralizing to other soldiers in the combat unit.   At a time when everyone is confronted with the task of mastering his own fear of threatening realities, it is not helpful to witness the spectacle of another man in one's own outfit trembling violently or screaming wildly, or sobbing over and over again an agitating thought like "We'll never get out of this alive."

Some evidence of the highly disturbing effect of seeing a man in one's own outfit overcome by fear is provided by the survey of combat troops in Italy.   Eighty-three per cent asserted that they had had the experience of seeing "A man's nerves 'crack up' at the front."   A very high percentage reported that this produced a disturbing effect on them, as shown by Table 4.

3. Among those who are predisposed to behavioral disorders are certain types of personalities who have developed abnormal psychological defenses against anxiety.   When confronted with the objective dangers of combat, their fear reactions may be minimal but they are likely to exhibit other kinds of reactions which are highly detrimental to others in the combat unit.   Some may react with rage rather than fear, and they are as likely to vent their rage against their leaders and comrades as they are to channelize it

against the enemy. Others may appear, on the surface, to be very cool and unemotional in the face of danger, but develop paranoid symptoms which often take the form of secretly making severe accusations against military leaders to other men in the unit or engaging in some other form of activity which tends to disrupt the functioning of the combat unit. Both the rage type of reaction and the

TABLE 4

REACTIONS TO WITNESSING EXTREME FEAR BREAKDOWN IN COMBAT
(Based on a Survey of 1,766 Combat Veterans in Rifle and
Heavy Weapons Companies in Italy, April 1944)

QUESTION: "What effect did seeing a man's nerves 'crack up' have on you?" Analysis of write-in answers*	Per cent
Made me nervous, jittery, or feel like "cracking up" myself	49
Made me feel depressed or lowered my morale	15
Bothered me at first but I got over it	4
Had no effect at the time but bothered me later	1
Made me resent the Army or the medics	1
Total negative reactions	70
Had no or little effect	17
Made me sorry for the man (or other favorable attitude toward the man)	9
Made me angry at the man (or other unfavorable attitude toward the man)	1
Miscellaneous neutral comments	2
Total neutral reactions	29
Made me mad or aggressive toward the enemy	1
Total positive reactions	1
Total	100

* Percentages are based upon the total number of write-in answers which made some reference to the effect of seeing a man's nerves "crack up." Twenty-six per cent of the men in the entire sample were not included in this analysis either because they checked the off-set answer ("I never saw a man's nerves 'crack up' at the front") or because they gave no answer or an irrelevant answer to the question. The summary categories "negative," "neutral," and "positive" reactions are based on an evaluation of the manifest content of the various types of answers. "Negative reactions" include all those answers which indicate interference with "good" combat motivation; "positive" reactions refer to answers which indicate increased motivation (S-177).

paranoid type are potentially a real danger to the unit since others in the unit are likely to be the target of an irrational attack. It would undoubtedly make for considerable insecurity among the men in a combat unit to have in their ranks a man who, in the heat of battle, might use his weapon against one of his own officers or men because he is unable to control his rage or because he suffers from persecutory delusions.

4. Men with psychoneurotic tendencies, in so far as they have

low tolerance for anxiety, are probably poor material for training in jobs which ultimately require a high level of performance in dangerous combat missions.   Fighter pilots, members of combat air crews, paratroopers, intelligence reconnaissance scouts, and other combat specialists are required to carry out tasks in which even a slight impairment of efficiency or a momentary blockage due to fear might jeopardize the lives of others and the outcome of a critical operation.   Disorganized responses due to fear may have similar catastrophic effects among front-line Infantry troops engaged in missions such as night patrols which require highly controlled activity on the part of every individual.   Hence even if mild psychoneurotics are accepted for military duty, it is necessary to exclude them from important types of combat assignments.   To some extent the classification of such cases as "limited service" at the induction station or at some early stage in their military career labeled them for automatic exclusion from critical combat jobs (in so far as the original classification was retained after subsequent medical examination).   Specific screening devices prior to training in combat specialties also were used as a means for eliminating men whose more subtle emotional disturbances may not have been noted earlier.

At most induction stations, the psychiatrist was able to spend only a few minutes with each of the hundreds of new selectees as they were shunted along the assembly line of medical examinations. If the psychiatrists were able to invest more time with each selectee they examined, it would be expected that a much higher proportion of psychologically unfit men would be screened for rejection from the Army or for labeling as "limited service."   In recognition of this situation, a special test was devised, known as the Neuropsychiatric Screening Adjunct (NSA).   This test was developed by the Research Branch in collaboration with the Surgeon General's Office on the basis of a large-scale research study comparing questionnaire responses of psychoneurotic patients in Army hospital wards with the responses of a cross section of soldiers in the United States.   A description of the studies from which the NSA was developed is presented in Chapter IX.

Within a short time after passing the induction station medical examination, the recruit reported to a reception center from which he was assigned to a training camp.   Throughout the training period, psychiatric screening of those who were psychologically unfit for combat duty continued on a more or less informal basis.   Men who developed behavioral disturbances in the course of adjusting to the strenuous Army training program or who showed unusually strong fear reactions in certain basic training activities involving some degree of danger were often sent by their officers to the psychiatrist. Informal screening of this kind occurred throughout later stages of training as well as during the period of combat duty and was occasionally supplemented by systematic psychiatric examination.[16]

Another aspect of eliminating men who were unable to control their fear reactions adequately when confronted with the objective dangers of combat was the use of screening devices by various specialized Army schools which trained men for skilled combat operations. The Air Force, especially, applied various diagnostic techniques in evaluating candidates for training in combat flying operations:

Flying cadets are first met by members of a regional cadet board whose duties are to eliminate immediately those men unsuitable because of readily apparent physical, mental, emotional, intellectual, or personal failings. Candidates who successfully pass this board are next sent to a reception center where a series of rigid psychological and psychiatric tests and examinations are given to determine fitness and adaptability for flying.
. . . Close checks are kept on the cadets during their training period to detect evidence of anxiety reactions as soon as they appear and to properly evaluate them.[17]

---

[16] After completing their training in the United States, most men who were qualified for overseas duty were sent to an Army center where they were processed for overseas shipment. At these centers or at the port of embarkation many men were once more examined by a psychiatrist as part of a general medical examination, in order to avoid burdening overseas theaters with the problems engendered by men who were suffering from psychological disturbances. This was probably an excellent stage for detecting low anxiety tolerance since a very high percentage of men, when faced with the immediate prospect of being sent to an active theater of war, developed a fairly high degree of anticipatory anxiety—a reaction commonly referred to by the men as "gangplank fever."
This situation might have been an excellent one for research oriented toward attempting to develop objective tests to discriminate between normal anxiety reactions and excessive anxiety, predictive of initial psychological failure under conditions of extreme danger. However, such a research program would have required a careful follow-up on the reactions to combat dangers of a large number of individuals—a requirement which was administratively difficult to meet.
In overseas theaters, the screening process was continued primarily by the practice of sending men with overt behavioral disorders through medical channels. From time to time systematic psychiatric examinations were carried out within a local command. It has been reported that a psychiatric screening program carried out at the stage when the men had already been subject to initial combat experience greatly reduced the rate of neuropsychiatric casualties in subsequent combat periods. As yet, insufficient data have appeared to substantiate this plausible claim.
[17] John M. Murray, "Disposition of Neuropsychiatric Cases in the Army Air Forces," *Manual of Military Neuropsychiatry*, edited by H. C. Solomon and P. T. Yakovlev (W. B. Saunders Co., Philadelphia, 1944), pp. 82–90.

Although the screening of air cadets may have been one of the best screening programs in the Army, apparently there were still considerable numbers of men who proved to be unable to cope with their fear and anxiety reactions when they were actually confronted with the realities of combat flying. This problem is highlighted in a report by three psychiatrists who studied the psychiatric problems of the 8th Air Force in Europe during its first year of combat operations:

There seems to be no apparent method of preventing this type of Psychological Failure except by eliminating susceptible personnel through some process of selection. It is recognized that there is no method of selection now in use which can pick those men who will show these ready fear reactions when they encounter combat flying. It seems doubtful if the natural stresses of flying training and peacetime flying or if any artificial set of tests can be relied upon to eliminate the men who will have insufficient emotional tolerance to combat flying.

If such is the case, the question arises as to what methods of selection could be utilized to make this prediction an accurate one. In view of the fact that the great majority of these cases occur within the first five combat missions, the most obvious method of selection would be to train candidates for air crew as gunners and send them on five combat missions. If they stood up to this trial emotionally, then they could start the specialized training for air crew. If they showed signs of fear or developed functional symptoms, they could be rejected. Such a method has obvious and important disadvantages such as transporting large groups of individuals to a combat theater for selection and then returning them to the Zone of Interior for training.

Another method, less accurate but more practical, would be to have each candidate make five parachute jumps, the last one to be a delayed drop. It is not known what correlation there might be between fear of parachute jumps and fear of combat flying, but it is probable that those men who are prone to show abnormal fear reactions and to become easily perplexed by problems of self-preservation would be uncovered by this method.[18]

In the training of paratroopers there was also the problem of eliminating men whose fear reactions might jeopardize crucial combat missions. One of the major procedures employed by the Parachute School at Fort Benning, Georgia, was the elimination of men who, at any stage of training, showed a marked fear reaction. Refusal to jump off a high tower or out of an airplane on a scheduled training jump as well as persistent inadequate motor control attributable to emotional disturbance while making the jumps were used as criteria for washing a man out of the training course. Like many other schools which train men for hazardous occupations, the Parachute School felt a need for some initial test which would make

[18] D. W. Hastings, D. G. Wright, and B. C. Glueck, *Psychiatric Experiences of the Eighth Air Force: First Year of Combat* (Josiah Macy Jr. Foundation, August 1944, 307 pp.). Cf. pp. 157–60.

it possible to eliminate at the outset those men who were prospective failures because of inability to master their fear reactions.

To meet this need, the Research Branch carried out an experimental study at the Parachute School, on the basis of which a screening device was developed for the purpose of making an initial selection of candidates for paratroop training. We shall describe this research study in some detail since it illustrates a number of methodological problems involved in the construction of objective screening devices. In addition, it exemplifies one of the ways in which an experimental approach may prove to be useful for the purpose of evaluating the aftereffects of a fear-eliciting situation in a training program designed to prepare men for a dangerous type of occupation.

Experimental Evaluation of an Objective Psychiatric Screening Device for Paratroop Training[19]

It is widely recognized that the type of screening device which is most likely to prove successful in predicting abnormal fear reactions in subsequent danger situations is one which employs a sample situation in which a fairly high degree of fear or anxiety is elicited. In order to make use of this approach in developing an objective test to predict subsequent psychological failure, it is necessary to find a reliable indicator of extreme fear or anxiety reactions elicited in the sample situation. In developing a screening device for paratroop training, a sample danger situation was utilized—requiring the candidates to make a "mock" parachute jump from a 34-foot tower. The major indicator of an extreme fear reaction to this situation was refusal to make the jump when ordered to do so. This clear-cut criterion was supplemented by ratings by qualified observers of the speed with which the man took off after he was ordered to jump, on the assumption that a slow performance due to hesitation is usually the result of fear.

Once a test situation has been selected and some behavioral indicator of fear or anxiety has been found to be applicable in that situation, it is necessary to evaluate the adequacy of the screening device. This involves two major research problems: (1) how well does the screening device differentiate men who fail to react adequately in future danger situations from those who succeed, i.e.,

---

[19] The material in this section is based on a Research Branch report which was prepared by John L. Finan under whose direction the study of paratroops was planned and carried out.

how accurate are the predictions made by the use of the particular screening device? (2) does the test situation in which fear is elicited have any deleterious effects upon those men who pass the test? If, for example, the fear-eliciting situation had a general traumatic aftereffect upon a large percentage of the men who passed the test so that their motivation to continue training was impaired, then the test would not be practical even if it were successful at predicting psychological failure. The purpose of an experimental evaluation of a screening device is to provide data which are relevant for determining the predictive success of the screening device and the favorable or unfavorable aftereffects of the test situation.

Background of the Study

Before describing the results of the experimental evaluation of the initial "mock-up" tower jump as a screening device for the elimination of potential psychological failures in paratroop training, the following brief sketch of the paratroop training course is provided as a background for the study.

The standard course of paratroop training as given by the Parachute School, Fort Benning, Georgia, consisted of four stages of one week each: A-stage was intended to build men up physically through rigorous calisthenics and running; B-stage taught the correct technique of jumping from a simulated airplane; C-stage trained men in managing the parachute during a series of jumps from a tower of 250 feet; in D-stage five "live" jumps were made from a plane.

The students were introduced to jumping from height during the second week (B-stage) when they were given their mock-up tower training. The mock-up tower is a structure 34 feet high which is used to train men to assume the correct body position to be assumed in jumping from a plane. A student taking this training climbed to the top of the tower where he was fixed in a harness attached by two "risers" or long straps to an inclined cable which runs alongside the tower. At a "tap-out" signal the man jumped from the door, fell about 12 feet and then he was "snubbed" when the risers suspending him were pulled taut against the cable, overhead. From this point the man rode down the cable to the point of release about 400 feet distant. That the mock-up tower was a fear-provoking situation to a good many men is shown by the fact that more than half of a group of qualified paratroopers stated, in answering a direct question, that it was more frightening to jump from the mock-up tower than from an airplane.

The Experimental Procedures

Two days before the beginning of formal training, or within a few days after the men had arrived at the school, the group of men randomly selected for the preliminary jump were assembled in the mock-up tower area where they were given two demonstration jumps to illustrate the technique of correct exiting. The men were told that they were to be given a preliminary jump as an orientation to the course of training. In the instruction it was emphasized that all men were expected to jump. Also, in order to avoid giving the impression that more attention was being paid to the jump group than to the no-jump group, it was stated that the men assembled to jump had not been specially chosen, and that their fellow students would also be given a preliminary jump if time and facilities permitted. Men in the no-jump group were told by their company officer that the schedule of their activities would not, unfortunately, permit a preliminary jump. Each man was given a single jump which was carefully noted by cadremen highly experienced in the observation of mock-up tower performance. Individual performance was rated as "fast," "medium," "slow," or "refused to jump." This relatively simple measure of speed of jumping was employed rather than a judgment of the more technical features of performance since it was not feasible to give more than a minimum of instruction in correct jumping technique. When the men had completed the jumping, they were reassembled and told that regardless of performance everyone would begin training two days later with an equal chance of success. No man, therefore, was disqualified on the basis of refusing to make the preliminary jump. Further, the early jump performance of the men was unknown to instructors rating them in the course of training which followed.

Results[20]

The Mock-up Tower Procedure as a Screening Device

How effective was the screening device as a predictor of success and failure in paratroop training? The following is a summary of data bearing on this problem.

---

[20] The experimental observations reported here were made during the period March 12–June 1, 1945 (S-216) on Parachute Training Classes 165, 166, 167, 168, 169, 170, 171, and 173. The size of these classes ranged approximately between 100 and 900 men. Only those students who had finished their processing and were actually assigned to a class participated in the experiment. Approximately a third of the men in the

Approximately 1,300 men were given a preliminary jump from the mock-up tower.   Thirty-seven men or approximately 3 per cent refused to jump.   These men, in spite of their refusal on the preliminary trial, were allowed to pursue the regular course of paratroop training with the same opportunity for succeeding as men who made the initial jump successfully.

CHART II

PERFORMANCE ON THE MOCK-UP TOWER SCREENING PROCEDURE IN RELATION TO SUBSEQUENT FAILURE IN THE PARATROOPER TRAINING COURSE

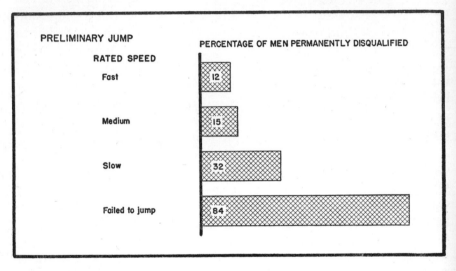

Data from S-216.

Eighty-four per cent, or 31 of the 37 preliminary jump refusals, failed in subsequent training in contrast to only 19 per cent failures among the men who were successful in making the preliminary jump.   None of the 31 men who failed in subsequent training got farther than B-stage; 45 per cent (14 men) were disqualified for insufficient determination to continue training; 35 per cent (11 men) refused to jump from the mock-up tower in B-stage training; the remaining 20 per cent (6 men) were dropped for miscellaneous rea-

classes studied were omitted from the experiment for some administrative reason such as late arrival, late processing, or for other reasons relating to the availability or status of the men.   The remaining two thirds composed the roster of men included in the experiment.   Depending on whether the last digit of his serial number was odd or even, each man was placed either in the early jump group or in the no-jump group. This was a purely random procedure of assigning the men and insured two approximately equal groups of similar background and experience.

sons such as "not adapted to parachute training," medical disability, etc.

From these results it appears that the selection ratio yielded by the preliminary mock-up tower procedure, although it involves only a small proportion of the men, would probably prove to be within the range of usefulness if it were necessary to screen thousands of recruits.

A more detailed analysis of the data in terms of speed of performance on the preliminary jump shows that even among men who were successful on the preliminary jump, the slowest men were more than twice as likely to fail in training as the men who made more rapid exits.   (See Chart II.)

About a fifth of the men who made the preliminary jump were rated as slow.   Of this group almost a third failed later in the training.   However, since two thirds of the same group succeeded in the later course of training, slow jump could not be used advantageously as a predictive index of success and failure unless supplemented by additional screening aids.

These results point to the need for more than one indicator in predicting psychological failure.   It is a frequent finding in a research designed to develop a screening technique that no single test is adequate to meet the needs for reducing the proportion of failures.   To achieve a level of prediction which is practical, it is necessary to discover additional predictive factors and to combine them into a weighted index on the basis of a multiple correlation analysis.   A supplementary study which was completed before the research program at the Parachute School was terminated, showed that certain background factors were related to failure in paratroop training and might have proved to be useful supplementary variables. Chart III provides illustrative results on mental ability, as measured by AGCT scores.

Age was another factor found to be slightly related to failure in paratroop training: 36 per cent of recruits over 22 years of age were permanently disqualified as against 24 per cent of those who were 18 to 21 years of age.   Other factors correlated with AGCT or with age (educational level, civilian occupational background, Army longevity, and marital status) were also found to be slightly related to success or failure in the paratroop training course.   If Research Branch studies at the Parachute School had not been discontinued at the end of the war, it might have been possible to construct an overall predictive index by making use of personality tests as well as the background factors we have just cited to supplement performance ratings on the mock-up tower screening procedure.

CHART III

RELATIONSHIP BETWEEN AGCT SCORES AND FAILURES IN PARATROOP TRAINING
(Based on a Study of Background Characteristics of 539 Recruits in
Paratrooper Training, March–June 1945)

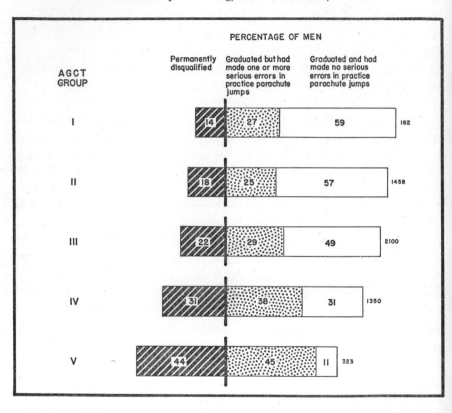

Data from S-216.
The numbers following the bars are the numbers of cases on which percentages are based.

Training Effects of the Mock-up Tower Procedure

In order to evaluate the overall usefulness of a fear-eliciting device like the mock-up tower procedure, it is necessary to know not only whether it yields a basis for predicting success and failure but also whether or not it has deleterious effects on men's progress in later training. Some of the training officers at the Parachute School expressed the point of view that giving men a jump too soon after their arrival at the school might interfere with subsequent training. There is the possibility that introducing a new student to a frightening situation in advance of a period during which he would normally be preparing himself psychologically, as well as gaining confidence through mastery of the technical training, may raise his anxiety to a higher level than would otherwise be the case. According to this argument, even those men who make the initial jump successfully might drop out of training at some later point in disproportion to men who were not given an early jump. Also, men who are forced from the tower without the usual week's training in general jumping technique may tend, on their first attempt, to make more and worse errors which may be more persistent and more difficult to correct than if the initial jump were given later.

It was necessary, therefore, to determine whether or not early exposure to the mock-tower procedure had unfavorable effects upon subsequent performance. An answer to this problem required setting up a group composed of men selected in advance to be *exactly comparable* to those who were given the preliminary jump, except that this control group was not given an early jump. As previously stated, selection was made solely on a random basis, and the two groups were found to be similar in terms of the background factors known to be related to paratroop success and failure such as age, AGCT, length of service in the Army, overseas service, and rural-urban status.

Possible effects of the preliminary mock-up jump procedure on later progress are, as suggested above, measurable in two ways: (1) in terms of any difference which may be found between the *proportions of men who drop out of training* in the two groups, either overall or in any stage of training and (2) in terms of any *differences in the men's B-stage performance on the mock-up tower*. Both of these measures were used:

1. The proportion of men permanently disqualified over the entire course of training in the two groups was approximately 19 per cent in both groups. Likewise, when the results were broken down into stages of training, no real differences between the two groups were found. Both groups showed the following percentages of disqualification: A-stage, 12 per cent; B-stage, 4 per cent; C-stage, 1 per cent; and D-stage, 2 per cent. No differences in type of disqualification were found. The proportions of men disqualified for "insufficient determination to continue training" were closely similar. The proportions of men who were disqualified for refusing to jump from the mock-up tower were not appreciably different. The preliminary jump had therefore no observable tendency to cause men to drop out of training.

2. Since both the jump and no-jump groups progressed to the B-stage of training without any disproportionate loss of men from either group, the mock-up tower performance of one group may be compared directly with that of the other.   The result shown in Chart IV compares the two groups in terms of "weak" performance[21] during routine mock-up tower training in B-stage.   The standard of rating distinguishes as faults only those features of performance considered by instructor-cadre to be of a serious nature.   The important fact (which may be seen in Chart IV) is that, whereas the jump group shows an initial residual advantage from the early jump, by the end of B-stage about the same level of efficiency of performance is achieved by both groups.[22]   It is concluded that giving men a preliminary jump at least does nothing to interfere with their subsequent mock-up tower training in B-stage.

This study of the effects of an early exposure to a fear-eliciting situation upon later performances in a similar training situation serves to illustrate the way in which experimental studies may prove to be useful in evaluating the effectiveness of precombat training procedures designed to minimize fear reactions to subsequent exposures to danger.   In the next section we shall discuss the problems involved in precombat training designed to control fear in combat but, in the absence of experimental studies of the type carried out to determine the aftereffects of the mock-up tower procedure, we shall be able to say very little about the effectiveness of such training.

Precombat Training Activities Related to Fear Control

In a sense, all aspects of the Army training program which develop effective combat skills serve to reduce the disruptive effects of fear reactions in combat, in so far as they provide soldiers with a set of habitual responses which are adaptive in danger situations.   There are two major aspects of training, however, which are most directly related to the control of fear in combat: training which prepared men to cope with specific kinds of danger situations and exposure to intense battle stimuli.

In their precombat training, the troops were given considerable

---

[21] The following behavior was considered to represent major errors: (1) refusal to jump from the mock-up tower (ideally this index of performance would be employed exclusively, but the number of mock-up tower refusals was not sufficiently large to permit comparison); (2) requiring assistance from the tower; (3) grabbing risers; (4) hesitating; (5) jumping out timidly, or falling out of the door; (6) placing both feet in the door and jumping; (7) showing obvious signs of fright.   Other faults relating more to the technique of jumping, such as keeping arms out or failing to turn the body, were classified as satisfactory-minus responses and are, for purposes of this presentation, pooled together with the satisfactory responses.

[22] The average numbers of jumps attempted by the two groups are as follows: for the jump group 5.4 trials, and for the no-jump group 5.6 trials on the mock-up tower during B-stage training.

practice in performing specific acts which would be adaptive in the face of specific dangers.   They were taught to disperse and "hit the dirt" when subjected to a sudden strafing attack by enemy aircraft; to crawl under machine gun fire; to roll away when confronted by an approaching tank; to "freeze" when a flare was set off at night; to dig a hasty slit trench from a prone position when pinned down under fire; to advance in rushes, running zigzag in a crouched posi-

CHART IV

SUBSEQUENT JUMP FAILURES AMONG PARATROOP TRAINEES WHO WERE GIVEN A PRELIMINARY PRACTICE JUMP AT THE BEGINNING OF THEIR TRAINING COMPARED WITH FAILURES AMONG THOSE GIVEN NO PRELIMINARY PRACTICE JUMP

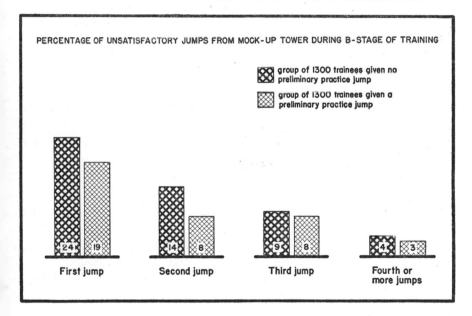

PERCENTAGE OF UNSATISFACTORY JUMPS FROM MOCK-UP TOWER DURING B-STAGE OF TRAINING

group of 1300 trainees given no preliminary practice jump

group of 1300 trainees given a preliminary practice jump

First jump	Second jump	Third jump	Fourth or more jumps
24 19	14 8	9 8	4 3

Data from S-216.
For definition of unsatisfactory jumps and for average number of jumps see footnotes 21 and 22. The number of cases in each group dropped slightly below 1,300 during the B-stage, as a small percentage of men were permanently disqualified.

tion toward an obstacle which provided cover when required to advance under fire; to "hit the dirt" at the sound of an approaching shell.

In some cases the men were drilled over and over again on certain act sequences which they were required to execute promptly and in a stereotyped way whenever the danger cue was given.   Gas-mask drill, for example, was practiced in this way; whenever a leader shouted the single word "gas," no matter what activity was in progress, the men were required to go through a highly routinized act sequence of putting on the gas mask.[23]   Drill of this type, when repeated sufficiently so that the response is "overlearned," tends to build up an automatic adaptive response to a source of combat danger.

Acquisition of an automatic habitual response to a danger cue is probably effective, to some extent, in counteracting the disruptive effects of fear in combat.   It is a plausible hypothesis that, as a result of such training, the correct act would tend to be performed as soon as the specific danger cue was given despite the competing response tendencies aroused by fear-eliciting stimuli.   Before the man had "time to think about it" he would automatically make the correct response, whereas if he had not been drilled in the habit, in his excited emotional state he might react in a maladaptive way.

Although repetitious drill designed to build up automatic reactions to specific danger cues may contribute to reducing the disruptive effects of fear, there are serious limitations upon the usefulness of this type of training for combat.   There are very few routine act sequences which would be generally adaptive, whenever a given kind of danger was encountered.   Most types of danger situations in combat require varying responses, depending upon the particular mission the man is assigned to carry out, the protective resources which happen to be available in his immediate vicinity, and other highly specific characteristics of the particular situation in which the danger occurs.

Most of the Army training for combat was designed to build up a repertoire of specific combat skills which the individual soldier could draw upon whenever they were needed in combat.   Rather than attempting to develop automatic reactions to combat dangers, training was designed to teach men to count on instructions from superiors or, if necessary, to exercise their own judgment about the best response to make when confronted by a given type of danger; it was also designed to provide practice in combat skills which were likely to be needed in order to react efficiently in danger situations, once the man knew what action he was going to take.   This type of preparation for combat would serve to reduce fear in combat in two major ways: (1) the general level of anxiety in combat would tend to

---

[23] Combat troops never had occasion to apply their gas-mask drill but, from reports on reactions to the introduction of gas on maneuvers, there is reason to expect that this training would have resulted in successful responses if gas warfare had occurred.

be reduced in so far as the men derived from their training a high degree of self-confidence about their ability to take care of themselves
and to handle almost any contingency that might threaten them
with sudden danger; and (2) the intensity of fear reactions in specific danger situations would tend to be reduced once the man began
to carry out a plan of action in a skilled manner.   The major problem in this type of training, from the standpoint of fear control, is
the danger that when the men are actually in battle and are confronted with a situation for which they have been trained, they will
be unable to apply their training because of their excited emotional
state.   Fear reactions are apt to interfere so seriously that the men
are unable to exercise good judgment or to carry out skillfully an
action which they have been trained to perform.   The major solution to this problem probably lies in training men to carry out combat activities under conditions which closely parallel those encountered in battle.   During the war, the Army introduced a number
of "battle inoculation" features into the training program.   By
1943, almost all men in basic training were being put through an
infiltration course which required crawling over rough ground for
about eighty yards under live machine-gun fire.   From time to
time Infantry troops were exposed to the sounds of near-by artillery
fire and took part in maneuvers which introduced realistic battle
stimuli.   This was done especially in combat training which troops
received overseas during preinvasion periods.

    There are a number of ways in which exposure to battle stimuli
during training would be expected to reduce the disruptive effects
of fear in battle: (1) a certain amount of adaptation to the extremely
loud noises and other intense stimuli probably takes place with repeated exposures so that when the stimuli are encountered in battle
they elicit less fear; (2) exposure to battle conditions during training enables the men to develop a realistic expectation of what combat is like, which would tend to increase motivation to acquire combat skills and would also tend to reduce anxiety about combat in
those men who, having heard a great deal about the horrors of war,
grossly overestimate the psychological shock of being exposed to
battle conditions; (3) in so far as the men obtain practice in making
decisions and in carrying out skilled activities (such as firing at
moving targets) in the presence of stimuli which elicit fear reactions,
this experience decreases the probability that fear reactions will interfere with successful performance in combat; (4) the experience

of being exposed to stimuli which elicit fear tends to mobilize the psychological defenses of the individual and as a result he may develop some personal techniques for coping with his emotional reactions—such as focusing his attention upon the details of his own combat mission as a form of distraction, frequently asserting to himself that he can take it, or some other type of action or verbalization which reduces anxiety.[24]

It is difficult to estimate the extent to which American troops were exposed to battle stimuli during their precombat training. It is probable that the majority of men who were sent into combat had been given relatively little exposure to battle stimuli other than small arms fire. Later in this chapter some research results will be presented which suggest that there may have been insufficient exposure to intense battle stimuli during precombat training.

Research Results on Factors Related to Precombat Training

It would be extremely valuable to know the extent to which each of the aspects of precombat training which were discussed in the preceding section contributed to the control of fear in combat. Systematic studies of the effectiveness of those Army training activities designed to reduce the disruptive effects of fear in combat would undoubtedly have furnished many useful insights into the conditions under which this type of psychological preparation for danger is of maximum effectiveness. In the absence of systematic research on these important aspects of fear control, it may be of some value to examine certain attitude data which bear indirectly upon these problems.

A cross-section survey of combat veterans in an Infantry division in the Southwest Pacific area provides some indirect evidence of a relationship between the intensity of fear reactions to combat and self-confidence in ability to perform well in combat. It was found that those men who reported the largest number of physiological symptoms of fear tended to show less confidence in their ability to perform successfully in combat, as indicated by their self-ratings on degree of self-confidence prior to going into combat for the first time, changes in self-confidence as a result of combat experience, and self-confidence about ability to take charge of a squad on a combat mis-

---

[24] Exposure to fear-eliciting stimuli during training may also have some detrimental effects which would tend to increase fears and anxieties in combat. Plans were made by the Research Branch for research studies to test hypotheses about the conditions under which exposure to battle stimuli is most effective. But the projected studies were not carried out. (See footnote 3.)

CHART V

RELATIONSHIP BETWEEN SELF-CONFIDENCE AND FEAR REACTIONS TO COMBAT
(Based on Questionnaire Responses of 1,350 Men in a Combat Division in the Southwest Pacific, January 1944)

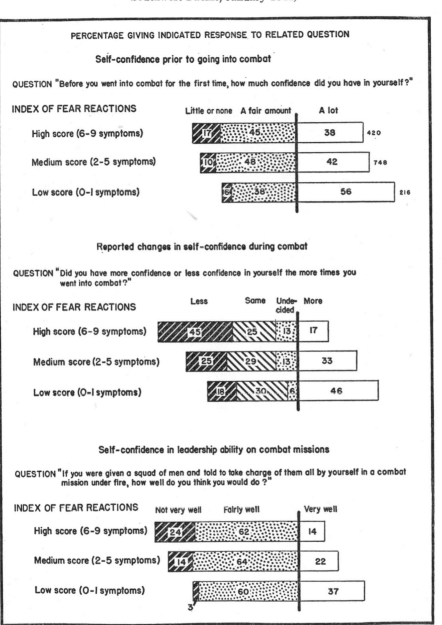

PERCENTAGE GIVING INDICATED RESPONSE TO RELATED QUESTION

Self-confidence prior to going into combat

QUESTION "Before you went into combat for the first time, how much confidence did you have in yourself?"

INDEX OF FEAR REACTIONS — Little or none / A fair amount / A lot

	Little or none	A fair amount	A lot	cases
High score (6-9 symptoms)	17	45	38	420
Medium score (2-5 symptoms)	10	48	42	748
Low score (0-1 symptoms)	6	38	56	216

Reported changes in self-confidence during combat

QUESTION "Did you have more confidence or less confidence in yourself the more times you went into combat?"

INDEX OF FEAR REACTIONS — Less / Same / Undecided / More

	Less	Same	Undecided	More
High score (6-9 symptoms)	45	25	13	17
Medium score (2-5 symptoms)	25	29	13	33
Low score (0-1 symptoms)	18	30	6	46

Self-confidence in leadership ability on combat missions

QUESTION "If you were given a squad of men and told to take charge of them all by yourself in a combat mission under fire, how well do you think you would do?"

INDEX OF FEAR REACTIONS — Not very well / Fairly well / Very well

	Not very well	Fairly well	Very well
High score (6-9 symptoms)	24	62	14
Medium score (2-5 symptoms)	14	64	22
Low score (0-1 symptoms)	3	60	37

Data from S-100.
The numbers following the bars are the numbers of cases on which percentages are based.

sion.   The relationship between degree of fear[25] in combat and each of the three indicators of self-confidence is shown graphically in Chart V.

From the type of correlational data presented in Chart V, it is unsafe to make any inferences about causal factors.[26] It may be useful, however, to point out some of the alternative hypotheses suggested by these results, since they have implications for further research on the problems of fear control.

1. First of all there is the possibility that lowered self-confidence is a consequence of having experienced intense fear reactions in combat: this hypothesis would be difficult to test and, although it would have practical implications for the treatment of men who had undergone intense fear experiences, it would have little direct bearing on the problems of precombat training.

2. A second possibility is that the relationship reflects some relatively persistent personality characteristic.   In other words, both intense fear reactions to danger and self-confidence about one's ability may be a function of some personality variable which had not undergone any pronounced change in the course of Army experience.   It is unnecessary to speculate upon the nature of the underlying personality trait that may be involved because in any case there is the implication that attitude items dealing with self-confidence may serve as an indicator of some factor which is predictive of fear reactions in danger situations.   This suggests that it may be worth while to test the usefulness of such attitude items for the prediction of subsequent reactions to danger.   If it were found that a low degree of self-confidence expressed during the precombat training period was predictive of intense fear reactions to combat, it would be possible to utilize this finding in the selection of personnel for important combat assignments or for leadership positions in combat units.

---

[25] The scores on the index of fear symptoms were determined by the number of physiological fear symptoms each man reported having experienced "sometimes" or "often," such as "violent pounding of the heart," "shaking or trembling all over," etc. (based on the question quoted in the footnote to Table 3).

[26] It should be recognized that the data in Chart V not only fail to indicate the causal sequence but are also of limited value as evidence of a correlation between fear reaction and self-confidence.   There is always the possibility that some extraneous attitude may have colored both the way in which fear reactions in combat were recalled and reported, and questionnaire responses to items on self-confidence.   For example, the correlation might simply reflect some factor like candidness in reporting about oneself, unwillingness for further service, or high anxiety originating from current personal problems other than those involved in facing combat danger.

3. A third possible interpretation of the relationship shown in Chart V is that it reflects a dynamic relationship between level of self-confidence prior to entering combat and fear reactions in combat. This would mean that by increasing the men's self-confidence about their abilities to perform well in combat, their subsequent fear reactions to combat would be reduced. If this hypothesis should prove to be true, it would have very direct implications for precombat training since it would point up the need for utilizing every available means for building up the men's self-confidence in their own abilities to perform their combat jobs. In evaluating whether or not a given unit needed more precombat training and in designing the training program itself, it would be necessary to take account not only of the men's performance with respect to necessary combat skills but also their *attitudes* with respect to the adequacy of their preparation for combat.

It is interesting to note at this point that from the survey of combat veterans in an Infantry division in the Southwest Pacific we find a relationship between self-ratings on the adequacy of training for the combat job and the index of fear reactions to combat.[27] The data are shown in Chart VI. This finding is consistent with the hypothesis which we have been discussing; it suggests that fear reactions in combat may be due, in part, to an attitudinal factor—the feeling that one has not had sufficient training for one's combat job. It should be recognized, however, that not very much weight can be given to the results in Chart VI as *evidence* for the hypothesis

---

[27] The following question on adequacy of training was used in this study: When you were first sent into combat, were you assigned to a job or duty for which

_____ You were thoroughly trained
_____ You had some, but not enough training
_____ You had no training

In the chart, the category "not enough training" combines the second and third choices. This was done because less than 6 per cent of the men checked the third choice ("You had no training"). The scores on the index of fear in combat were determined by the number of symptoms which the men reported having experienced "sometimes" or "often," such as "violent pounding of the heart," "shaking and trembling all over," etc. (based on the question quoted in the footnote to Table 3). In obtaining the data for the correlation, all cases where no answer was given to one or the other question were omitted. Several hundred cases in the original total sample were therefore excluded from the correlation table because they had failed to answer at least one of the parts to the fear symptom question and hence an accurate score could not be assigned to them. The "no answer" group on fear symptoms tended to respond to the question on training in the same way as the high score on fear symptoms group. This is not an unusual finding; it has been found in a number of Research Branch studies, on the basis of independent criteria, that it is the more emotionally disturbed men who tend to omit answering questions about fear or anxiety symptoms. (Cf. Chapter 9.)

since alternative interpretations of the relationship cannot be excluded.[28]

The Need for Fear-eliciting Battle Stimuli in Training Troops for Combat

One indication of the importance of exposing men to fear-eliciting battle stimuli during precombat training is provided by the criticisms and suggestions for training made by combat veterans, on the

CHART VI

RELATIONSHIP BETWEEN SELF-RATING ON ADEQUACY OF TRAINING AND
FEAR REACTIONS TO COMBAT

(Based on Questionnaire Responses of Combat Veterans in an Infantry
Division in the Southwest Pacific, January 1944)

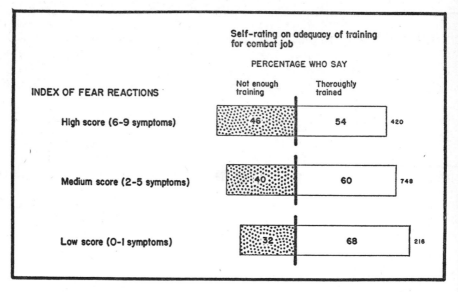

Data from S-100. See footnote 27 for explanation of ratings on adequacy of training and of the index of fear reactions.

The numbers following the bars are the numbers of cases on which percentages are based.

basis of their own experience in combat. From a number of attitude surveys there is evidence that combat veterans, in evaluating their own preparation for combat, felt that more exposure to battle stimuli prior to entering combat was one of the major deficiencies in their own training for combat.

Some data of this type are provided by the questionnaire results

[28] See footnote 26.

obtained from a study of 700 veterans of the North African campaign (summer 1943).[29]   In answer to a question on "the kind of training which lessens the initial shock of combat," the most frequent answers were as follows:

1. *Give men more training under live ammunition.*   This reply was given by about one third of the men.   A typical remark was: "Make it as real as possible, using real ammunition.   A few will get killed, but the others will learn.   They will know the score, that this is war and no picnic."

2. *Show what enemy weapons can do—so that men will know what to expect of them in combat.*   (Suggested by one fifth of the men.) A representative quotation expresses the suggestion this way: "Show them every enemy weapon and fire it.   Show them how it operates and what to expect.   [Show them] its deficiencies as well as its better qualities. . . .   Let them see German planes and hear their motors . . . so it makes a lasting impression."   Some men felt strongly that the high quality of German weapons was not adequately stressed during their training.   "[We need] to explain to our men the value of the enemies' weapons—not to underestimate them."   That this is not an isolated opinion is supported by the fact that 57 per cent of the men interviewed reported that they found German equipment "better than expected."   (Sixty-six per cent of the men, however, still believed American equipment superior to German.)

3. *Give men even more training in how to protect themselves from enemy weapons.*   (Suggested by 15 per cent of the men.)   The following statement typifies the type of concrete suggestion given: "More instruction on how to protect themselves from machine gun fire and how to dispose of machine gun nests."

These results are supplemented by studies of combat veterans in other combat areas.   An analysis has been made of the free-answer comments on deficiencies in precombat training obtained from a survey (in April 1944) of combat veterans who had fought in Sicily.[30] Approximately 40 per cent of the 500 combat infantrymen in the sample gave a write-in answer to the question: "What kind of training, if any, did you lack?"[31]   The proportions who gave each type

---

[29] S-66.

[30] S-100C.

[31] This question appeared in the questionnaire immediately following the question on adequacy of combat training quoted in footnote 27.   The percentages presented in the table give a total which is slightly more than 100 per cent due to the fact that some men mentioned more than one deficiency.

of response (based on the 200 cases who gave an answer) were as follows:

Type of deficiency mentioned	Per cent giving each answer
Training under fire, under realistic battle conditions	30
More training in specific weapons	27
More training in general	17
Amphibious and other types of tactics	14
Mountain training	12
Experience with artillery fire	4
Knowledge of enemy weapons and tactics	4
Physical endurance training	4
Miscellaneous	3

It will be noted that the most frequently mentioned deficiency in combat training was experience with live ammunition and realistic battle stimuli. The same sample of combat infantrymen gave similar answers to the question: "Is there any type of training you think new troops should be getting more of before being sent into your type of outfit as replacements?" More than one fourth of the men asserted that training under live ammunition was needed.

The same type of results is provided by a survey of 344 combat infantrymen in Italy.[32] Slightly more than half of the men gave an affirmative answer to the question: "Is there any particular kind of training you *did not* get that *you wish you had received* before you went into combat?" Once again, one of the most frequent types of answer written in by those who gave a "Yes" answer was "training under live ammunition, under realistic battle conditions." [33]

Another indication of how combat troops rated training under realistic battle conditions as compared to other types of training is provided by the responses of the same group of combat infantrymen to questions about the importance of four types of training activities. These responses are shown in Chart VII.

The results which we have presented on the responses of combat veterans to questions about deficiencies in their own training indicate that many men, on the basis of their own experience in combat,

---

[32] S-100A.

[33] It is probable that the majority of men in this sample had received their training *after* the infiltration course and other "battle inoculation" features had been introduced into the standard training program, whereas the preceding findings (for veterans of the North African and Sicilian campaigns) were obtained from men who had received their training *before* these features were introduced. It is interesting to note, therefore, that even after the Army introduced live ammunition into the training program, combat troops tended to feel that their training was deficient in this respect.

felt that there was a considerable need for exposure to live ammunition and realistic battle conditions in precombat training.   In the next section, on fear of enemy weapons, we shall present some findings which suggest that with increased exposure to actual combat conditions, the men's ratings of the dangerousness of weapons tended to correspond more closely to the actual effectiveness of the weapons and exaggerated fears of enemy weapons tended to be reduced.   It

CHART VII

COMBAT VETERANS' RATING OF THE IMPORTANCE OF VARIOUS TYPES OF TRAINING
(Based on Responses of 344 Combat Infantrymen in Italy, February 1944)

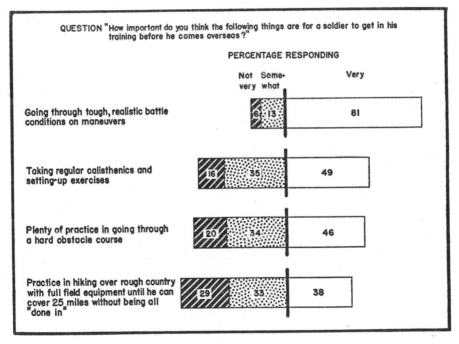

QUESTION "How important do you think the following things are for a soldier to get in his training before he comes overseas?"

PERCENTAGE RESPONDING

Not very   Some-what   Very

Going through tough, realistic battle conditions on maneuvers — 6 | 13 | 81

Taking regular calisthenics and setting-up exercises — 16 | 35 | 49

Plenty of practice in going through a hard obstacle course — 20 | 34 | 46

Practice in hiking over rough country with full field equipment until he can cover 25 miles without being all "done in" — 29 | 33 | 38

Data from S-100A.

is likely that this type of adjustment to sources of objective danger is one of the ways in which exposure to realistic battle stimuli serves to prepare men psychologically for combat.

Factors Affecting Fear of Enemy Weapons

Some suggestive material on the problems involved in preparing men to withstand fear-eliciting stimuli in battle is provided by two studies of attitudes of combat veterans toward enemy weapons. One of the primary purposes of these studies was to determine what characteristics of fear-eliciting weapons tend to be frightening.   The results, as will be shown in the tables given below, indicate that certain weapons elicited more fear than appears to be warranted by their actual degree of dangerousness.   There is evidence that these irrational fears of specific weapons were based on psychological factors of the type which would be subjected to modification by train-

TABLE 5

PERCENTAGES OF MEN EXPOSED TO EACH WEAPON WHO RATED IT
MOST FRIGHTENING*

BASED ON RESPONSES TO THE QUESTION: "What enemy weapon used against you
seemed most frightening to you?"

	Per cent
88 mm. gun	48
Dive bomber	20
Mortar	13
Horizontal bomber	12
Light machine gun	7
Strafing	5
Land mines	2
Rifle fire	0
Miscellaneous (booby traps, tank attack, heavy machine gun, etc.)	4

Data from S-66.
    * This table is to be read as follows: Of all men exposed to the 88 mm. gun, 48 per cent rated it as the most frightening weapon; of all men exposed to the dive bomber, 20 per cent rated it as the most frightening weapon; etc.   Those exposed to the 88 mm. gun were not in all cases the same men as those exposed to the dive bomber.   Since each percentage shown in the chart is calculated from a different base, depending on the number of men exposed to the weapon, they do not total exactly 100 per cent.   The same method of calculation is used in determining which weapons were rated "most dangerous."   This method of analysis includes all men, regardless of how many or how few of the weapons they had been exposed to.   An alternative method of analysis would be to use only men who had been exposed to all of the weapons and therefore had a more complete basis on which to judge dangerousness and frighteningness.   This could not be done because too few of the men had experienced all of the weapons.   A selection of the five more frequently experienced weapons was made: 88, mortar, bomber, land mine, and light machine gun.   The ratings of dangerousness and fearfulness were determined for all men who had been exposed to all five of these weapons.   The results obtained by this procedure parallel closely those obtained by the method used to compile the table above and the one which follows.   The exact number of cases on which each of the percentages in Tables 5 and 6 and Chart VIII is based is not available, as the punch cards and work sheets for S-66 have not been located.   The total sample includes somewhat more than 700 cases.

ing.   This suggests that inappropriate fear reactions to certain highly feared weapons could be avoided by adequate precombat training.

The first study was carried out in the summer of 1943.[34]   More than 700 enlisted men, most of whom had been evacuated from the North African theater because of combat wounds, were given a questionnaire dealing with their reactions to a variety of German weapons.   As shown in Table 5, almost half of the men believed

[34] S-66.

that the German 88 mm. gun was more frightening than any other German weapon used against them in the North African campaign. The next three weapons mentioned, in order of frequency, were the dive bomber, the mortar, and the horizontal bomber. The low frequencies for the remaining weapons do not necessarily mean that they were not feared, but only that they were rated as most frightening by relatively fewer men.

The men were asked what enemy weapon they thought most dangerous, in terms of the number of our men they believed it killed or wounded. The results are shown in Table 6. It will be seen that

TABLE 6

PERCENTAGES OF MEN EXPOSED TO EACH WEAPON WHO RATED IT
MOST DANGEROUS*

BASED ON RESPONSES TO THE QUESTION: "Judging from what you yourself saw, what weapon used by the enemy caused the most casualties (killed and wounded) among our men?"

	Per cent
88 mm. gun	62
Mortar	17
Light machine gun	6
Horizontal bomber	5
Dive bomber	4
Strafing	4
Land mines	2
Rifle fire	0
Miscellaneous (booby traps, tank attack, heavy machine guns, etc.)	2

Data from S-66.
* See footnote to Table 5.

in general the weapons which are considered most dangerous are also rated high in terms of fearfulness. The most important discrepancy is in the case of the dive bomber, which is considered most frightening by 20 per cent of the men although only 4 per cent of the men rated it most dangerous. Similarly, the horizontal bomber is rated most frightening by 12 per cent, but most dangerous by only 5 per cent of the men.

In addition to these two exceptions, the relationship between dangerousness and "frighteningness" is lessened by the fact that in many cases the men who rated a particular weapon as most frightening were not the same men who consider it most dangerous. Only 38 per cent of the individual men rated as most frightening the same weapon they rated most dangerous.   Hence it is evident that factors other than belief in the dangerousness of the weapon are involved in rating the fearfulness of enemy weapons.

The weapon which caused the greatest number of wounds among the men in the present study was the 88 mm. gun.   This was also rated as the most dangerous by a majority of the men.   But there is little correspondence in the list beyond this point.

The most common reasons men gave for fearing particular weapons are summarized below for the five most frequently feared weapons.   The percentage of men giving these reasons for each weapon is indicated in parentheses:

> *Mortar:* The mortar, the men say, is to be feared for its "deadly accuracy" (24 per cent) and because it "is right on top of you before you know it's coming" (19 per cent).
>
> *88 mm. gun:* The 88 is most frequently feared for its accuracy (21 per cent).   "They could hit a dime at a thousand yards with it."
>
> *Light machine gun:* The light machine gun impresses men with its "rapid rate of fire" (42 per cent).   As one man said "Our gun sounds like a slow motor boat, theirs like a buzz-saw."

The above reasons are seen to be more or less in line with casualty-inflicting characteristics that the weapons actually possess.   On the other hand, other types of characteristics were referred to in describing the fearfulness of air attacks:

> *Dive bomber:* The dive bomber is feared because of its "siren" and its "terrible shrieking noise" (48 per cent).
>
> *Horizontal bomber:* The horizontal bomber is feared because of its noise (21 per cent) and the fact that it leaves many men with a "feeling of helplessness—you can't fight back at it" (14 per cent).

The reasons most often given for fearing air attack had little or no relationship to the casualty inflicting characteristics of these weapons, but appear to have been of a purely "psychological" character.   This finding is consistent with Dollard's conclusion in his report based on interviews with combat veterans in the Abraham Lincoln Brigade who had fought in the Civil War in Spain:

"A weapon may be high on the list [of feared weapons] either because it is especially common and dangerous, perhaps the case with artillery shells, or because something about it arouses irrational fear, perhaps the case with air-bombing.   The machine gun should probably be high on the list because it is actually dangerous, but the men may feel that, though dangerous, it is in the realm of the familiar and that they know how to cope with it.[35]

There are some additional findings which provide supplementary information on this point. With more experience in combat the men appear to have become relatively more afraid of weapons with real striking power and less afraid of those which were objectively less effective. Men with the longest battle experience were found to be less likely than green troops to regard as most frightening a weapon like the dive bomber and more likely to regard as most frightening a weapon like the 88 mm. gun.[36] In Chart VIII the percentages of men considering artillery most frightening as contrasted with those who consider air attack most frightening are classified according to the length of time the individuals were in combat.

The threat of air attacks may have evoked exaggerated fear reactions among those who had been in combat for only a short time. As we have seen, the reasons men gave for fearing air attacks had little to do with casualty-inflicting effectiveness, unlike the reasons given for fear of artillery shelling. This finding, together with the results shown in Chart VIII, suggests the hypothesis that fears unwarranted by the objective effectiveness of a weapon are capable of being reduced by exposure to the sounds and other fear-eliciting stimuli which the weapon produces. The results from another study presented below suggest that this might also hold true even for weapons which are highly effective in inflicting casualties.

Before presenting the additional data on this point, it might be noted in passing that there is some indirect evidence that the retrospective reports which the men gave about the way they felt when they were in combat do provide some indication of their actual re-

---

[35] J. Dollard, *op. cit.*, p. 14

[36] The data were examined for the possibility that these results may reflect a decreased use of air attack by the enemy as the Tunisian campaign progressed. If this assumption were true, men who entered combat in the later phases should show less fear of air attack than those who had come in earlier. This was *not* borne out by the data. Neither did it turn out that men who were in combat for a very short period were relatively any more exposed to bombing than to artillery fire. Hence the statement as made above does not appear to be the result of the particular course of the African campaign, nor of any greater use of bombing on troops who were first entering combat. Our data are in conflict with results reported by the British who found that the "morale" weapons—dive bomber, and other forms of air attack—all showed increases in the number of dislikes (both absolute, and relative to other weapons) with increased experience, while the "wounding" weapons—machine guns, artillery and rifle—all showed decreases.

actions to combat.   As part of the study of the North African combat veterans, the responses of an additional small group of combat
psychiatric casualties (48 cases) were compared with those of the
700 wounded combat veterans on the following question: "Did this
[most frightening] weapon become more frightening or less frightening as time went on?"   Approximately one fourth of the group of

CHART VIII

RATINGS OF THE FEARFULNESS OF TWO ENEMY WEAPONS IN RELATION TO
LENGTH OF TIME IN COMBAT

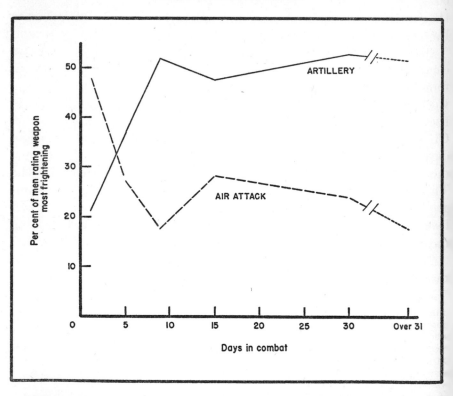

Data from S-66.   See footnote to Table 5.

combat psychiatric casualties reported that their fear of the weapon
which they had rated as most frightening was reduced ("Became
somewhat less frightening" or "Became much less frightening"), as
against nearly twice this proportion for the wounded group (46 per
cent).

Additional findings on fear of enemy weapons are provided by a
survey of combat veterans in France.   During September–October

1944, 842 wounded combat veterans were interviewed in four general hospitals in France and in a reconditioning center in England.[37] This study provides data which tend to bear out the main conclusion suggested by the earlier study of veterans of the North African campaign:[38] (1) fear of enemy weapons, in some cases, appears to have been disproportionate to the apparent dangerousness of the weapon —which implies that psychological factors play a role in augmenting fear of enemy weapons; and (2) fears of enemy weapons appear to have become more realistic as a result of exposure to actual combat conditions. These conclusions are suggested by a comparison of the reactions to two major enemy weapons, both of which were highly dangerous: the 88 mm. gun and the mortar.

At the time of the study both weapons were effective in inflicting casualties. It will be noted in Chart IX that approximately one fourth of the men in the sample reported that they had been wounded by the 88 mm. gun and the corresponding proportion for the mortar was 18 per cent. As shown by the additional results in Chart IX, the proportion of men who rated the 88 mm. as the most dangerous weapon is smaller than the proportion who rated it as the most fearful weapon, whereas the reverse is true for the mortar. This finding suggests that although the fear of the 88 mm. gun was grounded in its objective dangerousness, it evoked relatively greater fear response compared with its actual effectiveness, than did the mortar.[39]

There are some supplementary findings which indicate that there may have been a somewhat exaggerated fear of the 88 mm. gun due

[37] S-163. Approximately three fifths of the men sampled were in the general hospitals where they had been sent after evacuation from the fighting at the German border and the combat zone at Brest, France. The remaining two fifths were veterans who had been evacuated from France to England for extended hospitalization and reconditioning for further active duty. Though the men surveyed came from a large variety of units and their combat experiences varied considerably, they cannot be assumed to be a representative cross section of combat veterans. Since the survey was conducted among wounded men, infantrymen made up a disproportionate number of the veterans sampled.

[38] The survey in France did not provide an opportunity for checking specific findings of the previous study of North African veterans, with respect to exaggerated fears of aerial attacks. The majority of American troops in France during the post D Day period were never exposed to attacks by enemy aircraft; 87 per cent of the men in the sample asserted that they had never experienced aerial bombardment.

[39] Some indication of a psychological factor which may have been involved is to be found in the reasons the men gave in explaining their dislike of the weapon they feared most. One of the most frequent types of answers about the 88 mm. gun given in response to a question on reasons for fearing the weapon was: "the sounds it produces— when it goes off and when the shell is traveling through the air." In the case of the mortar, on the other hand, almost all of the reasons given for disliking the weapon were directly related to its effectiveness in causing casualties.

to the reputation which the weapon had acquired among combat troops who were fighting in France, which may not have been the case among troops in North Africa.

Research Branch personnel, from their interviews with combat soldiers during this period, reported that of all German artillery pieces, the 88 mm. gun was the only one which the men frequently mentioned by name and that this weapon appeared to have acquired the character of a "bogey." It was a favorite subject of stories and legends. This tends to be borne out by the results of a comparison

CHART IX

COMPARISON OF REACTIONS TO TWO ENEMY WEAPONS
(Based on a Survey of 842 Wounded Combat Veterans in the
European Theater, September–October 1944)

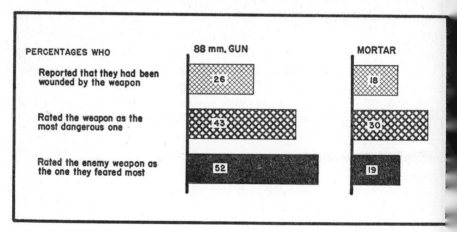

Data from S-163.

between the 142 men who reported that they had experienced very little or no exposure to the weapon and the 664 men who reported having been exposed to the weapon many times. Fifty-one per cent of the latter and 59 per cent of the former group rated the 88 mm. gun as the weapon they feared most. It appears, therefore, that the 88 mm. gun was highly feared even before the men had very much direct experience with artillery fire. Such was not the case with the mortar. Only 9 per cent of the 247 men with little exposure to the weapon rated it as the one they feared most as against 24 per cent of the 524 exposed to it many times.

The results shown in Chart X suggest that fear of the 88 mm. gun may have decreased in the course of continued exposure to combat

It will be noted that combat veterans who had served in actual combat for the longest period were less likely than other men to rate the 88 mm. gun as the most dangerous enemy weapon and were less likely to regard it as the most fearful enemy weapon.   In contrast to this, the mortar tended to be regarded as relatively more dangerous and more fearful with increased time in combat.

Apparently, with this sample of men, the 88 mm. actually caused

CHART X

CHANGES IN REACTIONS TO TWO ENEMY WEAPONS WITH INCREASED
EXPOSURE TO COMBAT
(Based on a Survey of Wounded Combat Veterans in the
European Theater, September–October, 1944)

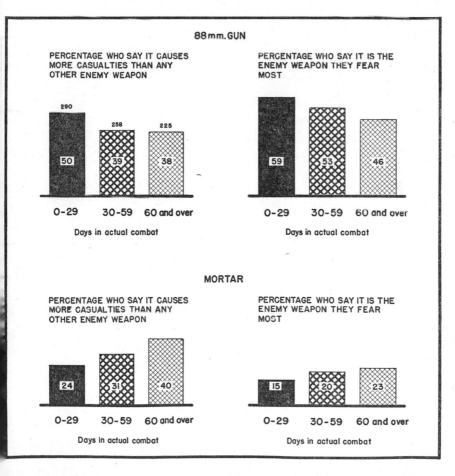

Data from S-163.
The numbers at the top of the bars are the numbers of cases in each subsample.

a decreasing proportion of casualties with increased time in combat. The proportions who said they were wounded by the 88 mm. and mortar respectively, by length of time in combat, were:

	PERCENTAGE WOUNDED BY	
Time in combat	*88 mm.*	*Mortar*
60 days or over	19	16
30 to 59 days	22	21
Under 30 days	35	12

Hence, in this sample, the decreasing proportions with time in combat, as shown in Chart X, who rated the 88 mm. as most fearful, as well as most dangerous, correspond with the decreasing proportions of 88 mm. casualties. This suggests "realism" in the responses, but it also must be noted in Chart X that even among the men with more than 60 days in combat the 88 mm. was most feared by 46 per cent and the mortar by only 23 per cent in spite of the fact that the two weapons were, according to this subsample, causing almost equal casualties.[40]

While controlled observations of the same group of men over a period of time are necessary in order to obtain clear-cut evidence of a true change in reactions to enemy weapons, the results in Chart X are of some interest when compared with the findings of the earlier study of veterans of the North African campaign. That study indicated that fear of aerial bombardment (which, from independent evidence, appeared to be an exaggerated fear) may have been reduced with increased time in combat while fear of artillery fire (a reaction to a more realistic source of danger) tended to increase. The study of combat veterans in France suggests a pattern similar in some respects. Fear of the 88 mm., while it was in large part a realistic fear, may have been somewhat exaggerated by the reputation the weapon had acquired; with increased exposure to combat conditions this fear appears to have decreased, though even among those longest exposed the 88 mm. was by far the most feared weapon. The mortar, on the other hand, appears to have been underestimated initially, and with increased time in combat fear of this weapon appears to have increased.

An obvious hypothesis suggested by these findings is that a learning process operates in combat which has the dual effect of decreasing fear reactions to exaggerated dangers and increasing fear re-

[40] When the data in Chart X are further broken down separately for men wounded by 88 mm., mortars, and other weapons, the same essential pattern of response to the questions on fright and danger, by time in combat, appears for each subgroup separately

actions to underestimated dangers. The extinction of emergency fear reactions to pseudo danger cues and the strengthening of these reactions in response to cues of genuine danger would be highly adaptive in an environment which contains a multitude of potential dangers.

It has been reported by many observers that men in combat develop considerable ability in discriminating among the various sounds emitted by projectiles traveling at varying heights and in varying trajectories which provide cues to one's proximity to the target. The acquisition of this type of discrimination in combat would facilitate adaptive reactions. It would be expected that if the men perceived relatively little evidence of actual damage accompanying certain recurrent sounds—which initially may have elicited an excited, emotional reaction—they would develop the ability to ignore these sounds. Other cues which may have been neutral, originally, would become effective in eliciting fear reactions if they occurred contiguously with perceptible damage and became a sign for danger. The acquisition of differential fear reactions to battle stimuli is probably also facilitated by experience in attempting to counteract various sources of danger: those dangers for which the men develop successful protective habits, such as taking cover, would tend to elicit less fear than those against which the men find themselves to be defenseless.

There are some results from the study of combat veterans in France which suggest that learning processes of this type may operate in the case of fear reactions to stimuli associated with certain enemy weapons. Of those men who had been under 88 mm. and artillery fire many times, approximately one out of every ten reported that the 88 mm. gun subsequently became less frightening than it was at first; the main "reasons" they gave, in explaining why the weapons became less frightening, were the following: (1) You get used to it. (2) You can hear it coming. (3) You can take cover and avoid it.

While the most important "real reason" may have been a relative decrease in the 88 mm's effect, compared with other weapons, these answers suggest that having the experience of escaping from danger by taking successful protective action and having practice in discriminating among sound cues can be critical factors in the reduction of fears of enemy weapons in combat.

CHAPTER 5

THE COMBAT REPLACEMENT [1]

Introduction

THE fact has already been noted that high casualty rates among combat personnel, together with an established system of replacing individuals rather than units, led to a constantly changing membership of the front-line combat unit. Many veteran outfits which had seen much fighting contained a relatively small proportion of men who had come overseas as original members. For example, in a survey of four Infantry divisions in Italy in April of 1945, only 34 per cent of the cross section of infantrymen in line companies said they had come overseas with their outfits, while the remainder had joined their divisions as replacements. [2] So ground combat is not to be thought of as having involved teams of men who had all trained together from the beginning. The normal turnover in the membership of combat outfits had several implications for the adjustments required of many combat soldiers. For one thing, it meant that many of them would first have to be assimilated to a pre-existing group. This process of assimilation was an important one, for we have seen that intragroup ties played a central role in combat motivation. Aside from the processes of social integration, the replacement also had to acquire for himself the practical knowledge and skills of battle so that he could function properly as a member of the team. The question arises as to how long it would take him to reach a peak of efficiency and, for that matter, whether *there was* in fact a peak of efficiency after which his value as a soldier decreased.

The present chapter will treat some of these problems arising from the replacement system. The assimilation of the replacement to a veteran outfit will first be discussed. In regard to this process, the fullest data are available for men joining veteran divisions during a

---

[1] By M. Brewster Smith. Special mention is due Robin M. Williams, Jr., whose ideas and suggestions have been used extensively.
[2] S-177, 1,766 cases.

period when they were not in combat. While this situation was by no means typical of the conditions under which all replacements joined their outfits, it is of some special interest since it permits a study of the processes of assimilation abstracted from the problems of the soldier's initial adjustments to combat. In contrast to the alternative case, in which the replacement first saw his new outfit in the lines, perhaps at night in the midst of a major offensive, it also represents the ideal way for the individual replacement system to operate. After exploring the data on the process of assimilation before combat, we will more briefly sketch the normal sequence of events for the replacement, from the replacement depot through his initial adjustments to combat. Some evidence in regard to the length of time it took the combat soldier to reach his peak of efficiency will be discussed in a final section. These final data will be relevant not only to an understanding of the adjustment of the replacement to combat but also to any general evaluation of the individual replacement system, which assured combat outfits a kind of formal immortality but tended to keep individuals in combat until the limit of their endurance was reached. While no attempt will be made to evaluate the many complex considerations involved in an appraisal of the individual replacement system as a whole, the question of the existence of a peak of efficiency is certainly one factor which would have to be taken into account in such an evaluation.

The Assimilation of Replacements to a Veteran Outfit Before Combat

The period of the winter and spring of 1944, when a vast force of combat troops was being assembled in England in preparation for the Normandy invasion, provided a unique natural laboratory for the study of the state of mind in which veteran and inexperienced soldiers awaited major action. Several veteran divisions which had seen varying amounts of action in the Mediterranean campaign were shipped to the British Isles to spearhead the coming invasion. Following customary practice their ranks were filled with new replacements, the divisions carrying "overstrength" beyond the complement normally authorized. A period of intensive preinvasion training was then instituted during which the replacements were to be assimilated, and in which the replenished units, together with many fresh divisions from the States, were to be welded into the most effective possible team for the crucial assault. Two of these replenished veteran Infantry divisions were among eleven divisions in which questionnaire surveys were conducted in England during this preinvasion period. The surveys were primarily intended to give the commanders concerned an appraisal of various aspects of the morale of the men in their immediate commands. However, the resulting data permit comparison of the attitudes of replacements in the veteran divisions with those of combat veterans in these same divisions, and also with the attitudes of men in completely inexperienced divisions. The surveys thus provide a coherent picture of some of the ways in which the attitudes of the new replacements were modified in interaction with their veteran organizations, and also give some indication of the gross effects of combat experience on the veterans.

One of the two veteran divisions which were surveyed in April of 1944 (Division A) was the same division which had been surveyed in the United States in December 1941 and which was discussed at length in Volume I, Chapter 2. Although it was a Regular Army division, the earlier study found that barely more than half of the enlisted men were from the Regular Army.[3] After repeatedly sending out cadre personnel to newly activated divisions in the intervening two-year period, the division probably retained a relatively small proportion of "old" Army men at the time of the later study. Nevertheless, the combat veterans did differ in background characteristics from men in the newer, inexperienced divisions and particularly from more recently recruited replacements, as an inspection of the numbers of cases in the tables of this chapter will indicate. The most notable difference between veterans and replacements in this division was in regard to rank: very few of the replacements were noncoms. Since factors such as rank may be related to the attitudes with which we are to be concerned, statistical controls are indispensable for any comparison of the attitudes of the various groups. Because Division A was the only veteran division surveyed with a questionnaire which obtained information on background characteristics, the findings from this division will be relied upon as the chief source of data for comparing veterans and replacements. Data from the second veteran division (Division B), which had seen somewhat heavier combat, will be used in supplementation.

An overall view of the answers of veterans and replacements in Division A, in comparison with those of men in inexperienced divisions freshly arrived overseas, reveals some striking differences in key attitudes. Chart I presents the data in a preliminary way.

[3] Cf. Chart II in Volume I, Chapter 2, "The Old Army and the New."

CHART I

COMPARISON OF ATTITUDES OF REPLACEMENT PRIVATES IN LINE INFANTRY
COMPANIES OF A VETERAN INFANTRY DIVISION WITH THOSE OF VETERAN
PRIVATES IN THE SAME COMPANIES AND OF ALL PRIVATES IN THE LINE
INFANTRY COMPANIES OF THREE INEXPERIENCED DIVISIONS
(European Theater, April–May 1944, S-129)

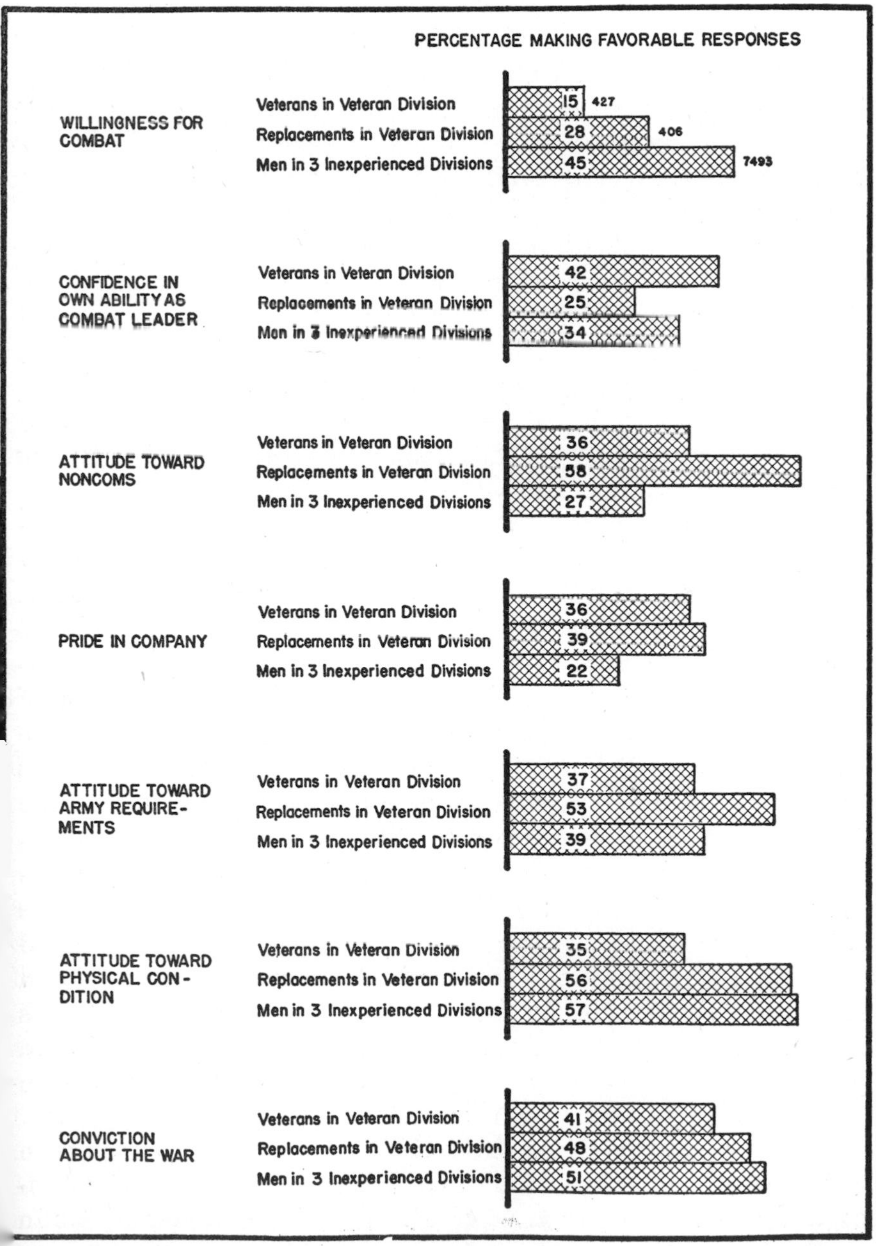

PERCENTAGE MAKING FAVORABLE RESPONSES

WILLINGNESS FOR COMBAT
- Veterans in Veteran Division — 15   427
- Replacements in Veteran Division — 28   406
- Men in 3 Inexperienced Divisions — 45   7493

CONFIDENCE IN OWN ABILITY AS COMBAT LEADER
- Veterans in Veteran Division — 42
- Replacements in Veteran Division — 25
- Men in 3 Inexperienced Divisions — 34

ATTITUDE TOWARD NONCOMS
- Veterans in Veteran Division — 36
- Replacements in Veteran Division — 58
- Men in 3 Inexperienced Divisions — 27

PRIDE IN COMPANY
- Veterans in Veteran Division — 36
- Replacements in Veteran Division — 39
- Men in 3 Inexperienced Divisions — 22

ATTITUDE TOWARD ARMY REQUIREMENTS
- Veterans in Veteran Division — 37
- Replacements in Veteran Division — 53
- Men in 3 Inexperienced Divisions — 39

ATTITUDE TOWARD PHYSICAL CONDITION
- Veterans in Veteran Division — 35
- Replacements in Veteran Division — 56
- Men in 3 Inexperienced Divisions — 57

CONVICTION ABOUT THE WAR
- Veterans in Veteran Division — 41
- Replacements in Veteran Division — 48
- Men in 3 Inexperienced Divisions — 51

Caution: The responses to a given question, here called favorable and discussed in
the text, permit one to compare the pattern of replies by the three types of troops on
a given question. Moreover the pattern on one question may be compared with that
on another. But no special significance is to be attached to the absolute length of the
bars in this chart. The absolute length is dependent on question wording and the
responses selected as favorable.

Since there were an insufficient number of replacement noncoms, the comparisons in this chart are restricted to privates and privates first class. For the sake of further homogeneity, only members of line Infantry companies are included, here and throughout the chapter. The inexperienced divisions selected for the comparisons were those which were surveyed at approximately the same time as Division A, with the questionnaire which included information on background characteristics. The various attitude areas represented in Chart I will each be treated in a separate subsection to follow; here each area is represented by a single question for the sake of graphic simplicity. The chart shows the proportion in each group who gave responses which were arbitrarily selected by inspection as favorable. The wording of the questions, as well as the designation of favorable responses, may be found in the table accompanying the subsection dealing with each content area.

As Chart I shows, the relationship of the responses of replacements to those of veterans and of members of inexperienced divisions differs for different questions. There appear to be at least four principal patterns:

1. In regard to willingness for combat, the replacements stand *intermediate* between the relatively unwilling veterans and the relatively more willing men in inexperienced divisions. As a convenient oversimplification, it could be said that in this respect the replacement who had joined a veteran division was already half a veteran without ever having been in combat.

2. In regard to feeling that they had enough training and experience to take charge of a group of men in combat, the replacements are the *lowest* of the three groups and the veterans are highest.

3. On some of the questions, the replacements were *more* likely to give favorable responses than either of the other groups. This was true of their attitudes toward their noncoms and toward Army requirements (thinking that most requirements "seemed necessary") In regard to pride in company they were at least as likely to be favorable as the veterans, and more so than men in inexperienced divisions.

4. On other questions, the replacements differed little or not at all from men in new divisions. Thus their attitudes toward their physical condition were similar to those of men in inexperienced outfits but different from those of veterans. In regard to their conviction about the war, the replacements differed slightly from the veterans but were essentially similar to the third group.

Several factors will be adduced in explanation of these divergent patterns. The differences between veterans on the one hand and men in inexperienced divisions on the other can for the most part be attributed in one way or another to the effects of combat experience on the veterans. The replacements, like the men in the new divisions, lacked battle experience, but the fact that they had joined a seasoned outfit appears to have been significant for their attitudes in at least two ways. In some respects they partially took over the attitudes of the veterans around them. This is most apparent in Chart I in regard to willingness for combat, though it will be shown later in the chapter that their attitudes responded in several other respects to the prevailing atmosphere in their companies. Secondly, as distinguished from men in green divisions, they seem to have reacted to the fact that their new outfit and its members had the prestige of combat experience. Thus they were especially likely to have confidence in their veteran noncoms, were likely to accept as necessary the requirements which their veteran leaders imposed on them, and were more likely than troops in green divisions to express a high degree of pride in their companies. At least partly for the same reason, however, they were less likely than either of the other groups to say they had enough training and experience to be able to do a good job of taking sole charge of a group of men in combat; they had the seasoned veterans in their companies to look up to for that.

The process of being assimilated to a veteran outfit thus involved effects on the replacements' attitudes of both favorable and unfavorable aspect. Some of the bitterness of the veterans appears to have been contagious. Counterbalancing this was the special significance to the replacement of being among proved veterans in an outfit that had made a name for itself. These effects will appear in greater detail in the sections that follow.

Willingness for combat. The responses of veterans, replacements, and members of untried divisions on two questions concerned with willingness for combat are compared in Table 1. The more detailed results for both questions are in agreement with the summary findings that were shown in Chart I for the first of them. The questions were sufficiently different so that the overall proportions of men checking favorable responses differed considerably for the two items, but on both of them combat veterans were markedly less likely to indicate willingness for combat than were men in new divisions, while replacements in the veterans' divisions were intermediate in their answers.

TABLE 1

WILLINGNESS FOR COMBAT AMONG ENLISTED VETERANS AND REPLACEMENTS IN LINE
INFANTRY COMPANIES OF TWO VETERAN INFANTRY DIVISIONS AND ENLISTED
MEN IN LINE INFANTRY COMPANIES OF THREE INEXPERIENCED DIVISIONS
(European Theater, April–May 1944. S-129)

	Number of cases	QUESTIONS: "Which of the following best tells the way you feel about getting into an actual battle zone?" Per cent making favorable responses*	"Which of the following best describes your own feeling about getting into combat against the Germans?" Per cent making favorable responses†
All Enlisted Men			
Veteran Division A			
Veterans	*605*	15	32
Replacements	*427*	28	56
Veteran Division B‡			
Veterans	*2,227*	12	14
Replacements	*983*	32	45
Inexperienced Divisions	*9,850*	48	70
Noncoms			
Veteran Division A			
Veterans	*178*	17	41
Inexperienced Divisions	*2,357*	57	81
Privates and Pfc's			
Veteran Division A			
Veterans	*427*	15	27
Replacements	*406*	28	57
Inexperienced Divisions	*7,493*	45	67
Married			
Veteran Division A			
Veterans	*76*	12	29
Replacements	*114*	30	59
Inexperienced Divisions	*1,999*	43	63
Unmarried, H.S. Graduate			
Veteran Division A			
Veterans	*94*	13	22
Replacements	*114*	22	51
Inexperienced Divisions	*1,418*	46	69
Unmarried, Others			
Veteran Division A			
Veterans	*257*	16	29
Replacements	*178*	30	57
Inexperienced Divisions	*4,076*	46	68

* The answer categories were as follows:

    __X__ I want very much to get into it just as soon as possible.
    __X__ I'm ready to go any time.
    __X__ I'd like to go before it's over, but I don't think I'm ready yet.
    _____ I hope I won't have to go but if I do I think I'll do all right.

The table also shows that these relationships hold when several background characteristics are simultaneously controlled as fully as the number of cases from Division A permits: rank, education, and marital status (which affords a partial control on age, with which it is correlated—the men were not asked how old they were). The breakdowns on education and marital status could be made only among privates. The data for noncoms omit replacements, since there were only 21 replacement noncoms. However, the contrast between veteran noncoms and noncoms in new divisions is as sharp as between the privates in spite of the fact that, in line with expectation, noncoms were somewhat more likely than privates to say they were willing for combat.

Data from Division B, also shown in the table, are in agreement with those from Division A. Replacements in Division B, as in Division A, were more likely than veterans and less likely than the men in new divisions to say they were relatively willing for combat. The differences are sufficiently great that it is unlikely that any of the factors that were controlled in Division A could account for them.

Two salient facts emerge from the table which warrant interpretative comment. One is the marked tendency of combat veterans to show less willingness for combat than either of the groups without combat experience. This difference is clearly attributable to the combat experience of the veterans. What the difference means, however, in terms of differences in effective combat motivation is probably more complex. A word of caution should be introduced here in accordance with findings which were discussed in Chapter 1. There it was shown that in terms of certain gross indexes of combat effectiveness, expressed willingness for combat turns out to be related to combat effectiveness *within* the veteran and replacement groups. In spite of this, the replacements as a whole do not seem to have shown a higher degree of combat effectiveness than the vet-

---

_____ I hope I won't have to go because I don't think I would do very well.

_____ No opinion.

The categories marked X were considered favorable. Privates' answers to this question were shown in Chart I.

† The answer categories were:

____X____ I'd like to get into the fight as soon as I can.
____X____ I'm ready to go when my turn comes.
_____ I'd just as soon stay out of combat if possible.
_____ I don't want to get into combat at all.

The categories marked X were considered favorable.

‡ Surveyed in January 1944 (S-128). Other divisions surveyed April–May 1944 (S-129).

erans.   The latter finding may be the result of a counterbalancing
of influences, a result of selective factors in regard to the veteran
group, or it may reflect a change in the meaning of "willing" responses with combat experience.

The second major fact appearing from the table, namely the intermediate standing of the replacements, could therefore reflect a
taking over by the replacements of veterans' attitudes at a relatively
superficial level rather than a deep change in their combat motivation.   The present data leave this question open, but they do
strongly suggest that becoming a replacement in a veteran outfit
caused a deterioration at some level in the men's willingness for
combat.   This does not seem to have been a matter of differences
in background characteristics; the relationship is but little reduced
when certain relevant background factors are controlled.   (The
possibility, of course, remains that yet other uncontrolled factors
may have made the difference.)   Neither can it have been a matter
of a general deterioration in the replacements' morale as a result of
their experiences prior to joining a unit, for it has been seen in Chart
I that in some aspects the morale of replacements in a veteran division was *higher* than that of the other groups.   The most obvious
interpretation is that to some extent the replacements took over the
attitudes of the combat veterans around them, whose views on combat would have for them high prestige.   Some additional evidence
that this occurred will be presented later.[4]

Self-confidence.   It was seen in Chart I that among privates, the
veterans in a veteran division were most likely to say they had had
enough training and experience to take charge of a group of men in
combat, replacements in a veteran division least likely, and men in
new divisions intermediate in this respect.   The responses to the
first question in Table 2 show that this pattern holds when several
background variables are controlled and also is true of Division B.
However it would be erroneous to interpret this pattern as applying
to general self-confidence in combat proficiency.   The second question in the table, at first glance, appears closely similar to the first
one: "If you were given a group of men and told to take charge of
them all by yourself under enemy fire, how well do you think you
would do?"   The differences between the responses of the three
groups to this question are much smaller than the differences on the
first question, however, and the veterans do not differ from the

---

[4] Cf. Chart II.

members of new divisions. However there remains a small but consistent tendency for the replacements to be less likely to give favorable answers.

The key to the difference in results for the two questions appears to lie in the fact that the first question brought in the factor of *experience* while the second did not. For the veterans, experience was their strong point, and also the point at which replacements in contact with them felt the greatest inferiority, standing as they did in the shadow of the veterans. The pattern of differences in the men's answers which resulted probably reflects real differences in the resources which the various groups had at their disposal. The second question may, however, give a fairer appraisal of the men's relative confidence in their ability as combat leaders. The tendency of replacements to be slightly less confident is probably to be attributed again to the contrast which they perceived between themselves and the veterans. The lack of difference between veterans and men in new divisions is more surprising. Perhaps such factors as increased realism about the nature of combat and accompanying reluctance to assume responsibility may have balanced the greater experience of the veterans.

It should be noted that veterans tended to interpret any question dealing with "readiness" for combat as implying in some degree a query as to "willingness" for combat. This halo effect seems to have entered into various questions in different proportions, and may account for some of the responses which are otherwise difficult to interpret. Thus the results for the third question in Table 2 seem anomalous. We find the veterans if anything *less* likely than either of the other groups to give the favorable answer when asked, "Do you feel that you are now trained and ready for combat, or do you need more training?" Certainly the veterans were not less prepared for combat than inexperienced men. An interpretation of this anomalous finding suggests itself from the character of the favorable answer category: "I'm ready for combat now." This was an admission which the reluctant veteran might indeed wish to avoid. The reluctance which most of them felt about going back to combat was a very central attitude for them, and one which in other instances than this seems to have colored their responses to questions ostensibly bearing primarily on other matters. Alternatively, the veteran's reluctance to call himself "trained and ready" may have reflected genuinely higher standards of training and prep-

TABLE 2

SELF-CONFIDENCE AMONG ENLISTED VETERANS AND REPLACEMENTS IN LINE
INFANTRY COMPANIES OF TWO VETERAN INFANTRY DIVISIONS AND ENLISTED
MEN IN LINE INFANTRY COMPANIES OF THREE INEXPERIENCED DIVISIONS
(European Theater, April–May 1944. S-129)

	Number of cases	QUESTIONS:		
		"Do you think you have been given enough training and experience so that you could do a good job of taking charge of a group of men on your own in combat?"	"If you were given a group of men and told to take charge of them all by yourself under enemy fire, how well do you think you would do?"	"Do you feel that you are now trained and ready for combat, or do you need more training?"
		*Per cent making favorable responses**	*Per cent making favorable responses†*	*Per cent making favorable responses‡*
All Enlisted Men				
Veteran Division A				
Veterans	605	49	66	29
Replacements	427	26	55	28
Veteran Division B§				
Veterans	2,227	57	67	24
Replacements	983	25	49	19
Inexperienced Divisions	9,850	41	66	35
Noncoms				
Veteran Division A				
Veterans	178	66	84	34
Inexperienced Divisions	2,357	62	86	44
Privates and Pfc's				
Veteran Division A				
Veterans	427	42	59	27
Replacements	406	25	54	29
Inexperienced Divisions	7,493	34	60	33
Married				
Veteran Division A				
Veterans	76	42	66	32
Replacements	114	20	54	26
Inexperienced Divisions	1,999	37	61	32
Unmarried, H.S. Graduate				
Veteran Division A				
Veterans	94	44	63	24
Replacements	114	30	57	25
Inexperienced Divisions	1,418	33	65	33
Unmarried, Others				
Veteran Division A				
Veterans	257	41	54	27
Replacements	178	25	53	33
Inexperienced Divisions	4,076	34	57	33

aration than those that characterized men in inexperienced divisions. The two interpretations are mutually compatible and may both contribute toward an account of the results.

Attitudes toward leaders. The case of attitudes toward noncoms is a striking instance of a situation in which the stimulus object was different for replacements in a veteran division as compared with members of inexperienced divisions. As we have seen, during the period of preinvasion training in the veteran division for which data are available, the large majority of noncoms were combat veterans. For the apprehensive new replacements, these were likely to be "the kind of noncoms one would want to serve under in combat." The results shown in Table 3 are therefore quite meaningful.

The table shows that replacements in Division A were much more likely than men in inexperienced divisions to say that all or most of their noncoms were the kind they would want to serve under in combat. When rank is controlled—taking due account of the understandable tendency of noncoms to think well of themselves—the replacements were fully twice as likely to give the favorable response. While the combat veterans also held their noncoms in higher esteem than did the men in green divisions, the highly favorable attitudes of the replacements cannot have been primarily the result of any kind of psychological osmosis since the veterans were less likely than the replacements to express favorable attitudes.

In so far as the especially favorable attitudes of replacements were due to their special respect for veteran noncoms, the fact that they exceeded veterans as well as men in new divisions in favorable re-

---

* The answer categories were as follows:

___X___ Have been given enough training and experience
_____ Have not been given quite enough training and experience
_____ Have not been given nearly enough training and experience

The category marked X was considered favorable. Privates' answers to this question were shown in Chart I.

† The answer categories were as follows:

___X___ Very well
___X___ Fairly well
_____ Not very well
_____ Not well at all

The categories marked X were considered favorable. In Division B, the phrase "squad of men" was used instead of "group of men" in the question.

‡ The answer categories were as follows:

___X___ I'm ready for combat now
_____ I need a little more of some kinds of training
_____ I need a lot more of some kinds of training

The category marked X was considered favorable.

§ Surveyed in January 1944 (S-128).

sponses is to be expected.   The prestige of combat experience was something that both private and noncom veterans shared, so while the veterans did tend to think well of their noncoms, they were less likely than replacements to stand in admiring awe of them.

The results for Division B, not shown in Table 3, are consistent with the findings for Division A: 64 per cent of the replacements as

TABLE 3

CONFIDENCE IN NONCOMS AMONG ENLISTED VETERANS AND REPLACEMENTS IN LINE INFANTRY COMPANIES OF A VETERAN INFANTRY DIVISION AND ENLISTED MEN IN LINE INFANTRY COMPANIES OF THREE INEXPERIENCED DIVISIONS
(European Theater, April–May 1944. S-129)

QUESTION: "How many of the noncoms in your outfit are the kind you would want to serve under in combat?"

| | PER CENT MAKING FAVORABLE RESPONSES* AMONG: | | |
	Veterans in a veteran division	Replacements in a veteran division	Men in inexperienced divisions
Noncoms	62 (178)	† (21)	53 (2,357)
Privates and Pfc's	36 (427)	58 (406)	25 (7,493)
Married	32 (76)	55 (114)	25 (1,999)
Unmarried, H.S. graduates	32 (94)	54 (114)	24 (1,418)
Unmarried, others	39 (257)	61 (178)	28 (4,076)
Total	44 (605)	58 (427)	33 (9,850)

Numbers in parentheses are the numbers of cases on which percentages are based.

* The answer categories were as follows:

```
  X     All of them are
  X     Most of them are
_____ About half of them are
_____ Few of them are
_____ None of them are
```

The categories marked X were considered favorable.   Privates' answers to this question were shown in Chart I.

† Too few cases to warrant reporting.

compared with 48 per cent of the veterans gave favorable answers, in contrast to 33 per cent of the men in new divisions.

No question on attitudes toward officers was asked of Division A or of the inexperienced divisions for which findings have been presented.   Results for Division B suggest that the pattern of relationships was similar to that for attitudes toward noncoms.   Fifty-five per cent of the replacements, as compared with 29 per cent of the veterans, said that all or most of the officers in their company were the kind they would want to serve under in combat.   This difference is too large to be easily attributable to uncontrolled background factors.

Thus the replacement in a veteran division seems to have had special reasons for favorable attitudes toward his leaders. Factors such as this might well tend to counterbalance the effects on his combat motivation of taking on some of his veteran associates' expressed reluctance to fight. The data, as we have noted, leave open the question as to the extent to which these effects are fundamental or primarily at the verbal level.

Attitudes toward company. Both veterans and replacements in the veteran divisions were more likely to say they felt very proud of their companies than were men in divisions which had yet to see combat, as the first column of Table 4 shows. Regarding the veterans, this difference might be expected; they had earned the right to be proud of their combat unit. The higher degree of pride on the part of replacements relative to men in new divisions cannot, however, be fully attributed to their having adopted the attitudes of the veterans, unless one assumes that they took the veterans' attitudes over *in toto*, since the replacements were fully as likely as the veterans to give the most favorable answer. An interpretation similar to that invoked to account for their highly favorable attitudes toward their noncoms seems most plausible. Both Divisions A and B had seen extensive combat at a time when relatively few units had played a part in the fighting war. Their prestige value to the insecure replacement awaiting a major invasion appears to have been considerable.

One might perhaps expect the veterans to have expressed even greater pride than the replacements. But there were certain factors peculiar to the veterans which were likely to diminish the pride they might otherwise have expressed concerning their battle-scarred outfits. They had some basis, for example, for feeling contemptuous toward the current garrison status of their outfit. The general complex of despair, anxiety, disillusionment, and anger which combat soldiers called "being browned off" could hardly have failed to color their responses. Or, their feeling of pride in the unit may have been diminished by the dilution of their outfits by new men who had not shared the significant experiences of the group. It is possible to make a rough test to see if the last-mentioned factor was important. In one of the Infantry divisions, the attitudes of veterans in Infantry companies which had taken on a relatively high proportion of replacements were compared with those of veterans

TABLE 4

ATTITUDES TOWARD COMPANY AMONG ENLISTED VETERANS AND REPLACEMENTS IN LINE INFANTRY COMPANIES OF TWO VETERAN INFANTRY DIVISIONS AND ENLISTED MEN IN LINE INFANTRY COMPANIES OF THREE INEXPERIENCED DIVISIONS
(European Theater, April–May 1944. S-129)

| | | QUESTIONS: | | |
| | | "Do you feel proud of your company or battery?" | "What sort of teamwork and cooperation is there among the men in your company or battery?" | "On the whole, how is the morale of the men in your company or battery?" |
	Number of cases	*Per cent making favorable responses**	*Per cent making favorable responses†*	*Per cent making favorable responses‡*
All Enlisted Men				
Veteran Division A				
Veterans	*605*	39	72	17
Replacements	*427*	40	82	30
Veteran Division B§				
Veterans	*2,227*	47	69	15
Replacements	*983*	53	85	37
Inexperienced Divisions	*9,850*	26	63	30
Noncoms				
Veteran Division A				
Veterans	*178*	46	76	26
Inexperienced Divisions	*2,357*	38	70	40
Privates and Pfc's				
Veteran Division A				
Veterans	*427*	36	69	14
Replacements	*406*	39	82	30
Inexperienced Divisions	*7,493*	22	61	27
Married				
Veteran Division A				
Veterans	*76*	45	62	10
Replacements	*114*	40	78	32
Inexperienced Divisions	*1,999*	22	59	24
Unmarried, H.S. Graduates				
Veteran Division A				
Veterans	*94*	32	70	16
Replacements	*114*	31	82	21
Inexperienced Divisions	*1,418*	16	60	23
Unmarried, Others				
Veteran Division A				
Veterans	*257*	35	71	14
Replacements	*178*	44	84	34
Inexperienced Divisions	*4,076*	25	63	30

in companies which had had to absorb relatively few of them.[5] Though some significant differences in other attitudes were found between these two groups, there was virtually no difference between them in the extent to which the veterans expressed pride in their company.[6] Although the difference in proportion of replacements in the two groups of companies was not extreme, this suggests that dilution of the company by replacements was not an important factor in keeping the veterans from expressing a higher degree of pride in outfit.

The second question on Table 4, in regard to teamwork and co-operation within the men's companies, confirms the previous findings in so far as both veterans and replacements were more likely than men in green divisions to give favorable responses. On this question, however, replacements were consistently more favorable than veterans. Here again the garrison status of the units at the time of survey may be relevant to the responses of the veterans. In

---

* The answer categories were as follows:

    __X__   Yes, very proud
    _____ Yes, fairly proud
    _____ No, not very proud
    _____ Undecided

The category marked X was considered favorable. Privates' answers to this question were shown in Chart I.

† The answer categories were as follows:

    __X__   Very good
    __X__   Fairly good
    _____ Not very good
    _____ Not good at all

The categories marked X were considered favorable.

‡ The answer categories were as follows:

    __X__   Very high
    __X__   Fairly high
    _____ Just so-so
    _____ Fairly low
    _____ Very low

The categories marked X were considered favorable.

§ Surveyed in January 1944 (S-128).

[5] Division B was used because of the large sample available. Of the 36 line companies, the 8 companies with 36 per cent or more replacements in the sample (average per cent replacements = 39 per cent, number of veterans = 442) were compared with the 9 companies with 25 per cent or less replacements (average per cent replacements = 21 per cent, number of veterans = 567). The sample was a cross section of each company. However, the grouping was in terms of the proportion of replacements in the sample, not in the population.

[6] Forty-nine per cent of veterans from companies with many replacements versus 48 per cent of veterans from companies with few replacements said they were "very proud."

a questionnaire administered to veteran infantrymen in Division B in November 1943,[7] the men were much more likely to say that there had been very good teamwork in battle than that teamwork was very good on the job at the time of the survey:

	QUESTIONS:	
	"What sort of teamwork and cooperation do the men in your company have on the job?"	"What sort of teamwork and cooperation did the men in your company show in actual battle?"
	Per cent making each answer	*Per cent making each answer*
Answer categories		
Very good	38	60
Fairly good	51	31
Not very good	9	6
Not good at all	2	2
No answer	—	1
Total	100	100
Number of cases	*431*	*431*

Again on the hypothesis that the veterans' reactions to their company might be colored unfavorably by the infusion of replacements, the responses of veterans in companies with high and low proportions of replacements were compared in the later survey.[8]   Veterans in companies with a smaller proportion of replacements in the sample were somewhat more likely to say that there was "very good" teamwork and cooperation than veterans in companies with a larger proportion of replacements (26 per cent versus 18 per cent respectively).   This reaction was not unique to the veterans, however. The replacements in the companies in which they were in smaller minority were also slightly more likely than replacements in the other group of companies to say teamwork was very good (39 per cent versus 32 per cent).[9]   And in both groups of companies, replacements gave a considerably more favorable rating than veterans. The most plausible interpretation would seem to be that the assimilation of large numbers of replacements into a company actually did impair to some extent its smoothness of functioning, and that this was recognized by both veterans and replacements.   The influx of

---

[7] S-91.

[8] See footnote 5 for characteristics of groups compared.

[9] Number of cases, 148 and 286 respectively.   The difference is of questionable reliability.

replacements therefore does not seem to have been a specific reason for the veterans' having had less favorable attitudes in this respect than the replacements.

The men's evaluations of the morale of their company—by which they usually tended to mean general well-being, satisfaction, and high spirits, rather than zeal or commitment to the cause—reflect the "browned-off" attitude on the part of the veterans which was

TABLE 5

ATTITUDES TOWARD ARMY REQUIREMENTS AMONG ENLISTED VETERANS AND
REPLACEMENTS IN LINE INFANTRY COMPANIES OF A VETERAN INFANTRY
DIVISION AND ENLISTED MEN IN LINE INFANTRY COMPANIES OF
THREE INEXPERIENCED DIVISIONS
(European Theater, April–May 1944. S-129)

QUESTION: "Do too many of the things you have to do seem unnecessary for making
your outfit or the Army run better?"

| | PER CENT MAKING FAVORABLE RESPONSES* AMONG: | | |
	Veterans in veteran division	Replacements in veteran division	Men in inexperienced divisions
Noncoms	44 (178)	† (21)	49 (2,357)
Privates and Pfc's	37 (427)	53 (406)	39 (7,493)
Married	37 (76)	57 (114)	37 (1,999)
Unmarried, H.S. graduates	32 (94)	39 (114)	30 (1,418)
Unmarried, others	39 (257)	60 (178)	43 (4,076)
Total	39 (605)	54 (427)	41 (9,850)

Numbers in parentheses are the numbers of cases on which percentages are based.

* The answer categories were as follows:

```
  X   Almost all of them seem necessary
  X   Some, but not too many, seem unnecessary
      Too many seem unnecessary
      Far too many seem unnecessary
```

The categories marked X were considered favorable. Privates' answers to this question were shown in Chart I.

† Too few cases to warrant reporting.

previously mentioned.   The question is also shown in Table 4. The veterans were considerably less likely than men in inexperienced divisions to say that the morale of the men in their company was high.   Interestingly enough, the replacements were no less likely than men in green divisions to say that the men in their company had high morale—in spite of the divergent testimony of their veteran associates.   One would expect that the replacements' answers to this question would be colored by the less favorable attitudes of

TABLE 6

ATTITUDES TOWARD PHYSICAL CONDITION AMONG ENLISTED VETERANS AND
REPLACEMENTS IN LINE INFANTRY COMPANIES OF TWO VETERAN INFANTRY
DIVISIONS AND ENLISTED MEN IN LINE COMPANIES OF
THREE INEXPERIENCED DIVISIONS
(European Theater, April–May 1944. S-129)

| | | QUESTIONS: | | |
| | | "Do you think that you are in good physical condition?" | "Do you think that you are in tough enough physical condition for going into combat?" | "If and when you get into combat, how well do you think you will stand up under battle conditions?" |
	Number of cases	Per cent making favorable responses*	Per cent making favorable responses†	Per cent making favorable responses‡
All Enlisted Men				
Veteran Division A				
Veterans	*605*	37	21	50
Replacements	*427*	57	32	64
Veteran Division B§				
Veterans	*2,227*	31	17	44
Replacements	*983*	61	34	70
Inexperienced Divisions	*9,850*	61	41	72
Noncoms				
Veteran Division A				
Veterans	*178*	41	26	68
Inexperienced Divisions	*2,357*	74	55	86
Privates and Pfc's				
Veteran Division A				
Veterans	*427*	35	19	43
Replacements	*406*	56	31	63
Inexperienced Divisions	*7,493*	57	36	68
Married				
Veteran Division A				
Veterans	*76*	28	19	39
Replacements	*114*	53	29	55
Inexperienced Divisions	*1,999*	53	33	65
Unmarried, H.S. Graduates				
Veteran Division A				
Veterans	*94*	38	24	48
Replacements	*114*	60	31	61
Inexperienced Divisions	*1,418*	64	40	72
Unmarried, Others				
Veteran Division A				
Veterans	*257*	36	18	42
Replacements	*178*	57	32	70
Inexperienced Divisions	*4,076*	57	37	68

the veterans. Evidence to be presented later makes it seem likely that the lack of difference between replacements and men in new divisions represents a counterbalancing of factors, the special grounds for higher morale on the part of replacements in veteran divisions being compensated by the influence of the lower morale of the veterans around them.

Attitudes toward Army requirements. The pattern of the men's attitudes toward Army requirements is much the same as in the case of their attitude toward their noncoms. This time, in the proportion who said that all or most of the things they had to do seemed necessary, the veterans did not differ from men in inexperienced divisions. The replacements in veteran divisions, on the other hand, were consistently more likely than others to accept demands upon them as necessary, as Table 5 shows. The results for Division B, not shown in the table, are in agreement, 47 per cent of the veterans but 59 per cent of the replacements giving favorable answers.

These findings appear to be another instance of the way in which the prestige of veteran status evoked a favorable reaction from the replacement thrust in the midst of a veteran organization. Since we have seen that the replacement tended to have high respect for his predominantly veteran leaders, it is not surprising that this should have led him to a more compliant attitude toward the demands and requirements they made on him.

Attitudes toward physical condition. Detailed findings on three questions presented in Table 6 confirm the preliminary finding that

---

* The answer categories were as follows:

_X_	Yes, very good
_X_	Yes, fairly good
____	No
____	Undecided

The categories marked *X* were considered favorable. Privates' answers to this question were shown in Chart I.

† The answer categories were as follows:

_X_	Yes
____	No
____	Undecided

The category marked *X* was considered favorable.

‡ The answer categories were as follows:

_X_	Very well
_X_	Fairly well
____	Not very well
____	Not well at all

The categories marked *X* were considered favorable.

§ Surveyed in January 1944 (S-128).

TABLE 7

CONVICTION ABOUT THE WAR AMONG ENLISTED VETERANS AND REPLACEMENTS IN
LINE INFANTRY COMPANIES OF TWO VETERAN INFANTRY DIVISIONS AND
ENLISTED MEN IN LINE INFANTRY COMPANIES OF
THREE INEXPERIENCED DIVISIONS

(European Theater, April–May 1944. S-129)

| | | QUESTIONS: | | |
| | | "Do you ever get the feeling that this war is not worth fighting?" | "How much do the things that this war is being fought over mean to you personally?" | "Which comes closest to your idea of how hard it is going to be to beat the Germans?" |
	Number of cases	*Per cent making favorable responses**	*Per cent making favorable responses†*	*Per cent making realistic responses‡*
All Enlisted Men				
Veteran Division A				
Veterans	*605*	41	62	67
Replacements	*427*	48	71	56
Veteran Division B§				
Veterans	*2,227*	—	67	76
Replacements	*983*	—	75	62
Inexperienced Divisions	*9,850*	53	74	54
Noncoms				
Veteran Division A				
Veterans	*178*	41	64	69
Inexperienced Divisions	*2,357*	59	80	51
Privates and Pfc's				
Veteran Division A				
Veterans	*427*	41	61	66
Replacements	*406*	48	71	56
Inexperienced Divisions	*7,493*	51	72	55
Married				
Veteran Division A				
Veterans	*76*	35	55	65
Replacements	*114*	49	76	55
Inexperienced Divisions	*1,999*	50	72	57
Unmarried, H.S. Graduates				
Veteran Division A				
Veterans	*94*	39	60	71
Replacements	*114*	40	65	59
Inexperienced Divisions	*1,418*	51	71	63
Unmarried, Others				
Veteran Division A				
Veterans	*257*	44	64	64
Replacements	*178*	51	72	55
Inexperienced Divisions	*4,076*	52	72	52

the main difference in attitudes toward physical condition was between combat veterans and all other men.   As Chapter 2 pointed
out, the poorer physical condition that veterans tended to report
probably involved both physical and motivational factors.   The
minor differences in pattern for the three questions are also of some
interest.   On the first question, which simply asked the men "Do
you think you are in good physical condition?" there were no conse-
quential differences between the replacements in either veteran
division and the men in inexperienced divisions.   The similarity in
the men's answers undoubtedly parallels similarity in the men's actual physical condition.   The remaining two questions asked for
an evaluation relative to the ordeal of combat which would put their
physique and stamina to the test.   On both of these questions there
was some tendency for the replacements to be slightly less likely
than men in new divisions to answer favorably.   The tendency on
one of the questions is slight, with minor inconsistencies; on the
other question, it is consistent for all subgroups.   As in the case of
willingness for combat, the replacements occupy an intermediate
position between the men in inexperienced outfits and the veterans.

This secondary pattern of differences suggests an interpretation
similar to that given for the replacements' intermediate standing on
willingness for combat.   The degree of reluctance for combat which
the replacements acquired from their veteran associates was a factor
tending to make them more prone than men in new divisions to use
their physical condition as an "out" and express doubts that they

---

* The answer categories were as follows:

	Very often
	Sometimes
_X_	Only once in a great while
_X_	Never

The categories marked X were considered favorable.   Privates' answers to this question were shown
in Chart I

† The answer categories were as follows:

	They mean everything to me
_X_	They mean quite a bit to me
	They don't mean very much to me
	Not sure whether they mean anything or not

The categories marked X were considered favorable.

‡ The answer categories were as follows:

	It will not be very hard
	It will be a tough job but our losses won't be too heavy
_X_	It will be a tough job with heavy losses of men and equipment

The category marked X was considered realistic.

§ Surveyed in January 1944 (S-128).   (One of the questions was not included in the questionnaire.)

were in tough enough shape for combat.   Or—which is not so very
different—they may have acquired from the veterans a more forbidding conception of the stress they would be called upon to withstand in combat, and were therefore more likely to doubt their endurance.   The differences between replacements and members of
new outfits remain minor, however, and the replacements' absolute
evaluation of their physical condition was apparently not influenced
by their having joined a veteran outfit.

Conviction about the war.   None of the three questions which were
asked the men concerning their beliefs and convictions about the
war revealed any effects of replacement status which differentiated
inexperienced men in veteran divisions from men in entirely new
outfits.   Table 7 does not show any consistent differences between
replacement and new division groups.   There were, however, consistent differences between the responses of the combat veterans
and both the other groups of men.

As the table shows, veterans were somewhat less likely than the
others to say that they rarely had the feeling that the war was not
worth fighting.   This finding for men in Division A is, incidentally,
in disagreement with data presented in Chapter 3, where it was
shown that the average pattern of response of combat veterans in
several divisions in both Europe and the Pacific to this question
was not significantly different from the pattern of response in the
same inexperienced divisions for which data are reported here.
Since Division A was the only veteran division in which it was possible to compare veterans and replacements on this question, little
weight can be attached to the slightly less favorable responses of
the veterans, which may have been fairly specific to Division A.
The second question, which asked the men how much the things the
war was being fought for meant to them, gave essentially the same
results.   Since matters of conviction about the war were probably
of relatively peripheral concern to most of the men, occasions in
which the veterans could convey their point of view on this subject
to the replacements may well have arisen less frequently than in
the case of matters more vital to their personal interests.

One of the reasons why veterans were perhaps less likely to express a high degree of ideological conviction may have been that
their experiences in combat left them with a keener awareness of
the personal costs of war.   If the untried infantrymen were more
likely than veterans to say that they rarely felt that the war was
not worth fighting principally because they had a distant and un-

derestimated conception of the price which would be exacted from them, who can say with certainty that their initial "faith in the cause" was really higher than that of the veterans? The third question in Table 7 shows, in line with expectations, that the veterans were more likely than the other groups to say that it would be "a tough job with heavy losses" to beat the Germans. The question as to whether this response was good or bad in terms of combat motivation has already been discussed in Chapter 3. The attitude it represents was associated with the veterans' greater reluctance for combat, yet the expectation of a long and tough war was realistic, and such favorable motivation as they retained in spite of their more grim outlook may have been less vulnerable than that of inexperienced men.

There is no indication, however, that being in a veteran outfit had any effect on the replacements' expectations about the difficulty of the job ahead. One would have expected, from the previous findings, that replacements would be more likely than men of new divisions to anticipate a tough job.

The psychological climate of a unit as a factor in the attitudes of replacements who join it. The intermediate standing of replacements between the combat veterans and the men in inexperienced divisions in regard to willingness for combat led to the interpretation that in some respects replacements tended to adopt the attitudes of the veterans around them. Fortunately, additional data are available for Division A which provide a partial check on this assumption. Some three months before the survey in April 1944, from which the data hitherto reported were drawn, the division had been surveyed with another questionnaire which included many of the same items. The January survey was made prior to the main influx of replacements into the companies of the division. It therefore provides information on the psychological climate prevailing in the subunits of the division at the time that the replacements were being assimilated. If the replacements' attitudes were affected by those of their veteran associates to any important extent, one would expect that replacements who joined companies in which strongly favorable attitudes prevailed would themselves come to have more favorable attitudes than those who joined companies in which the prevalent point of view of the veterans was unfavorable.

On a number of questions, the responses of combat veterans in the January survey were therefore determined separately for each of the 36 lettered Infantry companies of the division. For each ques-

CHART II

ATTITUDES OF REPLACEMENTS AND VETERANS IN INFANTRY LINE COMPANIES GROUPED ACCORDING TO THE RESPONSES WHICH VETERANS IN THE SAME COMPANIES HAD MADE TO THE SAME QUESTION THREE MONTHS PREVIOUSLY
(Division A, European Theater, April 1944, S-129, Grouped by Results from S-128, January 1944)

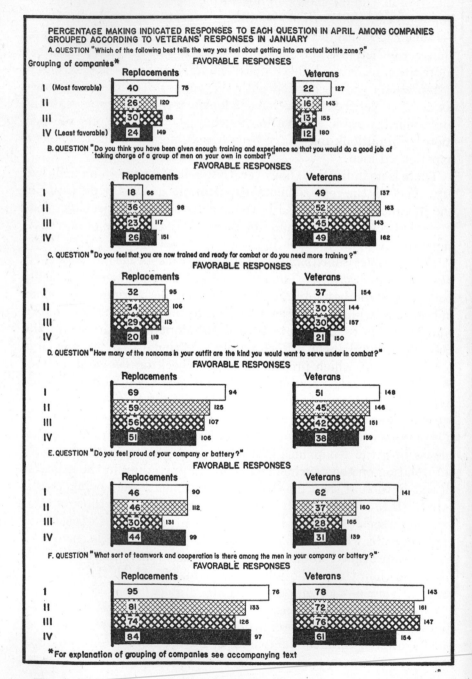

The numbers following the bars are the numbers of cases on which percentages are based.

CHART II (Continued)

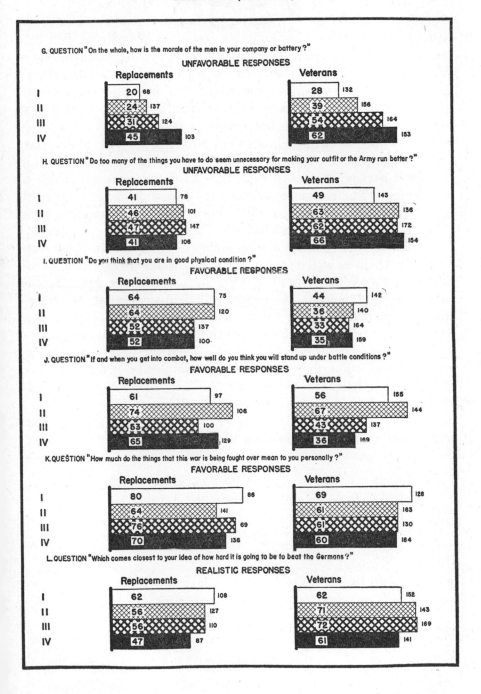

G. QUESTION "On the whole, how is the morale of the men in your company or battery?"

UNFAVORABLE RESPONSES

Replacements

I 20 | 68
II 24 | 137
III 31 | 124
IV 45 | 103

Veterans

I 28 | 132
II 39 | 156
III 54 | 164
IV 62 | 153

H. QUESTION "Do too many of the things you have to do seem unnecessary for making your outfit or the Army run better?"

UNFAVORABLE RESPONSES

Replacements

I 41 | 78
II 46 | 101
III 47 | 147
IV 41 | 106

Veterans

I 49 | 143
II 63 | 136
III 62 | 172
IV 66 | 154

I. QUESTION "Do you think that you are in good physical condition?"

FAVORABLE RESPONSES

Replacements

I 64 | 75
II 64 | 120
III 52 | 137
IV 52 | 100

Veterans

I 44 | 142
II 36 | 140
III 33 | 164
IV 35 | 159

J. QUESTION "If and when you get into combat, how well do you think you will stand up under battle conditions?"

FAVORABLE RESPONSES

Replacements

I 61 | 97
II 74 | 106
III 53 | 100
IV 65 | 129

Veterans

I 56 | 155
II 67 | 144
III 43 | 137
IV 36 | 169

K. QUESTION "How much do the things that this war is being fought over mean to you personally?"

FAVORABLE RESPONSES

Replacements

I 80 | 86
II 64 | 141
III 76 | 69
IV 70 | 136

Veterans

I 69 | 128
II 61 | 163
III 61 | 130
IV 60 | 184

L. QUESTION "Which comes closest to your idea of how hard it is going to be to beat the Germans?"

REALISTIC RESPONSES

Replacements

I 62 | 108
II 56 | 127
III 56 | 110
IV 47 | 87

Veterans

I 62 | 152
II 71 | 143
III 72 | 169
IV 61 | 141

tion, the companies were ranked according to the proportion of veterans in them who gave favorable responses,[10] and classified into four groups of nine companies each. The grouping was made independently for each question. In respect to each question, group I consisted of the 9 companies in which the proportion of veterans giving favorable responses was the highest, group IV included the 9 companies in which the proportion of veterans giving favorable responses was lowest, and groups II and III contained the 18 intermediate companies. The men's responses to the same questions in the April survey were then determined for the same groupings of companies. The responses of veterans and replacements in April by company, grouped according to the responses of veterans in these companies in January, are shown in Chart II.[11]

It is important to know the responses of veterans[12] in these companies in April, as well as those of the replacements in which we are primarily interested. They enable us to tell if the groupings of companies by the veterans' responses in January actually represent stable differences in the psychological atmosphere of the companies which in fact provided different psychological environments for the replacements or if, on the other hand, the initial differences were an artifact of question unreliability or sampling error or other factors. By simple statistical regression one would expect the differences between responses of veterans in group I and group IV companies to be smaller in April than in January. But unless the January pattern of differences for a question remained to some extent in April, there would be no reason to anticipate differences in the attitudes of

---

[10] The response categories arbitrarily singled out as favorable were the same as have been identified in Tables 1–7, with two exceptions. For these exceptions, see footnote 13.

[11] The basis on which the companies were grouped is shown in the following table which records the proportion of veterans giving the designated responses to each question in January. The companies were ranked for each question according to the percentage in each who gave the designated responses, and divided into four groups of nine companies for each question. Questions are identified by the letters assigned to them in Chart II.

Grouping of Companies	A		B		C		D		E		F		G		H		I		J		K		L	
	%	N	%	N	%	N	%	N	%	N	%	N	%	N	%	N	%	N	%	N	%	N	%	N
I	16	593	73	457	38	569	65	574	67	622	89	624	29	563	47	513	47	539	63	571	73	509	82	571
II	11	599	61	620	28	663	56	727	54	586	79	693	43	668	61	656	32	700	50	628	69	613	77	616
III	7	645	58	757	20	558	45	531	41	675	71	597	55	676	67	654	26	677	42	663	67	703	71	639
IV	3	645	47	647	14	691	33	649	27	598	60	567	76	574	73	655	14	564	30	619	54	656	61	655

[12] Not the same individuals as were surveyed in January. Samples were drawn by last digit of Army Serial Number to avoid questioning the same men twice.

the replacements in the different groups of companies, even if the attitudes of veterans were actually influential on the replacements.

Of course the attitudes of the veterans in a company were only one of several factors which could conceivably result in differential effects on the attitudes of replacements who joined it. The nature of the company leadership, for example, could produce similar effects on the attitudes of veteran and replacement members alike. In regard to some attitudes, one might expect leadership to be more important, and in regard to others, the attitudes of veterans in the company. However, the data themselves cannot prove that positive findings were the result of one or another of these influences. Positive findings are consistent with the hypothesis that the replacements were influenced by the veterans' attitudes, and they are a necessary consequence if this hypothesis is correct—except that the results may have been diluted by the effects of question unreliability.

In Chart II the relevant comparisons are presented for a number of questions, in the same order in which they were discussed in the previous sections.[13] The basis on which the companies were grouped for each question in terms of veterans' responses in January is summarized in footnote 11.

In regard to willingness for combat, the results for Question A on the chart are in agreement with our hypothesis. The pattern of responses of the veterans in April indicates a persistence over the three-month period of the attitudes elicited in January. The psychological atmosphere provided by the veterans' attitudes was therefore different for replacements who joined companies in one or another of the four groups. While the pattern of the replacements' responses is not fully consistent, the difference between the attitudes of those who joined companies in group I, in which the highest proportion of veterans were favorable, and the attitudes of those who joined group IV companies, in which the smallest proportion of veterans were favorable, is statistically significant. Forty per cent of the former as compared to 24 per cent of the latter indicated relatively high willingness for combat.

The findings in the earlier part of this chapter gave no particular

---

[13] The arbitrary designation of answer categories as "favorable," etc., was the same employed earlier in the chapter, except for Questions G and H, where the two least favorable categories were taken as "unfavorable." See Tables 1–7 for wording of answer categories and designation of favorable responses.

reason to expect the replacements' feelings of self-confidence to be markedly influenced by the attitudes of the veterans around them. Replacements in the four groups of companies did not differ consistently in regard to saying that they had been given enough training and experience to do a good job of taking charge of a group of men in combat, but this is not informative about the effect of the climate of veteran opinion in this area, since as Chart II shows (see Question B), the January differences in the veterans' attitudes turned out to be unstable. On Question C, which asked the men if they felt they were trained and ready for combat, there is some indication of differences in the expected direction. As the section on self-confidence suggested, this question appears to have touched indirectly on the sensitive point of the men's willingness for combat, and for that reason differences would perhaps be expected.

There are pronounced differences in their attitudes toward their noncoms between replacements who joined companies in which the veterans held their noncoms in high respect and those who joined units in which the noncoms were held in lower esteem. The veterans' attitudes on this score also seem to have been relatively stable. In this case, however, it seems probable that the attitudes of the veterans were less influential on the replacements than were the actual qualities of the noncoms which were presumably responsible for the differences in the veterans' attitudes. Taking this finding in conjunction with what has been said in the section on attitudes toward leaders, it can be said that while the replacements were in general more likely than veterans to be favorable to their noncoms, those who joined companies in which the veterans viewed their noncoms favorably were even more likely than others to have favorable attitudes.

In regard to pride in company and what the men had to say of the teamwork and cooperation that prevailed, there is little indication of difference in the attitudes of replacements entering companies in which the earlier attitudes of veterans had been favorable or unfavorable. But, as the chart shows (see Questions E and F), there was relatively little stable difference in the psychological atmosphere provided by the veterans in the companies as originally grouped. If, as earlier considerations suggested, the distinctive features of the replacements' pride in outfit developed primarily as a response to being in a prestigeful, battle-tested company rather than through adopting the veterans' attitudes, positive findings would not be expected here.

A striking and consistent pattern of differences again appears on the question asking the men to evaluate the morale of the men in their companies. It would indeed be a matter for surprise if the differences did not appear. The earlier finding that replacements were more likely than veterans to say that their company morale was high can thus be supplemented. Evidently the replacements were not merely projecting their own higher morale. While they consistently were more likely than veterans to make a favorable rating, they were sufficiently in touch with the psychological realities of their situation so that companies which ranked high in terms of the responses of the veterans also ranked high in terms of those of the replacements. The data also indicate a fair degree of stability in company morale as rated by the men.

The veterans' responses in regard to the necessity of Army requirements (Question H) showed little stability over the three-month period, so the lack of differences between replacements in the four groups of companies would be expected. On the same grounds, the absence of consistent patterns in the replacements' answers concerning their physical condition (Questions I and J) and their convictions about the war (Question K) is in line with expectations.

In regard to the final question on the chart, "Which comes closest to your idea of how hard it is going to be to beat the Germans?" there is a tendency of moderate reliability for replacements in the four groups of companies to differ in the same direction as the veterans surveyed in January. However, the differences in responses of veterans which were the basis of grouping the companies turned out to be highly unstable over the three-month period.

On three questions, then, unambiguous patterns in the replacements' responses paralleled patterns in the responses of the veterans in the same groups of companies: willingness for combat, attitude towards noncoms, and evaluation of the morale of men in the company. In the case of the last two of these, it seems likely that the results are best accounted for in terms of existing differences in company leadership and morale—though at the same time the veterans may well have helped to define the situation for the replacements. The agreement on patterns of response concerning willingness for combat is such as would have been expected if the replacements had to some extent adopted the attitudes of the veterans in their companies. Willingness—and reluctance—for combat is an attitude which one would expect to reveal influences of veterans on replacements if such occurred at all, since it was of immediate and vital concern to both veteran and replacement groups, and in an area in which the veteran could speak with especial prestige and authority.

The ways in which the process of assimilation to a veteran division affected the attitudes of new replacements thus appear to have stemmed primarily from the aura of prestige attaching to veteran status. On the one hand, the replacement tended to adopt some of the reluctance about going into combat that was expressed by the combat veterans whom he admired, and, on the other hand, the fact that most of his leaders were veterans assured them his respect and made him especially compliant to their requirements. In a number of respects, however, his point of view differed little from that of men awaiting combat in entirely inexperienced divisions.

The Career of a Replacement

The assimilation of replacements into veteran outfits before combat has been considered at length both because of the significance of the process and because of the amount of data available concerning it. By no means all replacements, however, had a chance to become fully assimilated before they were thrown into action. And even for those who were fortunate enough to join their units away from the front, the process of assimilation was not the whole story of being a replacement. The present section will, therefore, sketch some of the important aspects of the replacement's career. Since the data available leave much to be desired, the treatment will be brief.

The overseas career of the replacement began in one of the chain of replacement (or reinforcement) depots through which he filtered until he finally filled a requisition from some depleted combat unit. His experiences in the "repple depple" (replacement depot) are of some interest for the bearing they may have had on the significance to him of joining his combat outfit. Aside from variable sources of discomfort and dissatisfaction which were subject to correction as experience, time, and facilities permitted, there were certain apparently irreducible sources of psychological disturbance which remained a fairly constant feature of the experience of replacements in depots. These centered about the fact that replacements were casuals, who were handled in bulk without the benefit of permanent leaders from whom they could expect a measure of personal interest, and without the support of social ties and the security of having an established niche in some organization. The new replacement, fresh from training in the United States, who had never been assigned to a permanent unit, might not have expected anything different and might therefore have felt little special cause for dissatisfaction with depot life. Nevertheless, the contrast between the psychological environment of a replacement depot at its best and that of a permanent unit was great. The following comments, drawn from a survey of a small number of men in a replacement depot in the European theater (September 1944), probably reflect a minority reaction, yet the conditions to which they were reacting were of general significance:

We want to feel that we are a part of something. As a replacement we are apart from everything. You feel as if you were being pushed out of a place blindfolded. You feel totally useless and unimportant. They treat us like idiots and we don't disappoint them. "I don't know" is the rule.

Being a replacement is just like being an orphan. You are away from anybody you know and feel lost and lonesome.

The uncertainty of mail delivery to a transient population withheld another source of support normally available to the soldier overseas. Often a replacement would get no mail during the entire time he was in the replacement system; at best he received it irregularly and in batches. It was an important source of specific complaints of the men. In a survey made among new replacements from the mainland in replacement depots in the Pacific in June 1945, complaints about mail service were more frequent than about any other aspect of living conditions and facilities about which questions were asked.[14]

In contrast to the casual replacements were the cadre or permanent party of the depot. In their dealings with droves of replacements, the cadre could not avoid a degree of impersonality. The majority of new replacements probably took the situation more or less for granted. In the survey of the replacement system in the Pacific after the end of the European war but before the end of the Pacific war was in prospect, 63 per cent of the new replacements checked a favorable answer, "they have done all they could" in answer to the question, "Do you feel that the 'permanent party' at

---

[14] S-231.

this Replacement Depot have done all they could to help you?" [15] Those who indicated that "they could have done a little more" or "a lot more" were asked, "In what ways, if any, do you think they could have been more helpful?"   While their answers to this question are a minority view, they nevertheless probably reflect more general features of casual status which some took for granted.   The criticisms centered mainly on the attitude of the cadre—their lack of concern for the problems of replacements as individuals.   Such critical comments as the following reflect this:

Everyone is looked upon as a rookie.

They (the cadre) could of taken their time.   They tried to get through with us too fast so they would have a chance to set on their ass.

Or the following comments from combat replacements in a depot in Europe—the latter by a replacement officer:

Those cadres are no more experienced than we are. . . .   The cadres would be lost without that whistle.   Men three or four years in the Army are treated like two-year-olds.   Cadre treats us like dirt under their feet.

The only suggestion I would have is that officers in charge at depots have more interest in the men who pass through and try to treat them less like lumber.

A similar question asked of the cadre in the Pacific survey elicited a similar assortment of critical comments:

Casuals as a rule are forgotten men.   I would like to see as much as possible individual attention to their problems.

Let's have better treatment of the casuals by the cadre.   The general tendency is to figure that they can be run through like so many cattle.

Probably the most salient psychological characteristic of depot life for the replacement was that the situation led to a state of anxious uncertainty without opportunity for resolving the tension.

---

[15] S-231 (N = 1,276).   On a parallel question, about the same proportion of cadremen were favorable or critical and, as their written-in comments indicated, for the same reasons.   The question was: "Do you feel that the permanent party at this Replacement Depot are doing all they can to help the replacements (casuals) at this Depot?"

_____ They are doing all they can
_____ They could do a little more
_____ They could do a lot more

Sixty-seven per cent (N = 828) checked the first category.

The all-important questions, "When will I be sent into combat?" and "What outfit will they send me to?" could naturally not be answered ahead of time.   Besides these crucial questions, new replacements had a host of others, many concerned with "what will combat really be like?"   Some indication of the extent of uncertainty is shown by the fact that the sizable minority of 35 per cent of the new replacements in the Pacific checked "haven't any idea" in answer to the question, "Do you think you will be assigned to the same kind of Army job for which you are *now* classified?" [16]   A cadreman in one of the Pacific replacement depots described the situation vividly as it applied to relations between casuals and cadremen:

The principal hardship we all work under is *uncertainty!* It should be possible in dealing with men's questions to be able to approach the definite answer. Inability to do this hurts the morale of these replacements and casuals and thus they lose confidence in us and everything the depot stands for. It affects their work, their cooperative spirit, and makes the job of everyone doubly hard. Surely we can be able to tell a man that he will be paid within a certain time, and how long he will be here under certain conditions. It is the *little* things that count, these men are still soldiers but they will never do much to help improve themselves if they are unable to find out things they should know. Most of them feel: "Why take any interest, nobody knows a damn thing or what's going on or why around here!"

At best, the cadre could hardly answer the replacements' many questions to their full satisfaction.

Sometimes the replacement remained in one or another depot for weeks or months before being assigned to his permanent organization.   In a survey of a cross section of line infantrymen in combat divisions in Italy made in April 1945, 11 per cent of those who had joined their outfits as replacements said they had spent 3 months or more in a replacement depot before joining their combat unit, while an additional 30 per cent said they had spent from 1 to 3 months in a depot.[17]   At the time of the survey, 44 per cent of these replacements had already seen over 6 months of combat, so the figures reflect conditions in the replacement system which may have been changed by the time the survey was made.   Prolonged delay

---

[16] S-231.   1,276 cases.

[17] (S-177), 1,766 cases.   The question asked was: "How long were you at the Replacement Depot before you joined the outfit you went into combat with the last time?"

_____ I didn't go through a Replacement Depot	_____ 2 months up to 3 months
	_____ 3 months up to 4 months
_____ Less than 2 weeks	_____ 4 months up to 6 months
_____ 2 weeks up to 1 month	_____ Over 6 months
_____ 1 month up to 2 months	

within the depots of the replacement system can only have accentu-
ated the replacement's tendency toward feelings of being lost and
his uncertainty.   A comment by a former replacement in France
suggests some of the possible psychological effects:

Before I got out of the pool I practically got the willies.   I was in depots 5 weeks,
and in two different centers in that time.   After so long a man doesn't know
whether he's coming or going; he's unsettled and anxious and finally just doesn't
give a good goddam.

Among the group surveyed in Italy, however, no lasting effects of
prolonged stays in a replacement depot could be found in the men's
attitudes.   With education and time in combat held constant, the
attitudes of replacement privates who had spent less than a month
in a depot were compared with those of replacement privates who
had spent a longer period in one.   The two groups did not differ
appreciably or consistently in respect to such things as saying that
combat became more frightening, that they were more afraid or that
they were less afraid than other men, that they had confidence in
their officers, that they liked to work with the other fellows in their
company, that they had no use for a soldier who goes AWOL from
combat, or in the extent to which they reported psychoneurotic
symptoms.   However, it is possible that selective factors may have
operated to eliminate from combat and from the sample those who
had been most affected.   At any event, the lack of differences on a
questionnaire administered to the men after most of them had been
in combat for a period of months does not mean that there were no
immediate and short-run effects on the frame of mind in which the
men joined their units.

The sum of the replacement's experiences in the depots of the replacement system was therefore likely to make him welcome many
aspects of a permanent assignment—though by no means to welcome combat itself.   Even in this regard, however, the termination
of anxious uncertainty was probably in some respects a psychological
gain.   The new combat man could say to himself, for better or for
worse, "This is it."

There were, as we have noted, two general sorts of situations in
which the replacement could first join his outfit: while the outfit
was actively engaged with the enemy, or while it was withdrawn
from the line and in rest phase, training, or reserve.   Since the need
for replacements was heaviest during prolonged and costly action,
many men first joined their units during heavy combat in spite of

official attempts to avoid this procedure as much as possible. The conditions under which replacements joined their outfits naturally varied according to the character of the campaign. In Italy, a survey of a cross section of veteran infantrymen made in early April 1945 found that 64 per cent of the men said they had joined their outfit overseas as replacements. Of these men, half said they went into combat less than 3 days after they joined their outfit, as may be seen in Table 8. Probably most of this 33 per cent of the

TABLE 8

LENGTH OF TIME REPLACEMENTS WERE WITH THEIR OUTFIT BEFORE
ENTERING COMBAT

(Cross Section of Infantrymen in Line Companies of Four Infantry
Divisions, Italy, April 1945, S-177)

QUESTION: "How long were you with your present outfit before you went into action?"	Per cent in each category	
Original members of outfit	34	
Replacements	64	
With outfit less than 3 days before seeing action		33
With outfit 3 days up to 1 week before seeing action		12
With outfit 1 week up to 1 month before seeing action		12
With outfit over 1 month before seeing action		7
No answer	2	
Total	100	
Number of cases	1,766	

men joined their outfits in the line. At all events, neither they nor the additional 12 per cent who went into action within a week after joining their units had much opportunity to become integrated with their units before meeting the test of combat.

Some aspects of the assimilation of replacements into veteran units not in the line have already been discussed. The replacement who joined his unit in combat had two adjustments to make simultaneously: to his new outfit and to combat itself. Lacking established ties to buddies as well as experience in teamwork with them, he would appear to be at a distinct disadvantage in his first combat experience. The questionnaire data from Italy fail to show effects sufficiently enduring to appear in the men's responses after nearly half of the former replacements had been in combat for more than 6 months. With rank, education, and length of time in combat controlled, the replacements who had entered combat less than 3 days after joining their outfits were compared with those who had the benefit of a longer acclimation period on the same questions that were investigated in relation to the length of time the men had spent in a replacement depot.   With one exception discussed later,[18] no consistent differences appeared.   Since casualties may have had a selective effect, the possibility that there may still have been long-run effects on the men's attitudes cannot be completely ruled out.

But the data tell nothing about the magnitude of the more probable short-run effects, which could be important enough to a man seeing his first combat among strangers in the midst of the confusion of an offensive.   Replacements coming into the line at night or during a rapidly moving combat situation could enter combat without even the most elementary knowledge of their outfit and of the men they were supposed to work with.   This point was rather frequently mentioned by combat veterans in interviews, the following comment being illustrative:

These replacements should know the organization of the outfit.   We've had casualties come to us and when you ask them what company they're in they say 9th company or their outfit is "B" Company, 2d Battalion—and they don't know what regiment even.   (Battalion Aid Station Medic, France)

I have seen men killed or captured when even their squad leaders didn't know their names.   (Infantryman, Italy)

With the important exception that the replacement joining his outfit in combat had to make acquaintance with battle at the same time as he was establishing himself in his new outfit, the processes by which he was assimilated to his outfit probably did not differ greatly from those we have already discussed.   His respect for the old-timers as well as self-interest moved him to model his actions closely on theirs.   It was to the interest of the old-timers in turn to work the replacement into the unit as quickly and completely as possible.   This was the more acceptable for them as the insecure replacement offered little challenge to their acknowledged status.   Among a small random group of hospitalized wounded men who were surveyed in the European theater, 82 per cent of the former replacements who were asked whether or not the old-timers tried to pass on their experience and be helpful said "they did as much as they could," while 12 per cent said "they could have done a little

---

[18] See Table 9.

more than they did." [19] The testimony of combat veterans returned to the States at the end of the war is in agreement with this.
Eighty-eight per cent agreed with the statement, "When a replacement comes into an outfit during combat, the veterans usually try
to help him out all they can." [20]

One special type of replacement was not welcomed by the veterans: the replacement who came in with a noncom's rank, presumably
to take the place of a noncom casualty. Among five divisions surveyed in Europe and the Pacific, an average of only 39 per cent of
the veteran infantrymen said they had not had in their company
new replacements who came in as noncoms. Of those who indicated
that they had had experience with noncom replacements, an average of 55 per cent said they thought the practice was bad.[21] The
problem of replacements in grade was not peculiar to combat units,
but entailed more serious potential effects there. These men may
formerly have been cadremen at training centers in the States, or
casuals sent out from divisions still in the States. Later in the war,
in some theaters, many physically qualified men in noncombat units
overseas were retrained for combat duty, some of whom possessed
high ratings from their previous service jobs. The noncom replacement himself often felt insecure because he doubted his qualifications
for combat leadership. In some cases such noncoms requested to
be broken to the grade of private. From the point of view of members of the unit to which such a replacement was assigned, there was
the double objection that replacements in grade made it impossible
to reward by promotion deserving men within the unit, and that
the men in the unit could not have the confidence in replacement
noncoms that they would have had in battle-tested veterans of
their own unit.

---

[19] S-165, August 1944. One hundred and thirty had been replacements. The question was: "Do you think the men who had been in your outfit for some time tried to
pass on what they had learned and tried to be of help to the replacements?"

_____ They did as much as they could
_____ They could have done a little more than they did
_____ They could have done a great deal more than they did

[20] Combat veterans from a cross section of white enlisted men in continental United
States, November 1945 (S-234 B), 243 cases.

[21] S-91, European theater, November 1943, and S-100, Pacific theaters, March–April
1944. The figures presented are an unweighted average of the separate values for the
various divisions. The question was: "During combat, how did you feel about new
replacements who came in as noncoms?"

_____ This did not happen in my company
_____ I thought it was OK
_____ I did not care much one way or the other
_____ I thought it was bad

Under the pressure of necessity and the bonds formed by shared experience, the typical replacement may have been integrated fairly rapidly into his social group.   Such was the retrospective testimony of the group of hospitalized former combat replacements surveyed in the European theater,[22] though the sample was small and the question has unfortunate ambiguities:

How long was it after you arrived in your present outfit [23] before you felt you really belonged in the outfit and were an important part of it?

Answer categories	Per cent giving each answer
After the first day	14
After the first few days	33
After the first week	18
After several weeks	9
Never felt this way	13
No answer	13
Total	100
Number of cases	130

As has been said, most attitudes of the former replacements in the survey of infantrymen in Italy[24] were not distinguishable from those of the original members of units with equivalent rank, education, and combat time.   No major or consistent differences between the groups appeared in regard to whether or not the men said that they found combat more frightening the more they saw of it, that they got frightened or worried more often than most of the other men, that they had confidence in their officers as combat leaders, or that they often got the feeling that a battle was not worth the cost. There was practically no difference at all between the veterans and replacements, when the above controls were applied, in the number of items on a scale of psychoneurotic symptoms which they admitted.

There was, however, one indirect indication that the integration of the replacements with their units may not have been complete. As Table 9 shows, the men who joined their units as replacements were reliably less likely than men who came overseas with their outfits to say that they "don't have any use for a fellow who lets the other fellows down" by going AWOL.   This difference holds up

---

[22] S-165.

[23] The context clearly indicated that their *combat* outfit was the referent.

[24] S-177.

when differences in education and in combat time are controlled. It is somewhat surprising, in view of the fact that new replacements were generally more likely than veterans to express conformist attitudes. The most reasonable interpretation would seem to be that, even after much combat, the replacement did not have as strong ties to his buddies and outfit as the men who trained with the unit and came overseas with it.[25]

TABLE 9

ATTITUDES OF ORIGINAL MEMBERS OF UNITS AND OF REPLACEMENTS TOWARD
SOLDIERS WHO GO AWOL FROM THE FRONT
(Privates and Pfc's in Line Infantry Companies of Four Infantry Divisions,
Italy, April 1945, S-177)

QUESTION: "How do you feel about a soldier who goes AWOL from the front after being in the line a long time?"

| | PER CENT GIVING EACH ANSWER AMONG: | |
	Men who came overseas with their outfit	*Men who joined their outfit as replacements*
I don't have any use for a fellow who lets the other fellows down like that	30	22
He shouldn't let the other fellows down like that, but probably couldn't help it	41	49
He probably did his share, and they should go easy on him	18	18
It doesn't make any difference to me one way or the other	5	6
Something else*	4	3
No answer	2	2
Total	100	100
Number of cases	*405*	*903*

* Written-in answers.

Besides making a social adjustment, the replacement had, of course, to learn other complex adjustments to the combat situation in order to become an effective combat soldier. Replacements in general did not think as well of the training they had had before reaching combat as did original members of units. Data from the survey cited above show that among privates 32 per cent of the

[25] It might be argued that the men who came overseas with their unit but remained privates are a selected group, since the more able men and those with superior attitudes may have been more likely to become noncoms. If this is the case, the expected differences in terms of selection alone would be in the opposite direction from those found. Too few noncoms were included in the sample of replacements to make adequately controlled comparisons of noncoms possible.

original members said that their training had fitted them very well to do their part in combat operations, as compared with only 18 per cent of the replacements (Table 10). This considerable difference is independent of differences in education or combat experience as well as rank.[26]

The replacement who joined a unit in combat was at an initial disadvantage in regard to training in several ways. Most of the

TABLE 10

APPRAISAL OF TRAINING BY ORIGINAL MEMBERS OF UNITS AND REPLACEMENTS
(Privates and Pfc's in Line Infantry Companies of Four Infantry Divisions, Italy, April 1945, S-177)

QUESTION: "When you first went into combat, how well do you think your training had fitted you to do your part in combat operations?"

| | PER CENT GIVING EACH ANSWER AMONG: | |
	Men who came overseas with their outfit	*Men who joined their outfit as replacements*
Very well	32	18
Pretty well	36	34
Not so well	15	21
Not well at all	10	21
Undecided	6	6
No answer	1	—
Total	100	100
Number of cases	*405*	*903*

replacements had probably had briefer training than men who had trained with their combat division. They had had less opportunity in replacement training programs to gain experience in group operations. And, of course, they had not in the nature of the case had the chance to learn to function in close coordination with the men with whom they would be teamed in combat. Social integration with the combat team was relevant to combat performance as well as to individual adjustment.

In his first experiences with actual combat, the new replacement, like all green troops, was naturally prone to certain errors which the veterans had learned to avoid. The kinds of errors that he typically made are revealing of the psychological state in which he en-

---

[26] If the veterans who remained privates were in some sense a selected group, one would expect the differences which might result from such selection (by promotion of the more able, etc.) to be in the opposite direction from those actually observed.

tered combat. Among a sample of wounded veterans surveyed in a European hospital, men who had once been replacements themselves were in substantial agreement with men who had come to France with their outfits concerning the most common errors of the

TABLE 11

COMBAT ERRORS MOST COMMONLY MADE BY VETERANS AND REPLACEMENTS, AS REPORTED BY THEM

(Wounded Combat Veterans, European Theater, August 1944, S-165)

	QUESTIONS:			
	"From your experience, how often are the following errors made by new replacements?"		"From your experience, how often are the following errors made by old seasoned combat men?"	
	PER CENT SAYING "VERY OFTEN" AMONG MEN WHO:		PER CENT SAYING "VERY OFTEN" AMONG MEN WHO:	
	Came to France with their outfits	Came in as replacements	Came to France with their outfits	Came in as replacements
Bunching up	48	59	16	21
Talking loud or making noise at night	35	37	8	10
Shooting before they are able to see their target	27	25	4	5
Not taking advantage of available cover	26	24	4	13
Not moving fast enough when crossing open ground	22	20	8	9
Not being aggressive enough in the attack	22	18	3	6
Being overcautious	16	15	7	5
Not digging in when they should	17	15	10	11
Freezing	15	14	1	4
Number of cases	*147*	*130*	*147*	*130*

new men. (See Table 11.) Of a list of ten errors, the three most often checked as being frequent among new replacements were:

1. Bunching up (the tendency of men to huddle together in groups when under fire).
2. Talking or making noise at night.
3. Shooting before they are able to see their target.

The three errors least frequently cited were:

1. Freezing (becoming immobile in an exposed position, or failing to advance when under fire).

2. Being overcautious.

3. Not digging in when they should.

This pattern of reported errors appears to be meaningful. Bunching up under fire—gathering together for mutual psychological support—is a strong indication of feelings of insecurity. New replacements engaged in this practice in spite of its obvious dangers, and in spite of the emphasis in training doctrine upon dispersal under fire. The obvious irrationality of the action suggests the imperativeness of the motivation behind it. Talking loud or making noise at night reflects a lack of caution when the presence of the enemy was not obvious, which might be expected of men as yet imperfectly aware of the full character of their situation. Shooting before they are able to see their target, or being "trigger happy," is usually interpreted as a sign of improperly controlled anticipatory anxiety or nervousness, which was of course high among replacements.

The same veterans indicated that seasoned combat men made all these errors much less frequently. The greatest improvement between new and seasoned troops was reported on the three errors which were most frequently attributed to new replacements. Nevertheless, bunching up remained the most frequently reported error—another indication of the strength of the need of combat men for mutual support. Shooting before they are able to see their target, one of the more frequent errors reported of new men, was one of the errors least frequently attributed to seasoned troops. Apparently this manifestation of anticipatory anxiety was brought under control.

With the initial adjustments behind him, the career line of the individual replacement in combat becomes indistinguishable from that of any combat soldier. Additional combat experience brought with it greater knowledge and skill on the one hand, and the cumulative effects of combat stress on the other. The last section of this chapter will examine some data on the changes in overall effectiveness of the front-line soldier with time in combat. We will see that in the judgment of his immediate leaders, the value of an infantryman did not rise steadily as he acquired more combat experience, but attained a definite peak and then declined.

Combat Time and Combat Effectiveness

The individual replacement system made it possible to keep divisions in intermittent combat indefinitely. By the same token, it put to the test of unlimited combat the soldier who was lucky enough to avoid becoming a casualty. The relation of combat time to combat efficiency was therefore one of major importance.

Data showing the relationship between various attitudes and extended combat experience[27] cannot provide satisfactory evidence here. Perhaps the veteran soldier, though sour and embittered,

CHART III

VALUE TO PLATOON RELATED TO LENGTH OF TIME IN COMBAT, AMONG
REPLACEMENT NONCOMS AND RIFLEMEN WITH LESS THAN A
YEAR OF COMBAT EXPERIENCE IN LINE COMPANIES OF
TWO VETERAN INFANTRY DIVISIONS

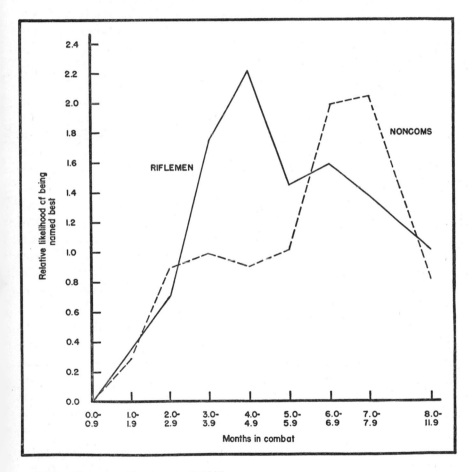

S-222. European Theater, April 1945.
Ratio of the proportion of "best men" with a given amount of combat experience to the proportion of all men with that amount of combat experience. See Table 12 for data and computations.

[27] Such as is presented, for example, in Chapter 3.

kept on increasing in actual fighting ability and hence in value to
his company.   Only a direct investigation of the problem, employing some adequate criterion of combat efficiency, could furnish the
relevant information.   Fortunately, a study was carried out in two
veteran Infantry divisions just before VE Day from which it is possible to draw tentative conclusions.   These divisions were admi-
rably suited for such a study since, at the time of the survey, each
had seen extensive action in the Mediterranean and European theaters.   Like all veteran divisions, each was composed of men with
widely varying lengths of combat experience.

The criterion of combat effectiveness used in this study was the
judgment of the men who were best qualified to rate individual combat performance: the platoon leaders.   In 87 rifle platoons of the
two divisions, the platoon leaders were asked to name the three noncoms and the three riflemen whom they would "hate most to lose"
in terms of their value to the platoon.   Once the names of these
best noncoms and riflemen were obtained, they were checked against
the men's records to determine how much combat experience they
had had.   It was then possible to compare the combat experience
of these best men with the combat experience of all noncoms and
privates in the two divisions.

This method had the advantage of requiring from the platoon
leaders the information that they were most competent to give.   Instead of asking them for their opinion about the relation of combat
time to combat efficiency, it simply asked them to identify the best
noncoms and riflemen in the platoon.   Personnel records then made
it possible to determine the relationship between time in combat and
effectiveness as measured by this criterion.

Chart III summarizes the findings for replacements who had been
in combat less than a year.[28]   The data for the chart are presented
in Table 12 together with the computations on which they were
based.   The chart shows the relationship between the number of
months noncoms and riflemen had spent in combat and their relative
likelihood of being rated "best" by their platoon leaders.   This like-

---

[28] Data are restricted to men who had been in combat less than a year because it
was likely that a considerable proportion of the men with longer combat service were
original members of the outfit.   One might well expect different factors to enter into
the rating of the combat performance of replacements and of original members.   Since
the data collected in the field do not permit separating the veteran combat men into
replacements and original members, findings are reported only for the more homogeneous group that can be assumed with some assurance to have joined their outfits
as replacements.   These comprise 87 per cent of the total sample.

TABLE 12

VALUE TO PLATOON RELATED TO LENGTH OF TIME IN COMBAT, AMONG REPLACEMENT NONCOMS AND RIFLEMEN WITH LESS THAN A YEAR OF COMBAT EXPERIENCE IN LINE COMPANIES OF TWO VETERAN INFANTRY DIVISIONS*

Months in combat	NONCOMS					RIFLEMEN				
	A† Number named among 3 best in platoon	B Per cent named among 3 best in platoon	C‡ Total number in line Infantry companies	D Total per cent in line Infantry companies	E Relative likelihood of being named "best" (B/D)	A† Number named among 3 best in platoon	B Per cent named among 3 best in platoon	C‡ Total number of privates and Pfc's in Infantry line companies	D Total per cent of privates and Pfc's in Infantry line companies	E Relative likelihood of being named "best" (B/D)
8.0–11.9	50	27.48	506	33.63	0.82	29	13.67	687	13.35	1.02
7.0– 7.9	37	20.33	150	9.96	2.04	17	8.02	300	5.83	1.38
6.0– 6.9	32	17.58	134	8.90	1.98	20	9.43	305	5.93	1.59
5.0– 5.9	14	7.69	113	7.51	1.02	18	8.49	304	5.91	1.44
4.0– 4.9	14	7.69	128	8.50	0.90	42	19.81	460	8.93	2.22
3.0– 3.9	14	7.69	117	7.77	0.99	46	21.71	637	12.38	1.75
2.0– 2.9	16	8.79	148	9.84	0.89	25	11.79	851	16.54	0.71
1.0– 1.9	5	2.75	141	9.37	0.29	15	7.08	1,078	20.95	0.34
0.0– 0.9	0	0.00	68	4.52	0.00	0	0.00	524	10.18	0.00
Total	182	100.00	1,505	100.00		212	100.00	5,146	100.00	

* S-222, European theater, April 1945.
† Platoon leaders were asked to name the three noncoms and the three riflemen whom they would "hate most to lose" in terms of their value to the platoon.
‡ Based on special reports prepared by the company personnel officers. Note that the data for privates and Pfc's are *not* restricted to riflemen.

lihood was computed as the ratio of the proportion of best men with a given amount of combat experience to the proportion of all men with that amount of combat experience.[29]

It will be readily seen that, for both noncoms and riflemen, the data indicate a definite peak in combat efficiency after which the relative likelihood of being rated "best" declines. The proportion of best riflemen reaches its peak among men who have been in combat four to five months, after which it begins to drop. The proportion of best noncoms reaches its highest point somewhat later, after six or eight months of combat, after which it also falls off. In both groups, men who have had more than eight months of combat time are apparently less likely than men with less time in combat to be rated as the best men in their outfits.

It is particularly significant that a peak of performance is indicated in the case of *both* riflemen and noncoms. Had the data been for riflemen alone, it might have been argued that the findings were an artifact of selective factors that were surely in operation. For example, a really good rifleman would be likely to be spotted in the course of time and promoted to be a noncom. Since the present data do not follow the same individuals through their combat careers, the expected result of promotions would be a falling off in the relative proportion of best riflemen with extensive combat experience. Such an argument, however, could hardly be applied to the case of the noncoms. Battlefield commissions were sufficiently rare that they can hardly have been a factor in accounting for the drop in the proportion of best noncoms after eight combat months. A genuine point of diminishing returns in combat experience is strongly suggested by the data.

There remains the possibility that a different sort of selective factor may have contributed to the results both for noncoms and riflemen. If the best soldiers were more likely to expose themselves to combat risks in carrying out their missions, it is possible that they may have suffered disproportionately high casualty rates. After eight months of combat, the surviving group may have been over-

---

[29] For the purposes of this analysis, two assumptions were made, each of which introduces approximations into the results. It was assumed that the 87 platoons surveyed were representative of the two divisions. The "best men" in the 87 platoons were thus compared with *all* corresponding men in line Infantry companies of the two divisions. Furthermore, in the case of the privates and Pfc's, data on combat time were not available for the divisions as a whole for riflemen separately. Consequently, the best riflemen were compared with all privates and Pfc's in line Infantry companies. Since riflemen account for most of these, the error introduced is probably not large.

loaded with cautious soldiers who had preserved their necks by not sticking them out. Such a factor may well have contributed to the curves that were obtained. It seems equally likely, however, that a counterbalancing factor was in operation. The testimony of combat veterans was usually to the effect that the inexperienced, reckless, poor soldier was most likely to become a casualty, not the good soldier.

Too much importance should not be attached to the different location of the peaks of the two curves. It is certainly not surprising that a soldier should learn to perform optimally the duties of a rifleman in shorter time than it took to make the best combat noncom. But the selective factor of promotion already mentioned would lead to the same result. Both for this reason and because of the approximations involved in the computations, the main conclusion warranted by the data is simply that combat efficiency appears to reach a peak after prolonged combat experience, after which it falls off.

This conclusion is of major importance. It represents a limitation inherent in the individual replacement system, whatever its other advantages. It also is in agreement with the discussion of combat motivation, where it was suggested that no set of motives or incentives remained permanently effective in indefinite combat.

A final tentative finding from Chart III adds something to our understanding of the process by which the replacement became a functioning member of his combat outfit. The men with less than a year's combat experience in the two divisions surveyed, it must be remembered, had necessarily joined their divisions as replacements, since the divisions had seen more than two years of combat. From the chart it may be seen, then, that by three months of combat experience the replacements can be said to have reached the average level of combat efficiency. By then both riflemen and noncoms included about the same proportion of best men that existed in the line companies of the division as a whole. After approximately that point, not only was the replacement a full-fledged combat man, but our data indicate that for the next several months he was even more likely to be valued as a combat soldier than were his more battle-scarred comrades.

CHAPTER 6

ATTITUDES OF GROUND COMBAT TROOPS TOWARD REAR ECHELONS AND THE HOME FRONT[1]

Introduction

RESENTMENTS of front-line fighters toward the large supporting base of the Army which never saw combat have been mentioned in several connections in the preceding chapters. Largely through the workings of a seemingly unintelligible fate, the most dangerous and arduous duty befell a small minority of all the men inducted into the Army, who in turn constituted a small minority of the total population of the nation at war. This fact, probably inherent in the nature of organized combat at the time of the Second World War (though potentially subject to a certain amount of mitigation), was of central importance to the minority who bore the brunt of actual combat. A study of their reactions to the more favored majority in the rear can throw light on some of the ways in which these men came to terms with their special position.

The present chapter is concerned solely with the attitudes of ground combat troops and of service troops in so far as they are relevant to the understanding of the former. The problem will not be treated in regard to the Air Forces, principally because little or no relevant data are available. But the Air Forces represented a radically different sort of setting from Ground Forces for the development of attitudes toward noncombat personnel. A word as to some of the key differences will indicate why one would not expect to find in the Air Forces the same sort of pattern of attitudes as in the Ground Forces, and will serve as a background for the consideration of Ground Forces data.

The distinction of front and rear, usually applicable in the Ground

---

[1] By M. Brewster Smith. In preparing this chapter, much use was made of notes and ideas by Robin M. Williams, Jr.

Forces, had no literal equivalent in the Air Forces. In the Ground Forces, Infantry companies served in danger and hardship at the front, Field Artillery batteries were located considerably to the rear in less danger and discomfort, while behind the artillery were service outfits in which the danger and discomfort were minimal. The usual Air Force fighter or bomber group, on the other hand, was based considerably back of the front in relative comfort and safety.[2] The fundamental split in kind of duty was not between forward and rear units, but between flying and ground personnel within the same group or squadron. Unlike the case of Ground Forces, the smallest combat outfit was quite evenly divided into men with each sort of duty. The ground personnel had a special tie to the flyers in their assignment as ground crews to specific planes. No ordnance outfit maintaining Ground Force equipment was in a position to sweat out the fate of the men who used the guns as the ground crews typically sweated out the missions of the air crew who manned their plane. There were also, of course, many purely service units in the Air Forces, with no more direct relationship to the flight crews than men in base sections had to front-line infantrymen. But the fact remains that while differences in danger in the Ground and Service Forces were associated with difference in unit of assignment, in hardship, and in geographical location, such was not the case in the Air Forces. The pattern of front-rear antagonisms to be discussed here is not to be generalized to the Air Forces.

Neither were the Air Forces integrated into the accompanying hierarchy of prestige which can be isolated with considerable degree of definiteness in the Ground Forces and their supporting service troops to the rear. The special factors which contributed to the elite status of Air Corps personnel [3] were largely of a different sort from the sources of status of the front-line infantryman. Combat experience also meant very different things on the ground and in the air. The kinds of status acquired in the Air Forces and Ground Forces were thus hardly comparable, and informal observation could discern no mutually recognized ranking of status between ground and air combat men. If we leave the Air Forces out of the picture, however, it will be seen that a fairly consistent patterned relationship emerged among ground and service troops in an active theater.

The discussion of the attitudes of ground combat troops toward

---

[2] There were, of course, local exceptions, especially in the case of fighter groups operating in close tactical support of ground troops.

[3] Cf. Chapter 7.

rear elements will begin with the finding, somewhat surprising in view of the general tenor of unsystematic accounts of front-rear antagonisms, that on the whole combat troops seem to have thought fairly well of the supporting job done by troops to the rear.   There were, however, some grievances, which will be examined as one source of feelings of antagonism.   Secondly, it will be noted that in spite of their relatively favorable attitude toward the supply job, front-line troops were typically resentful toward men in the rear echelons.   The available data are limited to the European and Mediterranean theaters, where there is reason to believe that there may have been greater resentment than in the Pacific.   This resentment is most easily interpreted as primarily a matter of resentful envy towards those who were getting the softer breaks.   To make their unfavored position more tolerable, combat men claimed higher status than those who were taking less punishment, and cherished feelings of fierce, often bitter, pride.   This higher status was allowed them by men in the rear, who shared the set of values on which the combat men's status claim was based.   Thus there developed, parallel to the front-rear distinctions, a status hierarchy which appears to have played an important role in channelizing the aggressive tensions felt between front and rear.   In spite of the pride felt by the front-line infantryman and his position at the top of the "pecking-order," we will finally see that he would nevertheless gladly have changed places with the men of whom he was so scornful to the rear. The reactions of pride and resentment overlaid the fundamental envy that combat men felt toward the green pastures of the rear, without supplanting it.

Finally, there will be a brief discussion of the combat men's feelings toward certain specific noncombatant groups, overseas and in the States: "Headquarters" and soldiers and civilians on the home front.

Attitudes of Combat Troops Toward the Supporting Job Done by Troops in the Rear Echelons

The way combat infantrymen felt about the kind of job service troops behind the front were doing in supporting their efforts is a good starting point for a discussion of the rear-echelon problem, since their judgment in this respect touched most closely their practical problems of daily existence at the front.   As long as they could feel confident that the service troops were generally doing their best, such resentment and scorn as combat men might feel toward rear troops was perhaps a luxury they could well afford without jeopardizing their feeling of being members of a strong and winning team with full backing.

Veteran Infantry officers and men in divisions in both Europe and the Pacific were asked if they felt while they were in combat that troops in the rear, in general, were doing as much as they could under the circumstances for the men who were doing the fighting. The results are shown in Chart I.

It will be seen from the chart that in each of the divisions at least a majority of the enlisted infantrymen said they felt that troops in the rear had done as much as they could. This is true in spite of the wide range of experience represented among the divisions: Division E, for example, was one which had seen particularly severe combat in the early days of the Mediterranean campaign, and one in which Research Branch interviewers were impressed by the degree of bitterness shown by the men. In each of the divisions, enlisted men were more favorable in their answers than officers, though their grounds for resentment of the rear might be expected to have been greater. Even among the officers, half or more in three of the divisions gave the favorable response.

The evidence suggests that the men's evaluation of the kind of support they got from the rear was colored to a relatively small extent by nonrational antagonisms and reflected to a considerable degree the objective supply conditions which they had experienced. As Chart I shows, differences between the divisions are fairly consistent for enlisted men and officers: in those divisions in which a high proportion of enlisted men were favorable, a high proportion of officers also tended to give favorable answers. Table 1 further shows that the divisions in which the performance of rear troops was rated the most highly also ranked highest in the proportion of officers and men saying they usually received the supplies they needed at the front. For the four divisions surveyed in the Pacific, the rank orders correspond perfectly for both officers and enlisted men. The one exception is Division E from the European theater; a second division from the European theater in which officers but not enlisted men were asked the two questions showed about the same results.

For the Pacific divisions, these data agree with what is known about the campaigns in which they took part. The Pacific division which showed the lowest proportion of favorable opinion was an outfit which had been through an especially grueling island campaign under poor supply conditions. At the other extreme, the

CHART I

ATTITUDES OF COMBAT INFANTRYMEN TOWARD THE JOB DONE BY REAR-ECHELON TROOPS

(Veteran Enlisted Infantrymen and Company Grade Infantry Officers in Five Divisions)

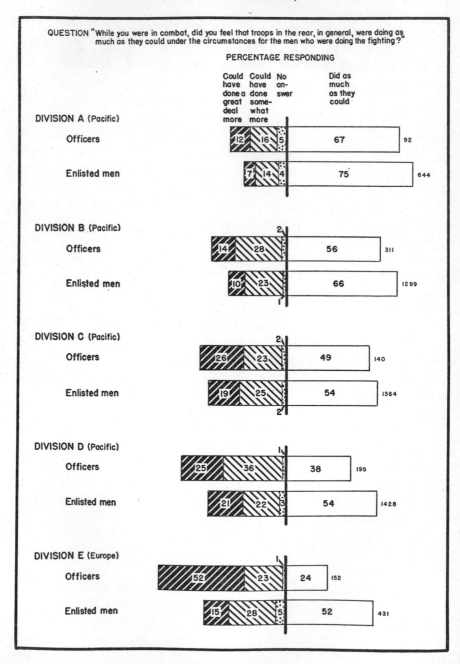

QUESTION "While you were in combat, did you feel that troops in the rear, in general, were doing as much as they could under the circumstances for the men who were doing the fighting?"

PERCENTAGE RESPONDING

Could have done a great deal more / Could have done somewhat more / No answer / Did as much as they could

DIVISION A (Pacific)
Officers — 12, 16, 5, 67 — 92
Enlisted men — 7, 14, 4, 75 — 644

DIVISION B (Pacific)
Officers — 14, 28, 2, 56 — 311
Enlisted men — 10, 23, 1, 66 — 1299

DIVISION C (Pacific)
Officers — 26, 23, 2, 49 — 140
Enlisted men — 19, 25, 2, 54 — 1364

DIVISION D (Pacific)
Officers — 25, 36, 1, 38 — 195
Enlisted men — 21, 22, 3, 54 — 1428

DIVISION E (Europe)
Officers — 52, 23, 1, 24 — 152
Enlisted men — 15, 28, 5, 52 — 431

Enlisted men from surveys S-100 (March–April 1944), and S-91 (November 1943); officers from S-101 (April 1944).

The numbers following the bars are the numbers of cases on which percentages are based.

division characterized by highest frequency of favorable attitudes had taken part in a campaign that lasted only a few days, with no gross supply deficiencies. The other Pacific divisions exhibited opinion differences which correspond roughly to the adequacy of supply which might have been expected under the known circumstances in which they fought. The divisions surveyed in Europe had taken part in the early campaigns in the Mediterranean area at a time when rear-echelon support of the front was probably less ade-

TABLE 1

ATTITUDES OF COMBAT INFANTRYMEN TOWARD ADEQUACY OF SUPPLY AND
REAR-ECHELON PERFORMANCE
(Veteran Enlisted Infantrymen and Company Grade Infantry
Officers in Five Divisions*)

| | PERCENTAGE OF ENLISTED MEN WHO SAID: | | PERCENTAGE OF OFFICERS WHO SAID: | |
	Rear-echelon troops did as much as they could†	*Supplies needed were usually received†*	*Rear-echelon troops did as much as they could*	*Supplies needed were usually received*
Division A (Pacific)	75	84 *(644)*	67	81 *(92)*
Division B (Pacific)	66	68 *(1,299)*	56	80 *(311)*
Division C (Pacific)	54	42 *(1,364)*	49	49 *(140)*
Division D (Pacific)	54	28 *(1,428)*	38	43 *(195)*
Division E (Europe)	52	52 *(431)*	24	50 *(152)*

The numbers in parentheses are the numbers of cases on which percentages are based.
* Data from same source as in Chart I.
† See Chart I for question.
‡ The question was: "Did supplies you wanted or needed at the front ever fail to reach you?"

   X   We usually got what we needed
          We often did not get what we needed
          We seldom got what we needed

quate than later in the campaigns on the mainland of Europe. However, it seems more likely that the somewhat divergent data from the European divisions reflect a different pattern of relations between front and rear in the two theaters, which will be discussed briefly at the beginning of the next section. In so far as men in Europe felt greater resentment toward rear-echelon troops on grounds other than the way they did their job, their appraisals of rear-echelon services may have been affected.

The reasons which the men gave for critical answers to the question under discussion (available only for men in the division which fought in Europe) support the view that combat soldiers were to a large extent reacting to the objective supply situation. While a majority of the men's comments referred to inadequacies in specific supply functions, a number of men had critical remarks to make about the good fortune and bad behavior of troops in the rear.   Such comments reflect the sort of antagonism which will be treated in the

TABLE 2

CRITICISMS OF REAR-ECHELON TROOPS BY COMBAT INFANTRYMEN
(Veteran Enlisted Infantrymen in a Division Which Fought in
North Africa and Sicily, April 1944)

QUESTION: "While you were in combat, did you feel that the noncombatant troops to the rear were doing as much as they could, under the circumstances, for the men who were doing the fighting?   If you do not think they were doing as much as they could, give an example."

	Percentage of comments falling in each category
Specific criticisms of various supply functions as inadequate	61
Food supply	*31*
Clothing, equipment, ammunition	*9*
PX rations	*8*
Water supply	*5*
Transport	*3*
Mail	*2*
Miscellaneous	*3*
General criticisms of lack of effort and efficiency of troops in rear	17
"They were inefficient"	*7*
"They did not do very much" or "did nothing"	*7*
"They think only of themselves"	*3*
Expressions of general resentment toward troops in the rear	20
"They should fight"	*9*
"They get the breaks"	*6*
"They didn't show us proper respect"	*3*
Miscellaneous	*2*
Irrelevant	2
Total	100
*Number of comments**	*291*
Number of men	*593*

S-100.
* Some men presumably made more than one comment.   Tally was not kept of the number of men making more than one comment.

next section.   Table 2 shows a classification of the comments of the men who were critical.   The pattern of answers by company grade officers in the two European divisions was quite similar, the majority of criticisms again being directed at specific inadequacies of supply rather than at the attitudes or behavior of rear-echelon men.   Pilfering, "picking over," or "short-stopping" of supplies came in for frequent mention in the latter category.

While, as has been seen, the majority of combat men surveyed seem to have had a favorable opinion of the supply job done by the rear echelons, there were some chronic sources of dissatisfaction and resentment which centered on supply.   The lack or inequitable distribution of minor luxuries, in addition to the pilfering of supplies, was a particular source of personal antagonisms toward the rear. Combat men in most theaters complained about the distribution of PX articles.   Distribution systems which frequently worked satisfactorily for the basic necessities of cigarettes and minimum toilet needs rarely could prevent the choicer items from being diverted from the front-line fighter to personnel nearer the chain of supply. Table 2 showed PX rations as the subject of relatively frequent complaint.   In Italy, where a specific question was asked on the subject, men from ground combat units were much less likely than men from rear service units to say that PX supplies were given out fairly, as Chart II indicates.   Two comments written on questionnaires in this survey may be cited by way of illustration:

I don't think that we received a fair distribution of articles such as pens, watches, knives, etc., while with my unit. Suggest that more of these articles be made available to combat troops instead of so many in the base sections.

PX rations by the time they have reached a rifle company have been picked over all down the line. It has ended up with shower slippers for a rifleman.

Combat men who had so few luxuries were particularly resentful of being deprived of ones to which they felt legitimately entitled.

An additional factor which may have heightened the amount of criticism of the supply situation, and at the same time provided a source of resentment toward civilians on the home front, was ill-advised publicity purporting to show how well supplied the troops were.   Articles and advertisements in newspapers and magazines, as well as letters from persons in the United States, often conveyed the impression that the public believed even the front-line GI to be invariably well supplied not only with essentials which in fact were often scarce, but also with the minor luxuries which the men never saw.   Sarcastic comment on such matters was a standard conversational topic among combat troops.   Of a sample of infantrymen and field artillerymen in Italy in early 1944, nearly half the men (44 per cent) said they had seen or heard news from the States about things the men overseas were said to be getting but which they were quite sure they were not getting.[4]

Veterans who had seen greater amounts of combat duty were not

CHART II

ATTITUDES OF FORWARD AND REAR GROUND TROOPS TOWARD DISTRIBUTION OF PX SUPPLIES

(Enlisted Men from Ground and Service Force Units, Italy, May 1945)

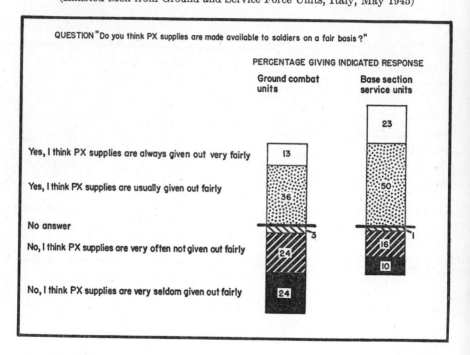

Survey of 747 enlisted men in Italy awaiting return to the United States. Men were returning as casuals, and represented a wide variety of organizations. Number of cases for the groups compared is not available.

significantly more likely than those with less combat duty to be critical of the kind of job men in rear areas were doing. This was true for the question which has been discussed, and also for a similar question asked of combat troops in Italy, among whom there was a much wider range of combat experience.[5] Apparently the men's

---

[4] (S-100). Survey of 1,171 enlisted combat veterans in Italy, February 1944. Men were surveyed in rest camp, and represented three Infantry divisions and three artillery brigades.

[5] (S-177). The second question, asked of 1,766 veterans of line Infantry companies in Italy in April 1945, was:

answers to these questions did not express a cumulative frustration or resentment on the part of the combat men.

Resentment and Envy Toward the Rear Echelons

The Prevalence of Resentment

Although the greater proportion of combat men tended to rate the general supply job done by rear-echelon troops favorably, this does not mean that only a small minority harbored any grudge against the rear echelons.   The evidence from the European campaigns is that the majority of combat men felt some degree of resentment.   Unfortunately, no questions bearing directly on front-rear resentments were asked in the Pacific.   In the absence of data, one can only conjecture about the extent to which the findings from Europe can be generalized to the other area.   There is some reason to expect that the conditions in Europe would have been the more conducive to resentment against the rear.   In both the European and Mediterranean theaters, there was usually a fairly definite front.[6]   Most of the supply troops worked in relative safety in the rear zones.   The campaigns were for the most part in civilized countries which had large cities and provided relatively comfortable living conditions for the troops behind the fighting lines.   Thus, when combat soldiers returned to the rear for hospitalization or on leave or pass, they saw the men in the supply services living in what seemed to be complete safety and comparatively great comfort.   In the Pacific, on the other hand, the supply troops with which the combat soldiers usually came into contact shared most of the discomforts and some of the dangers which the combat outfits experienced.   When everyone was on the same island, living under jungle conditions and subject to bombing raids and infiltration ground attacks, there was probably a greater community of experience and sentiment.   The far-removed groups in Brisbane or Honolulu, on

---

"On the whole, how hard do you think the rear echelons are trying to see that front-line troops get the supplies they need?"

_____ They are trying very hard
_____ They are trying pretty hard
_____ They are not trying so hard
_____ They are not trying at all

Sixty-four per cent said they are trying very hard or pretty hard.

[6] Of course there were exceptions.   It could hardly be said, for instance, that there was a rear echelon on the Anzio beachhead.   Nevertheless, small quotas of men were sent back to Naples from Anzio on leave.   In France, there were periods when front and rear became relatively meaningless because of infiltration tactics, local breakthrough operations, and encircling maneuvers.

the other hand, were probably too remote for the men at the front to give much thought to them.

Chart III shows that considerably more than half of the combat

CHART III

RESENTMENT OF COMBAT MEN TOWARD REAR-AREA TROOPS
(Enlisted Men in Ground and Service Force Units, European Theater,
April–May 1945)

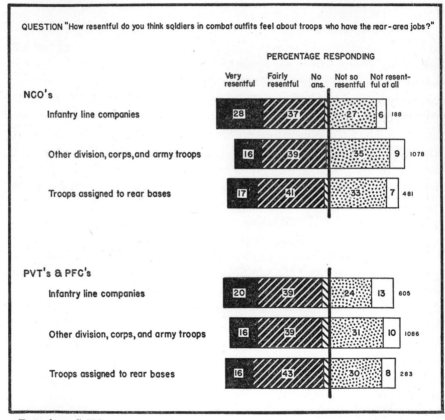

QUESTION "How resentful do you think soldiers in combat outfits feel about troops who have the rear-area jobs?"

Data from S-223.
The numbers following the bars are the numbers of cases on which percentages are based.

men in the European theater said that soldiers in combat outfits felt "fairly resentful" or "very resentful" about troops who had the rear-area jobs.[7]   A further interesting fact to be seen in the chart is that

---

[7] The direct question as to the respondent's own resentment toward the rear echelon was not asked, since the question was worded to be asked of a cross section of troops in the theater.   However, it is safe to assume that combat men in answering the question reflected their own attitudes to a considerable extent.

rear-echelon troops themselves were almost equally aware of the combat men's resentment.   Whether this was primarily a result of contacts with combat men or perhaps a projection of guilt feelings on their own part, it means that the rear-echelon problem was not restricted to the attitudes of combat men but also had its reflection in the awareness of men to the rear.   This is a necessary precondition to the reciprocal structuring of attitudes of forward and rear troops which will be noted later.

A slight tendency appears in the chart for men in intermediate echelons not involved in the front-line Infantry fighting, but still close to the front, to be less likely than either infantrymen or men in rear bases to say that soldiers in combat outfits felt resentful toward troops holding down rear-area jobs.   Although the differences are not statistically reliable, the chart shows that they occurred among both noncoms and privates.   When educational level is simultaneously controlled, the pattern of differences remains.   In Italy, where a similar question was asked, the intermediate group was again the least likely to indicate awareness of resentment of front-line troops toward rear-area soldiers.   As Chart IV shows, the men in service units attached to an army or corps were less than half as likely to say that most combat soldiers felt resentful as were men in line combat outfits, and significantly less likely to give the response than were men in service units assigned to rear bases.   The controls applied to the data for the European theater were not available for the Italian data, but the magnitude of the differences is such that one would expect them to hold up if rank and education had been controlled.   The chart also indicates that antagonism toward the rear echelon was widespread among combat men in Italy, as well as in the European theater.

The fact that fewer men in forward service units than in actual combat units said they were aware of resentment of combat troops toward the rear echelon is reasonable in terms of either of two mutually compatible assumptions: that the forward service troops themselves felt less resentment toward those further to the rear and were expressing to some degree their own attitudes, or that they were answering as men with rear-area jobs but were not aware of being the target of much antagonism on the part of combat men. The difference between forward and rear service troops is such as would be obtained if the far-rear troops were aware of being the principal target of the combat men's resentment, or if they felt more guilt about their Army role and were therefore more ready to attribute resentment against themselves to combat men.

In Italy there were special historical circumstances which made the far-rear base section a chosen target of resentment. During the spring of 1944, the major rear-area commander enforced exception-

CHART IV

RESENTMENT OF COMBAT MEN TOWARD REAR-AREA TROOPS
(Enlisted Men in Ground and Service Force Units, Mediterranean Theater,
May–June 1945)

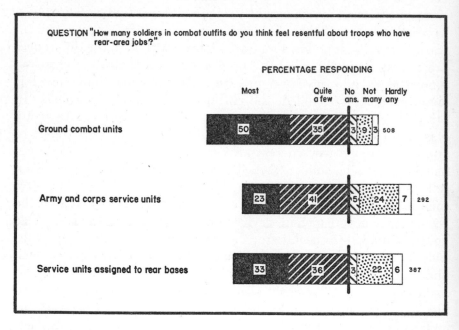

QUESTION "How many soldiers in combat outfits do you think feel resentful about troops who have rear-area jobs?"

PERCENTAGE RESPONDING

	Most	Quite a few	No ans.	Not many	Hardly any	
Ground combat units	50	35	3	9	3	508
Army and corps service units	23	41	5	24	7	292
Service units assigned to rear bases	33	36	3	22	6	387

Data from S-205.
The numbers following the bars are the numbers of cases on which percentages are based.

ally rigid military requirements of protocol, uniform, and saluting, with the result that a soldier just out of the lines from the Anzio beachhead on occasion spent his rare rest leave in detention for a missing button or an improperly typed pass.[8] Grievances of this sort, in addition to the more usual ones that rear soldiers lived in relative comfort and pre-empted the entertainment facilities, aroused intense bitterness on the part of combat men. Reforms

[8] Cf. Robert Neville, "What's Wrong With Our Army?" *Life*, Vol. 20 (February 25, 1946), p. 111.

were eventually instituted to alleviate many of the difficulties, but the residual bitterness was great enough that the name of the particular command remained a term of opprobrium to combat troops in the theater to the end of the war.   While the situation in Italy seems to have been exceptional, the same tendency for men in far-rear bases to be more aware than troops in intermediate echelons of front-line antagonism appeared in the European theater.

Among the sources of front-line resentment toward the rear echelon, specific grievances of combat troops about supply problems and about rear-area "chicken" have already been mentioned. While such essentially remediable complaints undoubtedly added fuel to the fire, it is likely that the feeling of the combat men that they had been arbitrarily singled out to take the punishment of war was more basic.   Men in Infantry line companies were less likely than all other ground troops to say that the Army was trying its best to see that no man got more than his fair share of the hard and dangerous jobs.   The data in Chart V show that other forward combat and service troops were little if at all less likely than men in rear bases to give the favorable response, whereas the combat infantry-men differed markedly from the others.   Infantry noncoms were somewhat more likely than privates to be favorable, but the relationship holds even when rank and education are controlled.   As one might expect, the greater the length of time men in Infantry line companies had served in combat, the more likely they were to say that the Army was not trying its best to distribute the dangerous duty fairly, and also to say that they often felt that their outfit was getting more than its fair share of the tough and dangerous duty.

This feeling of grievance was easily translated to a resentful envy of men more favorably situated.   It is an instance of the familiar mechanism whereby an unfortunate person feels that damaging the more fortunate person will improve his own position.   Such an implicit process was the easier for the combat man since he could think that if rear-echelon men were put into combat, he himself might then be relieved.   When combat infantrymen in Italy were asked "If you had a chance to change one thing in the Army, what would you change?" 20 per cent of the men who answered suggested that combat men be given a better break and rear-echelon and front-line troops be made to change places.[9]   The tone of many of these comments suggested that they reflected not only a desire for relief

---

[9] S-177, April 1945 (1,766 cases).   Twenty-eight per cent of the men failed to answer or made irrelevant or illegible remarks.

and a more equitable distribution of combat duty, but also a feeling that such a turnabout would "serve the bastards right."

For resentful envy to develop, conditions other than mere inequity of benefits and disadvantages are necessary. For one thing, it seems likely that the less fortunate group must be vividly aware of the existence of the more fortunate group. On this basis one might expect combat men in the Pacific to be less hostile toward the rear

CHART V

BELIEF IN ARMY'S EFFORT TO DISTRIBUTE DANGEROUS DUTY FAIRLY
(Enlisted Men in Ground and Service Force Units, European Theater,
April–May 1945)

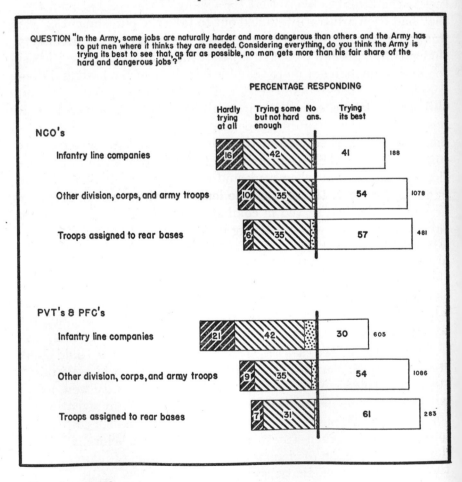

QUESTION "In the Army, some jobs are naturally harder and more dangerous than others and the Army has to put men where it thinks they are needed. Considering everything, do you think the Army is trying its best to see that, as far as possible, no man gets more than his fair share of the hard and dangerous jobs?"

PERCENTAGE RESPONDING

	Hardly trying at all	Trying some but not hard enough	No ans.	Trying its best	
NCO's					
Infantry line companies	16	42		41	188
Other division, corps, and army troops	10	35		54	1078
Troops assigned to rear bases	6	35		57	481
PVT's & PFC's					
Infantry line companies	21	42		30	605
Other division, corps, and army troops	9	35		54	1086
Troops assigned to rear bases	7	31		61	283

Data from S-223.
The numbers following the bars are the numbers of cases on which percentages are based.

echelon than men surveyed in Europe, where there was greater opportunity for contact with far-rear groups. Another probably necessary condition is that the favored person or group must seem similar enough to the unfortunate one so that the latter can imagine a change of places. For the infantryman, almost any other soldier met this condition. Maximum resentment is to be expected under these conditions when the disadvantaged group does not fully accept the *legitimacy* of the advantaged group's position: resentment then approaches "moral indignation." The combat man's powerlessness to change his situation could only add to his antagonism.

Unalloyed envy, however, could not be an entirely satisfactory attitude to the combat man. Since for the most part he could not hope realistically for a rear assignment, it suited him better to think of his unwelcome role as superior. His frank desire to serve in the rear was overlaid to some degree by feelings of pride and superiority. The resultant pattern of the combat man's feelings toward the rear, it will be suggested, was compounded of these elements of pride, envy, and resentment.

Compensations for Combat Duty: Status and the "Pecking-Order"

The general nature of the status compensations available to the combat men for the hard fate allotted to them is apparent from discussions in earlier chapters. The discussion in Volume I, Chapter 7 of the respect which men felt for the various Army branches indicated that men in the Army at large had a high regard for the infantryman, though they had little wish to be one. Some of the standards entering into the men's judgments of respect were examined in that connection. It was seen that they involved values commonly shared by men in our society, and that for this reason the respect which was claimed by men in the combat branches was also granted to them.

For ground combat troops and soldiers in the rear echelons overseas, there is some evidence that this more general pattern of group status and respect carried over and was developed into a hierarchy with the line infantryman and his closest associates in danger at the top. The evidence is less direct than could be wished, since the questions used asked the men in one instance to rate the job being done by various kinds of troops while the fighting was on, and in the other how much combat credit should be given to men in different kinds of units. Neither question asked the men specifically about their respect for men in the various groups. The data never-

theless seem to reflect the relative status of the groups.   Although
the first question asked for a rating of the job done by men in the
branch, real differences in combat performance can largely be ruled
out as a determinant of the men's answers, since the performance of
widely different kinds of units was basically incommensurable except
in terms of an arbitrary set of standards.   The data can be taken
as relevant in the present connection because of the close correspondence which they show with what is known of the general hierarchy
of respect for the different branches in the Army at large, and with

TABLE 3

COMBAT VETERANS' RATINGS OF THE JOB BEING DONE BY DIFFERENT
ARMY BRANCHES
(Company Grade Officers and Enlisted Men in Two Veteran Pacific
Infantry Divisions, March–April 1944)

QUESTION: "In general, how would you rate the job being done, while the fighting was
on, by each of the following kinds of U. S. troops?"

PERCENTAGE RATING THE JOB DONE BY EACH KIND OF
TROOPS AS GOOD* AMONG:

KIND OF TROOPS RATED	Infantry Units	Enlisted Men in: Field Artillery Units	Divisional Service Units	Officers in: Infantry and Field Artillery
Field Artillery	90	93	90	99
Medical Corps	86	83	87	95
Engineers	83	87	90	91
Ordnance	51	68	74	57
Quartermaster	41	58	68	48
Number of cases	*2,790*	*621*	*629*	*444*

Data for officers and enlisted men from S-101 and S-100, respectively, March–April 1944.
* Other answers provided were: "Poor" and "No opinion."

the prestige hierarchy found by informal observation among ground
troops overseas.

Results for the first question are available for both Infantry and
other divisional troops in two divisions in the Pacific.   Table 3
shows that both officers and enlisted men in the Infantry and artillery essentially agreed in their ratings, though, as one would expect,
the infantrymen were somewhat less lavish with favorable ratings.
The only difference in the rank order of the branches is that the infantrymen and the officers rated the medical corps higher than the
engineers, while the other groups shown did not.   If this should
represent a reliable difference, it can probably be attributed to the
special gratitude of infantrymen toward the company aid men and

litter bearers, with whom it was their lot to be in closer contact than was the case for men in other branches.

A somewhat similar pattern may be found in Table 1 of Chapter 2 which showed a ranking of types of units according to the amount of combat credit toward demobilization which men in various sorts of outfits said they should receive. That table has the advantages of including a variety of combat units, distinguishing between combat medics and medics in field hospitals, and specifying combat engineer units. There the rank order given by members of front-line combat outfits was, first, rifle and heavy weapons companies, aid men and other combat medics, combat engineer units, tank and tank destroyer companies; then reconnaissance platoons, Infantry cannon companies, chemical mortar companies, and field artillery batteries; and finally medics in field hospitals, division quartermaster troops, and regimental, division, army and corps headquarters troops. First came the units in close combat with the enemy, who were subject to heavy casualties; then came combat troops who did most of their fighting at a distance in greater safety; and finally came groups who were noncombatant and relatively safe.

Several factors can be provisionally isolated which appear to enter into the way combat men ranked different sorts of units in respect to how well they did their job or as to how much combat credit they should be allowed. First in importance would be exposure to danger from the enemy; in this respect the first group of units above are clearly differentiated from all others. But this alone is not sufficient. The men in the two Pacific divisions whose ratings were shown in Table 3 were also asked about how many battle casualties their present company had had since they first went into combat with it. Aside from the Infantry, 62 per cent of whom reported more than a quarter of their company to have been casualties, men from the different branches did not differ very much from each other in the proportion reporting heavy casualties. Men in field artillery batteries were, if anything, less likely to say that more than a quarter of their battery had become casualties than were division medics, engineers, or quartermaster troops.[10] Yet, as we have seen,

---

[10] The percentages reporting that more than a quarter of their unit had been casualties, and the number of cases, respectively, were: field artillery, 4 per cent, 620 cases; medics, 18 per cent, 203 cases; engineers, 8 per cent, 207 cases; quartermaster, 8 per cent, 67 cases. These results, though crude, may be peculiar to the Pacific fighting, in which there was little counter-battery artillery fire. Even in Europe, however, casualty rates in the artillery were more similar to those in divisional service units than to those in the Infantry—see, for example, the last section in Chapter 2.

field artillery troops were rated more highly with respect to their combat performance. A second factor involved in the judgment is required, and this would seem to be the degree to which the troops in question made a visible contribution to active combat. Field artillery, who fired at the enemy, were rated higher than service troops, who in many instances received as many enemy shells but fired none back. A minor third factor can perhaps also be distinguished, though it may well be merely a generalization from the first two: physical proximity to the front. Table 1 of Chapter 2 showed that troops in general would accord more combat credit to men in regimental headquarters than to men in division headquarters, and would give more to the latter than to men in army and corps headquarters. The danger from the enemy was normally negligible for all three groups. The farther forward troops were, however, the more closely they were connected with the fighting in the minds of troops farther to the rear.

Both tables also show the important fact that noncombat troops were in essential agreement with the combat men in the way they ranked the various sorts of units. In Table 3, it can be seen that the divisional service troops, like the Infantry and artillery, put artillery units first among the kinds of units which they were asked to rate in terms of the job they did "while the fighting was on," and they rated the service branches in the same rank order as the artillerymen did. Even when all men belonging to a specified service branch are eliminated from the rating of that branch, the rank order of the various service branches, as rated by the divisional service personnel, remains the same.

If, as has been suggested, the preceding data reflect the status hierarchy which developed in active theaters, they illustrate one source of compensation to the combat man for the bitter pill of his assignment. He could feel superior to those farther to the rear and feel sure of receiving their respect. The foregoing discussion of the factors involved in the men's ratings of the various branches also suggests grounds for the stability of the hierarchy and its general acceptance by men in groups having different status. The code of masculinity, discussed in Chapter 3, attached value and prestige to enduring danger and hardship, while the general orientation of social values toward the aim of fighting the war lent prestige to the persons most directly concerned with this aim. On both counts, the combat man could claim his role to be the superior one, and thereby with good face translate his envy of the rear-echelon soldier into scorn and superiority. During a war which the majority had in some sense accepted as inevitable and necessary, the combat soldier was the only person who could not be asked "What are *you* doing for the war?" He had no need to justify himself. He had also proved his manhood by withstanding the severest kinds of stress. Others might or might not be able to "take it"; he had proved that he could.

The rear-echelon man, on the other hand, might by the same considerations find his own position socially vulnerable. Especially when there was a real chance of his being transferred to combat duty, his fervent hopes of avoiding it could result in guilt feelings. During the last year of the European war, in both the European and Mediterranean theaters, this danger was not remote, since thousands of men from rear-echelon outfits were retrained as Infantry replacements. The threat of the "repple depple" (replacement depot) hung heavily over the heads of rear-echelon soldiers in these theaters. To invest combat men with prestige and to treat them with deference was a way of alleviating possible guilt feelings and reaffirming the common bond of shared values with them.

The status hierarchy, springing from many of the same sources as the combat man's resentful envy, served to channelize the expression of resentful attitudes of front to rear. Between groups of different status there grew up a fairly definite etiquette of permissible behavior of a sort which at the same time expressed the superiority of the higher-status group and gave direct or indirect vent to their aggressive tendencies. In the absence of systematic data, informal observations must be relied on to sketch a tentative picture. Mauldin has given a vivid description of one aspect of front-rear etiquette:

> While men in combat outfits kid each other around, they have a sort of family complex about it. No outsiders may join. Anybody who does a dangerous job in this war has his own particular kind of kidding among his own friends, and sometimes it doesn't even sound like kidding. . . . If a stranger comes up to a group when they are bulling, they ignore him. If he takes it upon himself to laugh at something funny they have said, they freeze their expressions, turn slowly around, stare at him until his stature has shrunk to about four inches, and he slinks away, and then they go back to their kidding again. It's like a group of prosperous businessmen telling a risqué joke and then glaring at the waiter who joins in the guffaws. Combat people are an exclusive set, and if they want to be that way, it is their privilege.[11]

The status hierarchy, with the front-line combat man at the top, was in some respects analogous to the barnyard pecking-order, with

11 Bill Mauldin, *Up Front* (Henry Holt and Co., New York, 1945), p. 58.

the men in groups at the top being entitled to a variety of arrogant and aggressive behavior toward men in inferior groups, in a nonreciprocal relationship. A tentative list of some of these "pecking" behaviors, drawn from informal field observation in the European and the Italian theaters, would include something like the following:

1. Men from groups near the top of the hierarchy were entitled to have much lower frustration tolerance than lower-status men. A combat man felt he could draw the line concerning what he would tolerate at a lower point than a noncombat man should and this was expected of him by others.
2. They were entitled to gripe in the presence of lower-status men, but not vice versa.
3. They assumed the right to talk back to officers and otherwise break the "caste" taboos when the officers belonged to low-status groups. This right was frequently but not universally recognized by low-status officers.
4. They had the right to adopt a scornful point of view.
5. They were entitled to be more aggressive than lower-status men in looking out for their own interests in a scarcity situation. For instance, men from combat units would sometimes steal jeeps from rear units and, although this was resented and punished if the offender was caught, it was nevertheless somewhat expected.
6. They had the right to criticize and make derogatory remarks about the job or outfit of a lower-status man, but not vice versa. This did not extend to personal remarks, but included the standard taunts such as sarcastic use of the term "commando"—"USO commandos" for troops in the states, "blue star commandos," etc., for service troops overseas.
7. They had the right to boast about their own outfit in the presence of lower-status men, but not vice versa.
8. They had the right to be distinctive in dress—to wear combat boots, to neglect rear-area uniform regulations (a frequent bone of contention with rear-echelon authorities), etc.

Given an established "pecking-order," aggressive behavior in an upward direction would violate the mores of the total group, and could be expected to result in disproportionate counteraggressive tendencies. The attitudes of combat men toward rear-echelon military police were a case in point. The MP in a rear area was near the bottom of the status hierarchy, yet he was required to enforce unwelcome restrictions on the behavior of combat men on pass and was endowed with the formal authority to carry out his prescriptions. This could result in great resentment from the combat men, which in many cases led to an embittered attitude on the part of the MP, in turn provoking further resentment. To quote Mauldin again,

Because he picks up a hundred soldiers a day and hears a hundred dirty cracks, none of them original or amusing, the garrison MP (overseas) is going to be soured on life in general and soldiers in particular, and he is going to be downright mean. When a peaceable guy like myself is rudely stopped by the MP who asks: "Where the hell is yer gawdam helmet?" I start to say truthfully that I forgot it, but he cuts me off, "Don't you gimme none of yer gawdam lip, dammit—I heard that one before." This goes on until I get sore and blow my top and he takes me to jail or gives me a ticket. . . .[12]

The front-line infantryman was, then, at the top of the hierarchy. For playing his unwanted role he was for the most part rewarded by the esteem of his more fortunate fellows. If the latter should fail to pay proper respect to his true merits, he could express himself

CHART VI

RELATION OF RESENTMENT TOWARD REAR ECHELON TO BELIEF IN IMPORTANCE OF RIFLEMAN'S JOB

(Veteran Enlisted Infantrymen in a Pacific Division, March–April 1944)

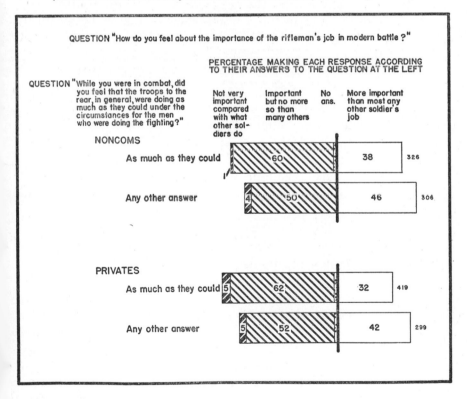

Data from S-100.

"Any other answer" included the check-list categories "Could have done somewhat more," and "Could have done a great deal more."

The numbers following the bars are the numbers of cases on which percentages are based.

[12] *Ibid.*, p. 192.

without compunction and at least feel the solace of aggrieved virtue. The extent to which resentments were associated with pride in high status remains in doubt.   There is some evidence from questionnaire surveys in support of the contention that the combat man's antagonism toward the rear echelon was related to a feeling of superior status.   Chart VI shows that, in one division which fought in the Pacific, the veteran infantrymen who were more critical of troops to the rear in regard to their supply functions, were also more likely to give the extreme response that the rifleman's job was "more important than most any other soldier's job" in modern battle.   This was true for men of all ranks and educational levels; men with differing amounts of education did not differ in their pattern of answers when rank was controlled.   This result, while it might be expected, is not logically required by the nature of the two questions.   Disparagement of the men in the rear areas seems to have been slightly associated with placing a higher value on the importance of the job of men at the front.

Preference for Rear-Echelon Jobs

It would be entirely misleading to conclude from the foregoing discussion of the combat man's resentment toward soldiers in the rear echelons and his feelings of superiority toward them that he often succeeded in selling himself on combat.   However superior the combat man may have felt toward the rear echelon, this feeling of superiority rarely supplanted frank eagerness on his part to change places and fill one of the rear jobs towards which he was so scornful.   The feeling of superiority made his position more tolerable, but did not make him want it.   Table 4 shows that of the veterans in line Infantry companies in two divisions, very few indeed would remain in the Infantry if it were up to them.   The largest number would prefer the Air Corps—a choice that is difficult to interpret in respect to whether or not it involved choosing another combat assignment.   But the choice next in frequency was the Quartermaster Corps—which it will be remembered ranked near the bottom in combat prestige.   Furthermore, among those men in the sample who chose to remain in the Infantry, 40 per cent were noncoms in the first three grades, as compared with 17 per cent of those choosing other branches.[13]   This result may be attributed to two main factors: (1) that the high noncoms were well selected as those who had a particularly strong loyalty to their jobs; (2) that

---

[13] 83 and 700 cases respectively, Division A (S-100).

many of the men who wanted to stay in the Infantry probably desired to do so not so much from pride in the "Queen of Battles" as to preserve valued ratings.

A survey of men returned to the United States under the rotation plan at about the time of the Normandy invasion gives essentially similar results for Infantry returnees.   It may be seen in Table 5

TABLE 4

BRANCH PREFERENCES OF COMBAT VETERANS IN INFANTRY RIFLE COMPANIES
(Veteran Enlisted Men in Rifle Companies of Two Pacific Divisions,
March–April 1944)

QUESTION: "If you had a choice, which one of these branches of
the Army would you like to be in?"

| BRANCH | PERCENTAGE CHOOSING EACH BRANCH AMONG MEN IN: | |
	Division A	*Division B*
Air Corps	32	26
Quartermaster Corps	21	18
Infantry	11	9
Coast Artillery and Anti-Aircraft	7	11
Ordnance Department	6	5
Transportation Corps	6	6
Military Police	3	8
Field Artillery	3	4
Armored Force	3	2
Engineers	2	3
Signal Corps	1	2
Chemical Warfare Service	*	*
Medical Department	*	1
No answer	5	5
Total	100	100
Number of cases	*783*	*649*

Data from S-100.
* Less than 0.5 per cent.

that only a minority did not want to change their branch, and the low-status but safe Quartermaster Corps and Military Police were the most frequently chosen branches.[14]

One must therefore conclude that the scorn in which combat men sometimes held such rear-echelon branches as the Quartermaster Corps was outweighted by the deep reluctance of most men to see more combat than they had to.   This is not surprising in view of

---

[14] The fact that few Infantry returnees chose the Air Corps is probably due to at least two things: under widely known reassignment policy, it was not then a realistic choice; and, these men, being returnees, had particular reason for feeling that they were through with combat and had little desire to be in a combat branch.

what has been suggested to have been the principal root of the overseas resentment-aggression pattern: the fundamental envy which combat troops felt toward those in more desirable assignments. With all said and done, this envy remained.   The infantryman who inveighed against the rear echelon and took manifest satisfaction in his higher status would usually have been only too glad to change boots with the lowly quartermaster.   It is not unlikely that in imagining such a change, moreover, the combat man could hope to retain much of his hard-won status.   Even as quartermaster, he

TABLE 5

BRANCH PREFERENCES OF INFANTRY RETURNEES
(Enlisted Infantry Returnees at Reassignment Center,
June–July 1944)

QUESTION: "If you wanted to change your branch at the time you were interviewed, what branch did you want to change to?"

	Percentage naming each branch:
Quartermaster Corps	23
Military Police	13
Ordnance Department	8
Transportation Corps	8
Signal Corps	3
Medical Department	3
Corps of Engineers	*
Other ASF branches	8
Any other AGF branch	7
Air Corps	5
Did not want to change branch	22
Total	100
Number of cases	*154*

Data from S-132.
* Less than 0.5 per cent.

would remain a combat veteran.   The status problems that arose when such shifts actually occurred will be encountered in Chapter 10, "Problems of Rotation and Reconversion."

Attitudes of Combat Men Toward Headquarters

The attitudes of combat men toward headquarters constituted in a sense a special case of their attitudes toward the rear echelon, since headquarters, to the men in the line, was always rear echelon.   In addition, headquarters was the source from which emanated the orders that kept a man in combat and determined deployment in battle.   In an active theater of operations, there was necessarily a great deal of decentralization of authority.   Ordinary practice in combat operations, for example, was for each successive level of command to specify tactical objectives, leaving the exact detailed plans for attaining them to the subordinate commanders.   Most soldiers overseas were probably aware of this general picture.   On the other hand, one consequence of the chain of command was that they rarely were directly concerned with such higher headquarters as theater, army, corps, or division: directives originating from these centers which affected them were as a rule digested and reissued by intermediate headquarters.   Such factors as the existence of personally dramatic commanders in particular high headquarters may have had an effect on the extent to which the higher headquarters impressed themselves on the men.

When combat men were asked how well they felt that headquarters understood their problems and needs, a considerable proportion gave critical answers.   Among infantrymen in one division which saw extensive fighting early in the Mediterranean campaign, 34 per cent said that when they were in combat they felt headquarters was very much aware of their needs, 43 per cent said "fairly well," while 20 per cent said "I felt that they did not know very much about our real problems and needs." [15]   A survey made of infantrymen in Italy a year and a half later showed 52 per cent saying that headquarters understood their problems and needs "very well" or "fairly well," and 38 per cent saying "not so well" or "not well at all." [16]   The proportion who gave manifestly unfavorable answers was in each case a minority.   In general, it seems likely that the men were reacting to "headquarters" in an unanalyzed way, grouping together the sources of authority to the rear, though any specific headquarters they might have had in mind was probably of a relatively low echelon.

Criticisms of headquarters elicited from combat men in other connections expressed resentment that headquarters was exempt from their hardships; resentment against "harassing" in the form of fre-

---

[15] S-91, November 1943, 431 cases.   The question was:

"When you were in combat, how well did you feel that headquarters understood your problems and needs?"

_____ I felt that they were very much aware of our needs.
_____ I felt that they were fairly well aware of our needs.
_____ I felt that they did not know very much about our real problems and needs.

[16] S-177, 1,766 cases.

quent reports, inspections, and regulations; and the feeling that "nobody who *really* understood what we have to put up with could keep us in the line like this"—essentially blaming headquarters for their situation. The fact that higher echelons were of necessity rearward echelons introduced an inevitable source of misunderstanding and resentment into the relations of front-line troops with higher commands.

CHART VII

ATTITUDES TOWARD HEADQUARTERS IN RELATION TO TIME IN COMBAT
(Enlisted Infantrymen in Line Companies, Italy, April 1945)

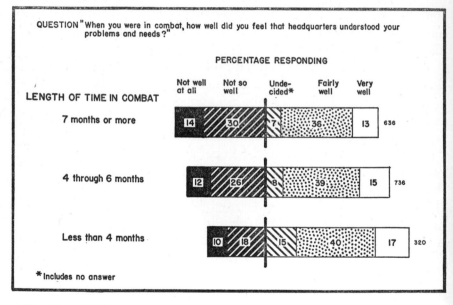

Data from S-177.
See footnote to Table 3 in Chapter 3 for the question concerning time in combat.
The numbers following the bars are the numbers of cases in which percentages are based.

As one might expect, men who had seen more combat were more likely than newer men to be critical of headquarters. Chart VII shows the data from the study of infantrymen in Italy. The considerable differences in response between new men and old-timers hold up when rank and educational level are controlled. This relationship to time in combat is probably indicative of the way in which the cumulative frustrations of combat augmented the men's resentment of the agency at whose behest they had to remain in the line.

Attitudes of Combat Men Toward Soldiers
Still in the United States

So far, we have been considering how combat men felt toward other groups of soldiers within the overseas theater.   Their attitudes toward soldiers and civilians back in the States had certain similarities, and may also conveniently be considered in this chapter.

Soldiers still in the States were the target of considerable outspoken sarcasm and bitterness on the part of all soldiers overseas, but particularly of the front-line combat man.   Table 6 shows that,

TABLE 6

ATTITUDES TOWARD SOLDIERS IN THE UNITED STATES
(Enlisted Men in Ground and Service Force Units, European Theater,
April–May 1945)

QUESTION: "How resentful do you yourself feel about troops who have jobs in the United States?"

	PERCENTAGE GIVING EACH ANSWER AMONG:		
ANSWER CATEGORIES	*Infantry line companies*	*Other division, corps, and army troops*	*Troops assigned to rear bases*
Very resentful	21 }51	15 }45	12 }40
Fairly resentful	30	30	28
Not so resentful	26	29	32
Not resentful at all	19	23	26
No answer	4	3	2
Total	100	100	100
Number of cases	*804*	*2,181*	*769*

Data from S-223.

in the European theater, men in Infantry line companies were somewhat more likely than men in rear units to say that they felt fairly resentful or very resentful about troops who had jobs in the United States.   This remains true when rank and education are controlled. As the table shows, however, the proportion making the extremely resentful response was a relatively small minority; the degree of bitterness felt by the men could easily be exaggerated.

A survey made in Italy at about the same time restricted the question specifically to soldiers who had never been overseas.[17]   The results found in Europe are supported by the fact that men in ground combat units were more likely than men in rear service outfits to

---

[17] On the question, "Do you think there are too many soldiers who have never been overseas?" 78 per cent of the ground combat troops checked "Yes, there are too many."

say that it bothered them very much that there were some soldiers who had never been overseas. (See Table 7.) Again only a minority checked the most critical category.

Too much emphasis should not be placed on the difference between combat and rear-area troops in regard to their resentment of soldiers still in the States. The difference is not large, and perhaps the similarity in attitudes is more striking than the difference. Among combat infantrymen, those who had been in combat for a very long time were more likely than others to say it bothered them that some soldiers had not been overseas, as the data in Chart VIII

TABLE 7

ATTITUDES TOWARD SOLDIERS IN THE UNITED STATES
(Enlisted Men in Ground and Service Force Units, Mediterranean Theater, May–June 1945)

QUESTION: "Does it bother you that there are some soldiers who have never been overseas?"

| ANSWER CATEGORIES | PERCENTAGE GIVING EACH ANSWER, AMONG MEN IN: | | |
	Ground combat units	Army and corps service units	Service units assigned to rear bases
It bothers me very much	38	19	24
It bothers me some	26	33	28
It bothers me a little	17	16	20
It does not bother me at all	17	31	27
No answer	2	1	1
Total	100	100	100
Number of cases	*508*	*292*	*387*

Data from S-205.

indicate. This finding is in accord with the reasonable supposition that the frustrations of combat would accumulate to result in a rising level of resentful envy toward men still enjoying the luxuries of a stateside existence. In the sample from the European theater, where the men had on the average seen much less combat, those who had served a long time overseas were only slightly more likely than other soldiers to say they resented soldiers in the United States.

It will be noted that in the Italian sample, even among the men who had seen seven months or more of combat, less than half gave the extreme unfavorable response. During the earlier phases of the war when only a few divisions were in actual combat in North Africa, Sicily, Italy, or the Pacific, men in these outfits may well have been more bitter at the seeming injustice of their lot.   As a wounded veteran of the three former campaigns put it:

Seems as though we could just name the outfits that were fighting on one hand. All the rest were in the States.   We were always hoping to be relieved.[18]

CHART VIII

ATTITUDES TOWARD SOLDIERS IN THE UNITED STATES IN RELATION TO
TIME IN COMBAT

(Enlisted Infantrymen in Line Companies, Italy, April 1945)

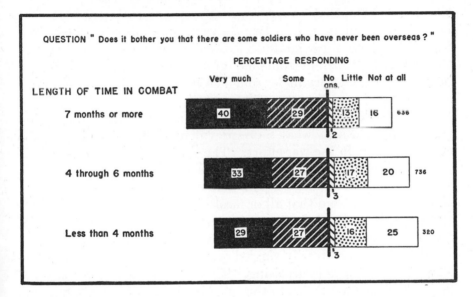

QUESTION " Does it bother you that there are some soldiers who have never been overseas ? "

Data from S-177.
See footnote to Table 3, Chapter 3 for the question concerning time in combat.
The numbers following the bars are the numbers of cases on which percentages are based.

A comment written at the end of a questionnaire early in 1944 by a private in the South Pacific expresses the extreme of bitterness:

Us guys over here that's left of the outfit are beat up with malaria and tropical ulcers.   We should have a chance to breathe a little fresh air for a while.   But I guess you better keep them USO boys back there or there won't be any USO.   If we have to we'll take another crack at the Japs.   There is nothing to look forward to anyway.

Such comments should not, however, be taken as typical of the attitudes of combat men in general.   As we have seen, many of them said they felt no resentment.

---

[18] Personal interview in hospital in the United States, made in spring of 1944.

Attitudes Toward Civilians on the Home Front

While there certainly was a great deal of outspoken criticism of civilians on the home front by soldiers overseas, the available data suggest that a surprisingly large proportion of the men felt rather favorably toward them. Two commonly reiterated complaints against civilians were that they were not doing all they should for the war—"Hell, they don't even know there's a war on"—and that they had no appreciation of what soldiers had done for them. Chart IX shows that on questions referring to each point, at least half of the combat men in two theaters gave answers which were favorable in manifest content. Also apparent from the chart is the finding that men in front-line Infantry companies or other combat units differed very little from men in rear-echelon units in their appraisal of the civilian war effort or civilian gratitude.

The data do suggest that resentments about civilian ingratitude may have been somewhat more prevalent than resentment about civilian laxness in the war effort. The proportions of men who said that all or most of the people back home had a real sense of gratitude and appreciation toward soldiers were consistently smaller than the proportions who said that all or most were doing all they should for the war effort. Since feelings of desertion and lack of appreciation might be expected to have been involved in the soldiers' perception of having been arbitrarily singled out to bear the real brunt of the war, this result is not surprising. That half or less of the men gave unfavorable answers even to this question is probably more remarkable.

On both of these questions, the more educated men tended to be somewhat more critical, but when education is controlled, men in forward elements still do not differ significantly from men in the rear. For the sample from the European theater, neither length of overseas service nor combat experience was significantly related to the men's responses.

While the general tenor of the men's answers about the civilian war effort was favorable, there is some evidence that a considerable proportion of the men who expressed anticivilian attitudes may have been reacting to stereotypes rather than to specific and known individuals. In both the European and Mediterranean theaters, the men were asked a question parallel to the one about the general civilian war effort, but concerning their own families and close

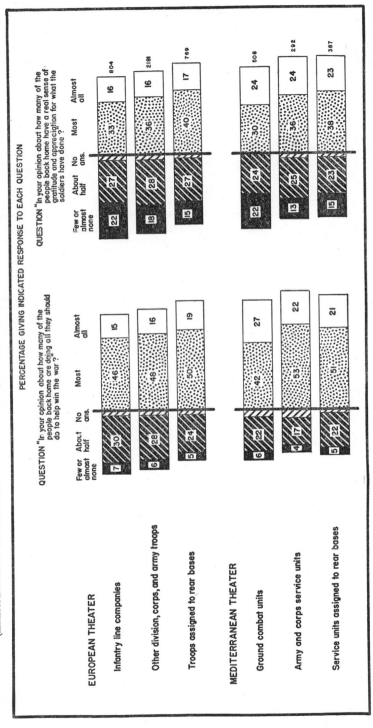

CHART IX

ATTITUDES TOWARD CIVILIANS

(Enlisted Men in Ground and Service Force Units, European and Mediterranean Theaters, April–June 1945)

PERCENTAGE GIVING INDICATED RESPONSE TO EACH QUESTION

QUESTION "In your opinion about how many of the people back home are doing all they should do to help win the war?"

QUESTION "In your opinion about how many of the people back home have a real sense of gratitude and appreciation for what the soldiers have done?"

EUROPEAN THEATER

Infantry line companies

Other division, corps, and army troops

Troops assigned to rear bases

MEDITERRANEAN THEATER

Ground combat units

Army and corps service units

Service units assigned to rear bases

Few or almost none   About half   No ans.   Most   Almost all

Data for the European and Mediterranean theaters are from S–223 (April–May 1945) and S–205 (May–June 1945), respectively. The numbers following the bars are the numbers of cases on which percentages are based.

friends.[19]   Chart X shows a comparison of the results of the two questions for cross sections of enlisted men in both theaters.   In the European theater, for which data on combat troops are available separately, the results for front-line infantrymen are nearly identical with the cross-section findings.   In both theaters, the troops in general were more likely to charge the public with not doing its share

CHART X

MEN'S ATTITUDES TOWARD THE GENERAL CIVILIAN WAR EFFORT, AS COMPARED TO THEIR ATTITUDES TOWARD THE WAR EFFORT OF THEIR FAMILY AND CLOSE FRIENDS
(Cross Section of Enlisted Men in European and Mediterranean Theaters, April–June 1945)

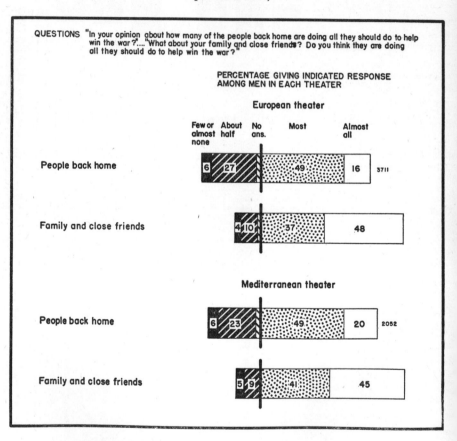

Data from S-223 and S-205.
The numbers following the bars are the numbers of cases on which percentages are based.

---

[19] The question did not specify close *civilian* friends, but in context one may be fairly sure that it was interpreted as intended, since it immediately followed the question on people at home.

than they were to say that their own family and friends had not done all they should do. Certainly the men's emotional ties to their friends and family would incline them to take a favorable view of what they were doing for the war. It may well be that these friends and relatives of overseas soldiers were actually somewhat more highly motivated than the rest of the population, because of their more personal involvement in the war effort. The increase in favorable response when the reference point was shifted to people whom the men knew intimately does nevertheless suggest that some elements of anticivilian feeling were relatively unstable.

The present data on soldiers' attitudes toward the home front thus fail to support the notion that a large proportion of combat men were violently anticivilian. Combat men did not differ much from men in the rear echelons in their feelings toward civilians. To the extent that resentment of people at home was a morale problem, it was not the special problem of the men whose personal contribution to the war was most immediate and, in one sense, greatest.

CHAPTER 7

MORALE ATTITUDES OF COMBAT FLYING PERSONNEL IN THE AIR CORPS[1]

Introduction

THIS chapter is the first of two which will deal with Air Corps combat flying personnel, a subpopulation of the Army which, though comparatively small numerically, played a major role in the military defeat of the Axis powers.

The foregoing chapters on ground combat have been concerned at some length with the situation of the infantryman and his fellows, describing characteristic attitudes and behavioral reactions to the sustained deprivations and harassments to which they were exposed. As would be expected from the sharp contrasts between aerial and ground warfare, combat personnel in the Air Corps differed in many essential ways from those in the Ground Forces.

The average infantryman, cast in his role through no choice of his own, was subjected to sustained danger in a chronically deprivational environment. In contrast, combat air crew members, while on their missions against enemy targets, were exposed to danger situations of comparatively short duration, alternating with longer periods, often days at a time, in a relatively danger-free environment, usually far behind the fighting lines. Although, from the point of view of the participants, aerial combat may have had some advantages over ground combat, the Air Corps combat situation was extremely harassing and in many squadrons the chances of survival were even lower than the average for combat infantrymen. But the important point is that it was, essentially, a type of combat of the men's own choosing, since 100 per cent of the combat personnel in the Air Corps had initially volunteered for combat flying duty.

Moreover, while there were marked cumulative psychological

---

[1] By Irving L. Janis. Extensive use was made of studies in the Eighth Air Force, for the design and analysis of which A. J. Jaffe, Arthur A. Lumsdaine, Marion Harper Lumsdaine, and Robin M. Williams, Jr., were mainly responsible.

effects of successive exposures to the stresses of aerial combat—as will be described in the next chapter—there was a definite termination point, as a consequence of the Air Corps practice of relieving combat air crew members from their combat assignment after they had completed a specified number of combat missions. Whereas most combat personnel in the Air Corps could look forward to a return to the United States if they survived the hazards of the required number of combat missions, those in the Ground Forces could expect only a continuation of their combat duty so long as they met the minimum physical requirements. Some indication of the tremendous difference in the objective situation with respect to return to the United States, the primary goal of so many American soldiers while they were overseas, is provided by the results of surveys of enlisted men who had been rotated to the United States, results which will be presented in the last section of this chapter. For example, it was found that 86 per cent of the enlisted Air Corps combat flying personnel rotated from the European and Mediterranean theaters had been overseas for less than 1 year whereas only 4 per cent of the rotated Ground Force combat personnel had been overseas for less than a year, the vast majority (90 per cent) having been overseas for 2 to 3 years or longer. (See Chart XII.)

As was described in the preceding chapter, the ground combat soldier, required to remain overseas for years and to undergo the stresses of sustained exposure to combat conditions, could and did take considerable satisfaction in his sheer toughness. No one, he felt, had to put up with so much for so long a period of time, and this gave him a feeling of a kind of superiority—a superiority which he never wanted in the first place and would gladly have relinquished if possible. Highly skilled performances were seldom required and, perhaps as a consequence, proportionately more endurance was demanded of him, since this demand would not jeopardize the efficiency of the total operation.

Combat air crew members, on the other hand, were not only able to take pride in their highly dangerous combat role but were, from the very beginning of their training, accorded elite status. Carefully selected and screened for the skilled jobs they were to perform in combat, Air Corps flying officers and enlisted men were recognized as a superior type of military personnel. As will be described later in this chapter, there was a definite demographic basis for this. For example, in cross sections of enlisted men in the Army as a whole, Research Branch surveys consistently show that well over one half of the men had not completed high school; among enlisted men in cross-section samples of Air Corps combat flying personnel, two thirds had graduated from high school, including a substantial proportion who had gone to college.

The status of combat flying personnel was further enhanced by the comparatively high rank which they were awarded, a form of recognition for their skill and exposure to danger which entailed concrete benefits and was highly prized in the Army.   Among mem-

CHART I

HIERARCHY OF ENLISTED GRADES IN HEAVY BOMBER CREWS AS COMPARED WITH A CROSS SECTION OF THE ENTIRE UNITED STATES ARMY

(Based on a Survey of 1,905 Men in Heavy Bomber Crews in the European Theater, June 1944, and a World-wide Cross-Section Survey of All Enlisted Men, June 1944)

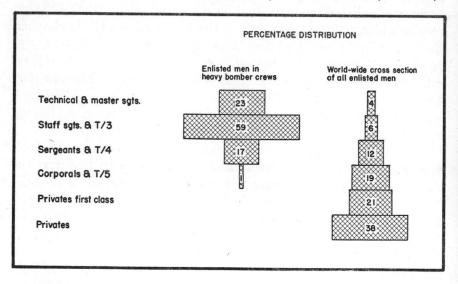

Data from S-135 and AGO 2 per cent sample.

bers of heavy bomber crews, 4 out of every 10 men were given commissioned officer status, and, in general, approximately 50 per cent of all combat flying personnel were officers.   Those members of combat air crews who were enlisted men—with whom most of the survey findings to be presented in this chapter are concerned—were also given high ratings as compared with enlisted men in ground combat units.   Chart I illustrates the fact that the rank distribution of enlisted men in combat flying crews was almost the reverse of the steep pyramid existing in the military system as a whole.

The picture presented by this chart is symptomatic of the differential treatment accorded to enlisted flying personnel as well as to flying officers, providing them with a secure sense of their elite status in the Army. And there was no lack of recognition from the general public of the courage of combat flying personnel and of their crucial contribution to the war effort.

This brief sketch of the differences between ground combat personnel and air combat flying personnel will be expanded in the remainder of this chapter. In Section I we shall present typical results from Research Branch surveys, in which morale attitudes of enlisted men in combat air crews are compared with those of enlisted men in combat Ground Force units. Section II will deal with some of the major characteristics of the Air Corps which may have been effective determinants of the comparatively favorable morale attitudes described in Section I. Attention will be focused primarily upon the practices of the Air Corps which appear to have played an important role in building favorable morale attitudes.

Our discussion will deal with only one type of Air Corps personnel, combat air crew members. Obviously the findings which we shall present cannot be regarded as applying to men in other types of jobs in the Air Corps. We have found that the morale attitudes of ground crews and service troops in the Air Corps differ in many ways from those of combat air crew members.

The type of survey data available does not warrant an attempt to give a systematic account of the morale attitudes of combat flying personnel or of the factors which are involved. For the most part the data are suggestive rather than conclusive. Hence the material in this chapter is limited to highlighting those special characteristics of the men and of their military organizations which are relevant for an understanding of the special problems of Air Corps combat personnel, many of which will be discussed in the next chapter. At the same time, the descriptive results may be of value in suggesting the types of organizational practices likely to have favorable consequences for the morale attitudes of combat personnel in general.

SECTION I

CHARACTERISTIC MORALE ATTITUDES OF COMBAT AIR CREW MEMBERS

Throughout the war it was widely reported by newspaper correspondents and other observers that morale was exceptionally high among combat airmen.   Bomber crews and fighter pilots have been consistently portrayed as men who were highly motivated to carry out the arduous demands of their organization, despite the extreme hazards to which they were exposed on combat missions.   This conception of Air Corps combat units as military organizations with high combat morale is supported by evidence from a number of attitude surveys in overseas theaters.

CHART II

JOB SATISFACTION AMONG COMBAT AIR CREW MEMBERS, INFANTRYMEN, AND ALL ENLISTED MEN

(Based on a Cross-Section Survey of Enlisted Men in the Pacific Ocean Areas, July 1945)

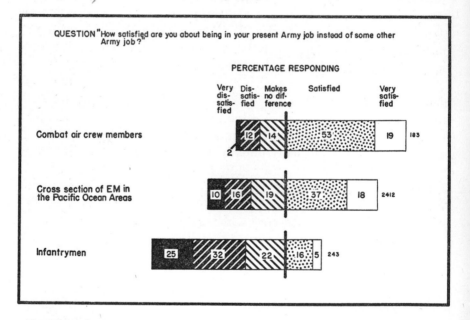

Data from S-232.

The numbers following the bars are the numbers of cases on which percentages are based.

The survey results show that a comparatively high proportion of combat flying personnel express: (1) Satisfaction with their combat assignment.   (2) Pride in their military organization.   (3) Willingness for combat.

We shall present survey results which typify the general findings of many Research Branch surveys, viz., that *combat flying personnel consistently tended to express relatively favorable attitudes as compared with men in other types of combat units.*   In presenting the compara-

CHART III

Attitudes Toward Job and Military Unit Among Enlisted Men in Combat Flying and Ground Units and Among All Enlisted Men

(Based on Surveys in Europe and the Pacific During the Early Months of 1944)

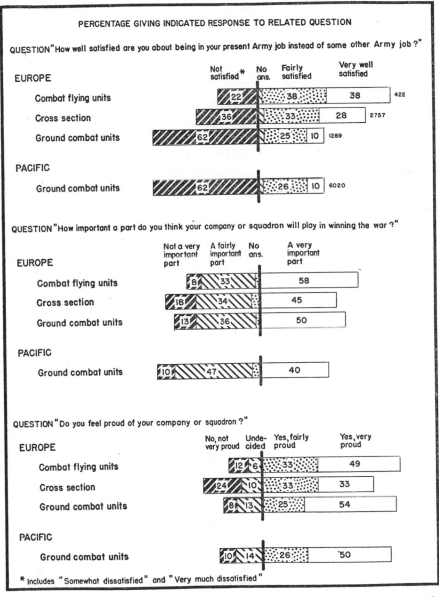

PERCENTAGE GIVING INDICATED RESPONSE TO RELATED QUESTION

QUESTION "How well satisfied are you about being in your present Army job instead of some other Army job?"

	Not satisfied*	No ans.	Fairly satisfied	Very well satisfied	
EUROPE					
Combat flying units	22		38	38	422
Cross section	36		33	28	2757
Ground combat units	62		25	10	1289
PACIFIC					
Ground combat units	62		26	10	6020

QUESTION "How important a part do you think your company or squadron will play in winning the war?"

	Not a very important part	A fairly important part	No ans.	A very important part
EUROPE				
Combat flying units	8	33		58
Cross section	18	34		45
Ground combat units	13	36		50
PACIFIC				
Ground combat units	10	47		40

QUESTION "Do you feel proud of your company or squadron?"

	No, not very proud	Unde-cided	Yes, fairly proud	Yes, very proud
EUROPE				
Combat flying units	12	6	33	49
Cross section	24	10	33	33
Ground combat units	8	13	25	54
PACIFIC				
Ground combat units	10	14	26	50

* Includes "Somewhat dissatisfied" and "Very much dissatisfied"

Data from S-116 and S-100. The majority of enlisted men in combat flying squadrons were combat air crew members but there was a minority of men in ground crews who could not be identified and eliminated from the sample. It is probable, however, that if a pure sample of combat air crew members had been available, the result would show exactly the same pattern since other surveys show that combat flying personnel tended to express slightly more favorable attitudes on these items than did the ground crews in combat flying squadrons. Figures shown for ground combat units in Europe are the average for two veteran Infantry divisions transferred from fighting in the Mediterranean; those for the Pacific are the average for combat veterans in four Infantry divisions.

tive data, no attempt has been made to hold constant the relevant background variables—such as age, rank, education—or other factors which may account for the differences. These variables will be discussed in Section II of this chapter which is devoted to the major factors which appear to underlie the favorable morale attitudes of combat flying personnel.

Job Satisfaction

Combat air crew members expressed a relatively high degree of satisfaction with their combat flying assignment. This is borne out by comparative results from a number of cross-section surveys in overseas theaters. Chart II presents typical findings from a survey in the Pacific Ocean Areas showing that enlisted men in combat air crews much more often expressed satisfaction with their job than did enlisted men in the Infantry. It will be observed that the proportion of favorable replies of combat air crew members exceeded the average for enlisted men in the entire theater, whereas the infantrymen were definitely below the average.

Similar findings on job satisfaction, obtained from a survey in the European theater, are shown in Chart III.

Attitudes Toward the Combat Unit

From surveys of overseas troops there appears a fairly consistent pattern which differentiates combat flying personnel from Ground Force combat troops. This pattern may be schematized in the following way:

Attitude variables	Combat air crew members	Ground combat troops
Satisfaction with their job	Above average	Below average
Evaluation of the importance of their military unit	Above average	Average or slightly above average
Pride in their military unit	Above average	Above average

The essential feature is that combat air crew members tended to be above the average for the Army in general in all three areas. Combat infantrymen tended to give a lower than average proportion of replies indicating job satisfaction but exhibited a high level of pride in their combat organization. While a sizable majority of combat infantrymen rated their own military organization as important in the war effort, they were somewhat less likely to do so than were combat air crew members.   Illustrative data are shown in Chart III.   While this particular set of results cannot be regarded as sufficient evidence for establishing the pattern which we have described, it does present the typical picture which appears from the results of other surveys based on smaller samples.

In Chart III it will be observed that a majority of men in combat flying units gave a favorable response to the question on importance of their own squadron.   When a similar question was asked in another survey about the importance of their type of outfit, a very high proportion of enlisted men in combat air crews gave a favorable response.   In June 1944 a cross section of all enlisted men in heavy bomber crews in the European theater (a sample of 1,869 men) were asked the following question: "How important a part do you think your type of outfit will play in winning the war?" Seventy-nine per cent answered "a very important part" and an additional 19 per cent answered "a fairly important part." [2]

Willingness for Combat

The results from a number of separate surveys indicate that there was a comparatively high degree of willingness for combat duty among combat airmen.   Before examining some of the detailed findings, it may be of value to keep in mind certain considerations related to motivation for combat in the Air Corps.   As will be described in the next section, only those men who had volunteered for a combat flying assignment were recruited for precombat air crew training by the Air Corps.   The fact that almost all combat flying personnel had originally volunteered for that type of assignment would lead one to expect that they were relatively highly motivated to engage in combat.   But, on the other hand, it has been pointed

---

[2] S-135.   The majority of men in a cross section of enlisted men in medium bomber crews in the European theater (a sample of 647 men) were also favorable, although the proportion is less than that found for men in heavy bomber crews: 61 per cent of the men in medium bomber crews answered "a very important part" and 37 per cent "a fairly important part."   But in a cross-section sample of enlisted men in light bomber crews in the European theater (384 men) only 34 per cent answered "a very important part" and 54 per cent "a fairly important part."   The low proportion in light bomber crews has very little effect on the average results for all enlisted combat flying personnel in the theater, however, since only a very small proportion of the total population of combat air crew members were in light bomber crews.   Presumably the small number of men in light bombers tended to feel that the types of missions they flew were of minor importance compared with those flown by heavy and medium bombers, the major types of bombers used in the European theater.   (Data for medium and light bomber crews are from S-150, July 1944.)

out by some observers that many volunteers for combat flying had extremely unrealistic, glamorized notions about aerial combat and sometimes suffered a cruel awakening when they developed a sharp awareness of the realities of combat flying in the course of their first few combat missions.   That this occurred in extreme forms in some cases and constituted a serious problem in the Air Corps is indicated by psychiatric discussions of the problem of "psychological failure" among men who were just beginning their tour of combat duty.[3] Hence, while it is to be expected that combat flyers, as a class of men who had originally volunteered for combat assignments, would show a high degree of willingness for combat, it is also to be expected that, to some extent, combat motivation decreased once the men were actually exposed to combat conditions.

There are no data at hand which are relevant for estimating the proportion of combat flyers who were relatively immune to the initial shock of exposure to actual combat conditions.   We have found, however, that in a cross section of combat air crews, the majority asserted that they would willingly volunteer for combat flying if they had to make the choice over again.

To the extent that verbal responses on an anonymous questionnaire may be assumed to be indicators of willingness for combat, the responses to the direct question shown in Table 1 support the conclusion that during a period of maximum effort (the preinvasion air assault), the vast majority of combat air crew members in the European theater, most of whom had had a considerable amount of combat experience, were willing to volunteer for combat flying duty.

The samples shown in Table 1 constitute a cross section of men in each of the various operational categories; the results are representative of all combat flying personnel in the European theater at the particular time when the survey was made.   Although the findings are limited to a single time period, they are consistent with additional findings at other time periods, lending some weight to the generalization that throughout the war the majority of combat air crews in the European theater tended to express willingness for combat.

In evaluating the "generalizability" of the data, it is important to consider the amount of combat experience of the men in our samples.   If, for example, the European theater at the time of the cross-

---

[3] Cf. D. W. Hastings, D. G. Wright, and B. C. Glueck, *Psychiatric Experiences of the Eighth Air Force: First Year of Combat* (Josiah Macy Jr. Foundation, August 1944, 307 pp.).

section survey had an unusually large proportion of men who had flown only a few missions, the results might overestimate willingness for combat among the general population of combat flying personnel, in so far as an undue proportion of the sample may not have been sufficiently exposed to combat.   As will be shown in Chapter

TABLE 1

WILLINGNESS TO VOLUNTEER FOR COMBAT FLYING DUTY

(Based on a Cross-Section Survey of Combat Air Crew Members in the European Theater, June–July 1944)

QUESTION: "If you were doing it over again, do you think you would choose to sign up for combat flying?" *

	Number of of cases	Per cent answering "Yes"
Heavy bomber crews		
Pilots	*351*	70
Enlisted gunners	*1,869*	63
All crew positions combined	*3,125*	66
Medium bomber crews		
Pilots	*242*	81
Enlisted gunners	*647*	77
All crew positions combined	*1,308*	79
Light bomber crews		
Pilots	*200*	91
Enlisted gunners	*384*	75
All crew positions combined	*629*	82
Fighter plane crews		
Pilots	*654*	93

Data from S-135, S-142 and S-150.
* The specific choices for this question were as follows:

_____ Yes, I'm pretty sure I would
_____ Yes, I think I would but I am not sure
_____ No, I don't think I would
_____ No, I'm sure I would not

In the table the first two choices are combined to give the total percentage who gave a "Yes" response. In the case of all the subsamples in the table, the major portion of the combined "Yes" percentage was due to the high percentage who gave the first choice.

8, there is a strong tendency for combat motivation to decline with successive exposures to combat.   Hence, if the samples were unrepresentative of men who had flown many missions, the results would tend to overestimate willingness for combat among a more general population of combat flyers.

It is important to note, therefore, that the men surveyed represent a wide range of combat experience.[4]   The samples were not heavily weighted with men who had a minimal amount of combat experience, as is illustrated by the following data for the samples of air crew members in the four major operational categories:

Fighter pilots: 87% had completed 30 or more combat flying hours.

Heavy bomber crews: 89% had completed 5 or more combat missions.

Medium bomber crews: 89% had completed 10 or more combat missions.

Light bomber crews: 83% had completed 10 or more combat missions.

Hence a potential source of serious overestimation of willingness for combat may be ruled out, in evaluating the results in Table 1.

The results in Table 1, showing that a majority of combat air crew members expressed willingness for combat, are in marked contrast to the general findings for men in ground combat units.   As was described in earlier chapters, the majority of infantrymen with combat experience were outspoken in their complaints about further combat duty.

To establish the differential between ground and air combat personnel, however, it is necessary to compare responses of the two groups to identical questions dealing with willingness for combat. Although comparative results from large-scale samples are not available, a number of small sample comparisons from the Pacific theater as well as from the European theater consistently show that combat veterans in air crews were more likely than those in Ground Force units to express willingness for combat.

The following are some typical comparative findings on attitudes related to willingness for combat, obtained from small sample studies:

---

[4] For more detail on the number of missions (or combat hours) completed by these samples see Chapter 8, Charts V, VII, and VIII and accompanying text.

So far as we know, no one has attempted the complex statistical analysis necessary to determine the distribution of combat exposure for all combat airmen in the European theater in World War II.   Hence we cannot determine the extent to which the distribution of combat exposure for our samples approximates those for the corresponding total populations.

In taking account of the range of combat exposure for the distributions shown in the tables, it should be borne in mind that, in general, almost all combat air crew members were affected by the policy of relieving men from flying combat status after they had completed a specified maximum number of missions (or combat hours), which constituted a tour of duty.   (Cf. the discussion of the tour of combat duty at the end of this chapter.)   Hence there was a ceiling on the total number of missions; this reduces the probability that any sizable proportion of combat flyers greatly exceeded the maximum number of missions flown by the men in our samples.

From a survey of enlisted men in the European theater, April 1945,[5] the responses of 302 combat infantrymen may be compared with those of 63 combat air crew members.   One of the questions asked of both groups was the following:

> Some soldiers feel they've already done their share in winning the war. Others feel they should do still more.   How do you personally feel about what you've done in this war?
>
> _____ I don't feel I've done my share yet
> _____ I feel I've already done my share, but I'm ready to do more, but not in a combat job
> _____ I feel I have done my share, but I'm ready to do more in any kind of job they assign me to
> _____ I feel I've already done my share and should be discharged

While 59 per cent of the combat infantrymen expressed unwillingness for future combat duty (i.e., gave the second or fourth category as their answer), only 25 per cent of the combat air crew members did so.

Another question, with less complicated response categories, was asked of both groups:

> After Germany's defeat, if you had to be stationed overseas until after Japan surrenders, which of the following would you prefer as an assignment?
>
> _____ Stay in ETO (as part of the forces occupying Germany)
> _____ Go to the Pacific, in my present kind of job
> _____ Go to the Pacific, but in a different kind of job than I now have
> _____ It doesn't make any difference to me

More than three quarters (78 per cent) of the combat infantrymen expressed a preference for avoiding duty in the active overseas theater (by giving the first category as their answer) as against only one third (32 per cent) of the combat air crew members.

From a survey of enlisted men in the Pacific Ocean Areas in July 1945,[6] the responses of 223 combat infantrymen may be compared with those of 183 combat air crew members.   The following question was asked of both groups: "Considering everything, how do you feel about further service in the Army?"   Of the combat infantrymen, 44 per cent answered "I should be discharged now," whereas 33 per cent of the men in combat flying units gave this answer.

---

[5] S-223.
[6] S-232.

CHART IV

ATTITUDE SCALE SCORES OF ENLISTED MEN IN THE UNITED STATES:
AIR CREW TRAINEES COMPARED WITH CROSS SECTIONS OF
ARMY GROUND FORCES AND ARMY SERVICE FORCES
(Based on a Survey in July 1943)

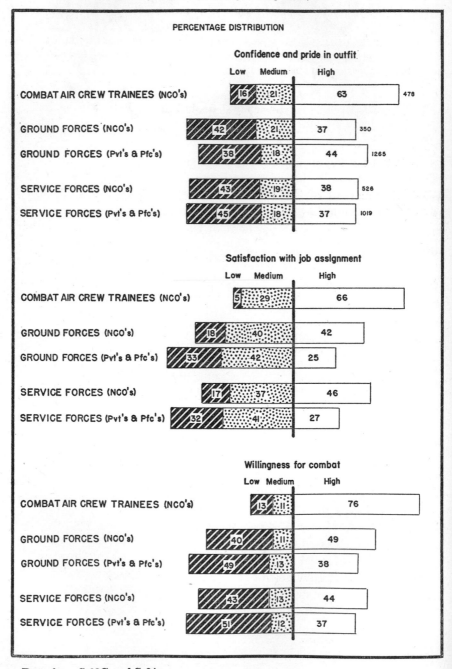

Data from S-63G and S-64.
The numbers following the bars are the numbers of cases on which percentages are based.

Only 17 per cent of the infantrymen asserted that they should not be discharged until after Japan was defeated whereas 34 per cent of the men in combat flying units gave this response. Since at the time of this survey knowledge of one's own Adjusted Service Rating score (under the Army Demobilization Plan) tended to be a major factor in determining attitudes toward further service, it is relevant to note that the median ASR score was the same for both groups (67 points) and there were equal proportions eligible for immediate discharge.

While results of the type which we have just cited are not conclusive, they support the general conclusion that willingness for combat tended to be higher among combat air crew members than among combat infantrymen. The findings presented so far serve to illustrate the general picture which consistently emerges from surveys in overseas theaters. Turning now to results for soldiers in the United States, we find the same pattern. Combat flying trainees, like the men in combat crews in active overseas theaters, appear to have had comparatively favorable attitudes with respect to the three important types of morale attitudes which have been discussed in this section: (1) Satisfaction with their job assignment. (2) Pride in their military organization. (3) Willingness for combat.

A number of surveys show that air crew trainees expressed more favorable morale attitudes than did men in Ground Force and Service Force units. The results in Chart IV provide illustrative findings for the three attitude areas with which we have been primarily concerned. Since the data are based upon scale scores, they summarize the results of many specific questions for each of the three attitude areas.[7]

---

[7] The specific questions used in the attitude scale on confidence and pride in outfit were:

Do you feel proud of your company (battery, squadron, troop)?
   Yes, very proud
   Yes, fairly proud
   No, not proud
   Undecided

Do the men in your company (battery, squadron, troop) cooperate, and work well together?
   All of the time
   Most of the time
   Often do not
   Almost never do
   Undecided

How many of the men in your company would you say are good all-around soldiers?
   All are
   Most are

It will be noted in Chart IV that when rank is held relatively constant the differences between combat air crew trainees and men in Ground and Service Forces still remain.   The attitude responses of the former tended to be more favorable than those of noncoms in Ground and Service Force units.   This point has an important bearing on the material to be presented in the next section, in which we shall describe some of the specific characteristics of the Air Corps which appear to have been effective factors underlying the comparatively favorable morale attitudes of Air Corps combat personnel. Since the relative favorableness of combat air crew trainees on the three morale attitude scales is not markedly reduced by limiting the comparisons to noncoms in Ground and Service Force units, it follows that the single factor of rank, important as it was shown to be in Volume I, Chapters 3 and 4, does not by itself account for the differentials in morale attitudes.   Rank is only one element in a constellation of factors which, when considered together, form the basis for the comparatively favorable morale attitudes of combat flying personnel.   It is this set of factors which we shall attempt to delineate in the next section.

        About half are, half are not
        Only a few are
        Almost none are
    Do you like to work with the other fellows in your company?
        With most of them
        With about half of them
        With only a few of them
        Undecided
    How do you think your company would show up under combat conditions?
        Very well
        Fairly well
        Not so well
        Poorly
        Undecided
    Do you feel proud of your Regiment?   (If you are not part of a Regiment answer this question for the largest unit to which you belong.)
        Yes, very proud
        Yes, fairly proud
        No, not proud
        Undecided
  The specific questions used in the attitude scale on satisfaction with job assignment were:
    How interested are you in your Army job?
        Very much interested
        A little but not much
        Not interested at all
    Would you change to some other Army job if given a chance?
        Yes
        No
        Undecided

SECTION II

FACTORS RELATED TO FAVORABLE MORALE ATTITUDES AMONG COMBAT FLYING PERSONNEL IN THE AIR CORPS

In this section we shall not attempt to describe all aspects of the complex social matrix underlying the morale attitudes of combat flying personnel. Rather, our attention will be focused primarily upon those distinctive features of combat Air Corps units which appear to have had a favorable effect upon morale attitudes. Our approach to the problem is, in a sense, a case study of a special type of military unit, and it may provide some insights into the kinds of policies and practices which facilitate high combat morale in general.

The various policies and practices to be described in this section may be classified conveniently under the following general headings:

How satisfied are you about being in your present Army job instead of some other Army job?
    Very satisfied
    Satisfied
    It does not make any difference to me
    Dissatisfied
    Very dissatisfied
Do you feel that everything possible has been done to place you in the Army job where you best fit?
    Yes
    No
    Undecided
On the whole, do you think the Army is giving you a chance to show what you can do?
    A very good chance
    A fairly good chance
    Not much of a chance
    No chance at all
    Undecided
The specific questions used in the attitude scale on willingness for combat were:
If it were up to you, what kind of outfit would you rather be in?
    In a combat outfit overseas
    In a noncombat outfit overseas
    In an outfit that will stay in the United States
If you were sent into actual fighting right now, how do you think you would do?
    I think I would do all right
    I think I would have trouble at first, but after a while I would be O.K.
    I don't think I would do very well
    I haven't any idea how I would do
Which of the following statements best tells the way you feel about getting into the fighting?
    I'm ready to go and I want to get into the real fighting soon
    I'd like to get in on the fighting before it's over, but I don't think I'm ready yet
    I hope I won't have to go, but if I do, I think I'll do all right
    I hope I won't have to go because I don't think I'll ever be good as a fighter
    None of the above fits me. My feeling is this: _____

(1) Personnel recruitment. (2) Status and prestige. (3) Officer-enlisted men relationships. (4) Characteristics of flying jobs. (5) Characteristics of the Air Corps combat situation.

Under each of these headings, many specific factors will be discussed. As was mentioned before, the type of data which is available does not warrant an attempt to determine the specific and general effects of each individual factor which we shall discuss. It is probable, however, that the total constellation of factors to which we shall refer accounts in a large degree for the differences in attitudes between combat flying personnel and men in other types of military organizations.

Personnel Recruitment

The Air Corps instituted personnel recruitment policies which had very favorable consequences for the demographic composition of Air Corps combat personnel. It is well known that during the period of the war when the Army was undergoing its most rapid phase of expansion (1941–1943), the Air Force received the major share of the "cream of the crop" from reception centers. In addition, within the Air Force itself, there was a formal selective process with respect to the recruitment of personnel for training in combat flying jobs. Men were accepted as aviation cadets for training as bombardier, navigator, or pilot only if they were at least 18 but no more than 27 years and 6 months of age.[8] In addition, they were required to pass a fairly rigorous physical examination[9] and mental qualifying examinations or educational requirements.

Similar standards were applied in the recruitment of enlisted air crew members, many of whom had met all of the requirements for aviation cadets but had been "washed out" of the cadet training course and thereupon accepted assignments as gunners in air crews. One of the most important features of the recruitment policy affecting all combat flying jobs was that only men who had volunteered for a combat flying job were accepted for training.

Obviously, these selective recruitment policies had marked demographic consequences which differentiated the Air Corps population from that of the Army in general. Some of the important ways in which the population of enlisted combat air crew members

[8] Army Regulations No. 615-100, "Enlisted Men: Aviation Cadets," War Department, Washington, November 5, 1942.

[9] As prescribed in AR 40-110 or AR 40-105, with modifications prescribed by the Commanding General, Army Air Forces.

differed from enlisted men in other types of Army units were the following:

Higher level of mental ability as measured by AGCT scores.

Higher average education level as indicated by highest school grade completed.

Higher proportion of younger men, i.e., under 25 years of age.

Higher proportion of men in good physical condition as indicated by the ratings of medical officers during the precombat period.

Higher proportion of men who volunteered for military service after Pearl Harbor.

Higher proportion of men who volunteered for a combat assignment.[10]

In publicity about the Air Corps, combat air crew members were represented as young, healthy, intelligent men whose willingness to volunteer for active combat duty reflected their courage and their desire for excitement and adventure.   Inasmuch as this stereotype was widely circulated throughout the American civilian population and since it had, to some extent, an objective demographic basis, the men who were assigned to air crew training were very much aware

---

[10] The objective population statistics which conclusively demonstrate the demographic differences are not available to us for publication.   We have consulted the relevant Army population data, however, and found that they verify the conclusions derived from cross-section survey results.

The following comparisons, based upon Research Branch cross-section survey results, serve to illustrate some of the differences between enlisted men who were Air Corps flying personnel and enlisted men in general.

Age: About half of all enlisted men in cross-section surveys of the Army were 25 years of age or older.   This proportion is approximately twice as large as that for enlisted men who were Air Corps flying personnel.

Education: As was mentioned in the introduction to this chapter, among the enlisted men in cross sections of the Army as a whole, well over half of the men had not completed high school.   Among enlisted men in samples of Air Corps combat flying personnel, two thirds had completed high school.

Proportion of volunteers: While there were fluctuations at various time periods in the ratio of volunteers to selectees, surveys consistently indicate that the proportion who volunteered for military service was almost twice as high among Air Corps enlisted flying personnel as among enlisted men in the Army as a whole.   In some samples of enlisted combat flying personnel, close to 50 per cent of the men had volunteered for military service.

Physical condition: As would be expected from the fact that no one with any physical defect was accepted for training in combat air crews, all of the men in surveys of Air Corps enlisted flying trainees in the United States reported that they had been classified as physically qualified for overseas duty.   In cross-section surveys of enlisted men in the United States, a sizable minority (varying between one fourth and one third of all enlisted men, at different time periods) reported that their current official medical classification was "limited service" or "physically unqualified for overseas duty."

of the fact that they represented a highly selected superior group of soldiers.

Thus, at the very beginning of their careers as air crew trainees, the recruitment standards of the Air Corps provided a basis for the men's conception of themselves as part of an elite military group. In this way the recruitment policy may have indirectly served to build up the men's pride in their military organization. It probably also tended to give the men a sense of personal achievement, simply by virtue of their having been included among the chosen few. This may have increased their job satisfaction and reinforced their motivation for making the grade in their subsequent military careers.

There is another way in which the recruitment policy of the Air Corps resulted in an increase in favorable attitudes among combat flying personnel. Certain of the demographic consequences of the recruitment policy are of the type which have been found to be related to favorable morale attitudes. In other words, the population selected for combat air crew jobs was more likely than the general population of soldiers to contain men with favorable morale attitudes.

For example, as has already been indicated, the average age of combat air crew members was substantially lower than the average age of the total Army population; it has been found that, in general, younger men were more likely than older men to express willingness for combat duty. Results from cross-section surveys indicate that men who were 30 years of age or older constituted the age group with the lowest motivation for combat. That the findings from cross-section surveys apply to Air Corps combat personnel is indicated by the results shown in Chart V.

These data are consistent with the notion that if the Air Corps had not held down the proportion of older men in combat air crews, a lower percentage of Air Corps combat personnel would have been found to express willingness for combat. In the same way, a number of other demographic consequences of the Air Corps selective recruitment policy probably tended to augment the proportion of men with favorable morale attitudes. The two factors which were most important in this respect were:

1. The high proportion of men in good physical condition (since this attribute has been found to be correlated with willingness for combat).

2. The high proportion of men who volunteered for their combat

assignment (since this factor, as was shown in Volume I, Chapter 7, is related to satisfaction with job assignment).[11]

Status and Prestige

Combat personnel in the Air Forces tended to think of themselves as members of an elite military group. This has already been mentioned as one of the indirect consequences of the relatively high

CHART V

RELATIONSHIP BETWEEN AGE AND WILLINGNESS FOR COMBAT DUTY AMONG
COMBAT AIR CREW MEMBERS
(Based on a Survey of Heavy Bomber Crews in the European Theater, June 1944)

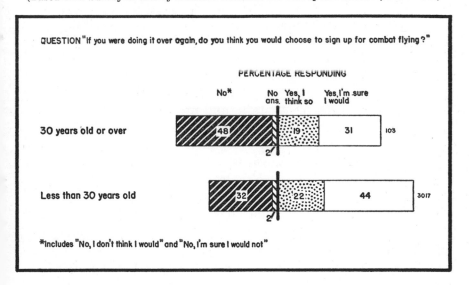

Data from S-135.
The numbers following the bars are the numbers of cases on which percentages are based.

standards set by the Air Corps in recruiting men for combat training, reinforcing the favorable publicity which the Air Corps enjoyed throughout the war. The Air Corps not only performed an excellent public relations job in gaining public recognition for men in its organization but also adopted certain policies and practices which

---

[11] The high proportion of men who volunteered for military service was another factor which probably tended to have the same general effect. But this factor does not necessarily represent higher initial willingness for military duty because, as was mentioned in Volume I, Chapter 4, many men volunteered when they were just one step ahead of the draft board in order to have the advantage of choosing their branch of service. In such cases, volunteering for the Army is indicative of a high initial preference for Air Corps duty.

tended to augment the status and prestige of Air Corps combat flying personnel.

Before discussing these factors, it is necessary to point out that during both the training period in the United States and the period of active combat duty overseas, combat air crew members were aware of the prestige and deference accorded to men in their type of Army job. Very early in their training, air cadets, as an elite group, were set apart from other types of personnel in the Army. For example, Army regulations specifically provided that: "So far as practicable, aviation cadets will be segregated from other enlisted men in all activities, including housing, messing, and hospitalization." [12]

Enlisted air crew members also shared in the elite position of men in Air Corps combat jobs. Enlisted men in the entire Air Force were conscious of the high degree of recognition accorded to their military organization by the public at large. Of all the enlisted men in the Air Forces, it was those in combat flying jobs who enjoyed the highest degree of status and prestige.

Of primary importance in increasing the status and prestige of Air Corps combat personnel were the policies and practices of the Air Corps with respect to promotions. As compared with other types of Army units, the Air Corps' Tables of Organization specified relatively high Army grades for men in combat flying jobs. The result was that combat flying personnel received much higher ratings than men in other types of combat organizations in the Army. First of all, as was mentioned earlier in this chapter, over 50 per cent of all combat air crew members were given officer status. This is in marked contrast to the proportion of officers in other types of Army units, since officers constituted less than 10 per cent of the total Army population. Hence an exceptionally high proportion of Air Corps combat personnel enjoyed the special privileges, the higher income and prestige that accrued to officers. In Volume I, Chapters 3, 4, and 8, it has been pointed out that officers tended to have more favorable attitudes, in general, than enlisted men. That this generalization applies to Air Corps combat personnel with respect to willingness for combat is indicated by the results in Chart VI.

As was shown in Chart I, even those members of combat air crews who did not receive commissioned officer status were given higher ratings as compared with men in other types of combat units. Almost all enlisted men in combat flying jobs were given the rank of

[12] AR 615-160, p. 7, Section IV, Para. 21b.

sergeant or higher, the vast majority being top three graders; whereas, in the Army as a whole, only about one enlisted man out of every four attained the rank of sergeant or higher.

There was a steady upgrading of officers in the course of their tour of combat duty as is illustrated by Chart VII.

Enlisted combat personnel were also upgraded while they were on combat duty. As is seen in Chart VIII, during the period cov-

CHART VI

RELATIONSHIP BETWEEN OFFICER VERSUS ENLISTED STATUS AND WILLINGNESS FOR COMBAT AMONG COMBAT AIR CREW MEMBERS

(Based on a Survey of Heavy Bomber Crews in the European Theater, June 1944)

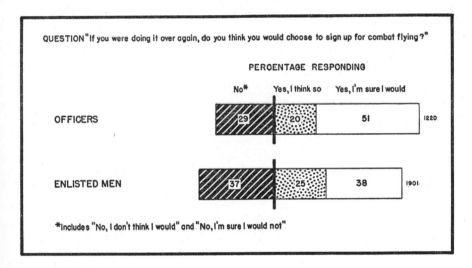

Data from S-135.

The numbers following the bars are the numbers of cases on which percentages are based.

ered by the June 1944 survey there was a definite increase in rank during the first half of the tour of combat duty although the promotion rate tended to level off during the second half.[13]   The majority of enlisted men appear to have received at least one promotion while on active combat duty.

[13] This situation may have been improved at a later period, when the Air Corps introduced the policy of withholding promotion to high noncom ranks until the men were on active combat duty. However, it appears from surveys of enlisted men in the United States that this change in policy gave rise to considerable dissatisfaction among enlisted air crew trainees, since they felt that they were being deprived of the rank that had been given to their predecessors. It is possible that an increased rate of promotion during the tour of combat duty may have compensated for this status deprivation during the training period.

Another factor which may have reinforced the prestige of combat flying personnel was the liberal policy of the Air Corps with respect to issuing awards and decorations.   While it may be true that American soldiers in World War II did not value awards and decorations

CHART VII

CHANGES IN THE DISTRIBUTION OF OFFICER GRADES WITH INCREASED NUMBER OF
COMBAT MISSIONS FLOWN
(Based on a Survey of 1,220 Officers in Heavy Bomber Crews in the
European Theater, June 1944)

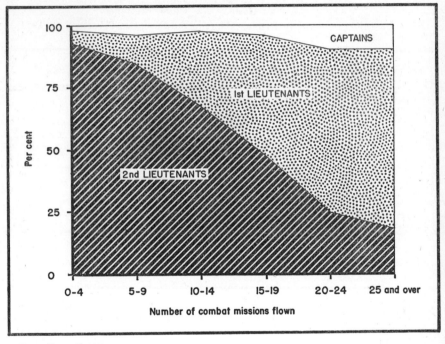

Data from S-135.

as highly as did men in other armies, there were relatively few who were indifferent about receiving this form of recognition for combat performance.[14]

In one survey of a cross section of enlisted men in the European theater (May 1945)[15] it was found that combat air crew members

[14] Late in the European war but before the Army demobilization plan was announced, the Air Corps introduced new rules which tended to cut down the number of awards and decorations.   There was a considerable amount of unfavorable comment from the combat flying personnel who were affected, which would appear to indicate that they were far from indifferent about the number of awards and decorations they received.
[15] S-205.

had the same average number of campaign stars as did combat ground troops.   But combat air crew members were found to have, in addition to campaign stars, an average of 530 awards and decorations per every 100 men.   Ground combat troops, while they had received more awards and decorations than noncombat Ground and Service Force troops in the theater, averaged only 39 awards and

CHART VIII

CHANGES IN THE DISTRIBUTION OF ENLISTED MEN'S GRADES WITH INCREASED
NUMBER OF COMBAT MISSIONS FLOWN

(Based on a Survey of 1,905 Enlisted Men in Heavy Bomber Crews in the
European Theater, June 1944)

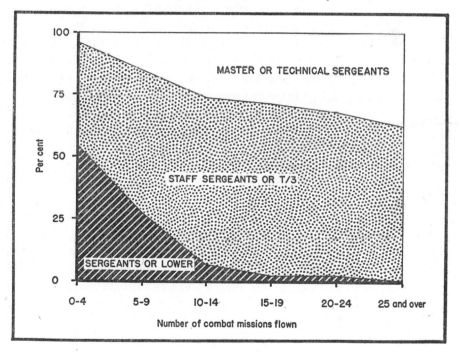

Data from S-135.

decorations per every 100 men.   Thus, according to this survey, the average number of awards for combat flying personnel was almost fourteen times higher than that for ground combat troops.

Awards and decorations took on a very special significance when the Army demobilization plan was put into effect inasmuch as each one contributed 5 points to a man's discharge point score.   But the tremendous differential between Air Corps and Ground Force combat personnel was reduced somewhat by the large numbers of retroactive awards given to Ground Force troops during the first few months after VE Day.   Nevertheless, the fact remains that while the war against Germany was going on, combat personnel in the Air Corps received many more awards and decorations than did men in other types of combat units.   While this may have had the effect of cheapening Air Force medals to some extent, it is likely that the overall effect was a positive boost to esprit de corps.

Officer-Enlisted Men Relationships

As was mentioned in Volume I, Chapter 8, enlisted members of combat air crews have been found to be somewhat less critical of their officers than were other types of enlisted personnel in the Air Corps.   The results of a number of comparative studies, most of them based on small samples, suggest that enlisted men in combat flying units tended to make fewer criticisms of their officers than did enlisted men in Ground and Service Force units.   Typical findings based on a fairly large sample are presented in Chart IX.[16]

There were several factors which probably tended to make for relatively favorable relationships between officers and enlisted men in combat flying units.   First of all, because an enlisted member of a combat air crew was accorded high status and prestige it is probable that he received more favorable treatment from his superior officers than did the average enlisted man.   In accordance with the general Air Corps practice of minimizing deprivations of combat flying personnel, they were subjected to fewer of the traditional military demands such as periodic inspections, military formations, and routine menial tasks.   It is probable, therefore, that enlisted men who were in combat air crews were less likely than those in other types of jobs to develop resentful attitudes toward their officers because of "too much chicken."

Interpersonal relationships between enlisted flying personnel and the officer in charge of their crew were strongly affected by the high

---

[16] The check-list categories for the questions shown in Chart IX were as follows:

Question A
_____ They have a good idea
_____ They have a fair idea
_____ They know little or nothing about my abilities

Question B
_____ Very well
_____ Fairly well
_____ Not so well
_____ Not well at all

degree of group identification which developed among combat air crews.   Air Corps psychiatrists have reported that in a typical air crew all of the members shared feelings of intense loyalty toward each other and that there was a high degree of mutual psychological dependence.[17]   From a survey of 1,563 officers and enlisted men in heavy bomber crews (June 1944)[18] there is indirect evidence of the

CHART IX

ENLISTED MEN'S ATTITUDES TOWARD SUPERIORS IN CHARGE OF THEIR WORK
(Based on a Cross-Section Survey of Enlisted Men in the European Theater,
January 1944)

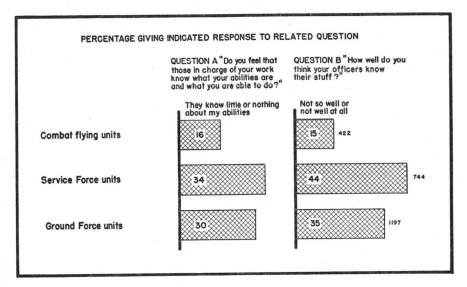

Data from S-116.
The numbers following the bars are the numbers of cases on which percentages are based.

strong desire of the men to stick with their own crew.   In answer to the question, "How important is it to you to fly your missions with the same crew rather than with different crews?" 88 per cent answered "Very important" and an additional 9 per cent answered "Important."   Only 3 per cent gave a negative response: "Not very important" or "Not important at all."

Group identification was undoubtedly a major source of personal motivation to perform the combat job as effectively as possible.

---

[17] Cf. R. R. Grinker and J. P. Spiegel, *Men Under Stress* (Blakiston, Philadelphia, 1945).
[18] S-135.   This question was asked of approximately half the entire sample.

The social integration of air crews may have been facilitated by the fact that ground officers rather than the crew leaders had some of the responsibility for inspecting enlisted men's billets, disciplining the men for off-duty offenses, and the like.

In the Ground Forces, the platoon leader and other company officers usually had a dual role with respect to the enlisted men under their command: they functioned, on the one hand, as the combat leader whose responsibility was analogous to that of a job supervisor, and, on the other hand, as the disciplinary authority responsible for maintaining conformity to Army rules and regulations. In combat Air Corps units, however, these two functions were divided to some extent among two entirely different sets of officers. In his combat job, the enlisted air crew member was under the supervision of an officer who was a member of his own combat crew. But disciplinary and administrative functions were often carried out by noncombat (ground) officers, who had little contact with the enlisted men under their authority while the men were actively engaged on their jobs. It is likely that some of the sources of impaired relationships between enlisted men and their combat leaders were eliminated, to the extent that disciplinary functions of aircraft commanders were limited to behavior on combat missions.

Characteristics of Flying Jobs

In addition to the prestige and status accorded to Air Corps combat flying jobs, there were a number of special characteristics of combat flying jobs which appear to have played an important role in the men's satisfaction with their combat assignment. We shall discuss several such factors which, although not directly tied up with policies and practices of the Air Corps, constitute an integral part of the context underlying high job satisfaction.

Skill level. The skill level of most combat flying jobs was much higher than that of the average Army job, and many men took considerable pride in performing the skilled operations involved. The sense of pride was undoubtedly augmented by the fact that the job was one requiring completion of highly specialized training before being assigned to it. This was especially the case for pilots, navigators, and bombardiers, all of whom were required to go through intensive technical training courses in order to be qualified to carry out their complex job functions. Also, a much higher proportion of enlisted men in combat flying jobs than in Service Force or Ground Force units had received Army specialized technical training. As a matter of fact, 100 per cent of the men in combat air crews had attended an Army Specialist School for training in their particular jobs. From a cross-section survey of enlisted men in the European theater (January 1944)[19] we find the following proportions of men reporting that they had attended an Army Specialist School: Service Force units (N = 744), 51%; Ground Force units (N = 1,197), 48%.

Psychological satisfaction from flying. Flying provided opportunities for certain kinds of psychological satisfactions which were lacking in other types of Army jobs. Since it involved exciting visual and kinesthetic experiences as well as the exercise of skills, flying was often regarded as a kind of sport. For many of the men, flying was fun—at least when there was no exposure to the dangers of enemy action. Moreover, as has been pointed out by Grinker and Spiegel, flying assignments—especially for a pilot—afforded unique opportunities for the symbolic gratification of personal motivations:

Nothing is so powerful and yet so responsive to delicate touch as modern aircraft. . . . The mastery of the power in the machine is a challenge which gives a justified sense of accomplishment when it has been successfully met. Furthermore, the flier increases his sense of power by identifying himself with his plane, which he feels as an extension of his own body. He thereby achieves a feeling of aggressive potency bordering on the unchallenged strength of a superman. This is well illustrated in Colonel Robert Scott's book, *God Is My Co-Pilot,* where, in an account of his flight over Mount Everest in a little P-43, the author describes how he felt that he had humbled this highest mountain and then patronizingly saluted his fallen opponent.
The flier's opportunity to master his environment and to dominate a powerful machine represents an attraction which is emotionally satisfying to the average young man in our civilization. Its appeal is universal and many respond to it out of a perfectly healthy interest. On the other hand, it is also a very satisfying compensation for feelings of inferiority. It is a purposeful and socially acceptable escape from and compensation for personal defeats among ground-bound humans. . . . Furthermore, this denial of weakness and dependence is highly exhibitionistic. The flier is universally recognized as someone daring and courageous with dash and glamour.[20]

Although psychological gratifications of this sort probably occurred mainly during precombat flight training, they may have served as incentives in the combat situation, increasing the motivation of some of the men to perform adequately on their combat flying assignment so as to maintain their flying status after the tour of

[19] S-116.
[20] Grinker and Spiegel, *op. cit.,* p. 5.

combat duty was completed.   There is little question, however, that the intense stresses engendered by the harassments of combat flying often outweighed satisfactions derived from flying in general. In the next chapter we shall discuss some of the major sources of stress, especially in connection with the marked decline in motivation for combat flying which occurred with increased number of combat missions flown.

Relevance for postwar civilian jobs.   To some extent, combat flying jobs provided relevant experience for a future career in civilian aviation—or at least this was widely thought to be the case.   Many men volunteered for combat flying jobs with this consideration in mind.

It is well known that, in contrast to officers in ground combat jobs, a comparatively high proportion of officers in combat flying jobs (especially pilots and navigators) counted upon using their Army training and experience in postwar jobs.   Enlisted men in the Air Corps were slightly more likely than enlisted men in Ground Force units to feel that the skills they acquired on their Army job would prove to be useful in future civilian work.   This is illustrated by the following results from a cross-section survey of enlisted men in the European theater (January 1944):[21]

Have you learned any skills or trades in the Army which you think you will use in the civilian work you expect to do?

Enlisted men in combat flying units (N = 422)—27% answered "Yes"

Enlisted men in Ground Force units (N = 1,197)—17% answered "Yes"

Characteristics of the Air Corps Combat Situation

In general, the environmental situation for Air Corps combat flying personnel was much less deprivational than that for combat ground troops.   Many air bases were located in relatively safe areas, far behind the fighting lines.   Between missions combat air crew members usually had more physical comforts and far more opportunity for relaxation, recreation, and amusements than did combat personnel in Ground Force units.   This was especially true in the European theater, where bomber bases were often situated in the British countryside, not far from a more or less normal civilian community.

---

[21] S-116.

The comparatively favorable character of the environmental situation of Air Corps combat personnel was further enhanced by certain policies and practices of the Air Corps.   Throughout the war, Air Force headquarters appears to have adhered to a policy of providing combat personnel under its command with as favorable environmental conditions as possible.   The widely publicized Air Force vacation centers in overseas theaters and the attractive Air Force redistribution centers at Atlantic City and Miami Beach were symptomatic of the overall command policy of treating combat flying personnel with a high degree of indulgence, deliberately giving them the "breaks" whenever circumstances permitted.   This policy was probably based on a realistic appraisal of the losses of highly trained personnel and expensive aircraft that would be entailed if airmen were given insufficient opportunities for rest and recuperation between missions.   By means of directives and formal recommendations, it was communicated through Air Force channels to all echelons of the organization.   Among the most important consequences, at the operational level, were a number of practices directly affecting the daily life situation of combat air crew members.   We shall describe three important factors which tended to reduce the deprivational character of Air Corps combat duty.

Work load and time off.   In general, work schedules for men on active combat flying duty were arranged so as to take account of the men's need for adequate rest and time off.   Air Corps combat units appear to have made a definite effort to avoid overworking their men (1) by spacing the combat missions to which any one crew was assigned so that there were rest intervals between missions, and (2) by giving the men relatively frequent leaves or passes which enabled them to have brief vacations from combat activities.

As will be shown in the next chapter, a heavy work load (as measured by the number of combat missions flown in 10 days or in some comparable short period of time) resulted in a high degree of physical fatigue.   There is some evidence which indicates that the actual work load of combat air crew members in the European theater rarely exceeded the range which the men regarded as optimal for efficient combat performance.

Results from a survey of fighter pilots in the European theater show that during a sample period of 7 days, the actual work load of fighter pilots was well below the maximum work load which the pilots themselves estimated to be the limit for optimal combat efficiency.   The value of these results is enhanced by the fact that the sample work-load period occurred at a time when air operations were at one of the highest peaks of activity, i.e., the period of Allied invasion of Continental Europe.   It is highly improbable that during less active periods the average work load would be found to be heavier than it was during the sample period covered by our study.

CHART X

A COMPARISON OF THE ACTUAL WORK LOAD OF FIGHTER PILOTS WITH THE
MAXIMUM OPTIMAL WORK LOAD AS ESTIMATED BY THE PILOTS
(Based on a Survey of 654 Fighter Pilots in the European Theater, June 1944)

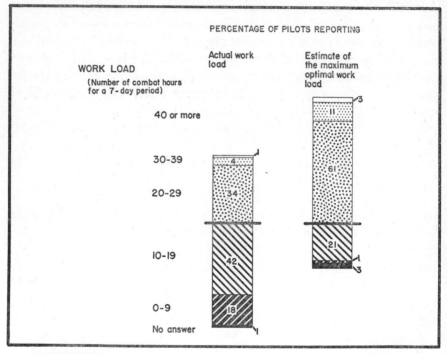

Data from S-142.

Hence the data in Chart X support the conclusion that the work load of fighter pilots rarely exceeded the maximum optimal work load as estimated by the men themselves.[22]

[22] Actual work-load data are based upon the answers of fighter pilots to the following question:
    "How much combat flying have you done in the past 7 days?"
        About _____ hours combat flying

It will be noted in Chart X that the majority of fighter pilots estimated that for a 7-day period, 20–29 flying hours was the maximum optimal work load, whereas during the sample 7-day period the actual work load of 60 per cent of the men was below 20 combat hours. Only 5 per cent of the men had a work load which exceeded 29 combat hours per 7 days.

We do not have comparable data on a sample work-load period for heavy, medium, and light bomber crews.   There are some findings, however, which tend to bear out the conclusion that combat air crew members were rarely subjected to excessive work loads.

Men in heavy bomber crews in the European theater were asked the following question: "About how many days in a row do you think a man in your job can fly on combat missions of the sort you have been on and keep his efficiency at a reasonably high level?" [20] Eighty-five per cent gave estimates within the range of 2 to 4 days in a row.   The men were also asked to specify "the greatest number of days in a row that you have flown on combat missions."   Almost three fourths of the men reported that they had never flown more than 4 days in a row, and more than half of the men reported that they had never flown more than 3 days in a row.   Only 6 per cent reported having flown on more than 6 consecutive days.

In evaluating these results it is necessary to bear in mind that the men in heavy bomber crews were not reporting on their actual work load during a sample period but rather on the heaviest consecutive work load to which they had ever been subjected at any time. Furthermore, since the survey was conducted in early June of 1944, the combat experience of all of the men occurred during the period of preinvasion bombing, which, as has already been mentioned, was one of the most active periods of air operations of the entire war. The results, therefore, provide evidence that heavy bomber crews were rarely given a consecutive work load which markedly exceeded

---

The data on estimates of the maximum optimal work load are based on the answers of fighter pilots to the following question:

"About how much combat flying *of the sort you have been doing recently* do you think a man in your job can do during a week's time and keep his efficiency at a reasonably high level?"

In my best judgment, about _____ combat hours

[20] S-135.

the men's own estimates of what the maximum should be for optimal combat efficiency.[24]

In addition to assigning work loads which gave the men an opportunity for rest and recuperation between combat missions, Air Corps combat units in ETO adhered to a relatively liberal policy with respect to granting leaves, passes, and furloughs.[25]

An indication of the frequency with which combat air crew members were given an opportunity of spending a period of free time away from their air base is provided by the following set of results, obtained from Air Corps surveys (June–July 1944) in the European theater:[26] (1) among heavy bomber crews 7 out of every 10 men received at least one leave or pass[27] during the month preceding the survey and 1 out of every 10 men received a furlough during that month; (2) among medium bomber crews and also among light bomber crews 8 out of every 10 men received at least one leave or pass during the preceding month and 1 out of every 10 men received a furlough during that month; (3) among fighter pilots 6 out of every 10 men received at least one leave during the preceding month.

Comparative data are not available for other types of combat personnel in the Army, but it is clear that combat troops in the Ground Forces were given much less opportunity, on the average, to spend a period of free time away from their military organization. One essential point for which comparative evidence is available is that a much higher proportion of men in combat flying units than in Ground Force and Service Force units expressed satisfaction about the amount of free time they were given. In a cross section survey of enlisted men in the European theater (January 1944),[28]

---

[24] The same conclusion applies to medium and light bomber crews. The results for medium and light bomber crews, based on the same two questions, show an even smaller deviation between the men's estimates of the number of consecutive daily missions for optimal performance and the heaviest consecutive work load which had ever been required of them.

[25] An additional indication of the effort of the Air Corps to facilitate vacations for air combat personnel is the fact that rest homes were set up in Europe which offered excellent recreational facilities and relatively luxurious living conditions. When combat air crew members were given a routine furlough they usually had a choice of spending it in an Air Corps rest home or elsewhere. The popularity of the rest homes is evidenced by answers to the following question, included in the survey of heavy bomber crews (June 1944) in the European theater: "If you were to be given seven days off as a furlough, after a certain number of missions, do you think you would prefer to spend your furlough time at one of the Air Corps rest homes or somewhere else on your own?" The proportion of heavy bomber crews who asserted that they would prefer to spend their furlough in an Air Corps rest home was higher than the proportion who asserted a preference for spending their furlough somewhere else.

[26] S-135, S-142, and S-150.

[27] Only leaves or passes which covered a minimum of 24 hours are included.

[28] S-116.

the following question was asked: "Are you getting about as much time off (furloughs and passes) as you should have under present circumstances?" Sixty-four per cent of the men in combat flying units expressed satisfaction[29] whereas only 47 per cent of the men in Ground Force units and 34 per cent in Service Force units did so.[30]

Medical attention. The Air Corps provided extensive medical facilities for combat flying personnel and established medical policies designed to avoid sending men on combat missions when they were ill or when they were suffering from some physical impairment. Adequate medical attention was an important feature of the combat situation for Air Corps flying personnel, since the men were not only exposed to the danger of being injured by enemy action but were also subject to various physical disorders resulting from exposure to high altitudes, extreme cold, rapid changes in air pressure, excessive vibration, and other flying conditions which are health hazards.

Survey results show that air crew members consistently expressed a high degree of satisfaction with the medical treatment they received while in combat. For example, from the survey of heavy bomber crews in the European theater (June 1944) we find that in response to the question, "All things considered, do you think that the practice in your outfit with respect to excusing men from missions for physical reasons is too strict, about right, or not strict enough?" a majority of the men (71 per cent) answered "about right." Only 10 per cent answered "too strict," 3 per cent "not strict enough," and 16 per cent "don't know." Similar results are obtained for the following question: "Have you personally observed any cases where a man you thought was physically unfit to fly a particular mission, and who wanted to be grounded that day, was required to fly anyway?" Only 5 per cent of the men in heavy bomber crews claimed that this had occurred "on a number of occasions"; 30 per cent asserted that they knew of one or two such cases, while 64 per cent stated that they never knew of any such cases. The vast majority of men in heavy bomber crews (82 per cent) expressed satisfaction with the medical service, in their responses to

---

[29] The first choice in the following check list for the question is used as the indicator of satisfaction:

_____ About as much as we should have
_____ Should have a bit more
_____ Should have a lot more

[30] Since this survey was made before the invasion of the European continent, most of the men in Ground Forces were undergoing precombat training. The results therefore do not apply to the combat situation.

the following question: "On the whole, how satisfied do you feel about the medical service you are getting?" [31]

The comparative results from a survey in the Central Pacific theater in Chart XI indicate that criticisms of medical treatment tended to occur less frequently among enlisted men in combat flying units than among a cross section of all enlisted men in the entire theater.[32]

CHART XI

CRITICISMS OF MEDICAL ATTENTION
(Based on a Survey of Enlisted Men in the Central Pacific Theater,
July–August 1945)

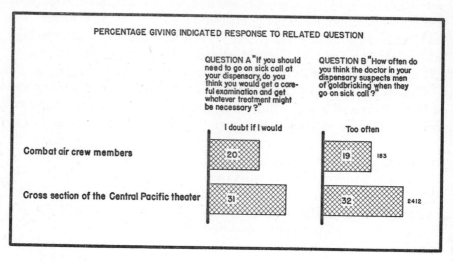

Data from S-232.

The numbers following the bars are the numbers of cases on which percentages are based.

---

[31] The first choice of the check list for this question was used as the indicator of satisfaction:

_____ About as good as it could be under the circumstances
_____ Could be improved but it wouldn't make too much difference to me
_____ Could be improved and it would help a lot if it were
_____ Uncertain

[32] The check-list categories for the questions shown in Chart XI were as follows:

Question A
_____ Yes, I am sure I would
_____ I think I would, but I am not sure
_____ I doubt if I would

Question B
_____ Too often
_____ About as often as necessary
_____ Not often enough
_____ As far as I know, the doctors never think the men on sick call are "goldbricking"

The tour of combat duty. Early in the war, Air Force Headquarters in the War Department advocated that all operational units engaged in combat establish a tour of combat duty, to be calculated on the basis of casualty figures, with the aim of giving men on combat flying duty what was deemed to be a reasonable chance of survival. Officially it was never admitted that the completion of any specified amount of aerial combat duty established a blanket right for transfer from operational flying status to a noncombat assignment. In actual practice, however, any man who did not wish to continue flying could usually secure grounding once he had completed the amount of combat duty regarded as a tour at the time. The required amount varied with the type of aircraft, the particular theater of operations, the stage of the war and the exigencies of the particular military situation.[33]

At the time of the survey of combat air crew members in the European theater (June 1944), the customary tours of duty were as follows:

Heavy bomber crews, 30 missions.[34]

Medium bomber crews, approximately 50 missions, but no definite number was clearly defined.

Light bomber crews, approximately 60 missions but no definite number was clearly defined.

Fighter pilots, 300 hours of combat flying.

The formal and informal practice of rotating combat flying personnel to the United States after they had completed their tour of combat duty was undoubtedly an important factor affecting morale attitudes in the Air Corps combat situation. In the next chapter we shall discuss in detail the variety of ways in which the tour of duty affected motivation for combat.

The essential point, in the present context, is that combat flying personnel could look forward to relief from combat duty and return to the United States if they survived the hazards of a specified number of combat missions. In ETO the tour policy provided an objec-

---

[33] In the fall of 1944 the War Department advocated that all overseas theaters discontinue the tour of duty system and replace it by individual evaluation of each combat air crew member in terms of his physical and psychological capacity to tolerate the stresses of combat missions. The War Department also recommended, however, that allowance be made for a transition period during which all men who had already begun their series of missions would be permitted to continue under the tour of duty system. In the case of almost all flying units the transition period lasted until the end of the war and hence the tour of duty system was not actually discontinued in practice.

[34] Later in 1944 the number was increased to 35 missions.

CHART XII

EXTENT OF OVERSEAS SERVICE BEFORE ROTATION OF AIR CORPS COMBAT FLYING PERSONNEL AS COMPARED WITH OTHER TYPES OF ARMY PERSONNEL

(Based on a Cross-Section Survey of Returnees in Redistribution Centers in the United States, March–April 1945)

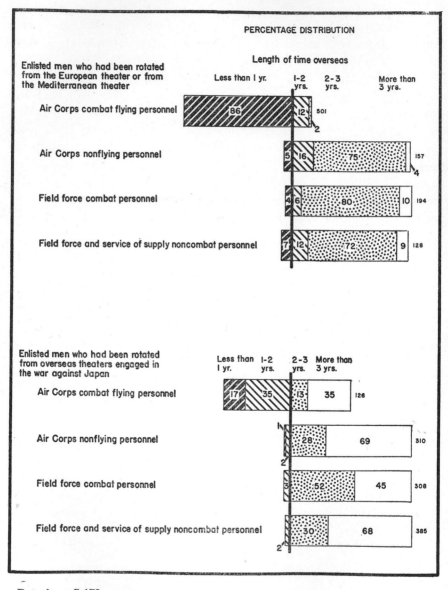

Data from S-172.

The samples are restricted to able-bodied returnees who had been rotated to the United States on the basis of long service overseas or extensive service under severe and hazardous combat conditions.

The numbers following the bars are the numbers of cases on which percentages are based.

tive basis for the expectations of combat flying personnel that they would be returned home from the overseas theater after six or seven months on active combat duty.

The results shown in Chart XII provide clear-cut evidence of the fact that combat flying personnel were rotated to the United States after a much shorter period of overseas service than were men in other types of Army jobs. Almost identical results were obtained from two additional surveys of rotational returnees covering different time periods.

CHAPTER 8

OBJECTIVE FACTORS RELATED TO MORALE ATTITUDES IN THE AERIAL COMBAT SITUATION[1]

SECTION I

PSYCHOLOGICAL EFFECTS OF SUCCESSIVE EXPOSURES TO AERIAL COMBAT

FRONT-LINE ground troops were exposed for days and weeks at a time to sustained combat harassment which fluctuated sporadically in intensity. The combat situation for Air Corps personnel was considerably different. Most combat flyers were subjected to brief, intense exposures lasting for only a few hours at a time, alternating with relatively long periods in a fairly safe environment. It is possible, therefore, to obtain fairly clear-cut measurements on the extent to which flyers were exposed to combat. For men in any given type of plane, the number of missions flown (or the number of combat flying hours) provides a reasonably good measure of combat exposure. With an adequate criterion of combat exposure it is possible to secure relatively precise information on the cumulative effects of exposure to the stresses of aerial combat.

From the extensive cross-section survey of combat flying personnel in the European theater carried out during the late spring and early summer of 1944, data are available on the relationships between various morale factors and amount of combat exposure, as indexed by the number of combat missions flown. These data show that *with increased number of combat missions flown, willingness for*

---

[1] By Irving L. Janis. Section I of this chapter is based primarily on a manuscript prepared by Robin M. Williams, Jr. In this chapter, as in Chapter 7, extensive use was made of studies in the Eighth Air Force, for the design and analysis of which Arthur A. Lumsdaine, Marion Harper Lumsdaine, and Robin M. Williams, Jr., were mainly responsible, along with A. J. Jaffe, to whom belongs the principal credit for designing the analysis of the objective data and for compiling these data from operational records.

combat flying tended to deteriorate markedly and symptoms of chronic tension and anxiety tended to increase.

Before presenting the detailed findings, there are certain methodological problems to be considered in connection with the use of the number of combat missions completed as the criterion for determining the amount of exposure to aerial combat.   It is well known that individual missions varied enormously in severity, as indicated by casualties and battle damage.   Also, there were trends and cycles in the intensity of combat.   Heavy bomber losses, for example, were extremely high in the early phases of the American air assault on Germany, then leveled off and finally dropped fairly steadily toward the end of the war in Europe.   Nevertheless, in surveying a cross section of men flying in a specific type of ship, the variations in severity of individual missions tend to average out.   Moreover, since the men studied had been flying their missions during a relatively short time span, the influence of trends in casualties is minimal.

There is some objective evidence supplied by the Statistical Control Section of the 8th Air Force which shows the trends during the period relevant for our study.   The data cover two major aspects of severity of aerial combat: dangerousness of the missions and work load.   The dangers of flying missions may be measured by two objective criteria: (1) casualty losses and (2) battle damage to the planes, whether by flak or by enemy fighters.   Charts I and II show that during the seven-month period preceding our study of the 8th Air Force, there was little change in the dangerousness of heavy bomber missions: battle damage increased slightly, but casualties among bomber crews decreased slightly.   Ninety-seven per cent of the men in our study began flying during the seven-month period covered by these tables.

Work load, which is defined as the amount of flying within a given period of time, may be measured by (1) the frequency of missions per unit of time and (2) the number of operational hours of combat flying per unit of time.   The data in Charts III and IV show that work load increased markedly during the seven-month period, reflecting the intensification of aerial bombardment before D Day.

It will be noted that in May 1944 the average crew flew over twice as many missions and over twice as many operational hours as it did in November 1943.   A more strenuous work load could imply inadequate rest periods between missions, fatigue and loss of sleep, which reinforce the usual strains of facing the hazards of combat fly-

CHART I

CREW LOSSES (MISSING AND KILLED IN ACTION, AND SERIOUSLY INJURED)
PER MONTH AS A PERCENTAGE OF SORTIES

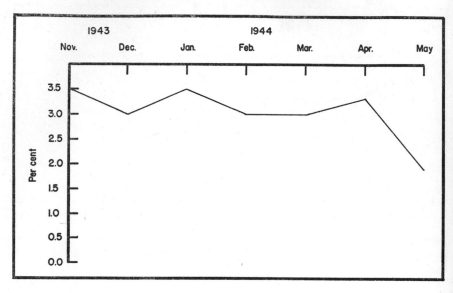

CHART II

PERCENTAGE OF SORTIES RECEIVING BATTLE DAMAGE, BY MONTH

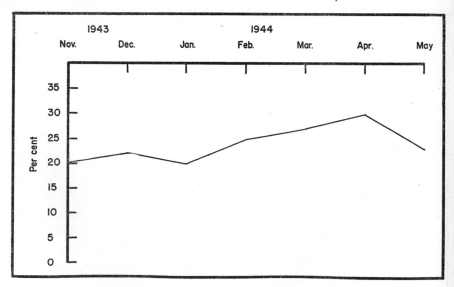

Data for Charts I and II from Research Branch Report ETO 19, June 1944.

CHART III

AVERAGE NUMBER OF OPERATIONAL HOURS FLOWN PER MONTH PER CREW
ASSIGNED TO OPERATIONAL GROUPS

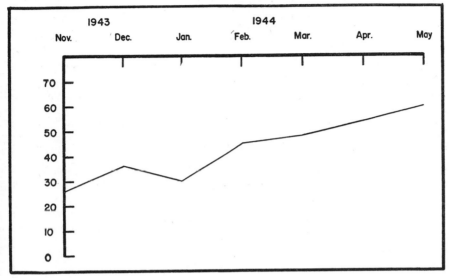

CHART IV

AVERAGE NUMBER OF SORTIES PER MONTH PER CREW ASSIGNED TO
OPERATIONAL GROUPS

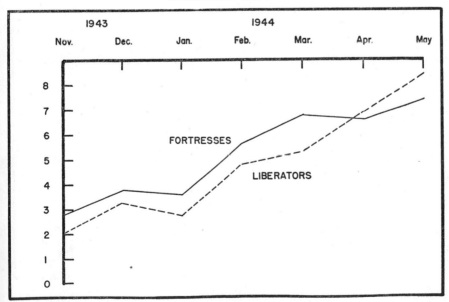

Data for Charts III and IV from Research Branch Report ETO 19, June 1944.

ing.[2] It is highly improbable, however, that the work-load trend was a source of spurious correlations in the findings which will be presented on the effects of increased number of combat missions.

The work load was constant for the two groups in the sense that at the time of the survey the heavy work load affected those who had flown few missions as well as those who had flown many missions. There is some slight possibility that the latter group may have been disturbed by the fact that during their tour of duty the work load had been stepped up. While experience of this kind might have given rise to some slight deterioration in combat morale, it is even more probable that there was a compensating effect upon those who had flown only a small number of missions. The newer men had flown their few missions under the conditions of a heavy work load, whereas those who had many missions to their credit had flown their earlier ones under the conditions of a more favorable work load. Therefore, if a heavy work load had any pronounced effect upon combat morale, we would be *underestimating* the higher morale of the newer men. Actually it is probably unduly meticulous to elaborate these compensating effects of the work-load trend since the relevant data, which will be presented in a subsequent section of this chapter, provide no evidence that increased work load had any substantial effect on the type of attitude responses with which we shall be concerned.

It appears to be safe to accept the relationships between amount of exposure to combat and various morale variables reported below, since the major potential sources of spurious correlations would not account for the results:

1. Despite the fact that the work load was not constant throughout the period during which the men had been flying their missions, there is no reasonable basis for assuming that this factor could account for correlations between impaired combat morale and number of combat missions flown.
2. The objective data in Charts I and II support the assumption that the average degree of dangerousness of each mission tended to be relatively constant, when the men in our study are grouped according to the number of missions they had flown.
3. When men who had flown many missions were compared with those who had flown few missions, no significant differences were found with respect to background characteristics such as education, age, etc.

---

[2] On the other hand, there are some grounds for expecting an added strain from anticipatory anxiety when missions are hazardous but widely spaced in time. But it is likely that the unfavorable consequences of a small work load interfere with morale and efficiency to a much lesser degree than the strain of a high work load—which entails more sustained exposure to combat without adequate opportunity for physical and psychological recuperation between missions. (See Section II of this chapter.)

4. There is no known selective factor which could account for lower morale among men who had flown a larger number of missions. It is true that not all men in any original population of flyers reached the stage where they had flown a large number of missions. Those who were combat casualties might possibly be considered to have had higher morale than those who survived to fly again, if one were to assume that combat casualties tended to be more frequent among men who, having higher morale, were more willing to take chances in combat. But there is no evidence that this occurred; differential selection must have been minor in comparison with the random selectivity which characterized the occurrence of casualties in aerial combat, where purely chance factors played such a great role. Moreover, the other major group of men withdrawn from the population of flyers with larger amounts of combat experience consisted of the nonbattle casualties. This group included a considerable proportion of psychoneurotic cases as well as men who had been suffering from physical disabilities. Elimination of nonbattle casualties does constitute a selective factor, but this factor tends to operate in the direction of removing men with lower morale. Hence if this factor affects our findings it would operate in the direction of decreasing the differences between men who had flown few missions and men who had flown many missions, since the proportion of low-morale men in the latter group would be underrepresented.

This section deals with two major effects of increased number of exposures to aerial combat: (1) Decrease in motivation for combat flying. (2) Increase in symptoms of tension and anxiety. The evidence is derived primarily from the survey of heavy bomber crews in the European theater and is supplemented by findings for medium and light bomber crews and fighter pilots. In the third part of this section, the tour of combat duty will be discussed, and some hypotheses on the role it may have played in sustaining combat motivation will be suggested.

Decrease in Motivation for Combat Flying

Increased exposure to aerial combat appears to be associated with a marked decrease in willingness for combat flying. Chart V presents the replies of heavy bomber crew members who had completed from 1 to 29 missions[3] to the question, "If you were doing it over

---

[3] There were in the sample 20 men who had flown no missions, too few to warrant inclusion in the chart. There were 41 men who had flown 30 missions or more. These were excluded from the chart not only because of the small number of cases but also because those who flew more than 30 missions are not comparable with the other men, inasmuch as many of them had volunteered to stay on for additional missions beyond the 30 missions required by the tour of duty. The results for the two extreme categories omitted from the chart were as follows:

	Yes	No	No answer
0 missions	95%	5%	
30 missions or over	68	29	3%

again, do you think you would choose to sign up for combat flying?"
The percentage of men who replied "Yes, I'm pretty sure I would"
or "Yes, I think I would but I'm not sure" decreases with increased
number of combat missions flown.   This relationship holds for both
officers and enlisted flyers and for all crew positions (i.e., navigators,
gunners, etc.).

CHART V

RELATIONSHIP BETWEEN NUMBER OF HEAVY BOMBER MISSIONS COMPLETED AND
WILLINGNESS TO VOLUNTEER FOR COMBAT FLYING
(Based on a Survey of Heavy Bomber Crews in the European Theater, June 1944)

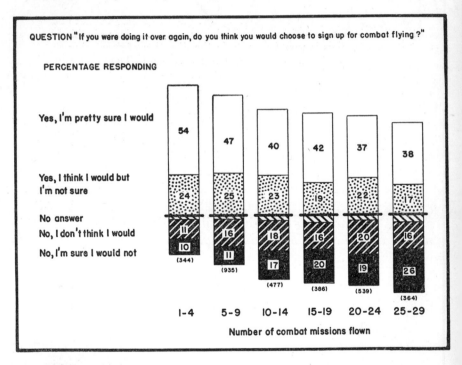

Data from S-135.
The numbers in parentheses at the bottom of the bars are the numbers of cases on
which percentages are based.

Additional evidence of the effects of successive combat exposures
on motivation for combat is provided by responses to the two questions dealing with willingness to undertake an *additional* series of
missions.

From Chart VI it appears that after the first few missions there
was a decrease in the proportion who gave verbal assent to the idea

CHART VI

RELATIONSHIP BETWEEN NUMBER OF HEAVY BOMBER MISSIONS COMPLETED AND WILLINGNESS TO VOLUNTEER FOR AN ADDITIONAL SERIES OF COMBAT MISSIONS
(Based on a Survey of Heavy Bomber Crews in the European Theater, June 1944)

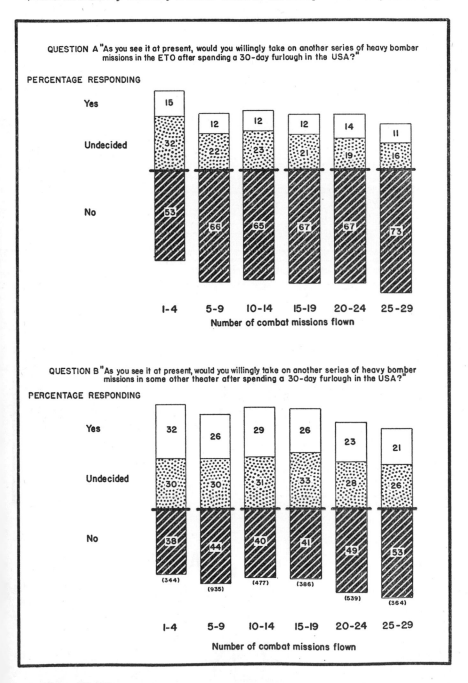

QUESTION A "As you see it at present, would you willingly take on another series of heavy bomber missions in the ETO after spending a 30-day furlough in the USA?"

PERCENTAGE RESPONDING

Number of combat missions flown

QUESTION B "As you see it at present, would you willingly take on another series of heavy bomber missions in some other theater after spending a 30-day furlough in the USA?"

PERCENTAGE RESPONDING

Number of combat missions flown

Data from S-135.

The numbers in parentheses at the bottom of the bars are the numbers of cases on which percentages are based.

of signing up for additional combat duty in the ETO.[4]   During the intermediate period in the tour of duty there was little change, but as the men approached the end of the required series of 30 missions there was another increase in the proportion who expressed definite unwillingness to undertake another series of missions.   This trend, shown by the results for Question A, is paralleled by the results for Question B on willingness for additional combat flying duty in some other overseas theater.[5]

Results from studies of flyers in medium bomber crews tend to confirm the relationship between number of combat missions flown and decreased motivation for combat.   Allowing for the difference in average number of missions completed, the results for medium bomber crews closely parallel those for heavy bomber crews on all three questions indicative of willingness for combat.   Chart VII, based on one of the three questions, shows that among medium bomber crews willingness to volunteer for another series of missions in the ETO decreases with increased number of combat missions flown.   This relationship was found to hold for all crew positions.

Among light bomber crews the relationship is less marked than among heavy and medium bomber crews.   The results, nevertheless, do tend to bear out the same general trend.   For example, in answer to the question on willingness to sign up for another series of missions in the ETO, the percentages answering "No" among light bomber crews were as follows (S-150):

---

[4] Positive responses to Questions A or B in Chart VI are probably indicative of much stronger motivation for combat than positive responses to the question in Chart V, since the former involve willingness to volunteer for a new series of missions after having already completed a large number of them.

[5] The proportion of combat flyers who asserted that they would be willing to take on another series of missions is significantly higher for "some other theater" than it is for the European theater.   This is attributable to the men's expectation that in some other theater, which for most men probably meant one of the Pacific theaters, the degree of dangerousness of combat missions would be somewhat less.   That this was a widespread attitude among flyers in the European theater is borne out by results from a separate survey of 847 men, representing a cross section of combat air crew members in the European theater (S-136) carried out during the same month as the survey from which the data in Chart VI are derived:

QUESTION: "All things considered, how do you think Air Force duty in ETO compares with Air Force duty in the Pacific with respect to the difficulty of combat flying?"

Much easier in the Pacific	20%	} 54%
Somewhat easier in the Pacific	34	
About as hard one place as the other	23	
Somewhat tougher in the Pacific	7	} 11%
Much tougher in the Pacific	4	
No opinion	12	

1–19 missions   35% ($N = 180$)
20–49 missions   41   ($N = 373$)

The relatively small decline in combat motivation among light bomber crews forms part of a consistent pattern.   In general, as will be seen in subsequent sections, light bomber crews do not show the effects of successive missions as markedly as do other types of combat crews.[6]   This is probably attributable to the lower degree of stress to which light bomber crews were exposed.

CHART VII

RELATIONSHIP BETWEEN NUMBER OF MEDIUM BOMBER MISSIONS COMPLETED AND
WILLINGNESS TO VOLUNTEER FOR AN ADDITIONAL SERIES OF COMBAT MISSIONS
(Based on a Survey of Medium Bomber Crews in the European Theater, July 1944)

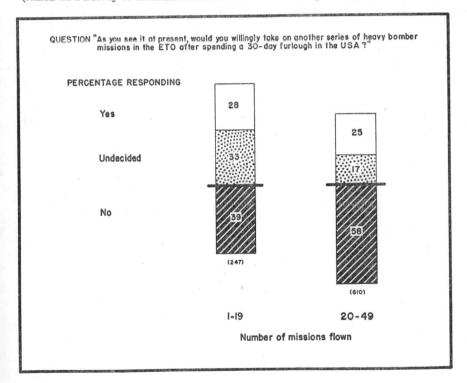

Data from S-150.
The numbers in parentheses at the bottom of the bars are the numbers of cases on which percentages are based.

---

[6] Among the members of light bomber crews, the decline in willingness for combat is much more marked among pilots than it is among enlisted members of the crew. This suggests that the strain of continual combat missions in light bombers may have affected primarily the pilots.

Among fighter pilots there is evidence of a decrease in willingness for combat with increased combat exposure, but it is not as clear-cut as in the case of heavy bomber crews. There was very little change with increased exposure to combat in responses to the question shown in Chart V, but there was a definite increase in the pro-

CHART VIII

RELATIONSHIP BETWEEN NUMBER OF COMBAT HOURS COMPLETED AND PREFERENCE
FOR THE LESS DANGEROUS (ESCORT) MISSIONS, AMONG FIGHTER PILOTS
(Based on a Survey of Fighter Pilots in the European Theater, June 1944)

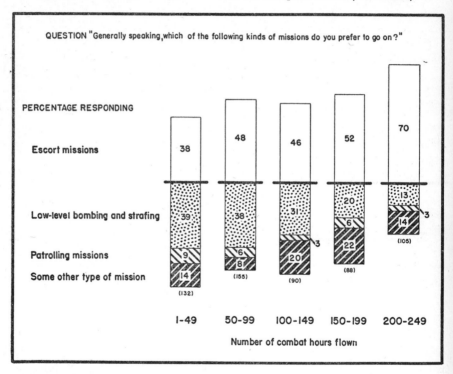

Data from S-142.
The numbers in parentheses at the bottom of the bars are the numbers of cases on which percentages are based.

portion of fighter pilots expressing unwillingness for an additional series of missions (Questions A and B in Chart VI). Of those who had flown 1–49 combat hours, 32 per cent answered "No" to the question on willingness for an additional series of combat missions in the ETO, and this proportion increased to 44 per cent among those who had flown 200–249 combat hours. Similarly, in answer to the question on willingness for another series of missions in some other theater, the proportion answering "No" increased from 15 per cent among those with 1–49 combat hours to 39 per cent among those with 200–249 combat hours.[7] The decline in combat motivation of fighter pilots with increased exposure to combat appears to be manifested more markedly in another way. As is shown in Chart VIII, there is a very pronounced trend toward preferring the safer escort missions to the more dangerous low-level bombing and strafing.[8]

Increase in Symptoms of Tension and Anxiety

As the men flew on successive missions, the cumulative strain was manifested by an increase in many symptoms of tension and anxiety. It has been widely recognized that many physical and behavioral symptoms are psychological effects of exposure to the stresses of combat. One of the commonest functional symptoms reflecting a high degree of anxiety is insomnia. Chart IX shows that among heavy bomber crews, with increasing number of missions flown, there was an increase in the proportion of men reporting difficulty in getting to sleep.

A similar relationship was found among medium bomber crews, where the percentage who reported that they "fairly often" or "very often" had difficulty in sleeping increased from 13 per cent among those who had flown less than 10 combat missions to 28 per cent among men who had flown 40–44 missions, and to 52 per cent among those who had flown 60–69 missions.

Among the light bomber crews there was no evidence of an association between insomnia and number of combat missions: men who had flown many missions were no more likely to report difficulty in sleeping than men with little combat experience. Again, lack of relationship in the case of light bombers is probably attributable to the lower degree of stress to which light bomber crews were exposed. Their missions were shorter and probably far less dangerous than those carried out by other types of combat air crews.

---

[7] Data from S-142.

[8] Sixty-five pilots who had flown 250 combat hours or more are excluded from Chart VIII because they are probably not comparable to the other pilots since 250 combat hours constituted the tour of combat duty at the time of the survey. However, the results for this group were almost identical with those for the group who had flown 200–249 combat hours: of those who had flown 250 or more combat hours, 69 per cent preferred escort missions; 14 per cent preferred low-level bombing and strafing; 2 per cent preferred patrolling; 15 per cent preferred some other type of mission.

Insomnia is only one of many symptoms which developed in the course of successive exposures to aerial combat.   On the basis of a study of 150 heavy bomber flyers who had completed their tour of combat duty successfully, Hastings, Wright and Glueck report that:

CHART IX

RELATIONSHIP BETWEEN AMOUNT OF COMBAT EXPERIENCE AND SLEEP DISTURBANCE
(Based on a Survey of Flyers in Heavy Bomber Crews in the European Theater,
June 1944)

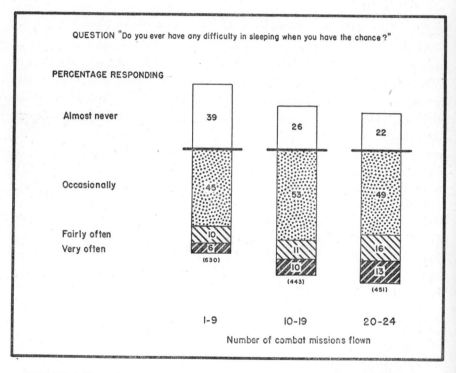

Data from S-135.   The question on sleep disturbance occurred in only one of the two forms of the questionnaire administered to heavy bomber crews.   Hence the results are based on only half as many cases as the results in other charts on attitudes of heavy bomber crews.   Only three categories with respect to the number of combat missions flown are used in this chart, rather than the six categories which appear in the other charts, because otherwise there would be under 100 cases in certain of the narrower class intervals.

The numbers in parentheses at the bottom of the bars are the numbers of cases on which percentages are based.

"The most frequent symptoms . . . include sleep loss, anorexia, weight loss, somatic symptoms of anxiety such as nausea, diarrhea, palpitation, frequency of micturition, tremors, faintness and so on, abnormal irritability and impatience, loss of interest and of concentration, loss of efficiency, depression, seclusiveness, and change in alcohol habits." [9]

Additional evidence indicative of the increase in anxiety symptoms engendered by aerial combat experience is provided by the results in Chart X based on a survey of air crews in a very heavy bombardment wing in the United States. Among those being trained for B-29 crews were a number of men who had had combat flying experience as members of medium bomber crews in the European theater. These men had been returned to the United States before they had completed their tour of combat duty in order to be trained and prepared for deployment to the Pacific as B-29 crews. In Chart X the NSA (Neuropsychiatric Screening Adjunct) scores of men who had had combat flying experience in the ETO are compared with those of men in the same military organization who had had no combat flying experience. Separate comparisons are made for officers and enlisted men, and in each case the groups with and without combat flying experience have been equated with respect to combat flying jobs. [10]

Scores on the NSA are based on a series of 15 questionnaire items which deal mainly with psychosomatic complaints. Validation studies of the NSA have shown that a low NSA score is indicative of marked psychoneurotic tendencies. [11]

---

[9] D. W. Hastings, D. G. Wright, and B. C. Glueck, *Psychiatric Experience of the Eighth Air Force: First Year of Combat* (Josiah Macy Jr. Foundation, August 1944), pp. 123–24.

[10] The job distributions for the samples shown in Chart X are as follows:

	Officers with combat flying experience	*Officers with no combat flying experience*
Airplane commanders	26%	26%
Pilots	23	23
Navigators	26	26
Bombadiers	25	25
Total	100%	100%
Number of cases	*198*	*396*

	Enlisted men with combat flying experience	*Enlisted men with no combat flying experience*
Radio operators	26%	26%
Tail gunners	20	20
CFC gunners	21	21
Blister gunners	33	33
Total	100%	100%
Number of cases	*171*	*342*

[11] See in Volume IV the discussion of "The Screening of Psychoneurotics in the Army."

In Chart X it will be observed that the proportion of officers with combat flying experience who obtained low and intermediate NSA scores is greater than the corresponding proportion of officers with no combat flying experience.   There is an even greater difference between the two groups of enlisted flying personnel.   It is conceivable that selective factors other than combat experience might have given rise to spurious differences in NSA scores.[12]   Nevertheless,

CHART X

NSA Scores of Flying Personnel with and Without Combat Flying Experience

(Based on a Survey of Officer and Enlisted Air Crew Members in One Very Heavy Bombardment, B-29, Wing in Training in the United States, May 1945)

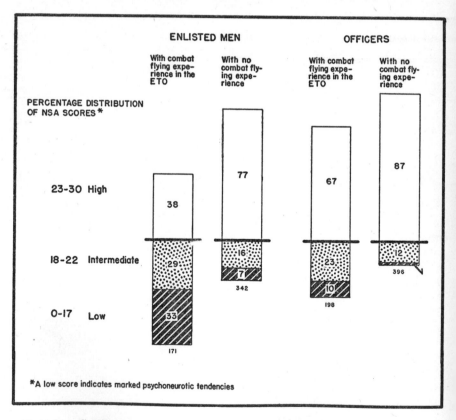

Data from S-207.

The numbers at the bottom of the bars are the numbers of cases on which percentages are based.

[12] For example, there is the possibility that those with combat flying experience in the B-29 wing might have been returned to the States because of psychoneurotic reactions in combat.   From the available information there appears to be no basis what-

the results in Chart X support the conclusion that combat flying experience engenders an increase in anxiety symptoms, as indicated by low NSA scores.

Table 1 and Chart XI present additional results from the study of B-29 air crew members. Those crew members with combat fly-

TABLE 1

RESPONSES OF FLYING PERSONNEL WITH AND WITHOUT COMBAT FLYING EXPERIENCE ON ITEMS INDICATIVE OF FLYING ANXIETIES

(Based on a Survey of Officer and Enlisted Air Crew Members in One Very Heavy Bombardment, B-29, Wing in Training in the United States, May 1945)

| | PER CENT ANSWERING "OFTEN" OR "SOMETIMES" BOTHERED BY SPECIFIC SOURCES OF FLYING ANXIETY | | | |
| | *Enlisted Men* | | *Officers* | |
	With combat flying experience in the ETO	With no combat flying experience	With combat flying experience in the ETO	With no combat flying experience
QUESTION A: "How often have you been bothered by any of the following thoughts?"				
The thought of ditching	58	43	54	40
The thought of crash landing	60	38	49	38
The thought of engine failure	67	44	61	47
The thought of fire on the ship	63	39	65	48
The thought of bailing out	58	37	42	37
The thought of getting lost	27	13	23	35
QUESTION B: "For each of the following items check how often it has bothered you."				
Flying over mountains	42	8	34	19
Flying over water	43	19	37	20
Take-offs	74	36	65	33
Landings	62	32	45	29
Trouble with pressurized cabins	23	17	22	15
Flying formation through heavy clouds	72	32	69	43
Night flying	49	13	43	24
Flying in bad weather	67	43	66	53
Number of cases	*171*	*342*	*198*	*396*

Data from S-207.

soever for assuming that there was a selective factor of this sort. On the contrary, the men with combat experience in this sample of B-29 crews were among a group of 500 out of a total of 900 who were picked for deployment to the Pacific via the United States on the basis of the excellence of their combat flying performances.

CHART XI

RESPONSES OF FLYING PERSONNEL WITH AND WITHOUT COMBAT FLYING
EXPERIENCE ON ITEMS INDICATIVE OF WILLINGNESS FOR
FUTURE COMBAT FLYING

(Based on a Survey of Officer and Enlisted Air Crew Members in One Very Heavy
Bombardment, B-29, Wing in Training in the United States, May 1945)

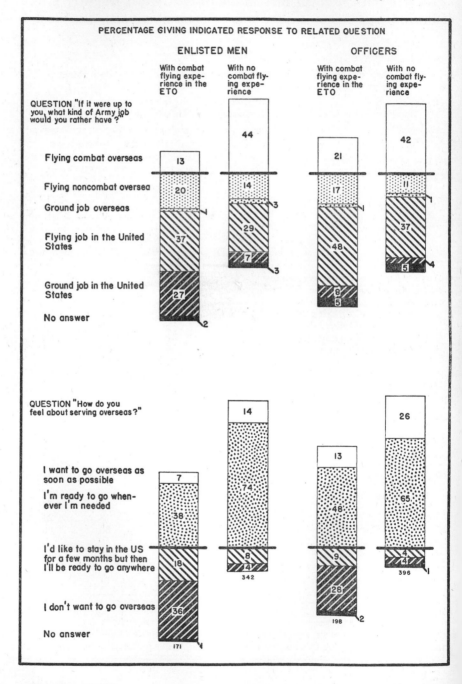

Data from S-207.

The numbers at the bottom of the bars are the numbers of cases on which percentages
are based.

ing experience in the ETO were more likely than those with no combat experience to assert that they had experienced various fears or anxieties in connection with flying. This is borne out by the results on 13 of the 14 relevant items contained in the questionnaire and shown in Table 1. To some extent, fears or anxieties about flying among those with combat experience may have persisted. In other words, there is some likelihood that despite the fact that the questions shown in Table 1 were worded in the past tense, the men's responses may have been indicative of their current anxieties about flying.

The findings presented in this section on the decrease in willingness for combat with increased number of combat missions flown are borne out by the results shown in Chart XI. Men with combat flying experience were less likely to express willingness for combat flying than those with no combat flying experience.

The June 1944 survey of combat flying personnel in the European theater did not include the NSA, but, as is shown in Chart XII, a single questionnaire item requiring self-ratings of general physical condition showed that with increased number of combat missions flown there was a decrease in the proportion reporting "good" or "very good" physical condition.

To some extent, of course, the men's estimates of their own physical condition reflect the physiological fatigue engendered by repeated combat activity. But self-ratings of physical condition have been found to be correlated with NSA scores based on psychosomatic complaints and other items which are predictive of psychoneurotic tendencies.[13] Hence the increased concern about health, shown in Chart XII, may be interpreted as symptomatic of an increase in anxiety reactions.

According to Hastings, Wright and Glueck,[14] symptoms of anxiety —such as nausea and vomiting, headache and dizziness, rapid heart and palpitations, weakness and easy fatigability—occur in only a small percentage of combat air crew members during the early missions of the tour of duty. But, during the latter part of the combat tour, a wide variety of anxiety symptoms develop in many men as a result of the stresses of combat flying duty. Hastings et al. report on the basis of a psychiatric study that among a group of 150 heavy bomber crew members who had successfully completed their tour of duty, 95 per cent had developed definite symptoms of "opera-

[13] Cf. the chapter on "The Screening of Psychoneurotics in the Army" in Volume IV.
[14] *Op. cit.*

tional fatigue," which is characterized by a group of behavioral symptoms: tenseness, irritability, hyperaggressiveness, impairment of motor dexterity due to fine or gross tremors, depression, and slowing of mental processes.

Among medium bomber crews surveyed by the Research Branch

CHART XII

RELATIONSHIP BETWEEN AMOUNT OF COMBAT EXPERIENCE AND SELF-RATING OF PHYSICAL CONDITION

(Based on a Survey of Heavy Bomber Crews in the European Theater, June 1944)

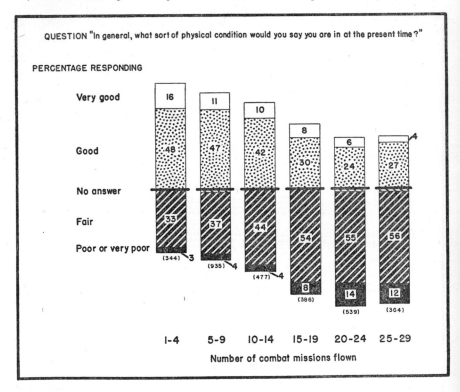

Data from S-135.

The numbers in parentheses at the bottom of the bars are the numbers of cases on which percentages are based.

the proportion of men reporting "good" or "very good" physical condition declines steadily with increased number of missions, from 73 per cent among those with less than 10 combat missions to 41 per cent among men who had flown 40–49 missions, and to 25 per cent among men who had flown 60–69 missions. A similar, though less marked, decline occurs among light bomber crews: from 70 per cent among men with less than 10 missions to 52 per cent among those with 40–49 missions.

In the case of fighter pilots, there is a steady decline from 84 per cent who report "good" or "very good" physical condition among pilots who had flown less than 50 combat hours to 55 per cent among pilots who had flown 200–249 hours.

CHART XIII

RELATIONSHIP BETWEEN SICK-CALL RATE AND NUMBER OF COMBAT MISSIONS FLOWN AMONG HEAVY BOMBER CREWS

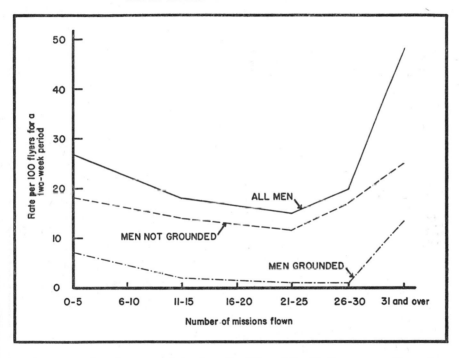

The data are based upon statistics from the Office of the Air Surgeon on all members of heavy bomber crews in the European theater during June 1944. Sick-call rates cover the two-week period of June 3 to June 16, 1944. Men who had flown 31 or more missions are included in this chart in order to show sick-call behavior after the tour of duty was completed.

For heavy bomber crews certain data were obtained through the Office of the Air Surgeon which give a basis for appraising the men's actual behavior with respect to their subjective concern about physical condition. The data, presented in Chart XIII, show that the proportion of combat crew members who requested medical examination (the sick-call rate) decreased after the first few missions, and then remained fairly stable until 30 missions had been flown. After

30 missions, there was an abrupt rise in the sick-call rate and an even sharper increase in the percentage of men removed from flying duty on medical recommendation.

The results on sick-call rates shown in Chart XIII cover the same time period (early June 1944) as the cross-section attitude data presented in Chart XII. It is readily seen that the trend in Chart XIII, which indicates the men's actual *behavior* with respect to physical symptoms, differs markedly from the trend in Chart XII, which indicates the men's *attitudes* toward their own physical condition. The discrepancies between the trends in the two charts provide some suggestive insights into the motivations of combat flyers.

During the early stages of the tour of combat duty, self-evaluation of physical condition deteriorated markedly. In so far as this attitude change reflects an increase in subjective concern about health and specific physical symptoms, it would be expected that a larger proportion of men would voluntarily present themselves for medical attention. But, instead, as shown in Chart XIII, the sick-call rate decreased slightly during this stage. Moreover, toward the end of the tour of combat duty, there appears to be a fairly stable attitude toward physical condition, i.e., there is little difference between those who flew 20–25 missions and those who flew 25–29 missions. If we were to extrapolate from this finding, we would expect little change in self-evaluations of physical condition after 20–24 missions. But Chart XIII shows that after 25 missions there is a gradual rise in the sick-call rate followed by a very sharp increase after 30 missions.

These findings suggest that the behavior of men in heavy bomber crews was strongly oriented toward the goal of completing the number of missions which constituted the tour of combat duty. To some extent sick call was avoided while the 30 missions were in progress, despite the increasing concern about health. Under normal conditions men with physical complaints had nothing to lose, in general, by bringing their health problems to the attention of medical officers. But for men in heavy bomber crews, temporary or permanent removal from flying status might be the consequence, and this would seriously interfere with achieving the goal of completing the tour of combat duty and being rotated back to the United States.

Identification with the combat crew undoubtedly gave rise to another powerful motivation which reinforced the avoidance of reporting physical complaints which might result in interference with the normal sequence of combat missions. Results have been cited in Chapter 7 which indicate that almost all men in heavy bomber crews preferred to fly with their own crews. If a man were to be grounded for a temporary physical disability, he might have to face the prospect of finishing his tour of combat duty later on as an isolated "black sheep" in a strange crew, separated from the original crew with whom strong bonds of friendship and loyalty had developed.

Under these conditions it is understandable that combat crew members would be reluctant to go on sick call while their tour of duty was in progress, despite increased concern about health. The contrast between the trend in Chart XIII (sick-call rate) and the trend in Chart XII (self-rating of physical condition) probably reflects the fact that there was a strong tendency to save up physical complaints until the tour of 30 combat missions was completed.

The Tour of Combat Duty

Whether or not it had been officially sanctioned by higher headquarters, there was a general expectation among heavy bomber crews that 30 missions constituted their tour of duty. A tangible indication of this fact is provided by answers to a specific question on the maximum number of missions a man should be required to fly. The majority of the men in the sample of heavy bomber crew members gave 25 to 30 missions as their estimate. Less than 2 per cent gave an estimate of more than 30 missions.

The sharp focus among men in the heavy bombers upon completion of the tour of duty would be almost sufficiently documented by a single fact, namely the widespread existence of the "Lucky Bastard" clubs. By the spring of 1944 it was common for bomber groups to award "Lucky Bastard" certificates to crew members after the completion of their thirtieth mission. This practice appears to have developed spontaneously among the men themselves and was not explicitly sanctioned by the high command. The certificates were usually elaborate affairs, made up after the fashion of a college diploma, with ornate lettering, seals, signatures, and ritualistic language which gave a pseudo-official air to the document. The document certified that such and such a person was thereby proclaimed a "Lucky Bastard" for having completed 30 missions through the "hazards of enemy flak and fighters."

Some reference has already been made in this chapter to the extremely important role which the tour of combat duty played in influencing the behavior and attitudes of the men.   Numerous interviews with combat air crew members have documented the importance of the tour of combat duty as a factor in the Air Corps combat situation.   In many ways the tour of duty was closely tied up with personal goals.   Most men realized that in order to maintain their elite status as combat flying personnel and to continue to receive the deference and the special rewards which accrued to that status, it was necessary to continue to accept each combat mission assigned to them until the required number had been flown.   Above all, almost every combat air crew member had the strong expectation that, once he had completed his tour of duty, he would gain the much desired reward of being returned to the United States as a veteran who had done his share in combat, or, at least, the reward of being transferred to the relative safety of ground duty overseas.

Many men in heavy bomber crews felt that 30 missions was their "debt to society"—that in order to do their share they must fulfill their "contract" by completing the quota.   This attitude was probably held all the more strongly at the time of the June 1944 survey of heavy bomber crews, since the number of required missions had shortly before been stepped up from 25 to 30.   There was a common phrase during this period among the combat crews: "We do 25 for ourselves and 5 for Jimmy," ("Jimmy" Doolittle being the commanding general to whom was imputed the responsibility for increasing the number of missions).   There was a tendency to regard every man lost on the last 5 missions as, in a sense, an unnecessary tragedy. As nonrational as this might have appeared to an impersonal and detached observer, it was an entirely understandable reaction among men whose whole life situation was permeated by the consciousness of recurrent exposure to danger and the desperate hope of personal survival in the face of relatively low odds.

Since the men conceived of a limited, definite amount of combat duty as satisfying the demands of their society upon them and since this conception was shared by their fellows and sanctioned by many of their leaders, it is to be expected that the completion of this share would remove a powerful block to escape responses.   In this context it is highly probable that the sharp increase in sick-call rate after the thirtieth mission, shown in Chart XIII, is a behavioral resultant of a considerable change in motivation.   After they reached the point which constituted their goal, the men no longer avoided taking an action which formerly would have interfered with the rapid completion of their tour of duty.   Rather, many men probably actively sought to call the attention of medical officers to their physical symptoms (and also to their psychological symptoms) to insure removal from operational status and prompt return to the United States.

Except for complaints about increases in the number of missions required, the only negative comments which combat crews made about the tour of duty system were centered upon reactions to the last few missions of the tour.   After they had finished their tour of combat duty, many men reported in personal interviews that the last 2 or 3 missions were the hardest of all to take.   Some men asserted that at times they wished they had not been told how many missions were required so that they could have avoided the intensified "sweating out" of their last missions.   The increase in anxiety on the last missions engendered by the realization that the final goal was almost at hand is another indication of the tremendous significance attached to completion of the required series of missions.

The realization that one was committed to flying a definite number of missions, which arose from the Air Corps practice of setting up a tour of combat duty, was undoubtedly a crucial morale factor affecting the entire motivational structure underlying willingness for combat flying.   The hypotheses which follow suggest some of the ways in which awareness of the tour of combat duty may have affected combat motivation.

1. The risks of combat, which at first are not sharply felt as applying to oneself, eventually become a central, dominating feature of the entire life situation.   In the course of successive missions, the combat crew member perceives again and again that planes in his own formation are vulnerable.   As he becomes aware of the cumulative losses of men in his own outfit, the potential danger to himself comes to be seen as a mathematical certainty: if a man flies long enough, he will surely be hit or will go down in combat.   One of the few sustaining thoughts to counteract the conception of combat flying as an almost suicidal assignment is the realization that there is a definite tour of duty and that the hope of surviving has, therefore, some basis in reality.

2. In the course of carrying out the series of combat missions, there is a gradual exhaustion of affectional resources.   For many flyers, the cumulative effect of losing comrades in combat results in sustained grief and chronic depressive feelings of profound loss.   At the same time the continuation of the separation from one's social and family milieu back home may give rise to a feeling of estrange-

ment, a sense of a growing chasm due to differences in experiences, and the absence of contact except through the rarified medium of letters. The conception of oneself as abandoned and devoid of affection from others, which tends to arise whenever there is prolonged separation from family and close friends, is probably heightened by the effect of repeatedly facing a hostile environment on combat missions and of meeting insistent demands from figures of authority. The hope of returning to one's home becomes a major feature of the emotional life in an environmental situation which engenders so much hopelessness. Without this hope, many men might have been psychologically incapacitated by severe emotional depression. The tour of duty may have played an important role in keeping alive the hope of returning home, not only by providing a realistic final goal but also by reinforcing the sense of accomplishment with each successive combat mission. The men could feel that they were actively working toward the achievement of their goal; as some of the men expressed it, "with each mission under your belt, you feel that much closer to home."

3. It was shown in the first part of this chapter that combat motivation deteriorated with successive combat missions. This is undoubtedly related to the cumulative effects of tension and anxiety described in the second part. There is probably a cycle of mounting physiological fatigue interacting with emotional disturbance: physical weariness, augmented by anxiety, results in physiological disturbances due to loss of sleep, poor digestion, and chronic tension. This leads to lowered physical stamina, which decreases the threshold of anxiety and once again leads to further increases in sleeplessness, etc.

As fatigue and anxiety increase there is an increased desire to escape from the combat situation, augmented by the sharpened awareness of the relatively low probability of survival and the depressive features described in the preceding paragraphs. At the same time, there is a weakening in some of the forces which counteract escape tendencies: (a) there is a curve of diminishing returns in prestige—beyond a certain point, additional combat missions may bring only slight increments in deference; (b) after a man has flown 15 or 20 missions, there is no longer a need for a man to prove himself; he knows that most of his comrades and the wider public will concede that he has shown himself capable of facing the test of hazardous combat and that he has contributed a larger share to the war effort than most other men.

Speaking schematically, we may say that with increased number of combat missions, the double approach-avoidance conflict undergoes a shift in the balance of forces; the set of motives which impel a man to escape from combat become stronger while the set of motives which impel him to continue in combat become weaker. Under these conditions there would be a strong tendency to evade combat assignments—by developing psychoneurotic symptoms or by malingering (e.g., deliberately catching a bad cold in order to be grounded) or even, in extreme desperation, by taking a chance on getting away with outright refusal to fly.

In this configuration of motivational conflict, the tour of duty may have played a crucial role in counteracting heightened escape tendencies. If a limited, definite amount of combat duty is regarded as the requirement for satisfying the demands of one's society, and if this conception is sanctioned by one's peers and fostered by one's leaders, the completion of this share tends to become a part of the individual's frame of reference for evaluating himself as a worth-while person. Thus the acceptance of a contractual commitment to a definite number of missions as the requirement for doing one's full share of combat duty may become incorporated into the individual's internalized sense of duty or conscience. This would tend to strengthen demands upon the self to "stick it out to the end." Moreover, the concept of a tour of duty implies the promise of relief from combat duty and return to the United States when the series of missions has been completed. This may function as an external reinforcement so that the flyer may be willing to undergo a definite increment of combat stress as an instrumental means for the attainment of the anticipated reward. Hence, the tour of combat duty may have been of critical importance in sustaining men in combat, especially at crucial times when tendencies to evade combat assignments had increased to a dangerously high level.

SECTION II

ATTITUDES RELATED TO REST AND RECREATION
BETWEEN COMBAT MISSIONS

The work activities of a combat air crew member were focused almost exclusively upon combat missions: engaging in preparatory activities (such as attending briefing sessions and checking equipment) prior to an assigned mission and then carrying out his job functions while flying on the mission. Needless to say, a day's work usually involved a high degree of tension and anxiety as well as physical fatigue. Under these conditions, adequate spacing of combat missions was necessary if the men were to have sufficient time for physical and psychological recuperation between their combat missions.

The work load of combat air crew members, as measured by the number of combat missions flown within a short period of time, is a fairly direct indicator of the amount of free time the men were given

TABLE 2

PERCENTAGE DISTRIBUTION OF MEN IN EACH WORK-LOAD GROUP ACCORDING TO
TOTAL NUMBER OF MISSIONS FLOWN
(Heavy Bomber Crews, ETO, June 1944)

WORK-LOAD GROUP (Number of combat missions flown in the past 10 days)	TOTAL NUMBER OF COMBAT MISSIONS FLOWN				
	Number of men	1–9	10–19	20–29	30 or more	Total
7 or more	189	30	39	30	1	100
6	293	43	29	27	1	100
5	461	39	33	26	2	100
4	580	43	26	29	2	100
3	624	52	23	25	—	100
2	455	43	24	33	—	100
1	297	41	25	34	—	100
0	189	32	35	33	—	100

Data from S-135.

between combat missions. In the survey of heavy bomber crews in the European theater, the men were asked to report the number of combat missions they had flown during the preceding 10 days. Comparisons between the men who had flown many missions and the men who had flown few missions during the 10 days provide an indication of the effects of the amount of free time available between missions.

In using this type of data for determining the effects of a heavy work load, it is necessary to exclude the possibility that the findings are attributable to differences in total number of missions flown, since, as was described in the preceding section, there are pronounced changes in attitudes with increased total number of missions flown. In order to check on this potential source of spurious results, the various work-load groups have been compared with respect to total number of missions flown. The results are shown in Table 2.

While there is some variation in the total number of missions flown by men in the various work-load groups, these variations do not form a consistent pattern. In general, there is no linear relationship between number of combat missions flown in the past 10 days and the total number of missions flown. The fact that men in the heavier work-load group did not have a larger total number of missions to their credit may be easily perceived in Table 2: (a) by comparing the group who flew 0 missions in the last 10 days with the group who flew 7 or more missions (i.e., the top row versus the bottom row) and (b) by comparing the groups who flew 1 and 2 missions in the past 10 days with the group who flew 6 missions in the past 10 days. The differentials among the work-load groups in questionnaire responses which we shall present are therefore not attributable to differences in total amount of exposure to aerial combat.

The most marked effect of a heavy work load appears to be a considerable reduction in the amount of sleep, as is shown in Chart XIV.[15] It will be observed that a large proportion of men with a light work load (0 to 3 missions in the 10-day period) reported that on the average they obtained 7 or more hours of sleep each night. The proportion declines rapidly as the work load increases, and in the group who had the heaviest work load only a very small proportion of the men reported that they obtained this amount of sleep. The parallel decrease in the proportion of men who expressed satisfaction with the amount of sleep they were getting suggests that the men felt this deprivation and were very much aware of the fatigue which resulted from it.

Earlier in this chapter it was shown that self-evaluations of general physical condition changed markedly with increased exposure to aerial combat. In so far as a heavy work load over a 10-day period gave rise only to temporary fatigue effects, we would expect

---

[15] The response categories for the questions shown in Chart XIV are as follows:

Question A:
　　About ＿＿＿＿ hours per day

Question B:
　　＿＿＿＿ Usually have enough time for sleep
　　＿＿＿＿ It would help a little if I had more time for sleep
　　＿＿＿＿ It would help a lot if I had more time for sleep

Questions A and B appeared in only one form of the questionnaire and hence the sample is approximately half as large as that shown in Table 2. The distribution of total number of combat missions flown for this smaller cross-section sample is almost identical with the results shown in Table 2.

very little change in self-rating of physical condition. In other words, a man would not be expected to lower the rating of his general physical condition simply because he was temporarily "all pooped out" from overworking. If, however, a heavy work load

CHART XIV

RELATIONSHIP BETWEEN WORK LOAD AND AMOUNT OF SLEEP
(Based on a Survey of Heavy Bomber Crews in the European Theater, June 1944)

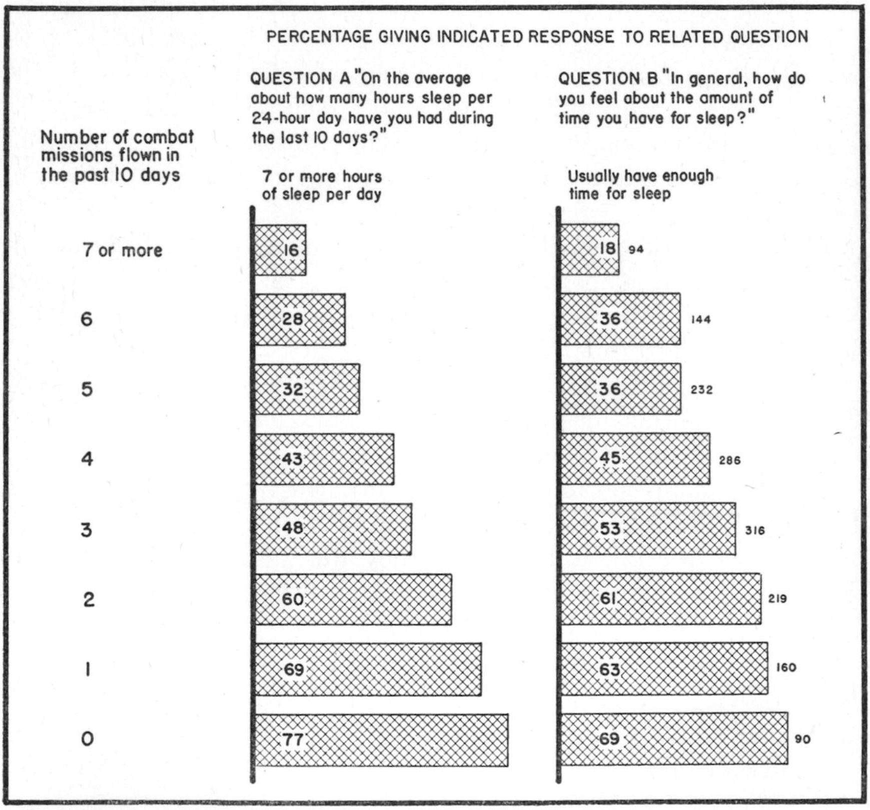

PERCENTAGE GIVING INDICATED RESPONSE TO RELATED QUESTION

QUESTION A "On the average about how many hours sleep per 24-hour day have you had during the last 10 days?"

QUESTION B "In general, how do you feel about the amount of time you have for sleep?"

Number of combat missions flown in the past 10 days

Number of combat missions flown in the past 10 days	7 or more hours of sleep per day	Usually have enough time for sleep
7 or more	16	18 — 94
6	28	36 — 144
5	32	36 — 232
4	43	45 — 286
3	48	53 — 316
2	60	61 — 219
1	69	63 — 160
0	77	69 — 90

Data from S-135.
The numbers following the bars are the numbers of cases on which percentages are based.

gave rise to sustained anxiety and tension, or to an actual physical symptom, a deterioration in attitude toward one's own physical condition would be expected.

When the various work-load groups are compared with respect to responses to the question on general physical condition ("In general, what sort of physical condition would you say you are in at the present time?") we find only a slight difference between those who had a light work load and those who had a heavy work load:

Number of combat missions flown in the past 10 days[16]	Per cent answering "good" or "very good physical condition"
7 or more	42
6	45
5	46
4	46
3	48
2	48
1	48
0	50

While there is a statistically significant difference between the extreme groups, the small magnitude of the difference suggests that a heavy work load had only a slight effect upon the men's appraisal of their general physical condition. It appears, therefore, that workload variations—within the range covered by this study—did not give rise to a pronounced increase in anxiety and tension comparable to the effects of successive exposures to aerial combat indicated by Chart XII. This tentative conclusion is further borne out by the fact that there is no difference between heavy and light work-load groups on responses to the question dealing with insomnia, whereas, as was shown in Chart IX, there was an increase in the reported occurrence of this symptom with increased total number of combat missions flown.

There is the possibility that the physical strain of an increased work load might result in a deterioration in combat morale. Analysis of the data provides no evidence, however, of any change in morale attitudes with heavier work load. Typical results are presented in Table 3. There are no substantial differences between men who were operating under a heavy work load and men who were operating under a light work load on questionnaire items dealing with any of the following aspects of combat morale: (1) Willingness for combat. (2) Attitude toward higher headquarters. (3) Evaluations of the worth-whileness of combat missions. (4) Belief in the importance of the unit. If increased work load gave rise to some form of generalized discontent, it would be expected that there would be a decline in at least one of the above types of attitudes. Since no definite changes are found for these attitudes when the

---

[16] The number of cases in each work-load group is given in Table 2, in which the distribution of total number of missions for the various work-load groups is shown.

TABLE 3

RELATIONSHIP BETWEEN WORK LOAD AND VARIOUS MORALE ATTITUDES*

(Based on a Survey of Heavy Bomber Crews in the ETO, June 1944)

Number of combat missions flown in past 10 days	Number of cases	QUESTION A: If you were doing it over again, do you think you would choose to sign up for combat flying? *Per cent answering "Yes"*	QUESTION B: Would you willingly take on another series of heavy bomber missions in the ETO? *Per cent answering "Yes"*	QUESTION C: How well do you feel that higher headquarters understand your problems and needs? *Per cent answering "They are fairly well" or "very much aware of our needs"*	QUESTION D: Have you ever had the feeling that a particular mission wasn't worth the cost? *Per cent answering "No, never"*	QUESTION E: How important a part do you think your type of outfit will play in winning the war? *Per cent answering "A very important part"*
7 or more	189	64	28	73	29	82
6	293	68	22	76	33	77
5	461	66	26	77	30	76
4	580	66	24	74	34	74
3	624	66	23	76	33	75
2	455	66	28	74	33	78
1	297	66	28	76	29	80
0	189	63	38	73	29	78

Data from S-135.

* The complete wording of the attitude questions and their check lists will be found in Chapter 7, Chart III, and Chapter 8, Charts V, VI, and XV. The check-list items for Question D are: No, never; Yes, sometimes; Yes, quite often.

work load varies from 1 to 7 or more missions per 10 days, it is probable that there is very little deterioration in these attitudes as a result of the usual variations in the work load for a 10-day period. Moreover, there are additional data which suggest that work-load variations within a shorter time period do not affect morale attitudes; there are no differences in attitudes among groups of men who had flown 0, 1, 2, or 3 missions in the 3 days preceding the survey.

It is necessary to take account of certain limitations of the data in interpreting these findings. First of all, it does not follow from these findings that work loads could be increased beyond the range studied without producing a deterioration in morale attitudes; there is undoubtedly a critical point (e.g., 10 to 12 missions per 10 days) beyond which pronounced negative effects would occur. Secondly, it is possible that a change in morale attitudes might have been detected if a more refined measure of work load had been available— e.g., an index which would take account of the number of successive days on which combat missions were flown in addition to the number of missions flown over a 10- and 20-day period. But so far as the present data go, they do not support the conclusion that a heavy work load—within the brief time limits studied—affected morale attitudes.[17]

We turn now to another problem in connection with free time between missions, a problem which, although of minor significance, appears to have been a source of dissatisfaction among combat air crew members. When a combat crew was not scheduled for a combat mission, it was often possible to notify the men on the preceding day. This advance notification of a "stand-down" was undoubt-

---

[17] From a correlational analysis of the type employed here, one cannot give much weight to negative results as evidence that there is no relationship between the two variables since: (a) the questionnaire items may not be sufficiently sensitive to detect the changes that accompany increased work load or (b) some uncontrolled factor may obscure the actual relationship (for example, the light work-load groups might possibly have been assigned fewer missions because they had been exposed to more dangerous and more difficult missions than the heavy work-load groups; unknown selective factors of this kind could obscure the effects of increased work load).

Even if the results are accepted at face value, it is still possible that a heavy load may have had an unfavorable effect upon morale attitudes which was counteracted by the satisfaction of accomplishing many combat missions in a short period of time. Despite the added strain of an increased work load, combat morale may have been sustained by the intense motivation of the men to achieve the goal of completing their tour of combat duty. A heavy work load may have been psychologically rewarding to the men in the sense that they realized that the more rapidly they completed the required number of combat missions, the sooner they would be rotated back to the United States. Thus the policy of setting up a definite tour of combat duty for heavy bomber crew members may have counteracted the potential decline in morale attitudes which might otherwise have resulted from increased work load.

edly of value to the men since it tended to reduce anticipatory anxiety and tension that usually accompanied the expectation of being
scheduled for a combat mission.   Moreover, if the men were to
have some free time on the following day, knowing about it in advance enabled them to work out plans for their time off—arranging
for transportation to a nearby town, making a date with a girl friend,
arranging a get-together with friends in other outfits, etc.   Hence
the practice of giving the men advance notice of stand-downs facilitated the utilization of opportunities for recreation and tension-
reducing distractions.

There appears to have been considerable variation from unit to
unit in the frequency with which the men were given advance stand-
down notice.   In some heavy bomber groups, three fourths of the
men reported that they were usually not given advance notice; in
other groups, an equally high proportion reported that they were
given such notice at least half of the times when they were not
scheduled to fly the next day.

There is little question but that combat air crew members were
dissatisfied if their unit was one of those which—in the eyes of the
men—failed to provide them with advance notice of stand-downs as
often as possible.   Only a very small percentage of the combat air
crew members (11 per cent) expressed indifference ("doesn't make
much difference to me") in answer to the question: "How much difference does it make for you personally to know about this [stand-
downs] the day before?"   Moreover, as would be expected if the
men were genuinely interested in having advance notice of time off,
there is a high correlation between the reported occurrence of advance stand-down notice and the men's satisfaction with it.[18]

Approximately half of the men in each of three cross sections
(heavy, medium, and light bombers) expressed dissatisfaction about
the frequency of advance stand-down notice and, as would be ex-

---

[18] Of the 805 men who reported that they were usually not told of stand-downs in
advance, 86 per cent expressed dissatisfaction in answer to a direct question on whether
or not they felt that they were being given advance notification as much as possible.
Only 14 per cent of the men who reported that they usually received advance notification expressed dissatisfaction.   In interpreting the results it should be recognized that
the occurrence of advance notification was recorded from the men's own responses to
a questionnaire item.   There is always the possibility that answers to a question of
this sort may have been influenced by the degree of satisfaction, but it is unlikely that
this subjective factor alone accounts for the high correlation.   It was found that, in
general, in any given unit there was agreement on the part of a large majority of the
men on their reports of the frequency of occurrence of advance notice.   The question
on the frequency of advance notice appears, therefore, to reflect the actual conditions
in the unit rather than the men's attitudes.

pected from the correlations just mentioned, the majority of these cases were from units in which a high proportion of the men reported that they were usually not given advance notice.

Evidence that this source of dissatisfaction bears some relation to attitudes toward the military organization is presented in Chart XV.

CHART XV

RELATIONSHIP BETWEEN DEGREE OF SATISFACTION WITH ADVANCE NOTIFICATION OF
STAND-DOWNS AND ATTITUDE TOWARD HIGHER HEADQUARTERS
(Based on a Survey of Heavy Bomber Crews in the European Theater, June 1944)

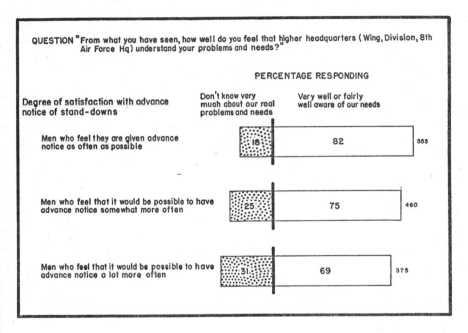

Data from S-135.
The numbers following the bars are the numbers of cases on which percentages are based.

The results suggest that the men who were dissatisfied with the lack of advance stand-down notice may have tended, to some extent, to blame higher headquarters for indifference toward the needs of combat crews.[19] It might be expected that when men are working on dangerous jobs which require irregular cycles of work and free time, the lack of advance notice of changes in the work schedules would give rise to specific dissatisfactions which would contribute to the

[19] The results in Chart XV cannot be regarded as unequivocal evidence for this conclusion since other attitudinal factors may account for the slight correlation.

development of a generalized attitude of resentment toward the authorities who appear to be responsible.

There are similar findings with respect to advance notice of leaves and passes. Combat air crew members were given frequent leaves and passes which usually involved at least several days of free time away from the military environment. These much-needed vacations were highly prized by the men and elaborate plans were often made for them.

There appears to have been considerable variation from unit to unit with respect to the reported occurrence of advance notice of leaves and passes. In some groups, for example, a majority of the men reported that they were given at least several days' advance notice, and in others the majority reported that they were usually given no advance notice.

A majority of heavy bomber crew members expressed dissatisfaction with the way in which leaves and passes were administered in general; one of the most frequent types of written-in comments was the complaint that leaves and passes were too unpredictable. Lack of advance notice as a source of dissatisfaction with the administration of leaves and passes is also suggested by the fact that men who reported that they received no advance notice were more likely than others to express dissatisfaction about the way in which leaves and passes were administered in their units.[20] Moreover, those men who reported no advance notice of leaves and passes were slightly more likely than those who reported at least several days' advance notice to express a negative attitude toward higher headquarters; 26 per cent versus 15 per cent, respectively, asserted that higher headquarters "don't know very much about our real problems and needs."

Lack of advance notice of free time tended in some instances to reinforce a conception of higher authorities as remote, detached persons who were indifferent to the welfare of the men. Consequently the practice of providing advance notice of time off as often as possible may have been important, not simply in facilitating the men's utilization of their free time, but also in maintaining favorable atti-

---

[20] Of those who reported that they were usually given no advance notice of leaves and passes (N = 836), 76 per cent responded "It could be somewhat better" or "It could be a lot better" to the question: "How do you feel about the present practice in your outfit with respect to the granting of leaves and passes?" Among those who reported that they were usually given at least several days' advance notice (N = 460), 60 per cent gave these answers.

tudes toward higher headquarters.   In so far as the data provide some evidence for this relationship, they are in agreement with research findings in the field of industrial morale which show that policies and practices which facilitate the advantageous utilization of employees' free time give rise to more favorable attitudes toward management.

SECTION III

ATTITUDES RELATED TO DIFFERENTIALS IN COMBAT FLYING CONDITIONS FOR VARIOUS TYPES OF AIRCRAFT

There were considerable differences in the entire combat situation, depending upon whether a man flew in a heavy, medium, or light bomber or in a fighter plane.   Some indication of the differentials in the conditions of combat flying is provided by the criticisms made about the various types of aircraft to which the men had been assigned.   Among heavy bomber crews, many more criticisms came from men who flew in the B-24 than from those who flew in the B-17. That the former tended to be more critical of their plane than the latter is shown by the following results:[21]

QUESTION: "Do you think you have the best type of airplane for the particular job which you have to do?"

	Number of cases	PER CENT ANSWERING: *No*	*Uncertain*	*Yes*	*Total*
B-24 crew members	*1,333*	16	8	76	100
B-17 crew members	*1,792*	4	4	92	100

The following excerpts illustrate the types of free-answer criticisms written in by men who flew in the B-24:

The main objection to the B-24 as a combat plane is the poor design with regard to space for personnel movement.   Everything is cramped in front of the waist, with no chance of fast or easy movement in combat situations.   It is poor for bailing out of for the same reasons.

I personally don't feel that the B-24 is a good ship from the standpoint of accurate bombing and precise navigation because of its poor visibility characteristics.

Men who are picked to fly B-24's should be picked for their physical abilities; there should be no pilots under 160 lbs., because the physical strain of formation flying is too much.

---

[21] Data from S-135.

As these quotations indicate, the major complaints tended to be: crowded working space in the nose of the plane, low visibility, and the strain and difficulty of flying B-24's in formation.

A somewhat different type of criticism was made by medium bomber crews. The comments made by men who flew in the B-26 tended to center upon the inappropriate type of missions in which their plane was employed. Forty per cent of the officers and 30 per cent of the enlisted men in medium bomber crews answered "Yes" to the question: "In your judgment is your ship now being used in any kinds of combat assignments for which it is *not* well suited?" [22] The most frequent criticism (mentioned by two thirds of the men who wrote in comments in answer to a supplementary question) was the use of medium bombers for night missions.

Night flying. The B-26 is not a night or instrument ship. Forget about night flying. I dread it. Let the RAF do it.

Night missions—which seem senseless as bombing and navigation is far worse than day. Enemy fighters have golden chance. Flak more accurate.

Other criticisms asserted that the B-26 was being misused because it was employed for low-level bombing, long-range missions, and pinpoint precision bombing. Unlike the men in B-24 crews, those who flew in the B-26 made few criticisms of specific features of the design of their plane in response to a question on improvements needed in their type of ship.

A substantial proportion of men in light bomber (A-20) crews made criticisms of both types. Forty per cent asserted that modifications in the design of their plane were needed to improve combat efficiency; most of the written-in comments stressed the inadequate speed and maneuverability of the A-20. Criticisms in terms of the misuse of their plane were also frequent among light bomber crews. More than 50 per cent of the officers and 30 per cent of the gunners asserted that the A-20 was being misused.[23] The major criticisms referred to the inefficiency of employing light bombers for medium altitude and precision bombing.

Medium altitude bombing. We don't have the bomb load, our speed is sacrificed, and the six fixed fifties in the nose have still to be used.

Havocs do not appear to be readily adaptable to precision bombing, and yet their results are judged on that basis in this theater.

---

[22] S-150.
[23] S-150.

Medium altitude. They say P-47's are carrying 2,000 pounds . . . so why send a bigger ship when a fighter could do it?

As might be expected, among the crews in each type of aircraft those who were most critical of their own type of plane were most likely to express dissatisfaction about their combat flying assignment. Illustrative results, based on the sample of heavy bomber crews, are shown in Chart XVI.

CHART XVI

RELATIONSHIP BETWEEN MEN'S EVALUATION OF THEIR OWN TYPE OF PLANE AND SATISFACTION WITH THEIR COMBAT FLYING ASSIGNMENT
(Based on a Survey of Heavy Bomber Crews in the European Theater, June 1944)

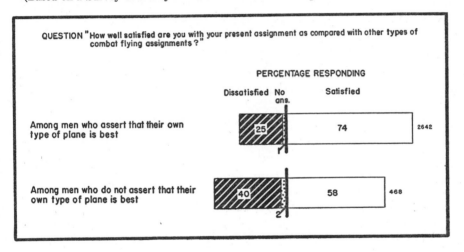

Data from S-135.
The numbers following the bars are the numbers of cases on which percentages are based.

We have seen that somewhat different types of criticisms about their plane were made by the men in heavy, medium, and light bomber crews. These criticisms reflect the differentials in combat flying conditions to which crews in the various types of aircraft were exposed. Missions in different types of aircraft differed in many important respects: the duration of the flight, the type of target which was attacked, the amount and type of antiaircraft action to which the plane was exposed, the extent to which evasive action could be taken, etc. These differences in the conditions of combat flying in various types of aircraft may have had markedly differential effects upon morale attitudes, especially because of the differences in the amounts of fatigue and anxiety elicited.

Survey results show that on many attitude items there are significant differences among men who flew in the various types of aircraft. The data do not show the extent to which these differences in attitudes are attributable to any of the many factors which differentiated the combat flying conditions of the different types of aircraft. Nevertheless, when the differences in attitudes among crews in various types of aircraft are examined, certain patterns emerge which are suggestive of possible effects upon motivation for combat of various combat flying conditions.

Section I of the preceding chapter described the relatively favorable morale attitudes of combat flying personnel in general, as compared with ground combat troops and with general cross sections of the Army as a whole. Nevertheless, there are marked differences among various subgroups of airmen. If the attitude responses of combat air crew members are broken down by type of aircraft, we find a fairly consistent rank order: (1) Fighter pilots. (2) Light bomber crews. (3) Medium bomber crews. (4) Heavy bomber crews.

This rank order, with fighter pilots expressing the most favorable attitudes and heavy bomber crews expressing the least favorable attitudes, may be conveniently referred to in terms of the size of the aircraft in which the men flew, since the rank order based on differences in attitudes happens to correspond to a ranking from the smallest to the largest plane.[24] As is seen in Chart XVII, this rank order tends to occur in the case of four attitude items which are indicators of motivation for combat:[25]

----

[24] The phrase "size of aircraft" will be used as a purely descriptive term to designate the particular rank order under discussion. The use of this term is a matter of convenience and does not imply that size of aircraft is, in itself, an effective variable which accounts for differences in attitudes.

[25] The complete wording of the questions and check-list responses used in Chart XVII is as follows:

Question A:
> If you were doing it over again, do you think you would choose to sign up for combat flying?
>> Yes, I'm pretty sure I would
>> Yes, I think I would, but I'm not sure
>> No, I don't think I would
>> No, I'm sure I would not

Question B:
> How well satisfied are you with your present assignment, as compared with other types of combat flying assignments?
>> Better satisfied than I would be with any other combat flying assignment
>> As well satisfied as I would be with any other
>> Would be better satisfied in some other type of combat flying assignment.
>> (What type of assignment?)

1. Willingness to volunteer for combat.

2. Satisfaction with combat assignment.

3. Willingness to volunteer for an additional series of combat missions in the ETO.

4. Willingness to volunteer for an additional series of combat missions in some other theater.

For the first two items, A and B, the rank order corresponding to size of aircraft is unequivocal. In the case of the latter, there are statistically significant differences between successive groups, i.e., for each of the following comparisons: fighter pilots versus light bomber crews; light bomber crews versus medium bomber crews; medium bomber crews versus heavy bomber crews. For the two additional items (C and D), the rank order does not completely correspond since fighter pilots do not differ significantly from light bomber crews. But if these two groups are combined and compared with medium and heavy bomber crews, the difference is statistically significant. Self-rating of physical condition is another attitude variable which is relevant to consider since it has been found in other studies to be related both to motivation for combat and to psychoneurotic reactions. The results on self-ratings of physical condition in Chart XVII show that the rank order of the four types of air crews corresponds to the size of aircraft with the exception that medium and heavy bomber crews do not differ.

There is thus a relationship between the men's motivation for combat and the size of the aircraft in which they flew. Before attempting to interpret this relationship in terms of differences in

---

Question C:

    As you see it at present, would you willingly take on another series of missions in the ETO after spending a 30-day furlough in the USA?

        Yes
        No
        Undecided

Question D:

    As you see it at present, would you willingly take on another series of missions in some other theater after spending a 30-day furlough in the USA?

        Yes
        No
        Undecided

Question E:

    In general, what sort of physical condition would you say you are in at the present time?

        Very good physical condition
        Good physical condition
        Fair physical condition
        Poor physical condition
        Very poor physical condition

CHART XVII

ATTITUDES INDICATIVE OF MOTIVATION FOR COMBAT AMONG COMBAT AIR CREWS IN FOUR TYPES OF AIRCRAFT

(Based on Surveys of Officers and Enlisted Men in Various Types of Air Crews in the European Theater, June 1944)

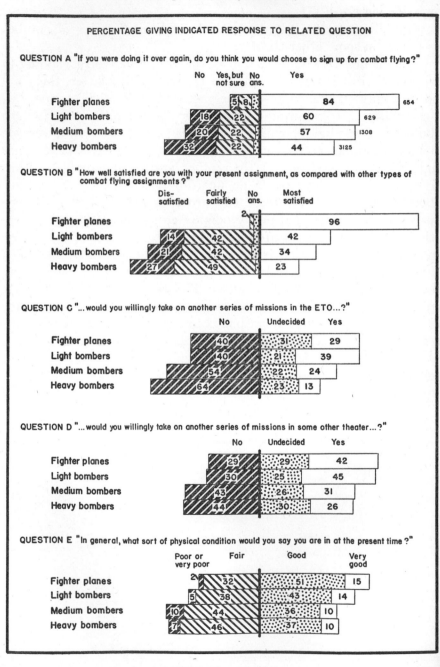

PERCENTAGE GIVING INDICATED RESPONSE TO RELATED QUESTION

QUESTION A "If you were doing it over again, do you think you would choose to sign up for combat flying?"

	No	Yes, but not sure	No ans.	Yes	
Fighter planes		5	8	84	654
Light bombers	18		22	60	629
Medium bombers	20		22	57	1308
Heavy bombers	32		22	44	3125

QUESTION B "How well satisfied are you with your present assignment, as compared with other types of combat flying assignments?"

	Dis-satisfied	Fairly satisfied	No ans.	Most satisfied
Fighter planes			2	96
Light bombers	14	42		42
Medium bombers	21	42		34
Heavy bombers	27	49		23

QUESTION C "...would you willingly take on another series of missions in the ETO...?"

	No	Undecided	Yes
Fighter planes	40	31	29
Light bombers	40	21	39
Medium bombers	54	22	24
Heavy bombers	64	23	13

QUESTION D "...would you willingly take on another series of missions in some other theater...?"

	No	Undecided	Yes
Fighter planes	29	29	42
Light bombers	30	25	45
Medium bombers	43	26	31
Heavy bombers	44	30	26

QUESTION E "In general, what sort of physical condition would you say you are in at the present time?"

	Poor or very poor	Fair	Good	Very good
Fighter planes	2	32	51	15
Light bombers	5	38	43	14
Medium bombers	10	44	36	10
Heavy bombers	7	46	37	10

Data from S-135, S-142, and S-150. For complete wording of questions and check-list responses, see footnote to accompanying text.

The numbers following the bars are the numbers of cases on which percentages are based.

combat flying conditions, it is necessary to exclude the possibility that the results are due to differences in Army rank or in the type of flying job which existed among crews in the four types of aircraft. For example, in heavy bomber crews, only 1 out of every 10 men was a pilot and only 4 out of every 10 men were officers, whereas 100 per cent of the men who flew in fighter planes were pilots and officers.[26]

The two factors—rank and type of flying job—are held relatively constant in the comparisons presented in Chart XVIII by limiting the samples to pilots in each of the four types of aircraft. It will be observed that in the case of all five of the attitude items which are indicative of motivation for combat, the rank order tends to correspond to the size of the aircraft in which the pilots fly. In three of the attitude items (Questions A, B, and C) there is a definite correspondence to this rank order. For the other two attitude items (Questions D and E) the rank order is not clear-cut, but there is a statistically significant difference between the responses of: (a) pilots in the two smaller types of aircraft (fighter planes and light bombers) and (b) pilots in the two larger types of aircraft (medium and heavy bombers). Hence, of the five attitude questions relevant to combat motivation, three show a definite relationship between pilots' attitudes and the size of their aircraft, while the remaining two attitude questions deviate only slightly. The results in Chart XVIII indicate that the relationship is not attributable to variations in the distribution of Army rank or type of flying job (pilots, navigators, gunners, etc.) among flying personnel in the four types of aircraft.

If this relationship were to be interpreted solely on the basis of the differences among pilots shown in Chart XVIII, one might be inclined to hypothesize that the degree of responsibility for other crew members is the effective variable. This interpretation is plausible because the size-of-aircraft rank order is identical with a rank order

---

[26] The distribution of Army rank or grade in each of the four samples is shown in the following table:

	Number of cases	Majors or captains	1st Lts.	2nd Lts. and flight officers	Noncommissioned officers
Fighter pilots	*654*	12%	40%	48%	0%
Light bomber crews	*629*	8	19	13	60
Medium bomber crews	*1,308*	4	25	17	54
Heavy bomber crews	*3,125*	2	14	24	60

It will be noted that the main difference is between fighter pilots and the other three types of combat crews. There is no consistent trend corresponding to the rank order of aircraft size.

CHART XVIII

ATTITUDES INDICATIVE OF MOTIVATION FOR COMBAT AMONG PILOTS IN FOUR TYPES OF AIRCRAFT

(Based on Surveys of Combat Pilots in the European Theater, June 1944)

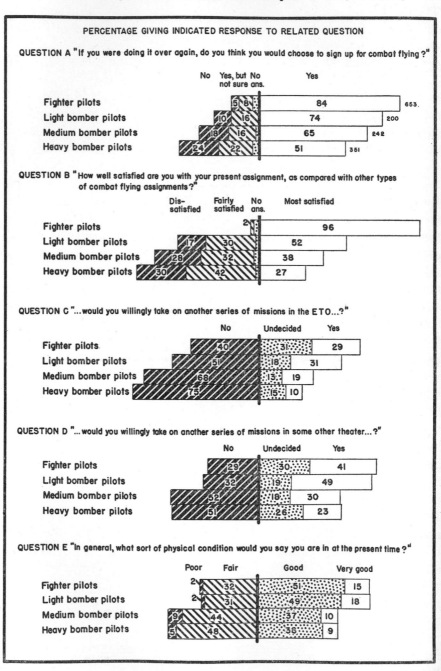

PERCENTAGE GIVING INDICATED RESPONSE TO RELATED QUESTION

QUESTION A "If you were doing it over again, do you think you would choose to sign up for combat flying?"

	No	Yes, but No not sure ans.	Yes	
Fighter pilots	5	8	84	653
Light bomber pilots	10	16	74	200
Medium bomber pilots	18	16	65	242
Heavy bomber pilots	24	22	51	351

QUESTION B "How well satisfied are you with your present assignment, as compared with other types of combat flying assignments?"

	Dis-satisfied	Fairly satisfied	No ans.	Most satisfied
Fighter pilots			2	96
Light bomber pilots	17	30		52
Medium bomber pilots	28	32		38
Heavy bomber pilots	30	42		27

QUESTION C "...would you willingly take on another series of missions in the ETO...?"

	No	Undecided	Yes
Fighter pilots	40	31	29
Light bomber pilots	51	18	31
Medium bomber pilots	68	13	19
Heavy bomber pilots	75	15	10

QUESTION D "...would you willingly take on another series of missions in some other theater...?"

	No	Undecided	Yes
Fighter pilots	29	30	41
Light bomber pilots	32	19	49
Medium bomber pilots	52	18	30
Heavy bomber pilots	51	26	23

QUESTION E "In general, what sort of physical condition would you say you are in at the present time?"

	Poor	Fair	Good	Very good
Fighter pilots	2	32	51	15
Light bomber pilots	2	31	49	18
Medium bomber pilots	9	44	37	10
Heavy bomber pilots	5	48	38	9

Data from S-135, S-142 and S-150. For complete wording of questions and check-list responses, see footnote to text accompanying Chart XVII.

The numbers following the bars are the numbers of cases on which percentages are based.

in terms of the number of combat air crew members who were directly dependent upon the skill and good judgment of the pilot. The fighter pilot was alone in his plane.   He had the responsibility of cooperating with other pilots in his squadron in the tactics of meeting the enemy, but, so far as the fate of his own plane was concerned, he was on his own and had only himself to worry about.   In interviews, fighter pilots often mentioned this and explicitly referred to the burden of responsibility for other men in the crew as a reason for preferring their own assignment.   The light bomber pilot had two other men in his ships; the medium bomber pilot was responsible for five others; the heavy bomber pilot was the commander of a crew of nine others.

It is possible that pilots who had a larger number of men in their crews may have experienced more psychological stress on their combat missions because of the increased responsibility, and this may have resulted in reduced motivation for combat.   But this interpretation does not satisfactorily account for the relationship between size of aircraft and motivation for combat in the light of the additional results presented in Chart XIX.

While the differences among enlisted men in the three types of bomber crews (Chart XIX) are not as clear-cut and consistent as those for pilots (Chart XVIII), they do tend to show the same relationship between size of aircraft and motivation for combat: (a) in the case of all five attitude questions, the proportion of enlisted men who express favorable attitudes is significantly higher for light bomber crews than for heavy bomber crews; (b) on two of the questions (Questions C and D) the medium bomber group definitely is in an intermediate position between the light and heavy bomber groups; (c) on three attitude questions (Questions A, B, and E) the medium bomber crews are not in an intermediate position but this deviation is significant only in the case of one of them (Question E). In general, the results in Chart XIX tend to bear out the data presented in Chart XVIII in indicating that with Army rank and type of flying job held relatively constant, there is a relationship between size of aircraft and motivation for combat.   However, since the results for enlisted crew members tend to parallel the corresponding results for pilots, it is clear that the relationship cannot be explained solely on the basis of the increased degree of responsibility of pilots in the larger aircraft.   Thus the relationship may be due to some factor or set of factors which affect all of the combat air crew members in the larger ships.

CHART XIX

ATTITUDES INDICATIVE OF MOTIVATION FOR COMBAT AMONG ENLISTED MEN IN THREE TYPES OF AIRCRAFT

(Based on Surveys of Enlisted Men in Combat Air Crews in the European Theater, June 1944)

PERCENTAGE GIVING INDICATED RESPONSE TO RELATED QUESTION

QUESTION A "If you were doing it over again, do you think you would choose to sign up for combat flying?"

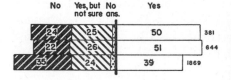

	No	Yes, but not sure	No ans.	Yes	
EM in light bomber crews	24	25		50	381
EM in medium bomber crews	22	26		51	644
EM in heavy bomber crews	35	24		39	1869

QUESTION B "How well satisfied are you with your present assignment, as compared with other types of combat flying assignments?"

	Dis-satisfied	Fairly satisfied	No ans.	Most satisfied
EM in light bomber crews	11	51		35
EM in medium bomber crews	9	52		36
EM in heavy bomber crews	20	55		24

QUESTION C "...would you willingly take on another series of missions in the ETO...?"

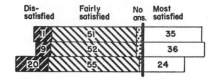

	No	Undecided	Yes
EM in light bomber crews	33	23	44
EM in medium bomber crews	45	26	29
EM in heavy bomber crews	59	26	15

QUESTION D "...would you willingly take on another series of missions in some other theater...?"

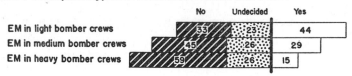

	No	Undecided	Yes
EM in light bomber crews	29	30	41
EM in medium bomber crews	38	28	34
EM in heavy bomber crews	39	32	29

QUESTION E "In general, what sort of physical condition would you say you are in at the present time?"

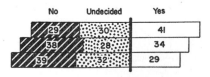

	Poor	Fair	Good	Very good
EM in light bomber crews	7	41	39	13
EM in medium bomber crews	15	44	34	7
EM in heavy bomber crews	7	46	37	10

Data from S-135 and S-150. For complete wording of questions and check-list responses, see footnote to text accompanying Chart XVII.

The numbers following the bars are the numbers of cases on which percentages are based.

One possibility to consider is that the differences are attributable to differences in amount of exposure to aerial combat. As we have seen earlier in this chapter, with increased number of missions flown in any given type of aircraft there appears to be a marked decline in motivation for combat. But in view of the differences in types of missions to which they were assigned, it is not very meaningful to compare total number of missions flown by crews in one type of aircraft with the total flown by crews in another type of aircraft. In any case, the factor of frequency of combat missions could not be adduced to explain the differences in attitudes because, as would be expected from the number of missions specified for their tour of combat duty, the men in our sample of heavy bomber crews flew the fewest total number of missions. The average number of missions

TABLE 4

AIR FORCE BATTLE CASUALTY RATES IN THE EUROPEAN THEATER DURING THE SIX-MONTH PERIOD, JANUARY THROUGH JUNE 1944

	CASUALTY RATES PER 1,000 PER 6 MONTHS		
COMBAT AIR CREWS IN:	*Killed or missing in action*	*Wounded or injured in action*	*Total casualties*
Fighter planes	484	39	523
Medium bombers	238	112	350
Heavy bombers	712	175	887

flown by men in the sample of medium bomber crews was greater than that for the sample of light bomber crews and it was the fighter pilots who flew the greatest number of missions.

Clearly, the differences in the character of the missions flown rather than in the absolute frequency of missions must be taken into account. Of primary importance were the differentials in the chances for survival in flying combat missions in one type of aircraft as against another.

Table 4 shows the casualty rates for fighter pilots, medium bomber crews, and heavy bomber crews, based on data obtained from the Office of the Air Surgeon. (Rates for light bomber crews were not obtainable, but members of the Air Surgeon's statistical section indicated in informal conversation that the casualty rates were probably lower for light bomber crews than for medium bomber crews.) Since the casualty rates are for the period of January through June 1944, they cover the period during which the men surveyed in June

1944 had been flying.   It will be observed in Table 4 that although the casualty rate was highest for heavy bomber crews, the rank order in terms of casualty rates does not correspond to the size of aircraft rank order.[27]

It is highly probable that the objective degree of dangerousness to which the men were exposed had an effect upon their motivation for combat.   To some extent, this would explain the finding that heavy bomber crews appear to show lower motivation for combat than men in other types of aircraft.[28]   Nevertheless, it is useful to consider the ways in which objective danger was perceived by the men flying in various types of aircraft.   We shall, therefore, discuss some of the specific conditions of combat flying which may have resulted in greater psychological stress among men flying in the heavier types of aircraft than among those in the lighter types of aircraft.

One possibility is that heavy bomber crews may have been more aware of their vulnerability to enemy fire.   The necessity to fly in rigid formation and the restrictions upon evasive action when exposed to flak and enemy fighter attacks are conditions which probably tended to augment anxiety reactions in all of the members of the crew.

In interviews, men who flew in heavy bombers often asserted that they sweated out antiaircraft attacks on almost every one of their missions; they sometimes explicitly stated that they felt extremely tense when their ship was exposed to flak while flying in formation because they realized that nothing could be done about it.   Men in the smaller ships, which had greater maneuverability and often oper-

---

[27] Fighter pilots manifested a consistently higher degree of motivation for combat than did the men in medium and light bomber crews, whereas the casualty rate for fighter pilots was much higher than for the other two types of aircraft.   This discrepancy may have been the consequence of special selection factors.   First of all, after initial pilot training, those who had volunteered to be fighter pilots rather than bomber pilots may have been more highly motivated to participate actively in aerial warfare (to be a "hot" pilot).   Secondly, there was a special administrative policy which was applied only to fighter pilots.   All fighter pilots were systematically examined throughout the entire period that they were on operational duty; as soon as any slight physical impairment or any anxiety reaction to combat flying was detected, the man was immediately removed from combat duty as a fighter pilot.   (In some cases the disqualified fighter pilot was transferred to another combat assignment as a bomber pilot.)   The continual selection process probably resulted in the elimination of the fighter pilots who were most likely to manifest a decline in motivation for combat.   These selective factors may account, to a large extent, for our findings which show that fighter pilots on active combat duty had higher motivation for combat than any other type of combat flying personnel.

[28] The heavy bomber crews were surveyed before D Day and all the others were surveyed after D Day.   It may be that psychological reactions to the launching and first weeks of the invasion of Europe had considerable influence on the attitudes of combat air crews.

ated in looser formations, were perhaps less frequently exposed to this kind of situation.

Prolonged inactivity is another factor which may have tended to augment the feeling of helplessness on combat missions:

"There is a special type of physical strain connected with flying which is felt most keenly by the pilots although also to some extent by other members of the crew. This is due to the immobility on long flights. They are required to sit in uncomfortable postures for many hours with little opportunity to move about. During much of this time they are under severe emotional strain, which becomes registered as muscular tension. Yet there is no way in which they can adequately relieve this muscular tension as long as they are in the plane. Gunners who can move around in the plane have only a few moments of actual activity suitable for release of tension and during the remainder of the time build up large quantities of tension anticipatory to the battle." [29]

There were considerable differences among the four types of aircraft crews in the degree of activity on combat missions. It is probable that the larger the plane, the less opportunity there was for engaging in the kind of overt, concentrated activity which would serve to release tension and to distract attention away from anxiety cues. In general, a fighter pilot flew on relatively short combat missions and, as the sole flyer in his plane, was continuously occupied with the activities involved in operating and maneuvering his plane and in carrying out assaults upon his targets. But in the larger planes, missions were of much longer duration. Also, with a larger number of men in the crew, there was increased specialization of function, and concomitantly, a greater proportion of inactivity. Hence the relationship between size of aircraft and motivation for combat may be attributable in part to the increased tension on combat missions arising from prolonged inactivity.

This hypothesis is in accord with a widely accepted principle of emotional behavior: the less opportunity there is for the release of motor tension and for concentration of attention upon a distracting task in a situation of stress, the greater the degree of anxiety elicited by that situation. There is reason to believe that this principle applies to the Air Corps combat situation. Many incidents have been reported about nonrational acts of airmen on their combat missions (e.g., gunners firing at flak bursts) which served no apparent

---

[29] R. R. Grinker and J. P. Spiegel, *Men Under Stress* (Blakiston, Philadelphia, 1945), p. 29.

function except to relieve the strain of inactivity. In interviews, combat flying personnel often reported that they felt most anxious on their combat missions when they were "just sitting and waiting to see what would happen" and least anxious when they were so busy that they "didn't have time to think about it."

Summary

The first section of this chapter dealt with some of the psychological effects of successive exposures to aerial combat. Evidence was presented which indicates that with increased number of combat missions flown there was a decrease in willingness for combat flying and an increase in symptoms of chronic tension and anxiety. In addition, it was shown that there was a marked discrepancy between the trend in the men's *attitudes* toward their own physical condition and the trend in their actual *behavior* with respect to physical symptoms as measured by sick-call rates. This finding was interpreted in terms of the goal of finishing the tour of combat duty and a number of hypotheses were presented on the ways in which the Air Corps policy of specifying a tour of combat duty may have affected the motivational structure underlying willingness for combat flying.

Several problems in connection with rest and recreation between combat missions were discussed in the second section. From the available evidence it was shown that the primary effect of a heavy work load (as measured by number of combat missions flown in a 10-day period) appeared to have been physical fatigue due to insufficient time for rest and recuperation between missions. The results provided no evidence of any changes in morale attitudes when the work load was varied from 1 to 7 or more missions per 10 days. Results were presented on another factor connected with rest and recreation: advance notice of time off. Some findings were presented which suggest that this factor may have been important in the Air Corps combat situation, not simply in facilitating the men's utilization of their free time but also in maintaining favorable attitudes toward higher headquarters.

In the third section comparisons were made of the attitude responses of combat crews in various types of aircraft. A number of hypotheses were formulated, in terms of differentials in the conditions of combat flying which may account for attitude differences on items indicative of motivation for combat.

CHAPTER 9

PSYCHONEUROTIC SYMPTOMS IN THE ARMY[1]

Introduction

FROM time to time reference has been made in these volumes to problems which may be thought of as falling within the field of psychiatry. The discussion of men in combat, in earlier chapters of this volume, devoted a good deal of attention to their fear and anxiety reactions. In Volume I the discussion of men's adjustment to the Army immediately raised the question of their preliminary adjustments and how these affected their reactions to the Army.

It is the purpose of this chapter to offer a systematic review, so far as the data permit, of soldiers' emotional reactions to some of the major types of situations which were encountered in the Army. That is, though not all men went through every phase of Army service, the typical Army cycle may be thought of as a sequence of induction, training, overseas duty, combat, return to the United States, and finally return to civilian life. The earlier stages of this cycle, through combat, have already been analyzed in some detail, and the two later stages will be discussed in chapters to follow. Our interest here is not so much on these situations themselves as it is on abstracting from them their implications for the emotional stability of the men involved in them and in putting these together for a kind of panoramic view of the Army cycle from this standpoint.[2] Obviously, this is not, nor is it intended to be, a discussion of either the history or the findings of military psychiatry in World War II. These subjects are treated elsewhere by persons more qualified by

---

[1] By Shirley A. Star. Other analysts of the Research Branch staff who did major work in this area were Arnold M. Rose, Robin M. Williams, Jr., and Irving L. Janis. Louis Gutman was primarily responsible for the techniques used in deriving the tests discussed in this chapter. The techniques themselves are discussed in Volume IV.

[2] The final stage of this cycle—return to civilian life—is one for which we have only the indirect data presented in Chapter 13 so far as the problems of emotional adjustment are concerned.

training and experience and the interested reader is referred to their work.[3]

Our purpose, then, is to trace the changing incidence of psychoneurotic stresses through the idealized sequence of situations in the Army. In doing so, we shall employ test scores as indices of psychoneurotic tendency and deal with changes in them. The significance of changes in these test scores, of course, depends upon the extent to which they are valid and reliable. We may anticipate the next several sections of this chapter by saying that the available data indicate that these scores have sufficient validity and reliability so that changes in scores—even though the comparisons are drawn from studies made at different points in time and with samples differing in demographic characteristics—can be attributed to the changed Army career situation involved and not to structural weaknesses of the indices.

The reader who is not concerned with the evidence bearing on these technical points can turn at once to the substantive portion of this chapter beginning with Section II headed "Variations in the Incidence of Symptoms Associated with Stages of the Army Cycle." Before coming to this section, we shall discuss (1) the indices used and the data relating to their validity, (2) the extent to which test scores had the same meaning for different subgroups of the population, and (3) the extent to which test scores had the same meaning at different points in time.

SECTION I

THE INDICES OF PSYCHONEUROTIC TENDENCIES

In the course of its work, the Research Branch was asked by the Surgeon General's Office to develop a paper-and-pencil test to be used in psychiatric screening. That some of the standard attitude items used as indicators of general adjustment to the Army were actually predictive of subsequent psychiatric breakdown was evident from sample studies initiated in the fall of 1943.

In Volume I, Chapter 4, there appears an extensive comparison of factors in the pre-Army experience of Army psychiatric patients in the United States and of a cross section of enlisted men. Evidence was shown there that psychiatric patients had distinctly less

---

[3] See, for example, R. R. Grinker and J. P. Spiegel, *Men Under Stress* and *War Neuroses* (Blakiston, Philadelphia, 1945) and E. A. Strecker and K. E. Appel, *Psychiatry in Modern Warfare* (The Macmillan Company, New York, 1945).

favorable attitudes on several standard items reflecting general adjustment to the Army than did the cross section of soldiers. The same was true of AWOL's in stockades as compared with the cross section—as might be expected if the attitude variables were to meet any test of validity. With respect to questions reflecting adjustment to the Army, however, it was particularly needful to study attitudes of an unselected group of men and trace their *subsequent* behavior in the Army. Would items on adjustment discriminate significantly, for example, between men destined *eventually* to be segregated as psychoneurotic and men not so destined?

This was checked on the basis of a survey made on a cross section of new Infantry recruits in the autumn of 1943. These men had been in the Army only a few weeks, having been sent directly to a division for training without going through the usual replacement training center. This division was followed for several months by a research team which was detached from Washington to remain with it. By the following March, approximately six months after the initial study, 73 men in the sample whose attitudes were studied in the autumn had been diagnosed as psychoneurotic by the division medical staff. These psychoneurotics were matched with 730 men who had the same characteristics by education, age, and marital status; and the attitudes of the two groups as of the previous autumn were compared. Results are shown in Table 1.

While many questions of the type shown in Table 1 discriminated significantly between men who were destined for psychiatric treatment and other men, it was felt necessary to develop a still better diagnostic set of items for general use in the Army. The relatively high discriminating value of items like the report on physical condition indicated, in particular, the need for more explicit investigation of psychosomatic complaints as useful in screening tests.

The test that the Research Branch was developing for the Surgeon General for screening at induction stations[4] obviously could not use items based on Army experience. In developing this test, in use at all induction stations since 1944, a good deal of data bearing on the reported incidence in the Army population of symptoms frequently associated with psychoneurosis was accumulated. The potential usefulness of these data in analyzing other attitudinal and motivational problems of the Army was immediately apparent and led to the development of abridged versions of the Neuropsychiatric

---

[4] The construction of this test is described in detail in Volume IV in the chapter on "The Screening of Psychoneurotics in the Army."

TABLE 1

ATTITUDE RESPONSES OF A GROUP OF MEN SUBSEQUENTLY DIAGNOSED AS
PSYCHONEUROTIC COMPARED WITH AN EQUATED NORMAL CONTROL GROUP
(Trainees in an Infantry Division in the United States, Autumn 1943)

	73 trainees subsequently diagnosed as psychoneurotics	730 "normal" trainees equated for education, age, and marital condition	Difference
Personal Esprit			
"What kind of physical condition are you in?"			
Percentage answering "poor"	47	13	34
"In general, how would you say you feel most of the time, in good spirits or low spirits?"			
Percentage answering "low spirits"	41	18	23
"Do you usually feel sure of yourself when you face new jobs and situations or do you usually have some doubts about your ability to handle them?"			
Percentage answering "a lot of doubts"	52	36	16
"How much homesickness do you feel?"			
Percentage answering "quite a lot" or "a good deal"	67	58	9
"In general what sort of time do you have in the Army?"			
Percentage answering "I have a pretty rotten time"	34	26	8
"Do you ever worry about whether you will be injured in combat before the war is over?"			
Percentage answering "a great deal"	19	11	8
Personal Commitment			
"Do you feel it was fair for you to be drafted when you were?"			
Percentage giving reasons why "I should never have been drafted"	32	12	20
"If it were up to you to choose, do you think you could do more for your country as a soldier or as a worker in a war job?"			
Percentage answering "as a worker in a war job"	74	58	16
Complaints About Army Job or About Army in General			
"Do you usually feel that what you are doing in the Army is worth while or not?"			
Percentage answering "not worth while"	44	25	19

TABLE 1 (Continued)

	73 trainees subsequently diagnosed as psycho-neurotics	730 "normal" trainees equated for education, age, and marital condition	Difference
"Do you feel that the Army is trying to control you and other soldiers more strictly and in more ways than it needs to?"			
Percentage answering "yes"	52	40	12
"Do you think the Army is piling too much work on you?"			
Percentage answering "a little too much" or "a lot too much"	60	49	11
"How well satisfied are you about being in your present Army job instead of some other Army job?"			
Percentage answering "dissatisfied" or "very dissatisfied"	60	49	11
"How much of your training or duty time is used in doing things that do not seem important to you?"			
Percentage answering "a lot of it"	36	26	10
"In general how well do you think the Army is run?"			
Percentage answering "very poorly"	14	6	8
"How do you feel about medical attention in the Army?"			
Percentage answering "rather poor" or "very poor"	54	47	7

Data from S-70.

Screening Adjunct (as the induction station screening test was called officially) which could be more conveniently included in studies whose primary interest was directed to other sets of problems. The data collected in these later studies are the data with which we shall be primarily concerned in analyzing differentials in reported symptoms under the varying conditions in which soldiers lived, so it is necessary to describe briefly the alternative tests we shall be using.

Altogether, three tests will be referred to here, the full test and two abridged versions of it. Thus we have:

1. *The Anxiety Symptoms Index*, based on five of the more common signs of anxiety included in the NSA, viz., nervousness, insomnia, tremors, sweaty hands, and stomach disturbances.

2. *The Psychosomatic Symptoms Index,* made up of six of the questions used in the NSA, two of which were also used in the Anxiety Symptoms Index. These symptoms were tremors, stomach disturbances, fainting spells, nightmares, shortness of breath, and pressure in the head.

3. *The Neuropsychiatric Screening Adjunct (NSA),* which contains fifteen items,[5] including, in addition to those employed in the other indexes, questions about health problems generally, dizzy spells, accelerated heartbeat, nail biting, cold sweats, and sick headaches.

It should be readily apparent that all of the questions have a roughly similar content, the subjectively experienced incidence of psychosomatic complaints.[6] The distinction in name among the three tests is introduced primarily for convenience in referring to them and is not meant to imply any real differences in the behavior being indexed by them.

By comparing the score distributions of each of these indices which occurred in a cross section of white enlisted men with no overseas service with those of a sample of hospitalized white psychoneurotic patients with no overseas service drawn from the same universe,[7] each score distribution was dichotomized. The phrase critical scores will be used to indicate those scores which occurred relatively

---

[5] "NSA" is customarily employed as an abbreviation for the entire "Neuropsychiatric Screening Adjunct." Here, and hereafter, however, we are referring only to the part of the Adjunct which is numerically scored. See the chapter on "The Screening of Psychoneurotics in the Army" in Volume IV for an exact statement of the composition of the test.

[6] Most of the questions took the form of:

Are you ever bothered by _____
Have you ever been bothered by _____

_____ Often
_____ Sometimes
_____ Never

See the chapter on "The Screening of Psychoneurotics in the Army" in Volume IV for their exact wording.

[7] The sample of hospitalized psychoneurotic patients was obtained by sampling patients in station hospitals at all of the camps visited in securing the cross section. Since a station hospital served only the camp in which it was located, the psychoneurotics may safely be taken as coming from the same universe as the cross section represents. And since station hospitals functioned as the clearinghouse from which psychoneurotics were treated and returned to full duty, assigned to special rehabilitation training, referred to other hospitals for further treatment, or discharged from the Army, the sample may reasonably be regarded as representative of psychoneurotics in the Army who were hospitalized before serving outside the United States. It does, however, omit such psychoneurotics as were never hospitalized, e.g., those who received only outpatient treatment.

more frequently among the psychoneurotic group than among the cross section representing the universe from which the patients came, while other scores (that is, those which occurred relatively more frequently in the total population than in the psychoneurotic subgroup) are referred to as noncritical.[8]

As might be expected from their similar and, indeed, overlapping content, the three indices gave very similar results. By this classi-

TABLE 2

INTERRELATION OF THE NSA, ANXIETY SYMPTOMS INDEX, AND PSYCHOSOMATIC SYMPTOMS INDEX

(White Enlisted Men with No Overseas Service, Cross Section and Hospitalized Psychoneurotic Patients, January–February 1944)

CLASSIFICATION OF SCORES:	NSA AND ANXIETY SYMPTOMS INDEX		NSA AND PSYCHOSOMATIC SYMPTOMS INDEX		ANXIETY SYMPTOMS INDEX AND PSYCHOSOMATIC SYMPTOMS INDEX	
	Cross section	Psycho-neurotic patients	Cross section	Psycho-neurotic patients	Cross section	Psycho-neurotic patients
Received critical scores on both tests	24%	86%	23%	83%	23%	80%
Received critical score on first test only	3	4	4	7	10	8
Received critical score on second test only	9	2	9	2	9	5
Received critical score on neither test	64	8	64	8	58	7
Total	100%	100%	100%	100%	100%	100%
Number of cases	3,501	563	3,501	563	3,501	563
Correlation:						
Fourfold	.72	.70	.69	.60	.57	.45
Pearsonian	.89	.83	.85	.84	.75	.62

Data from S-99.

fication into critical and noncritical scores, the relationship between each pair of tests has been reduced to a fourfold table, as shown in Table 2. As we see here, from 81 to 88 per cent of the cross section of white enlisted men with no overseas service and from 87 to 94 per cent of the psychoneurotic group were placed consistently into either the critical or noncritical score group by both tests in any

---

[8] Operationally speaking, critical scores are those at or below the point of intersection of the frequency polygons of the score distributions of the cross section and the psychoneurotic group. See Volume IV.

pair. In other words, the use of one test rather than another affected the scores of only a small minority of the men. The actual correlations for these fourfold classifications, as well as the correlations of the full score distributions, are also shown in Table 2, although, in view of the lack of independence of the several scores, these are not too meaningful. As a final note on the substitutability of one score for another, we may mention that 78 per cent of the cross section and 86 per cent of the psychoneurotic patients received the same classification whatever index was used; that is, they were classified into the critical group or into the noncritical group by all three indices considered simultaneously.

TABLE 3

COMPARATIVE DISCRIMINATION OF THE NSA, ANXIETY SYMPTOMS INDEX, AND PSYCHOSOMATIC SYMPTOMS INDEX AMONG WHITE ENLISTED MEN WITH NO OVERSEAS SERVICE, CROSS SECTION AND PSYCHONEUROTICS COMPARED
(January–February 1944)

| | PERCENTAGES RECEIVING CRITICAL SCORES ON GIVEN TEST: | | |
Test	Cross section	Psychoneurotic trainees in rehabilitation centers	Psychoneurotic patients in station hospitals
NSA	27	87	90
Anxiety Symptoms Index	33	89	88
Psychosomatic Symptoms Index	32	82	85
Number of cases	*3,501*	*313*	*563*

Data from S-99.

The data in Table 2 indicate, as well, the degree of success of each of these indices in discriminating between men who had become ineffective because of psychoneurotic symptoms and men who had not, under the conditions of Army training and duty in the United States, before being subjected to the further stresses involved in overseas and, particularly, combat service. As may be seen, either in this table or in Table 3, where these data are more conveniently summarized, the NSA distinguished somewhat more sharply than the two shorter indices between the psychoneurotics and the cross section, primarily because its greater range of scores permitted finer subdivision. As between the two shorter forms, the Anxiety Symptoms Index was, perhaps, slightly superior to the Psychosomatic Symptoms Index.

In Table 3, in addition to the scores of the cross section and of the hospitalized psychoneurotics, the scores of a group of psychoneurotics who were felt to be salvageable for Army duty and therefore transferred from hospitals to special training centers are also reported. The lack of any essential difference between the scores of this last group and the scores of hospitalized psychoneurotics suggests that the indices were about as efficient in selecting milder psychoneurotics as in distinguishing more extreme types, though these data are not to be regarded as conclusive since they were collected when the rehabilitation training centers were newly established and the men surveyed were recent arrivals who, up to that point, had been hopeful of discharge from the Army.

The absolute size of the proportion receiving critical scores in a cross section population is not particularly meaningful.[9] True, it represents the proportion of men who reported a rate of psychosomatic anxiety symptoms at a level more usually characteristic of psychoneurotics, but their reasons for doing so might have been manifold. The group would include men whose symptoms were later to culminate in breakdown, but it would also include chronic physical complainers, hypochondriacs, and men with mild or compensated psychoneuroses who were to go through their training with little or no overt difficulty. Moreover, it might also include men whose symptoms derived from actual organic disorders, and who might, in fact, have been classified for only limited Army service on that account. And more than that, the group would contain some men whose poor scores reflected merely some individual variations in judgment in deciding which answer category best described them, or outright misunderstanding of the questions. Finally, there may have been a few men who were deliberately malingering and purposively exaggerating their symptoms, though, since these are replies to anonymous questionnaires, there would seem to be little incentive to malingering.[10]

If, however, the absolute size of the proportion receiving critical scores is interpretable to only a limited extent, its relative size has a clearer significance. For, if we compare matched groups of men, differing only in their situation or in the time when they were surveyed, then differences between them can be taken as reflecting true changes in the general level of anxiety being experienced by the

---

[9] It has, however, a practical importance so far as screening procedures are concerned. This aspect is discussed in Volume IV.

[10] A study designed to permit the follow-up of men whose scores were known, in order to arrive at some estimates of the relative size of these subgroups, was begun but never completed because of the sudden ending of the war.

group. This would be the case because the matching process can be extended to exclude, in large part, differences in the proportion with organic defects and will also tend to control any variations in tendency to misinterpret the questions. Moreover, the factor of malingering may be discounted; since there is little point to malingering in replies to anonymous questionnaires, the proportion who nevertheless do so may be expected to remain fairly constant or, at worst, to vary with the general intelligence level which in itself is not likely to vary much between educationally matched groups.

Compositional Variations in the Incidence of Symptoms

Among men in training in the United States scores vary primarily with three background factors: age, education, and physical condition. As we see in Table 4, the proportion receiving critical scores

TABLE 4

PROPORTIONS RECEIVING CRITICAL SCORES ON THE ANXIETY SYMPTOMS INDEX AT VARIOUS AGE-EDUCATION LEVELS

(Cross Section of White Enlisted Men with No Overseas Service, January–February 1944)

| AGE | PERCENTAGES RECEIVING CRITICAL SCORES AMONG MEN WHO HAD: | | |
	Attended Grade School Only	Attended High School, But Did Not Graduate	Graduated from High School
30 and over	51 *(494)*	43 *(441)*	35 *(431)*
25–29	51 *(405)*	41 *(484)*	31 *(838)*
20–24	41 *(453)*	34 *(629)*	24 *(1,213)*
Under 20	35 *(153)*	25 *(443)*	18 *(785)*

The numbers in parentheses are the numbers of cases on which percentages are based. Data from S-95 and S-99.

rose steadily with age and declined steadily with education. That these relationships were not a function of the internal correlation between age and physical condition is shown in Table 5, where the same relationships between scores and age and education hold within the group classified as fit for general service. Within the limited service group, age differences, perhaps because of the small number of cases at any age, hold less well especially at the lower educational levels. From these data, it may also be seen that at any age-education level, those who were not fit for general service received poorer scores on the average.

These compositional differences in the frequency with which symptoms were reported are clear enough, but the question is what do they imply? That is to say, can these differences be interpreted as reflecting actual differences in the level of emotional stability among the various groups, or do they indicate merely that the kinds of errors which make the tests less than perfect indicators of the criterion of psychoneurotic tendencies were unequally operative in different kinds of populations? Let us look at each of the three variables from this point of view.

As far as the higher level of symptoms among limited service men

TABLE 5

PROPORTIONS RECEIVING CRITICAL SCORES ON THE ANXIETY SYMPTOMS INDEX AT VARIOUS AGE-EDUCATION LEVELS, AMONG LIMITED SERVICE AND GENERAL SERVICE MEN

(Cross Section of White Enlisted Men with No Overseas Service, January–February 1944)

AGE-EDUCATION LEVEL	PROPORTIONS RECEIVING CRITICAL SCORES AMONG:	
	Men not classified as limited service*	Men classified as limited service*
High school graduates and over		
30 and over	33 (433)	46 (98)
25–29	28 (659)	42 (179)
20–24	23 (1,022)	31 (191)
Under 20	16 (711)	24 (74)
Some high school but did not graduate		
30 and over	44 (355)	37 (86)
25–29	39 (395)	49 (89)
20–24	34 (536)	31 (93)
Under 20	24 (411)	41 (32)
Grade school only		
30 and over	50 (359)	55 (135)
25–29	49 (321)	57 (84)
20–24	41 (381)	43 (72)
Under 20	32 (131)	50 (22)

Data from S-95 and S-99.

The numbers in parentheses are the numbers of cases on which percentages are based.

* This classification is based on men's answers to the question, "Has the Army at any time classified you as a limited service man?" The answers to this question were:

Yes, I was classified as limited service by the Army	17% of cross section
No, I was never classified as limited service by the Army	66
I don't know whether the Army has ever classified me as limited service or not	17
	100% $N = 6,869$

In the table above, those who said "No" and those who said "Don't know" are combined to make up the group which is designated "not classified as limited service." Actually, the men who answered "Don't know" appeared to show as many symptoms as the limited service group, or more, so this procedure is a conservative estimate of the differences between limited and nonlimited service personnel.

is concerned, the question may be put as: Would a group of men such as these, in less than perfect health, report a larger number of symptoms simply because of their physical condition, or can these differences be interpreted as implying greater emotional instability among the limited service men? We know, of course, that the limited service group contained men who were so classified because they were judged by psychiatrists to be too unstable to be good risks for overseas or combat duty,[11] so to this extent, at least, the score differences reported were reflecting actual differences in the incidence of emotional disturbances in the two groups. But whether the score differences reflect merely this last fact or reflect as well some tendency for this test to fail to distinguish men in poor physical condition from men in poor psychiatric condition is difficult to say.

There is some evidence on this point, however. In this survey of soldiers, 27 per cent of the general service men received critical scores on the NSA as compared with 42 per cent of the limited service men, a difference of 15 per cent. Yet, in a study of men being examined at induction stations, the difference in proportions receiving critical scores between men accepted for either general or limited service and men rejected on physical, nonpsychiatric grounds was only about 5 per cent.[12] If we assume that men with rejectable defects would be even more prone to report symptoms than men whose defects led to their classification as limited service, then we would expect even less than a 5 per cent difference between general service and limited service men. In other words, it would seem that only a small part of the 15 per cent difference between general and limited service men can be traced to a failure of the test to distinguish between men whose symptoms were organic in origin and those whose symptoms were primarily psychogenic.

On the other hand, it must be remembered that these data were collected at induction stations, not in the Army itself. While it cannot be completely documented with existing data, there is fairly conclusive evidence, as will be discussed more fully in a later section, that there was a rather general rise in the reporting of psychosomatic symptoms in the transition from civilian to Army life. To the extent that this increase represents a rather natural response to the

---

[11] The concept of limited service included both men disqualified for overseas service and men limited to noncombat duty overseas. The practice, adopted later, of classifying men into qualified or disqualified for overseas service was not quite equivalent, since men classified for limited overseas service were classified "limited service" in the one case and "qualified for overseas service" in the other.

[12] See Volume IV.

greater physical exertion which Army training required as over against the usually less physically active civilian life,[13] it might well result in a proportionately higher increase among those with less physical stamina and thus account in part for the differences between the general and limited service men. Or it may be that the

TABLE 6

THE AGE-EDUCATION DISTRIBUTION OF WHITE ENLISTED MEN WITH NO OVERSEAS SERVICE

(Cross Section and Hospitalized Psychoneurotics Compared, January–February 1944)

AGE-EDUCATION LEVEL*	WHITE ENLISTED MEN WITH NO OVERSEAS SERVICE		
	Cross section %	Psychoneurotic patients in Army hospitals %	Ratio of psychoneurotics to cross section†
High school graduation or more			
30 and over	7.7	9.2	119
25–29	12.2	6.2	51
20–24	18.0	5.3	29
Under 20	11.4	3.6	32
Some high school, but not graduation			
30 and over	6.4	13.7	214
25–29	7.0	7.3	104
20–24	9.2	9.1	99
Under 20	6.4	5.9	92
Grade school only			
30 and over	7.0	19.9	284
25–29	5.9	9.2	156
20–24	6.6	8.5	129
Under 20	2.2	2.1	95
Total	100.0	100.0	
Number of cases	6,869	563	

Data from S-95 and S-99.
* These distributions are affected slightly by the omission of illiterates from the sample.
† See footnote 15.

physical demands made by the Army called forth anxiety reactions in the less fit. It is obvious, then, that the data at hand are not sufficient to establish the effect of the possession of actual organic defects on responses to supposedly psychosomatic indices. At the same time, it is also clear that such variation in scores as might be attributable to this source of error is relatively small.

---

[13] This is, of course, not the only possible interpretation of the change in responses. See below for a discussion of its possible significance.

The rising incidence of reported psychosomatic symptoms with age at first suggests an interpretation paralleling the one above in terms of physical condition. That is, it is easy enough to assume that even within the group classified fit for general duty there were variations in general health and physical endurance. Older men might be expected, by and large, to have poorer health and lower endurance if for no other reason than that they tended, upon induction, to be more out of condition than the younger men. Then, if we continue to assume a relationship between general physical level and incidence of vague physical complaints, the age differences in scores on the Anxiety Symptoms Index might be rather summarily dismissed as signifying no more than this. But that more than this is involved is underlined by the result obtained in every study of psychoneurotics in the Army: They were always found to contain a disproportionate number of older men;[14] and this is true even among combat breakdowns who, psychiatrists are generally agreed, are typically individuals who would not break down under ordinary conditions but are responding to conditions of unendurable emotional stress.

In fact, if we examine the age-education distributions of the cross section of white enlisted men with no overseas service and the hospitalized psychoneurotics from among their number, as shown in Table 6, it is at once apparent that there is an excess of psychoneurotics in exactly those classes in which the Anxiety Symptoms Index was shown to select relatively higher proportions—among older men and among less well educated men. This is most easily seen by examining the relative ratios[15] of psychoneurotics to the cross section at each age-education level, presented in this table, in conjunction with the proportions of each age and education group receiving crit-

---

[14] It should be remembered, when we refer to the demographic characteristics of psychoneurotics in the Army, that we are not describing all the men whose personalities psychiatrists would diagnose as psychoneurotic, but rather we are limited to those types who found it impossible to go on functioning in the Army environment. These statistics should not, therefore, be generalized into comparative rates of psychoneurosis in the male population generally.

[15] These figures, given in the last column of Table 6, are simply the proportion of psychoneurotics in a given category divided by the proportion of the cross section in that category, the ratio then being multiplied by 100 to keep it in the same dimension as percentages. It may be variously interpreted without changing the general conclusion arrived at in the text. If we assume that the cross section is an approximate representation of the unselected Army population before any psychoneurotics were removed from it, then this ratio times k would be the proportion of any age-education group which is psychoneurotic, where k equals the proportion of psychoneurotics in the population as a whole. Thus, if we assume that one tenth of the population is psychoneurotic, these figures indicate that 3 per cent of the high school graduates

ical scores on the Anxiety Symptoms Index which were given earlier in Table 4. This relationship is presented graphically in Chart I.

Simple inspection of this diagram indicates that the relationship is very close. When we look at the relationship within any single age group (shown in Chart II), it is obvious that it tends to be linear; the three points when joined forming almost a straight line in each age group except for men under 20. This pattern of educational differences indicates that they are almost entirely a function of the differential psychoneurotic rates. The correlation is lowered by variations in symptomatology as between age groups of a given educational level. Inspection of the four age group observations making up an educational level, portrayed in Chart III, indicates that the group of men age 30 and over tends at each educational level to have an even higher incidence of psychoneurosis than we would have expected from the incidence of symptoms reported. Nevertheless, the correlation between the relative incidence of psychoneurosis and the proportions with a critical number of anxiety symptoms is .84 ± .08, which means that about 70 per cent of the variation in reported psychosomatic symptoms among age-education classes is attributable to variations in the actual incidence of psychoneurosis among these groups.

We may take it, then, that we have an instrument which reflects rather well variations in the general incidence of psychoneurotic disturbance in the population. Before turning to an examination of the major situations in which there were marked changes in psychological tension among enlisted men in the Army, however, we must now raise the question of whether the indices employed were as efficient at other times during the war as they were in the period we have been discussing up to now.

---

under 20 years of age and 28 per cent of the men 30 and over with only grade school education are psychoneurotic. On the other hand, we may assume that the cross section is already completely selected and contains no psychoneurotics. In this case, the figures in the last column, when multiplied by $k/1-k$, represent the number of psychoneurotics per 100 nonpsychoneurotics. Under these assumptions and again assuming one tenth of the population to be psychoneurotic, the correction factor is one ninth and these relative ratios could be converted to show about 4 psychoneurotics per 100 normals in the young, educated group and 32 per 100 in the older, less educated group. Actually, the cross section is more reasonably to be regarded as falling somewhere between the two extreme assumptions discussed. An assumption along these lines could be made and would require only the introduction of a more complex correction factor without any alteration of the relative figures shown in the table.

No assumption about the actual proportion of psychoneurotics in the population has been introduced, simply because it is a most difficult attribute to estimate and, being a constant, would not at all affect the relative differences shown here nor the computation of the correlation discussed later.

CHART I

THE RELATIONSHIP BETWEEN THE PROPORTIONS RECEIVING CRITICAL
SCORES OF THE ANXIETY SYMPTOMS INDEX AND THE INCIDENCE OF
PSYCHONEUROSIS WITHIN AGE-EDUCATIONAL LEVELS
(White Enlisted Men with No Overseas Service, January–February 1944)

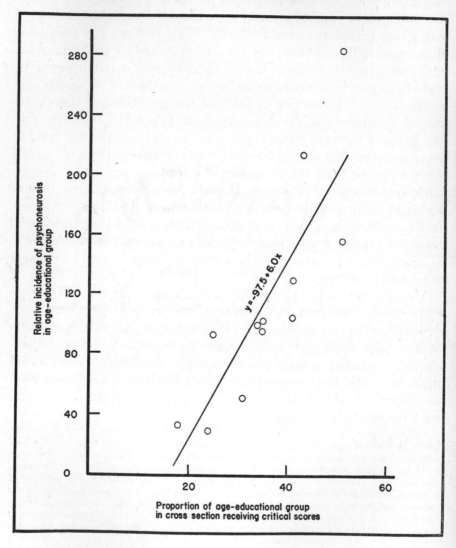

Data from Tables 4 and 6.

CHART II

THE RELATIONSHIP OF EDUCATIONAL VARIATIONS IN THE PROPORTIONS RECEIVING CRITICAL SCORES ON THE ANXIETY SYMPTOMS INDEX TO EDUCATIONAL VARIATIONS IN THE INCIDENCE OF PSYCHONEUROSIS, AGE HELD CONSTANT

(White Enlisted Men with No Overseas Service, January–February 1944)

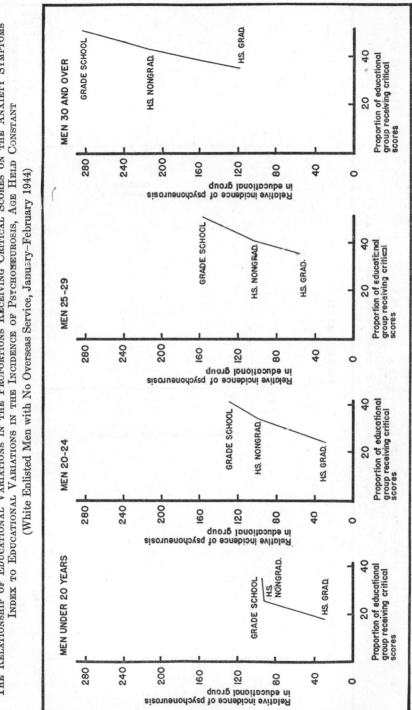

Data from Tables 4 and 6.

CHART III

The Relationship of Age Variations in the Proportions Receiving Critical Scores on the Anxiety Symptoms Index to Age Variations in the Incidence of Psychoneurosis, Educational Level Held Constant

(White Enlisted Men with No Overseas Service, January–February 1944)

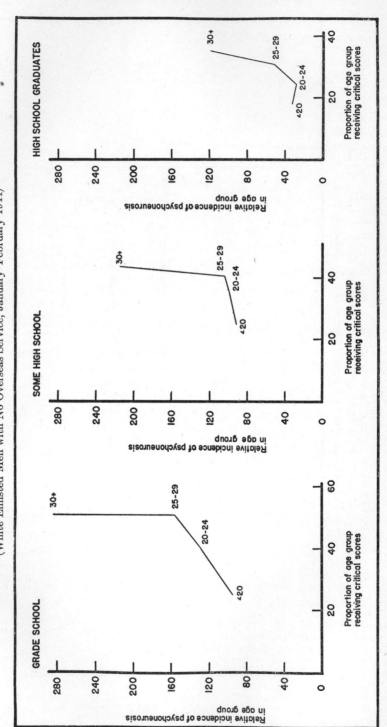

Data from Tables 4 and 6.

Variations in the Incidence of Symptoms Through Time

At least among troops in the United States, the level of anxiety did not fluctuate in the last months of the war. As shown in Table 7, in four studies made between November 1944 and July 1945, which furnish, therefore, observations before and after VE Day, there are no differences in the reporting of anxiety symptoms among white enlisted men with no overseas service.[16] While there are progres-

TABLE 7

CHANGES THROUGH TIME IN THE PROPORTIONS RECEIVING CRITICAL SCORES ON THE
ANXIETY SYMPTOMS INDEX
(Cross Section of White Enlisted Men with No Overseas Service)

Date of survey	Number of cases	Proportions receiving critical scores
January–February 1944	6,869	33
November 1944	1,989	43
Early June 1945	4,659	46
Late June 1945	937	42
Early July 1945	3,159	46

Data from S-95 and S-99, S-157, S-205, S-215, and S-218.

sive differences in the composition of samples of men with no overseas service, standardization to eliminate these variations would not change this result.

On the other hand, these data also indicate an apparent increase in anxiety symptoms at all four of these time periods as compared with the time of the first study in early 1944.[17] But, though this difference might seem to suggest a generally lower level of emotional disturbance before D Day as compared with after it, this explanation does not seem quite plausible in view of the fact that troops in training in early 1944 could anticipate combat duty in the Italian

[16] Even the small increases noted in early June and early July can be traced to the mechanics of scoring. Because of the NSA's original function as a practical screening test, it was imperative that no man should escape psychiatric evaluation simply by failure to answer the questions. The test was, therefore, scored in such a way that a large proportion of unanswered questions led automatically to a critical score. In these two surveys, the questions in the Anxiety Symptoms Index came near the end of a long and unusually difficult questionnaire, and extensive analysis of the individual items indicates that the somewhat poorer scores are a result of greater nonresponse on these surveys as compared with the others.

[17] The most obvious explanation of this difference, viz., that it represents the deterioration in test efficiency to be expected as between the original study in which the test was developed and a repetition, does not hold in this case since the item selection and scoring were determined prior to the first study.

or Pacific campaigns, then under way, even without the opening of the European front.   If we are to assume that the intensification of the war represented by the coming of D Day resulted in increased anxiety reactions among men in training, then it is only reasonable to suppose as well that VE Day, signifying the closing of one phase of the war, would have had a reassuring effect; but this was not the case, as we have just seen.

There is at least one alternative theory which would account for the observed difference in other terms, though unfortunately it must remain largely speculative.   Since we know that physical standards for overseas duty were revised generally downward as the war went on, it follows that when we apparently control the factor of physical condition, there still remains the element of deterioration of physical standards which has not been controlled.   When we examine the proportion receiving critical scores on the Anxiety Symptoms Index in early 1944 as compared with just after VE Day,[18] it is true that more men received critical scores in 1945 even holding age, education, and physical condition constant (see Table 8).   But these differences can be accounted for under the assumption of the deterioration of standards as follows: Let us take the 1944 group of physically fit men as representing the more rigidly defined group, both because it excludes men who were fit only for limited overseas duty and because physical standards were higher at that time, and take the 1945 group of unfit men as the more purely unfit group in that men fit for limited overseas service were excluded and, with the lower physical standards prevailing, some men classified unfit in 1944 would be excluded from this group.   If we further assume that the scores made by these two groups represent the way clearly fit and unfit men answered the Anxiety Symptom Index at both time periods, then all we have to do to account for the higher scores of the men classified as fit in 1945 is to assume that they consist of about two thirds fit men by 1944 standards and one third unfit men.   By following these assumptions we can reproduce almost exactly the proportions receiving critical scores among the physically fit in 1945 (see Table 8).   In a similar fashion, the scores of the unfit in 1944 can be accounted for by assuming that they consist in equal parts of fit men who answer as do the fit in 1944 and unfit men who answer as do the unfit men in 1945.   That these assumptions are not too

---

[18] Strictly speaking, the comparison should be made between the two 1944 studies, for it is the later 1944 study in which the increase is first noted.   But the sample in this study is so small that we have turned to the next observation after it.

TABLE 8

INCIDENCE OF ANXIETY SYMPTOMS IN JANUARY-FEBRUARY 1944 AS COMPARED WITH JUNE 1945

(Cross Sections of White Enlisted Men with No Overseas Service)

AGE-EDUCATION LEVEL	PERCENTAGES RECEIVING CRITICAL SCORES				PHYSICALLY FIT 1945		PHYSICALLY UNFIT 1944	
	Physically fit*		Physically unfit*		Hypothetical proportions receiving critical scores†	Deviation of hypothetical from actual score	Hypothetical proportions receiving critical scores	Deviation of hypothetical from actual score†
	1944	1945	1944	1945				
High school graduation or more								
30 and over	27 (364)	39 (294)	46 (98)	59 (254)	38	1	43	3
25–29	23 (564)	39 (454)	42 (179)	64 (183)	36	3	43	−1
20–24	20 (913)	30 (529)	31 (191)	52 (172)	30	0	36	−5
Under 20	16 (650)	12 (357)	24 (74)	47 (32)	26	−14	31	−7
Some high school, but not graduation								
30 and over	36 (241)	53 (148)	37 (86)	67 (120)	46	7	52	−15
25–29	34 (296)	50 (172)	49 (89)	64 (72)	44	6	49	0
20–24	30 (433)	47 (156)	31 (93)	75 (69)	45	2	52	−21
Under 20	20 (329)	20 (187)	41 (32)	43 (21)	27	−7	31	10
Grade school only								
30 and over	44 (219)	50 (119)	55 (135)	74 (184)	54	−4	59	−4
25–29	44 (217)	66 (106)	57 (84)	80 (54)	56	10	62	−5
20–24	38 (279)	53 (83)	43 (72)	72 (46)	49	4	55	−12
Under 20	24 (79)	36 (50)	50 (22)	67 (9)	38	−2	46	4

Data from S-95 and S-99 and from S-205.

The numbers in parentheses are the numbers of cases on which percentages are based.

* Based for 1944 on the question, "Has the Army as physically fit for overseas duty?" In 1945, the question used was, "As far as you know, are you now classified by the Army at any time classified you as a limited service man?" Even without the introduction of a change in physical standards for overseas duty between the two time periods, these questions, as pointed out previously, do not measure quite the same thing because men who were fit only for limited service duties overseas are classified limited service in the one case and physically fit in the other. In this table, men who did not know their classification (1,130 in 1944 and 838 in 1945) have been omitted.

† In order to correct for a deterioration in physical standards between the two time periods, the assumption is being made that of the physically fit in 1945 two thirds are men who answered like the fit in 1944 and one third are men who answered like the unfit in 1945. For the physically unfit, it is assumed that in 1944 they consisted equally of men who answered like the 1944 physically fit and of men who answered like the 1945 physically unfit. See text for further discussion.

absurd is suggested by the fact that, if we extrapolate the proportions unfit in our samples, we get roughly 700,000 limited service men among those who had not yet served overseas in 1944 as compared with about 500,000 in 1945. In other words, between those two time periods there appears to have been a reclassification to physically fit for overseas duty of almost a third of the men classified as limited service in 1944. While some of these men were undoubtedly discharged rather than reclassified, these discharges were probably more than compensated for by the continued drafting of men for limited duty only.

If these assumptions are correct, then the differences in Anxiety Symptoms scores noted in early 1944 as compared with those noted in later periods may be attributed to changes in composition not fully reflected in the objective statistics. That is to say, shipment overseas increased the proportion of physically unfit men in the United States despite the fact that the lowered physical standards and the shift in usage from "limited service" to "unfit for overseas service" both made for a decline in the total number of physically unfit men in the Army. (It will be recalled that in January–February 1944, 17 per cent of the white enlisted men with no overseas service said they were classified "limited service." By June 1945, 27 per cent said they were classified "unfit for overseas duty.") If, as seems reasonable, this unfit group was more highly selected in 1945 than in 1944, and if the selective process of shipment overseas also operated to increase the proportion of marginally fit men among the fit group that had never served overseas, then we have accounted for the apparent shift in scores. Though this argument remains in large part inferential, it seems reasonable to suppose that part, at least, of the difference in anxiety scores between early and late 1944 was attributable to the revision in physical standards which accompanied the man-power demands of the European front. It should be emphasized, however, that even if this were the case it still would not mean that there was not an increased proportion of emotionally disturbed men in the part of the Army remaining in the United States. Rather, it would simply trace the source of this increase to a concealed change in the composition of the population of men with no overseas service instead of to differences in the adjustment of similar individuals at different times.

Unfortunately, we do not have sufficient data to make any statement about how the scores of men serving overseas changed through time. Although it appears likely that the emotional reactions of men in the United States were not, in the large, affected by the course of the war, it does not necessarily follow that the same would be true of men who were closer to the war fronts. But since we do not have studies of psychosomatic symptoms made in the same overseas area at different points of time, there is little we can do but note the problem.

SECTION II

VARIATIONS IN THE INCIDENCE OF SYMPTOMS ASSOCIATED WITH STAGES OF THE ARMY CYCLE

Now that we have seen that we have an index of anxiety which was sensitive enough to reflect changes in the general level of tension and which remained relatively uninfluenced in the United States by the course of events, let us see what situations in the Army were accompanied by a rising level of symptoms. The materials extend to three of these type situations: Getting used to the Army, serving overseas, and facing the threats of combat. Each of these will be treated in turn.

The Impact of the Army on New Recruits

The data which we shall review tend to show that, among troops stationed in the United States, there is little evidence of changes in anxiety symptoms with increasing time in the Army—except for an initial rise early in the soldier's Army career.

The proportion of men receiving critical scores at induction stations was considerably smaller than the proportion found among men in early stages of training. In a check of NSA performance at all induction stations in the United States for the month of August 1945, it was found that only 7 per cent of the literate men accepted for service in the Armed Forces received critical scores.[19] On the

---

[19] While the use of the month of August, the only month for which full records are available, means the inclusion of large numbers of men examined and inducted after the cessation of hostilities, it is not likely that the course of the war changed these proportions very greatly. Small spot checks made earlier showed proportions in the same range. For example, the Chicago Induction Station reported, for the month of October 1944, and again for the first half of March 1945, that 7 per cent of the men found acceptable for service received critical scores, and for one week in February 1945, at the New York Induction Station, the proportion was 12 per cent. If we break the August 1945 figures down into time periods related to the course of events we get:

other hand, in late June 1945, close to a quarter of the men under 20 years of age with 3 months or less service in the Army received scores in this range.[20]

At first glance, it appears that the precipitation of men,into the strange and, to many, fearful world of the Army brought about a heightened anxiety. Certainly, the very great physical exertion required of men in basic training, and the use of punishment, threats of punishment, and fear as major techniques of imposing military discipline and producing conformity to the military system, as well as the bewilderment, confusion, and often resentment, which were the new recruits' first reactions to the Army, all contributed to producing tension. Moreover, not only the aches and pains of unaccustomed hiking and exercise, but the narrowing of interests which the transition to the Army milieu represented would be expected to bring about a greater preoccupation with bodily functions and a consequent rise in psychosomatic complaining. Nor should it be forgotten that being ill, "going on sick call," was practically the only legitimate means of avoiding onerous training and duty, an arrangement which itself might be expected to encourage men's discovery of physical symptoms in themselves.

But, though this increase in emotional disturbance is so in line with theoretical expectations and impressionistic observations as almost not to require detailed demonstration, we should point out the circumstances which make the data just offered something less than precise documentation of this point. First, the induction station data are based on all men inducted into service, which means that they include the scores of men selected for service with the Navy and Marine Corps as well as the Army. There is some reason to believe that the Army received a disproportionate share of the

Date of examination	Stage of war	Percentage receiving critical scores on NSA among men acceptable for induction
August 1–9	War going on, atomic bomb dropped, but no rumors of peace	6
August 10–14	Japanese peace offer rumored, then being discussed	7
August 15–31	Japanese surrender accepted, cessation of hostilities	9

[20] The late June figures are the only ones, aside from the early January–February 1944 study, available for comparison since this was the only other full-scale study in which the complete NSA was asked. (Only the NSA score is available for induction stations.) The group of men under 20 with 3 months or less service is selected as the closest approximation possible to the August 1945 induction station population.

borderline fit men, a fact which would make the proportion receiving critical scores at induction stations somewhat higher than the 7 per cent reported if the data were limited to men later inducted into the Army.

More serious, perhaps, is the difference in test conditions. In the one case, men filled out the NSA as part of their preinduction physical examination; it was an official document to which they signed their names. If they had discussed procedures with any of their previously inducted friends, they knew that they were going to be quizzed again by doctors about these and similar symptoms and perhaps believed their answers could be proved true or false by physical examination. In the other case, the NSA was filled out as part of a questionnaire administered anonymously, with great stress being placed on assuring men that their answers could not and would not be traced to them. It might therefore be assumed that men would be more cautious in attributing symptoms to themselves in an induction station setting, even if the induction examination setting offered greater incentive to malingering than did the survey situation when men were already in the Army.[21]

Fortunately, there is some evidence bearing on this point, even though it may not entirely reproduce the problem situation. Three times studies were made in which two comparable groups of men answered the NSA, one group under conditions of anonymity and the other being instructed to sign their names. Two of these studies were made among men in the Army and the NSA was included as part of a longer questionnaire, the administration being conducted exactly as an ordinary study except that in each case one group of men were asked to sign their names. The third study was made in one induction station as part of the preliminary testing prior to the adoption of the NSA.[22] The preliminary form used in this last instance was very similar to the final form later adopted, and administered in much the same way. About all that was lacking in this setting in comparison with the later induction station procedure was the prior word-of-mouth knowledge which many men had that such a test was part of the examination process and that a psychiatrist

---

[21] It should not be assumed that a reluctance to go into the Army and a test whose intent was fairly clear necessarily added up to malingering. Men were frequently ambivalent about it. On the one hand, they might prefer to stay out of military service; but, on the other, rejection, especially for psychiatric reasons, often took on overtones of personal disgrace.

[22] See Volume IV.

would ask them about their answers to it. Each of these three studies was based on about 400 men, evenly divided between the anonymous and the identified groups.

In each case, differences of about 4 per cent in the proportions receiving critical scores were found, the identified group consistently making the better scores. This difference was in no case significant, nor would it have been if the three samples had been pooled. These three replications, while suggestive, are of course not sufficient to establish the existence of a tendency for anonymous individuals to claim more psychosomatic disturbances than identified individuals. But even if we assume such a tendency did exist to the extent of the 4 per cent differences observed in these three studies and to that difference add a reasonable amount to take care of the inclusion of Naval and Marine personnel in the induction station data, we would still have to conclude that there was a significant increase in the incidence of symptoms expressive of anxiety during the period of transition from civilian life to the early weeks of Army training.

This general increase appeared to level off after about 6 months' service, and reports of symptomatology showed little change thereafter with continued service in the United States. As shown in Table 9, reports of anxiety symptoms were higher among men with 6 months' to 1 year's service than among men with less service at every age-education level. For men with over 6 months' service, there were no longevity-related differences in anxieties among men under 25 years of age, while in the older group, symptoms appeared to decline with increasing longevity. The data presented in Table 9 have been limited to men classified fit for general duty; although the data for limited service men appear to follow the patterns just described, the number of cases in any one cell is so small that they have been omitted.[23]

The relationships presented in Table 9 are, however, static ones from which we are attempting to infer something of how men's reactions changed with increased Army experience. Ideally speaking, what we need are successive observations of the responses of a cohort of men who entered the Army all at once and who continued to serve in the United States with no changes in composition through discharges and selective shipment overseas. Since in fact we could

---

[23] The reader will recall that the criterion used in the 1944 data is general service, while fitness for overseas service is employed in 1946. This fact, together with the change in physical standards through time already discussed, probably accounts for the differences between apparently comparable longevity groups.

not follow such a group of men through time, we have substituted the observation at a given moment in time of groups of men for whom varying amounts of time in the Army had elapsed. But in order to be reasonably secure in using this ex post facto approach, we should, of course, be able to assume that the groups of men successively entering the Army represented equivalent cohorts and that attrition of these groups by discharges and shipment overseas either affected all groups equally or, if it occurred unequally, operated

TABLE 9

PROPORTIONS RECEIVING CRITICAL SCORES ON THE ANXIETY SYMPTOMS INDEX IN
RELATION TO LENGTH OF ARMY SERVICE

(Two Cross Sections of White Enlisted Men with No Overseas Service:
Those Classified Fit for General Duty in January–February 1944
and Those Fit for Overseas Duty in June 1945)

	PERCENTAGES RECEIVING CRITICAL SCORES AMONG:			
	Men under 25 years of age		Men 25 and over	
	Less than high school graduate	High school graduate or more	Less than high school graduate	High school graduate or more
LENGTH OF ARMY SERVICE				
January–February 1944				
Over 2 years	29 *(132)*	19 *(149)*	31 *(262)*	20 *(250)*
Over 1 year to 2 years	29 *(595)*	20 *(783)*	40 *(465)*	25 *(397)*
Over 6 months to 1 year	29 *(244)*	19 *(449)*	47 *(147)*	29 *(180)*
6 months or less	24 *(149)*	10 *(182)*	42 *(99)*	25 *(101)*
June 1945				
Over 3 years	41 *(17)*	28 *(29)*	42 *(168)*	35 *(229)*
Over 2 years to 3 years	43 *(127)*	25 *(314)*	60 *(170)*	40 *(242)*
Over 6 months to 2 years	37 *(109)*	24 *(296)*	61 *(133)*	46 *(189)*
6 months or less	28 *(175)*	13 *(247)*	51 *(84)*	37 *(93)*

Data from S-99 and S-205.
The numbers in parentheses are the numbers of cases on which percentages are based.

randomly so that only the size and not the composition of the affected groups was altered.

On the contrary, we know in this case that neither assumption can be maintained. As we recall the constantly changing Selective Service policies—shifts in age limit, shifts in policy regarding the drafting of fathers and the deferment of industrial workers, revisions of physical standards and of policies affecting the induction of limited service men, to mention a few—it is clear that the men inducted in one 6-month period might have differed radically from the men entering the Army in the succeeding 6 months. Even though we may correct for such things as variations in the age of inductees at different periods, there is, as we have seen, no way of making precise allowance for the subtler differences, such as changes in physical standards.

Perhaps the group most affected by such factors as these is the group with greatest longevity in the Army. In the data just presented for 1944, for example, men with over 2 years of service entered the Army during or before January 1942, which means that they were comprised largely of old Regular Army men and pre-Pearl Harbor inductees and volunteers. It is well known that men inducted during the prewar period were a group selected under higher physical and psychiatric standards than were ever used again during the war, while volunteers at the time of Pearl Harbor and men who chose to join the Regular Army in peacetime may well have been psychologically very different from the average run of men who entered the Army involuntarily.[24]

Moreover, the two major attrition factors—discharge and shipment overseas—also affected the composition of the longevity groups. Army policy was that men physically qualified for overseas service who had not yet served overseas should not remain in the United States over a year.[25] There were large exceptions to this policy, especially in the first years of the war when the bulk of the Army was still in the United States. But even as early as the January 1944 study, men physically fit for overseas duty and with long service who were still in the United States were beginning to be an anomalous group consisting in good part of men considered irreplaceable in skilled positions. And, of course, the proportion of men discharged from any original cohort would vary directly with the length of time that cohort had been in the Army. Since the bulk of discharges were medical, and a large proportion of these for psychiatric reasons, their effect was to make the longer-service groups more psychiatrically select than the shorter-service groups.

These considerations apply with even more force to the older men in the long service group. As is generally known, psychoneurotic

---

[24] Of men classified by Selective Service from November 1940 through September 1941, 78 per cent were deferred for nonmedical reasons, and of the 22 per cent considered for induction over half were rejected on physical grounds. See Selective Service System, *Medical Statistics Bulletin No. 2*, "Causes of Rejection and Incidence of Defects," Washington, August 1943.

[25] See, for example, War Department Circular 100, 1944, "Enlisted Men—Utilization of Manpower Based on Physical Capacity": "It is contrary to War Department policy to permit an enlisted man physically qualified for general service and under 38 years of age to remain at a fixed installation or activity of the Zone of the Interior in excess of 1 year, unless he shall have served overseas."

and other disease rates were higher among the older men so that the composition of this group would have been more greatly altered through discharges than the group of younger men.   And it is probable that older men being considered for induction under the peacetime Selective Service operations were subject to even more rigid scrutiny than the younger men.

Considerations like these lead to the conclusion that neither set of data in Table 9 by itself can be interpreted as representing the effect of Army service on psychoneurotic manifestations.   However, if we look at the two sets of observations in relation to each other, certain inferences can be made.   It has already been pointed out that each shows the same pattern of longevity-selected differences.   That is, at both time periods, the differences among younger men were essentially a difference between men with 6 months or less of service and men in all other longevity groups; and at both time periods older men showed an initial rise in symptoms after 6 months of service, followed by a progressive decline.   The form in which these data were collected does not permit the adjustment of the longevity groups at the later period to correspond exactly to what those shown for the earlier study would have been after the sixteen months elapsing between studies; still there is enough overlapping to make it most suggestive that we do find the same relationships.   For, in the later study, the apparent decline in symptoms among older men is found after longer service than in the first study.   In fact, the older men showing the lowest incidence of critical scores at the later date are in just about the longevity groups that the older men with fewest symptoms in the first study would have been in by the later date.   In other words, the decline in symptoms noted is associated with a particular group of men rather than with some phase of Army experience.   It would seem, then, that *there is little evidence for changes in anxiety symptoms with continuing Army service except for the initial rise after 6 months of service which is consistently present for all groups in both these studies.*

Reactions in the Face of Overseas Service

As might be anticipated from the comparisons in Volume I, Chapter 5, of general attitudes of soldiers overseas and at home, the problem of making such comparisons as to anxiety symptoms is fraught with many complications.   No simple, clean-cut conclusion emerges from our data.   European data reveal very little higher level of anxiety responses than United States data; Pacific data indicate a somewhat higher level than European data. But differences in timing of the surveys, as well as the fact that mental health was a factor in the selection of men for overseas service, make generalizations dangerous. Further data do suggest, however, some increase in anxiety symptoms with greater amount of overseas service.

As we have already suggested, the rise in symptoms from the early phase of Army training to all later periods probably repre-

TABLE 10

PROPORTIONS RECEIVING CRITICAL SCORES ON THE ANXIETY SYMPTOMS INDEX
AMONG INFANTRY REPLACEMENTS IN TRAINING IN COMPARISON WITH A
CROSS SECTION OF WHITE ENLISTED MEN WITH NO OVERSEAS
SERVICE, CLASSIFIED FIT FOR OVERSEAS SERVICE
(June 1945)

| | PERCENTAGES RECEIVING CRITICAL SCORES | |
	Infantry replacements	Cross section
High school graduates or more		
25 years or more	50 *(295)*	43 *(918)*
20–24 years	43 *(121)*	33 *(598)*
Under 20 years	20 *(156)*	17 *(409)*
Some high school, but not graduation		
25 years or more	62 *(132)*	55 *(453)*
20–24 years	59 *(56)*	52 *(204)*
Under 20 years	40 *(134)*	34 *(204)*
Grade school only		
25 years or more	70 *(143)*	65 *(430)*
20–24 years	65 *(63)*	60 *(131)*
Under 20 years	49 *(73)*	51 *(96)*

Data from S-205.
The numbers in parentheses are the numbers of cases on which percentages are based.

sented in part the end of an adjustment process whose beginnings were reflected in the increase in psychosomatic manifestations during the transition from civilian life to early days in the Army. But at least one other factor may also have been contributing to this rise, namely, anticipatory anxieties about going overseas. The expectation of imminent shipment overseas was most widespread among the men who had recently completed their Army training, that is, the men whom we have just shown to be most characterized by psychosomatic complaints. Army psychiatrists became very familiar with the phenomenon of a vast increase in mild psychoneurotic manifestations among troops being processed for shipment overseas, so familiar in fact, that the name "gangplank fever" was coined for it.[26]

While it was not possible to conduct studies among troops once they were alerted for movement overseas, something of the effect of anticipatory fears may be seen in the reactions of men being trained as Infantry replacements.   Among these men, as compared with the cross section, higher proportions in 8 of the 9 age-education levels shown in Table 10 reported a critical number of psychosomatic symptoms.   Though these differences are small, their substantial consistency, as well as the fact that in an earlier study the same differences were found as between men in Infantry divisions in training and other men, indicates that they are significant.

However, the experience of being stationed overseas did not necessarily result in increased psychosomatic complaining.   If we compare the Anxiety Symptoms scores of a cross section of the troops in the European theater with those of men in the United States eligible for overseas service (see Table 11), we find that, for the most part, the troops in the ETO scored somewhere between the January–February 1944 and the June 1945 United States samples.   This is entirely what we would expect if there had been no general shift in scores among men after leaving the United States, for some of the men left under the relatively higher physical standards prevailing for overseas duty in 1944 while others were selected under later standards.   That is, in the light of our previous discussion it seems reasonable to conclude that the June 1945 sample contained a higher proportion of marginally fit men than either the European or the earlier United States samples.   The European sample, in turn, would contain a lower proportion of the marginally fit than the later United States sample but would exceed the earlier United States observations in this respect, if only because it was made up of men who were in part selected under the earlier higher standards for overseas shipment and in part under the later downward revisions.   In addition to this, the European data on the incidence of anxiety symptoms might be expected to be higher than the United States January–February 1944 figures, since the latter exclude the scores of men later sent overseas for limited duty while these men are included in the European data, a fact which itself would lead to ap-

---

[26] Such behavior was so common that Army directives specified that "mild psychoneuroses transient in character" should not be considered as disqualifying men for either overseas or combat duty.   War Department Circular No. 164, Washington, 1944, "Enlisted Men—Use of Manpower Based on Physical Capacity."

parently higher proportions with critical scores among the men in Europe.   From these data, then, it appears that the emotional responses of men in Europe differed little, if at all, from those of men in the United States.[27]

One fact, however, mars the generality of this finding.   The European data were collected at an atypical period of the war, during the

TABLE 11

THE INCIDENCE OF ANXIETY SYMPTOMS AMONG MEN IN THE EUROPEAN
THEATER AS COMPARED WITH TROOPS IN THE UNITED STATES

	PERCENTAGES RECEIVING CRITICAL SCORES		
AGE-EDUCATIONAL LEVEL	Cross section of nonlimited service troops with no overseas service, United States, January–February 1944	Cross section of European theater, April 1945	Cross section of troops with no overseas service fit for overseas duty, United States, June 1945
High school graduation or more			
30 years and over	33 *(433)*	39 *(329)*	43 *(383)*
25–29 years	28 *(659)*	36 *(514)*	43 *(535)*
20–24 years	23 *(1,022)*	30 *(948)*	33 *(598)*
Under 20 years	16 *(711)*	33 *(153)*	17 *(409)*
Some high school, but not graduation			
30 years and over	44 *(355)*	49 *(265)*	56 *(216)*
25–29 years	39 *(395)*	49 *(367)*	53 *(237)*
20–24 years	34 *(536)*	44 *(536)*	52 *(204)*
Under 20 years	24 *(411)*	37 *(145)*	34 *(204)*
Grade school only			
30 years and over	50 *(359)*	59 *(280)*	63 *(245)*
25–29 years	49 *(321)*	56 *(280)*	69 *(185)*
20–24 years	41 *(381)*	49 *(323)*	60 *(131)*
Under 20 years	32 *(131)*	60 *(82)*	51 *(96)*

Data from S-95 and S-99, S-223, and S-205.
The numbers in parentheses are the numbers of cases on which percentages are based.

period when the allied armies were advancing rapidly and the sense of imminent victory was in the air.   It is possible that enough enthusiasm and feelings of relief were generated during this period to lower the level of expressed anxiety from what it formerly had been.   Although we were able to show that the course of the war did not seem to affect the reported symptoms of men with no overseas service,

[27] The seeming exception to this generalization in the "under 20 years" group, whose scores exceed those in either of the United States samples, is attributable to the large proportion of combat men among them, whose emotional responses changed radically. See below for further discussion of the anxiety symptoms of combat men.

this conclusion cannot simply be broadened, without evidence, to extend to the reactions of men who were so much closer to the combat zones.   Since we have only this one observation of the anxiety symptoms of men in Europe, there is little possibility of deciding definitely whether the similarities observed between the European and United States data were peculiar to this time period or whether they were the usual case.

Certainly, there was a difference between the incidence of psychosomatic symptoms men reported in this European study and those

TABLE 12

INCIDENCE OF ANXIETY SYMPTOMS AMONG OVERSEAS TROOPS
EUROPE AND PACIFIC COMPARED

| | PERCENTAGES RECEIVING CRITICAL SCORES | |
| | Cross section of Central and Western Pacific, July–August 1945 | Cross section of European theater, April 1945 |
AGE–EDUCATION LEVEL		
High school graduation or more		
30 years and over	60 *(198)*	39 *(329)*
25–29 years	48 *(295)*	36 *(514)*
Under 25 years	40 *(427)*	30 *(1,101)*
Some high school but not graduation		
30 years and over	62 *(109)*	49 *(265)*
25–29 years	59 *(150)*	49 *(367)*
Under 25 years	55 *(267)*	43 *(681)*
Grade school only		
30 years and over	77 *(154)*	59 *(280)*
25–29 years	68 *(190)*	56 *(280)*
Under 25 years	60 *(175)*	51 *(405)*

Data from S-232 and S-223.
The numbers in parentheses are the numbers of cases on which percentages are based.

reported by men in the Central and Western Pacific in a study made at a later date.   As the data in Table 12 indicate, a higher proportion of men in every age and education group, among troops stationed in the Pacific, reported a frequency of symptoms at or beyond the critical level.   The date of the study in the Pacific was shortly before VJ Day, but the unexpectedness of that event makes it unlikely that the men in the Pacific had as much of a sense of the imminence of the war's end as did the men in Europe.   No selection factor is known which could have operated to send the relatively less stable individuals to the Pacific and the more stable men to Europe. It therefore follows that these observed differences must be attributed either to such differences in the stage of the war as it was psychologically perceived or to differences in the conditions of service between the two areas.   In general, Pacific service varied from European service in involving relative isolation from civilization and from civilian populations and living in tropical or semitropical climates, with all that such weather implies; and conditions like these may have exacted a greater psychological toll from the men stationed in the Pacific than was the case in the European environment.

At any rate, it was commonly felt that overseas service anywhere had a deleterious effect on emotional stability, so much so that men in each locality had their own terms to refer to the condition—in Europe, for instance, they spoke of being "ETO-happy," while in the Pacific men often referred to becoming "rock-" or "island-happy."   It is certainly true that, in Europe at least, the men who had been there longest, among men in noncombat jobs, were somewhat more likely to report anxiety symptoms than were men who had spent less time overseas.   (See Table 13.)

TABLE 13

EFFECT OF LENGTH OF OVERSEAS SERVICE ON ANXIETY SYMPTOMS AMONG NONCOMBAT MEN IN EUROPE, APRIL 1945, AND CROSS SECTION OF CENTRAL AND WESTERN PACIFIC

(July–August 1945)

	PERCENTAGES RECEIVING CRITICAL SCORES ON THE ANXIETY SYMPTOMS INDEX	
	Men overseas 1 year or less	Men overseas over 1 year
NONCOMBAT MEN IN EUROPE		
High school graduate or more		
25 years and over	29 (276)	34 (272)
Under 25 years	22 (367)	33 (234)
Less than high school graduate		
25 years and over	51 (311)	52 (343)
Under 25 years	37 (275)	41 (247)
ALL MEN IN CENTRAL AND WESTERN PACIFIC		
High school graduate or more		
25 years and over	51 (161)	53 (332)
Under 25 years	38 (185)	42 (242)
Less than high school graduate		
25 years and over	64 (208)	68 (395)
Under 25 years	58 (175)	57 (267)

Data from S-223 and S-232.
The numbers in parentheses are the numbers of cases on which percentages are based.

The data from the study in the Central and Western Pacific areas, also shown in Table 13, tend to support this conclusion though they show a much less clear-cut picture of difference between men with less and more overseas service.   However, it should be noted that it was not possible to exclude men with combat experience from this sample.   Combat men experienced a sharp increase in anxiety symptoms, irrespective of the amount of time they had spent overseas, and had on the average spent less time overseas than noncombat men.   Their inclusion would therefore tend to diminish the differences between the two longevity groups.   And, as suggested before, in the Pacific, the exact location in which men served may have been relatively more important than in Europe.   It was not possible from the information contained in this study and with the relatively small sample involved to control the factor of where men spent their time, e.g., in the relative comfort of Oahu or the discomfort of Saipan and Iwo Jima, which may well be complicating the reported differences.

When we recall that the men with longest service overseas left the United States earliest or were, in other words, selected under more rigid physical standards than later departures, we might have expected that as a more select group these men would have had, if anything, a smaller proportion of maladjusted men among them at the outset.   It therefore appears highly probable that the rather more frequent incidence of psychosomatic symptoms among men with greater amounts of overseas service represented a real though slight change in the responses of men as they continued to serve overseas rather than simply a reflection of initial differences between groups of men who went overseas at different times.[28]

Reactions to Combat

If it is difficult to draw conclusions about the effects of overseas service in general, the same is not true about the effects of actual combat.   There can be no doubt about the high level of anxiety symptoms among combat troops, both on the ground and in the air.

---

[28] The factors of selection which operated through time—primarily rotation of men with long periods of service overseas back to the United States and the return of men who became unfit for overseas duty—all worked in the direction of removing the most unstable individuals from the overseas population.   These selections would affect the greater longevity group more than the group with less service overseas, and would, therefore, tend to reduce the difference between the longevity groups.   However, the number of men eliminated through these channels, especially among noncombat men, was not large enough to alter the proportions significantly.

Combat, of course, remains the major experience of Army life most conducive to anxiety. Several chapters have already been devoted to the reactions of Ground and Air Force men in combat and these have gone at some length into the great emotional tensions engendered by combat participation. However, the analysis there presented may perhaps be rounded out by the rather systematic materials about combat anxiety reactions which have been collected by means of the various psychosomatic indices.

TABLE 14

ANXIETY SYMPTOMS OF INFANTRYMEN IN TRAINING IN THE UNITED STATES AND
OVERSEAS BEFORE AND AFTER COMBAT
(United States and Central Pacific, June 1945)

	PERCENTAGES RECEIVING CRITICAL SCORES ON THE ANXIETY SYMPTOMS INDEX		
AGE-EDUCATION LEVEL	Infantry replacements in training in the United States	Fresh replacements newly arrived in Central Pacific	Veteran replacements about to return to combat in Pacific after hospitalization
High school graduate or more			
25 years or more	48 (*347*)	54 (*56*)	71 (*65*)
20–24 years	39 (*150*)	41 (*88*)	71 (*55*)
Under 20 years	17 (*237*)	31 (*196*)	—
Som high school but not graduation			
25 years or more	60 (*180*)	67 (*48*)	80 (*49*)
20–24 years	53 (*81*)	58 (*76*)	83 (*35*)
Under 20 years	36 (*210*)	39 (*168*)	—
Grade school only			
25 years or more	67 (*188*)	71 (*68*)	83 (*69*)
20–24 years	62 (*81*)	47 (*120*)	86 (*49*)
Under 20 years	44 (*121*)	42 (*99*)	—

Data from S-205.
The numbers in parentheses are the numbers of cases on which percentages are based.

It may be seen, in Table 14, how a greater proportion of Infantry replacements who had just arrived in the Pacific and were awaiting assignment to combat units reported the typical anxiety symptoms as compared with men still in the United States being trained for use as Infantry replacements. Of course, this increased level of tension reflected many factors, among them the strangeness and uncertainty of their present situation as well as their anticipation of what combat would be like. However, the increase is small, especially when it is compared with the much higher level of anxiety reported by combat infantrymen in the area who were about to be reassigned to combat units after hospitalization for wounds or illnesses.

In general, the closer men approached to combat, the more likely they were to experience fear reactions. As shown in Table 15, men who had undergone air raids or buzz bomb attacks in Europe were more often subject to psychosomatic symptoms than men who had no personal experience with enemy fire. Men who had been subjected to closer range enemy fire—rifle fire, mortars, artillery—indi-

TABLE 15

Effect of Nearness to Combat on Anxiety Symptoms
(Europe, April 1945)

AGE-EDUCATION LEVEL	PERCENTAGES RECEIVING CRITICAL SCORES			
	Men never under enemy fire*	Men under long-range fire only*	Men under close-range fire*	Men in actual combat*
High school graduate and over				
30 years and over	38 (79)	33 (101)	38 (61)	47 (88)
25–29 years	23 (109)	29 (119)	35 (79)	47 (207)
Under 25 years	20 (246)	30 (205)	27 (150)	36 (500)
Some high school but not graduation				
30 years and over	54 (63)	41 (69)	58 (50)	48 (83)
25–29 years	42 (69)	48 (65)	51 (53)	52 (180)
Under 25 years	34 (152)	40 (97)	43 (81)	47 (351)
Grade school only				
30 years and over	57 (62)	50 (54)	60 (42)	63 (122)
25–29 years	43 (56)	77 (30)	56 (41)	57 (153)
Under 25 years	40 (81)	45 (53)	48 (58)	57 (213)

Data from S-223.
The numbers in parentheses are the numbers of cases on which percentages are based.
* Based on men's answers to the following questions:

"Have you ever been in actual combat or under enemy fire in this war?"

_____ No, I have not been in combat nor under any kind of enemy fire from the ground or air.
_____ I have not been in actual combat, but I have been under some kind of enemy fire.
_____ I have been in actual combat with the enemy.

The first and last groups in the table represent the first and last responses to this question. The middle two groups have been obtained by splitting men who gave the middle answer according to their answers to this question:

"On the list below, check all the kinds of enemy fire you yourself have been under."

_____ Enemy bombing raids
_____ Buzz bombs
_____ Strafing from enemy planes
_____ Enemy artillery or mortar fire
_____ Enemy rifle fire
_____ Anything else. (What? _____)

Those who indicated that they had been under artillery, mortar, or rifle fire are classified as under close-range fire, all others are regarded as long-range.

cate a somewhat higher level of disturbance, while men who had been in actual combat were, of course, most likely to have these emotional reactions.

The impact of combat on the infantryman's emotional adjustment is most clearly apparent in a study of four divisions made in Italy in April 1945, while fighting was still going on. In this study, men were asked the questions which make up the Psychosomatic Complaints Index. But instead of asking them in the general form usually employed (that is, "Are you ever bothered by . . . ?" or

TABLE 16

PROPORTIONS OF INFANTRYMEN RECEIVING CRITICAL SCORES ON THE
PSYCHOSOMATIC SYMPTOMS INDEX PRIOR TO COMBAT

| | PERCENTAGES RECEIVING CRITICAL SCORES | | |
AGE-EDUCATION LEVEL	*Infantrymen in divisions in training in United States January–February 1944*	*Infantrymen in training in United States as replacements June 1945*	*Combat infantrymen in 4 divisions in Italy April 1945*
25 years or more			
High school graduate or more	25 (65)	37 (57)	34 (188)
Some high school but not graduate	51 (64)	43 (53)	34 (244)
Grade school only	49 (47)	61 (31)	47 (251)
Under 25 years			
High school graduate or more	32 (69)	20 (50)	23 (376)
Some high school but not graduate	43 (77)	34 (44)	37 (348)
Grade school only	51 (51)	47 (19)	53 (358)

Data from S-99, S-205, and S-177.
The numbers in parentheses are the numbers of cases on which percentages are based.

"Have you ever been bothered by . . . ?") the questions were asked in two forms. In the first instance, each question was preceded by the phrase, "During your civilian and military life, but before you went on active combat duty . . ." The questions were then repeated in the form of "Since you have been on active combat duty . . ." The men were thus asked to evaluate both their present symptoms and their precombat symptoms.

There are, of course, serious theoretical objections to the use of this retrospective approach to obtain an estimate of men's psychosomatic symptoms prior to their combat experience in order to secure a base line from which to measure the combat-induced changes. Most especially, it is always possible that men's recall will be faulty and be strongly colored by their current emotional state. But in view of the impracticality of more adequate approaches to the problem, this method was attempted. Fortunately, in this case, the results for relatively large groups of men did not seem to be seriously affected by biases in recall, though there was, of course, no such assurance in the case of any individual. If we compare the combat infantrymen's reports of their precombat symptoms with the symptoms of infantrymen still in training, there were, as may be seen in Table 16, no essential differences.

With this assurance that our base line is relatively reliable, we may compare the precombat anxiety symptoms of infantrymen with the

TABLE 17

THE INCIDENCE OF PSYCHOSOMATIC SYMPTOMS AMONG COMBAT INFANTRYMEN
(Retrospective Reports of Precombat Symptoms Compared with
Current Postcombat Reports, Italy, April 1945)

AGE-EDUCATION LEVEL	Number of cases	PERCENTAGES RECEIVING CRITICAL SCORES ON THE PSYCHOSOMATIC SYMPTOMS INDEX	
		Retrospective form	Postcombat form
25 and over			
High school graduates	*188*	34	56
Some high school	*244*	34	56
Grade school	*251*	47	61
Under 25 years			
High school graduates	*376*	23	51
Some high school	*348*	37	55
Grade school	*358*	53	68

Data from S-177.

symptoms they reported at the time of the study, that is, since going on combat duty. As shown in Table 17, there was after combat a marked increase in the proportion of men experiencing many anxiety symptoms.

A similar increase in symptoms among combat infantrymen may be noted in every study made, even when the questions contained no explicit reference to the combat experience. Among combat infantrymen in four divisions in the Pacific area, a significantly higher proportion of the men in each division reported psychosomatic disturbances at or beyond the critical score as compared with men with no combat experience (Table 18).

Combat exposure had the same effect on air crews as it did on the men who did their fighting on the ground. In Table 19, the anxiety

TABLE 18

ANXIETY SYMPTOMS AND CERTAIN RELATED FACTORS AMONG COMBAT INFANTRYMEN
IN FOUR DIVISIONS IN THE SOUTH AND CENTRAL PACIFIC AREAS
(March–April 1944)

	DIVISION A S. Pacific	DIVISION B S. Pacific	DIVISION C Cen. Pacific	DIVISION D Cen. Pacific
Percentages receiving critical scores on the Anxiety Symptoms Index	79	63	56	44
Percentages overseas 18 months or more	89	77	71	6
Median number of days in combat	55	31	19	3
Rank order of number of battle casualties to date	3	1	2	4
Percentages hospitalized since coming overseas	79	65	27	32
Percentages who have had malaria	66	41	2	2
Percentages reporting complete turnover of company officers since first combat	43	15	10	4
Number of cases	*1,420*	*1,388*	*1,298*	*643*

Data from S-100.

symptoms of bomber crews who returned to the United States after completing a tour of duty[29] are compared with those of bomber crews in training, and a similar increase in symptoms among combat air men is apparent. The differences between officers and enlisted

TABLE 19

INCIDENCE OF ANXIETY SYMPTOMS AMONG BOMBER CREWS WHO HAVE
COMPLETED A TOUR OF COMBAT DUTY
(November 1944)

	PERCENTAGE RECEIVING CRITICAL SCORES	
	Enlisted men	*Officers*
AAF bomber crews returned to United States after completion of tour of duty in:		
European Theater	60 *(234)*	33 *(66)*
Mediterranean Theater	65 *(132)*	19 *(220)*
AAF flyers in training in United States	23 *(344)*	6 *(300)*

Data from S-157.
The numbers in parentheses are the numbers of cases on which percentages are based.

[29] Men whose return to the United States after conclusion of a tour of duty was complicated by "operational fatigue" or other medical secondary reasons for their return, have been excluded to make these data a conservative estimate of the increase in symptoms among the combat-exposed.

men which also appear in this table reflect in part the higher educational level of officers and in part the effect of the careful program of selection of candidates for officer training in the Air Forces.

Perhaps more interesting than the fact that each of the four Pacific divisions studied contained a relatively higher proportion of disturbed men than noncombat troops did were the wide differences between the divisions with respect to the incidence of those symptoms. As the other data in Table 18 show, the division with the highest level of anxiety was also the division which had been overseas longest, had the most exposure to combat, had the highest illness rate, especially malaria, and had been subjected to the greatest turnover of officers. On the other hand its battle casualty rate was low in comparison with the other divisions. Not shown, because the information is not available, are the differences in the kind of combat in which each division participated, or in the kind of surroundings in which the divisions spent their time between combat engagements. In other words, in addition to the mere fact of combat exposure there were a host of other factors often unique to a particular outfit's history which affected the general level of psychological tension prevailing among the men in that unit. The combination of all these and, no doubt, other factors together made up what may be thought of as the atmosphere prevailing in an outfit, and its influence was so strong that controlling simultaneously on the factors of incidence of malaria and other illnesses and amount of exposure to combat did not serve to reduce substantially the differences between divisions.

It is noteworthy, however, that a static relationship between amount of combat exposure and the incidence of psychosomatic symptoms did not reveal a very sharp tendency for the level of anxiety to increase with increased exposure to combat. For example, among the four divisions in Italy, the following results were obtained:[30]

Time in combat	Percentages receiving critical scores on the current postcombat form of the Psychosomatic Symptoms Index
Over 9 months	62 (309)
6 to 9 months	55 (619)
3 to 6 months	57 (605)
1 to 3 months	58 (137)
1 month or less	54 (56)

Similarly, among each of the Pacific divisions studied a small statis-

[30] Data from S-177. The numbers in parentheses are the numbers of cases on which percentages are based.

tically insignificant increase in symptoms among the men with the most time in combat was noted.   It must, however, be recalled that combat was itself the most radical of selection factors.   The men with the most combat experience represented only the survivors from a much larger group whose numbers had been reduced by rotation, psychiatric breakdown, sickness, wounds, and death.   In view of the fact that the attrition of combat men would lead one to expect that those who survived as old combat men would represent, by and large, the most stable of the original cohort, they could reasonably have been expected to have fewer symptoms than the less selected groups.   In the light of this fact, the slight increase of symptoms among men with the most time in combat takes on greater importance and may well be assumed to be underestimating the tendency for anxieties to increase with continued exposure to combat.

Something of the effect of this selection may be seen in comparing the four Italian divisions with a random sample of psychiatric battle casualties from them.   The four divisions were surveyed during holding action just prior to their going into an offensive, while the psychiatric casualties from them represented casualties from their immediately prior and immediately following combat experience. The psychiatric casualties were surveyed at a point in the line of evacuation through which all psychiatric casualties passed, so that they constituted an unselected sample of all the psychiatric combat breakdowns in these divisions in the time period which the study covered.

A comparison of the amount of combat service in the two groups clearly indicates that psychiatric breakdowns tended to occur disproportionately among the newest combat men.   The rate of breakdowns declined gradually from the group with a month or less of combat service up to the group with the most combat experience in which the rate showed an upward turn.   (See Table 20.)   This change of direction in the trend of the psychiatric breakdown rate is significant by at least one statistical test,[31] and is made the more plausible by one weakness in the design of the study.   This is that many of the cases of psychiatric casualties were gathered a month or two before the cross section and should really be compared with a cross section which averaged somewhat less combat experience than shown here.   This source of error was not large enough to

---

[31] The test employed was the significance of the difference in proportions of men with over 9 months of combat time among men who had 6 months or more of combat service.

affect the general pattern shown, but its correction could only increase the tendency of the group with most combat experience to deviate in the unexpected direction.

These data tend to support the interpretation which has frequently been advanced that early combat breakdowns represent the reactions of men who would ordinarily be considered psychogenically predisposed.   Once these had been weeded out, the psychiatric rate was regarded as leveling off until the mounting tensions of combat brought a rise in breakdowns among men who would usu-

TABLE 20

COMBAT EXPERIENCE OF INFANTRYMEN IN FOUR DIVISIONS
(Cross Sections of Divisions and of Psychiatric Casualties from Them, Italy, April 1945)

Percentage distribution of time in combat	Cross section	Psychiatric casualties	Relative ratio of psychiatric casualties to cross section
Over 9 months	17.9%	19.0%	1.1
6 to 9 months	35.9	25.7	0.7
3 to 6 months	35.1	29.9	0.9
1 to 3 months	7.9	15.8	2.0
1 month or less	3.2	9.6	3.0
Total	100.0%	100.0%	
Number of cases	1,726	311	

Data from S-177.

ally be regarded as within the normal ranges.   Some further evidence for this interpretation comes from the fact that in the cross section of these four divisions the new combat men were most likely to report that they had a large number of anxiety symptoms prior to combat, while the group with most combat service seemed to have had about the same level of precombat difficulties as the middle groups in terms of combat experience, who were lowest in psychiatric rates:

Time in combat	Relative psychiatric rate (from Table 20)	Percentages receiving critical scores on the retrospective precombat form of the Psychosomatic Symptoms Index
Over 9 months	3	39 (309)
6 to 9 months	5	35 (619)
3 to 6 months	4	38 (605)
1 to 3 months	2	47 (137)
1 month or less	1 (highest)	52 (56)

On the other hand, this perfect rank correlation between the incidence of psychiatric combat breakdowns and the incidence of symptoms prior to combat, as they are retrospectively reported, suggests one of two things: (1) If we assume that these retrospective reports are trustworthy, and in the large they appeared to be, then the implication is that in this instance the men with most combat experience were somewhat more predisposed than men with somewhat less combat experience; or (2) that these retrospective reports were to some extent colored by men's current states of tension and thus reflected the variations in rate of breakdown to be anticipated.   But

TABLE 21

INCIDENCE OF PSYCHOSOMATIC SYMPTOMS AMONG CROSS SECTIONS AND
COMPARABLE PSYCHONEUROTIC GROUPS

POPULATION	PERCENTAGES RECEIVING CRITICAL SCORES ON THE PSYCHOSOMATIC SYMPTOMS INDEX		
	Cross section	Psychoneurotics	Difference
Infantrymen with no overseas service, January–February 1944	41 *(373)*	86 *(127)*	45
Combat infantrymen in 4 divisions in Italy, April 1945			
Retrospective report of symptoms before combat	38 *(1,726)*	64 *(311)*	26
Current postcombat report	57 *(1,726)*	73 *(311)*	16

Data from S-99 and S-177.
The numbers in parentheses are the numbers of cases on which percentages are based.

if these data are too imprecise to permit any final conclusion about the tendency for psychiatric rates to begin rising again with prolonged combat exposure, they do make clear the early attrition as a result of which old combat men were a psychiatrically select group in general, though the particular sample under consideration may not have been.

It should be apparent, however, that the incidence of psychosomatic symptoms in the combat situation had a somewhat altered meaning.   Even though we speak of the early combat breakdowns as representing the more predisposed individuals, it is obvious that the most predisposed among them were less maladjusted than the men who did not survive this far in the life history of the soldier but broke down while still in training in the United States.   As we might expect, then, the psychoneurotic casualties in these divisions did not show as high a level of psychosomatic symptomatology as did the psychoneurotic patients in the United States.   More important, however, the fear and anxiety implicit in combat brought forth psychosomatic manifestations in so many men that these served less and less to discriminate between men who were labeled psychiatric casualties and those who were not (Table 21).   And the data throughout this section have clearly reflected the very high level of anxiety manifested by combat men as compared with other soldiers.

*   *   *

We have seen, in summary fashion, the experiences in the Army which were most disturbing to men as these were reflected in their psychosomatic symptoms.   While in many cases our data were suggestive rather than final, taken together they permit the tentative generalization that transition from one phase of the Army cycle to another was marked by a rise in the level of psychoneurotic symptoms.

CHAPTER 10

PROBLEMS OF ROTATION AND RECONVERSION[1]

A TOPIC of paramount interest to men stationed overseas was the question of coming home. Men wanted very much to come home; they believed that they could be replaced without impairing the war effort; and, whether they were stationed in the cold of the Aleutians, in the heat of India, or in a more temperate climate, they felt that eighteen months to two years of overseas service was all that men could stand.

All through the war there were, of course, ways in which soldiers serving overseas might be sent home, but there never was, on an Army-wide basis, the adoption of the system the men so desired of a limited and defined amount of overseas service. Briefly, there were several ways in which soldiers serving overseas might be sent home during the war. First of all, men might be given temporary duty in the United States or emergency furloughs home, in which case they spent a few weeks in the United States and then returned to their overseas theaters. Other men returned from overseas with their units, primarily when the contraction of formerly active combat theaters made units of their type no longer needed. Some of the men in these units were later sent on to other theaters, while other men remained in the United States until the end of the war. This mode of return was more common in the earlier years of the war, for example, when the campaign in the Aleutians ended, or when it was decided that an attack on the Panama Canal was improbable. A host of men returned as hospital patients; these represented the more seriously ill or injured, since men whose early recovery and restoration to duty could be expected were usually

---

[1] By Shirley A. Star. Major Research Branch studies in this area were directed by John A. Clausen, Robert N. Ford, Clarence Glick, H. Ashley Weeks, and William W. McPeak. Ford's preliminary organization of the materials for this chapter has facilitated the final presentation.

hospitalized overseas. A large proportion of the patients sent to the United States were discharged after hospitalization.

The bulk of returnees who were retained in the Army and assigned to duty in the United States returned either as men no longer physically fit for overseas duty or under the rotation and tour of duty plans. The system of tours of duty, which was described in Chapter 7, applied only to combat flying personnel, and it fixed, for most practical purposes, a prescribed amount of duty in any area at any time, after which men were returned to duty in the United States. The establishment of this policy for flyers undoubtedly intensified the widespread feeling among soldiers that a limited amount of overseas duty for all personnel was both just and practicable. The Army, on the other hand, officially maintained that there was neither the man power nor the shipping to institute such a plan. Instead, in 1943, the War Department announced the policy of rotation for nonflying personnel which was a compromise plan offering some hope of returning to the United States, after long service overseas, without assuring it.

As rotation policy was first fully formulated in early 1944, only men with the longest service overseas were eligible. Each theater was assigned a monthly quota which the theater commander in turn distributed among his units, to be filled from among men who had a given amount of service, the amount of service necessary for eligibility varying from theater to theater. It was clearly stated, however, that "eligibility [in terms of length of service] does not bestow the right to be relieved from an overseas theater, but only establishes a basis for selection. . . ." [2] Methods of selection from among those eligible were not clearly defined, though as guiding principles the official circular declared:[3]

The purpose of the rotation of personnel is to:

a. Insure the efficiency of a command by replacing those who do not require hospitalization, but whose morale or health has been adversely affected by prolonged periods of duty under severe conditions.

b. Return to the United States experienced personnel for use in training and in the formation of new units, or for other purposes.

c. Return . . . personnel considered by the theater commander as deserving of such return.

---

[2] War Department Circular No. 58, February 9, 1944, "Rotation or Return of Military Personnel on Duty Outside Continental United States."
[3] *Ibid.*

Actually, the selection methods employed varied all the way from choice by lot to the use of rotation quotas to send home the least useful members of an outfit, a practice which could be justified under (a) above.

That the rotation system was not a solution to the desires of the men for a fixed span of duty may be inferred from the rather low quotas permitted. At one time, for example, when the rotation quota was fixed at 1 per cent of total strength per month, men in the South Pacific rather bitterly estimated that it would take over eight years for all the men then in the area to be sent home. Moreover, later modifications in the directives dealing with rotation revised the original provision that rotated personnel be selected only from among those with long service, and made length of service only one consideration:

> Within an element of an oversea command selection of individuals for rotation will be based on conduct record of individual, nature of duty performed, length of continuous oversea service, physical condition of the individual including effect of any wound received. Preference in selection will be given to those individuals who have been longest in combat or who have served under the most hazardous and severe conditions. Consideration will be given to individuals who do not require hospitalization but whose morale or health would be adversely affected by continued periods of duty under severe conditions. . . . The privilege of rotation is reserved for the most deserving individuals.[4]

In general, however, rotational quotas still were filled from among men with long service, though throughout the war the quotas remained so low as to make the rotation system a far cry from the fixed tour of duty plan which the air crews had, and which all other men coveted.

If the rotation policy was not altogether a success with the men serving overseas, permitting as it did only a trickle of men to be relieved in each area, nevertheless the gradual accumulation in the United States of men returned from overseas created a difficult series of problems for the Army. The numerical size of the problem may be seen from the fact that of the over a million and a quarter men returned to the United States up to VE Day, about half a million were on duty in the United States at VE Day,[5] and they made

[4] War Department Circular No. 8, January 6, 1945, "Rotation; Temporary Duty for Purposes of Rehabilitation, Recuperation, and Recovery; and Return for Reassignment of Military Personnel as Individuals on Duty outside the Continental United States."

[5] The difference is largely attributable to the return overseas of men who came back on temporary furloughs, the hospitalization or discharge of most of those returning as patients and some of those returning in other ways, and to a much lesser extent to the reassignment of returnees to overseas theaters.

up almost a quarter of the Army's United States strength.   Nor was this a phenomenon merely of the late stages of the war; by the beginning of 1944 there were almost a quarter of a million returnees on duty in the United States, though the problem of their absorption was simplified by the fact that only about one man in fifteen was a returnee at that time.

But these statistics alone do not begin to suggest the nature of the difficulties created by the presence of this large group of overseas veterans.   As we shall see, these men had great prestige both with the public and with other enlisted men in the United States by virtue of their overseas experience.   It followed from this that their problems and discontents were potentially contagious, so that not only numerically but also strategically they became one of the foremost administrative problems of the military establishment in the United States.   While, as the next section will show, in certain important respects returnees were not a group representative of the men serving overseas, nevertheless the materials which follow have historical interest as a case study of a major Army problem.   They may also be used, with some caution, to throw light on the more general problem of how men with high status and deference expectations react to situations which do not realize their desires.   To understand these problems fully we must turn first to what these men were like, what sort of treatment they expected from the Army, and to the Army's policies with regard to them.   It is only in this light that the adjustment of returnees to domestic service can be made clear.

Who Were the Returnees?[6]

It would be convenient if we could regard the returnees as representative of men with long overseas service, for then the points to be made in this chapter might perhaps be generalized into some conclusions regarding the effects of long overseas service.   Quite the contrary, however, although returnees were, by and large, veterans of long periods of overseas service, they were in several important respects not representative of the men serving overseas.

Among the returnees there were a large proportion of men who

---

[6] It should be clear that in discussing returnees we are primarily concerned with those men who remained on active duty in the Army and who remained in the United States after having been returned from overseas.   This means that the large group of returned hospital patients as well as the men who made temporary visits to the United States are excluded.   The returnees discussed here are largely rotational and permanent limited assignment returns, and to a lesser extent men who returned with their units.

had been sent home because they were no longer physically or mentally fit for service abroad; these men, returned for permanent limited assignment, were an obviously nonrandom selection from among the men overseas. Even among the men who came back on rotation—men who might have been expected to be typical of the long service group from which they came—this selection process may be noted, for one third of a cross section of rotational returnees on duty in the United States in June 1945 reported that they had been classified as physically disqualified for overseas service. This inclusion of so many unfit men in the returnee group cannot be attributed to a winnowing process by which physically fit returnees were sent back overseas, leaving a high proportion of disqualified men among those remaining in the United States. Army policies dictated that, as far as possible, men who had already served overseas should not be sent overseas again while physically fit men who had not been overseas were available. Although there were occasional exceptions to this policy, regulations were even more definite that returnees should not be reassigned overseas until after a minimum of 6 months' service in the United States.[7] Yet, a comparison of those back in the United States less than 6 months with those back longer, among the cross section of rotational returnees just referred to, indicates that the proportion of unfit men was no higher among those who had been in the United States over 6 months than it was among returnees who had less than the minimum period of domestic service.

Beyond the undoubtedly high proportion of men in poor physical condition among them, returnees as a group were rather morbidly preoccupied with their health and physical condition. A survey in the summer of 1944 of rotational returnees just debarking in the United States[8] found that among these men, who were just off the boat and about to return home for their first visits in many months, 55 per cent felt that their physical condition had deteriorated since going overseas and only 29 per cent felt sure that they would be in shape to take up another Army assignment without some amount of medical attention. And in the same survey, responses of rotational returnees just back from their furloughs and awaiting their new assignments indicated that these attitudes had not changed at all during their time at home. These data, shown in Table 1, sug-

---

[7] War Department Circular No. 17, January 1945, "Rotation—Additional Tours of Duty in Overseas Commands."

[8] S-132.

gest that these attitudes toward health were not so transient a phenomenon as to disappear after a three weeks' rest.   Moreover, these
attitudes persisted even after medical examination, classification,
and assignment to duties in the United States.   For example, in
the June 1945 survey,[9] close to half (42 per cent) of those who had
been classified fit for overseas duty felt that this classification was
not suitable for them.[10]

TABLE 1

ATTITUDES OF ROTATIONAL RETURNEES TOWARD THEIR HEALTH, JUNE–JULY 1944

	Rotational returnees about to go home on furlough	Rotational returnees just back from furlough
"Are you in better or worse physical condition now than you were just before you went overseas?"		
Percentage responding:		
Better	6	2
About the same	39	41
Worse	55	57
Total	100	100
"Do you feel you will need medical attention before you will be in shape to take up a permanent assignment?"		
Percentage responding:		
Yes, a good deal	8	7
Yes, some	38	30
No, none	29	33
I'm not sure	25	30
Total	100	100
Number of cases	*539*	*414*

Data from S-132.

As this description suggests, the men selected for return to the
United States were not a particularly stable group.   In fact, if we
look at the anxiety symptoms reported by returnees from Europe
in comparison with the symptoms of men of similar age, education,
and combat experience still serving in Europe and surveyed at the
time, it is clear that the returnee group, even those returning under
the rotation plan, included a disproportionate number of emotion-

---

[9] S-205.
[10] Of course this response reflected in part reluctance for another tour of overseas duty.

ally disturbed individuals, and this is equally true of returnees who had had combat service and those who had not (Chart I).

The data in Chart I also indicate that at this particular time, among men returning from Europe, rotational returnees had a

CHART I

ANXIETY SYMPTOMS SCORES OF RETURNEES FROM EUROPE COMPARED WITH THOSE OF MEN STILL IN EUROPE, STANDARDIZED FOR AGE AND EDUCATION ON THE BASIS OF THE COMPOSITION OF THE ARMY IN EUROPE

(Returnees at Reassignment Centers, April and June 1945)

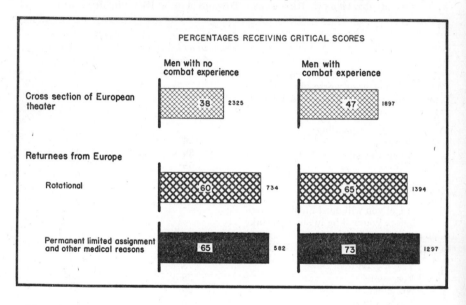

Data for Europe from S-223, April 1945. Data for returnees from S-172 and S-211, June 1945. Both studies of returnees give approximately the same results; they have been pooled here for greater reliability. The figures shown are standardized by applying the age-education rates of symptoms within each of the six groups presented in the chart to the age-education distribution in the cross section of the European theater.

The numbers following the bars are the numbers of cases on which percentages are based.

somewhat lower incidence of anxiety symptoms than the men being returned for limited assignments or for similar medical reasons,[11] a group which included a number of men whose incapacity for further overseas service was emotional in origin. It is noteworthy, however—and is further evidence that rotational returnees were a

---

[11] These data, as noted before, exclude returning hospital patients. These medical cases were all able-bodied men, evacuated for a variety of reasons. They also include a few men originally returned as patients who had recovered and were being started back on the road to further Army duty.

selected group—that this difference between rotational and medical returnees was not found among returnees from other areas. (See Table 2.) The slight change in the proportion of European returnees receiving critical scores in this table as compared with Chart I is, of course, attributable to the different bases of standardization employed.

While the foregoing data fail to control the fact that returnees had on the average more overseas service than men serving in the

TABLE 2

ANXIETY SYMPTOMS AMONG RETURNEES AT REASSIGNMENT CENTERS
CLASSIFIED BY AREA OF OVERSEAS SERVICE
(Standardized for Age and Education on the Basis of the
Entire Sample of Returnees,* April and June 1945)

| | PERCENTAGES RECEIVING CRITICAL SCORES ON THE ANXIETY SYMPTOMS INDEX | |
	Men with no combat experience	Men with combat experience
European returnees		
Rotational	60 (734)	67 (1,394)
Permanent limited assignment and other medical reasons	66 (582)	74 (1,297)
Pacific returnees		
Rotational	70 (900)	76 (584)
Permanent limited assignment and other medical reasons	70 (484)	73 (333)
Returnees from all other areas		
Rotational	63 (1,286)	—
Permanent limited assignment and other medical reasons	62 (289)	—

Data from S-172 and S-211.
Numbers in parentheses are the numbers of cases on which percentages are based.
* The age-education rates of symptoms within each of the ten groups shown in this table have been applied to the age-education distribution among these returnees generally.

theater, the variation in anxiety symptoms associated with increased service overseas was slight, as may be recalled from the previous chapter. It is not surprising then that, when each of the four main types of returnees from Europe was compared with a group of men serving in Europe selected to match the returnees precisely in age, education, and length of overseas service, each group of returnees showed a much higher incidence of anxiety and psychosomatic symptoms than did the men from whose number the returnees were drawn.

The foregoing data suggest very strongly that the rotation system was often used as a convenient means of eliminating the least desirable men from overseas theaters. Any channel for return of men to the United States would offer a temptation to the commanding officer to improve the efficiency of his outfit by pruning it of its weakest members, and in this case, it will be remembered, the directives dealing with rotation explicitly sanctioned this procedure by advising return of men whose emotional or physical condition had markedly deteriorated.

It has sometimes been suggested, alternatively, that the widespread emotional disturbances among returnees were rather the result than the cause of their return. Many psychiatrists have noted that even men who had served arduously were likely to feel a certain amount of guilt when they returned to the United States. Besides this feeling that they were deserting their buddies, returnees often had a feeling of being psychologically deserted themselves once they were separated from the close group with whom they had lived and worked for so long and from whom they had drawn psychological support. Among the newly arrived returnees sampled in the summer of 1944,[12] three fifths said they missed being with their old outfit. Moreover, many returnees found all sorts of vague disappointments in their long-dreamt-of return home. In spring 1944, two fifths of a sample of 810 returnees[13] said being back in the United States did not seem as good as they expected it to be[14]—perhaps in part because of these feelings of guilt and desertion and in part because the actuality did not correspond with the overidealized picture of home they had built up for themselves.

While processes such as these no doubt played their part in perpetuating emotional disturbances in some returnees and, perhaps, even in touching off neurotic reactions in others, it seems doubtful that they alone can account for the contrast in anxiety between returnees and other men. In the first place, joy and relief were the dominant emotions of the men returning to the States. In a survey in June 1945 of returnees at reassignment centers after their fur-

---

[12] S-132.

[13] S-105.

[14] The question was "On the whole, how does it feel to be back in the United States?"

It seems better than I expected it to be	24%
It seems just about the way I expected it to be	33
It does not seem as good as I expected it to be	43
	100%
	$N = 810$

loughs home,[15] men were asked: "Knowing what you do now, how do you feel about having come back to the U. S.?" Almost all of them said they were glad they did come back:

	Percentage giving each response
I wish I hadn't come back	2
I would rather have come back just for a furlough and then returned to my old outfit overseas	7
I am glad I came back	88
Something else	2
No answer	1
	100
	$N = 2,052$

It may be objected that this observation was made rather late in the war. However, an earlier study made in November 1944 [16] indicated that among the returnees assigned to duty in the United States two thirds said they were glad they had returned. A similar sample of returnees surveyed in June 1945 [17] yielded the same proportion. The assigned returnees had, of course, been back home for much longer than those at reassignment centers. The difference between newly arrived and assigned returnees in the proportion saying they were glad to be back suggests that some of the initial enthusiasm of returnees wore off as they became accustomed to being back and, as we shall see later, as they encountered disillusioning experiences. Nevertheless, the high and apparently invariant proportion of the *assigned* returnees who expressed no regrets over their return casts doubt on the seriousness of any guilt or deprivational reactions they may have felt. After intensive analysis of psychoneurotic combat returnees, Grinker and Spiegel came to somewhat the same conclusion.[18] They point out that the ambivalence felt between joy and relief at being home on the one hand, and guilt, loss, and disappointment on the other, was one in which the former emotions usually triumphed, and it was the exceptional case rather than the rule in which this conflict was serious enough to engender anxiety symptoms.

---

[15] S-211.

[16] S-157.

[17] S-213.

[18] R. R. Grinker and J. P. Spiegel, *Men Under Stress* (Blakiston, Philadelphia, 1945), Part IV, "The Reactions after Combat."

In addition to the psychiatric testimony on this point, we have the fact noted previously that rotational returnees from Europe were somewhat more stable than other classes of returnees, while no such difference characterized returnees from other areas. This finding is most plausibly explained by assuming that returnees were, by and large, a special selection from among men overseas, but that the degree of selection varied from time to time and from place to place.

Although returnees generally must therefore be regarded as an atypical group, there were certain attitudes, important to understanding the reactions of returnees, which are not to be attributed solely to the large number of emotionally disturbed men among the returnees, even though their presence may well have intensified these attitudes. Primarily, the complex of attitudes characterizing returnees is implied simply by saying that these men were veterans. For this is a double-barreled term: to the Army, a veteran is a seasoned, experienced soldier; while to the general public, a veteran is an ex-soldier. There is, of course, a relation between these two meanings since a soldier must ordinarily become an Army veteran before he can anticipate discharge, so that ex-soldiers are usually veterans in both senses of the word. However, from the standpoint of attitude, very different things are implied.

As experienced soldiers, returnees expected that their achievements would be recognized. They were not raw recruits, they were men who had put their Army training to the use for which it was intended, and they felt entitled, on that account, to deference from civilians and less seasoned soldiers alike. The returnees themselves, of course, tended to deny their status cravings when questioned about them directly. As may be seen in Table 3, only 25 per cent of a group of returnees newly arrived in the United States, in comparison with men who hadn't served overseas, said that they expected civilians to look up to them. The proportions who said they expected such deference from officers and from enlisted men who had not served overseas were 16 and 22 per cent, respectively. However, it must be remembered that the very use of the word "expect" mingled the dimensions of the returnee's desires and his perhaps more realistic or even cynical predictions of what would eventuate, so that, even on the surface, these questions cannot be taken as an accurate reflection of the extent to which returnees felt respect was due them.

More important than this technical matter of question wording is the inhibition against violating the American democratic dogma of equality which is necessarily involved in baldly asserting that one should be treated better than someone else. Time and again, in interviewing discharged veterans, it was noted how these men would preface their discussion of the essentially preferential treatment

TABLE 3

THE TREATMENT WHICH RETURNEES EXPECTED AND EXPERIENCED
(Returnees at Four Debarkation Centers and a Reassignment Station,
June–July 1944)

	PERCENTAGES GIVING INDICATED RESPONSES:	
	Expectation*	*Experience*†
QUESTION: "As an overseas veteran how do you expect to be (how have you been) treated by civilians?"		
I expect to be (I think I was) looked up to more than enlisted men who haven't been overseas	25	44
I expect to be (I think I was) treated just the same as enlisted men who haven't been overseas	70	50
I expect to be (I think I was) looked down upon more than enlisted men who haven't been overseas	5	6
	100	100
QUESTION: "As an overseas veteran how do you expect to be (how have you been) treated by enlisted men who haven't been overseas?"		
I expect to be (I think I have been) looked up to because I've been overseas	22	37
I expect to be (I think I have been) treated just the same as enlisted men who haven't been overseas	71	57
I expect to be (I think I have been) looked down upon by enlisted men who haven't been overseas	7	6
	100	100
QUESTION: "As an overseas veteran, what sort of treatment do you expect to get (have you gotten) from officers who haven't been overseas?"		
I expect to be (I think I have been) treated better than enlisted men who haven't been overseas	16	32
I expect to be (I think I have been) treated just the same as enlisted men who haven't been overseas	71	61
I expect to be (I think I have been) treated worse than enlisted men who haven't been overseas	13	7
	100	100
Number of cases	*1,000*	*636*

Data from S-132.

* In the expectation form these questions were asked of returnees at debarkation centers on their first or second day in the United States.

† Returnees at a reassignment station, where men report after the furloughs home and before being assigned to regular Army duties, were asked these questions in terms of their experience.

they wanted with the assertion that they "just wanted to be treated like everyone else," many of them, in fact, carefully explained that the particular concessions they asked for were necessary to bring them up to equality with men who had not gone to war.[19]   Similarly, many of the comments made by returnees indicate that they were counting on recognition whether or not they were aware of it or willing to admit it.   For instance, one returnee said, "People here don't know what war really is and therefore they don't respect a returning soldier like they should."   And another returnee, writing his suggestion of how returnees should be treated recommended, somewhat contradictorily: "Treat him humanly and squarely.   Forget his combat overseas.   Do not pamper him.   Be considerate and try to eliminate all his fears.   Show him the possibility of a good future."

Perhaps the clearest evidence that returnees did expect to be recognized as the seasoned soldiers they were and treated accordingly comes from their own views on how the Army could best utilize them.   When returnees were asked to write freely on the topic of "the best use the Army could make of men returned from overseas," [20] the two leading suggestions—leaving aside the proposal that returnees be discharged—proposed by two fifths and one fifth of the men replying, respectively, were, first that they be used as instructors or cadre men to pass along their practical knowledge to soldiers who hadn't been overseas yet, and, second, that they be given permanent assignments in the United States, at least until all men who had not yet done so went overseas.   It is apparent from these proposals that the returnees did consider themselves both technically and morally superior to the men who had not done so much in the war as they had.

It may be noted here, in anticipation of a later section, that returnees did in fact have high prestige among men who had never left the States, although it was not unmixed with conflict and resentment and did not satisfy the returnees' status demands.   As the parallel data in Table 3 show, large minorities of returnees just back from their furloughs home conceded that they were given deference or better treatment by civilians and Army personnel, although at this time their contacts with Army personnel in the United States had been limited to the officers and men in charge of their processing, and to social and casual contacts.   As we shall see in the section on

[19] See Chapter 13 for a further discussion of these data.
[20] S-132, June–July 1944.   Survey of 1,000 returnees at four debarkation centers.

relations with personnel who had not served overseas, when returnees and nonoverseas men were put into daily working relationships, attitudes were somewhat modified.

But, if returnees were experienced soldiers with some claim to consideration because of their experience, this experience also formed the basis of their feeling that they had performed their part of the war to the best of their ability and should now be permitted to retire from the war. In June 1945, just after VE Day, two thirds of the returnees on duty in the United States and not eligible for discharge under the point system reported themselves as unwilling to go overseas again while another fifth asserted that they would be willing to go when needed.[21] This latter answer, however, may be considered as frequently an evasive one. As early as June 1944, just after the launching of the European invasion, almost none of the returnees when surveyed were willing to believe that they would in fact be needed overseas again. At that time close to 3,000 returnees were asked: "Do you believe there are enough enlisted men still in the United States who haven't yet been overseas so that returning overseas veterans won't need to go overseas again?" Only 3 per cent said they didn't believe there would be enough, 19 per cent weren't sure, and 78 per cent said they believed there were enough enlisted men to relieve veterans of the need for another tour of overseas duty.[22] Significantly enough, the returnees who said they were willing to go overseas again if needed did not in the main believe that they would actually be needed. As shown in Table 4, two thirds of the returnees who took this position with respect to overseas service believed that there were enough enlisted men in the United States so that returnees would not be needed overseas again.

We must recognize that, in line with the general attitudes of limited commitment to the war which existed,[23] most returnees regarded it as a matter of simple justice that they should not be sent overseas again until eligible men who had not served overseas did as much as they had. From this point of view it seems likely that most of the returnees who said they were willing to go when needed, believing as they did that they would not be needed, were really little, if any, more willing to go overseas again than were the returnees who flatly said "No."

The major difference between the answers of returnees back an

---

[21] S-205.
[22] S-132.
[23] See Volume I, Chapter 9.

average of six months and returnees who had not been back in the United States long enough to have been assigned to regular duties, was a tendency for the returnees who had been back for some time to shift away from the position that they would be ready to go overseas after a few months in the United States, to the statement that they were ready to go overseas whenever they were needed. (See Table 5.) To some extent this shift, like the small decrease in the proportion unwilling to go overseas, may reflect an improvement in

TABLE 4

RETURNEES' BELIEFS AS TO THE NECESSITY OF ANOTHER TOUR OF OVERSEAS DUTY, CLASSIFIED BY THEIR WILLINGNESS TO SERVE OVERSEAS AGAIN
(Survey of Debarkation, Reception, and Reassignment Centers, June–July 1944)

| | PERCENTAGES GIVING STATED RESPONSE AMONG MEN WHO SAY THEY: | | | |
	Don't want to go overseas again	*Would like to stay in U. S. for a few months, then ready to go*	*Are ready to go whenever needed*	*Want to get overseas again as soon as possible*
QUESTION: "Do you believe there are enough enlisted men still in the U. S. who haven't yet been overseas, so that returning veterans won't need to go overseas again?"				
Yes, I believe there are enough	85	67	66	41
I'm not sure	14	27	28	39
No, I don't believe there are enough	1	6	6	20
Total	100	100	100	100
Number of cases	*1,862*	*571*	*285*	*52*

Data from S-132.

attitudes toward further service as a result of a longer period of relief from overseas rigors. But we should not lose sight of the fact that some of the men surveyed at reassignment centers were discharged rather than given regular assignments, which would itself account for at least a part of the apparent improvement of attitudes among assigned returnees. Moreover, it is noteworthy that the shift is primarily from one delaying response, best adapted to men who have been home only a short time, to another response which has been shown to be in large part evasive.

As is also shown in Table 5, over 90 per cent of the returnees who were not eligible for discharge just after VE Day frankly stated that they felt they had done their share, and almost three fifths of them stated that they should be discharged.   Though it is not shown in this table, the fact is that among the veterans who said they were ready to do more, less than half felt that they should stay in the Army until the end of the war.   The comparison made in this table

TABLE 5

ATTITUDES TOWARD FURTHER SERVICE AMONG RETURNEES, JUNE 1945
(Excludes Men Eligible for Discharge under the Point System)

| | PERCENTAGES GIVING STATED RESPONSE AMONG: | | | |
| | *Rotational returnees* | | *All other returnees** | |
	At reassignment centers†	At regular Army camps‡	At reassignment centers	At regular Army camps
QUESTION: "How do you feel about serving overseas again?"				
I want to get overseas again as soon as possible	1	7	2	7
I'm ready to go whenever I'm needed	9	20	12	22
I'd like to stay in the U. S. for a few months, but then I'll be ready to go anywhere	19	8	11	6
I don't want to go overseas again	71	65	75	65
	100	100	100	100
QUESTION: "How do you feel about what you've done in this war?"				
I feel I've already done my share and should be discharged	61	58	61	57
I feel I've already done my share, but I'm ready to do more	35	37	32	35
I don't feel I've done my share yet	4	5	7	8
	100	100	100	100
Number of cases	*669*	*1,027*	*597*	*986*

Reassignment center sample from S-211, others from S-213.
 * This group is made up of the permanent limited service and other medical returnees in the case of the reassignment centers group. Among returnees in Army camps this group includes in addition men who returned home when their outfits were removed from a theater as unneeded there.
 † These are returnees who have been in the United States about a month, most of which time was spent on furloughs home. At reassignment centers these new returnees were examined, classified, and disposed of, either being discharged or given a regular assignment in the United States.
 ‡ These are returnees, back an average of six months, on regular assignments.

between returnees who had not yet served in the United States as returnees and those who had done so, again indicates that their contact with the United States garrison situation had little effect on returnees' attitudes toward further service.

These attitudes were in no sense peculiar either to returnees or to the post VE Day period of the war. As the analysis in Volume I, Chapter 9, made clear, by the time of VE Day, men with any sizable amount of Army service, whether they were then serving overseas or had never served overseas, held similar views of their role in the war. The evidence presented did suggest that there was some increase with VE Day in the "done my share" feeling among men with no overseas service. But, as far as returnees were concerned, almost all of them had felt before VE Day that they had done their share and hence VE Day increased only the proportion who felt justified in wanting immediate discharge. As might be inferred from the fact that returnees had felt they had done their share long before VE Day, attitudes toward serving overseas again did not change with VE Day; in fact, the study made a year before the post VE Day survey showed identical responses on the question of going overseas.

Although these attitudes were not entirely unique to returnees, all circumstances combined to make them the group most typical of this frame of mind. As a group, they were characterized disproportionately by all the traits shown in this earlier chapter to be associated with the feeling of being finished with the war and the Army; that is, returnees had, by and large, long periods of overseas service, many of them were combat veterans, and they were older and in poorer physical condition than the soldiers generally.

Moreover, it was psychologically very difficult for the returnee not to feel this way, for he had, in a sense, come to the end of the Army cycle. In the ordinary course of events men entering the Army expected first to be trained, then to go overseas to use their training, and finally to come home and get out of the Army. The returnee had completed this cycle up to the point of getting out of the Army, though it deviated from the ideal typical cycle in that his return home had preceded the end of the war. Nevertheless, with the attitudes toward personal participation in the war which prevailed, this was not of great moment to the returnee who could only feel that his cycle of service was complete and he should, therefore, be out of the Army.

What Happened to the Returnee

Retention in the Army

The most crucial Army policy affecting returnees was, of course, the decision to retain them in the Army.   From the description just given it might be said that many returnees were of questionable usefulness to the Army.   Although all of them had valuable experience, there were many among them whose physical or emotional state made their utilization difficult, and almost all of them were psychologically finished with the Army.   If these had been the only considerations to take into account, the Army might have dealt with returnees to their satisfaction and with little loss to the Army by being liberal with discharges to them.   Nevertheless, at some point, the decision was made to retain them in general.[24]   For the most part, rather than being explicitly enunciated, this policy decision was implicit in directives which specified procedures for reassigning returnees, types of jobs to which they should be assigned, etc.   Yet there can be little question that the subject of discharging returnees did receive official attention, for directives were issued making exceptions of certain classes of returnees—most notably, at certain periods, combat men fit only for permanent limited assignment as a result of battle wounds could be discharged at their own request—and the general subject of handling returnees came in for a good deal of official concern.

But, in the nature of the way the decision was implemented, no official document which incorporates the reasons for the policy of keeping returnees in the Army is accessible.   The explanation of this course of action must, therefore, remain speculative, but it seems highly likely that the decision stemmed primarily from concern over man-power needs and a fear that discharged returnees would deleteriously affect these needs in several ways.   In the first place, returnees were becoming a problem calling for policy action just at the time when the Army was combing all domestic establishments for physically fit men who had not served overseas.   These men were to be sent overseas as rapidly as possible, and it was thought that they could be replaced from among the physically

---

[24] Returnees eligible for discharge under provisions applicable to the whole Army were, of course, not retained.   Many returnees were eligible for discharge under medical and other provisions, and they were discharged, but this did not constitute a policy of discharging *returnees*.

unfit and returnees.[25] Then too, the physically fit among the returnees were a potential source of overseas replacements, even though it was a source to be used only if other sources were exhausted. It is probable that the extreme reluctance of returnees to remain in the Army either to replace men fit for overseas duty or to go overseas again themselves was not considered a strong enough reason to alter these policies, for the Army by this time was quite well aware that almost all men served reluctantly and yet complied with what was demanded of them. More immediately, it might well have been assumed that a policy of discharging returnees would have a serious harmful effect on the morale of men still overseas. They too wanted to come home, and there were many complaints about the unfairness of rotation which returned some men but left overseas others with as much or more overseas service. If return to the United States had been made tantamount to discharge from the Army, it is easy to believe that these reactions would have been intensified, perhaps even to the point where they would have seriously interfered with the prosecution of the war. Some observers have reported that even the existence of the possibility of another tour of overseas duty for returnees served to temper the desire for rotation among overseas personnel. If rotation had become even a guarantee that no more overseas service would be required of a man, let alone a guarantee of discharge from the Army, it might have created difficult problems of morale.

Finally, it is quite possible that the Army considered what the effect on public opinion would be if large numbers of unmarried or young or physically fit returnees were discharged at a time when Selective Service was forced to order the induction of fathers to fill Army needs. Whether public reaction to the discharge of veterans would in fact have been unfavorable is a matter of speculation, but the Army may well have feared that it might have been and so have proceeded cautiously.

Early Phases of the Returnees' Adjustment

At any rate, the general policy of retaining returnees in the Army led to the further question of what to do with them. There were, in any case, immediate problems of troop management when returnees landed in the United States. In the belief that the first impressions would have much to do with the returnees' outlook, an

[25] See ASF Circular No. 193, June 1944, "Enlisted Men—Utilization of Manpower Based on Physical Capacity."

attempt was made to make them as pleasant as possible. It is a little difficult to describe the processing of returnees briefly and accurately since procedures evolved gradually as experience in handling returnees accumulated. In general, however, at the time of the study of returnees made in the summer of 1944, the procedures were about as follows: men went from their boats to a debarkation center where they were usually met by a band. The debarkation centers served primarily to get men away from the congested port areas while transportation for them was being arranged. Usually arrangements were made within forty-eight hours to send men to the reception station nearest their home. Here at the reception station there was again some ceremony in meeting men; they were issued clothing and pay and allowed within twenty-four hours to depart for their furloughs home. After their furlough home, usually three weeks, returnees went to redistribution stations or reassignment centers.

The military purpose of the redistribution and reassignment centers was to examine and classify the soldier and determine his next assignment. However, it was also desired that the orientation and reindoctrination deemed necessary to prepare returnees for their new assignment be "carried on without haste in an environment characterized by mental and physical relaxation and comfort." [26] The Army Air Forces quite early took over several resort hotels and used them as redistribution stations. Here the Air Force returnee enjoyed a two-week vacation while going through the necessary processing, and he could bring his wife along at nominal expense. Somewhat later, Ground and Service Forces adopted the same system of giving returnees a taste of a pleasant Army "environment" as a kind of "decompression" period, but they did not have enough hotels in operation during most of the war. This meant that many of their returnees were processed through reassignment centers, which were modifications of the usual Army camp setup and in which facilities were not ordinarily provided for wives to accompany their husbands.

There can be little question that these special efforts to make the necessary processing an agreeable experience were well received by the returnees. They were, of course, delighted to be home, but this does not necessarily mean that they would not have been critical if they had been badly handled. This was not the case, however.

[26] War Department Circular No. 303, July 1944, "Army Ground Forces and Army Service Forces Redistribution Stations."

Surveys made at debarkation centers, reception stations, and redistribution and reassignment stations brought forth numerous voluntary compliments about the smoothness of procedure and consideration given returnees, as well as quantitative data which point to the same conclusion.   For example:[27]

76 per cent said they were "very well satisfied" or "fairly well satisfied" with the way they were handled on the boat coming back.[a]

Only 11 per cent were dissatisfied with the "welcome home" they were given after landing.[c]

85 per cent said they understood the necessity for their stop at a debarkation center, even though this stop was not known to most men ahead of time.[b]

Despite their impatience to be home, 85 per cent said they had found enough interesting things to do at the debarkation center to avoid boredom.[b]

Even though there was great traffic congestion in the port and debarkation center areas, over 90 per cent were on their way to reception stations within two days of their landing.[b]

Two thirds found the trip from the port area to their reception stations "comfortable enough."[b]

And even though there was much to be attended to at the reception station—men had to have their clothing checked, get service ribbons, draw their pay, find their baggage, get records brought up to date, receive instructions, arrange transportation home—still, 76 per cent said they started from the reception station on their furloughs in less than 24 hours.[c]

After their furloughs home, there was a similar favorable reaction to the redistribution stations.   Over 80 per cent of 4,676 returnees surveyed at 12 redistribution stations in March and April 1945 [28] gave unqualified approval to the idea of having such stations for returnees, and the overwhelming majority felt that the treatment they received from the personnel of the station was better than that which they had encountered in most Army installations.   As one returnee, enjoying the luxury of a resort hotel, put it, "This isn't the Army, but don't change it."   Even the returnees who were sent to the Army post type of redistribution station reacted favorably, although there were sometimes objections to the dual system.   (See Table 6.)

But, running through these new and, for the most part, enjoyable experiences was a great deal of concern with the reassignment process.   Pleasant though three-week furloughs home and two-week vacations at resort hotels might be, these were temporary.   The assignment a returnee was given, on the other hand, while not necessarily permanent, would cover a much longer period of his military

---

[27] These results are all from S-132, a survey made in June–July 1944 of:

    a. 1,000 returnees at four debarkation centers

    b. 1,134 returnees at three reception stations

    c. 636 returnees at one reassignment center

[28] S-172.

service.   Moreover, the classification and assignment process was something the returnee had been through before.   At this point, his experiences as a returnee began to duplicate his earlier Army experience, and in the earlier case the eventual outcome of the assignment he was given had been a tour of overseas duty.   So, since the

TABLE 6

REACTIONS OF RETURNEES TO REDISTRIBUTION STATIONS, MARCH–APRIL 1945

| | PERCENTAGES GIVING EACH RESPONSE AMONG: | | |
| | Men in hotel-type stations | | Men in post-type stations |
	Air Forces	Ground and Service Forces	Ground and Service Forces
QUESTION: "On the whole, what do you think of the idea of having such redistribution stations as this one for returning soldiers?"			
It is a good idea in all ways	88	89	83
It is a good idea in most ways, but not in other ways	12	10	16
It is a poor idea in most ways but not in other ways	*	*	1
It is a poor idea in all ways	*	1	*
Total	100	100	100
QUESTION: "How does the treatment you get from Army personnel here compare with the treatment you received from Army personnel in most other installations you have been in?"			
It is better here	81	85	73
It is about the same	19	14	26
It is worse here	*	1	1
Total	100	100	100
Number of cases	1,838	2,414	424
Number of stations	4	6	2

Data from S-172.
* Less than 0.5 per cent.

assignment he drew might determine not only what he was doing but where, once he was settled back into the Army routine, it took on tremendous importance.

So great was the returnees' concern that, when asked at debarkation and reception centers what it was that they wished they had been told more about, three fourths answered "about the assignment we might get after our furlough" (see Table 7).   It may be noted that this response was made by men newly home and eager to go on their furloughs, two thirds of whom said they did not have a definite idea of what processing they still had to go through before they could depart. Nevertheless, they were concerned far more about their coming assignments than about the immediate details of pre-furlough processing. In fact, when directly questioned, two thirds of these returnees said they had been worrying about the

TABLE 7

INFORMATION DESIRED BY RETURNEES AT DEBARKATION CENTERS,
RECEPTION STATIONS, JUNE–JULY 1944

| | PERCENTAGE GIVING EACH RESPONSE AMONG RETURNEES AT: | |
	Debarkation centers	*Reception stations*
QUESTION: "Which of the following do you wish the Army had told you about on the boat?"*		
About where we would go after we landed	7	†
About processing we have to go through before we actually go on our furlough	21	31
About the assignments we might get after our furlough	76	84
About what has been happening on the home front since we left the U. S.	19	23
Total‡	123	138
Number of cases	*1,000*	*1,134*

Data from S-132.

* The question was asked in this form at debarkation centers. At reception stations the wording was "Which of the following do you wish the Army had told you about or more about at the debarkation center?"

† This category was inapplicable and therefore omitted from the check list in the reception station questionnaire.

‡ Adds to more than 100 per cent since men were instructed to check as many categories as they wished.

kind of assignment they would get. In similar fashion, when returnees at reception stations—90 per cent of whom had said they knew little or nothing about the processing they would be going through at the reassignment centers after their furloughs—were asked to write out the things they would like to know about the reassignment center, almost all of them answered, not in terms of the specific aspects of processing or the steps leading up to their next assignment, but in terms of the nature or location of these assignments. (See Table 8.)

Finding Job Assignments for Returnees

The returnees' fear of being sent overseas again did not become a fact for most of them during the course of the war.   As we have mentioned earlier, the general policy was that men who had returned from overseas should not be sent overseas again until physically qualified men with no overseas service had been sent, and in any case not until they had spent a minimum of six months in the United States.   Unquestionably some returnees did go overseas again,

TABLE 8

INFORMATION ABOUT REASSIGNMENT CENTERS WHICH RETURNEES AT
RECEPTION STATIONS DESIRED*

Information desired	Per cent of men answering:
Nature or location of assignment	
What kind of an assignment will I get?	52
Where will I be stationed?	18
Will I go overseas again?	5
Details of processing	
What's going to happen when we get there?	17
How long will I be there?	13
Miscellaneous	5
No information desired	11
Total†	121
Number of cases	1,134

Data from S-132.
* Based on men's freely written answers to the question, "What things would you like to know about the reassignment center that you don't know now?"
† Adds to more than 100 per cent since some men requested more than one type of information.

especially those who came back when their units were withdrawn from contracting theaters and who remained with their units when these were reassigned overseas again.   Nevertheless, the high proportion of men not physically qualified for overseas service among them, as well as the unexpectedly early ending of the war, made another tour of duty for returnees the exception rather than the rule.

This general practice of not sending the returnees overseas again was probably a wise one from the standpoint of returnees' attitudes. As we have seen, returnees did not want to go overseas again, and there is little question that they would have deeply resented the threat to them of double exposure to overseas service when there were some who had not gone through it for the first time. As one returnee put it:

I won't say anything if I'm called again, but it sure would be a blow to my morale to go back again and say goodbye to these guys who have not been over, who are sitting here fat, dumb and happy, waving a flag to the poor guys going over again and saying "get one for me."

But this policy meant that the easiest solution to the job assignment problem, viz., to assign returnees to retraining in preparation for another tour of overseas duty, could not be fully adopted. Instead, assignments that called for relatively permanent duty in the United States were needed.

The assignment most favored by returnees, as we have pointed out in another context, was that of instructor or training cadreman. On the face of it, this would seem to be an excellent use to make of returnees, for they had practical experience in overseas and combat conditions and had much to teach new recruits. The Army early saw the advantage of this and tried, as much as possible, to place returnees in the instructor jobs.[29] Nevertheless, this policy did not work out in practice as well as it sounded, nor was it, by itself, a sufficient source of assignments to take care of all returnees. In the first place, many returnees were not suited to such assignments; they had neither the physical stamina, nor the training, nor the ability to teach. Many of them were emotionally unstable and most unenthusiastic about the Army and especially about garrison discipline—hardly qualities to be desired in instructors. Moreover, many returnees who did become instructors soon found themselves at war with the training program. It was their frequent claim that the training program was impractical or out of date, and their orders to follow the training manuals—more informally characterized as "teaching by the book"—created much friction. The returnee instructor's frequent point of view is summed up in this not untypical comment of an ex-combat man who was instructing in an Infantry Replacement Training Center.

I do not agree with this kind of training. There has been pitifully small or no progress toward jungle training. All overseas men know we can't fight by the book!!! Much training in U. S. is very useless—no practical jungle training whatever—wrong psychology in dealing with recruits.

---

[29] See for example ASF Circular No. 193, June 1944, "Enlisted Men—Utilization of Manpower Based on Physical Capacity" which provided: "Personnel returned from overseas will be utilized to the maximum extent to replace instructor and trainer personnel."

While some of the returnees' criticisms of recruit training may have been justified, in general they showed a lack of perspective on training needs. Training programs generally were designed, not to train troops for desert warfare, jungle warfare, or arctic warfare, but to give a generalized foundation on which specialized training for a particular terrain could be built rapidly. Getting the returnee to add his localized experience, as far as this was possible, might serve a valuable purpose in making the training more real and immediate to the recruit, but the returnee tended to want to train his men for exactly what he had gone through.

Though these difficulties existed, some returnees could be and were utilized in instructor assignments. But even if all returnees had been ideally suited to such assignments, they could not all have been so assigned. As we have pointed out, there was in the United States by VE Day one returnee to every three men who had not been overseas and not all of the nonoverseas men were in training, so that returnees far outnumbered the existing needs for instructors.

The other major group of jobs to which returnees could be assigned were the permanent party and housekeeping assignments. These assignments were relatively safe from the possibility of another tour of overseas duty, but, aside from a few specialized jobs among them, they were typically little-skilled, low-status kinds of work—routine clerical jobs, orderlies, prisoner-of-war guards, cooks, etc., come under this heading.

Air Force returnees were normally retained within Air Forces, though a good deal of job reclassification was called for. For example, among enlisted returnees in Air Forces who had held flying jobs overseas, two fifths reported in November 1944 that they no longer held flying assignments, while in June 1945 three fourths of the flying enlisted returnees surveyed said they were now in ground jobs. Ground Force returnees, on the other hand, were quite often shifted to branches of the Service Forces in the effort to find appropriate assignments for them. As the data in Table 9 show, of returnee infantrymen on duty in the United States in June 1945 and not imminently to be discharged, over half had been reassigned to Service Forces, while most of the remainder had been retained in their original branch. For other Ground Force returnees, the proportion of Service Force conversions was almost as high. Non Infantry Ground Force returnees who were assigned to Infantry came almost exclusively from among Coast Artillery and Antiaircraft Artillery returnees who came back with their outfits for the express purpose of such conversion when it was realized that there would not be a need for their original units. Even among Service Force returnees, a large percentage were shifted from their original branch to another service branch. In these data, the small proportion who report a shift to Air Forces are primarily men performing Service Force type jobs at Air Force installations, and for some of the Service Force returnees this should not really be interpreted as a change of branch.

TABLE 9

ACTUAL CHANGES OF BRANCH AMONG RETURNEES

(Assigned Returnees at Army Posts, June 1945—Excludes Men Eligible for
Discharge Under Point System)

| | PERCENTAGE NOW IN EACH TYPE OF BRANCH ASSIGNMENT AMONG: | | | |
| | Returnees in given branch of Ground Forces overseas | | | Returnees in Service Force branches overseas |
PRESENT BRANCH ASSIGNMENT	Infantry	Field artillery, armored force, tank destroyer	Coast and antiaircraft artillery	
Same branch as overseas	34	39	3	45
Different branch than overseas				
Air Forces	8	7	9	13
Service Force branches	56	47	43	40
Ground Force branches	2	7	45	2
Infantry	—	7	38	2
Other	2	*	7	*
Total	100	100	100	100
Number of cases	*221*	*56*	*148*	*720*

Data from S-205.
* Less than 0.5 per cent.

These changes of branch were not necessarily contrary to the returnees' wishes. As a matter of fact, a survey of a small sample of returnees at a reassignment center in the summer of 1944 showed that two thirds of the Infantry returnees wished to switch to the Service Forces, a larger proportion than actually were switched. Less than a quarter of the Service Force returnees, on the other hand, desired to switch to some other Service Force branch, though almost twice as many were so transferred. The leading preferences among the men who wished to change branches were for the Quartermaster Corps and the Corps of Military Police, the traditionally "soft job" branches as viewed by men who had not served in them.

It is, indeed, noteworthy that these veterans did not share the recruits' desire to get into the glamorous Air Corps.[30]   (See Table 10.)

All this changing of branch implied, of course, a shift to jobs for which the men had not originally been trained, and such shifts of job also occurred extensively even where men remained in their old branch, as, for example, in the Air Forces.   Whether men were to be used as instructors or as permanent party or in other jobs, a certain amount of retraining was necessary.   And for returnees who were earmarked for eventual use overseas and those for whom assign-

TABLE 10

DESIRE TO CHANGE BRANCH AMONG RETURNEES AT A REASSIGNMENT CENTER,
JUNE–JULY 1944

| | PERCENTAGE WITH GIVEN BRANCH PREFERENCE AMONG: | | | |
| | Men in Ground Force branches | | | Men in Service Force branches |
BRANCH PREFERENCE	Infantry	Field artillery, armored force, tank destroyer	Coast and antiaircraft artillery	
Do not wish to change branch	22	33	48	73
Wish to change to:				
Air Corps	5	10	2	4
A Ground Force branch	7	2	7	1
A Service Force branch	66	55	43	22
Total	100	100	100	100
Number of cases	*156*	*53*	*129*	*293*

Data from S-132.

ments were not available, training served as a convenient way of occupying their time.   For this combination of reasons, a vast amount of retraining of returnees was done.   About two out of three returnees reported having received some sort of training since their return to the United States, and three fifths of all returnees said they had taken or were taking a retake of basic training, either the standard program or a condensed course designed for returnees and other men being converted to new branches.

Returnees did not react favorably to this program of training, for they were and thought of themselves as being experienced soldiers,

---

[30] Some data on branch preferences and branch status in relation to job satisfaction were presented in Volume I, Chapter 7.   The meaning of these branch preferences among returnees will be discussed presently.

and did not relish being put through basic training again as if they were a bunch of raw recruits. In June 1945, two thirds of the returnees who had been given this refresher type of training said that they got little or nothing out of it. And even among the returnees who had been given specialist or technical training, three fifths said it was of little or no use to them. There can be little question that there was a certain lack of imagination in the conduct of training for the returnees, as an official memorandum to commanding generals from the General Staff section in charge of training acknowledges:

1. Numerous complaints individually filed or recorded in Inspector General reports indicate that in many instances, little or no individual consideration or thought is given to redeployment or conversion training of individuals returned from overseas. Examples of mishandling of this personnel include requiring infantry battle-experienced soldiers to qualify in an infiltration course and other repetitious training.

3. It is desired that the following policies be immediately adopted in the training of personnel returned from overseas:
   a. Individuals being trained . . . will not be trained together with inexperienced replacements. Every effort will be made to create in the mind of the returned soldier the feeling that he is being given further training and *not* basic training.[31]

Nevertheless, though the returnees resented it, there were at times good reasons for requiring even the repetition of basic training. For example, one classification and assignment officer, interviewed in the course of a survey, described his difficulties with a group of returnees he was trying to convert to instructors and cadre in the same branch in which they had served overseas. He held that many changes had occurred in the training program since these men had been trained and sent overseas and he was, therefore, requiring them to take the refresher training course. As he said, "I know they don't know the program, because they were sent out from this very post thirty months ago when we were just starting to train men here and didn't know ourselves what to teach them. These returnees hate to take training, but I don't know what else to do with them."

Perhaps for reasons like those cited by the officer just quoted, as well as the job shifting which went on even when men remained in the same branch, or perhaps because nothing else could be found to

---

[31] War Department General Staff, Organization and Training Division G-3, Memorandum for Commanding Generals, Army Service Forces, Army Air Forces, Army Ground Forces. Subject: Training of the Overseas Returnees, WDGCT 333 (February 5, 1945).

do with them, returnees who remained in the branches they had served in overseas were just as likely as the converted returnees to report that they had been given training since their return, but they were no more likely to dislike it than were the men to whom it was new (Table 11).

TABLE 11

RETRAINING OF RETURNEES AND THEIR ATTITUDES TOWARD IT, JUNE 1945
(Excludes Returnees Eligible for Discharge Under the Point System)

TYPE OF TRAINING TAKEN OR IN PROCESS SINCE RETURN	PERCENTAGE REPORTING GIVEN TYPE OF TRAINING AMONG:		PERCENTAGE SAYING THEY GOT LITTLE OR NOTHING OUT OF TRAINING AMONG MEN WHO HAVE COMPLETED GIVEN TYPE OF TRAINING AMONG:	
	Returnees serving in same branch as overseas	*Returnees serving in branch other than their overseas branch*	*Returnees in same branch as formerly*	*Returnees in new branches*
None	29	30		
Basic training, either repeat of complete course or condensed refresher version	52	66	70	69
Specialist or technical training	39	21	58	57
Total*	120	117		
Number of cases	*1,203*	*729*		

Data from S-213.
* Adds to more than 100 per cent since men could report more than one type of training.

The dislike of training which the returnees generally exhibited may be traced not only to its inconsistency with their conception of themselves as trained, experienced veterans but to the kinds of jobs to which they were assigned after they had completed training. As we have pointed out earlier, there were relatively few instructor jobs available and only a small number of technically skilled jobs, usually filled by men already trained for them. The bulk of assignments available for Ground and Service Force returnees, at least, were unskilled, routine, and usually uninteresting jobs whose main virtue was that they were permanent garrison jobs and gave promise to returnees of relief from further overseas service. There is little wonder that the returnees in jobs like these could find, in retrospect, little justification for the added training.

Returnees' Adjustment to Their Jobs

As we have just implied, returnees were not particularly happy with the job assignments they eventually drew. As the data in Table 12 show, returnees were less satisfied with their branch and job assignments than were men with no overseas service who held similar rank in the same force of the Army.

In view of the central importance to their overall adjustment of men's attitudes toward what they were doing in the Army, it is worth while to devote some attention to the major factors in returnees' dissatisfaction. The general factors making for job satis-

TABLE 12

BRANCH AND JOB SATISFACTION AMONG RETURNEES AND MEN WITH
NO OVERSEAS SERVICE, JUNE 1945
(Excludes Men Eligible for Discharge Under the Point System)

PRESENT ASSIGNMENT AND RANK	PER CENT DISSATISFIED WITH PRESENT BRANCH ASSIGNMENT* AMONG:		PER CENT DISSATISFIED WITH PRESENT JOB† AMONG:	
	Returnees	Men with no overseas service	Returnees	Men with no overseas service
AAF: First 3 graders	27 (567)	11 (89)	42	15
Sergeants	23 (117)	24 (101)	32	25
Corporals	38 (134)	29 (121)	33	24
Privates and Pfc's	36 (119)	24 (366)	28	35
ASF: First 3 graders	40 (157)	14 (70)	40	22
Sergeants	40 (187)	27 (115)	38	33
Corporals	48 (228)	38 (166)	46	33
Privates and Pfc's	54 (314)	40 (360)	47	39
AGF: First 3 graders	51 (43)	58 (19)	49	31
Sergeants	45 (40)	32 (22)	38	23
Corporals	49 (32)	47 (45)	44	37
Privates and Pfc's	70 (79)	51 (488)	63	46

Data from S-213.
Numbers in parentheses are the numbers of cases on which percentages are based.
* The question asked was: "How do you feel about being in your present arm or branch?"

_____	Very well satisfied
_____	Fairly well satisfied
_X_	Somewhat dissatisfied
_X_	Very dissatisfied

† The question asked was: "How satisfied or dissatisfied are you with your present Army job?"

_____	Very satisfied
_____	Satisfied
_X_	Dissatisfied
_X_	Very dissatisfied
_____	Undecided

faction or dissatisfaction among enlisted men have been thoroughly analyzed in Volume I, Chapter 7, and there is no need to repeat them here.   It is, however, necessary to point out the respects in which returnees were exceptions to the generalizations about job satisfaction made earlier, as well as to discuss briefly some of the major influences on returnees' attitudes which did not operate or operated less extensively for other men.

It may have been noticed in the table presented above that although dissatisfaction with branch tended to decrease as rank increased, formal status was not so consistently associated with job satisfaction among returnees.   In fact, in neither case was the relationship among returnees as sharp as among men with no overseas service, although the discussion in Volume I, Chapter 7, has served to emphasize what a crucial part rank played in the satisfaction of most men.   The reasons for this difference between returnees and men with overseas service probably lie primarily in the differential meaning of rank as between the two groups.   For the men serving overseas as well as the men serving in the United States, the rank held was generally a concomitant of the job performed, so that by knowing a man's rank certain things about his status, work, and working conditions could be inferred.   Returnees, on the other hand, had attained their rank in their jobs overseas, and they might or might not find themselves after their return in jobs which carried with them the conditions usually implied by their rank.   This situation followed from the Army's decision to avoid demoting returnees.   Many returnees held high rank, while the formal tables of organization called for lower ranking men in many of the jobs to which they could be assigned.   Modifications in procedure were, therefore, introduced to permit units to carry an excessive number of higher ranking returnees in their ranks up to a certain percentage over their normal allotment of such grades.   And returnees being retrained or for whom assignments were being sought were also generally allowed to hold their rank while they attempted to qualify for jobs appropriate to their rank.

There is little question that returnees would have looked on any other policy as a bitter injustice.   The majority felt there was little to justify their being kept in the Army and their reactions would undoubtedly have been even worse if they found, upon their return, that the reward for their long service overseas was demotion.   Nevertheless, the jobs which existed for returnees were not the most desirable jobs, so returnees found themselves occupying jobs that were defined as beneath their rank even though they held their former rank and pay. This was better than losing their rank as well, but it was an uneasy situation. As long as returnees outranked their jobs, the theoretical possibility of demotion, made the more real by the Army's reputation for sudden changes of policy, was there to bother the returnee. And, more important than this fear, perhaps, was the injury done to the returnee's conception of himself when he was forced into a status lower than he expected, not only from his rank but from his assumption that returnees should receive deference, consideration, and jobs worthy of their experience.

Another way in which returnees differed from other men was shown earlier: their preference for serving in branches typified by the Corps of Military Police and the Quartermaster Corps and in the lack of desire to be in the Air Corps. Those returnee preferences were gathered in a context in which the men were actually in the process of being reclassified and reassigned, while the general analysis of branch preferences among enlisted men used the preferences they expressed when most of them had no reason to expect reassignment. It may be, therefore, that the answers of returnees were conditioned by the real possibilities confronting them and that their low choice of the Air Corps represents their realization that such transfers were seldom made. Yet, taken all together, the branch preferences of returnees appear to indicate more than this. In fact, they suggest very strongly that the considerations which determined recruits' preferences were not the important ones to returnees. Returnees tended to choose branches which other men ranked low in prestige, importance, and general desirability, but which they thought of as having the most safety and the least work. One appeal which the Air Corps had for the new recruit—the opportunity to learn new skills which would be useful in civilian life—was largely lacking in the case of returnees, both because returnees generally regarded themselves as already trained and because they were subjectively, if not actually, close to discharge from the Army. Moreover, to men who had already been overseas, the Air Corps, like the Infantry, was more likely to symbolize the probability of more overseas service than an opportunity to learn. All of these facts lead to the conclusion that returnees were primarily motivated to select what they thought were the least dangerous and least onerous positions in which to weather out whatever further service the Army demanded from them. The fact that Service Force returnees were not particularly anxious to make any change implies that, once the avoidance of danger motive was fulfilled, returnees, like other men, preferred to go on doing the work with which they were already familiar.

Nevertheless, the reassignment of returnees to branches other than those they had served in overseas did not meet with their approval in practice, even though, as we have shown earlier, a great many returnees had thought they favored such moves.   The data in Table 13 compare men who were serving in the same branch in

TABLE 13

SATISFACTION WITH BRANCH AND JOB ASSIGNMENTS AMONG RETURNEES WHO CHANGED BRANCH AND RETURNEES WHO DID NOT, JUNE 1945

PRESENT ASSIGNMENT	PER CENT DISSATISFIED WITH PRESENT BRANCH ASSIGNMENT		PER CENT DISSATISFIED WITH PRESENT JOB AMONG:	
	Returnees serving in same branch as overseas	*Returnees serving in different branch than overseas*	*Returnees serving in same branch as overseas*	*Returnees serving in different branch than overseas*
AAF	26 *(797)*	44 *(139)*	37	39
ASF	37 *(353)*	52 *(532)*	47	44
AGF	52 *(100)*	63 *(95)*	42	44

Data from S-213.
Numbers in parentheses are the numbers of cases on which percentages are based.

which they had served overseas with men who were serving in new branches.   As we see, the men in new branches were more frequently dissatisfied with their branch assignments, though attitudes toward their jobs were not particularly different between the two groups. Nor did it matter what branches the transferees had originally come from: infantrymen transferred to Army Service Force branches (and it will be remembered a majority of them wished to make this change) were just as dissatisfied as were men transferred within the Service Force branches, most of whom had not desired the change.[32]

As the foregoing data suggest, branch satisfaction and job satisfaction were not quite the same thing, even though they were highly related.   Very few returnees liked their branches if they did not

[32] These two findings—how many wished to change branch as over against how many of those who did change were satisfied—come from two separate studies made at different points of time, but there is no evidence to suggest that anything had happened to alter the branch preferences of new returnees between the two studies.   Only if these two items had been ascertained for the same group of men could we determine definitively whether transferees who had desired their transfer were as dissatisfied as involuntary transferees.

like their jobs, but, especially in the Air and Service Forces, there were a sizable number who were satisfied with their branches and objected only to the particular jobs they held:

	AAF	ASF	AGF
Satisfied with both job and branch	45%	36%	35%
Satisfied with branch but not with job	25	17	7
Satisfied with job but not with branch	7	8	11
Not satisfied with either	23	39	47
	100%	100%	100%
Number of cases	*936*	*885*	*195*

In so far as branch and job satisfaction did have a common core, it will be seen that they both related to the same job factors. There were, however, other aspects to dislike of branch, especially when it was an unfamiliar branch, besides the factors of job frustration. There was, for example, in branch transferring, a loss of contact with men who had shared precisely the same kind of experience and spoke exactly the same language. The question of status was also involved in at least two ways. In Chart II it may be seen that, except in Ground Forces where the bulk of new trainees were concentrated at this time, men with no overseas service had as much rank as the returnees who were transferees to this branch, while returnees who had always been in this branch had much more rank than the other two groups. This strongly suggests that the returnee transferees could look upon themselves as being put into a status inferior to that usually occupied by returnees and no better than that of nonreturnees. Beyond this difference in rank, there were no particular differences between returnee transferees and nontransferees in such factors as whether they had jobs which used their experience or whether they were being trained or used in unskilled jobs; nevertheless the difference between the two groups in attitudes toward branch still persists when the factor of rank is controlled. On the other hand, transferees and nontransferees of equal rank had about the same attitudes toward their jobs (see Table 14).

Besides the probability that individual status deprivation was associated with branch transfer, there was also the fact that returnees who changed branches usually shifted to branches with lower prestige than those they had been in. Something of the effect of this could also have been seen from the data in Table 14; for transferees to Air Force, the most prestigeful arm of service, while less

CHART II

PERCENTAGES HOLDING RANK OF SERGEANT OR ABOVE AMONG RETURNEES
WHO CHANGED BRANCH, RETURNEES WHO DID NOT, AND MEN WITH NO
OVERSEAS SERVICE, CLASSIFIED BY FORCE

(United States, June 1945)

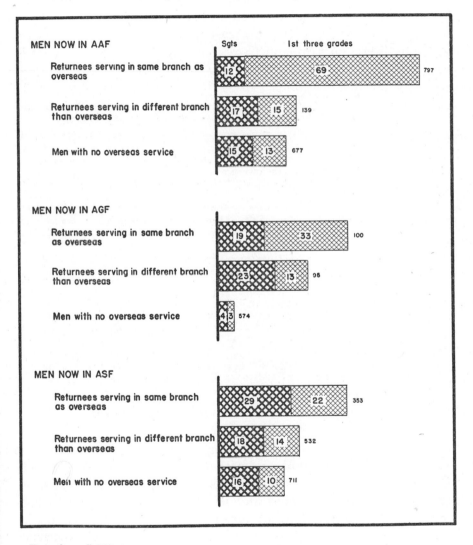

Data from S-213.
The numbers following the bars are the numbers of cases on which percentages are
based.

satisfied with their branch than men who had always been in Air Force, were more satisfied than transferees to the less valued branches.

If we turn now to the more specific job aspects of branch and job dissatisfaction, we find, as shown in Table 15, that the main factors making for good job adjustment among returnees were just those which the earlier discussion of Army policies in assigning returnees indicated were most difficult to establish by Army action. That is,

TABLE 14

BRANCH AND JOB SATISFACTION AMONG RETURNEES WHO CHANGED BRANCH AND RETURNEES WHO DID NOT, CLASSIFIED BY RANK AND FORCE

PRESENT ASSIGNMENT AND RANK	PER CENT DISSATISFIED WITH PRESENT BRANCH ASSIGNMENT AMONG:		PER CENT DISSATISFIED WITH PRESENT JOB AMONG:	
	Returnees serving in same branch as overseas	*Returnees serving in different branch than overseas*	*Returnees serving in same branch as overseas*	*Returnees serving in different branch than overseas*
AAF: All Sergeants	25 *(639)*	40 *(43)*	50	48
Corporals	33 *(89)*	48 *(48)*	46	48
Privates & Pfc's	31 *(67)*	42 *(48)*	34	43
ASF: All Sergeants	32 *(180)*	45 *(164)*	51	52
Corporals	35 *(95)*	54 *(133)*	60	62
Privates & Pfc's	51 *(78)*	55 *(236)*	60	61
AGF: All Sergeants	50 *(52)*	45 *(34)*	52	42
Corporals	38 *(16)*	59 *(17)*	41	59
Privates & Pfc's	61 *(32)*	77 *(44)*	57	77

Data from S-213.
Numbers in parentheses are the numbers of cases on which percentages are based.

returnees who held regular jobs, doing work they had done overseas, with little shifting around, and with a subjective assurance in them that they would not be sent overseas again, tended to report satisfaction with their branches and jobs. Conversely, the returnees being trained or for whom no jobs had yet been found, those who had been transferred to work unrelated to their previous experience or who felt the work they were doing required no skill, and those who thought another overseas tour was likely, all tended not to be satisfied. These data are not completely objective reports of job status. For example, it is easy to imagine that a combat rifleman converted to a rifle instructor might have said in response to these questions either that he had done this kind of work overseas or that he had never done this kind of work before, and no doubt his choice would have been influenced by whether or not he liked his new assignment. Nevertheless, there would seem to be little question that the relationships portrayed in the data cannot be entirely attributed to subjective evaluations of job characteristics. We can only conclude that many of the necessities of returnee placement, dictated by the decision to utilize them somehow, were exactly the factors making returnees so dissatisfied with their lot.

In the discussion so far, we have said very little about how the job problem among returnees was affected by the fact that returnees were not typical of the bulk of the men in the Army. It would be an easy answer if the returnees' adjustment difficulties could be simply attributed to their initial emotional instability, and certainly in some cases this was true, as witness the following statements of three returnees, one from each of the forces, whose job difficulties, it is reasonable to suppose, were inherent in their personality difficulties and would have pursued them from job to job:

A mess sergeant: I can't stand it nervously. Get all tore up over details. Mess inspection last week was too much for me. Now the C.O. is going to get me a new job. I was not this way before going overseas, I was just high strung.

A flight gunner instructor: I thought I could maybe get to some field where I wouldn't have to fly in a B-24, but they sent me to a field as a flight gunner instructor. I'm nervous as hell when I fly and I'm scared to tell them about it as I may lose my rank.

An instructor in Infantry: I asked to get out of Infantry and to be put at a quiet job at a quiet post. I can't stand gunfire or the sight of marching troops anymore.

Nevertheless, this is a point so easy to dramatize that it is in danger of being overemphasized. As the more reliable data in Table 16 show, it is true that emotional stability is related to branch and job satisfaction, but the differences between the more stable and the less stable men are not nearly as large as some of the differences related to objectively differing job characteristics previously discussed.

We may conclude then that while for some job adjustments were complicated by the psychological state of the men involved, this was not the sole, nor even the major, factor in the job problems in which returnees were involved.

On the other hand, the real and persistent job adjustment difficulties of the returnees must be evaluated in the context of the satisfaction returnees derived from being home and safe, whatever else hap-

TABLE 15

SOME FACTORS IN BRANCH AND JOB SATISFACTION AMONG RETURNEES
CLASSIFIED BY FORCE
(Excludes Men Eligible for Discharge Under the Point System)

FACTOR*	PER CENT SATISFIED WITH BRANCH ASSIGNMENT:			PER CENT SATISFIED WITH JOB ASSIGNMENT:		
	AAF	*ASF*	*AGF*	*AAF*	*ASF*	*AGF*
Job status						
Has regular job	72 *(520)*	57 *(654)*	59 *(121)*	63	51	61
Taking training	79 *(304)*	49 *(71)*	17 *(43)*	44	24	14
No regular duties	59 *(82)*	36 *(112)*	8 *(24)*	19	13	8
Nature of work (among men who have jobs)						
Did this kind of work overseas	81 *(227)*	66 *(202)*	56 *(43)*	76	66	68
Not the work done overseas but related to previous Army or civilian experience	78 *(98)*	67 *(97)*	44 *(23)*	51	67	52
Never did this kind of work before return	67 *(408)*	47 *(408)*	46 *(104)*	50	39	43
Job turnover (among men who have jobs)						
Had only one job	77 *(314)*	60 *(330)*	59 *(83)*	73	57	61
Had several similar jobs	74 *(92)*	55 *(128)*	43 *(21)*	64	49	64
Had several dissimilar jobs requiring different skills	53 *(96)*	57 *(107)*	24 *(21)*	38	42	45
Had several dissimilar jobs none of which required skills	55 *(121)*	33 *(158)*	24 *(25)*	29	23	47
Expectation of overseas service (among men fit for it)						
Fairly or very sure of not being sent again	72 *(140)*	63 *(43)*	56 *(18)*	52	56	59
Chances about fifty-fifty or undecided	75 *(378)*	63 *(167)*	46 *(52)*	52	45	41
Fairly or very sure of being sent again	73 *(165)*	44 *(66)*	48 *(42)*	49	35	44

Data from S-213.
Numbers in parentheses are the numbers of cases on which percentages are based.
* The questions asked:

What is your main Army duty at present?

_____ I am working on a regular job
_____ I am taking training or going to school
_____ I don't have any regular duties now

Check all of the following things that are true about your present Army job:

_____ I don't have a job at this post yet
_____ I never did this work until after I came back to the United States
_____ I did this kind of work overseas
_____ I did this kind of work in the Army before I went overseas
_____ I did this kind of work in civilian life

pened. As we saw earlier, the majority of returnees remained glad they had come home even after they had been working on their new assignments and had, presumably, gone through the sorts of experiences we have been describing. Indeed, as the data in Table 17

TABLE 16

RELATION OF ANXIETY SYMPTOMS TO BRANCH AND JOB SATISFACTION AMONG RETURNEES

(Excludes Men Eligible for Discharge Under the Point System)

	PER CENT SATISFIED WITH BRANCH ASSIGNMENT AMONG MEN WITH:		PER CENT SATISFIED WITH PRESENT JOB AMONG MEN WITH:	
	*Critical number of anxiety symptoms**	*Less than critical number of anxiety symptoms*	*Critical number of anxiety symptoms*	*Less than critical number of anxiety symptoms*
AAF	48 *(657)*	62 *(300)*	68	78
ASF	41 *(650)*	51 *(246)*	50	62
AGF	37 *(130)*	57 *(72)*	34	60

Data from S-213.
Numbers in parentheses are the numbers of cases on which percentages are based.
* The measure being used is the Index of Anxiety Symptoms. See Chapter 9.

serve to emphasize, the proportion of returnees who were glad they came back did decline as we move from those in the most desirable types of reassignment to those in the least fortunate positions. But, even at the bottom of the heap, among returnees for whom no regular assignments had been found, only a minority regretted their return, and such factors in their adjustment, yet to be described, as the respect which they got or failed to get were not at all related to the relief they felt, whatever else happened, to be back in the United States.

Two further factors in returnee adjustment may best be examined

Since you came back from overseas, have you done pretty much the same kind of work all the time, or have you been shifted around from job to job?

_____ I have been in training most of the time since I got back
_____ I have had one kind of job all the time since I got back
_____ I have had different jobs, but they were a lot alike
_____ I have had several jobs that used entirely different skills
_____ I have had different jobs but none of them required much special skill or training

Regardless of what you want to do, do you think you actually will be sent to some overseas theater again?

_____ I am very sure I'll be sent over again
_____ I am fairly sure I'll be sent over again
_____ The chances are about fifty-fifty
_____ I am fairly sure I'll not be sent over again
_____ I am very sure I'll not be sent over again
_____ Undecided

through data from a survey made in November 1944 of samples of returnees and men with no overseas service in Air Forces, Infantry, and two Service Force branches, the Corps of Engineers and the Quartermaster Corps.[33] Since most returnees who were reassigned

TABLE 17

EFFECT OF WORK STATUS ON RETURNEES' ATTITUDES TOWARD BEING BACK, JUNE 1945

(Excludes Men Eligible for Discharge Under the Point System)

Work status*	Per cent who said they were glad they came back to the United States
Men who are now doing work they did overseas	77 (*394*)
Men who are now doing work related to their pre-overseas experience	72 (*152*)
Men who are now doing work they never did before, but have done little shifting or shifted only between skilled jobs	70 (*609*)
Men who are now doing work they never did before and who have been shifted around among various unskilled jobs	61 (*140*)
Men who are in training	58 (*379*)
Men who have no regular assignments	54 (*342*)

Data from S-213.
Numbers in parentheses are the numbers of cases on which percentages are based.
* Based on a cross tabulation of the first three questions shown in the footnote to Table 15.

to the Ground Forces were to be found in the Infantry, the first two of these samples may be taken as adequately representing returnees who were assigned to Air Forces and Ground Forces. As for the returnees in Service Force branches, the two branches selected offer some interesting contrasts, being in many respects the two extremes to be found within the Service Forces,[34] and it is probably safe to

[33] S-157.

[34] At the time of this study, returnees in each of these two branches were made up about equally of men who had served in it overseas and men transferred to it since their return. However, two thirds of the transferees to the Quartermaster Corps had come from the Ground Forces, primarily Infantry, while a like number of the transferees to the Engineers had come from other Service Force branches. This difference is not simply a historical accident but reflects a difference in the type of jobs within each branch and the type of men assigned to them. The Army classification program had devised a physical profile plan whereby men were classified into one of three major groups on the basis of their physical condition, and quotas of men were assigned to each of the Service Force branches in accordance with an analysis of the physical requirements of the jobs each branch performed. On this basis, among Service Force branches, ASF Circular No. 175, "Classification and Assignment Based upon Physical Capacity or Stamina," provided that the Corps of Engineers get the largest quota of men from the best physical group (65 per cent of its men were to be in this physical condition) while the Quartermaster Corps was given the largest quota of men from the poorest group (80 per cent of its men). In other words, the Quartermaster Corps was a branch to which returnees in poor physical condition were sent in order to find non-

assume that the picture for the whole Service Forces lay somewhere between them.

The Desire to Be Stationed Near Home

Returnees strongly desired to be assigned to posts relatively near their homes.   Both because they had been away so long and because they tended to be older and married, home had a strong appeal to these men.   However, since the Army camps were concentrated in the South and West while the centers of population are in the North and East, it was not possible for returnees to be assigned routinely

TABLE 18

RETURNEES' DESIRE TO BE STATIONED NEAR HOME
(Assigned Returnees, November 1944)

	Number of cases	Per cent saying they were told officially that they would be assigned to duty at a station near their homes*	Per cent saying that, even considering the needs of the Army, they had not been assigned as close to home as possible†
Air Forces	*1,427*	34	58
Infantry	*870*	40	64
Engineers	*800*	44	59
Quartermaster	*906*	54	68

Data from S-157.
* The question asked was: "Were you ever told officially that you would be assigned to duty near your home?"

_____ No
_____ Yes

† The question asked was: "Considering the needs of the Army, would you say you have been assigned as close to home as is possible?"

_____ I've never thought about it
_____ Yes
_____ No

to posts close to their homes.   In the Air Forces, returnees were allowed to indicate three bases where they would prefer to be placed and were told that they would be placed there if it were at all possible, but no such policy existed in the Ground and Service Forces. Nonetheless, the impression soon grew up among returnees that they had been promised placement near home and that this promise had not been kept.   As we see in Table 18, from a third of the returnees in the Air Forces to over half the returnees in the Quartermaster

taxing jobs for them.   Perhaps not unrelated to the foregoing difference is the fact that the Corps of Engineers was one of the most prestigeful of the Service Force branches while the Quartermaster Corps ranked near the bottom.

Corps felt this promise had been made to them,[35] while a clear majority of men in all four branches felt that they had not been put as close to home as they could have been.

The actual fact was that returnees generally were not stationed any closer to home than were other troops. The median number of hours of travel required to reach the place where they would spend their furloughs were reported as:

	Returnees	Men with no overseas service
Air Force	40 hours	40 hours
Infantry	38	29
Engineers	29	31
Quartermaster	25	25

But though returnees and nonoverseas men were equally distant from their homes, returnees were much more likely to be resentful of their placement at a distance from home. In Table 19 it is shown that there was some relationship between the actual distance from home and men's feeling that they had not been placed near enough, but it may also be noted that returnees were more critical of their placement than other men at whatever their distance from home, and that the only returnee group in which the majority were consistently satisfied was that within six hours of home.

The reasons for the greater resentment on the part of returnees were only in part traceable to what many of them regarded as an unkept promise. It is true that returnees who admitted that they had no official promise of placement near home were less likely to resent their location than were men who felt they had been assured of such an assignment. And, of course, nonoverseas men could not advance the argument that such promises had been made to them. Nevertheless, excluding those men fortunate enough to have made living arrangements near their station for their wives, returnees who agreed that no promise had been made were more critical of their

---

[35] Oddly enough, in a survey made just a few months earlier (S-132, June–July 1944) of returnees just arriving in this country, less than 5 per cent said they had been told officially that they would be assigned to duty near home, which would seem to indicate that the misapprehension developed after their return. And most of the returnees in the later study who said such promises had been made them did say that they were already in the United States when they were told this. It is possible that some of them misinterpreted the explanation given that they would go to a *reception station* near their homes before going on furlough—a procedure adopted in order to save them transportation costs and which had no bearing on their ultimate assignment. It is also possible that some men were told they would be assigned near home by persons who did not have the authority to give such assurance.

TABLE 19

REACTIONS TO DISTANCE FROM HOME, NOVEMBER 1944

PER CENT SAYING THEY HAD NOT BEEN STATIONED AS CLOSE TO HOME AS POSSIBLE CONSIDERING THE NEEDS OF THE ARMY

DISTANCE FROM HOME*	Air Force		Infantry		Engineers		Quartermaster	
	Returnees	Non-returnees	Returnees	Non-returnees	Returnees	Non-returnees	Returnees	Non-returnees
72 hours or over	77 (199)	65 (153)	77 (171)	67 (45)	77 (162)	65 (71)	85 (32)	68 (22)
36–72 hours	71 (567)	57 (386)	67 (257)	50 (78)	76 (179)	63 (111)	77 (238)	54 (99)
18–36 hours	54 (325)	45 (205)	64 (311)	58 (222)	69 (160)	45 (77)	73 (298)	47 (106)
6–18 hours	33 (225)	36 (104)	45 (74)	33 (61)	51 (183)	12 (82)	61 (250)	35 (92)
6 hours or less	16 (86)	21 (33)	17 (29)	16 (19)	17 (85)	11 (47)	27 (51)	11 (36)

Data from S-157.

Numbers in parentheses are the numbers of cases on which percentages are based.

* Based on written-in answers to the question, "About how long would it take to reach the place where you would spend your furlough?"

location than were nonoverseas men of the same marital condition. (See Table 20.) Much of the explanation goes back, once again, not to a belief that promises had been made and broken, but to the returnee's conception of himself and to the nature of returnee assignments.

In this matter of being near home, the returnees generally depended on two main lines of justification. On the one hand, the

TABLE 20

RELATION OF PROMISE OF ASSIGNMENT NEAR HOME TO SATISFACTION WITH LOCATION
(Returnees and Nonreturnees, Classified by Marital Status)

| | PERCENTAGES SAYING THEY HAVE NOT BEEN STATIONED AS NEAR HOME AS POSSIBLE AMONG: | | |
| | *Returnees* | | *Nonreturnees* |
MARITAL CONDITION AND BRANCH OF SERVICE	Who say they *were* promised placement near home	Who say they *were not* promised placement near home	
Married men whose wives are living near their camp:			
Air Force	74 *(190)*	41 *(261)*	46 *(158)*
Infantry	88 *(48)*	54 *(61)*	43 *(95)*
Engineers	61 *(51)*	39 *(77)*	45 *(63)*
Quartermaster	78 *(72)*	48 *(75)*	41 *(68)*
Married men whose wives are not living near their camp:			
Air Force	83 *(89)*	62 *(109)*	49 *(162)*
Infantry	81 *(47)*	57 *(88)*	56 *(163)*
Engineers	68 *(93)*	54 *(88)*	51 *(151)*
Quartermaster	82 *(90)*	71 *(79)*	55 *(117)*
Single men:			
Air Force	73 *(316)*	45 *(462)*	54 *(573)*
Infantry	82 *(238)*	50 *(388)*	48 *(174)*
Engineers	67 *(194)*	59 *(297)*	42 *(183)*
Quartermaster	75 *(310)*	56 *(280)*	36 *(176)*

Data from S-157.
Numbers in parentheses are the numbers of cases on which percentages are based.

kind of jobs they did were not usually specialized and they had their counterparts all over the country, so it seemed reasonable to the returnees that they should be able to do these jobs somewhere nearer home. Especially when the jobs they did get had so little else to recommend them, and returnees were well aware that often at the camps to which they were sent they represented just so much surplus man power creating difficult problems of absorption for the command, the pleasure of being near home could be regarded as partial compensation for these unexpected unpalatable features of their returnee status.   In the words of one returnee, "When I arrived at station there were already too many of my MOS [Military Occupational Specialty] here, so that being the case I feel they could have sent me much closer home even if the same condition existed there." On the other hand, though, this was one of the privileges which many returnees felt they had earned by their service overseas, quite apart from and long before they became aware of the returnee job situation.   As an ex-combat man just in process of assignment said, "Too little attention is given to the Ground Force men desiring to be near home.   They seem to get the worst assignments even though some of these men had it tougher overseas than the others."   Implicit in the returnees' yearning for assignment near home, there was not only their desire that special status be accorded them but an indirect expression of their tendency to regard themselves as rightfully finished with the Army as well.   They were not so much concerned with what they were doing in the Army as with being out of the Army and back home.   Since they were kept in the Army, being near home was as close as they could come to their real wish.

The data on this point present an interesting paradox, however. If we turn first to the relationship between job adjustment and actual distance from home (see Table 21) we see that, with the exception of Air Force men, who in any case tend to be fairly well satisfied with their jobs, returnees at a distance from home tended to be somewhat more dissatisfied with their jobs than those stationed closer to home.   However, except for the sample of returnees in the Corps of Engineers, the relationship is essentially a difference between men within six hours of home and all other men.   When we turn to nonreturnees, the relationship is even less marked; only in the two Service Force branches is there a suggestion of such a relationship, and in neither of them is the difference significant.   The relationship between job adjustment and men's *satisfaction* with their nearness to home was, however, as shown in Table 22, much more clearcut and about as marked in the nonreturnee group as in the returnee group.

As these data indicate, the way men felt about their location, which was itself in part a function of the distance from home at which they were located, was more closely related to job adjustment than was their actual location.   This would tend to suggest that men dissatisfied with their jobs found other things like their distance from home to be dissatisfied about as well, rather than that the actual proximity to home was an important determining factor in job

TABLE 21

RELATION OF DISTANCE FROM HOME TO JOB ADJUSTMENT, NOVEMBER 1944

PER CENT WITH RELATIVELY LOW JOB ADJUSTMENT*

DISTANCE FROM HOME	Returnees				Nonreturnees			
	Air Force	Infantry	Engineers	Quarter-master	Air Force	Infantry	Engineers	Quarter-master
72 hours or over	14 (199)	33 (131)	49 (162)	56 (32)	13 (153)	16 (45)	27 (71)	73 (22)
36–72 hours	17 (567)	35 (257)	46 (179)	55 (238)	14 (386)	35 (78)	49 (111)	46 (99)
18–36 hours	14 (325)	42 (311)	43 (160)	51 (298)	21 (205)	38 (222)	32 (77)	45 (106)
6–18 hours	14 (225)	28 (74)	39 (183)	59 (250)	13 (104)	26 (61)	28 (82)	48 (92)
6 hours or less	17 (86)	17 (29)	32 (85)	41 (51)	15 (33)	37 (19)	26 (47)	25 (36)

Data from S-157.
Numbers in parentheses are the numbers of cases on which percentages are based.
* Based on an index of three questions:

How do you feel about the importance of the work you are doing right now as compared with other jobs you might be doing in the Army?
___ It is important as any other job I could do
___ It is fairly important, but I could do more important work
___ It hardly seems important at all

Does the Army job you now have give you a chance to use your skill and experience?
___ A very good chance   ___ No chance at all
___ A fairly good chance   ___ Undecided
___ Not much of a chance

Would you change to some other Army job if given a chance?
___ Yes
___ No
___ Undecided

The low job adjustment group is defined as those men who said that their jobs were not as important as other jobs they could do and did not give them much or any chance to use their skill and experience, and that they either would change jobs or were undecided.

satisfaction.   There is some evidence that this latter factor played some part, especially where returnees were concerned, but it does not seem to have been a basic concern.

Relations with Personnel Who Had not Served Overseas

Returnees were prone to feel that they were discriminated against, were not appreciated, and were not given the deference to which they were entitled.   As Chart III shows, the majority of returnees

TABLE 22

RELATION OF SATISFACTION WITH DISTANCE FROM HOME TO JOB ADJUSTMENT, NOVEMBER 1944

| | PER CENT WITH LOW JOB ADJUSTMENT* | | | |
| | Returnees | | Men with no overseas service | |
	Men who feel they are stationed as close to home as possible	Men who feel they are not stationed as close to home as possible	Men who feel they are stationed as close to home as possible	Men who feel they are not stationed as close to home as possible
Air Force	11 (354)	20 (827)	12 (208)	17 (459)
Infantry	24 (112)	41 (551)	23 (92)	38 (222)
Engineers	29 (165)	49 (476)	26 (120)	45 (168)
Quartermaster	34 (129)	60 (611)	33 (86)	59 (156)

Data from S-157.
Numbers in parentheses are the numbers of cases on which percentages are based.
* See footnote to Table 21.

felt that their contributions went unrecognized by men who had not been overseas.   And in similar fashion, returnees were likely to insist that the nonoverseas men got the better jobs, while men who had not been overseas tended to disagree with them:

PER CENT SAYING THE BETTER JOBS WERE
HELD BY NONOVERSEAS PERSONNEL[36]

	Returnees	Nonreturnees
Air Force	29	7
Infantry	27	10
Engineers	44	10
Quartermaster	55	15

[36] The question asked was: "Who have the better jobs in your outfit—enlisted men who haven't been overseas or those who have?"

_____ Enlisted men who have been overseas
_____ Enlisted men who haven't been overseas
_____ There isn't much difference
_____ I haven't been in this outfit long enough to know

CHART III

DEFERENCE GIVEN RETURNEES, AS RETURNEES AND NONOVERSEAS MEN VIEWED IT
(November 1944)

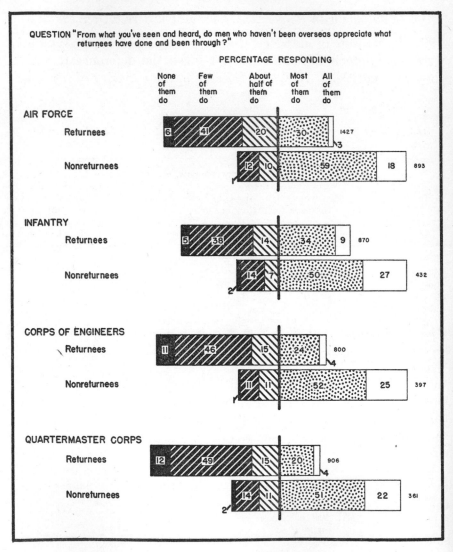

Data from S-157.
The numbers following the bars are the numbers of cases on which percentages are based.

Nonreturnees did not usually claim that returnees got the better jobs; they tended to assert simply that there was no appreciable difference in the kinds of assignments returnees and nonreturnees were given.

As the foregoing chart shows, nonoverseas men did not share the returnees' point of view on this matter, but believed that the returnees were adequately recognized.   It is clear that the returnees' deference demands were greater than the nonoverseas men realized, though in part the answers of the latter group must be taken as defensive, since in giving an unfavorable response they would, in effect, be criticizing themselves.   The attitudes of nonoverseas men might simply be taken as implying that the nonoverseas men felt that returnees were not entitled to much special recognition and were getting as much as they deserved, if it were not for the fact that other evidence exists to suggest that nonoverseas personnel did in fact accord the returnees high status, though their relationships were not unmixed with conflicts.   The respect for the returnees' superior experience may be inferred from the choices men made, as shown in Table 23, for men in the Corps of Engineers, though the same thing might have been shown for any of the other branches as well.   As we see here, a majority of men with no overseas service expressed a preference that their leaders, both officers and noncoms, come at least in part from the returnee group.   They were, however, less likely to want to be in an outfit in which their fellow enlisted men were returnees, a fact which has a double-barreled implication: on the one hand it may have represented the respect given returnees by new recruits who did not feel they had enough experience to belong to a returnee outfit, but on the other hand it also involved some of the conflicts between the two types of personnel which will be discussed later.

Returnees, however, were far more decided in their preferences for an all-returnee society.   If we take the three choices shown in the foregoing table—that is, preferences in officers, noncoms and fellow enlisted men—as defining an all-returnee group, it may be said that three fifths of the returnees gave this as their choice.   The choices of nonreturnees did not cluster to anything like this extent; the highest proportion choosing any one possible combination was only 13 per cent and this was the group of men who consistently had no preferences about the composition of their outfit.   However, the second most frequent choice was to be in an all-returnee outfit, and this was closely followed by a preference for returnee leaders, but either mixed or all nonoverseas fellow enlisted men.

It may be said, then, that in general nonoverseas men respected returnees and often wished to associate with them, but returnees preferred to keep to themselves. The reasons for the returnees' tendency toward exclusiveness may be broadly classified into two main groups: on the one hand, the returnees' general estrangement from the United States milieu, and, on the other, the more specific difficulties which arose between returnees and men with no overseas service.

TABLE 23

PREFERENCE FOR RETURNEE LEADERS AND ASSOCIATES AMONG RETURNEES AND NONOVERSEAS MEN

(Corps of Engineers, November 1944)

DESIRED COMPOSITION	PERCENTAGES CHOOSING GIVEN COMPOSITION OF OFFICERS* AMONG:		PERCENTAGES CHOOSING GIVEN COMPOSITION OF NONCOMS† AMONG:		PERCENTAGES CHOOSING GIVEN COMPOSITION OF OTHER ENLISTED MEN IN COMPANY‡ AMONG:	
	Returnees	*Non-returnees*	*Returnees*	*Non-returnees*	*Returnees*	*Non-returnees*
Returnees	79	49	81	39	69	15
Some of both	7	21	7	26	13	34
Don't care one way or the other	13	25	11	26	15	23
Nonreturnees	1	5	1	9	3	28
Total	100	100	100	100	100	100
Number of cases	*800*	*397*	*800*	*397*	*800*	*397*

Data from S-157.

* Based on the question: "In general would you rather have officers who have served overseas or officers who haven't been overseas?"

_____ Would rather have officers who have served overseas
_____ Would rather have officers who haven't been overseas
_____ Would rather have some of both
_____ It doesn't matter to me one way or another

† Based on the question: "In general would you rather have noncoms who have served overseas or noncoms who haven't been overseas?"

_____ Would rather have noncoms who have served overseas
_____ Would rather have noncoms who haven't been overseas
_____ Would rather have some of both
_____ It doesn't matter to me one way or another

‡ Based on the question: "If it were up to you would you rather be in a company made up mostly of overseas men, or would you prefer being in a company made up mostly of men who haven't been overseas?"

_____ Would rather be in a company made up mostly of overseas men
_____ Would rather be in a company made up mostly of men who haven't been overseas
_____ Would rather have some of both
_____ It doesn't matter to me one way or another

To turn first to the more general aspect of the problem, it is obvious that the environment of the military establishment in the United States was quite different from that overseas. Returnees found themselves not only in an atmosphere they were no longer used to, but among men who had not shared their experiences and did not speak their language. It has become a shibboleth among men who served overseas, and especially the combat men among them, that "no one who hasn't been through it can possibly understand what it's like." Attitudes like these as well as the objectively disappointing aspects of their duty in the United States operated to prevent returnees from fully reassimilating themselves to the domestic Army.

TABLE 24

FEELING OF ESTRANGEMENT AMONG RETURNEES, NOVEMBER 1944

| | PER CENT SAYING THAT THEY DO NOT FEEL THEY REALLY BELONG IN THEIR PRESENT COMPANY AND ARE AN IMPORTANT PART OF IT* | |
	Returnees	*Nonoverseas men*
Air Force	34	15
Infantry	50	34
Engineers	58	41
Quartermaster	72	61

Data from S-157.
 * Based on the question: "Do you feel you really belong in your company (battery, squadron) and are an important part of it?"

_____ Very much so
_____ Fairly much so
_____ Not very much
_____ Not at all

At the time of the survey made in November 1944, returnees in each of the branches surveyed, who had on the average been back in the United States for eight months, were less likely than men who had never been overseas to report that they felt integrated into their present units (see Table 24), in spite of the fact that these returnees had been in their present units as long as or even longer than the men with no overseas service. In part, of course, this sentiment, as the very differences between the branches imply, reflected the low esteem in which men held their present branch and job assignments, but some of this reaction is attributable to the greater prestige men gave to overseas units rather than to the particular frustrations they had encountered as returnees. This tendency to identify themselves with their overseas units to the disparagement of their domestic units was reflected in the importance which returnees placed on being permitted to continue to wear the insignia of their old units, and itself helped to keep the returnee psychologically aloof from his milieu.

One aspect of the United States environment which returnees found particularly distasteful was the emphasis given to forms of military courtesy and the "customs of the service" which tended to be more rigorously observed in the garrison situations in the States than in the usually less formal overseas situations from which the returnees had come. Returnees generally expressed more criticism of the enforcement of discipline and officer-enlisted men relationships than did men who had never been overseas, as is shown in Table 25. It is of some interest to note that while the foregoing statement is in any case historically true of the particular men who came back as returnees, there is some reason to believe that this finding has greater generality in that the same pattern of differences between returnees and nonreturnees is found when the comparisons are limited to only those men whose scores on the Index of Anxiety Symptoms make it unreasonable to hypothesize that personality disturbances were at the root of their criticisms. For example, if we limit our attention only to those men who had less than a critical number of anxiety symptoms, the proportions objecting to military discipline (the first item in Table 25) still remain higher among returnees than among men with no overseas service:

	Returnees	Nonreturnees
Air Force	45 (676)	34 (591)
Infantry	40 (269)	31 (217)
Engineers	58 (261)	33 (230)
Quartermaster	69 (314)	65 (188)

The whole question of garrison discipline was one of the subjects extensively written about by returnees in the morale questionnaire basic to the above data. In fact, the desire to escape from "chicken" and the "too GI" atmosphere was the most frequently advanced explanation given by the small number of returnees who expressed willingness to go overseas again.

In addition to these general reactions against the circumstances surrounding their service in the United States, returnees did not always look with favor upon or get along smoothly with their associates who had not been overseas. Returnees' attitudes toward

TABLE 25

ATTITUDES TOWARD ASPECTS OF THE GARRISON SITUATION, RETURNEES AND NONRETURNEES, NOVEMBER 1944

PER CENT WHO SAY THAT:*	AIR FORCE		INFANTRY		ENGINEERS		QUARTERMASTER	
	Returnees	Non-returnees	Returnees	Non-returnees	Returnees	Non-returnees	Returnees	Non-returnees
Military control and discipline at their post is too strict and a lot of it is unnecessary	51	36	47	41	65	41	72	67
Passes are tougher to get than is necessary	22	16	32	31	30	18	40	32
Military Police treat returnees worse than other men who haven't been overseas	33	6	30	9	25	5	22	8
Officers get far too many privileges as compared with enlisted men	52	43	44	35	47	25	54	44
Few or none of their officers try to look out for the welfare of enlisted men	60	47	44	36	54	33	46	41
Number of cases	*1,427*	*893*	*370*	*432*	*800*	*397*	*906*	*361*

TABLE 25 (Continued)

Data from S-157.

* The questions paraphrased here are:

What do you think of the military control and discipline at this post?

_____ It's too strict but most of it is necessary
_____ It's too strict and a lot of it is unnecessary
_____ It's about right
_____ It's not strict enough

How are the passes in your outfit?

_____ Tougher to get than is necessary
_____ Tough, but there are some good reasons for it
_____ About right

From what you've seen or heard, do you feel M.P.'s treat returnees better or worse than men who haven't been overseas?

_____ M.P.'s treat returnees better
_____ M.P.'s treat returnees and men who haven't been overseas about the same
_____ M.P.'s treat returnees worse

Considering their responsibilities, how do you feel about the privileges that officers get compared with enlisted men?

_____ Far too many privileges compared with enlisted men
_____ A few too many privileges compared with enlisted men
_____ About the right number of privileges
_____ Too few privileges

How many of your present officers are the kind that always try to look out for the welfare of enlisted men?

_____ None
_____ Few
_____ About half
_____ Most
_____ All
_____ Don't know

men who had not yet served overseas differed rather sharply depending on whether the nonoverseas men were men still in training who could reasonably be expected to be sent overseas, or men who had completed training and were occupying garrison-type jobs, and their attitudes were in turn reciprocated at least in part.   Toward the trainees, the returnees' attitudes were almost fatherly; they frequently expressed concern for the trainees' welfare and apprehension that they were not getting the training and information they would need for their overseas duty.   These trainees were about to confront experiences which the returnees had had to endure, so the returnees found it fairly easy to identify themselves with them.   A quite typical expression of returnee sentiments toward these trainees may be seen in the following comment of a returnee:

I was in a Machine Gun Co. (overseas) and we use to get men into it that didn't know a thing about the weapon.   So how about getting off their fanny and doing something about it for these men.

Many trainees in turn looked up to the returnees, as the apprentice would to the master.

Where the other group of nonoverseas personnel was concerned, however, a different series of reactions took place.   These men who were working rather than training in the United States were frequently the target of bitter attacks by the returnees.   In part, this was a continuation of the reactions of overseas troops to men who had escaped the experience; it will be remembered that in an earlier chapter troops overseas were shown to be quite hostile to the men they frequently characterized as the "U.S.O. Commandos."   The overseas men's point of view was a kind of invidious resentment of men who had been fortunate enough to escape their experience, but who were, by that escape, in a sense responsible for their enduring it.   By their reasoning, if the men not overseas had been the ones sent over, then those over there might have been the lucky ones who remained in the States.   These resentments continued when the overseas men returned to the States and in much the same context. These attitudes were most frequently expressed by the returnees in justification of their unwillingness to go overseas again or their feeling that they had done their share as long as these fully trained men, usually characterized with various derogatory epithets, had not gone overseas.   Especially since the returnees were not definitely assured that they would never go overseas again, the presence of these post-trainees who had never been over acted as a goad to keep both their fear and their resentment alive.

At the same time, there were in the United States situation some added sources of conflict between the returnees and this particular group of nonreturnees. These post-trainees held, by and large, the same general type of jobs that returnees were ultimately given, but since the returnees were relative newcomers, the nonoverseas men were likely to be holding the more desirable jobs. So these post-trainees were an easily identifiable element in the job frustrations of the returnees, and their shipment overseas not only seemed called for by simple justice, but appeared as a means of improving the returnees' situation.

These post-trainees, on the other hand, were aware of their good fortune to date and of the returnees' resentment of it, and felt some guilt in the situation, as well as a defensiveness and counterresentment. It was a frequent defense of theirs that the individual was not responsible for what happened to him in the Army, so the men who hadn't been sent overseas should not be blamed for it.[37] Some of them had, moreover, one real grievance against the returnees: as we have had occasion to discuss earlier, the excessive rank among returnees created some administrative difficulties and, though the returnees were usually protected in their rank, this sometimes meant that the nonoverseas men were reduced in grade or blocked from promotion in order to leave the returnees in their grades.

Much of the foregoing description rests on personal interview materials and freely written comments, but this description may be documented, at least partially, by more objective data. In Table 26 the answers of returnees and nonoverseas returnees to two statements about relationships between returnees and nonreturnees are shown. As a rough approximation of the trainee post-trainee distinction, the men with no overseas service have been divided into those with a year or less of service and those with longer service. As we see here, the post-trainees were as likely to recognize the overseas personnel's resentment of men who had not seen active service as the returnees were to admit it, while the trainees, who were not the target of this resentment, were not as aware of it. On the other hand, trainees were likely to identify themselves with returnees in equally accepting the idea that the veteran had a right to his superior status, as indexed by his being justified in directing anger toward men who had done less than he had, but the post-trainees who were

---

[37] Such rationalizations reached their peak in the occasional objection to the point system as unfairly discriminating against nonoverseas personnel by giving points for combat and overseas service, since the men "unfortunate" enough to have been kept in the United States didn't get the opportunity to earn such points.

somewhat guiltily aware that they were the group "who didn't go through what he did" were more likely to take the self-defensive position of denying that veterans were rightfully entitled to such expressions of superiority.

In spite of resentments on both sides, the fact is that when both groups were queried about how returnees and nonoverseas men got along, a majority of the nonoverseas men described the situation as one in which returnees and nonreturnees got along very well, while returnees, looking at presumably the same situation, were less likely to view the relations so favorably.   (See Table 27.)   Since the question was not one which attributed blame to either side in case rela-

TABLE 26

RETURNEE-NONRETURNEE RESENTMENTS, CROSS SECTION, NOVEMBER 1945

| | PERCENTAGES AGREEING WITH STATEMENT AMONG: | | |
| | Men with no overseas service | | Returnees |
STATEMENT	1 year or less in Army	Over 1 year in Army	
Most men who were under enemy fire in this war resent the soldiers who did not see action	32	50	49
A soldier who has seen a lot of the war has a right to get sore whenever he is annoyed by a person who didn't go through what he did	52	39	54
Number of cases	*149*	*412*	*473*

Data from S-234.

tionships were not good, there is little reason to infer that the non-overseas men's answers represent a kind of defensive response, although this is, of course, possible.   Rather, it would appear that these data are more consistent with the view that relationships between the two groups were not particularly characterized by overt hostilities but were a source of subjective tensions to the returnees of which the nonoverseas men were often unaware.

A good example of the kind of situation which returnees would regard unfavorably while nonoverseas men, who were less aware of the returnees' deference needs, might see no difficulties in it, is found in working and command relationships between returnees and nonreturnees in which nonoverseas men were in the superordinate positions.   While the nonoverseas man, trained for and experienced in his role, was not very likely to see this as any different from his similar relationships with other nonreturnees, returnees frequently regarded it as an affront to be put in a position subordinate to men whom they regarded as clearly their inferiors in experience and status. In the words of a returnee flying officer: "It's pretty bad working under men who have been commissioned much after I was and who have less flying experience."

TABLE 27

RELATIONS BETWEEN RETURNEES AND NONRETURNEES AS BOTH GROUPS
REPORT THEM, NOVEMBER 1944

		QUESTION: "From what you have seen or heard, how well do returnees and enlisted men who haven't been overseas get along together?"					
		PERCENTAGES RESPONDING:					
		Not well at all	*Not so well*	*Fairly well*	*Very well*	*Total per cent*	*Number of cases*
Air Force	Returnees	2	10	62	26	100	*1,427*
	Nonreturnees	1	2	42	55	100	*893*
Infantry	Returnees	5	15	54	26	100	*870*
	Nonreturnees	1	1	39	59	100	*432*
Engineers	Returnees	5	15	54	26	100	*800*
	Nonreturnees	1	2	42	55	100	*397*
Quartermaster	Returnees	7	19	55	19	100	*906*
	Nonreturnees	1	2	44	53	100	*361*

Data from S-157.

For a variety of reasons, then, returnees adjusted better when they were relatively isolated from contacts with men who had not served overseas. In Table 28, returnees have been classified, according to their outfit composition, into those in which the commanding officer and a majority of the noncoms were returnees and those in which both the commanding officer and a majority of noncoms were men who had never served overseas. Other outfits, in which either the officer or a majority of noncoms, but not both, were returnees are classified as mixed. Since, in general, outfits with returnee noncoms were made up of returnee enlisted men and outfits with nonoverseas noncoms consisted primarily of nonoverseas men, this additional compositional factor has not been controlled, but the data may be taken as roughly contrasting the attitudes of returnees in predominantly returnee outfits with those of returnees in predominantly nonreturnee outfits. As we see from these comparisons, returnees who lived and worked in a returnee atmosphere were less likely to feel estranged from their outfits, less likely to be dissatisfied with their jobs, less critical of the treatment and deference given returnees, less hostile toward nonoverseas personnel, and less critical of their officers than returnees in predominantly nonreturnee units.

These data certainly support the conclusion that returnees felt more at home, were happier, and believed they got better breaks when they stayed among their own kind and were not subjected to dealings with superiors they belittled because of lack of overseas experience, but there remains the question of how much basis in fact there was for these subjective reactions.   Certainly, as a simple matter of logic, it would follow that in an all-returnee outfit there would be no men who had not been overseas to compete with returnees or block them from the more desirable jobs in the unit, while returnees who entered a predominantly nonreturnee outfit would find such men in most of the top positions.   It is probable that returnee officers and noncoms, who would, as returnees, share the prejudices of other returnees against men who had not been overseas, did favor returnees in assignment and promotion.

It is even possible that counterprejudices operated in the assignments made by nonreturnee officers, who were sometimes irritated with the injustices they had to do men who had done their work well in order to preserve returnees' rank.   But, objectively speaking, those returnees who were in nonreturnee outfits would often be themselves in desirable positions (for example, one such situation would be an outfit in training which had some returnee instructors), while some all-returnee outfits were simply temporary organizations (casual companies) of returnees for whom no assignments existed. In other words, the known facts do not lead simply and clearly to the conclusion that returnees in all-returnee outfits were objectively better off.

On the other hand, the returnees' subjective evaluation of the situation was shared by men who had not served overseas.   As shown in Table 29, nonreturnees in predominantly returnee outfits were, like the returnees in these outfits, more likely to feel that returnees got jobs which were worthy of their experience, that returnees were not discriminated against in favor of nonoverseas personnel, and that the United States training program was being enriched by their practical overseas experience.   In part, this agreement between returnees and nonreturnees suggests that there was

TABLE 28

EFFECT OF OUTFIT COMPOSITION* ON RETURNEE ATTITUDES,† NOVEMBER 1944

	Air Force	Infantry	Engineers	Quarter-master
Per cent who do not feel they really belong in their present outfit and are an important part of it among:				
Returnees in predominantly returnee outfits	21 *(292)*	41 *(299)*	49 *(190)*	36 *(47)*
Returnees in mixed outfits	32 *(427)*	50 *(306)*	49 *(167)*	56 *(173)*
Returnees in predominantly nonreturnee outfits	45 *(313)*	58 *(135)*	68 *(234)*	82 *(369)*
Per cent with relatively low job adjustment among:				
Returnees in predominantly returnee outfits	7	31	43	17
Returnees in mixed outfits	15	37	40	45
Returnees in predominantly nonreturnee outfits	26	41	51	66
Per cent who feel that few or no returnees get jobs that make use of their overseas experience among:				
Returnees in predominantly returnee outfits	13	44	63	60
Returnees in mixed outfits	28	49	65	72
Returnees in predominantly nonreturnee outfits	33	59	75	76
Per cent who feel that the training in the U. S. is not making use of what has been learned from overseas experience among:				
Returnees in predominantly returnee outfits	12	30	25	34
Returnees in mixed outfits	18	39	35	34
Returnees in predominantly nonreturnee outfits	28	48	40	48
Per cent who feel that enlisted men who haven't been overseas get the better jobs in their outfits among:				
Returnees in predominantly returnee outfits	13	17	35	47
Returnees in mixed outfits	42	33	48	60
Returnees in predominantly nonreturnee outfits	44	50	64	65
Per cent who feel that few or none of their officers try to look out for the welfare of enlisted men among:				
Returnees in predominantly returnee outfits	53	39	57	40
Returnees in mixed outfits	59	50	53	46
Returnees in predominantly nonreturnee outfits	65	52	59	59

some basis in fact as well as in attitude for the returnees' preference
for and greater comfort in their own outfits.   But these data may
not be taken as sure corroboration of this point, since they may be,
at least in part, simply evidence that the attitudes of returnees
affected the opinions of the nonreturnees around them as well.

Data from S-157.

Numbers in parentheses are the numbers of cases on which percentages are based.

* The outfit classification used in this table is based on a cross tabulation of two questions:

Has the C.O. of your company (battery, squadron) served overseas in this war?

_____ Yes
_____ No
_____ Don't know

About how many of the noncoms in the permanent cadre of your company (battery, squadron) have
served overseas in this war?

_____ Almost all of them have served overseas in this war
_____ About three fourths of them have
_____ About half of them have
_____ About one fourth of them have
_____ Almost none of them have
_____ I haven't been in this outfit long enough to know

Men who reported that their C.O. and half or more of their noncoms had served overseas are classified
as being in predominantly returnee outfits; men who said that their C.O. had not served overseas and
less than half of their noncoms had are classified as being in predominantly nonreturnee outfits.   Men
who weren't sure of the overseas service of their noncoms and/or C.O. were excluded from consideration,
while the remainder are classified as being in mixed outfits.

† The attitude questions summarized in this table are:

Do you feel you really belong in your company (battery, squadron) and are an important part of it?

_____ Very much so
_____ Fairly much so
___X___ Not very much
___X___ Not at all

From what you have seen or heard, do returnees get jobs that make use of their overseas experience?

_____ All of them do   ___X___ Few of them do
_____ Most of them do   ___X___ None of them do
_____ About half of them do   _____ Don't know

Do you think training here in the U. S. is now making use of what has been learned from overseas
experience?

_____ Yes, most of the training does
_____ Yes, some of the training does
___X___ No, not very much of the training does
___X___ No, none of the training does
_____ Don't know

Who have the better jobs in your outfit—enlisted men who have been overseas or those who haven't?

___X___ Enlisted men who have been overseas
_____ Enlisted men who haven't been overseas
_____ There isn't much difference
_____ I haven't been in this outfit long enough to know

How many of your present officers are the kind that always try to look out for the welfare of enlisted men?

___X___ None
___X___ Few
_____ About half
_____ Most
_____ All
_____ Don't know

The job adjustment data presented are based on an index of three questions described in the footnote
to Table 21.

TABLE 29

EFFECT OF OUTFIT COMPOSITION ON ATTITUDES OF NONRETURNEES TOWARD ISSUES
INVOLVING RETURNEES,* NOVEMBER 1944

	Air Force	Infantry	Engineers	Quarter-master
Per cent who feel that few or no re-turnees get jobs that make use of their overseas experience among:				
Nonreturnees in predominantly returnee outfits	24 *(102)*	53 *(53)*	55 *(51)*	60 *(15)*
Nonreturnees in mixed outfits	32 *(243)*	46 *(176)*	47 *(115)*	63 *(80)*
Nonreturnees in predominantly nonreturnee outfits	42 *(143)*	62 *(97)*	59 *(102)*	73 *(111)*
Per cent who feel that the training in U. S. is not making use of what has been learned from overseas experience among:				
Nonreturnees in predominantly returnee outfits	6	26	15	13
Nonreturnees in mixed outfits	9	27	17	32
Nonreturnees in predominantly nonreturnee outfits	15	30	20	32
Per cent who feel that enlisted men who haven't been overseas get the better jobs in their outfits among:				
Nonreturnees in predominantly returnee outfits	8	6	8	7
Nonreturnees in mixed outfits	8	10	13	23
Nonreturnees in predominantly nonreturnee outfits	14	18	13	18

Data from S-157.
Numbers in parentheses are the numbers of cases on which percentages are based.
* See footnotes to Table 28.

Conclusion

Here then we have the returnees, in broad outline at least. They were men who came back, after long service overseas, often in poor physical condition and emotionally disturbed, often, in fact, selected for return for just these reasons. They came back expecting consideration and recognition for their services and often felt these services were already sufficient to justify their retirement from active service. They met a reception which, in its early phases, lived up to their expectations, but the basic difficulties began when the returnees were faced with the prospect of again going through all that they had gone through before when they had been trained.

Because the Army's need of these men was in part a prediction of what man-power needs in the Pacific would prove to be (needs which never materialized) rather than an immediacy, the returnees' basic unwillingness to start out in the Army again in an almost "rookie" status—to go through a hard training period, to learn new jobs, to accept garrison discipline—was reinforced by the returnees' awareness that their presence was a burden to the Army which tried constantly, but never fully successfully, to find ways of utilizing returnees. Returnees knew that large numbers of their kind were sitting around camps where no present assignments could be found for them, they knew that training was sometimes used as a temporary solution to the lack of suitable jobs, and they suspected that their training would often not be needed in the jobs they got. The jobs made available to them, as a result of the Army's decision to protect returnees for as long as possible from completing their repetition of the Army cycle with another tour of overseas duty, were often frustrating, and, though a necessary part of maintaining a military establishment, seemed unimportant and beneath the status of a returnee. They found further sources of dissatisfaction in working under men who had not been overseas, who were by that fact, in the returnee scale of values, inferior to the returnees in experience and status. And they resented the failure to accord them privileged treatment, not only in discharges and in job assignments, but in such matters as being stationed near home, and in the relaxation for them of the normally required degree of compliance with military forms.

Both by disposition and because of the situation in which they found themselves, then, returnees were a disgruntled group. Because they had great prestige with the public and with new recruits, whose training they were often in charge of, their discontents had repercussions in a wider area than simply the returnee group itself. Perhaps the one saving feature of everything that happened to the returnees was that for most of them, nothing that happened was as bad as being overseas. By way of conclusion and to put the returnee problem in its proper perspective, let us emphasize again that, whatever their objective circumstances, only a minority of returnees ever got so completely fed up as to wish they had never come back to the United States or had returned only for a brief furlough.

CHAPTER 11

THE POINT SYSTEM FOR REDEPLOYMENT AND DISCHARGE[1]

I N PLANNING for demobilization, the Army faced a problem unprecedented in American history.

With the defeat of Germany, it would be possible to release several million soldiers. Yet prudence required the assumption that another year or more might elapse before the capitulation of Japan. The Army had to assume that the invasion of the Japanese homeland would be necessary, with a long and costly campaign of extermination similar to those on the Pacific islands. For this invasion and for the supply lines stretching around the world to it, millions of soldiers would still be required.

To keep all men in the service was both unnecessary and politically unthinkable. Some would have to be discharged. Who should these be?

There were two schools of thought. One school of thought, which had particularly strong representation in Army Ground Forces, tended to see the problem as one of preserving intact, at all cost, the combat fighting teams. This meant discharging mainly service troops, limited service men, and soldiers not yet fully trained. The combat veterans, especially the experienced noncoms, were obviously the core of our magnificent fighting machine.

Another school of thought, also arguing on the basis of military efficiency, held that the men of longest service would be so disaffected by a policy which rewarded the men who had made the least sacrifice that the morale of the combat teams would be as much endangered by retaining such men as by discharging some of them. Furthermore, they pointed out, the Army did have a large

---

[1] By Samuel A. Stouffer. The principal liaison officer representing the Research Branch in the negotiations leading to adoption of the point system was Lieutenant Colonel Lyle M. Spencer. An important part in planning the first surveys was played by John A. Clausen. The principal technical responsibility in 1944–1945 was in the hands of Louis Guttman. Shirley A. Star was chief analyst of the surveys after VE Day on attitudes toward the redeployment program.

surplus of combat veterans, hence those of longest experience probably could be released without serious detriment other than a small delay for reorganization of units. Moreover, they questioned the necessarily superior military efficiency of men who had been in combat an extremely long time.[2]

Proponents of the first point of view had an additional argument which had a special plausibility. If discharges were made on the basis of entire units, the Army would not be open to the charges of favoritism to individuals. If an individual's record were taken into account, there was too much chance of a scandal, particularly if the Army yielded to political pressure to discharge certain individuals or certain categories of individuals without respect to military need. It was admitted that the replacement system had operated so that a given unit was likely to contain personnel with a very wide range of service and that a unit discharge system would give new replacements in demobilized outfits a head start in civilian life over the combat veterans in outfits retained. But this was advanced as the lesser of two evils.

If the individual discharge system were to be adopted, the simplest formula was "first in, first out." At this point, the Research Branch entered the picture. Lieutenant Colonel Lyle M. Spencer, representing General Osborn, became the liaison officer of the Information and Education Division with the Special Planning Division of the War Department General Staff which was drawing the redeployment plans. Spencer proposed, as a result of conferences with his colleagues in the Research Branch, that the temper of the soldiers themselves be discreetly sounded out. This was authorized in the fall of 1943.

Research Behind the Point System

After some extensive pretesting in the United States, a survey was made in the United States and six overseas areas of representative cross sections of enlisted men. Over twenty thousand soldiers were included in the study. Four possible factors were explicitly considered: (1) Length of time in the Army, (2) age, (3) overseas service, (4) dependency. To determine the relative importance of these factors in the soldiers' minds, the method of paired comparisons was used. Each factor was compared with each other. The question was as follows:

---

[2] In Chapter 5 of this volume some evidence tending to confirm this point is shown. See especially Chart III.

(a) After the war when the Army starts releasing soldiers back to civilian life, which of these two groups of men do you think should be released *first?*   (Check *only one*)

     _____ Men with dependents
           or
     _____ Men over 30 years of age

(b) Which of *these* two groups of men should be released *first?*   (Check *only one*)

     _____ Men who have been in the Army longest
           or
     _____ Men with dependents

(c) Which of *these* two groups of men should be released *first?*   (Check *only one*)

     _____ Men over 30 years of age
           or
     _____ Men who have served overseas

(d) Which of *these* two groups of men should be released *first?*

     _____ Men who have served overseas
           or
     _____ Men who have been in the Army longest

(e) Which of *these* two groups of men should be released *first?*   (Check *only one*)

     _____ Men over 30 years of age
           or
     _____ Men who have been in the Army longest

(f) Which of *these* two groups of men do you think should be released *first?*   (Check *only one*)

     _____ Men with dependents
           or
     _____ Men who have served overseas

Approximately 90 per cent of the respondents were completely internally consistent in their six check marks.   To be consistent, a man had to check one of the alternatives (for example, overseas service) three times, another twice, another once, and one not at all.[3]   By cross tabulation, a table for each overseas area and the United States could be constructed, as illustrated by Table 1 for the Central Pacific.   This table, based on 5,115 consistent answers, shows that among 54 per cent of the men overseas service was first choice for determining priority of discharge, while among 38 per cent of the men dependency was first choice.   Longevity in the Army or age were negligible as first choices.   Among second choices,

---

[3] An example of an inconsistent choice would be preferring longevity to dependency, and also preferring dependency to overseas service, and preferring overseas service to longevity.

overseas service again led, with dependency and longevity tied, and with longevity decidedly preferred to age. In third choices, longevity led age, and in last choices, as was necessary from internal consistency, age was most frequent.

A summary of the first choices in the various samples is presented

TABLE 1

PRIORITY OF DEMOBILIZATION CHOICES AMONG MEN IN CENTRAL PACIFIC, MARCH 1944

(Based on 5,115 Consistent Answers)

	PERCENTAGE CHECKING A GIVEN ITEM			
	0 times	1 time	2 times	3 times
Overseas service	1	6	39	54
Dependents	11	25	26	38
Longevity in Army	26	43	26	5
Age	62	26	9	3
Total	100	100	100	100

Data from S-125.

in Table 2. This represents the proportions of men checking a given category in *all three* of the comparisons in which it appeared. The uniformity from area to area in first choices is quite notable.

It was obvious that in the minds of the men, mere length of time in the Army ranked very low in importance as compared with over-

TABLE 2

PERCENTAGE OF MEN GIVING FIRST PRIORITY TO A GIVEN FACTOR IN DEMOBILIZATION, UNITED STATES AND OVERSEAS AREAS

(Winter and Spring of 1943–1944)

	United States	ETO	Central Pacific	South Pacific	South-west Pacific	India-Burma	Alaska
Overseas service	48	47	54	56	54	48	45
Dependents	45	47	38	38	40	47	42
Longevity in Army	3	3	5	3	3	2	7
Age	4	3	3	3	3	3	6
Total	100	100	100	100	100	100	100
Number of consistent answers	*3,594*	*2,510*	*5,115*	*2,116*	*2,942*	*999*	*1,419*
Source of data	S-95	S-92	S-125	S-124	S-93	S-127	S-133
Date of study	2/44	11/43	3/44	2/44	11/43	3/44	4/44

seas service and dependency. This was true even among soldiers in the United States.

In this study men were also asked: "Do you think there is some other group of soldiers besides those listed above that should be let out of the Army first?" Men were invited to write in their free responses. Not over a third of the men did so, but it was clear that the original paired comparisons which had been pretested in the United States and not overseas had omitted one category high on the priority list of overseas soldiers. That was combat. Many of the men overseas wanted to make a distinction between men in combat and men not in combat and give priority to the former. Combat experience was first on the list of write-ins in all overseas areas except India-Burma and Alaska. Second on the write-in list was physical disability, and a very low third was type of civilian job. (Since any demobilization plan would handle medical discharges independently of other priorities, physical disability had been purposely omitted from the original list.)

After studying the data of the type summarized in Tables 1 and 2, General Osborn decided to put all of the influence of the Information and Education Division behind a system which would (a) establish priorities on an individual, not a unit, basis and (b) take into account the explicit preferences of the soldiers themselves, in so far as the latter was consistent with military necessity. In the Research Branch the idea of a simple score card and point system was developed, and Lieutenant Colonel Spencer kept in constant contact with the Special Planning Division of the War Department throughout the subsequent discussions.

On the basis of soldier preferences, the Information and Education Division recommended a point system which would take into account combat (measured by length of time in a combat zone and by number of Purple Hearts awarded), number of months of overseas service, number of children, and length of time in the Army. After lengthy discussions, the War Department accepted the outlines of this proposal (leaving to a future date the setting of the exact number of points for each category and the method of determining such a factor as "combat service"). This decision was announced to the public in September 1944. The War Department announcement said:

The simplest plan of demobilization would have been to return . . . surplus units to this country and discharge their personnel intact. Such a method, however, would operate with great unfairness to many individuals who have had long and arduous service but are not assigned to one of the units declared surplus.

If only units in Europe were considered, this basis of expediency would work unfairly to units long in the Pacific or at outpost bases in the American theater. It would operate unfairly to men who have seen extended combat in Europe and the Pacific and have been returned to this country for reassignment. It would release men only recently assigned as replacements to units long in combat and would discriminate against veterans of many campaigns in units not selected to return.

Consequently, it was determined that the fairest method of selection would be through the selection of men as individuals rather than by units, with the selection governed by thoroughly impartial standards.

For the standards, the War Department went to the soldiers themselves. Experts were sent into the field to obtain a cross section of the sentiments of enlisted men. Thousands of soldiers, both in this country and overseas, were interviewed to learn their views on the kind of selective process they believed should determine the men to be returned to civilian life. Opinions expressed by soldiers themselves became the accepted principle of the plan.[4]

Two weeks later President Roosevelt, in an address to the nation, defended the plan as one "based on the wishes of the soldiers themselves."[5] In spite of the fact that an election campaign was on and much of the press was highly critical of the administration, an OWI digest of editorial opinions on the point system showed that out of more than a hundred editorials examined, all but one or two greeted the announcement favorably, most of them with enthusiasm.

It was decided that the actual points to be assigned would not be announced until after the surrender of Germany. Between September 1944 and the defeat of Germany there followed several months in which there was much argument in the Special Planning Division as to the assignment of points. The four factors—longevity in the Army, overseas service, combat, and parenthood—had been publicly announced, but it was thought still possible by opponents of the plan to obtain the benefit of claiming soldier endorsement and still manipulate the weights so that overseas service and combat service actually would count negligibly toward total score. The Information and Education Division, always recognizing that military necessity should come first, held that either the final points must have the effect of approximating the priorities desired by the majority of soldiers or else the reasons why this was impossible in terms of military necessity should be frankly admitted by the Army.

To provide more specific basis than the earlier studies afforded for estimating relative weights, the Research Branch had undertaken

---

[4] *New York Times*, September 7, 1944.
[5] *New York Times*, September 24, 1944.

another world-wide survey in August 1944.[6] This study, unlike the previous one, included combat service as an explicit category. As will be evident, combat service was high on the priority list, and length of time in the Army was very low.   Table 3 shows the distribution of responses to two simple check lists.   The questions were introduced as follows (cont. on page 527):

TABLE 3

PREFERRED PRIORITY OF DISCHARGE AMONG ENLISTED MEN QUERIED IN
AUGUST 1944

	PERCENTAGE SAYING INDICATED GROUP SHOULD BE DISCHARGED FIRST:			
	Overseas combat men	*Overseas noncombat men*	*United States men*	*World (weighted average by estimated strength)*
Men who have seen the most combat	55	36	23	30
Married men with children	18	23	33	29
Men who have been overseas longest	14	22	17	17
Men who have been in Army longest	4	6	7	6
Men over 35	3	5	7	7
Key men for getting civilian industry running	3	5	9	7
Others (what)	3	3	4	4
	100	100	100	100
Number of cases	*1,644*	*1,970*	*2,462*	*6,076*

	PERCENTAGE SAYING INDICATED GROUP SHOULD BE DISCHARGED LAST:			
Men who have been in Army shortest time, whether they have been overseas or not	29	32	27	28
Men who have not been overseas, no matter how long they have been in the Army	46	29	8	21
Men who are not married	7	10	19	16
Men under 25	6	14	21	15
None of these groups	10	13	23	18
Some others	2	2	2	2
	100	100	100	100

Data from S-145.

[6] In the August 1944 survey, comprising a sample of 6,273 men, Air Force men were not included, since at that time the plans were to use a different system of discharge in the Air Forces.   The field work was completed before the War Department announcement of the point system in September.

The War Department would like enlisted men's opinions on who should get out of the Army first after the war. Those men physically disabled from combat or disease will of course be let out first. But after that group, who should be picked?

Suppose that just one thing could be considered in deciding who should be let out of the Army first. Which *one* of these groups should be let out first? (Check list shown in Table 3.) Which *one* of the following groups should be let out *last?* (Check list shown in Table 3.)

Combat led the list, as shown in Table 3, with 30 per cent first preferences, with married men with children a close second. Very few (only 6 per cent) would give first preference to men in the Army longest, but 28 per cent thought that men in the Army the shortest time should be let out last.

Table 3 shows also that preferences were related, as perhaps would be expected, to the respondent's own characteristics. The preferences as to first discharges expressed by men in the United States, when tabulated by specific categories, further illustrate this point:

Percentage saying married men with children should be let out first, among:

Married men with children	60%
Married men without children	37
Single men	24

Percentage saying men who have been in the Army longest should be let out first, among:

Men in Army over 3 years	21%
Men in Army 2 to 3 years	9
Men in Army 1 to 2 years	4
Men in Army under 1 year	2

Percentage saying men over 35 should be let out first, among:

Men 35 and over	35%
Men 30 to 34	11
Men 20 to 29	2
Men under 20	4

Data like these (and similar results had been found in the surveys made the previous winter and spring) made it obvious that no point system could satisfy every soldier. The concern of the Information and Education Division was, of course, that any system of points adopted for weighting the announced four factors of combat, over-seas service, parenthood, and longevity in the Army be designed to minimize, not eliminate, feelings of injustice.

In the August 1944 survey a more elaborate system of paired comparisons was used than in the earlier survey. Ten questions were introduced as follows:

Below we want you to pick one man out of each group of three men. Check the one you think should be let out first. Read each question carefully, then put a check mark in front of the man you pick to get out first.

A sample question was the following:

Here are three men of the same age, all overseas the same length of time— check the one you would want to have let out first.

_____ A single man, through two campaigns of combat
_____ A married man, with no children, through one campaign of combat
_____ A married man with 2 children, not in combat

Relatively few men checked the middle category on any of the ten questions; hence, the analysis was confined to a comparison of the responses of those checking the extremes. The theory behind the tabulation was that if approximately the same number of men endorsed each of the extreme categories, the two categories could be said to have about equal weight in the minds of the men. For example, among men checking extreme categories in the illustrative example, 45 per cent voted for the single man, through two campaigns of combat, while 55 per cent voted for the married man with two children, not in combat. Hence, it would seem that the weights adopted would minimize dissatisfaction if two campaigns of combat counted about the same as two children, or only a little less.

A high degree of internal consistency on such intricate hypothetical choices was hardly to be expected. For example, comparing men of the same age and longevity in the Army, 52 per cent of the men rated 18 months overseas as more important than two children in determining priorities, whereas 60 per cent of the men rated two campaigns as worth more than 18 months overseas. In spite of the fact that the direct question gave two children a slight edge over two campaigns, the two indirect questions indicated a reverse preference.

In general, however, the differences were of such an order that it was possible to reconcile them fairly well, and the information was of crucial importance, especially to counteract staff pressures to reduce overseas and combat credit almost to the vanishing point.[7]

---

[7] A mathematical formula to reconcile the discrepancies, such as illustrated above, was worked out by Louis Guttman and subsequently published. See Louis Guttman, "An Approach for Quantifying Paired Comparisons and Rank Order," *Annals of Mathematical Statistics*, XVII, No. 2 (June 1946), 144–63.

When the Special Planning Division, taking into account military necessity as interpreted by the combat arms, adopted a tentative set of weights for the four factors, it was found by the Research Branch that this set of weights gave disproportionately large credit for sheer longevity in the Army and for parenthood, as compared with the August 1944 expression by the men. A special computation was made for a representative sample of enlisted men whose characteristics were known, and it was found that the correlation was quite high between the total scores assigned by this tentative system of weights and the total scores assigned by a system of weights more closely approximating the expressed wishes of the men. In fact, among the 20 per cent of men with the highest scores by *either* system of calculation, 90 per cent had the highest scores in *both* systems. One reason for this close correspondence was the fact that men longest in the Army tended also to come in for the greatest overseas credit. The Information and Education Division therefore endorsed the tentative scale of points, with minor modifications, and this was the scale announced after VE Day, namely:

Length of time in the Army	1 point per month
Length of time overseas	1 point per month
Combat	5 points per campaign star or combat decoration, including Purple Heart
Parenthood	12 points per child under 18, up to three

It was anticipated that the most serious weakness in the system would be the credit for combat, not only because of its inadequacy in total points but also because of the method by which it would be determined.

Serious study was given to alternative methods of determining combat. The fairest method, perhaps—length of time in combat, which was proposed by the Information and Education Division— was deemed impracticable because of the inadequacy of records and because of the real difficulty of defining "in combat." The method adopted, based on campaign stars, was recognized as unfair to combat men since many noncombatants were awarded these stars also, but the Special Planning Division decided that this was the only practicable procedure which also had the virtue of simplicity and objectivity.

To increase the combat credit, it was decided also to give 5 points for each decoration received, including the Purple Heart for wounds. This decision, made at a time when it was thought that the Air

Forces would be discharged on a different basis from the rest of the Army, was to lead eventually to some feelings of injustice. When Air Forces were blanketed in under a uniform point system, the numerous decorations of flying personnel gave these men priorities which were particularly to be resented by veterans of ground combat.

In view of the mounting hostility to the Army among enlisted men (documented in Volume I, Chapter 5) and in view of the widespread cynicism about Army promises, the Research Branch awaited VE Day with considerable misgivings. Careful plans were laid to study the actual workings of the point system in the Army after it went into effect, in order to inform the War Department of ways in which the redeployment program was miscarrying, if that should be the case. It was important to know (a) how well the Army was keeping its promises in the field and if not, why not, and (b) what modifications would be needed in the point system upon the defeat of Japan, which was not expected to transpire for a year after the defeat of Germany.

Initial Reactions to the Point System

Promptly after VE Day, the Army released throughout the world a motion-picture film describing the redeployment plan and the point system. The first reaction which the War Department received was telephone calls and letters from members of Congress asking that the point system be changed to let out men over 30 or men in the United States with long service or other categories in which the sons of some importunate constituents fell. To this, the War Department replied firmly, taking the position that while no system would please everybody, the soldiers as a whole would resent modifications giving preference to certain groups, especially men who had not seen overseas service. The correctness of this stand was soon to be justified when the Research Branch completed a poll, made in early June 1945, of a representative cross section of soldiers throughout the world.

In spite of skepticism about Army promises, the reaction of soldiers to the fairness of the point system was decidedly favorable. Seldom in the entire experience of the Research Branch had such a vote of confidence been given to an Army policy.

Sixty-nine per cent said the plan was "very good" or "fairly good," 5 per cent replied they "did not know enough about it to say," 17 per cent said it was "not so good," and only 9 per cent said it was "not good at all." [8] When the point scale was announced after VE Day, it was also stated that 85 points had been adopted as an arbitrary cutting point and that men with 85 points or over would be the first to be relieved from active duty. Such men in America (except for a limited number in scarce categories) would be discharged as soon as possible, those in the Pacific would be brought home as soon as replacements were made available, and those in Europe would be redeployed to special units which would not come home immediately but would follow the units to be transferred from Europe to the Pacific.

Chart I shows the responses of various classes of enlisted men, as of early June 1945. As would be expected, the men with 85 points or over were the most favorable, while taken as a whole the men with 30 to 59 points were least favorable. Even among this group, however, 65 per cent said the point system was "good" or "fairly good."

As had been feared, the greatest opposition to the point system was among the combat men, many of whom felt that the method of computing combat credit did not give them sufficient advantage over noncombat men in the same theater. Among men who had been in combat but had acquired less than 30 points, 43 per cent said that the point system was "not so good" or "not good at all." Only 18 per cent of the men with less than 30 points who had not been overseas made this response. In free comments the combat men expressed themselves with considerable affect. Such a result had been anticipated. In ETO, for example, the average field force combat veteran had 3 campaign stars, no more than the average field force veteran who had not seen combat (the latter had been overseas longer, on the average). Even the average comzone man in the rear areas in ETO had 2 campaign stars. Consequently, the more campaigns the combat veteran had been through, the more critical he was of the point system; whereas, the more campaign stars the noncombat soldier had, the less critical he was. The percentages saying the point system was "not so good" or "not good at all" among combat and noncombat men in ETO, equated for number of points for "combat" credit, were as follows (p. 533):

---

[8] A scale and intensity analysis using the methods illustrated in Volume I, Chapter 5, and described in detail in Volume IV, showed that there was little intensity of feeling among the opposition and strong intensity of feeling among those favorable.

CHART I

ATTITUDES TOWARD THE POINT SYSTEM
(World-wide Cross Section of Enlisted Men, June 1945)

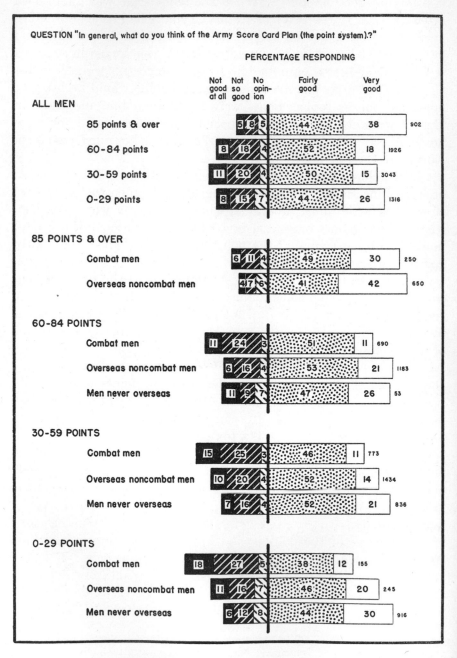

QUESTION "In general, what do you think of the Army Score Card Plan (the point system)?"

PERCENTAGE RESPONDING

Data from S-205. "Combat men" and "overseas noncombat men" comprise men overseas and returnees from overseas.

The numbers following the bars are the numbers of cases on which percentages are based.

	Combat men	Noncombat men
25 points	53%	14%
20 points	45	28
15 points	42	23
10 points	41	26
5 points	30	32
No combat credit	—	40

Among the combat veterans in the world-wide cross section there was a sharp difference in attitudes as between Air Force veterans and Ground Force veterans. Among the former, whose point scores were inflated by numerous decorations, a third had 85 points or over, while among the latter only a ninth had 85 points or over. It is not surprising, therefore, to find that among Air Force combat men only 11 per cent thought the point system "not so good" or "not good at all" as compared with 37 per cent among Ground Force combat men as a whole.

By and large, the unfavorable responses among men in any category were in the minority. Table 4 compares responses by marital

TABLE 4

PERCENTAGES OF MEN, BY AGE AND MARITAL CONDITION, WHO SAID THE
POINT SYSTEM WAS "NOT SO GOOD" OR "NOT GOOD AT ALL"
(World-wide Cross Section, June 1945)

| | | | POINT SCORE | | |
	0–29	30–59	60–84	85 & over	Total
Percentages					
All men	23	31	26	13	26
Fathers	19	26	21	9	22
Married, no children	28	35	29	16	30
Single	22	31	24	14	25
30 and over	31	35	25	14	29
25 to 29	21	28	27	11	24
Under 25	20	30	25	15	22
Number of cases					
All men	1,316	3,043	1,926	902	7,187
Fathers	207	686	377	191	1,461
Married, no children	238	660	382	155	1,435
Single	870	1,697	1,167	557	4,291
30 and over	215	817	537	244	1,813
25 to 29	211	808	756	402	2,177
Under 25	874	1,375	604	234	3,087

Data from S-205.

condition and age.　As would be expected, fathers were most favorable.　Married men without children tended to be more critical than single men.　Older men tended to be somewhat more critical than younger men.　There were no overall significant differences in response by length of time in the Army.　Negroes tended to be somewhat less favorable than whites, but only slightly more unfavorable (27 per cent as against 25 per cent), the main difference by race being the larger number of Negroes in the "no opinion" category (10 per cent as against 4 per cent).

At once, the Research Branch addressed itself to the task of studying the attitudes of soldiers toward the actual redeployment and demobilization process.　It was recognized that unless the Army machinery operated reasonably smoothly, the Army's publicity both to the soldiers and the civilian public could boomerang sharply.

Attitudes Toward Early Stages of the Actual Demobilization Process

In mid July 1945 a survey was made in the United States of a cross section of enlisted men with 85 points or more and of company grade officers in units which had such enlisted men.　On July 31, 1945, a report of this survey was given to the General Staff and the Secretary of War.

The summary of this report[9] read as follows:

ATTITUDES TOWARD DEMOBILIZATION OPERATIONS

(Survey of attitudes of U. S. enlisted men with at
least 85 points, supplemented by data secured
from their company grade officers)

Soldiers with 85 points or more, stationed in continental U. S., constitute a special morale problem.

However small numerically this group of men may be, compared with worldwide Army strength, it is a "visible" and important group, mostly veterans of overseas combat.　Attitudes of the American people toward the Army's good faith in carrying out the demobilization plan, which had such a favorable initial reception, will be determined to a considerable extent by what they hear in letters, press comments, and congressional hearings about these particular soldiers.　Furthermore, the rest of the soldiers in the Army also will judge the Army's good faith by its works, and Army morale will rise or fall depending on that judgment.

Main Findings

Although *four out of five* enlisted men in the U. S. with over 85 points think the point system is a good plan, *two out of three*—surveyed in late July 1945—think the Army is not carrying it out well.

---
[9] Report B-164 based on S-218 and S-219.

Nearly half of the men think the Army's way of deciding *when* a man with enough points for discharge can be released is "not fair at all" or "not so fair." They are particularly critical of the method used by local commanders of determining "essentiality." Two fifths of them have Army assignments which they say "hardly seem important at all" and a fourth say they are not kept busy.

58% of the high-point men in AAF and 33% of them in AGF and ASF say that their officers have *not told them anything* about why they are not being separated faster.

Only 7% in AAF and 13% in AGF and ASF have been given a reason for delay which they accept as justifiable.

On the good side of the ledger is the fact that criticism of favoritism or partiality on the part of unit commanders is almost nonexistent.

Company grade officers of the units containing one or more men with at least 85 points when queried tend to admit that they themselves do not know what the story is or tend to be critical of current policies. Half of the officers think shortage of replacements is a factor, and a fourth of the officers think "no real effort is being made" to get replacements. A fourth of the officers also think that discharge of 85 point men is being delayed "because unit commanders are trying to hold their good men." In free comments, officers are particularly critical of alleged lack of clear statement of policies and alleged local abuses of "essentiality."

Actually, the Army is ahead of schedule in its release of men above the critical score. And some confusion and error is to be expected in the initial months of the operation of any new program. However, this report underlines the need for immediate staff study of procedures for improving the present machinery, with the objectives of:

1. Clarifying and coordinating the directives issued at various echelons, from the top down.

2. Eliminating the basis for allegations as to waste of man power and abuse of "essentiality."

3. Informing officers at the unit level exactly what the facts are as they apply to men in their units.

4. Insuring that at the earliest opportunity, every enlisted man with 85 points or over has a personal interview with his commanding officer, following a careful study of his case by that officer.

In addition to numerous statistical tables documenting the conclusions in the summary, the text of the report contained free comments written by men with 85 points and over.

A sample of these comments reveals something of the flavor of the reactions of these men who were disgruntled:

Letting men out of the Army after VE Day has become a joke. The Army let a lot of men out at first just to keep their word with the American people. Why let men get out as soon as they hit the States with 95 points when some of us got back four months ago, have 95–115 points and still can't get out?

I thought the point system was very good prior to May 12. Since my discharge was turned down I am completely disgusted with the Army. Any rookie that can type poorly can replace me. What does the word essential mean? As I said before, I know a lot who are called essential here that could be replaced by unexperienced men. Why hold us? I've been overseas 39 months, then I get a dirty deal like this.

The point system is near to perfect if it were worked right as possible. Most of the eligible men in this unit are ex-infantrymen who were returned to U. S. on rotation a few months ago. Is it reasonable that these men be held as "essential" while men with no more points and possibly less points are being released? It's pretty damned rough to sit and watch men who came into the Army after you were overseas walking out to go to the Separation Center, especially Air Forces.

My officers say they haven't been authorized to release anyone. I think somebody is pulling a fast one. There are 30 men in my Co. all of whom have over 100 points and no effort has been made to release any of them.

Ground Force men transferred to the Air Corps are stuck. We just sit here and watch men with air medals, clusters, etc., get out with only 6 months to a year service. I have been overseas 3 years with 92 points. If the critical score is 85, why am I here? Why am I kept in the dark? Isn't 3 years and combat enough?

The point system is fine but the "essential" business sure knocks the heck out of it. A lot of us are stuck. Any 15-year-old could do what I'm doing and learn it in 2 or 3 days. I have plenty of points but am classified essential and held. Certainly something should be done about men being called essential.

My MOS keeps me in but most of us here with 85 points or over aren't doing a damn thing except waiting to get out. I don't intend to do a damn thing for the Army, for I am convinced my job is not important enough to warrant my being held over.

To be truthful about it, I don't think anybody knows anything in this field. Officers and all. And they don't care who gets what.

I've been replaced six weeks ago and the other day I was interviewed to be reassigned again. For some unknown reason this camp doesn't like to release men. When you do try to find the reason you run up against a stone wall.

There seems to be a lack of knowledge or cooperation in higher Hq. somewhere. The Army should either say that all men with 85 points will get out or raise the level higher.

The point system is a fair system, but every unit has a different way of working it. I think every unit should be forced to adhere to a hard and fast rule in discharging men.

It seems as though us guys that came back a few months before the point system went into effect and we were reassigned here in the States, are just a forgotten group.

All any soldier knows is what he reads in papers and hears on radios. So I have to believe the separation centers are too crowded at the present time. But that can continue indefinitely.

Too much stress is being placed on MOS titles. Classifications are made to fit the TO not the actual duty assignments.

I think it's unfair the way they are discharging men. I know we're nonessential because we're at a field where they train men in the same category I'm in and I've always noticed an excess of radio operators all the time. It seems unfair to me that on some posts they discharge them with just a little over the critical score and then in other places you got to have the highest points.

I have 92 points and have just been laying on my ass for three months doing nothing.

I think things stink as far as this Service Command is concerned. In plain words, I think we are taking a general fucking because other service commands let men out. But what can we small people do about it?

The officers in my company are not interested in whether men with critical scores get out or not.

If the C.O. of a field would give some definite information that could be depended upon. Nothing definite in 4 months has been told us. No one to talk to that would give us information.

This field don't give a damn what happens to us. We have 119 returnees doing details as ACU men, with at least 75% of them having 120 points and over. I'll be damned if that's fair. The point system still is a good idea but there should be an investigation at certain fields to see how they are running it. I have 147 points. Men on this field with 80 to 90 points have been discharged. Yet other men with 125 points and over can't even get a civil answer as to why we can't get discharged.

I'm stuck because of the Army's lack of foresight in not setting up a sufficient number of separation centers to facilitate the discharge of those men eligible.

Frankly we are being held just to give goldbricking officers a job which keeps them from going overseas.

A lot of fellows with even more points than myself deserve to be let out before me, but at least they could let me do some kind of work that I would be interested in and want to do.

Some places have discharged practically all men with 85 points or more, whereas this place has discharged virtually no men at all. I don't know what to think.

You have to have at least 115 points to get out of the Army at this post.

Separation centers seem to have been caught with their pants down. Should have been avoided, with proper planning.

Why aren't we told what we can expect? Getting information about what is going to happen is just about impossible. The result is: A person eligible for discharge is under such a strain he isn't worth much to himself or the Army.

The "essential list" is all fouled up. I have 102 points. I have been a radio operator for 10 years and I am assigned to a carpenter shop where the main product is fly traps for the mess halls. Of course, not being a carpenter, I do not actually construct the traps. I read newspapers or magazines 9/10 of the time and sweep the floor the remaining 1/10.

One of the basic reasons for establishing the point system was to reduce to a minimum the possibilities of favoritism operating at any stage in the pipe line for release. It is interesting to note that, in spite of the bitterness which many of the 85 point men felt about the *delay* in getting out, the charge of *favoritism* was almost non-existent.

The following question was asked the men:

If in your company (battery, squadron) some men with at least 85 points were released and some men were kept in, how was it done? What *one thing* do you think was most important in deciding who got out and who stayed in?

The percentage checking each response category was as follows:

None have been released	40%
They let out the men with the very highest point scores	24
They let out some men but we don't know how they chose them	15
They let out the men in the least important jobs	9
They let out the men they could get replacements for	5
They let out the men the officers wanted to get rid of	1
They let out the men who were special favorites of the officers	1
Miscellaneous and no answer	5
	100%

Some of the delay was undoubtedly inevitable. It could not be expected that a vast machine like the Army could execute a demobilization operation with anything like the speed and smoothness desired by those entitled to get out and straining at the leash. The responses of company grade officers in units having men with 85 points and over pointed out many of the problems and gave those charged with administration of the program information about specific aspects of the job which needed attention at the top—not the least of which was clarification of purpose for the benefit of the junior officers themselves.

did not contain questions which could serve as indexes of trends in soldier opinion revealing shifts toward or away from German ideology. However, it is of interest to note that a survey of a cross section of men stationed in Germany in September 1945 (N = 1,700),[11] did show a substantial number of men who admitted holding opinions in accord with the German point of view on a number of significant items. Some of the findings were reported in the press during the latter part of January and early February of 1946. The more striking of the findings released at that time are listed here.

51% of the men thought that, although Hitler was wrong in leading the Germans into war, he did do Germany a lot of good before the war.

24% thought the Germans had a very good or fairly good argument when they said that since Germany was the most efficient country in Europe, she had the right to be the controlling influence in Europe.

22% thought the Germans had some good reasons "for being down on the Jews." An additional 10 per cent were undecided.

20% thought there was some truth in the argument that the Germans had to go to war sooner or later because they needed more land to raise enough food to feed themselves. An additional 11 per cent were undecided.

19% thought that Germany had "a good deal" or "some" justification for starting the war. An additional 11 per cent were undecided.

The data presented earlier which showed a shift to more favorable attitudes toward the Germans suggest that there may have been a positive trend in the opinions found in the September survey. However it would be necessary to have repeated surveys using the same questions put to comparable groups of men before we could determine the existence of any trend.

In addition to its regular wartime information and propaganda efforts to orient the soldiers as to the nature of the enemy, the Army made a special effort to prepare the men for their proper conduct in Germany. The peak of this effort was just about the time of the Armistice. All the various media were utilized to convince the soldier of the necessity for humane but firm and distant conduct in his dealings with the German civilians, and of the danger both immediate and long range in being "taken in" by the Germans and in becoming familiar and friendly in his relations with them. In

[11] S-237.

addition, the men were warned of penalties in store for those who violated regulations against fraternization.

Unfortunately there are no systematic studies of the effectiveness of the antifraternization program as such. We do not know how much it restrained the soldiers' actions in this respect. However, to judge from the findings of surveys and from reported difficulties of enforcement, it does not appear to have been very effective.

One difficulty perhaps was the fact that the approach was almost entirely negative. There was a distinct lack of an attempt to outline in positive terms the mission of the Army in its occupation functions, of the broad significance of this mission, and of what this meant for the conduct of each man in the job of occupation.

While the Army information and orientation efforts contained little in the way of outlining an occupation policy and program, there was a considerable amount of discussion in the news about proposals such as the Morganthau Plan. It is interesting that the tough peace policy attitudes of the men showed the least change of any of the attitudes with respect to Germans and Germany which were studied.

Throughout the analysis of the data in April and August, attention was given to determining what differences, if any, existed in the attitudes of different groups of men. It is interesting to note that few differences were found and they were so slight that they were unimportant. Men with combat experience were slightly less inclined to express attitudes of hatred and dislike toward Germans and slightly more inclined to fraternize than noncombat men. Otherwise their attitudes were similar to those of other men. The men with high school and college training were slightly more inclined to have definite opinions favoring a firm policy of control of Germany than were the less educated men. Neither age nor length of time overseas showed any significant relationship to any of the attitudes toward Germans.

Summary of Findings on Shifts in Attitudes Toward the Germans

It seems fair to conclude that during the four months following VE Day American soldiers showed a tendency to lose much of the relatively moderate amount of antipathy they bore toward the Germans and to show an increase in favorable attitudes toward them. They showed a tendency increasingly to violate the regulations forbidding personal contact. As time went on, the amount of such contacts increased. With increasing contacts there was a correlated increase in the proportion of favorable attitudes toward Germans. There is some evidence that a substantial number of the men entertained opinions that accorded with the German point of view, although the existence of a trend in this respect is not known from present information.

On the other hand, in their thinking about Germany as an abstract national symbol of force and about what should be a general policy with respect to her, the men showed practically no change in their overwhelming support for a tough policy. This is not inconsistent with American behavior in other situations in which attitudes toward people in personal relations are divorced from and very different from attitudes toward the same people as members of certain groups or institutions (Catholics, Labor, Big Business, etc.). Nor is it inconsistent with what appears to be a growing tendency to regard massive social forces as independent of the wills and purposes of individual persons.

PART 2.   Attitudes Toward Our Allies

When the Research Branch was making its forecasts in the summer of 1944, it was anticipated that following the cessation of hostilities with Germany our soldiers would show an increase in negative, hostile attitudes toward our major Allies. The basis for such a prediction was the assumption that tensions had accumulated but were suppressed during the struggle against the common enemy only to come to the surface after his defeat. Tendencies to blame England for involving us in the war, and accusations that she let us bear the brunt of the tough fighting and that she was not sincere in wanting a just and permanent peace, were anticipated. Increasing suspicion as to Russian good faith and hostility toward her were also expected. In liberated countries (e.g., France), friction with and ill will toward the people and resentments over alleged exploitation of Americans by the citizens were expected to increase sharply.

The present section will summarize the available evidence on changes in attitudes toward our English, Russian, and French Allies.

Attitudes Toward the English and Russians

Surveys of American troops at home and in Europe at intervals throughout the war showed that for the most part a substantial majority of our soldiers entertained a favorable attitude toward the English and the Russian people and maintained a rather high level

CHART V

OPINIONS ABOUT OUR BRITISH AND RUSSIAN ALLIES

(Responses of Soldiers in Europe, April and August 1945, Compared with Responses of Soldiers in the United States, July 1943)

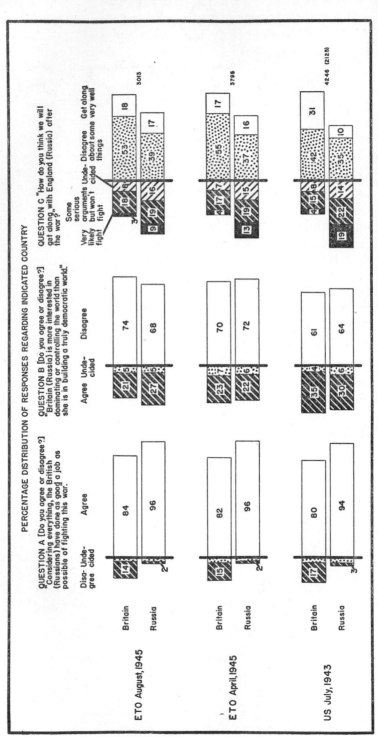

PERCENTAGE DISTRIBUTION OF RESPONSES REGARDING INDICATED COUNTRY

QUESTION A [Do you agree or disagree?] "Considering everything, the British (Russians) have done as good a job as possible of fighting this war."

QUESTION B [Do you agree or disagree?] "Britain (Russia) is more interested in dominating or controlling the world than she is in building a truly democratic world."

QUESTION C "How do you think we will get along with England (Russia) after the war?"

Data for ETO from S-235 and S-223; for the United States, Questions A and B from S-64 and Question C from S-63E. In the United States survey, the wording for Question A was, "The English (Russians) are doing as good a job as possible of fighting this war, considering everything."

of confidence in their war effort.[12]   In general there were slightly greater admiration for, and confidence in the war effort of, the Russians than the English, while the postwar intentions of the English and our future relations with them were viewed with somewhat more confidence than was the case with the Russians.

Our special interest, in this chapter, is to determine whether or not there were large and significant shifts in these attitudes after the end of the combat period in Europe.   As Chart V shows, the shifts were small.

An additional question calling for an expression of a generally favorable or unfavorable opinion was asked about the English people, but unfortunately not about the Russian people in the cross-section surveys reported here.   Hence no comparisons can be made except for a special survey made of a cross section of troops stationed in Berlin in which the same question was asked about English, Russian, French, and German people.   These results are presented below.   But first it may be noted that the replies from various cross sections in ETO[13] to the question, "What sort of an opinion do you have of the English people?" showed a uniformly favorable attitude. No significant change appeared during the four months following VE Day.

	Number of cases	Percentage of men holding "very favorable" or "fairly favorable" opinion of the English people
November 1943	3,002	73
January 1944	2,754	74
April 1945	3,795	72
August 1945	3,013	75

Some idea of the probable relative position of the Russians, had the question been put to the cross sections, is found in the replies on the survey of a cross section of the troops stationed in Berlin, August 1945 (N = 700).[14]   The same question as that quoted above was asked for each national group reported below:

---

[12] United States troops in the Middle Eastern theater who were in rather constant contact with British troops for an extended period showed a somewhat different picture. When they were surveyed in the late autumn of 1943, their preponderant attitudes were those of dislike and antagonism.   They did, however, express admiration for and confidence in the British war effort.   Their attitudes toward the Russian soldiers, as people, some of whom they had met in Teheran and other places, were rather more favorable than toward the British.

[13] S-92, S-116, S-223, and S-235.

[14] S-237B.

	Percentage of men holding "very favorable" or "fairly favorable" opinion
Of the British people	85
Of the Russian people	61
Of the German people	59
Of the French people	42

In general, it can be said that there was no significant change in attitudes toward our English and Russian Allies during the four-month period immediately following the German surrender. To this extent the predictions were not borne out. It should be added, however, that the data cover a short time period. That exposure to contact and to postwar disputes may have lessened respect for the Russians is suggested by the fact that the Berlin sample showed considerably more skepticism about getting along with Russia after the war than did the August total cross section.

Attitudes Toward the French

In the case of the French, our predictions of an increase in negative reactions were borne out. The responses to questions about the French people in April were favorable in about the same proportions as were the responses about the English. However, by August the proportion reporting favorable reactions to the French was, as we saw in Chart III, even less than the proportion who said they had favorable opinions of the German people.

Chart VI shows a generally sharp decline in favorableness of opinion about the French in the August as compared with the April survey. These findings raise the question of why the predictions were in error with respect to the English and Russians and correct with respect to the French. In the absence of any adequate statistical data to answer such questions, we can only conjecture what the answers might be.

In the first place, the information and orientation programs designed to foster favorable attitudes toward our Allies were directed largely at attitudes toward the British and the Russians throughout most of the war. Tests of the impact of various parts of these programs showed that they had small but slightly positive effects. News of the English and Russian war effort naturally bulked larger and was more impressive than what could be reported about French efforts under German occupation. There were no special post VE Day programs to encourage favorable attitudes toward the Allies

CHART VI

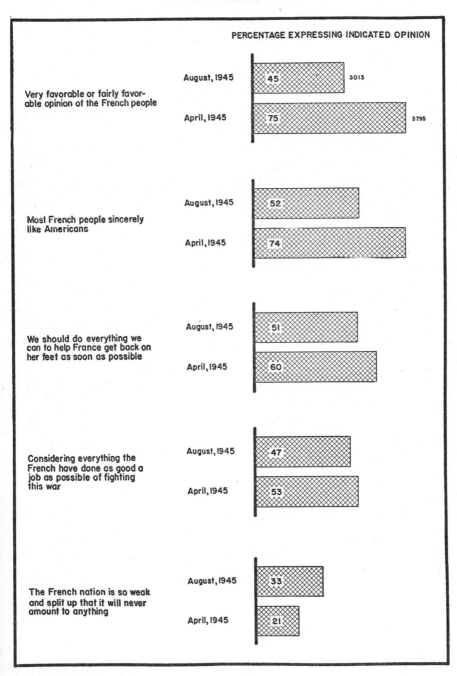

Data from S-235 and S-223.
The numbers following the bars are the numbers of cases on which percentages are based.

except for a small effort with respect to the French. Somewhat tardily the Army published a booklet designed to answer "gripes" about the French. Due to the curtailment of Research Branch personnel and facilities after VJ Day, no test was made of the impact of this material. It is very unlikely that it had much effect, since it came very late and was probably not widely distributed or used.

In the second place, it is quite possible that had more careful attention been given, when making the predictions, to such factors as immediacy of contact, discrepancy between expected response and actual response, and strength or weakness of the potential target, all operating in conjunction, we should have come nearer expecting what did happen. In concrete terms, this would have meant that more attention would have been given to the fact that contacts with the French were going to be of a more immediate and recent character than those with the British or the Russians. Moreover, it would have been important to recognize that this closer, more recent contact would be experienced in a situation in which expectations of being treated like a guest and a liberator were frustrated in actuality because of French inability and indisposition. Also, the alleged sharpness of the French in business dealings and their alleged uncleanliness would often stand in contrast to unexpected German deference and friendliness, as well as German cleanliness.

France as a symbol was weak, defeated, inadequate, and, in spite of all rational explanations of her defeat, anything but admirable. With these considerations in mind, it is not hard to see why, if negative hostile attitudes toward "Allies" emerged, the French would be the most likely target. The probabilities of such an occurrence would have been even more evident had sufficient weight been given in the prediction to the effect of World War I attitudes brought back by the veterans of 1917–1918.

Finally, we need to take the time factor into account. The predictions were not limited to a four-month period after the fighting was over, and a later survey may have shown some decline in favorable attitudes toward the English or Russians or both, particularly after more exposure to the news of diplomatic wrangling which characterized our later relations.

PART 3. Attitudes Toward the Army
and Further Service

It was predicted that with the end of the fighting in Europe there would be a rapid loss of motivation for further service and an in-

crease in preoccupation with individualistic concerns accompanied
by a rise in resentments and negative attitudes toward the Army.
Under these conditions morale would deteriorate and discipline
would become a serious problem.   The available evidence on these
reactions seems to bear out the predictions reasonably well.

As already shown in Chart I, the period following VE Day was
marked by a sharp increase of feeling among the men that they had
done their share in the war and should be sent home and discharged.
This trend characterized men of relatively short terms of service
overseas as well as those who had seen a great deal of overseas service.   These attitudes increased notwithstanding the fact that an
overwhelming majority favored a tough peace policy which would
require many troops to supervise and implement.

Those observers who were in Europe during the summer of 1945
were impressed with the intense, singleminded preoccupation of the
troops with the question of how soon they could get home and back
to civilian life.   Their impatience soon began to manifest itself in
criticisms of the redeployment system for establishing priorities for
shipment home and discharge.   The point system, described in the
preceding chapter, was based on what the men themselves had said
were the proper factors to take into account in establishing priorities.   When the plan was announced it had received the approval
of a large majority.   In ETO the percentage who said the point system was "very good" or "fairly good" dropped from 67 per cent in
May 1945 and 66 per cent in late July to 54 per cent in late August
after the defeat of Japan; although further cross tabulation shows
that the shift was related, not so much to criticism of the fairness of
the point system as such, as to the alleged slowness of the Army in
getting the troops home.   The point system, of course, merely established the priority of discharge, not the rate of discharge.

The marked loss of motivation for further service and lowered interest in what was involved in completing the job was shown further
in the reactions of the men toward the post VE Day information and
orientation program.   Interviews with officers and men and observations during June, July, and August in the various assembly areas
and staging areas all resulted in the same general reports, namely,
that it was extremely difficult to interest the men in any kind of discussions, lectures, or other information materials except those dealing with demobilization, aids and opportunities for returning veterans, and problems of readjustment to civilian life.   Even among
those units who were officially informed that they were classified as

units to be redeployed to the Pacific, there was little or no interest before VJ Day in discussing the situations and problems they would confront in the Orient.   Men in such units were constantly discussing their chances of being reclassified as a unit and sent to the United States or of getting transferred out of the unit and placed in one slated for the trip home.   This general attitude showed itself well before the atomic bomb was dropped on Hiroshima and was merely intensified during and after the period of the Japanese collapse.

It should be noted that the personal concerns were almost exclusively centered around "getting out."   They did not go beyond, into increased worries about personal problems to be faced after discharge.   These longer-range considerations will be discussed in the next chapter.   The aim here is merely to point out the important shift of motivation and interest from the collective job to be done to the individual problem of how to get home and out of the Army.

As might be expected, the shift noted above was accompanied by an appreciable increase in feelings of dissatisfaction and resentment toward the Army and of having a raw deal from the Army.   Chart VII shows this trend during the four months following VE Day.   It is clear that attitudes regarded as favorable toward the Army as well as important to good morale and discipline deteriorated appreciably during the period studied.   The progressive deterioration of morale and discipline is further evidenced by news reports of mass meetings, demonstrations, appeals to Congress and the like which reached their peak in January 1946.[15]

One of the more important general preventive actions proposed in the 1944 memorandum was an intensive information and orientation program emphasizing that the defeat of Germany, while a long stride ahead, was not the end of the war; that there was a well-prepared and fair plan for demobilization; and that demobilization would at best be very slow until after the defeat of Japan.   Considerable effort was made in this direction.   Feature stories in *Stars and Stripes*, discussion pamphlets, radio programs, films, and other similar types of materials were widely distributed.   Wisely or unwisely, the main emphasis in these materials was on clarifying for the soldier the redeployment plan—how it was set up and how it would operate—rather than on the magnitude of the job remaining to be done.

The apparent result was to give men a good idea of the plan and

---

[15] As illustrations see reports in *Time Magazine*, January 21, 1946, pp. 21–22, and May 6, 1946, p. 24.

CHART VII

CHANGES IN ATTITUDES TOWARD THE ARMY, APRIL 1945 TO AUGUST 1945

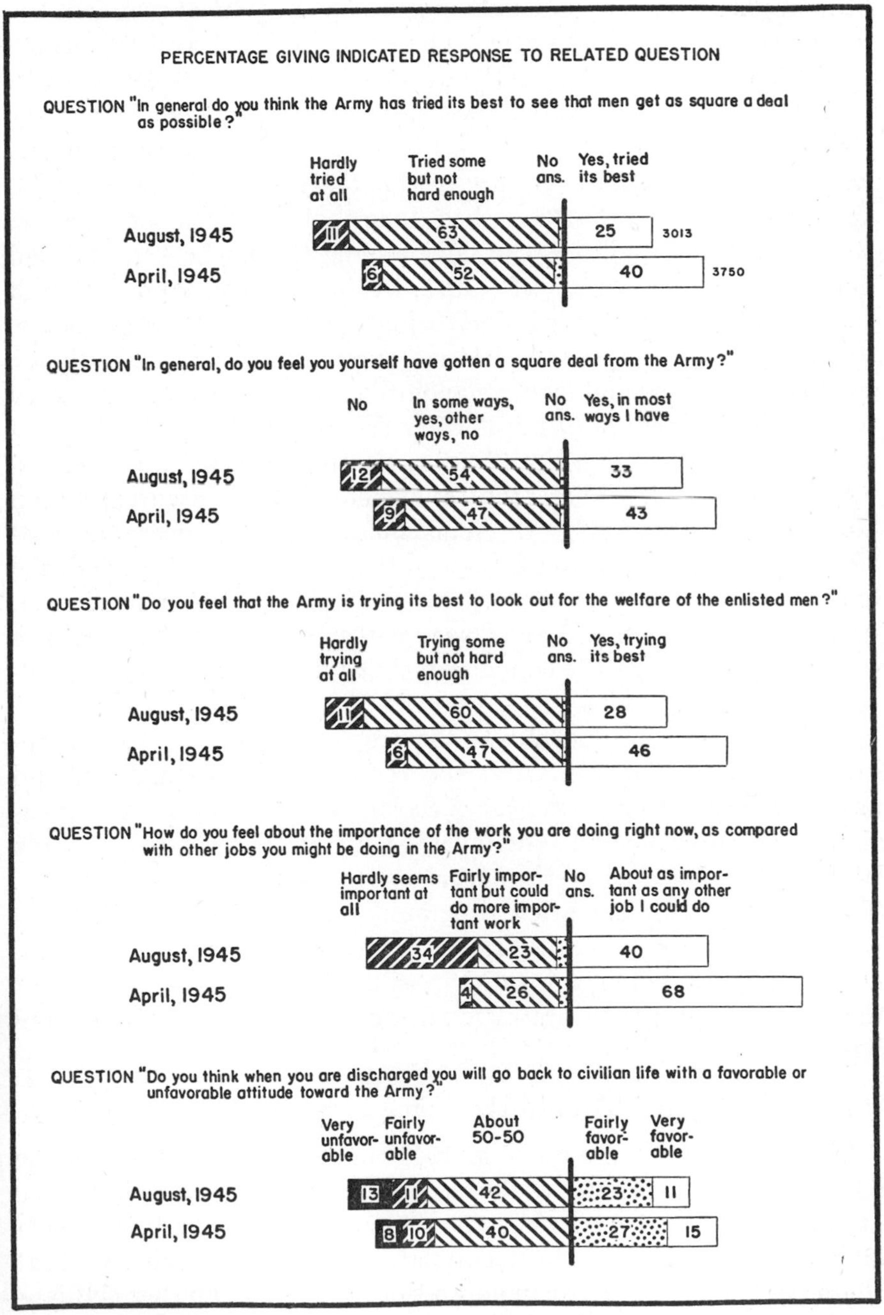

PERCENTAGE GIVING INDICATED RESPONSE TO RELATED QUESTION

QUESTION "In general do you think the Army has tried its best to see that men get as square a deal as possible?"

	Hardly tried at all	Tried some but not hard enough	No ans.	Yes, tried its best	
August, 1945	11	63		25	3013
April, 1945	6	52		40	3750

QUESTION "In general, do you feel you yourself have gotten a square deal from the Army?"

	No	In some ways, yes, other ways, no	No ans.	Yes, in most ways I have
August, 1945	12	54		33
April, 1945	9	47		43

QUESTION "Do you feel that the Army is trying its best to look out for the welfare of the enlisted men?"

	Hardly trying at all	Trying some but not hard enough	No ans.	Yes, trying its best
August, 1945	11	60		28
April, 1945	6	47		46

QUESTION "How do you feel about the importance of the work you are doing right now, as compared with other jobs you might be doing in the Army?"

	Hardly seems important at all	Fairly important but could do more important work	No ans.	About as important as any other job I could do
August, 1945	34	23		40
April, 1945	4	26		68

QUESTION "Do you think when you are discharged you will go back to civilian life with a favorable or unfavorable attitude toward the Army?"

	Very unfavorable	Fairly unfavorable	About 50-50	Fairly favorable	Very favorable
August, 1945	13	11	42	23	11
April, 1945	8	10	40	27	15

Data from S-235 and S-223.

The numbers following the bars are the numbers of cases on which percentages are based.

how it would work and a favorable attitude toward it; but there was little apparent effect on the willingness on the part of men in ETO for further service in the war.   For example, the July 1945 survey in ETO showed that among the men who had read the Army Talks pamphlet, *Two Down and One to Go*, 45 per cent said they had a very clear idea about the redeployment plan.   Among those who had not read it, only 22 per cent gave this reply.   On the other hand, the proportion who felt they had done their share in the war and should be discharged was the same among those who had and had not read the pamphlet.   Of course, by August, the capitulation of Japan was a major factor in increasing the motivation to get home.

Another proposal in the 1944 memorandum had to do with the relations of officers and men, and pointed specifically to the necessity for a stringent policy of minimizing the abuse of officer privileges and increased attention by officers to the interests, welfare, and dignity of their men.   The extent of systematic and intensive action along this line is not known.   While no research on officer-men relations was permitted in the European theater during this period, the evidence in the news, observations, and finally the action taken, under pressure, by the War Department in setting up the Doolittle committee, supports the conclusion that this became a major problem.

A third general proposal was the preparation of large-scale programs of education, athletics, and recreation (including arts and crafts and sight-seeing tours).   A comprehensive plan for an educational program was set up and initiated.   However, conditions made it difficult to execute and the actual operation was extremely spotty. The athletics and recreation programs never really got under way on anything like the scale proposed.   If the war with Japan had continued as expected, it is quite possible that the program planned for Europe would have stabilized in quite a different fashion from what it did.

PART 4.   Attitudes Toward the Home Front

The predictions were made in 1944 that following the end of the fighting in Europe there would be an appreciable increase in hostile attitudes toward civilians in general "back home," and toward specific groups in the American population.   It was anticipated that there would be an increase in expressions of the feeling that civilians made no real sacrifices and that they had no real appreciation of what the soldier went through and would forget all about him now that the danger was past.   It was further expected that expressions of resentments and hostility towards such groups as Labor, Business, Jews, Negroes, etc., would be more frequent.   These predictions were only partly borne out in the four-month period studied; and it

CHART VIII

CHANGES IN ATTITUDES TOWARD THE HOME FRONT
(European Theater, April and August 1945)

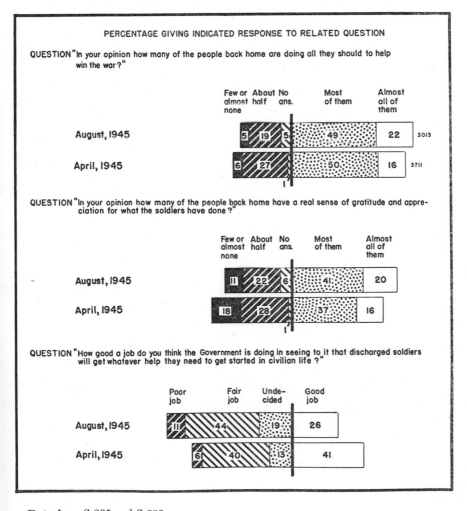

PERCENTAGE GIVING INDICATED RESPONSE TO RELATED QUESTION

QUESTION "In your opinion how many of the people back home are doing all they should to help win the war?"

	Few or almost none	About half	No ans.	Most of them	Almost all of them	
August, 1945	5	19	5	49	22	3013
April, 1945	6	27		50	16	3711

QUESTION "In your opinion how many of the people back home have a real sense of gratitude and appreciation for what the soldiers have done?"

	Few or almost none	About half	No ans.	Most of them	Almost all of them
August, 1945	11	22	6	41	20
April, 1945	18	28		37	16

QUESTION "How good a job do you think the Government is doing in seeing to it that discharged soldiers will get whatever help they need to get started in civilian life?"

	Poor job	Fair job	Unde- cided	Good job
August, 1945	11	44	19	26
April, 1945	6	40	13	41

Data from S-235 and S-223.
The numbers following the bars are the numbers of cases on which percentages are based.

is interesting to find that the negative attitudes appeared only in the context of "a square deal for the soldier when he got out."

As Chart VIII shows, the reactions toward civilians in general actually appeared to be slightly more favorable in August than they were in April. However, when questions about the home front were asked which involved the soldier's anxieties about his postwar problems and help he felt he would need in re-establishing himself in civilian life, there was evidence of a moderate increase in negative reaction. This is seen not only in Chart VIII but in other data. For example, when asked "About how many of the U. S. government leaders do you think will try to see to it that discharged soldiers get a square deal?" the percentage answering "most of them" dropped from 47 in April to 39 in August. A parallel question as to leaders in business and industry showed a drop from 31 to 24 per cent, and a parallel question as to leaders of labor unions showed a drop from 34 to 27 per cent.

If, however, the questions were not worded to involve problems specific to the men as soldiers there were no important changes, and expressions of negative attitudes toward specific groups failed to show any increase in hostile feeling. For example, the following question was asked (later facetiously called in the Research Branch the "Walt Whitman question"):

America is made up of a great many different kinds and groups of people.
There are city people and country people. There are Northerners and Southerners and Westerners. There are Catholics, Jews, and Protestants. There are Poles, Italians, Mexicans, Scotch, and many other nationalities. There are people whose skin color is white, black, yellow, brown, and red.
There are big business and little business men, factory workers, clerks, and farmers. There are business leaders, labor leaders, government leaders, farm leaders. There are Republicans, Democrats, Communists, Socialists, and Independents.
Some of these different groups always get along well together; others sometimes don't get along so well.

    a. Are there any kinds or groups of people in America that you feel will have a harder time getting along together after the war than they did before the war? (Check one)

        _____ No
        _____ Yes (What groups? _____)

    b. Are there any kinds or groups of people in America that you personally dislike very much? (Check one)

        _____ No
        _____ Yes (What groups? _____)

c. Are there any kinds or groups of people in America that you think have taken advantage of the war to further their own selfish interests? (Check one)

_____ No
_____ Yes   (What groups? _____)

The results are summarized in Table 3. The category most frequently mentioned, in free-answer write-ins, as having a harder time getting along after the war was Negroes; the categories ranked first

TABLE 3

PERCENTAGES OF MEN IN EUROPEAN THEATER WHO EXPRESSED INDICATED ATTITUDE TOWARD SPECIFIC GROUPS IN AMERICA

| | ARE THERE ANY KINDS OR GROUPS OF PEOPLE IN AMERICA THAT | | | | | |
| | Have taken selfish advantage of this war? | | Will have greater difficulty getting along after the war? | | You dislike personally? | |
	April 1945	August 1945	April 1945	August 1945	April 1945	August 1945
"No"	34	35	42	40	60	59
' Yes," but name no specific group	6	5	2	2	1	1
"Yes," and name a specific group*	47	41	46	42	29	25
Negroes	*6*	*7*	*34*	*32*	*14*	*12*
Jews	*11*	*9*	*5*	*4*	*8*	*8*
Labor or Labor Unions	*9*	*7*	*3*	*2*	*3*	*1*
Communists, Reds, etc.	*7*	*1*	*1*	*1*	*2*	*2*
Business	*19*	*17*	*3*	*3*	*1*	*1*
Other, unclassified	*7*	*5*	*6*	*7*	*7*	*5*
No answer	13	19	10	16	10	15
Total	100	100	100	100	100	100
Number of cases	*3,711*	*3,013*	*3,711*	*3,013*	*3,711*	*3,013*

Data from S-223 and S-235.
* This percentage is less than the sum of percentages mentioning particular groups because some men mentioned more than one group.

and second, respectively, in terms of dislike were Negroes and Jews (though only by small minorities); the category thought most to have taken selfish advantage of the war was "business." There were no marked shifts of any kind between the April and August surveys.

The results reported in this section together with the reported trends in attitudes toward the Army suggest the following interpretation:

1. With the sharp decline in motivation for further service, the men's attention was increasingly focused on getting home, out of the Army and re-established in civilian life.

2. The most immediate, obvious frustration to these desires was the Army itself.   Hence a good deal of hostility was directed toward the Army and its leaders.

3. Hostility toward civilians was not generalized.   What increases in hostile attitudes were expressed appeared only when questions focused attention on those groups[16] which had a vital relevance to the soldiers' dominant desires to get back into civilian life on reasonably favorable terms.

Throughout the war the Information and Education Division devoted a part of its program to maintaining attitudes of confidence and good will on the part of the soldier toward the civilian groups at home.   Toward the end of the war in Europe there was an intensification of these efforts along lines suggested in the Research Branch prediction memorandum.   Special weekly supplements to *Stars and Stripes* carried news and feature articles designed to demonstrate to the soldier that he was being backed up at home, that he was appreciated and not forgotten, that all civilian groups were doing their share, that the stories of fantastic profits and wages and work stoppages were untrue of the vast majority of Americans, and so forth.   Discussion materials, radio programs, and films carried the same type of material.

The impact of these materials on soldier attitudes is not known. It is quite possible that the cumulative effect was moderately successful in fostering favorable attitudes or at least in acting as a partial brake on hostile tendencies.

PART 5.   Attitudes Toward the War
            and the Future

Disillusionment and cynicism about the worth-whileness of the war and pessimism about the future—these were attitudes which it

---

[16] It is quite possible that had questions involving other groups in the context of "a square deal for the discharged soldier" been asked, expressions of increased hostility might have been registered against them as well.   The anxiety of the soldier about his future economic security and opportunities was a central one and any group which appeared to threaten this future would very likely become a target of hostile attitudes.

was predicted would become increasingly frequent among American soldiers in Europe after the fighting was over. They were attitudes said to characterize many veterans of World War I, not only American veterans but those of other countries as well. This section is concerned with the question of the extent to which there was any increase in the frequency of these attitudes among American soldiers in ETO during the four months following VE Day. Included in the section are data on the following questions:

a. Was there an increase of cynicism as to reasons for our entry into the war and our peace aims and disillusionment as to the worthwhileness of the war?

b. Was there an increase of opinion favoring a return to an isolationist policy?

Was the War Worth While?

One question, which was analyzed in some detail in Volume I, Chapter 6, indicates an appreciable trend toward a greater willingness to admit doubts and skepticism about the worth-whileness of the war. This is shown in Chart IX. In July of 1943, about one fifth of the troops of a cross-section sample in the United States said they "sometimes" or "very often" felt the war was not worth fighting. In January 1944, 5 months before D Day, about one third of the troops in the British Isles gave those responses. The same proportion gave the same responses 16 months later, just before VE Day. During the 4 months following VE Day, the proportion jumped to almost half the men, who said they "sometimes" or "very often" felt the war was not worth fighting. The nearest approach to that proportion found during the war was among certain Infantry divisions after very punishing combat experiences.

On the other hand, there was relatively slight shift in expressions of cynicism as to the reasons for entry into the war or as to our war aims.

In April and again in August, the men were asked the following questions about why we got into the war.

Read the two statements below and check which one you think is the more important reason why we got into the war. (Check one)

_____ We got into this war because "Big Business" in the United States was looking for more profits.
_____ We got into this war because we were attacked.

Now read these two statements and check which one you think is the more important reason why we got into the war.   (Check one)

———— We got into this war to destroy Nazism and Fascism.
———— We got into this war because "Big Business" in the United States was looking for more profits.

Now check which one of these two statements you think is the more important reason why we got into the war.   (Check one)

———— We got into this war to destroy Nazism and Fascism.
———— We got into this war because we were attacked.

The question aimed to discriminate between those who thought our principal reason was (1) self-defense, or (2) to destroy Nazism and Fascism, or (3) the "cynical" reason of economic imperialism.

The results given below indicate no increase in the frequency with which men chose the "cynical" reason.

CHART IX

INCREASES IN ADMISSION OF SKEPTICISM ABOUT THE WAR

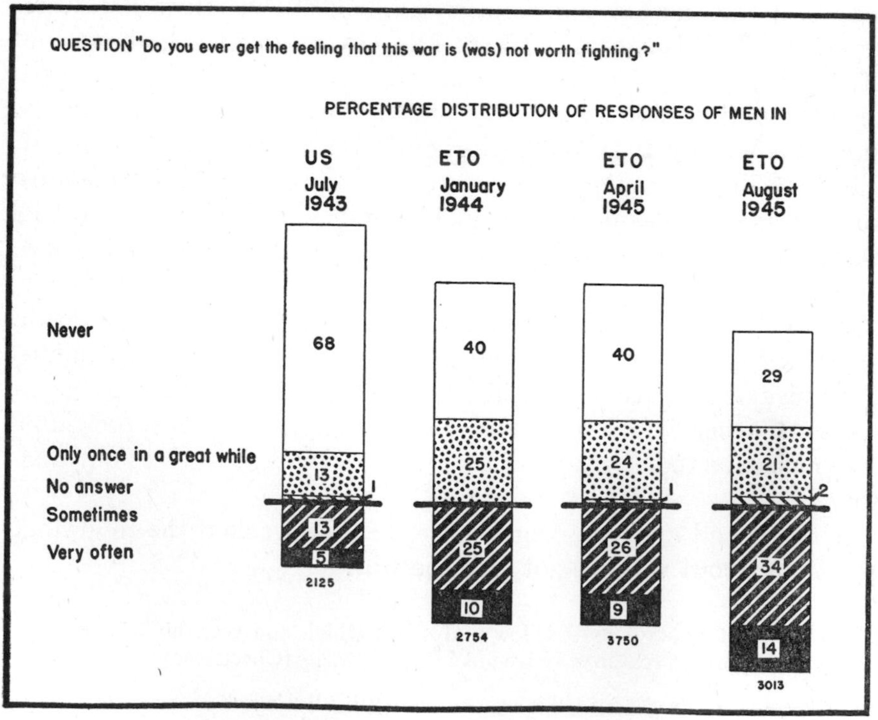

QUESTION "Do you ever get the feeling that this war is (was) not worth fighting?"

PERCENTAGE DISTRIBUTION OF RESPONSES OF MEN IN

| US July 1943 | ETO January 1944 | ETO April 1945 | ETO August 1945 |

Never — 68 / 40 / 40 / 29
Only once in a great while — 13 / 25 / 24 / 21
No answer — 1 / / 1 / 2
Sometimes — 13 / 25 / 26 / 34
Very often — 5 / 10 / 9 / 14

2125 / 2754 / 3750 / 3013

Data from S-63E, S-116, S-223 and S-235.
The numbers at the bottom of the bars are the numbers of cases on which percentages are based.

	April 1945	*August 1945*
To destroy Nazism and Fascism	38	36
Because we were attacked	37	37
Because of "Big Business" interests	11	12
Indeterminate, inconsistent, or no answer	14	15
Total	100	100
Number of cases	*3,750*	*3,013*

A similar question was asked about our peace aims.

Read the two statements below and check the one which you think should be the more important peace aim for the United States.   (Check one)

_____ To see that the nations organize to prevent wars in the future.
_____ To see that the United States is so strong that no nations would dare attack us.

Now read these two statements and check the one you think should be the more important peace aim for the United States.   (Check one)

_____ To see that the people in all countries have the right to govern themselves.
_____ To see that the nations organize to prevent wars in the future.

Now check which one of these two statements should be the more important peace aim for the United States.   (Check one)

_____ To see that the people in all countries have the right to govern themselves.
_____ To see that the United States is so strong that no nations would dare attack us.

This question was designed to discriminate between those who felt our most important peace aim should be: (1) An "idealistic" democratic aim, or (2) to establish an international organization to prevent wars, or (3) an aim of nationalistic self-defense.

Here again the results do not indicate any marked shift in the pre-

_____

[17] Each reason was paired against the other two.   There were some men who did not make all three choices or who made inconsistent choices.

dominant opinion supporting our officially announced peace policy
of establishing a world organization to prevent wars in the future.

	THE PERCENTAGES CONSIST- ENTLY[18] RATING EACH AS THE MOST IMPORTANT AIM OF THE THREE WERE AS FOLLOWS:	
	April 1945	*August 1945*
To see that nations organize to prevent wars	47	42
To see that all countries have the right to govern themselves	23	24
To see that the United States is so strong that no nations would dare attack us	21	24
Indeterminate, inconsistent, or no answer	9	10
Total	100	100
Number of cases	*3,750*	*3,013*

Not only was it the dominant opinion that we should make our
chief aim in the peace to see that nations organized to prevent war,
but the large majority of the men continued to believe that "our
government leaders are trying to do everything they can to see that
war will be prevented in the future." [19]   (Seventy per cent in April
and 72 per cent in August said they believed this to be so.)

From the foregoing tables it can be concluded that while there was
a certain amount of "cynicism" or confusion about our reasons for
entering the war, and a certain amount of "isolationist nationalism"
or confusion about what our peace aims should be, these attitudes
did not become more frequent during the four months after the fighting with Germany stopped.

Internationalism or Isolationism after the War

As was shown in Volume I, Chapter 9, only a minority of the soldiers thought that another war could be avoided during the next 25
years.   In Europe, in April and August 1945, the proportions who
thought that it could were 24 per cent and 21 per cent respectively.

There were decided majorities in favor of a policy of internationalism after the war and there was little change in these majorities

[18] Each aim was paired against the other two.   There were some men who did not
make all three choices or who made inconsistent choices.

[19] Exact wording of the question: "Do you think our Government leaders are trying
to do everything they can to see to it that wars will be prevented in the future?"
(Answer categories: Yes, No, Undecided.)

between April and August.   The percentages of men affirming a particular viewpoint were as follows:[20]

	April 1945	*August 1945*
After the war a permanent organization of nations should be set up to settle quarrels between countries and try to prevent wars	86	89
There should be an international police force under the direction of the international organization	65	63
The best way for the United States to try to keep out of wars in the future would be to join a strong permanent international organization	73	68
The United States should join such an organization even if it meant that this organization would have some say about how we deal with other countries	63	58
Number of cases	1,917	3,013

Data from S-223A and S-235.

It is important to note, however, that while the great majority of men continued to favor a policy of internationalism in principle, they tended to show a decreasing willingness to favor certain pro-

---

[20] The exact wording of the questions asked was:

After the war do you think the different countries (like the United States, Russia, England, China, France, etc.) should set up a permanent organization of nations to try to settle quarrels between countries and try to prevent war?   (Check one)

_____ Should be set up
_____ Should not be set up
_____ Undecided

After the war do you think there should be a special force of soldiers from the Armies of a number of different countries that could be sent any place the international organization decided they were needed?   (Check one)

_____ Yes, there should be an international Army of that kind
_____ No, there should not be an international Army of that kind
_____ Undecided

Which do you think would be the best way for the United States to try to keep out of war in the future?   (Check one)

_____ Stay out of world affairs
_____ Join a strong permanent organization of nations
_____ Some other way (How? _____)
_____ Undecided

Do you think the United States should join a strong permanent organization of nations, even if it means that this organization would have some say about how the United States deals with other countries?   (Check one)

_____ Yes, I think the U. S. should join
_____ No, I don't think the U. S. should join
_____ Undecided

posals for concrete American aid in postwar recovery. For example:

> After the war, some of our Allies will need help in feeding their people. Do you think the United States should send food to these countries even if it meant that we would have to keep on rationing food in our country for a while to do it?

> *Percentages answering*
> *"should":*
>
> August 1945   49
> April 1945   58

> After the war some of our Allies will need money and materials to help them get back on their feet. Do you think we should let them have money and materials to help them get back on their feet, even if it meant that we should have to pay higher taxes for it?"

> *Percentages answering*
> *"should":*
>
> August 1945   29
> April 1945   38

In evaluating these responses about postwar American aid to Europe, one must note that the views expressed just before the end of the fighting about future conditions in the United States were certainly not highly optimistic. Responses to a number of questions dealing with anticipated future conditions in the United States suggest this lack of optimism but show little shift from April to August. The percentages of men giving the indicated responses were as follows:[21]

---

[21] Exact wordings of the questions used here are given below:

Do you expect we probably shall have a widespread depression in the United States within 10 years after the war is over, or do you think we probably will avoid having one? (Check one)

   ————— We will probably have a depression
   ————— We will probably avoid having one
   ————— Undecided

After the war is over, do you think the United States will be a better place or worse place to live in than it was before the war? (Check one)

   ————— Worse after the war than before the war
   ————— Same after the war as before the war
   ————— Better after the war than before the war
   ————— Undecided

After the war do you think that most soldiers will find it easy or hard to get the kind of jobs they want? (Check one)

   ————— Very easy
   ————— Fairly easy
   ————— Fairly hard
   ————— Very hard
   ————— Undecided

	April 1945	*August 1945*
We could probably avoid a widespread depression in the United States after the war	28	25
After the war, the United States will be a better place in which to live than it was before the war	35	34
After the war most soldiers will find it "very easy" or "fairly easy" to get the kind of jobs they want	20	16
Number of cases	*3,750*	*3,013*

What, then, can be said about the direction of soldiers' orientation as to the meaning of the war and as to the future which was to come out of it?   It has been pointed out in Volume I, Chapter 9, on the orientation of American soldiers toward the war, that the average soldier did not appear to have a vigorous, well articulated set of ideas and conceptions which placed the war in any meaningful context and gave it purpose, beyond the recognition of the necessity of self-defense and of getting through with a disagreeable job in order to get back home as quickly as possible.   However, it is also true that, confronted by different types of reasons and aims, they voted down the cynical reasons for entering the war and narrow nationalistic peace aims, in favor of reasonably positive and constructive but realistic ones.

We went to war to defend ourselves against attack and to destroy a social system which was inimical to our peace and security.   We should aim to build an international system which will make wars less likely to occur, and this country should take an active part in such a world organization even if it means some limitation on our sovereignty.   These were the beliefs and sentiments men would subscribe to when presented in general terms and as alternatives to more cynical and less constructive ones.   Moreover, they believed the leaders in their government were sincerely working for the ends which they, the soldiers, subscribed to as important.

On the other hand, when the issues were stated in more specific and concrete terms rather than in general terms, what appeared to be a good constructive orientation showed up as a rather weak verbal one.   The proportion of men willing to aid in rehabilitating our Allies—never a majority—decreased appreciably in a short time after hostilities ceased.   The desirable aims for controlling international conflict did not appear to carry much faith behind them and the minority belief that another major war could be avoided in the near future did not gain any ground in the period studied.

Nor was there any evidence of change in the minority who entertained optimistic beliefs in a "better world" within the United States.

If one adds to these findings the fact that the only major change found in this series of data was the considerable increase in those willing to admit doubts about whether the war was worth while, it seems reasonable to conclude that if disillusion, cynicism, and pessimism did not increase during the period studied, at least a state of mind continued which was not very well fortified against such a trend.

Measures recommended for combating expected reactions of disillusionment and pessimism were outlined in the 1944 memorandum quoted at the beginning of this chapter. The efforts which were made consisted largely of furnishing news and information regarding (a) the plans being made to assure the returning soldier of reasonable economic security and opportunity and (b) the attempts of government leaders to cooperate actively with leaders of other nations in setting up an international organization designed to reduce the threat of war. The effects of such information materials cannot be determined from available data. Whatever the effects may have been, the men did not manifest great optimism about the future which was to emerge from the war.

Conclusion

To sum up the findings in this chapter, we see that some of the predictions made in the 1944 memorandum were completely borne out; others were not. In general, expectations about the increase in friendliness toward the Germans and the difficulties of expecting a nonfraternization policy to succeed were fully realized. Likewise, the psychological letdown at the end of hostilities with respect to further sacrifice had many of the consequences expected, particularly in so far as it was accompanied by an increase in aggression against the Army. Except in the case of the French, our Allies did not in the period immediately following VE Day become targets of increased dislike. The forecast was particularly inadequate in not anticipating that the French, rather than the British or Russians as well, would be the primary targets. The forecast also appeared to overestimate substantially the increase in hostility toward the home front and skepticism about the war. The increase in hostility to the home front was small and was manifest only on those items referring directly to the home front's relations with soldiers. The increase in skepticism about the war, while in evidence, did not involve any marked retreat to isolationism, although there was some falling off of support of the idea of postwar American aid to Allies if it were to involve any substantial sacrifices on our part. In retrospect, it appears that in our forecasts more account should have been taken of the fact, indeed well known to the Research Branch in 1944, that the soldiers had no very pronounced expectations of anything coming out of the war except the negative one of defeating aggression. Hence, a strong reaction of disillusionment after VE Day hardly should have been anticipated—one cannot be disillusioned if his initial expectations are not particularly high.

The predictions were not limited to a specific time period, such as four months following VE Day. It is quite possible that over a longer period some attitudes toward our Allies or toward the home front and specific civilian groups would have shown more pronounced shifts. Due to curtailment in Research Branch activities following VJ Day, there was not time nor staff to continue trend studies except on a very limited scale.

The predictions, it must be emphasized, were not made simply as a matter of scientific interest. They were made to be used as a basis for planning measures to counteract the anticipated problems. Some measures were planned and some action taken, as we have pointed out. For example, there can be little doubt that the publication of the point system for determining priorities for demobilization, with the emphasis on how it was derived from the men's own opinions, and the early initiation of operation of the system, blunted what could easily have been rather explosive attitudes of resentment and feelings of injustice among soldiers. Other efforts to counteract predicted trends were made and probably curbed certain potential trends to some extent.

When all reservations and qualifications are taken into account and all errors are noted, the predictions still remain a fairly accurate forecast of the state of mind of the troops in Europe following the German defeat. These predictions, together with the recommendations for preventive and remedial action, constitute a suggestion of the potential value of this kind of analysis in the field of democratic management and leadership.

CHAPTER 13

THE SOLDIER BECOMES A VETERAN[1]

D ETAILED study of the veteran was outside the scope of the Research Branch and hence falls outside the scope of these volumes.

From time to time, however, the Research Branch asked occasional questions about soldiers' postwar expectations, some of which have been illustrated in the preceding chapter. One intensive survey of a small sample of discharged veterans,[2] a few months before the end of the war, foreshadowed some of the postwar problems. For the historical record, it seems appropriate to conclude Volume II by looking briefly at the attitudes of the soldier as he faced his return to civilian status.

Perhaps the single most striking fact about the evidence available is the absence of any pronounced tendency either for personal bitterness or for social action.

The soldiers, as previous chapters have shown, were eager to get out of the Army as soon as possible. As Chapter 5 in Volume I made clear, the majority of men had accumulated a large amount of negativism toward the Army. Partly, perhaps, because they could so readily make the Army the target of their aggressions, there was little end-of-the-war evidence of strong aggression or bitterness toward civilian society. Nor, as we have seen suggested in the preceding chapter, was there a general sense of bitterness associated with disillusionment about the value of the war. This lack of emotional "letdown" seems best explained by the fact that there were very few illusions to be shattered, as Chapter 9 in Volume I has made evident. After the attack at Pearl Harbor the war was accepted as

---

[1] By Leonard S. Cottrell, Jr., and Samuel A. Stouffer. The main surveys of postwar job plans of soldiers were carried out under the direction of John A. Clausen. Other anticipated postwar problems of soldiers were largely studied in the Research Branch under Cottrell's direction. The survey of discharged veterans, quoted at some length in Section III, was directed by Shirley A. Star of the Research Branch and Eleanor Maccoby of the Division of Program Surveys, Department of Agriculture.

[2] Made jointly by the Research Branch and by the Division of Program Surveys in the Bureau of Agricultural Economics.

unpleasant, but necessary; the inevitable victory had been won; now back to civilian work.

When the soldier thought of the postwar world, he tended to think in terms of his own job and his chances to compete either for security or advancement, not in terms of social action to improve conditions. The soldier did not come home to reform America—there was little trace of any such attitude in responses at any period of the war. Soldiers intended, as veterans, to assert some preferential claims, but they had little desire for or expectation of social changes in the United States except the kind of technological changes which would promote a higher standard of living for themselves as well as others. As we have seen earlier, there was considerable skepticism about our ability to keep out of another war and a strong hope that some kind of international machinery might be set up to preserve the peace. But the soldier was mainly thinking about himself and his family, not about his country or the world.

These findings are in striking contrast to the expectations of those who anticipated deep-seated personal bitterness and disillusionment, manifesting itself either in widespread psychiatric breakdowns or in aggressive hostility against civilian society and institutions.   True, there were examples of both manifestations, but by and large the evidence from men still in the Army pointed rather to an individualistic motivation to get back on the same civilian paths from which the war was a detour.

While the attitudes of men about to be discharged did not, by and large, foreshadow alarming tensions in civilian life, it is possible that tensions greater than have developed in the years since 1945 might have become manifest, but for two facts.   One was the fact of relatively full employment—the depression expected by many experts did not materialize.   The other was the GI bill, whose billions in veteran benefits certainly cushioned the transition to normal peacetime pursuits.

In this chapter, we shall look first at some of the soldiers' expressions with respect to their personal future; next, we shall review briefly their attitudes toward American society; and, finally, we shall quote from a research document based on intensive interviews with men after their discharge from the Army.

SECTION I

VIEWING ONE'S PERSONAL FUTURE AS A CIVILIAN

Only about 3 per cent of the men, in various surveys in the closing year of the war, indicated a desire to remain in the Army for a career, though about as many more thought that they might re-enlist at some time after discharge if there were a severe depression and difficulty in getting civilian jobs.

The civilian orientation of the overwhelming majority, in their future plans, was manifested on all surveys. Central to these plans was the question of a job, or further schooling. It cannot be said that there was an overweening anxiety about future jobs. But, as Chart I, based on a survey in May 1945 shows, there were many who expressed concern about future work—and in all surveys, of which this is merely illustrative, concern about future jobs led the list in personal anxieties. In Chart I we see, for example, that a fifth of the men said they "worried a lot" about what kind of work they would do after the war, while nearly half of the men said they "worried a little."

It is interesting to note that men tended to be more optimistic about their personal chances of employment than about chances of employment for veterans in general:

Percentage who thought *most soldiers* would find it "very hard" or "fairly hard" to get the kind of jobs they wanted after the war   79%

Percentage who thought they *personally* would find it "very hard" or "fairly hard" to get the kind of jobs they wanted after the war   46%

In the background of the thinking of many was the probability of a postwar depression, which had been widely predicted, even by many expert economists. In the June 1945 study, 56 per cent anticipated a widespread depression, 15 per cent were undecided, and 29 per cent thought we would probably avoid having one.

As early as the summer of 1943, the Research Branch was undertaking studies of the postwar plans of soldiers. The first survey was made at the request of the special committee appointed by the President to advise him on legislation which eventuated in the GI bill. The data provided by the Research Branch were used by that committee in its estimates of future costs. At the same time, there

CHART I

FREQUENCY WITH WHICH SOLDIERS REPORTED SOME ANXIETIES AS WAR NEARED END, JUNE 1945

(Cross Sections of Overseas Returnees in the United States and Soldiers Who Had Not Been Overseas)

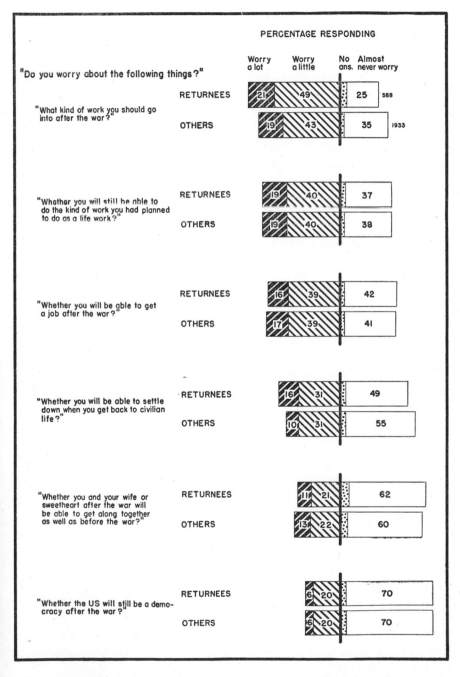

Data from S-212.

The numbers following the bars are the numbers of cases on which percentages are based.

were needs within and without the War Department for detailed information about the vocational aspirations of soldiers. The Education Branch of the Information and Education Division was drawing blueprints for an educational program within the Army to be greatly accelerated in the year or more expected to elapse between the surrender of Germany and the surrender of Japan and needed data to estimate the areas in which in-service educational courses would be needed. The Veterans Administration, the Office of Education, the Departments of Agriculture, Commerce, and Labor all had concerns with soldiers' postwar plans and urged the Research Branch to obtain for them information which would be helpful in planning.

The most extensive study of soldiers' postwar plans was based on a world-wide cross section of 4,000 officers and 23,000 enlisted men (19,000 white and 4,000 Negro) made in the summer of 1944. This study showed that almost two thirds of the men (64 per cent) appeared at the time of the survey to have definite job or educational plans. An additional sixth (16 per cent) had fairly clear-cut but less definite plans. The remainder (18 per cent) had no clear-cut plans and were undecided as to what they wanted to do. The distribution of these men as to their postwar plans is shown in Chart II for all officers and enlisted men and in Table 1 for white officers, white enlisted men, and Negro enlisted men separately.

Behind this chart and table lay some of the most intricate and technically difficult statistical analysis ever attempted by the Research Branch. The questionnaires eventually used were pretested and revised several times on samples themselves running into several thousand cases, and hundreds of informal personal interviews also were made in order to frame questions which would separate decided plans from mere aspirations and wishful thinking. Because of the importance to future social research of this experience in attempting to discover the structure of a man's future aspirations, a considerable section of Volume IV is devoted to a detailed analysis of the techniques used, and also compares the responses of two samples of soldiers as to their plans with the actual experience of the soldiers a few months after separation from the Army.[3]

In reporting the data in Table 1, the Research Branch sought to walk the narrow path of reasonable caution. On the one hand, it was obvious from the analysis that substantial minorities had only vague or tentative plans. On the other hand, it was necessary as a

---

[3] The analysis of the follow-up studies was made in the Veterans Administration.

practical engineering job to make some specific estimates—and this responsibility was not dodged.   To quote from one of the reports:[4]

The postwar expectations of the men represent what some men may have a chance to do next month or six months from now and what other men will not have a chance to do for several years.   Over a million men have already been separated from the Army and before the major demobilization begins many more men will have been discharged.

There are elements of uncertainty in the postwar plans of all men in the Army and basic uncertainties or inconsistencies in the plans of many.   The primary concern of most men in uniform is to "win the war and get home again."   But

CHART II

POST-SEPARATION PLANS OF SOLDIERS, SUMMER 1944
(World-wide Cross Section of 27,000 Officers and Enlisted Men)

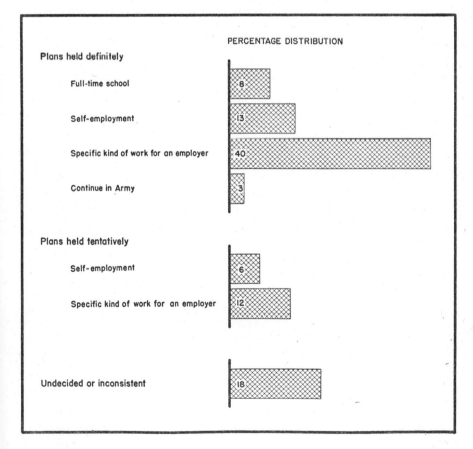

Data from S-106 and S-145.

_____

[4] *Postwar Occupational Plans of Soldiers*, Research Branch Report B-129.

most soldiers have nevertheless done a good deal of thinking about their job prospects when the war is won.

Asked the question: "Up to now, how much had you thought about exactly what you will want to do after the war?" three fourths of the men surveyed said: "I had thought a good deal about it." Another fifth said they "had thought some about it" and only 5 per cent said they "had hardly thought about it." In their answers to this question there was little difference between officers and enlisted men, between men in the States and men overseas, between whites and Negroes.

TABLE 1

POST-SEPARATION PLANS OF OFFICERS AND OF WHITE AND NEGRO ENLISTED MEN
(World-wide Cross Section, Summer 1944)

	PERCENTAGE DISTRIBUTION			
	All officers and enlisted men	*White officers of company grade*	*White enlisted men*	*Negro enlisted men*
Plans held definitely	64	67	65	51
Full-time school	*8*	*12*	*7*	*5*
Self-employment	*13*	*13*	*13*	*11*
Specific kind of work for an employer	*40*	*32*	*43*	*34*
Continue in Army	*3*	*10*	*2*	*1*
Plans held tentatively	18	19	17	28
Self-employment	*6*	*3*	*6*	*7*
Specific kind of work for an employer	*12*	*16*	*11*	*21*
Undecided or inconsistent*	18	14	18	21
	100	100	100	100
Size of sample	*27,000*	*4,000*	*19,000*	*4,000*

Data from S-106 and S-145.
* Most of the men considering but not definitely planning to go to full-time school or to remain in the Army expressed conflicting job plans, and are included in the "undecided or inconsistent group." This "undecided" group also included about 10 per cent of all officers and enlisted men who had fairly definite expectations of working for an employer even though undecided about any specific job.

Not all of the men surveyed had come to a definite decision in their thinking about postwar job prospects. Somewhat less than two thirds, in fact, expressed definite expectations of doing a particular kind of work after the war. The rest of the men divided almost evenly into those who expressed tentative plans to follow a particular postwar occupation and those who reported themselves undecided or who expressed markedly inconsistent plans.

The men classified as having definite plans are those whose answers to the whole series of questions about their postwar job plans reflect a single plan consistently and without reservations. It is more accurate to say that their plans are definitely expressed than to say that they are definite plans, for some of these men have not thought through the problems of carrying out their plans. The men classified as having tentative plans—i.e., plans held tentatively—are men whose present expectations are now tending more strongly toward one type of work than toward another, but they may at the same time be seriously consider-

At the same time that the Research Branch was studying the operation of the redeployment and demobilization program, at home and abroad, it also was studying attitudes of soldiers in advance of the expected revision of the point system upon the defeat of Japan.

Attitudes Toward Post VJ Day Revision of the Point System

The point system, as has been explained, was developed in response to the expectation that there would be a long gap between the defeat of Germany and the defeat of Japan. It was fully expected that the system would be considerably revised after VJ Day.

In mid July 1945 a world-wide survey went into the field to determine specifically what changes the majority of the soldiers would want, or would tolerate, in the point system after VJ Day. The war against Japan proceeded toward success with unexpected rapidity and the Information and Education Division was advised in July that any data bearing on revision of the point system after VJ Day would need to be submitted before the middle of August.

Arrangements were made with the overseas research staffs to cable back in a special abbreviated code the results of the mid July survey as soon as tabulations were completed in a theater. At the end of the first week in August these tabulations were consolidated and on August 9, 1945, a report was carried directly to the Chief of Staff.

This report, which will be quoted in full, marshaled facts, point for point, bearing on issues which had been debated, sometimes hotly, before the Special Planning Committee.

Incredible as it seemed at the time to many in the Information and Education Division, there was a strong sentiment within the War Department for eliminating combat credit entirely after VJ Day. The Research Branch's own very frank reports of criticisms of the point system were cited in support. In vain did representatives of the Information and Education Division argue that the research reports were being misinterpreted. The position was taken that the combat men would be better satisfied if points were given for the Purple Heart and decorations for bravery only, and, until actual data were forthcoming from the mid July survey, the Division was not successful in making the point that the complaint from combat troops was based on desire for more credit, not less.

Various other schemes for modifying the point system were advanced after VE Day—one of those most strongly supported being a proposal to abandon the point system and let sheer length of service determine priority of discharge. This would remove the relative advantage of overseas and combat service and give long-service men in the United States a "break."

Since, after VJ Day, the concept of military necessity would lose most of its cogency, it seemed to some on the staff more essential than ever that any changes in the point system deviate not too far from the wishes of the majority of the men. The Information and Education Division preferred no changes at all to changes which could not be defended publicly in the same terms as originally used to justify the point system.

On August 9, 1945, then, the report quoted below was given to General Marshall within a few days of the final decision as to the VJ point system:

OPINIONS OF SOLDIERS THROUGHOUT THE WORLD ABOUT A
POST VJ DAY POINT SYSTEM

This report, made at the request of the Special Planning Division, War Department Special Staff, records the opinions of a world-wide cross section of enlisted men with respect to a post VJ Day point system. The survey was made in the two-week period ending July 24, 1945. Results are based on the opinions of men with less than 85 points, since it is assumed that most men with 85 points or more will have been released by VJ Day and plans for post VJ Day release would not be relevant to them.

Summary

On the whole, men favor the present point system by a decisive majority, as has been previously reported.[10] Looking ahead to the period after the defeat of Japan, the majority want the point system retained in general outline and vote *against* discharging special categories of troops outside of the point system, if it would delay discharges under the point system. While the men want the point system retained, there are some changes which would be desired by substantial numbers and probably be acceptable to the majority.

Weights for Present Factors

More men vote to keep the weights unchanged after VJ Day for any given factor now in the score card than vote to raise or lower the weights. However, there is sufficient demand for an increase in overseas credit to justify giving serious consideration to raising it. There is considerable support for raising overseas, combat, and longevity credit relative to parenthood credit. The men are almost unanimous against lowering credit after VJ Day for overseas, combat, and longevity.

Method of Determining Combat Credit

While combat men are dissatisfied with the method of awarding campaign stars, the evidence shows that they would strongly resent eliminating campaign stars from combat credit. A special study in ETO shows that there would be general

---

[10] Report B-159, *World-wide Attitudes Toward Further Service and Redeployment.*

approval of giving points for the Combat Infantryman's Badge—men who are not entitled to this badge voting for the idea as well as those who wear the badge.

Parenthood and Dependency

Although more men would revise parenthood credit downward than upward, the majority would go along with a plan to give credit for every child instead of just the first three. Even more would favor giving points for dependents other than children. There is less support for the idea of giving additional points for wives, about half of those with opinions approving and half disapproving.

Credit for Age

The majority favor giving credit for age. The optimum credit would appear to be about one point per year beginning at age eighteen.

Discharge of Various Categories Outside of the Point System

There would be general opposition to discharging various categories of men outside of the point system—unless it did not very much delay other men getting out under the point system. There would be somewhat less opposition to blanket discharges of men who have been in the Army a long time or men over thirty-five than to discharges of fathers, men not physically qualified for overseas duty, or men who have been in the Army too short a time to complete their training. Substitution after VJ Day of the "first in, first out" plan for the point system is voted down, by nearly two to one, among those with opinions. A third of the men are so strongly opposed to the "first in, first out" idea that they say they would be "burned up about it."

Detailed statistics documenting these findings are presented below.

Detailed Findings

Opinions About Changing Weights for the Present Four Factors

(*World-wide cross section*)

	Would not change points	No opinion	Would raise points	Would lower points	Total
Overseas credit	46%	15%	35%	4%	100%
Combat credit	60	16	20	4	100
Longevity credit	60	19	19	2	100
Parenthood credit	48	16	15	21	100

Since only a minority vote to raise or lower the points for any one factor after VJ Day, these data would support the proposition to leave the present weights unchanged after VJ Day.

If, however, any change in weights is contemplated, the data give some important indications of what changes might conceivably be acceptable and what would not.

If only one weight were to be changed, an increase in the *overseas credit* would probably be the most acceptable. A further cross tabulation of the above data shows, for example, that 43% of those with opinions believe that twelve months overseas should have more weight than one child, while only 10% believe that one child should have more weight than twelve months overseas. The rest are content with the present relative weights of the two factors. Three fifths of those who would raise overseas credit would raise it to two points per month.

Any cut in combat credit or longevity credit would be directly contrary to the overwhelming opinion of the men.

A minority (21%) favors the outright cutting of credit for parenthood. As can be shown by detailed cross tabulations, an even larger proportion would favor readjusting points so that overseas, combat, and longevity credit would have a higher ratio to parenthood credit than is the case now. This could be accomplished, of course, either by raising overseas, combat, and longevity credit, or by lowering parenthood credit. It is unlikely, however, that parenthood credit could be cut now without severe psychological hazard.

Method of Determining Combat Credit

As previous reports have shown,[11] there is much disaffection among combat men overseas over the use of campaign stars for calculating combat credit.[12] However, this must *not* be interpreted as forecasting a willingness to dispense with credit for campaign stars after VJ Day. To the contrary. As the table previously reported shows, only 4% of the men in the world-wide cross section would *lower* the present credit for campaign stars and decorations. Even among troops in the U. S. who are not entitled to campaign stars only 7% would lower the credit.

In other words, there is practically unanimity on not lowering combat credit. A special study (made only in ETO) shows that only 17% of a representative cross section of men in the European theater would oppose *adding* credit for the Combat Infantryman's Badge. The opposition among field force combat veterans is 9%, field force noncombat veterans 18%, air force men 19%, and comzone men 26%. This is about as high a consensus as will be obtained in the Army for any proposal and strongly supports the wisdom of considering the inclusion of the Combat Infantryman's Badge in the point system. Some numerically small groups who have been exposed to enemy fire might still be dissatisfied, but it should reduce to a minimum the present large volume of protests from the men who have done the main fighting on the ground.

Another special study made on August 7, 1945, of a battalion of Category II Infantry veterans just shipped to the U. S. shows that very few of them would react favorably to a plan which would give points for the Purple Heart and for decorations that were given for outstanding bravery in action but which would not give points for other decorations or campaign stars.

---

[11] Report B-159, *World-wide Attitudes Toward Further Service and Redeployment.*

[12] For example, a special study in ETO shows that a cross section of men interviewed in July 1945 would like to see higher credit given to some classes of troops with campaign stars than to other troops with campaign stars. Entitled to the *highest* credit, in the men's opinion, would be rifle and heavy weapons companies, tank and tank destroyer companies, combat engineer units, aid men and other combat medics. *Next* would come recon platoons, air force combat crews, field artillery batteries, cannon companies, and chemical mortar outfits. *Last* would come medics in field hospitals, regimental headquarters troops, division headquarters troops, division quartermaster troops, and, at the bottom, army and corps headquarters troops. But only a small minority would deny combat credit to units facing the least hazard. Sixty per cent of the men in the ETO cross section said they wanted time in combat counted in the point score *in addition* to credit for campaign stars and decorations. Only 3 per cent would reduce credit for campaign stars and decorations.

QUESTION: "Below are several plans which could be used after VJ Day for giving points for combat. If you had to choose, which one of these plans would you rather have used?"

	First Choice
A. The present plan of giving points for campaign stars and decorations	40%
B. Points would be given for campaign stars, but not for decorations	5
C. Points would be given for the Purple Heart and for decorations which were given for outstanding bravery in action, but not for other decorations or for campaign stars	4
D. Points would be given for time in combat, but not for campaign stars or decorations	36
E. I don't care which of these plans is used	15
Total	100%

This shows that several times as many men favored the present plan as favored Plan C. The men also were asked to indicate their second choice. If those who voted for Plan D, which is popular but impracticable, are redistributed according to their second choices, it will be seen that the present method of computing campaign stars is still decisively preferred to Plans B or C by this sample of Infantry veterans.[13]

Prefer:	First choice of men who preferred A, B, C, and E, plus the second choices of the men who preferred Plan D
A. The present plan of giving points and campaign stars for decorations	63%
B. Points would be given for campaign stars but not for decorations	10
C. Points would be given for the Purple Heart and for decorations which were given for outstanding bravery in action, but not for other decorations or for campaign stars	11
D. I don't care which of these plans is used	16
Total	100%

The present method of figuring combat credit is clearly defective, and even with the addition of the Combat Infantryman's Badge (and, possibly, similar badges for medical aid men and the like), complaints must be expected. But the world-wide data, plus the supplementary small-sample information just reported, show that such complaints would be insignificant as compared with the morale damage which can be predicted if credit for campaign stars and decorations were to be lowered or eliminated.

Parenthood and Dependency

As has been shown, there is considerable resentment against the high points for parenthood credit. A majority would favor giving points for dependents other

---

[13] Quite similar figures are obtained from samples of Class II Air Force and Service Force troops just shipped to the U. S., with even greater preference for the present system.

than wife or children, and a smaller majority would favor giving points for every child, instead of just the first three. Attitudes toward giving points for being married, even without children, are quite evenly divided, with those opposed being quite strong in their opposition. (Data based on world-wide cross section.)

QUESTION: "How would you feel about giving points after VJ Day for . . ."

	Dependents other than wife or children	Every child instead of only the first three	Being married, even if there are no children
A fine idea—I would favor it very much	40%	39%	30%
A pretty good idea	23	16	16
I wouldn't care one way or the other	14	13	14
Not such a good idea	15	18	19
A poor idea—I would be burned up about it	8	14	21
	100%	100%	100%

Overseas men are much stronger in their opposition to proposals that points be given for additional children or wives than are men in the U. S. who have not been overseas.

Credit for Age

Relatively few men are opposed to adding age to the point system after VJ Day.

QUESTION: "How would you feel about giving points after VJ Day for age?"

	World-wide cross section
A fine idea—I would favor it very much	44%
A pretty good idea	20
I wouldn't care one way or the other	12
Not such a good idea	15
A poor idea—I would be burned up about it	9
	100%

The proper point credit for age, if it is to conform with men's opinions, would apparently be to give one point per year of age. This is tested indirectly by such questions as the following:

QUESTION: "Here are two men, *both* are *married*, *both* have *never served overseas*. Which of them should get out of the Army first after VJ Day?"

	World-wide cross section
Martin, who is 25 years old in the Army 4 years	47%
Clark, who is 35 years old in the Army 3 years	53
	100%

Since the vote splits approximately 50–50, this would indicate that ten years of age and one year in the Army are approximately equated. If the overwhelming majority had voted for letting Martin out first, this would have meant that the men thought a year in the Army should count *more* than ten years of age. The opposite would be true if the vote had been for Clark. Similar paired comparisons showed that a two-to-one majority rated a year overseas or two campaigns as worth more than ten years of age, while a majority voted to give less credit for a child than for ten years of age. This, of course, reflects inconsistency in the point system, which in the judgment of the men now underrates overseas and combat credit as compared with parenthood credit. Such discrepancies would tend to become reconciled, if overseas credit is raised and combat credit either is raised or is extended by including the Combat Infantryman's Badge.

Only 12% would start age credit at age thirty-five. The largest proportion favored starting at age eighteen.

Favor starting at 18	41%
Favor starting at 25	15
Favor starting at 30	10
Favor starting at 35	12
Don't care	22
	100%

Discharge of Various Categories Outside of the Point System

In general, the great majority of the men either would oppose the discharge of special categories of men outside the point system or favor it *only* if it did not very much delay other men getting out under the point system. Relatively more approval is given to letting out men with long service or men over thirty-five than to other categories.

(Percentage Distribution in World-wide Cross Section)

Plan to release after VJ Day outside of the point system all men who . . .	Would favor it even if it delayed other men under the point system	Would favor it only *if it did not very much delay* other men getting out under the point system	Would not favor it at all	No opinion	Total
have been in the Army four or five years or longer	32%	48%	19%	1%	100%
are over 35 years of age	22	53	24	1	100
are fathers	17	41	41	1	100
are not physically qualified for overseas duty	15	41	43	1	100
have been in the Army too short a time to complete their training	3	17	79	1	100

When soldiers throughout the world were asked directly what they would think of substituting for the point system the "first in, first out" plan—letting men out of the Army in the same order as they came in—the men with opinions voted against it by nearly two to one. It should be noted that 32% checked the extreme category "A poor idea—I would be burned up about it."

	World-wide cross section
A fine idea—I would favor it very much	20%
A pretty good idea	13
I wouldn't care one way or the other	7
Not such a good idea	28
A poor idea—I would be burned up about it	32
	100%

How This Study Was Made

For this study, five large representative cross sections of enlisted men were surveyed, anonymously, in the last two weeks of July 1945. The samples comprise representative cross sections of soldiers in (1) the European Theater of Operations, (2) Pacific Ocean Areas, including the Marianas and Okinawa, (3) India-Burma, (4) overseas returnees in the United States, and (5) men without overseas service. These data permit an accurate report for each of the areas covered, and with proper weighting and some allowance for error in filling in gaps for commands not fully covered, also permit an estimate of opinion on a world-wide basis which is reliable with an error probably not exceeding 5%.

The research report quoted above played a part in the War Department's decision to leave the point system intact after VJ Day. It was felt that the capitulation of Japan was so near at hand that any recalculation of point scores should not be undertaken unless overwhelmingly sought by the men.   This was a keen disappointment to some of the revisionists in the War Department who were working to reduce or eliminate overseas and combat credit.   It was also a disappointment, though perhaps a lesser one, to the Information and Education Division, which would have preferred an increase in credit for overseas service and the addition of the Combat Infantryman's Badge to the elements counting toward combat credit.

On August 14, 1945, President Truman announced the surrender of Japan, and the War Department promptly announced its decision to retain the point system as originally set up.

Concluding Comments

As demobilization proceeded, critics of the Army in and out of uniform formed a swelling chorus of discontent over the alleged slowness with which the Army was discharging men.   Congressional pressure was heavy, not only to speed up the process, but also to let out favored categories of men. The War Department lowered the critical score from 85 points to 80 points in September, 60 points in October, and 50 points by the end of December. All available shipping was jammed with returning troops.

Although in retrospect history may find that the greatest American Army ever created was broken up too rapidly, history also will record the irresistible political pressure to "bring the boys home" and the impatience of the soldiers themselves, some units of whom behaved in a manner hardly describable in terms other than mutiny. In the waves of criticism over the slowness of demobilization, the point system came in for at least some share of disapprobation. The point system merely established an objective basis for *priority* of discharge; it had nothing to do with the *rate* of discharge. But it is not surprising if the two concepts became confused in the minds of the public or even in the minds of some of the soldiers.

In early June 1945, shortly after the points were first announced, it will be remembered that only 19 per cent of the men said that the point system was "not so good" or "not good at all." By mid July the proportion went up to 28 per cent and among those still left in the Army by November 1945, to 42 per cent. At no time, however, did those disapproving constitute a majority, even in the post VJ Day period when almost every expression about the Army, as shown in Volume I, Chapter 5, was negative by a decisive proportion.

There can be little doubt that opinions as to the fairness of the point system were confused by frustrations in not getting out of the Army faster. In mid July, for example, when the 26 per cent who thought the point system was "not so good" or "not good at all" were cross tabulated on another item, it was found that among this 26 per cent a third believed that "the point system itself was a good idea but the Army is carrying it out badly." The same was true for 2 out of 5 among the 42 per cent who, still in the Army, disapproved by November. However, one should hasten to add that there was at no time evidence that more than a minute proportion of the men thought the system was abused by personal favoritism. In view of the general tenseness of the situation, it is unpleasant to contemplate what would have happened if the system or its administration had opened the gates to special privilege.

There can be little doubt that the Army took a considerable gamble with destiny in adopting a system of demobilization of individuals rather than of units. If men were robots, the arguments advanced by Army Ground Forces for discharge by units—in order to keep veteran combat organizations intact—would have had much plausibility. Even robots wear out, however, and as previous chapters of this volume have shown, the efficiency as well as the morale of the men exposed to long, protracted ground combat was at very least questionable. The Air Forces recognized such facts by putting a limit on the number of combat missions men had to fly. Ground Forces recognized no such limits, although some ground troops had been sent home on rotation.

In the official history of Ground Forces[14] the havoc played in one division in Europe by transfer out of its 85 point men after VE Day is described in some detail. The facts in general were, however, that of all the men with combat experience in Ground units throughout the world, only 1 man in 9 had 85 points or more. It is true that many of these were key men, but it is also true that there were replacements with combat experience available who could have taken their places and, indeed, many more such men than any current estimates for the Pacific war required.

If the veterans under MacArthur preparing for the invasion of Japan had heard of the wholesale discharge at home of millions of men, including new recruits who had never left the States, it can only be conjectured how enthusiastic they would have been about finishing the job alone. The planned invasion of Japan might have had to be delayed somewhat to permit absorption of replacements and training of new key men if the cutting point under the point system had dropped too far below 85 points. But unless the evidence accumulated throughout these volumes is to be disregarded, there is a possibility that the morale situation would have been explosive, if men whose sacrifice was small had been released by the millions, ahead of men whose sacrifice had been greatest.

There are "ifs" which history cannot definitively answer. In taking its calculated risks, the Army won its gamble. One cannot say for certain what would have happened, after VJ Day as well as before, if there had not been an objective method of demobilization which the majority of the men regarded as fair in principle. Because "military efficiency" is not independent of "morale," there are grounds for believing that the War Department chose correctly when it broke all precedent and went to the enlisted men for their opinions before promulgating its redeployment and demobilization policy.

---

[14] *United States Army in World War II—The Army Ground Forces* (Washington, 1947), pp. 496–98.

CHAPTER 12

THE AFTERMATH OF HOSTILITIES[1]

IN THE summer of 1944 a document was prepared in the Research Branch forecasting the problems which would arise as an aftermath of hostilities. This chapter presents that document exactly as written and compares the forecasts with the facts as to what happened, using as data primarily the attitudes of soldiers in Europe with whom the predictions were mainly concerned.

SECTION I

THE FORECAST

The summer of 1944 was one of great optimism. With the Normandy landings and Saint Lo behind us and our armies racing across France, many of the more sanguine were wagering that the Germans would acknowledge defeat by early fall and even the more sober prophets were willing to concede that a collapse of the Wehrmacht by Christmas was not out of the question. Under such conditions it was quite natural that those responsible for planning Army policies and programs for the post VE Day phase of the European theater operations should turn their attention concretely and realistically to the problems that would have to be met during that next period.

The Information and Education Division had to consider what the major needs of the Army would be with respect to an information, orientation, and education program. It also had to consider what kind of problems would require research and to design that research. The situation required the best possible forecasts of the kinds of problems which would confront the command after the capitulation of the German war machine.

It was decided that since the personnel of the Research Branch

---

[1] By Leonard S. Cottrell, Jr. The 1944 memorandum forecasting problems expected upon the defeat of the Germans was drafted by Cottrell, on the basis of Research Branch discussions. With the collaboration of the analytical staff in ETO he was also responsible for planning the April 1945 and August 1945 surveys which provide the principal factual basis for this chapter.

had been constantly engaged in the systematic study of troop reactions, they should be in a good position to make some reasonably intelligent predictions about what the reactions of troops would be after the fighting was over in Europe.   Consequently, certain of the research staff were assigned the task of outlining the major morale and discipline problems of the post VE Day period and suggesting ways and means of meeting these problems through the I and E program.   Needless to say, this was a challenging and difficult assignment.   It required a good deal of general social psychological knowledge and insight as well as the accumulated specific knowledge about troop reactions, plus the ability to construct imaginatively the main outlines of the situation as it would appear to our troops at that time.

In some respects the predictions were deductions from general sociological propositions, like the following:

1. In general, people are able to suppress their individualistic concerns and interests which handicap them in the performance of their parts in a collective enterprise under the following conditions:

   a. When they are aware of a significant personal stake in the goals of the group effort and of the necessity for total group effort to achieve those goals; or
   b. When they identify their own safety and welfare with that of the group and are aware of a threat to the security of the group.
   c. When they are aware of the nature and significance of their roles in the collective enterprise.
   d. When they are aware of the negative effects of failure to subordinate individualistic interests to group purposes and efforts.

2. Similarly people generally are able to suppress intragroup antagonisms which undermine the unity and efficiency of the group, when they are aware of the handicaps these antagonisms present in the achievement of group goals or in maintaining the security of the group against external threat.
3. The conditions stated above are basic to what is recognized as good discipline —"the cheerful and understanding subordination of the individual to the good of the team."
4. When the conditions outlined above do not obtain, it is still possible to secure group discipline by coercive measures.   But an army or any other group which has to rely on such measures to any great extent is highly vulnerable to stresses and strains.
5. When collective goals are achieved or abandoned or outer threats are removed, the hitherto suppressed individualistic concerns and interests and the latent internal antagonisms reassert themselves and cease to be subordinated to group interests.   Under such conditions, the problem of group discipline and unity becomes acute.

Also involved was thinking specific to American culture, like the following:

In their training experiences, Americans for the most part have emphasized for them the relatively great importance of individual striving for individual interests, goals, rights, privileges, etc., with a corresponding relatively slight emphasis on the duties, responsibilities, and obligations to the interests and welfare of the community. This relative emphasis and corresponding hierarchy of values by which we orient our efforts leads us when confronted by demands and requests to ask automatically "What is there in it for me?" and to be wary of becoming a "sucker." If the answer indicates a fairly obvious and immediate individual reward, we are interested. If it indicates something concerning the general welfare which does not obviously touch us as individuals, we will give it a verbal blessing but take no serious action to make more than a perfunctory response. Certainly the wholehearted commitment of the individual to collective ends is not one of our basic cultural traits. And anything more than a very limited commitment to causes representing general and rather remote values is virtually impossible for the average American.

Also involved was the kind of knowledge about the attitudes of American soldiers which Research Branch surveys had documented and which has been reviewed in the present volumes.

There was nothing especially new about the general formulations or the specific formulations about American culture or even about the American soldier. Most of the propositions were known not only to social scientists but also to practicing politicians and skillful leaders generally. It is probably true, however, that social scientists have not often used them in making explicit predictions about group changes.

Many of the specific predictions were not deductions from theory but were ad hoc applications of "common sense," fortified by some historical knowledge of the reactions of soldiers upon the cessation of World War I.

The reader may now peruse the original document. Following this reading, he will have the opportunity to see what specific predictions turned out to be right and what turned out to be wrong. Actually, of course, the unexpectedly quick capitulation of Japan after the defeat of Germany made some of the problems of the redeployment period discussed in the forecast much less important than they would have been if a year had elapsed between the two surrenders.

Post-Armistice Morale Problems in United States Army [2]

Introduction

The end of hostilities in Europe will bring changes in the mental condition of troops which will present special problems to the command and to those responsible

---

[2] Submitted to the Director of the Information and Education Division of the War Department, August 11, 1944. The first draft was completed July 15, 1944. It was prepared by Leonard S. Cottrell, Jr.

for Army information and orientation. This fact points to the urgent need for anticipating as far as possible what the problems are likely to be and preparing to deal with them before they become serious threats to morale.

The purpose of this outline is to set forth the more important problem reactions troops are likely to show following the cessation of hostilities in Europe and to propose measures for counteracting them.

The history of warfare has proved repeatedly that as long as there is an outside threat to a group or a collective goal to be achieved, internal antagonisms and individualist concerns are subordinated to the safety and interests of the whole group. But when the outer threats are removed or the collective goal achieved or abandoned, the individual concerns and the internal antagonisms come to the surface. Then the unity of the group may become seriously weakened.

This historic fact plus a careful study of research data on veteran combat troops who participated in campaigns in the Mediterranean and Pacific theaters and reports of the reactions of soldiers after the Armistice in 1918 furnish a reasonably sound basis for predicting what the probable reactions of troops in Europe will be following the collapse of Germany. These reactions are listed in sections I–III of this outline, and suggestions for action programs to correct them are continued in section IV.

It will be noted that these reactions are for the most part "problem" reactions. This does not mean that there will be no healthy, desirable reaction. On the contrary, there will be many such. However, by taking positive steps to counteract the "problem" reactions, the desirable ones will be reinforced at the same time the "problems" are being met.

It should also be remembered that all of the men will not show all of the reactions listed. All of the reactions listed, however, are likely to be present in sufficient amounts to warrant attention.

One further point is that these reactions are not inevitable. By constructive, skillful leadership and proper orientation, they can be effectively reduced.

The outline is organized as follows:

    I. Probable early reactions of troops upon receipt of news of cessation of hostilities.
   II. Probable later reactions developing during interim between cessation of hostilities and reassignment of troops.
 III. Probable later reactions of troops following reassignment for:
     A. Active duty in another theater
     B. Occupation duty in Europe
     C. Return to United States to be held as strategic reserve
     D. Demobilization
       1. Men with no disabilities
       2. Men with disabilities
  IV. Suggestions for action programs

I. *Early General Reactions*

When news comes of the cessation of hostilities in Europe, the troops in Europe will probably show the following early reactions:

1. The thrill of being victorious.
2. A desire for "celebrating" (wine, women, song, hell raising).
3. A general feeling of relief that their tough part of the war is over and they have survived it.
4. These will be followed immediately by a rapidly growing feeling of: "Well,

they don't need us here any more so let's get the hell home." (Meantime it should be remembered that the Pacific and CBI troops, still having tough going, will react to the news with the feeling, "Now they can really send us plenty of help to clean this job up fast.")

5. Very shortly there will be the reaction, "I wonder what is going to happen to me now. Will I go home, stay here, or be sent to another theater?"

II. *Later General Reactions*

During the interim between the big news of the cessation of hostilities in Europe and the reassignment of duties, certain deeper reactions will probably set in, following the first reactions of victory, relief and uncertainty. The more significant "problem" reactions likely to occur among many of the men are:

1. General war weariness and revulsion against the destruction of war. Manifestations:
   (a) Feeling the war was not worth while
   (b) Nothing good will come out of the war and
   (c) General depression and "don't give a damn" attitudes
   These attitudes will be aggravated by news of Allied bickering and of conflict and problems at home.
2. A sharp reduction in motivations of duty and self-sacrifice for the country and an accompanying increased preoccupation with individualistic concerns. Manifestations:
   (a) An increase of the feeling, "I have done my share, now let someone else do something for a change."
   (b) Increased eagerness to get home and out of the Army.
   (c) Increased concern about job opportunities.
   (d) Increased resentment at being at a disadvantage in the scramble for jobs.
   (e) Resentment at apparent inequality of sacrifice for the war effort.
   (f) Increased anxiety about welfare of family, fidelity of wives and sweethearts.
   (g) Increased feeling of being forgotten and unappreciated by the people back home.
   (h) Decreased feeling of loyalty to the Army and its leaders.
   (i) Increased demands for a "square deal for the soldier."
3. A decrease in feelings of aggression toward the enemy. Manifestations:
   (a) An increased sense of identification with the people of enemy country.
   (b) A resentment against those at home who voice extreme vindictive sentiments.
   (c) Increased disregard and violation of the nonfraternization policy. (Added December 1944.)
4. An increase of feelings of aggression toward:
   (a) The Army and Army authorities. Manifestations:
      (i) Army discipline regarded as unreasonable and uncalled for.
      (ii) Army leaders regarded as having no interest in the welfare of the men.
      (iii) Increased resentment at differential treatment and privileges accorded officers and men.
      (iv) Increased infractions, insubordination, AWOL, goldbricking, and uncooperativeness.
      (v) Increased tension between units, especially between combat and service units.

(b) Government officials and politicians.   Manifestations:
    (i) Blaming them for getting us into the war.
    (ii) Accusing them of being dupes of our Allies.
    (iii) Accusing them of running the war inefficiently.
    (iv) Accusing them of prolonging overseas service for selfish purposes.
    (v) Accusing them of having no effective plan for aiding soldiers after the war.
    (vi) Accusing them of not being sincerely concerned with plans to prevent war in the future.
    (vii) Resentment at their speeches about the horrors and sacrifices of the war.   "Only men who have been through it know what it's like."
(c) Civilians in general and special civilian groups.   Manifestations:
    (i) Increased bitterness and resentment about the inequality of sacrifice in the war and of advantages after the war.
    (ii) Resentment at being forgotten and not appreciated by home population.
    (iii) Resentment at credit received by civilian groups for their contribution to the war effort.
    (iv) Increased hostility toward such groups as: (1) Labor Unions.   (2) Jews.   (3) Negroes.   (4) Big Business.
(d) Allies.   Manifestations:
    (i) Increased tendency to blame England for getting us into their war.
    (ii) Increased assertions that Americans did the tough fighting and British troops were spared.
    (iii) Complaints that American troops are used to preserve British Empire.
    (iv) Complaints that British troops are being sent home or sent to best or easiest fronts, or occupation posts, and Americans do the dirty work.
    (v) Cynicism and disillusionment about sincerity of Allied efforts to establish permanent peace.
    (vi) Hostility toward civilians in occupied or liberated territories because of difference in languages, customs, reactions toward American troops, and overcharging troops for services rendered.
    (vii) Suspicious of political and military intentions of Russia.
    (viii) Brawls between American and Allied troops.

III. *Reactions Following Reassignment of Troops*

Reassignment of duties will result in the following groupings of troops.   Many of the reactions cited above will remain common to all groups but with different emphasis on different types of reaction.   In addition, each group will present some specific problems not found in other groups.

A. Troops assigned to active duty in another theater.
    1. Those troops will be marked by having in the most acute form more of the reactions listed under section II.   In addition there will be:
    2. Bitter reaction of "Why do we have to be the goats?"
    3. Depressive and pessimistic doubts about surviving another campaign.
    4. Resentment at troops who will go home and catch the cream while they will be doing the dirty work—forgotten.
    5. Strong feeling of: "The least they could do would be to send us over by way of the U. S. and give us a furlough before going on to the next campaign."

B. Troops assigned to occupation duty in Europe.
   1. These troops will react in much the same way as those in III A.
   2. Reaction III A 3 will not be present unless there is considerable amount of mopping up of Nazi underground and guerrilla resistance to contend with.   Nor will III A 5 be present.
   3. There is likely to be an increasing demand for reducing military training.
   4. Increasing demands for more definite information on how long their overseas duty is to last.
C. Troops to be sent to the United States and held in the Army as strategic reserve.
   1. During the interim between the news of cessation and news of being sent to the United States, reaction in section II will be manifested in common with other troops.
   2. Upon receipt of news of their assignment, reactions of relief and satisfaction with their good luck compared with groups A and B will overshadow other reactions.
   3. With the time lag there will be reactions of frustration at delay in getting shipped home.
   4. Some demand for III B 3.
   5. Upon arrival at posts in the United States there will be a sharp rise in: II 1; II 2; II 4; and III B 3.
D. Troops to be demobilized.
   1. Men with no disabilities
      (a) Same as III C 1–5.
      (b) Anxiety about jobs.
      (c) Anxiety about fitting back into civilian jobs, family and social relations.
      (d) Emergence of aggressive groups to champion the "rights of the soldiers."
   2. Men with disabilities
      (a) Much the same as D (1), aggravated by actual impairment of abilities and by hypersensitivity about handicaps.

IV. *Suggestions for Action Programs*

   A. Prepare an information and orientation program that will minimize the armistice in Europe as a terminal point in the war; stress the relatively small amount of immediate demobilization that will take place; and stress the fairness of whatever demobilization does take place.
   1. As pointed out earlier, the removal of an outside threat or the achievement of a common goal allows individualistic concerns and inner antagonisms to emerge and weaken the unity and morale of our Army.   The appearance of reactions listed in sections I and II will, therefore, result from the fact that many soldiers will regard the cessation of hostilities in Europe as an end of their part in the war.   Thus the problem is to reap as much as possible of the morale benefits of victory and at the same time to minimize the armistice in Europe as a terminal point in the war.
   2. While the reactions in I and II cannot be prevented entirely, their intensity can be materially reduced by mentally conditioning the soldier to regard the armistice as an important milestone marking great progress but not the completion of the job by any means.   Men must be conditioned to see the necessity for further duty and to expect reassignment. This suggests that well in advance of the cessation of European hostilities

there should be an all-out effort in information and orientation to drive home the following themes:

(a) Germany is about ripe now for the all-out knock-out punch.

(b) The defeat of Germany will mark a long stride toward cleaning up the war.   Stress the idea of "Two down and one to go."

(c) It will mean that the Allies can turn their whole fighting force to knocking out Japan.

(d) With our full force turned on Japan the last part of the war should go much faster than the first part.

(e) However, it will not be a pushover.

(f) Until the defeat of Japan only a relatively small part of the Army will be demobilized.

(g) While we are defeating Japan there will also be the job of maintaining order in Europe and seeing that friendly and antifascist elements are restored to power.   Otherwise we shall have to do the job all over again.

(h) Even after the defeat of Japan there will be the job of restoring and maintaining order in the Orient.

(i) Whatever demobilization is done will be
  (i) done slowly
  (ii) done on an absolutely just and fair basis (explanation of the basis on which priorities for demobilization will be determined).

3. The themes outlined above should also be worked into materials prepared for use in orientation discussion hours.

4. The plan for personnel readjustment should be explained as most equitable possible in view of military necessity and necessity of continuing war against Japan.

B. Develop plans of action and materials for information and orientation that are designed to counteract the specific problem reactions.

While the measures suggested under A should reduce the frequency and intensity of reactions listed in section I and II, they will not be sufficient. It is necessary to plan additional measures to counteract the specific reactions as they appear after the fighting stops.   Listed below under each of the probable reactions are recommended steps to be taken.

1. Problems presented by general war weariness and revulsion against the destruction of war.   (See reactions listed above under II 1.)

(a) Much of this reaction will be due to fatigue and general letdown. Direct action should include adequate provisions for:
  (i) Rest, with a gradual transition to garrison discipline for combat troops
  (ii) Full and varied recreation and entertainment
  (iii) A wide variety of education programs
  (iv) Sight-seeing

(b) Information and orientation material in the media that present with punch and convictions.
  (i) The magnitude of the job the Army has done.
  (ii) The kind of America and world we have kept the Germans from forcing on us.
  (iii) Factual material on conditions at home.
  (iv) The rights, privileges, and responsibilities of returning veterans.
  (v) Significance of contemporary world events.

(c) Orientation discussion hours using material prepared along the lines suggested in (b).

(d) Emphasize the news of progress made by the United States government and Allies in planning for the postwar world.

2. Problems presented by a sharp reduction in motivations of duty and self-sacrifice for the country and an accompanying increase in preoccupation with individualistic concern. (See reactions listed above under II 2.) This calls for:

(a) Continued emphasis in the media of the themes:
   (i) The job is not yet finished.
   (ii) A man's share in the job is done only when the job is finished.
   (iii) The job will be finished faster if everyone pitches in and does his share.

(b) Emphasis in the media on the themes of reassurance:
   (i) Adequate provisions are being made to assure the future security and opportunities of service men when they go back home. (Caution should be used in not overplaying this theme.)
      Report of actual successful operation of the rehabilitation of discharged men.
      Reports of specific actions by government, business, industry, and labor in providing for returned service men.
   (ii) The people back home are still doing the job of production to finish the job.
   (iii) The people back home are more and more aware of the tough job their soldiers have done and are doing.
      Human-interest stories which clearly demonstrate the affection, admiration, and appreciation the people at home have for their soldiers. (Not too Hollywood.)

(c) Orientation discussions based on materials prepared along lines suggested in (a) and (b).

3. Problems presented by a decrease in feelings of aggression toward the enemy. (See reactions listed under II 3.)

(a) Emphasis in the media on themes:
   (i) The existence of thousands of local and national Nazi and militaristic leaders who must be routed out before the future is safe.
   (ii) The distorted education and beliefs of the German people and the necessity of reeducating them before they can be trusted to govern themselves.

(b) Orientation discussion hours on what to do with the Germans based on materials prepared on themes in (a).

4. Problems presented by an increase of feelings of resentment and aggression toward:

(a) The Army and Army authorities
(b) Government officials and politicians
(c) Civilians in general and special civilian groups
(d) Our Allies

(See reactions listed under II 4.)

Before discussing specific ways for counteracting these reactions of aggression it is necessary to consider some of the important sources of resentment and aggression which have to be recognized in planning a program.

First, there is the fact that the necessity of military service itself has interrupted and frustrated the goals and interests and satisfactions of the men's civilian life. These frustrations produce resentment.

Second, Army life itself, its discipline, its apparent lack of concern for the individual, its privations are frequently frustrating to the individual and engender aggressive reaction.

Third, the feeling of inequality of sacrifice produces resentment and aggressive reactions.

Fourth, the conviction that the entrance of the United States into the war was unnecessary and that we got into it by blundering or by deliberate design of our leaders is still more than half believed by some people and is a source of resentment.

Fifth, the conviction that we were dragged in by our British Allies is still entertained by some and is a source of resentment.

Sixth, the suspicion that we were maneuvered into the war by certain groups for reasons of their own, that our stated war aims are not sincerely held goals by those in power, and that the war will really accomplish little is a latent belief among many which is or can reasonably become a source of aggression.

These various sources may be regarded as a reservoir of resentment and of aggressive reactions which are latent threats to the unity of purpose and action of the Army. They are minimized as disintegrative forces by a strong conviction of the existence of an outside threat and the necessity of accomplishing the common goal of winning the war.

It is obvious, therefore, that the potential reactions listed under II 4, a–d can best be dealt with by:

(i) An adequate job of holding the attention of the soldier on the importance of completing the job of winning the war and on the threats represented by the remnant fascist elements in Europe and by an undefeated Japan.

(ii) Convincing the soldier that it is necessary for all forces to be devoted to completing the job and that by this concentration the job will be completed more rapidly.

(iii) Reassuring him of the validity of our war aims and the worthiness of these aims.

(iv) Reassuring him of the possibility of achieving these aims.

(v) Reassuring him of the security of his own future in the postwar period.

In addition to these general measures certain specific ones should be planned.

(4a) To deal with an increase of feelings of aggression toward the Army and Army authorities.

(i) Suggestions under IV B 1 (a) i–iv, are relevant here.

(ii) Special attention by all officers to the welfare of their men with respect to housing, mess, clothing, medical care, personal problems. (This theme should be emphasized.)

(iii) Stringent measures by higher commanders to see that the obvious resentment-producing differentials in food, facilities, comforts, privileges between officers and men resulting from the flagrant misuse of the privileges of rank are minimized. (This theme should be emphasized.)

(iv) Regimental commanders should hold a series of discussions with junior officers on good leadership practices for the transition period.

(v) Explanations to the men of the reasons for garrison discipline even though fighting has stopped.

(vi) As soon as possible after the Armistice a well planned large-scale competitive athletic program at all levels should be initiated with emphasis on mass participation. This should include instruction in sports skills and utilization of sports celebrities, whether in or out of the Army. The competition should extend to higher levels to permit spectator interest. This higher echelon competition should, if possible, be carried to Army, Theaters, Inter-Service, and Inter-Allied stages. A large-scale intensive publicity campaign should introduce and accompany the program and everything possible should be done to stir up competitive spirit between, and spectator interest in, all echelons of competition. Lavish publicity, both by the press and the radio, should be enlisted to encourage participation and to provide entertainment. Broadcasting facilities should be employed wherever possible to bring the higher level competition to the personnel of the organizations competing.

(vii) A similar program of arts and crafts, music and theater, as well as increased library facilities should be organized simultaneously with the sports program to take care of those individuals who are not primarily interested in athletics.

(viii) Events should be planned which are designed to provide expression of mutual respect of different branches for one another. (E.g., a dance or reception held by a service outfit in honor of a combat outfit at which spokesmen of the two outfits express appropriate sentiments in brief soldierly style.)

(ix) News and feature articles which dramatize the concern high commanders have for the soldier's welfare.

(4b) To deal with an increase of feelings of aggression toward government officials and politicians.

(i) News and feature articles emphasizing the progress the government is making in planning and implementing an organization for peace.

(ii) The same kind of material on progress in providing for the future security and opportunities of the men in the service. Include reports of actual successful operation of rehabilitation.

(iii) Emphasize news that demonstrates the government has not forgotten that the speedy prosecution of the war is its number one job.

(4c) To deal with an increase in feelings of aggression toward civilians in general and toward civilian groups.

(i) Emphasis on suggestions in IV B 2 (b), (i)–(iii).

(ii) Feature personal human-interest stories of heroism, devotion to duty, loyalty, etc. of: Negro soldiers, Jewish soldiers, Soldiers with a labor background, Soldiers with business management background.

(iii) Emphasize that in spite of the publicized frictions, the vast majority of people back home did a production job that surprised the world.

(4d) To deal with an increase in feelings of aggression toward our Allies.

(i) Emphasis on news and information that show our Allies are doing their part in the war. Continue present policy of picturing what the situation might have been had England not stood against Germany after Dunkirk and had the Russian Army accepted defeat in the dark days of 1941 and 1942.

(ii) Feature personalized materials which picture the people in Allied countries possessing admirable characteristics and as being like ourselves in important respects.

(iii) Information showing the Allies to be cooperating with us in planning a stable peace.

C. Develop supplementary plans adapted to needs of troops with differential assignments outlined in III.

    1. For troops assigned to active duty in another theater.

        (a) Intensive application of all measures outlined in IV A and B that are feasible.

        (b) While they are waiting to be moved out of Europe, give them good rest areas and the best facilities for rest recreation, organize sightseeing tours, etc.

        (c) Emphasize that they are selected for further duty because of superior quality.

        (d) Explain the necessity for and process of the conversion of units.

    2. For troops assigned to occupation duty in Europe.

        (a) Intensive application of all measures outlined in IV A and B that are feasible.

        (b) Institute as early as possible a large-scale education program.

        (c) News stories of the tough job troops in the Pacific are doing.

    3. For troops to be sent to the United States and held in the Army as strategic reserve.

        (a) Intensive application of all measures outlined in IV A and B that are feasible.

        (b) Institute as early as possible a large-scale education program for them while they are waiting to be returned to the United States.

        (c) Focus attention on their light duty compared with that of the combat and occupation troops.

        (d) Explain the necessity for and process of the conversion of units.

    4. For troops to be demobilized.

        (a) Men with no disabilities.

            (i) Intensive application of all measures outlined in IV A and B that are feasible.

            (ii) Institute as early as possible a large-scale education program.

            (iii) Include a carefully prepared discussion program designed to give a constructive orientation to problems of American life.

            (iv) Vocational guidance to assist in job adjustment.

            (v) A well-oiled system set up well in advance for handling a man all the way back to his home and job that will furnish the best possible guidance and aid with a minimum of fruitless delay and confusion.

            (vi) Emphasize that the war has been destructive of our wealth and resources, that there will be problems in getting back on a sound economic basis again; that the soldiers coming back will have a large responsibility for helping to rebuild their country into the fine place to live they want it to be; that they must be prepared to take this responsibility.

        (b) Men with handicaps.

            (i) The same general program outlined in IV C 4 (a)

            (ii) Special provisions for general guidance and assistance

            (iii) Provisions for special vocational training for those who need it.

        (c) A campaign of advice to civilians on how to behave toward returned veterans, both handicapped and nonhandicapped. If possible this should be worked out by able men who have been through the experience of being returned veterans.

SECTION II

THE FACTS

The basic orientation from which the forecast drew both its specific predictions and its recommendations for action was the proposition that when threats to the security of a group are removed, or collectively held objectives and goals are achieved or abandoned, the unity of the group and its control over its members tend to weaken; the subordination of individual interests to the welfare and interests of the group is replaced by the predominance of individualistic concerns and motivations.

The American Army was not expected to be an exception to this

CHART I

SHIFTS IN ATTITUDES OF ENLISTED MEN IN EUROPEAN THEATER
(April 1945 to August 1945)

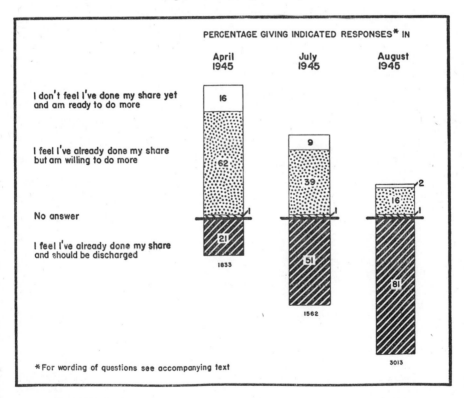

Data from S-223, S-218 and S-235.

The numbers at the bottom of the bars are the numbers of cases on which percentages are based.

general sociological proposition.   The readers of these volumes already know the broad outlines of what happened after VE Day. To illustrate the overall "letdown" we may look at Chart I, which graphs replies of soldiers to the following question, clearly reflecting a profound shift in orientation and motivation following the end of the fighting in Europe on May 5, 1945:[3]

A. Some soldiers feel they've already done their share in winning the war. Others feel they should still do more. How do you personally feel about what you've done in this war?
(Asked of a cross section of troops in Europe surveyed April 5 to May 5, 1945.)

B. How do you feel about what you've done in this war?
(Asked of a cross section of troops in Europe surveyed July 10–24, 1945.)

C. Although the war is over, there is still a big job for the Army to do in occupying the defeated countries and in completing the job of demobilization. How do you feel about further service on these jobs?
(Asked of a cross section of troops in Europe surveyed August 14–24, 1945.)

The April and August surveys in Europe were explicitly designed to elicit facts on subjects considered in the forecast made in the preceding summer.   They constitute the main source material of this chapter, though supplemented at various points by other studies. The dates of these two surveys should be kept clearly in mind.   The April survey was made in the last two weeks in April 1945—just *before* the German surrender.[4]   The August survey was made in late

---

[3] The answer categories to Questions B and C are as given in Chart I. The categories to Question A were as follows (percentages giving each reply are shown):

I don't feel I've done my share yet	16
I feel I've already done my share, but I'm ready to do more, but not in a combat job	35
I feel I've already done my share, but I'm ready to do more in any kind of job they assign me to	27
I feel I've already done my share and should be discharged	21
No answer	1

The second and third categories were combined for presentation in the chart. It is quite likely that the slight variations in wording of the questions and the differences in categories would account for some of the differences, but it is very unlikely they would account for anywhere near the difference found. In this connection it should be noted that Question C was deliberately loaded in such a way as to encourage replies indicating willingness for further service.

[4] In all, this cross section included 5,628 men. The questionnaire was broken into three forms, each administered to a cross section: Form A to a cross section of 1,917, Form B to 1,833, and Form C to 1,878. Nearly all questions asked appeared on two of the three forms. Hence for any one question the sample would be around 3,700 men.

August 1945—just *after* the official announcement of the Japanese surrender.[5]   The original plan was to make the second survey several months after the German surrender but well in advance of a Japanese surrender.   The sudden collapse of Japanese resistance made this impossible.   However it is our opinion that the impact of the Japanese defeat merely served to accentuate the trends which set in after VE Day (see, for example, Chart I).

It would have been highly desirable to conduct one or two more trend surveys, say in December 1945 and February 1946, in order to make a more complete recording of attitude changes after the fighting was over.   However, the end of the war with Japan brought sharp curtailment of research staff and facilities which made further large-scale studies of this type not feasible.   To judge from the news in late 1945 and early 1946, many of the reactions noted in this report became even more acute in the later phases of the demobilization period.

What, then, were the important specific changes in attitudes among American troops following the German surrender?   And to what extent were the predictions made of their reactions borne out?

In the following pages we shall discuss the extent of change in the following areas: (1) Attitudes toward the Germans and Germany. (2) Attitudes toward our Allies.   (3) Attitudes toward the Army and further service.   (4) Attitudes toward the home front and special civilian groups.   (5) Attitudes toward the war and the future.

These were the attitudes which were regarded as having an important bearing on morale and discipline and hence were the main objects of efforts to anticipate and control.

In the case of each of the five attitude areas the discussion includes a very brief summary of the predictions made and shows the research findings on the changes which actually took place during the period covered by the surveys.

---

[5] The size of this sample was 3,013 men.   In order to be sure that changes were not due to changes in composition of the Army a "matched" sample was drawn from the 3,013 returns so as to make it comparable to the April survey with respect to: educational status, marital status, combat experience, ratings, proportion of air and ground troops, length of time in the Army, and length of time overseas.   On the last two factors listed, the matching allowed for the four months of elapsed time between the two surveys.   The size of the matched sample is 2,648 men.   When the matched sample was compared with the total sample of 3,013 on the attitudes studied, the results were so nearly the same that the entire sample was used in the comparisons noted in this chapter.   The changes in attitudes were not due to changes in composition of the Army.

PART 1.   Attitudes Toward the Germans
           and Germany

It was predicted that there would be a general decrease in feelings
of hostility toward the Germans and an increase in more positive,
friendly attitudes.   In a special memorandum on the problems of
enforcing the nonfraternization policy[6] submitted in December 1944,
it was predicted that there would be a strong tendency toward
friendly contact with German civilians and a consequent increase in
violations of the regulations against such contact.   It was felt that
these shifts would result in some tendency to identify with the Germans and that this would mean an increased receptivity to the
German point of view.   It was not held that all men would show
these tendencies, but that these reactions would be found with sufficient frequency to warrant attention.

General Attitudes Toward Germans

As Chart II shows, during the four-month period between the two
surveys there was an appreciable shift in attitude among American
soldiers in the direction of less hostility toward and a more favorable opinion of German people.   There was also an increase in the
tendency to regard a majority of Germans as capable of being educated for a democratic society and of becoming a trustworthy
nation.

Additional information obtained in August, but not in April,
shows that at the time of the August survey there were slightly more
men who said they had favorable opinions of the German people
than there were who had such opinions of the French people.[7]   (See
Chart III.)   In another form of question men were asked, "Leaving
aside for the moment the fact that they are our enemies or our allies,
which one of the following do you like best, just as people?"   The
results were:

English people	48%
German people	23
French people	16
No answer	13
	100%

---

[6] Also prepared by Leonard S. Cottrell, Jr.

[7] Further data and some discussion about this finding are presented in the discussion
of "Attitudes Toward the French" in Part 2 of this section.

CHART II

Changes in Attitudes Toward Germans
(Cross Sections of Soldiers in European Theater, April 1945 and August 1945)

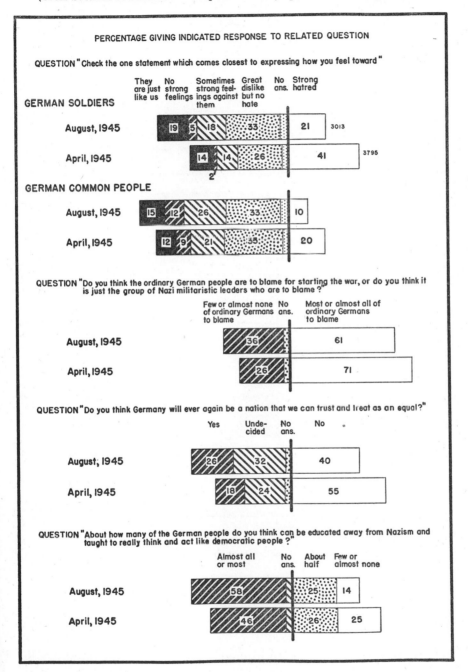

PERCENTAGE GIVING INDICATED RESPONSE TO RELATED QUESTION

QUESTION "Check the one statement which comes closest to expressing how you feel toward"

GERMAN SOLDIERS

They are just like us / No strong feelings / Sometimes strong feelings against them / Great dislike but no hate / No ans. / Strong hatred

August, 1945 — 19 | 5 | 18 | 33 | 21 — 3013

April, 1945 — 14 | 14 | 26 | 41 — 3795 (2)

GERMAN COMMON PEOPLE

August, 1945 — 15 | 12 | 26 | 33 | 10

April, 1945 — 12 | 9 | 21 | 35 | 20

QUESTION "Do you think the ordinary German people are to blame for starting the war, or do you think it is just the group of Nazi militaristic leaders who are to blame?"

Few or almost none of ordinary Germans to blame / No ans. / Most or almost all of ordinary Germans to blame

August, 1945 — 36 | 61

April, 1945 — 26 | 71

QUESTION "Do you think Germany will ever again be a nation that we can trust and treat as an equal?"

Yes / Undecided / No ans. / No

August, 1945 — 26 | 32 | 40

April, 1945 — 18 | 24 | 55

QUESTION "About how many of the German people do you think can be educated away from Nazism and taught to really think and act like democratic people?"

Almost all or most / No ans. / About half / Few or almost none

August, 1945 — 58 | 25 | 14

April, 1945 — 46 | 26 | 25

Data from S-223 and S-235.

The numbers following the bars are the numbers of cases on which percentages are based.

Attitudes Toward Specific Policies with Respect to Germany

It is clear from the foregoing data that there was an appreciable shift in the predicted direction of less hostility and more friendliness toward German people.   However, it is interesting and significant to note that on matters of specific policy in dealing with Germany

CHART III

COMPARISON OF OPINIONS ABOUT ENGLISH, GERMANS, AND FRENCH
(European Theater, August 1945)

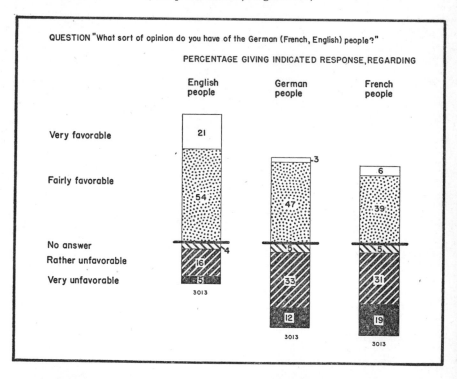

Data from S-235.
The numbers at the bottom of the bars are the numbers of cases on which percentages are based.

as a nation, there was either no significant change or a small increase in opinion favoring a policy of firm control.   The only statistically significant (though small) shifts toward greater leniency were with respect to the punishment of the "little Nazi leaders," breaking Germany into small states, and providing emergency relief for Germans needing food, clothing, etc.   The results are shown in Table 1.

TABLE 1

ATTITUDES OF ENLISTED MEN IN EUROPE TOWARD SPECIFIC POLICIES WITH
RESPECT TO GERMANY, APRIL 1945 AND AUGUST 1945

QUESTION: "Do you think the United Nations should keep an occupation force in Germany for some years after the war, even if it means that the United States will have to furnish a considerable number of troops in order to do it?"

	PER CENT OF MEN GIVING INDICATED ANSWERS IN:	
	April 1945	*August 1945*
Yes	65	75
Not sure	19	16
No	16	9
	100	100

QUESTION:* "Do you think the United Nations should or should not . . . ?"

	PER CENT SAYING WE SHOULD	
	April 1945	*August 1945*
Kill or put in prison for life all big-shot Nazi leaders	93	95
Closely supervise and inspect the German schools and colleges for some years to come	89	93
Make German labor rebuild devastated areas in other countries at POW wages	75	81
Prevent Germans from rebuilding their chemical, steel, and automotive industries	45	51
Kill or put in prison for life all the little Nazi leaders who held lower positions	78	75
Break Germany up into small states	56	49
Give emergency relief in such things as food, clothing, fuel, medical aid, where Germans cannot supply these things themselves	43	52
Number of cases	*3,795*	*3,013*

Data from S-223 and S-235.
* This list of questions was prefaced as follows: "There are listed below a number of things that might be done with Germany. After each item, draw a circle around the answer which shows whether you yourself think each thing should or should not be done. If you have no opinion on a particular item, then just circle the words don't know."

Fraternization with German Civilians and Its Relation to Attitudes

The nonfraternization policy of strictly forbidding all dealings with Germans except on official business was the center of considerable controversy from the time it was proposed until it was abandoned in most of its essential features July 14, 1945. In its detailed memorandum, mentioned above, the Research Branch predicted that the regulation could be enforced only with great difficulty, if at all.

There were reports that even during the heavy fighting in the border cities of Germany, the nonfraternization order was being violated very frequently. During April 13–18, 1945, the Research Branch sent experienced interviewers and observers into several cities along the Rhine, all of which had been recently taken, to interview officers and enlisted men on the problem of fraternization. The interviewers reported that fraternization of certain types, chiefly involving German women, was occurring on a fairly extensive scale and that the officers in charge were extremely dubious about being able to enforce the rules against it, particularly after hostilities ceased.

In the survey made during April 1945 (N = 3,795), 26 per cent of the men said they thought there would be "a good many" Germans with whom it would be all right for American soldiers to be friendly after the fighting was over.[8] An additional 44 per cent thought there would be "a few." Only 16 per cent were sure there would be none. Eleven per cent were undecided, and 3 per cent did not answer the question.

In answer to another question[9] in the same survey, 14 per cent said they thought a soldier should receive no punishment if he fraternized with a German civilian while the fighting was still going on, and 45 per cent thought there should be no punishment for fraternization after the fighting was over.

The theater command finally decided to relax the restrictions, first removing the ban against friendly contact with young children and on July 14, 1945 permitting Army personnel "to engage in conversation with adult Germans on the streets and in public places."

From what has been said so far on the fraternization situation, it is not surprising that reported contacts with German civilians increased markedly during the period between the two surveys. (See Table 2.)

---

[8] Question: "After the fighting with Germany is over, do you think there will be any German civilians that it would be all right for American soldiers to be friendly with?"

_____ Yes, there will be a good many
_____ There will be a few
_____ No, there will be none
_____ Undecided

[9] Question: "Check what you think should be done to a soldier if he does these things":

   a. If a soldier fraternizes with a German civilian while the fighting with Germany is still going on

      _____ The soldier should be punished severely
      _____ He should be punished some, but not severely
      _____ He should not be punished at all

   b. The same question for the case when the fighting with Germany would be over.

TABLE 2

AMOUNT OF CONTACTS WITH GERMAN GIRLS AND OLDER GERMAN CIVILIANS,
REPORTED BY SOLDIERS IN GERMANY, APRIL 1945 AND AUGUST 1945

QUESTIONS: "How many of the American soldiers (in that part of Germany you have
been in) do you think have had some friendly contact with German girls?
(For example, talking, joking, or flirting with them, etc.)"
"How many of the American soldiers there do you think have had some
friendly contact with older German civilians?   (For example, talking with
them, passing the time of day, etc.)"

| | PERCENTAGE GIVING INDICATED REPLY CONCERNING CONTACT WITH* | | | |
| | German girls in | | Older German civilians in | |
	April 1945	August 1945	April 1945	August 1945
"Almost all" or "most" of them have	18	57	6	31
"About half" of them have	11	14	6	16
"Few" or "almost none" of them have	68	27	82	52
No answer	3	2	6	1
Number of cases	*1,505*	*2,343*	*1,505*	*2,343*

Data from S-223 and S-235.
* These figures include only those men who said they had spent some time in Germany (79 per cent
of the April sample and 76 per cent of the August sample).   In April the questions were asked on only
one form of the questionnaire given to a cross section of 1,917.

The reports by men in the August survey of their own contacts
indicate that the proportions having personal contacts (not on official business) within a given three-day time interval increased with
length of time spent in Germany.   The percentages reporting contacts in the three days previous to the survey were:[10]

Among men who had been in Germany	With German girls	With older German civilians
4 months or more	51%	42%
Less than 4 months	33	24

In general, the first contacts of fraternization were with girls, the
earlier contacts being transitory sexual relations.   As time went on,
more stable liaisons with girls were established.   These relations, in
turn, frequently led to contacts with the girls' families and friends.
Among those reporting contacts with girls, almost eight in ten report
also having contact with older German civilians.

How was contact related to attitudes?   As Chart IV shows, the

---

[10] These data are available for the August survey only.

more frequent and intense the contacts with older German civilians, the more favorable were the opinions toward the German people The same pattern of relationship holds if contacts with German girls is the sorting variable.   Such data do not, of course, permit the conclusion that contacts produced more favorable attitudes, though this is quite possible.   The relationship could be the result of those with initially more favorable attitudes seeking more frequent contacts.   Probably both factors are operating.

CHART IV

OPINIONS OF GERMAN PEOPLE AS RELATED TO FREQUENCY OF CONTACT
WITH OLDER GERMAN CIVILIANS
(European Theater, August 1945)

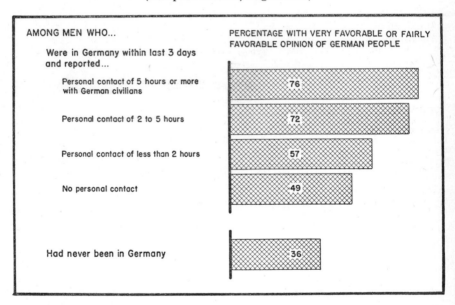

Data from S-235.

On the other hand, frequency or intensity of contact was not associated with significant differentials in the percentage of men who thought we should prevent Germany from rebuilding her basic industries or who held other "be tough with Germany" attitudes which were illustrated in Table 1.

It will be recalled that there were predictions that after VE Day some soldiers would show tendencies toward identification with the Germans.   One evidence of identification with another person is the acceptance of his point of view.   The surveys under discussion here

ing alternative courses of action.   Among the men classified as undecided or inconsistent are some who expect to work for an employer but say they will take the first job to come along, others who are considering two alternative jobs or employment statuses without being able to decide between them, and still others who express markedly inconsistent plans in answer to different questions in the series asked.

In Table III,[5] officers and enlisted men are classified by the definiteness with which they express their various post-separation employment plans.

A comparison between prospective employment status and previous civilian status points to an apparent decrease in the number of students, a considerable increase in the number of men self-employed and some decrease in the number who will enter the labor market as employees.   The shifts indicated by such a comparison, however, require more careful inspection.   They require inspection both from the point of view of the predictive value of the data and from that of the specific groups into which men have been classified.

Aspiring to a higher employment status than one has is a trait traditionally possessed in high degree by Americans.   The soldiers surveyed are, in this sense, typical of their countrymen.   Unfortunately, this complicates the problem of predicting what the men are most likely to do when they leave the Army, for some men have allowed their aspirations unduly to color their reported expectations of postwar employment.   This is particularly true of many of the men with only tentative plans.   Had these men been interviewed at length some of them would probably have admitted that they were voicing their aspirations and not real expectations in their answers to the questionnaire.   One would hesitate to predict that they will actually do the things they are planning or hoping to do.   Prediction, in the strict sense of the word, would require the evaluation of plans now held both in the light of the individual's qualifications to carry out such plans and in the light of prospective opportunities.   Moreover, such prediction would be subject to continuing re-evaluations as individuals and conditions change and develop.   Thus the data reported in Table III [5] should not be regarded at this time as predictions but as elements which must be considered in making predictions.

In the present chapter one can do no more than illustrate the kind of detailed information made available from these studies.   Let us take one small segment only—namely, the plans of soldiers for farming.   These plans were summarized in a 52-page report prepared by the Research Branch in December 1944.[6]   Here is illustrated the complexity of the analytical work of separating definite plans from wishful thinking and also the kind of information made available as to specific aspects of the problem.

The main findings in the report were summarized as follows:

1. *Number of Officers and Enlisted Men Planning to Farm*

(a) *Overall estimate*

Surveys of the postwar occupational plans of officers and enlisted men in the United States and overseas lead to an estimate of about 800,000 men in the Army

---

[5] Presented as Table 1 in this chapter.

[6] *Soldiers' Plans for Farming After They Leave the Army*, Research Branch Report B-131.   In preparing this report, the Research Branch worked in close cooperation with the Bureau of Agricultural Economics, in the Department of Agriculture.

alone with plans to farm as of summer 1944. Shifts in the plans of men not definitely decided but now considering full-time farming as a postwar occupation might lower this figure to 650,000 or might raise it as high as 1,000,000 although the latter seems unlikely. The estimate of 800,000 prospective farmers corresponds roughly with the number of officers and enlisted men who left farming to enter the Army. Also planning to return to farms will be a number of men from the other services and some civilian war workers who left farms only to take advantage of temporary opportunities in war industry.

Separate surveys were conducted of officers, white enlisted men, and Negro enlisted men. These groups are considered in order of the magnitudes of their prospective contributions of personnel to farming after the war.

(b) *White enlisted men*

Among a group approximating in most respects a cross section of white enlisted men (except illiterates) in the Army, ten per cent of the men reported that they were seriously considering farming as a full-time occupation after the war. Included in this ten per cent are nearly eight per cent with fairly definite and consistent plans for farming and slightly over two per cent who are either considering some alternative occupation or are somewhat uncertain that they will farm.

In addition to men seriously considering farming as a full-time occupation after the war, another fifteen per cent of all white enlisted men surveyed say that they "may do some farming" although most of these men have fairly definite plans to do something else.

Another six per cent of all white enlisted men surveyed express interest in part-time farming. Slightly under one per cent name part-time farming as their primary postwar plan, while for the other five per cent interest in part-time farming is secondary to plans for a steady job off the farm.

Making certain assumptions as to the proportion of unrepresented illiterates who expect to farm, it is estimated that the proportion of white enlisted men who will leave the Army expecting to farm will not be less than nine per cent nor more than thirteen per cent. An intermediate estimate of eleven per cent is arrived at. For an Army of six and three quarter million white enlisted men the "best estimate" of prospective farmers is thus about 750,000.

(c) *Negro enlisted men*

Slightly less than ten per cent of the Negro soldiers surveyed reported that they were seriously considering farming after the war, with seven per cent quite definitely decided and three per cent relatively less sure. It is estimated that if present plans are sustained, between eight and nine per cent of Negro enlisted men will leave the Army planning to farm. These would number about 60,000 of the 700,000 Negro enlisted men in the Army.

(d) *Officers*

Relatively few officers either come from or plan to go into farming as a full-time occupation. Approximately two per cent are seriously considering full-time farming. It is to be expected that from 10,000 to 15,000 officers will turn to agriculture for full-time employment after the war if current plans are sustained.

2. *Previous Experience of Men Planning to Farm*

Nearly nine out of ten men with definite plans to farm after the war report at least one year's full-time farming experience. Only two per cent report no previous farming experience. Even among men with relatively vague plans to farm, a considerable majority have had some previous farming experience.

The farming experience of men seriously considering full-time farming after the war was most often gained on family farms or as hired workers, but more than a fourth of these men say they were operators of farms before the war.

3. *Regional Distribution of Prospective Farmers*

In general, the men who expect to farm after the war will be distributed among the several regions of the United States in the same proportions as were men farming just prior to their induction into the Army. In large part this is indicated by the fact that men who farmed before the war and expect to farm after the war are planning to return to their former region of residence.

4. *Type of Farming Planned*

The principal products or crops that prospective farmers expect to raise correspond in general with the patterns of farming in the regions to which they expect to go. By and large, the men who expect to farm and who farmed previously will go back to the same type of farming they were engaged in.

5. *Plans for Obtaining a Farm*

Nearly two thirds of the men who plan definitely to farm say that they have in mind the particular farm they expect to operate or work on. Included in this group are men who say they own farms, men who expect to work on family farms, and men who say they already know which farm they expect to rent or buy. Most of the men not returning to family farms regard themselves as potential operators, as evidenced by the fact that only five per cent of the white enlisted men and ten per cent of the Negro enlisted men who are quite sure they will farm say they expect to work for wages.

6. *Availability of Family Farms*

More than half of the men planning definitely to farm after the war report that their fathers are farm operators (although less than one fourth expect to work on their family's farm). Negro enlisted men are slightly more apt to plan to return to their families' farms.

7. *Plans for Operating a Farm*

Most prospective farmers regard themselves as potential operators. Three fourths of the white enlisted men who feel sure they will farm can be said to have definite, consistent plans for operating a farm either by themselves or with relatives. These comprise six per cent of all white enlisted men surveyed. Another two per cent of the white enlisted men surveyed say they may try to operate a farm, but are not sure. Among Negro enlisted men, four per cent have definite plans for operating a farm either by themselves or with a relative and another two per cent have relatively less definite plans to operate a farm. Although a slight majority of the prospective farm operators say they will have at least half of the money they will need to get started with, many are planning very small investments.

8. *Interest in New Land Areas*

Approximately one sixth of the white enlisted men quite sure they will farm say that they would want to go to a new land area to farm if such areas are opened for settlement. Nearly a third of the Negro enlisted men say they would want to go to a new land area. Unless the location and character of any new land area can be explicitly described, however, it seems unlikely that any accurate estimate can be given of the number of potential migrants to that area.

9. *Interpretation*

A prediction of the number of soldiers who will actually farm after the war cannot be made solely from the expectations of the men. If industrial employment offers plenty of jobs at attractive wages, some men who now expect to farm may be induced to turn to industry. On the other hand, considerable industrial unemployment would help send into farming not only most of the men seriously considering farming but also some of those with only vague plans to farm.

The intermediate estimate of the proportion of soldiers who will leave the Army expecting to farm corresponds roughly with the proportion who were farming just prior to induction. This does not mean, however, that the nation's farms will be able to absorb all the men planning to return to them. Rural areas have normally produced more young men and women than can efficiently be utilized on the farm. A certain proportion of young men on farms at the time of their induction would probably have left the farms within a year or two even without the draft and the war. Moreover, the war has led to a decrease in the number of farms in operation, accompanied by an *increase* in farm production, the latter achieved through more efficient use of labor and less underemployment. It is unlikely that gains in efficiency will be entirely lost after the war; with increasing availability of farm machinery still greater efficiency may in fact be expected. Therefore, a return to farming of as large a proportion of enlisted men as now contemplate returning would probably give rise to acute problems in the agricultural economy.

10. *Potential Dangers*

Two potential dangers are indicated. (1) Most of these prospective farmers say they expect to be farm operators. Within the predicted group of approximately 800,000 veterans who may leave the Army expecting to farm, at least 125,000 are intent on operating a farm yet do not have a particular farm in mind. Another 150,000 more or less say they know which farm they expect to rent or buy; but many of these men may find either that they will face competition from other men who have the same farm in mind or that the farm has been incorporated in someone else's holdings. The wartime trend toward fewer, more efficient farms means both that there will be fewer good farms available and that competition will be much stiffer for the new farmer who plans something more than subsistence farming. (2) Many of the men who plan to operate farms say they expect to invest less capital than would be required to stock and equip a farm and provide adequate operating expenses. There is a danger that a large number may attempt to farm on submarginal lands where their chances of success will be slight. The Army has a responsibility to see that every man who plans to farm is aware of the problems he would face on an inadequately financed or a submarginal farm.

The overall estimates of the proportion planning to farm after leaving the Army were based on tabulations illustrated in Tables 2 and 3. We see in Table 2 that 30.6 per cent of the white enlisted men expressed at least some vague interest in farming. Only 7.7 per cent, however, planned definitely to farm full time (Group A), while smaller proportions had some serious intentions to farm full time (Groups B and C). Vague plans for full-time farming were registered by 14.8 per cent (Group D).

An illustration of how cross tabulations were used to evaluate in-

tensity of interest in farming in Groups A, B, C, and D respectively
is shown by Table 2.   Among men who said they planned definitely
to farm, three fourths said they expected to make farming their life

TABLE 2

PERCENTAGE OF WHITE ENLISTED MEN WHO PLAN TO FARM AFTER LEAVING THE
ARMY, BY DEGREE OF DEFINITENESS OF PLAN

Plans for Farming		Per Cent of White Enlisted Men
Seriously considering full-time farming		10.1
(A) Plan definitely to farm full time	7.7	
(B) Think they will probably farm but considering		
an alternative plan	1.0	
(C) May farm, but relatively uncertain	1.4	
Have vague plans to farm full time (Group D)		14.8
Have plans for part-time farming		5.7
(E) Have farming as primary interest	.8	
(F) Have farming as secondary interest	4.9	
No apparent plan to farm		69.4
		100.0

Data from S-106.

work, while all but 3 per cent of the remainder in this group said
they expected to work on a farm but might change later.

At the other end of Table 2, among those whose responses to other
questions had indicated vague plans to farm, only 2 per cent said

TABLE 3

ATTITUDE TOWARD MAKING FARMING THEIR LIFE WORK AMONG MEN
CONSIDERING FULL-TIME FARMING AS POSTWAR OCCUPATION

ATTITUDE TOWARD FARMING AS LIFE WORK	GROUP A Plan Definitely To Farm %	GROUP B Think They Will Probably Farm %	GROUP C Say They May Farm %	GROUP D Vague Plans To Farm %
Expect to make farming life work	73	51	13	2
Expect to work on farm but might change later	24	39	50	13
Expect to work on farm only if can't get other job	1	6	26	46
No answer to question	2	4	11	39
	100	100	100	100
Number of respondents	1,190	146	221	2,258

Data from S-106.

they expected to make farming their life work and only 13 per cent more said they expected to work on a farm but might change later.

As the cautious summary already quoted pointed out, there were many contingencies making predictions precarious from soldiers' expressed intentions about farming. Particularly, it was anticipated that "if industrial employment offers plenty of jobs at attractive wages, some men who now expect to farm may be induced to turn to industry. On the other hand, considerable industrial unemployment would help send into farming not only most of the men seriously considering farming but also some of those with only vague plans to farm."

A sample survey of the American labor force made by the Bureau of the Census in August 1946 reported that 8.2 per cent of all employed veterans were in agriculture.[7] Hence, the actual experience turned out to be nearer the minimum than the maximum expectations, a result no doubt related to the general level of industrial employment. As compared with some popular expectations of a vast back-to-the-farm movement on the part of veterans, the forecasts made by the Research Branch studies proved to be remarkably reliable.

In the same manner, analyses were carried out in other areas involving job plans. In addition to the reports already cited the Research Branch published the following: *Postwar Migration Plans of Soldiers*, Report B-128. *Soldiers' Plans to Own Businesses After They Leave the Army*, Report B-130. *Soldiers' Plans for Government Jobs After They Leave the Army*, Report B-132. *Postwar Educational Plans of Soldiers*, Report B-133.

For more detailed analyses the reader is referred to these reports, which were unrestricted and should be in most large libraries, as well as to the methodological discussion in Volume IV, by John A. Clausen, who had the major responsibility for studies of the postwar plans of soldiers.

In general, we have seen that the majority of soldiers had pretty definite plans as to what they would do after the war, but that there was a minority—perhaps as large as two fifths—who were not sure as to their intentions. While anxiety about future jobs was high on the list of worries which the soldier expressed as the war neared its close, a basic optimism is apparent from the figures, already cited, which show that the percentage who thought jobs would be hard to

---

[7] "Employment Statistics, August 1946," Bureau of Census, *Current Population Reports*, Series P-50, No. 1, July 11, 1947.

come by, for veterans in general, was nearly twice as high as the percentage who thought a job would be hard to come by for one's self personally.

In considering the psychological climate in which the soldier viewed his personal future, one must remember that, except for those seriously disabled, the Army experience was not necessarily a handicap to a future career and could be conceived as advantageous in two ways: (a) in terms of claims for GI bill benefits and veteran's preference, especially in government employment, and (b) in terms of intrinsic values of Army experience in teaching something which might be useful in civilian life. With respect to the first point, soldiers expected preferential treatment as civilians and thought they deserved it. In the June 1945 survey, for example, two thirds thought veterans should be given first choice of jobs that were open.[8] With respect to the second point, there is little available data adding up the pro's and con's of Army experience.

To those who liked to work with subtle hypotheses about the effects of various kinds of Army service on the personality, data of the type assembled in the Research Branch often were disappointing. To cite one illustration out of many: In the last year of the war, the Experimental Section of the Research Branch made surveys in the United States, ETO, Italy, the Pacific, India-Burma, and China to ascertain what the soldiers preferred to read in *Yank*, the Army magazine. There were numerous and intricate theories as to how overseas service and combat service might have altered the basic personality structure of soldiers in ways which would alter their reading interests. The survey, which showed specially prepared mock-ups of *Yank* and sought, by the best interviewing techniques known, to elicit information about what a sample of 8,713 men liked and what they disliked, was remarkably unexciting in its findings. To the surprise of almost everybody connected with the planning of this ambitious study, differences in what men liked or disliked in *Yank*, from theater to theater and in the United States, tended to be negligible. Men overseas, as would be expected, tended to value news in *Yank* about happenings in the United States more than did men at home and men overseas tended to be more enthusiastic than men at home about letters to the editor.[9] But the kinds of cartoons,

---

[8] S-212.

[9] As noted in Volume I, Chapter 8, letters to the editor in some overseas theaters often provided a safety valve for pent-up complaints against the command, which were likely to be more numerous overseas than at home.

pictures, humor, and stories which men preferred did not differ. *Sad Sack*, the soldier who was always getting the short end of the stick, pin-up girls, humor and sex in general had the same kinds of popularity among soldiers stationed all over the world.   For general feature stories, military topics were preferred to civilian topics by about two thirds of the men everywhere, with slight variations from theater to theater, but there was everywhere keen interest in the postwar plans of the nation, more than three fourths of the men in all theaters and the United States saying that they read at least one *Yank* story a month on postwar plans.   Similarly, when combat and noncombat men were compared, there were very few differences in reading tastes or preferences, except that returnees to the United States who had been in combat were a little more likely than other soldiers (32 per cent as against 23 per cent) to prefer civilian to military topics.[10]   The findings of this study, when paralleled, as they were, by comparable evidence as to similarity overseas and in the United States of preferences for different kinds of magazines and different kinds of radio programs, certainly were not indicative of any deep-seated sea change in basic interests or personality.

There can be no doubt that many men learned new skills in the Army or acquired useful experience in leadership.   This has been discussed in Volume I, Chapter 7, on "Job Assignment and Job Satisfaction."   They also had experiences in enduring privations and dangers and in the acquisition of patience which presumably had carryover values to civilian life.   Aggression against the Army was so strong at the end of the war, however (as documented in Volume I, Chapter 5), that it was rather difficult to induce men to admit that their Army experience had been especially valuable, even though in retrospect as veterans they might eventually find it valuable, at least in some respects.   The majority tended to add it up negatively while still in the Army.

For example, in November 1945, the Research Branch queried a representative cross section of men in the United States as to the value of their Army experience.   Men with less than a year in the Army were excluded from the tabulation, as were those who had been in the Army more than 3 years.[11]   This sample of men, 1 to 3

---

[10] These data are summarized in *Yank Reading Preferences Among Enlisted Men in Four Overseas Theaters and the United States*, Research Branch Report B-147.

[11] The latter were excluded because they included two widely different groups, those who were remaining in the Army of their own accord though eligible for discharge and those who were eligible for discharge but whose discharge had been delayed, much to their dissatisfaction.

years in the Army, was about evenly divided between returnees from overseas and men who had not been overseas.

As Chart III shows, the majority agreed with the statement, "On the whole, I think the Army has hurt me more than it has helped

CHART III

ATTITUDES TOWARD VALUE OF ARMY EXPERIENCE

(Enlisted Men in the United States—Returnees and Others—Who Had Been in the Army 1 to 3 Years, November 1945)

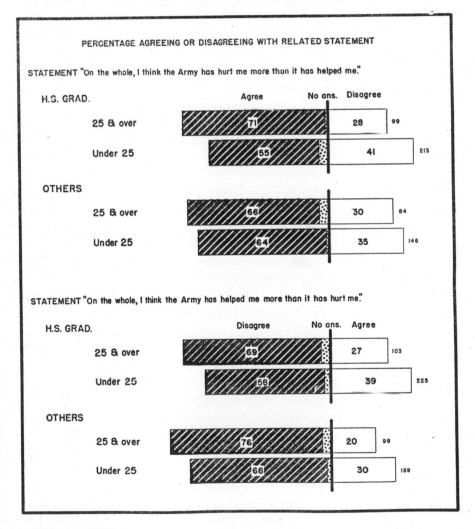

Data from S-234.

The numbers following the bars are the numbers of cases on which percentages are based.

me." A matched sample disagreed, in about the same proportions, with the statement, "On the whole I think the Army has helped me more than it has hurt me." As Chart III shows, the men under 25 were more likely to view their experience favorably than the men 25 and over. Educational differences were not marked, though in three of the four comparisons shown in Chart III the better educated were a little more likely to be favorable than the less educated —in contrast with a general tendency of the better educated, as shown in Volume I, Chapter 4, to be more critical of the Army than other men.

Overseas combat men and noncombat men and men who did not go overseas responded very nearly the same.

There were few specific items on which the majority would say they had improved as a result of Army experience, and there were a good many on which the majority claimed to have deteriorated. These responses must not be taken too seriously as findings of opinion, and certainly not as findings of fact. Most soldiers were "fed up" with the Army and negative evaluations at this period of their experience were, therefore, perhaps inevitable. What the same men would have said a year after discharge, there is no way of knowing.

One must be cautious, in any case, about interpreting absolute proportions agreeing or disagreeing with a specific statement as indicative of the general attitude toward the area covered by the statement. If, as was true, 81 per cent agreed with the statement, "My experiences in the Army have made me more nervous and restless" while only 15 per cent in a matched parallel sample agreed with the reverse statement, "My experiences in the Army have made me less nervous and restless," we should not take the exact figures too seriously. We can say, however, that the men were probably more likely to feel that the Army had made them more nervous and restless than that it had, for example, decreased their faith in God. Only 18 per cent of the men said that their Army experience had decreased their faith in God, while 60 per cent in a parallel sample said that their Army experience had increased their faith in God.

As Chart III showed, the younger men were more likely than the older men to add up their Army experience as more helpful than hurtful. Consistent with this response, we see that men under 25 were *more* likely than older men to think their Army experience had made them "more patient, considerate, and able to work with other men" (51 per cent as against 33 per cent among men 25 and over); the younger men were *more* likely than older men to say that their experience had made them "more self-confident" (51 per cent as against 33 per cent); and were *less* likely to say that they had become "more bitter and cynical" (37 per cent as against 59 per cent).

On the other hand, the balance was not entirely one-sided. The younger men were even more likely than the older men to report learning "bad habits" in the Army (64 per cent as against 38 per cent). It may be noted that the acquisition of "bad habits" may be a mere function of aging in civilian society, as well as military society, in these younger age groups. Specifically, 65 per cent of the younger men as compared with 37 per cent of the older men said that they did more drinking than before they came into the Army and 44 per cent of the younger as compared with 22 per cent of the older said that they were less religious than when they entered the Army.

Let us turn next to a brief résumé of the soldiers' attitudes toward postwar civilian society.

SECTION II

ATTITUDES TOWARD CIVILIAN SOCIETY

Early in the war, the Research Branch initiated what was expected to be a series of studies of attitudes of soldiers toward what was called "the home front." The first survey was made in January 1943, among a representative cross section of troops in the United States, at the explicit request of a member of the President's secretariat in the White House. When the report of this survey was completed, the Director of the Information and Education Division was ordered by his superior at Headquarters, Army Service Forces, to suppress the report and to make no further studies of this subject during the war. The reasons given were twofold: (a) The findings might be embarrassing to the War Department if reported attitudes of troops toward elements in civilian life could be used as arguments against War Department policies with respect to civilian production of war materials, and (b) the findings might, if revealed, lead to criticism in Congress to the effect that the War Department was stirring up unrest among the men sampled.

Not until the end of the war was the ban lifted sufficiently to permit some further questioning on attitudes toward civilians, though more general questions on the future of the country and of international relations were permitted in various surveys.

The study made in January 1943, declassified at the end of the war, showed on the whole moderately favorable attitudes toward civilians.[12]   For example:

In general, do you think civilians are trying to do everything they possibly can to back up the Armed Forces?

	Percentages responding were:
Almost all are	32
A good many are	46
Some, but not many are	15
Hardly any are	3
No answer	4
	100

In general do you think that civilians are taking the war seriously enough?

	Percentages responding were:
Almost all are	20
A good many are	34
Some, but not many are	31
Hardly any are	11
No answer	4
	100

Marginal percentages like these, of course, must be read with caution, but there was no important component of American civilian society which came in for strong criticism from the majority.   A series of questions of the following type was asked:

How much do you think farmers are doing to win the war?

_____ They are doing all they can
_____ They are doing quite a bit but could do more
_____ They are not doing nearly as much as they could
_____ No opinion

Percentages responding "they are not doing nearly as much as they could" with respect to various categories of civilians were as follows:

Labor union leaders	41%
Owners and managers of companies making war materials	12
Workers in companies making war materials	10
Farmers	3

In spite of some highly publicized strikes, 36 per cent thought that American business and American labor were working as well together

[12] Planning Survey V.   The sample comprised 3,474 cases.

on the job of producing materials for war as they possibly could; 43 per cent thought they were working well together but could do better, and only 17 per cent checked "they are not working as well together as they should." (There were 3 per cent with no opinion.)

Nor was there any suggestion of a tidal wave of soldier sentiment to "take over the country" after the war:

Some people have made the suggestion that "after the war the soldiers should take over the country and run it." What do you think of this idea?

	Percentages responding were:
I am strongly in favor of it	6
I am not exactly in favor of it, but it might be a good idea	16
I am not exactly against it, but it doesn't seem to be a good idea	27
I am strongly against it	41
No opinion	10
	100

It is interesting, also, to note that among the soldiers in January 1943 those who thought that after the war civilians would be better off than before the war (37 per cent) were only slightly more numerous than those who thought that after the war soldiers would be better off than before the war (34 per cent).

As the war came to an end, further data became available on attitudes toward civilians. Some of these findings have been noted in Chapter 12, which pointed out that in Europe in August 1945 the prevailing soldier sentiment was not unfavorable toward civilians back home—in fact sentiment was somewhat more favorable in August than in the preceding April. Three soldiers out of four said that "almost all" or "most" civilians had been doing all they could to complete the winning of the war and two out of three believed that "almost all" or "most" civilians back home had "a real sense of gratitude and appreciation for what the soldier had done."

The studies in Europe, summarized in Chapter 12, did show, however, a not inconsiderable hostility to some special groups in America. Actually, sentiment among soldiers overseas at the war's end was no different essentially from sentiment among soldiers at home in this respect. Chart IV shows that while only a third or less of the soldiers were willing to name a group which they disliked very much, nearly half named a group which they thought had "taken

CHART IV

EVIDENCES OF HOSTILITY TOWARD SPECIFIC GROUPS IN AMERICA, SUMMER 1945
(Among Returnees from Overseas, Soldiers in ETO, and Soldiers in the
United States Who Had Not Gone Overseas)

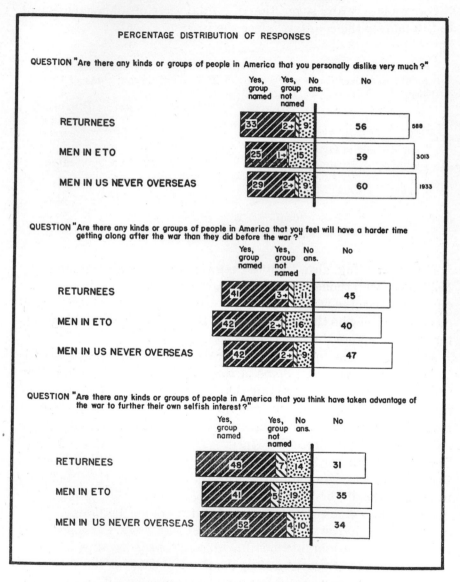

Men in ETO from S-235.   Others from S-212.

The numbers following the bars are the numbers of cases on which percentages are based.

advantage of the war to further their own selfish interests."[13]   As shown in Chapter 12, Table 3, the two groups "disliked" most were Negroes and Jews; the one group which accounted for almost all the answers as to which would have greater difficulty getting along after the war was Negroes; and the group most frequently cited as taking selfish advantage of the war was "Business," with Jews, Negroes, and Labor some distance behind.

Further analyses of these data show that the better educated (high school graduates and above) were about as likely as others to deny feelings of hostility and occasionally more likely than others to name the objects of hostility.   This finding has to be treated guardedly, as the questions as worded may have been somewhat difficult for men at low educational levels to comprehend fully and, as usually was the case with such questions, the "no answers" among the less educated were more frequent.   It is recognized that there is resistance to admitting oneself to be hostile or prejudiced, and the indirect and rather complicated form of the questions was deliberately chosen to provide a permissive format for the expression of antagonism by those who could leap the hurdle of comprehensibility.   In ETO, 26 per cent of the high school graduates and college men named a group which they personally disliked very much, as did 25 per cent of the lesser educated.   Among the better educated 10 per cent named Negroes, 8 per cent named Jews, with other responses scattering.   Among the less educated 14 per cent named Negroes, 7 per cent named Jews, with other responses likewise scattering.[14]

There are some supplementary data which further suggest that, contrary to what some believers in education might hope for, there was rather little difference between educational levels in attitudes toward minorities.   In Volume I, Chapter 10, there are several sources which indicate that, when region was held constant, educational differences were slight in attitudes of white soldiers toward segregation of Negroes in the Army.   (For example, see Chart XIV in that chapter.)

If we are dealing with folk beliefs, such as in the innate inferiority of the Negro, we are likely to find the better educated much more liberal than the less educated and, to a lesser degree, this tends also to be true when we are dealing with statements broadly reflecting the American creed.   For example, in 1943, the better educated

---

[13] The full wording of the questions on which Chart IV is based appears in the text describing Table 3 in Chapter 12.

[14] Free answers were not separately punched and tabulated for the United States data.

from the North were more likely than the less educated from the North to respond ' more" to the question, "Do you think that after the war Negroes should have more rights and privileges or less rights and privileges than they had before the war?" The educational differences among Southern whites were less, but in the same direction. Percentages checking "more" rights and privileges were:[15]

Northern whites		
High school graduates and college	31%	*(1,441)*
Others	17	*(1,934)*
Southern whites		
High school graduates and college	14	*(546)*
Others	11	*(857)*

On the other hand, if we are dealing with attitudes which reflect personal threats by minorities to majority status, there is some reason to expect that the group which feels the most threat (or potential threat) would express the greatest antagonism. For example, in a study of white Air Corps ground crew men in 1942,[16] men were asked, "Would you have any personal objection to working in the same ground crew with Negro soldiers?" The better educated Southern white enlisted men (who presumably would have more to lose in terms of customary status by working side by side with Negroes, unless the whites were officers) were much more likely than the less educated Southern whites to say that they would object. Educational differences in response of Northerners were negligible:

	Percentages saying they would object to working in the same ground crews with Negro soldiers	
Northern whites		
High school graduates and college	43	*(1,271)*
Others	45	*(706)*
Southern whites		
High school graduates and college	76	*(405)*
Others	57	*(260)*

Such findings are not inconsistent with findings of civilian polls, which also tend to show that the better educated and higher income groups, though more likely to hold ideologically liberal attitudes, are just about as likely as others to exhibit prejudice in the face of

[15] S-32.
[16] Planning Survey III.

personal status threats.   If the status deprivation suffered by the
better educated or higher income group would be greater, in a given
situation, than that suffered by others, the better educated or higher
income group might be expected to exhibit more hostility than
others.[17]

In War Department studies there was no systematic effort to ascertain the extent of anti-Semitism in the Army.   The ETO study
at the end of the war showed, as has been indicated, that 8 per cent
of the better educated and 7 per cent of the less educated wrote in
"Jews" as the group in America whom they disliked most.   Civilian
polls have shown that the proportions of respondents making answers which could be classified as anti-Semitic vary enormously depending on the wording of the question.   There is also evidence
from civilian polls that anti-Semitism, when indicated by responses
to questions of a broad ideological character, is more prevalent in
lower than higher educational or income groups but that, when indicated by responses to questions relating to personal involvement, it
is likely to be more prevalent among whatever groups feel most immediately or potentially threatened—which in the case of anti-
Semitism can in some situations be the white-collar urban dwellers.
A question which seemed to fall somewhere between these two types
was asked of soldiers by the Research Branch in January 1943,[18]
namely: "Do you think American Jewish people are doing their
share to help win the war?"   When urban and rural residence was
held constant there were no significant differences in response by

---

[17] To cite an illustration from civilian polls: In 1946 a cross section of Minnesota
people was asked: "Supposing a Negro family moved into your neighborhood, would
you treat them as you do other neighbors, would you try to have them moved out,
would you yourself move out or wouldn't you care?"   Percentage responses by economic class were reported as follows (as reported by the Minnesota poll):

	Below average economic status	Average	Above average economic status
Treat them as other neighbors	40%	36%	31%
Wouldn't care	31	24	21
Depends	10	12	15
Move out	2	11	7
Move them out	9	10	17
Undecided	8	7	9
	100%	100%	100%

Other questions of the same type on other polls seem to suggest the same tendency.
There is some evidence that *within* a given economic bracket, the better educated
seem to be somewhat more liberal than others; but education and economic status are
highly correlated.
[18] Planning Survey V.

education, but the urban respondents were more likely to have explicit opinions than rural respondents within each educational group. Percentages responding were:

| | HIGH SCHOOL GRADUATES AND COLLEGE | | OTHERS | |
	Rural	*Urban*	*Rural*	*Urban*
They are doing all they can	17%	22%	19%	20%
They are doing quite a bit, but could do more	24	24	25	25
They are not doing nearly as much as they could	24	30	23	29
No opinion	34	22	31	24
No answer	1	2	2	2
	100%	100%	100%	100%
Number of cases	*400*	*954*	*839*	*1,182*

The "no opinion" category was explicitly presented in the questionnaire. When those with "no opinion" or "no answers" are eliminated, the rural-urban differences are slight, though in each educational group the urban soldiers were a little more likely to check "they are not doing nearly as much as they should" than were rural soldiers. (High school and college: urban 40 per cent, rural 37 per cent; others: urban 39 per cent, rural 35 per cent.)[19]

The general picture which emerges from the rather scanty data available from Research Branch studies is one of some aggression toward certain minority groups, but by no means involving large numbers of the respondents. Toward American civilians in general, there were various manifestations of hostility but in no sense a preponderance of sentiment indicating generalized resentment toward civilian society. And toward the structure of American life as they knew it there was certainly no evidence of desire for drastic institutional changes.

Midway in the war, in July 1943, men were asked whether "we ought to have everything in this country the same as it was before the war or do you think there are some things that should be changed?" A fourth of the men thought a lot of things should be changed, a fourth thought hardly anything should be changed, a

---

[19] For a survey of civilian polls and of other studies of group prejudice see: Robin M. Williams, *The Reduction of Intergroup Tensions* (Social Science Research Council, New York, 1947), Bulletin 57, and Arnold M. Rose, *Studies in Reduction of Prejudice* (American Council on Race Relations, Chicago, 1947). The *Public Opinion Quarterly* and *Opinion News* regularly summarize digests of poll data.

half took a middle view that some things should be changed.[20]   That there was little thinking about needed changes is indicated by the fact that, although men were explicitly asked to indicate what changes they desired, only a third of the men did so.   Practically none of them suggested basic economic or political or social changes. Responses were very scattering, the most frequent favoring a larger standing Army and/or compulsory military training.   When asked whether in fact there would be lasting changes in America as a result of the war, the majority answered affirmatively, but when asked what changes they expected, half of the men expressed no opinion. The largest group of specific comments dealt with changes in terms of new inventions in such fields as aviation and plastics.

In the summer of 1945 a similar inquiry was made with a new set of questions in Europe and the United States.   Results are shown in Chart V.   About half of the men thought there should be at least a few changes, and about three fifths expected at least a few changes. Differences in response on expectations as between returnees from overseas, men in Europe, and men who had not gone overseas were negligible; on desire for changes, the men in Europe were more likely to vote for "a few changes" than the other samples.   Further breakdown of the data in Chart V shows that the main educational differences, as might be expected, were in the "undecided category." The better educated were less likely to be undecided and were more likely to desire and expect "a few changes."

Just as in the earlier study, there was almost no evidence of desire for drastic overhauling of American social, economic, or political life. There was little consensus and essentially a lack of articulate opinion other than slogan thinking in the free answers which were contributed.   The changes desired were phrased in general terms like "eliminate unemployment," "prevent strikes," "cut out bureaucracy and government spending," "help the veterans," "control big business," "clean up rotten politics," "have compulsory military training," "cut out race prejudice," "control the niggers."

When the men were questioned on what changes they actually expected, there was more agreement than on what changes they desired, but the expected changes had little apparent relation to the expressions of desire.   As in the 1943 study, most of the men who stated their expectations mentioned technological changes—improvements in methods of transportation, communication, and pro-

---

[20] S-63E.

duction, and improved consumer goods of the type mentioned in the national advertising found in popular magazines.

In view of such attitudes it is hardly surprising if soldiers did not visualize membership in veterans' organizations after the war primarily as an agency for promoting general political or economic reforms.   All studies in which questions about potential membership in veterans' organizations were asked indicated a majority expectation of joining them and also indicated as major objectives, in the minds of the men, the protection of veterans' rights and provi-

CHART V

Opinions About Postwar Changes in American Life, 1945

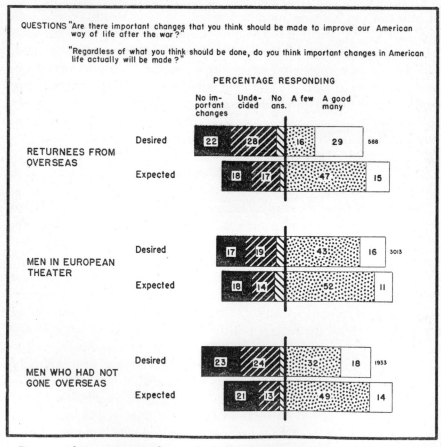

QUESTIONS "Are there important changes that you think should be made to improve our American way of life after the war?"

"Regardless of what you think should be done, do you think important changes in American life actually will be made?"

PERCENTAGE RESPONDING

	No important changes	Undecided	No ans.	A few	A good many

RETURNEES FROM OVERSEAS
Desired: 22 | 28 | 16 | 29 | 588
Expected: 18 | 17 | 47 | 15

MEN IN EUROPEAN THEATER
Desired: 17 | 19 | 43 | 16 | 3013
Expected: 18 | 14 | 52 | 11

MEN WHO HAD NOT GONE OVERSEAS
Desired: 23 | 24 | 32 | 18 | 1933
Expected: 21 | 13 | 49 | 14

Returnees from overseas and men who had not gone overseas from S-212, June 1945. Men in the European theater from S-235, August 1945.

The numbers following the bars are the numbers of cases on which percentages are based.

sion of personal help. A study made in the European theater in April 1945 will serve as a typical illustration of these expectations, as the war neared its end.[21]

Eighty-five out of a hundred of the 3,711 soldiers in this survey thought veterans' organizations were a good idea, 12 out of a hundred had no opinion, and only 3 per cent thought they were a poor idea.

TABLE 4

WHAT MEN THOUGHT VETERANS' ORGANIZATIONS SHOULD AIM TO DO AFTER THE WAR

(Cross Section of ETO Enlisted Men, April 1945)

QUESTION: "If you think there should be some sort of veterans' organization after the war, what are the two or three main things you think it should try to do or work for?"

	Percentage distribution of answers among those making replies
Protect veterans' rights, see that they get a "square deal," better conditions, bonus, or etc.	42
Provide personal help directly for veterans and their families—advice, aid in getting jobs, financial help for the needy, etc.	42
Work to prevent future wars, assure peace, influence foreign policy, etc.	29
Promote improvements of general conditions, for everyone (not just veterans)—promote good government, national prosperity, democracy, social programs, etc.	20
Have social activities—dances, parties, etc. to "keep the boys together"	9
Take part in politics directly as a group	6
Promote a large military force or compulsory military training	5
Miscellaneous other answers	13
Total	166*
Number of cases	*3,711*

Data from S-223.
* The percentages add to more than 100 because some men listed more than one item.

About 55 per cent indicated that they definitely planned to join some veterans' organization after the war, 44 per cent were undecided or had no opinion, and only 11 per cent said that they would not join.

In response to an open-ended question as to the two or three main things which a veterans' organization should try to do or work for, only 51 per cent of the men volunteered responses. These free an-

---

[21] S-223.

swers are summarized in Table 4.   They add to more than 100 per cent because of multiple replies.   First on the list were the protection of veterans' rights (mentioned by 42 per cent) and provision of personal help (mentioned by 42 per cent).   Another 9 per cent mentioned social activities—dances, parties, etc.   Only 6 per cent explicitly mentioned taking part in politics directly as a group, but 29 per cent had general ideas about veterans' organizations working to prevent future wars and influencing foreign policy, and 20 per cent suggested promotion of improvements in general conditions in America—good government, national prosperity, democracy, etc. Special note was made of explicit antilabor bias, but only 1 per cent made comments of the type "buck the power of labor unions"— such comments are included along with a wide variety of others in the "miscellaneous" category in Table 4.

It is quite clear that the orientation tended to be more in terms of one's personal future than in terms of anxiety about need for changes in the American social, political, or economic institutions.   As to the wider stage of international relations after the war, there was, as Volume I, Chapter 9, on "The Orientation of Soldiers Toward the War" has described in some detail, a widespread skepticism about the possibility of avoiding another war, and there was strong support both for keeping America's defenses strong (at least two thirds of the men, whenever and wherever surveyed, favored compulsory military training) and for establishing an effective international organization to keep the peace.   As Table 4 showed, 29 per cent of those who commented on their conception of the aims of veterans' organizations mentioned work to prevent future wars.

As the preceding chapter indicated, there was no marked reversion toward isolationism among soldiers in Europe upon the end of hostilities.   Troops at home—those who had not been overseas and those who had returned from overseas—were nearly unanimous, when surveyed in June 1945, in their support of a permanent organization of nations to settle disputes and try to prevent wars. Eighty-six per cent were definitely in favor and only 3 per cent definitely opposed.[22]

When it came to America making sacrifices in behalf of such an organization or of our former allies, however, there was less evidence of enthusiasm.

Less than two thirds of the men thought that the United States should join a permanent organization if it meant that such an or-

[22] S-212.

ganization would have some say about how the United States deals with foreign countries.   About the same proportion felt that we should send needed food to our allies after the war if it meant continuation of rationing, but only 40 per cent thought we should help them with money and materials if it meant higher taxes for us.

Returnees from overseas were somewhat less likely to favor international cooperation at some cost to America than were men who had not been overseas.   This is shown in Chart VI.   In all instances, as further tabulations show, the better educated were somewhat more favorable than the less educated toward membership in an international organization and postwar aid to allies.

During the war there was some hopeful discussion of the possibility that direct contact of Americans overseas with the soldiers and citizens of our allies would promote good feeling and stronger internationalism.   Against this was the fact that, after the honeymoon of first welcome of American troops to allied soil, the reaction was almost inevitably accompanied by tensions.   The longer troops stayed, the more occasions for mutual resentment would arise, the less the initial attractions of new experience would compensate, and the more soldiers' frustrations at being kept away from home could turn upon the most immediately available objects.[23]   In Chapter 12 it was observed that attitudes toward the French apparently deteriorated sharply with time (see Chart VI in that chapter, for example).   On the other hand a variety of studies, a portion of which was reported in Chapter 12, showed relatively little shift in attitudes toward England or the British people.   It should be noted that, unless a shift is very large, it is not easy to interpret it correctly with data not based on repeated observations of the same *individual* respondents.   Such panel studies were not made.   Studies which show a deterioration with length of time in the theater could conceivably reflect different attitudes which men old in the theater or men new in the theater had upon arrival.   Likewise, comparisons of two studies made of cross sections of men overseas at different time points could reveal shifts in average response without necessarily reflecting deterioration of *individual* responses, since the initial attitudes of the men in the different cross sections may have differed in the same way as the attitudes as of the time of study.

When a sample of 4,676 returnees from overseas was questioned

---

[23] A perceptive theoretical discussion of the psychological factors involved is seen in M. Brewster Smith, "Did War Service Produce International-Mindedness?" *Harvard Educational Review*, xv (October 1945), 250–57.

CHART VI

ATTITUDES TOWARD INTERNATIONAL ORGANIZATION AND POSTWAR AID TO ALLIES, JUNE 1945

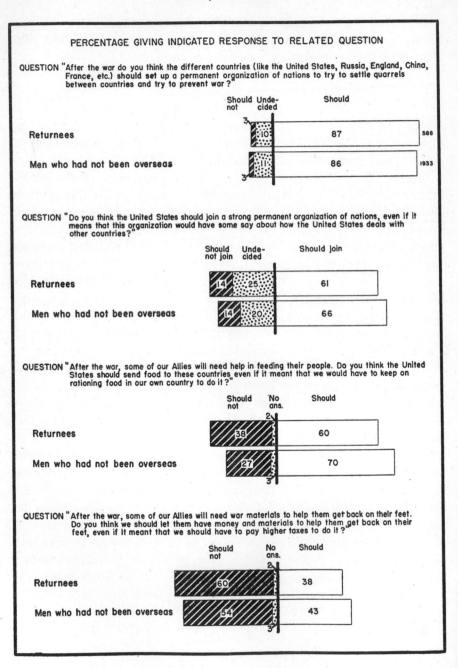

PERCENTAGE GIVING INDICATED RESPONSE TO RELATED QUESTION

QUESTION "After the war do you think the different countries (like the United States, Russia, England, China, France, etc.) should set up a permanent organization of nations to try to settle quarrels between countries and try to prevent war?"

	Should not	Unde-cided	Should	
Returnees	3	10	87	588
Men who had not been overseas	3	11	86	1933

QUESTION "Do you think the United States should join a strong permanent organization of nations, even if it means that this organization would have some say about how the United States deals with other countries?"

	Should not join	Unde-cided	Should join
Returnees	14	25	61
Men who had not been overseas	14	20	66

QUESTION "After the war, some of our Allies will need help in feeding their people. Do you think the United States should send food to these countries even if it meant that we would have to keep on rationing food in our own country to do it?"

	Should not	No ans.	Should
Returnees	38	2	60
Men who had not been overseas	27	3	70

QUESTION "After the war, some of our Allies will need war materials to help them get back on their feet. Do you think we should let them have money and materials to help them get back on their feet, even if it meant that we should have to pay higher taxes to do it?"

	Should not	No ans.	Should
Returnees	60	2	38
Men who had not been overseas	54	3	43

Data from S-212.

The numbers following the bars are the numbers of cases on which percentages are based.

soon after their return, at redistribution stations in the United States, in March through May 1945,[24] it was possible to get some data which throw a rather interesting light on how men viewed our allies, after contact with them. They were asked, for example, "Do you think the United States is doing her share in helping win the war?" Check-list categories were: "Doing more than her share," "doing her share," "doing less than her share," and "undecided." Exactly the same question was asked by substituting, in turn, England, France, Russia, and China.

The ethnocentrism of the American soldier home from overseas is reflected in the fact that three out of four thought the United States was "doing more than her share" while almost all of the remainder thought the United States was "doing her share"; yet no such vote was given to the war effort of any allied country. There were many who checked the "undecided" category, and if we compare only the responses of those with definite opinions we find the following distribution:

	Not doing her share	Doing her share	Doing more than her share	Total	
United States	—	22%	78%	100%	(4,541)
Russia	1%	77	22	100	(3,686)
China	25	67	8	100	(3,148)
England	29	66	5	100	(3,917)
France	36	62	2	100	(3,088)

It was possible to sort out men in the sample who said that they had some contact with civilians in England, France, and China, respectively. Those who said they had not gotten to know some civilians in a given country at least fairly well were sorted again according to whether they reported seeing at least something of soldiers of that country.[25] Thus, with respect to England, for example, it was possible to compare attitudes toward England's war effort according to (1) whether the respondent got to know at least

---

[24] S-172.

[25] The sorting questions were:

"Below is a list of countries you may or may not have been in while overseas. Show by checking after each country how many *civilians* you got to know at least fairly well." (The check-list categories were "A lot," "Some but not many," and "None.")

"Now, show by checking after each country how much you saw of soldiers belonging to the Armies of these countries." (The check-list categories were "A lot," "Some but not much," and "None.")

some British civilians fairly well, (2) whether his contacts were limited to British soldiers, or (3) whether he had neither civilian nor military contacts of any consequence. The results are shown in Chart VII.

First, it will be noted by looking at the left-hand bars in Chart VII that, as would be expected, the proportion of men who were undecided or had no opinion about a given country was greatest among those with fewest contacts.

Second, it will be noted by looking at the right-hand bars (percentage distribution of responses among those who had definite opinions as to whether a given country was or was not doing her share in the war) that, in the case of England and France, men with contacts with British or French civilians or soldiers were only slightly more unfavorable than those without contacts. China was a different story, however. Relatively few soldiers had had contacts with either Chinese civilians or Chinese soldiers, but those who had were highly critical of the Chinese war effort. For example, among high school graduates, 62 per cent of those reporting contact with Chinese civilians said China was not doing her share, as did 53 per cent of those with contacts limited to Chinese soldiers. But among high school graduates with little or no contact with Chinese, only 27 per cent said China was not doing her share. The contrasts depending on acquaintance with China were even sharper in the case of the less educated. Clearly, the fact that among returnees as a whole China ranked ahead of England and France was made possible by the views of China held by the great majority who had not been there.

Third, it will be noted in Chart VII that in any set of comparisons the better educated were less likely to be undecided in their opinions and that, among men holding opinions, the better educated were consistently a little less enthusiastic than others about the contribution of any of these countries, including our own, to the war effort.

One should remember that, in expressions about our allies, soldiers made discriminations depending on the subject matter. For example, in spite of their relatively high respect for the Russian war effort, they were more likely to anticipate postwar trouble with Russia than with any other country. Next to Russia as an anticipated postwar troublemaker was England, while few anticipated serious postwar disagreements with France or China. The responses to questions about postwar relations with England, France, and China, when broken down by extent of personal contacts,

CHART VII

RESPECT FOR ALLIED WAR EFFORT, AS RELATED TO CONTACT WITH
ALLIED NATIONALS, BY EDUCATION

(Enlisted Men Returned from Overseas Theaters, Surveyed in Redistribution
Stations in the United States, March, April, and May 1945)

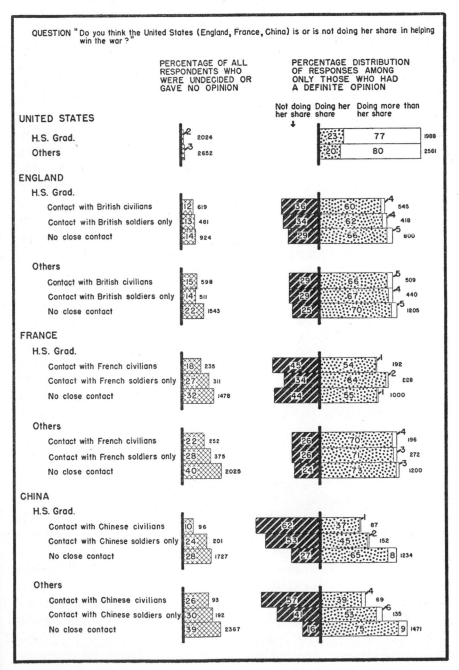

Data from S-172.

The numbers following the bars are the numbers of cases on which percentages are based.

showed the same type of pattern as is seen in Chart VII. Those who had contacts with allied nationals were a little more likely than others (much more likely in the case of China) to anticipate serious postwar disagreements.

Data such as those summarized in Chart VII highlight other findings reported in this section which suggested that the American soldier came home from the war pretty well satisfied with the United States. He had some prejudices against civilians in this country, and some criticisms to make of the government and of the civilian contribution to the war effort. But, by and large, he was not in a mood to crusade for any very fundamental changes in the American way of life. He had some skepticisms about our allies (apparently not lessened by personal contact) and he tended to have his doubts about future peace. As was shown in Volume I, Chapter 9, when asked who would be to blame for another war he almost never thought America would be to blame. His doubts about our allies may have led him to be a little wary about America making too many postwar sacrifices in their behalf, but he supported, strongly, the idea of an international organization to maintain peace.

SECTION III

AGAIN IN CIVILIAN CLOTHES

The first two sections of this chapter have reviewed data from studies made in the Army which might foreshadow, to greater or less degree, attitudes and behavior of veterans after they had returned to peacetime pursuits. What happened afterwards, as was pointed out at the beginning of this chapter, is a story which must be told someday mainly from data other than that assembled by the Research Branch. Only by way of supplementing, on a very small scale during the war, the information of the type already reported in this chapter, did the Research Branch undertake direct study of attitudes of discharged veterans. In December 1944, eight months before the end of the war, the Research Branch initiated and arranged for the financing of intensive interviewing of a small sample of men already discharged from the Army. The field work was done by the Division of Program Surveys, Bureau of Agricultural Economics, and the analysis was a joint responsibility of the Research Branch and that Division.[26] Like the studies made

---

[26] Extensity of coverage was sacrificed to thoroughness of individual interviews, each of which was personally conducted, usually in the veteran's home, and lasted from

within the Army, this civilian survey provided something of a preview of veterans' early adjustment, and it will be briefly reviewed.[27]

Since most of the million soldiers who had been discharged by the end of 1944 were men who had been separated from the Army for medical (including psychiatric) reasons, it was feared in advance that the study might prove quite unrepresentative of problems to be encountered after the war, when millions of able-bodied men returned to civilian life. Particularly it was realized that if, as some accounts in the press might have led one to expect, the study should indicate extreme nervousness and irritability among those already discharged, the results would need to be handled with more than ordinary caution. Many instances of failure to readapt to civilian ways did, indeed, turn up in the study. However, its most striking finding was the evidence of relatively satisfactory adjustment to civilian ways which the majority of men were experiencing. As the summary of the survey reported: "Personal readjustment problems of varying degrees of intensity are disclosed by the veterans in this study. But the 'typical' veteran pictured in some quarters as a bitter, hardened individual does not emerge from this survey."

In Section I of this chapter it was reported that when men still in the Army late in 1945 were asked to add up their Army experience, the majority felt that the experience had done them more harm than good. Among discharged veterans in the December 1944 study, just as in the Army study, more men reported undesirable than desirable changes:

Do you feel that Army life changed you?

Report undesirable changes only	37%
Report both undesirable and desirable changes	20
Report no changes	14
Report desirable changes only	22
Opinions not ascertained	7
	100%

one to two hours. The sample comprised 301 former enlisted men, veterans of overseas service, living in seven midwestern cities—Cincinnati, Toledo, Saint Louis, Minneapolis, Saint Paul, Indianapolis, and Milwaukee. All were white. All had been honorably discharged for disability, half of them having seen combat. Veterans with extreme disabilities, such as loss of sight or limbs, were not included in the sample, as they were felt to have special problems requiring separate study.

[27] Except where other sources are specifically indicated, the data in this section are from the report of this study, "Veterans' Readjustment to Civilian Life," Division of Program Surveys, Bureau of Agricultural Economics, United States Department of Agriculture, March 1945, Washington, D. C. A briefer condensed version of the report was issued in July 1945.

By informal and nondirective methods the interviewers sought to ascertain the kinds of changes which veterans thought they had experienced. The answers are classified below in order of frequency, the percentages adding to more than the total proportion of men reporting changes, since many men mentioned more than one change:

Undesirable changes:

More nervous, high-strung, restless, jumpy, tense, can't concentrate, want to be "on the go"	41%
More irritable, short-tempered, quarrelsome, belligerent	17
Sadder, more solemn, depressed, lacking pep, "older," no longer carefree	10
Harder, more bitter, cynical, critical, self-centered	9
More dependent, have trouble making their own decisions	8
More withdrawn, less social, shy	7
"Dumber," intellectually narrower, less well-informed	2
Wilder, less moral, more given to drinking and gambling	2

Desirable changes:

Intellectually broadened, think deeper, understand things or people better	16
Quieter, more settled, less given to running around or drinking	13
More independent, responsible, ambitious	12
More affectionate, appreciative, considerate	8
More spartan, more self-controlled, able to endure difficulties and discipline	5
More social, like being with people more	4

Each of the above percentages probably represents a minimum estimate of the number who have noticed the change indicated, as they are derived from comments made in response to general questions. If the veterans had been asked directly about each specific trait, the percentage reporting these changes would most likely have been larger.

Independent evidence that the proportions of veterans who thought the war had affected their lives deleteriously was larger than the proportion who thought the war had affected their lives favorably is provided by a survey reported by the National Opinion Research Center in February 1947.[28] This survey made of a representative cross section of the American population a year and a half after the end of the war, asked: "Has your own life been changed a great deal because of war?" If the respondent answered "Yes," he was asked: "Would you say that the war has generally made your life better or worse?" Replies were summarized as follows, in percentages:

---

[28] "How Has the War Changed People's Lives?" *Opinion News*, February 18, 1947.

	Veterans	Nonveterans
Life worse	48%	35%
Life changed, but don't know whether better or worse	6	3
Life better	24	9
No change	21	52
No answer	1	1
	100%	100%

These data indicate, as might be expected, that the veterans were much more likely than the nonveterans to report that the war had changed their lives a great deal. They agree with the findings of the Research Branch in its studies of soldiers and in the intensive study of discharged veterans made in December 1944 in showing that more veterans thought they were worse off than better off. It is of special interest to note that in the NORC study 24 per cent of the veterans as compared with only 9 per cent of the nonveterans thought that the war had made their life generally better.[29]

Some of the problems of adjustment faced by the veterans who had been discharged before the end of the war were necessarily different from those later encountered. For example, some of those interviewed in December frankly admitted feelings of guilt because of not being in uniform and others may have had similar feelings which they were unable or unwilling to verbalize. A good many, including combat veterans discharged because of wounds, were either belligerent or bitter because civilians confused them with 4F's who never got into the Army. When asked what advice they would give about how ex-servicemen should be treated, 34 per cent volunteered comments like "Recognize his honorable discharge button," "Don't comment as though he were a slacker," "Don't act as if he had no right to be back." This was the largest single block of suggestions except for "Don't ask him about his war experiences" (mentioned by 40 per cent of the men). A typical expression of irritation was the following:

If you have a disability such as a leg or arm off, it's all right. But anything they can't see they don't consider you disabled. They say, "What's wrong with you?" and I say, "So and so." They say "You look all right." About that time I have my own ideas what I would like to do to them.

---

[29] The NORC figure of 24 per cent for veterans cannot be compared exactly with the 22 per cent reported in the veterans' study of December 1944 because of differences in the method of asking the questions. It is worth noting, however, that the two figures are of the same general order of magnitude.

While the veteran discharged in wartime had advantages in getting employment in war industry which may have been greater than those enjoyed by men discharged after the war, he also found himself in competition with some civilians who seemed mainly concerned with making money out of the war. About half of the December 1944 sample expressed some form of resentment against civilians, mainly because civilians did not seem war-minded, seemed profit-bent, and were not so badly off as expected. A sample comment from a critical veteran:

We were over there and we heard how tough it was and we thought people were starving. We thought they had it worse than they did. That's why I probably have this feeling, like when I hear someone complain about not getting tires or something, I think "You civilian."

About a third of these men studied in 1944 expressed a feeling of being estranged from civilian life. This was doubtless experienced also by many veterans upon discharge after the war, but the transition was perhaps more difficult for the man separated earlier because the country was still at war. One man out of six mentioned the fact that old friends and acquaintances were no longer around, many if not most of them still being away at war. Also, there were personally uncomfortable changes associated with shortages of food and gasoline, high prices, rationing, etc. And there was the embarrassment, already mentioned, of having to explain why one had been discharged. Such factors combined to make coming home a letdown for a good many men.

Every guy thinks it will be the greatest thing in the world, but somehow I didn't quite get the thrill I thought I would get.

But the majority, even in December 1944, did not indicate any sense of estrangement from civilian society, even if they expressed minor irritations. And among only a few, less than a fifth, did feelings take the form of strong expressions about society's indebtedness to the veteran. Completely untypical was the remark of a disaffected veteran who said:

When you come back they treat you just like scum. They act just like you was the unlucky guy that got the dirty end, and that's just too bad. We figured we had done something and we find out we won't be shown any partiality. If you ever get the boys all together they probably will kill all the civilians. They [the civilians] aren't worth anything anyway.

About two men in five expressed moderate feelings like the following:

A veteran's entitled to a job. They should do everything possible to make a job for them. If they get jobs they will feel all right about everything else.

I think a veteran should be given all the opportunity he possibly can. But I don't believe they should be carried around on a pillow.

The rest of the men, two out of five, either had little feeling about society's indebtedness to the veteran or else did not express it, in spite of a good deal of probing in the informal interviews.

The majority believed that the discharged serviceman, as of 1944, was getting a square deal. In this sample 58 per cent said so flatly; another 28 per cent answered "in some ways yes, in others no"; 3 per cent had no opinion. Only 11 per cent offered an unqualified "no." As would be expected with injured and psychoneurotic dischargees, there were a good many complaints about the way the Veterans Administration had calculated their allotments for service-connected disabilities. Among a few who felt that they were now receiving an adequate allotment, there was apprehension about the future.

It is the future that worries me. As long as I'm this way I'm satisfied with my pension. But if I lose my job I'll need more.

When asked what they thought veterans should do about it if they didn't get a square deal after the war was over, only 8 per cent suggested resort to violent action. Almost all of them counted on successful political pressure through veterans' organizations.

To the veterans studied in December 1944, as well as to the soldiers studied while still in the Army, a steady job represented the keystone of security. Respondents in this veterans' sample were classified as to their own employability on the basis of a series of questions. This was summarized as follows: Able to work full time, 73 per cent; able to work only part time, 11 per cent; not able to work, 12 per cent; and employability not ascertained, 4 per cent. About 9 out of 10 had made attempts to find employment, and on the whole the men were more optimistic than pessimistic. When asked, "Do you think being a veteran makes it easier or harder to get a job?" the percentage distribution of responses was:

Harder	8%
It depends	17
Easier now, but harder later	6
No difference	15
Easier	47
Don't know	7
	100%

Of those working, only one out of six reported himself as dissatisfied with his present job, though a third of the men had held at least two different jobs since discharge. The main reasons given for shifting jobs were related to health rather than to dissatisfaction with pay or management. In the eyes of the veterans in this study, the two most desirable characteristics of a job were security and suitability to their physical condition. High pay was mentioned rather infrequently, though in cases where comparison with prewar wages was possible veterans were earning substantially more than before they went into the service. A majority said that they were satisfied with their present wage scale, although almost a third said that they found their pay envelopes slimmer than stories heard while in the Army had led them to expect. As one man said: "Overseas the average soldier is told that the war worker is making millions. You don't get near as much as you expected."

More than four veterans out of five favored some degree of job preference for veterans, but only a minority of these proposed special employment status for all veterans without limitations. Responses to a series of questions resulted in the following tabulation:

Favored preference for all veterans		76%
Over everyone	*25%*	
Over employees without much seniority; over people who gained disproportionately from the war; over 4F's	*9*	
Over people without dependents	*9*	
Over equally or less qualified people	*8*	
Over women	*4*	
Over other special groups	*7*	
Kind of preference not specified	*14*	
Favored preference for some veterans only (disabled, combat, married, etc.)		7
Opposed preference		6
No opinions or conflicting opinions		11
		100%

No systematic attempt was made in the December 1944 study to probe into the intimacy of the veterans' adjustments with their families, since the necessary line of questioning would have gone beyond the bounds of what is usually considered propriety in a government-sponsored inquiry.   Almost all of the single veterans were at this time living with their parents and practically all of the men who had been married before entering the Army or afterwards were living with their wives, often in parental homes.   The relatively few whose marriages had failed since their return to civilian life were divided in assessing the blame, some taking the blame themselves and some blaming their wives.   Among the latter several complained that their wives had been "running around" while they were in the Army.

The attitudes of the December 1944 sample of veterans toward America and the postwar world were in no significant way different from attitudes of men still in the Army as reviewed in Section II of this chapter.   The basic complacency of the majority, in spite of the feeling that their Army experience was more of a liability than an asset, already has been portrayed.   They were not reformers. In recommending what activities veterans' organizations should engage in, they placed first on the list provision of personal help and counseling; second was social activities and recreation; third was political protection of veterans' rights.   Only 13 per cent suggested the need for veterans' organizations to influence national policies on issues larger than veterans' rights.

There was some evidence of hostility toward labor unions and toward minority groups like Negroes and Jews.   About half of the men criticized labor unions for striking for higher pay during the war while they were in the Army drawing soldiers' wages.   A fifth of the men said that their outlook on organized labor had become less favorable as a result of the war; almost none had become more favorable; the rest reported their viewpoint unchanged, or had no opinion.   But among the veterans interviewed, there had been little clash with unions and only 2 per cent of the men expressed resentment over having to join unions in order to get their jobs. Only 6 per cent of the men predicted trouble with labor or between labor and management after the war.

A much higher proportion of men, however, predicted trouble with minority groups.   Over half predicted trouble with Negroes and a sixth predicted trouble with Jews.   The effect of Army experience on ethnic tolerance was, as might be expected, difficult to ascertain. There were some who felt that tolerance had been promoted by interracial contact in the Army:

I saw what these boys did on the Burma road. I had closer contact with them
in the hospital and all. It explodes a lot of things you hear. You realize they
have the same abilities—they just haven't had any breaks.

But a larger group seemed to have reinforced their pre-Army attitudes while in the service. Negroes made poor soldiers, these veterans said, or somehow managed to avoid combat and stay in safe
jobs behind the lines. The social acceptance of colored servicemen
overseas frequently was mentioned with some indignation. An
example:

They went with English girls. We practically had a war over there. Our men
were supposed to be given a 24-hour pass and we were going to town and wipe
every Negro out, but some of the officers said we had a war of our own to fight first.

Further questioning of the one in six veterans who expected trouble between Jews and non-Jews after the war indicated that such
men were usually themselves anti-Semitic. Stereotyped criticisms
of Jews came to the fore: They own too large a proportion of business, profiteer at the expense of non-Jews, and dodge the draft. If
they do get in the Army, they land safe jobs and get a disproportionate share of discharges. Some veterans illustrated their anti-Semitism directly by their Army experience. Others claimed to have
developed a more favorable attitude as a result of contact in the
Army, but such men often were ambivalent.

There were some Jews [in the Army] that were real white men and they were
swell, but back here they are a separate race all by themselves.

While the full employment and high wages of wartime helped to
minimize concern of the veterans with broad social and economic
problems of the country, there did hang over the future the specter
of a possible end-of-the-war depression. For the solution of problems like unemployment, the majority looked to the government
rather than to business. Fifty-six per cent thought the government
should have more say than business in such problems, while another
9 per cent thought likewise but qualified their answers with reservations. Only 13 per cent thought business should have more say
than government in solving problems like unemployment, and another 8 per cent thought the same but with reservations. The rest
either thought government and business should share the responsibility equally or had no opinion. Some men in their detailed comments favored giving business the first chance, letting the govern-

ment step in only if private interests failed.   But the most common sentiment was, "If there aren't enough jobs to go around, the government should *make* enough jobs to go around."

About the war itself, and the future of peace, there was little in the attitudes of these veterans suggesting either lofty idealism or disillusionment.   In describing our war aims, the usual sloganlike sentiments described in Volume I, Chapter 9, on orientation of the soldiers, appeared.   The majority thought we were fighting for "freedom," to avoid invasion or dictatorship at home.   About one man in eight said we were fighting for positive aims like a better world or to end wars.   At the other extreme, about one in eight was openly cynical of ideals; some thought we were being exploited by our allies (England and Russia, especially); some thought we were fighting for the benefit of special groups, like capitalists, Jews, politicians; and some thought we were in the war for no reason at all.   The large majority considered the war both unavoidable and unlikely to yield gains beyond preserving what they thought was the American way of life.   That, in spite of irritations and frustrations, was cherished enough to cause the majority to say the war was worth while.

The combination of liberal benefits under the GI bill and a continuation of employment at a high level in the postwar period provided an almost ideal situation for the reabsorption into civilian life of the millions of men who laid down their arms at the end of the war.   In spite of the fact that the psychological climate among men in the Army seemed conducive to a reasonably smooth transition for the majority of soldiers, it is possible to conjecture that severe tensions might have developed but for the GI benefits and the economic prosperity.   This, however, is one of the *ifs* of history, for there can be no conclusive answer.

One of the last surveys made in the Research Branch before it went under its new peacetime leadership was a study in December 1945 of 2,477 men getting their discharges at five northeastern separation centers.[30]   Their names and addresses were taken and it was possible for the Veterans Administration to locate and requestion 88 per cent of them in 1946—three to four months after they had filled out their Research Branch questionnaires.   This study was not concerned with psychological problems of adjustment, but merely with the extent to which the men had difficulties in carrying out the plans for jobs and schooling which they announced while

---

[30] S-240.

still in uniform.   Since data from this study, as well as from a similar study made a few months earlier, are reviewed in some detail in
the analysis of problems of prediction in Volume IV, they need not
be elaborated here.

The Veterans Administration's follow-up of the December 1945
study of separatees indicated that within three to four months of
discharge about two thirds of the veterans had been able to carry
out their predischarge educational or job plans or still expected to
carry them out.   Reasons given by the minority who had not been
able to carry out their plans were classified as follows:[31]

Impersonal conditions and problems		71%
Unavailability of desired job	*23%*	
Financial problems (lack of capital, inabil- ity to borrow)	*14*	
Shortages, market conditions, etc.	*17*	
Delayed decisions (application pending, awaiting job opening)	*5*	
Unable to get education or training desired	*11*	
Other	*1*	
Personal problems or considerations		29
Re-evaluation of abilities or opportunities	*20*	
Own illness or poor physical condition	*4*	
Family crisis or problems	*4*	
Other	*1*	
Total		100%

Although a good many were not carrying out their Army plans,
about 85 per cent were actually working at the same job they expected to have or at a different job, or were attending school, or
were pretty well settled as to what they would do.

From the standpoint of America's future, possibly the most remarkable single aspect of the program for veterans' aid was its broad
provision for a continuation of interrupted education, either full
time or part time or on the basis of on-the-job vocational training.
In the study made in the Army in the summer of 1944,[32] before the
educational provisions of the GI bill were widely known, it was estimated that about 8 per cent of the soldiers would go back to full-
time school.   As the provisions became more widely known, and,
especially, as the monetary allowances were increased by Congress
to a level much higher than originally intended, the Veterans Ad-

[31] From "Educational Plans of Veterans," Research Service, Veterans Administration, May 1946, Washington, D. C.
[32] S-106 and S-145.

ministration in 1946 raised the estimate to a minimum of 10 per cent. This meant, counting Navy and Marine Corps veterans as well as Army veterans, that about a million and a half men and women would eventually get full-time schooling with government aid, more than a million of whom would be in colleges and universities. To these must be added an even larger number who would receive aid for part-time schooling or on-the-job training.

In the sample of December 1945 separatees surveyed by the Research Branch, 9 per cent expressed definite or tentative plans for full-time school, while an additional 5 per cent were giving it some consideration. At the time of the follow-up on the same men three to four months later, 10 per cent actually were in full-time school or still definitely planning to enroll.

There was a good deal of talk as the war neared its end about the restlessness of the veteran and his possible inability to reintegrate himself in the life of the community. Would he wander around the country? Or would he settle down in a community and become a part of it?

On the first question, the Research Branch studies made in the summer of 1944 indicated that at least 80 per cent of the soldiers expected to reside most of their first five years out of the Army in the same state of the Union as they lived when they entered the Army. A study made by the Bureau of the Census shows that as of April 1, 1947, nearly two years after the end of the war, 85 per cent of the veterans actually were living in their home states. In fact, in the age group 18 to 34 years, which included most of the soldiers, 72 per cent were living in their home county—little different from the comparable figure of 74 per cent among nonveterans in the same age group.[33]

There are as yet no satisfactory postwar data on the reabsorption of the veteran into the civic and social institutions of the community to which he went to live after the war. Many veterans may have had difficulties, may have been socially maladjusted upon re-

[33] See Bureau of the Census, *Current Population Reports*, Series P-20, No. 14, April 15, 1948, and P-25, No. 5, November 25, 1947. The Research Branch study made in the Army in 1944 predicted that such long distance change of residence as occurred would result in population increases in the Pacific states and smaller increases in the New England and East North Central states, with losses elsewhere, especially in the South and in the West North Central states. The Bureau of the Census reports that the small migration of veterans which occurred followed the predicted pattern quite closely. There was a slight net increase in the Middle Atlantic states, where the Army data predicted no net increase or possibly a very slight decrease. In each of the other nine Census grand divisions the direction of net movement was correctly predicted from the analysis of the soldiers' responses a year before the war's end.

turn just as many of them were maladjusted while in uniform.   But surveys conducted in the Army late in the war left no doubt as to their intentions to take an active part in the affairs of their communities.   As we have seen, they were not reformers and, above all, not revolutionaries.   First and foremost, in the tradition of American individualism they were looking out for postwar jobs or for postwar education leading to better jobs.   At the same time, also in the American tradition, they were expecting to be "joiners"—in

TABLE 5

REPORTED ACTIVITY OF PARTICIPATION IN SPECIFIED ORGANIZATIONS
BEFORE THE WAR AND INTENTIONS TO PARTICIPATE
AFTER THE WAR, CLASSIFIED BY EDUCATION
(European Theater, April 1945)

| | PERCENTAGE CHECKING EACH ORGANIZATION AMONG: | | | |
| | Not high school graduates | | High school graduates or college | |
	Were active before the the war	Intended to be active after the war	Were active before the the war	Intended to be active after the war
Church	62	69	72	78
Labor unions	30	35	24	29
Fraternal order	7	8	21	25
Civic club	7	10	14	25
Businessmen's club	6	14	11	31
Farmers' organization	16	19	10	11
Forum or discussion club	2	5	8	16
Political party	4	11	7	21
Veterans' organization	3	50	2	60
Other	4	3	11	6
None	18	8	13	4
No answer	4	5	2	2
Number of cases	*1,939*	*1,939*	*1,750*	*1,750*

Data from S-223.

fact, to be more active in local community organizations than before the war.

Table 5, while singularly inaccurate, without doubt, as a picture of the extent of men's actual social participation before the war, is a revealing illustrative document.   It is based on responses of a cross section of 3,711 enlisted men in the European theater in April 1945, just before the German surrender.   The men were asked to look over a list of organizations and put a check mark opposite each of those in which they took an *active* part *before* they went into the Army.   Then they were asked to look over a similar list and check each of those in which they thought they would take an *active* part *after* they got out of the Army. Responses in Table 5, are tabulated separately by educational level.

Of course, it is necessary to discount the reported extent of prewar active participation—that 72 per cent of the better educated or 62 per cent of the less educated were really active in church organizations is quite unlikely except by a most implausible stretching of the vague term "active." But what is important to note in this table is not the reported facts but rather the attitudes reflected in the reporting. Whether the men were as fully integrated into the life of their home community as they wanted to believe is less important than the fact that they wanted to believe it and that they expected to be even more active after the war than before the war.

Whatever their antagonism to labor unions, more of the men at both educational levels, rather than less, expected to belong to labor unions after the war than before. More of them expected to join civic clubs and political organizations. And among the high school graduates or college men, nearly a third expected to belong to businessmen's clubs. Some of this expected increase could conceivably be a mere function of aging, but the general pattern of Table 5 remains essentially the same when age is held constant by further tabulation.

Books are likely to be written about the shattering experience of Army life. It is true that some men were physically ruined by the war and others bear scars which will never disappear. Others broke emotionally under the strain. But, unless the data reviewed in this chapter are to be largely disregarded, there has seemed little reason for doubting the reabsorption of the vast majority of American soldiers into the normal patterns of American life. These millions of young men, responses from samples of whom have been recorded in these volumes, gave their sweat and often their blood to winning a war which they accepted without enthusiasm as unavoidable. Loving American freedom, they chafed under the authoritarianism and social customs of an institution, which, though alien to democratic ways of life, was an agency for preserving those ways of life. The job done, they wanted to get out, get home, and by and large resume where they had left off. They had their prejudices, some of them bad by ideal standards. Although they were not postwar isolationists, they had plenty of ethnocentrism. From some points of view they were too complacent in their unreadiness to sponsor big social or political changes in the United States. There would be agreement on one fact: though our armies crossed all the seas and lived on all the continents, the men whose attitudes provided the data for these volumes came home, as they went out, indubitably American.

A P P E N D I X

SURVEYS MADE BY RESEARCH BRANCH AND ITS OVERSEAS COUNTERPARTS

··

Data in charts and tables of Volumes I and II are normally keyed to a survey number. Following is a list of surveys conducted. Pretests, some of which involved substantial samples, are omitted from this list, as are surveys of civilian personnel.

The numbering system for designating studies was changed at the beginning of 1943. The new numbering system was started arbitrarily at S-29.

Most surveys covered a considerable variety of topics; hence it is almost impossible to devise an adequate description in a single line for a given survey. The sample size indicated represents the total number of soldiers completing questionnaires (rounded to the nearest 100). Frequently several forms of questionnaires were used on a single survey and different subsamples of soldiers might receive different questionnaires, depending on the study design. Hence, the number of cases available on a particular topic is not necessarily as large as the aggregate number of respondents on the survey.

Survey designation	*Location*	*Date*	*Principal topics*	*Approximate sample size*
Planning Survey I	US	Dec '41	Attitudes in one division	1900
Special Survey I	US	Mar '42	Attitudes of new recruits	400
Special Survey II	US	Apr '42	Physical conditioning	1100
Planning Survey II	US	May '42	Attitudes in 3 divisions	4000
Panel Survey I	US	July '42	Radio listening	3000
Planning Survey III	US	Aug '42	Attitudes in Air Corps	5000
Special Survey III	US	June–Aug '42	Experimental studies of film on China	4000
Planning Survey IV	US	Oct '42	Attitudes toward medical care	5500
Panel Survey II	US	Sept–Oct '42	Attitudes toward allies	5600
Special Survey IV	ETO	Sept '42	Attitudes toward the British	3700

Survey designation	Location	Date	Principal topics	Approximate sample size
Special Survey V	US	Nov–Dec '44	Experimental study of "Prelude to War"	3400
Special Survey VI	Bermuda	Nov '42	Attitudes of soldiers stationed in Bermuda	300
Special Survey VII	US	Nov '42	Attitudes toward the war	2900
Planning Survey V	US	Dec '42	Attitudes toward civilians	3500
S-29	ETO	Jan '43	Leisure-time activities	2400
S-30	ETO	July '43	Attitudes toward Army jobs, etc.	3000
S-32	US	Mar '43	Attitudes of and toward Negroes	12,200
S-33	US	Jan '43	Attitudes of WAC recruits	100
S-35	US	Jan '43	Leisure-time activities	4300
S-36	US	Feb '43	Attitudes of Special Service officers	100
S-37	US	Jan '43	Transportation problems	900
S-38 and S-43	US	Feb '43	Experimental studies of film "Battle of Britain"	5600
S-40	US	Apr '43	Attitudes of officers and EM	5300
S-41	US	Mar '43	Savings and insurance	900
S-42	US	Apr '43	Attitudes of Special Service officers	100
S-44	US	Apr '43	Attitudes toward branch of service	4400
S-45	Middle East	May '43	Attitudes toward war and overseas service	2300
S-47	US	Apr '43	Attitudes of AWOL's and others, compared	1300
S-48	Middle East	July–Aug '43	Attitudes toward allies, etc.	1400
S-49 & S-55	US	May '43	Experimental studies of films "Nazis Strike" and "Divide and Conquer"	1200
S-50	US	Feb '43	Attitudes in Special Service School	1800
S-51	Southwest Pacific	Aug '43	Attitudes toward Special Services	4000
S-53, S-67, S-73	US	May–Aug '43	Studies of educational news reels	1600
S-54	US	June '43	Attitudes of WACS	300
S-60	US & overseas	Sept '43 Apr '44	Follow-up study of Infantry recruits	3900
S-63 A to G and S-64	US	July–Sept '43	Omnibus study of attitudes	18,100
S-66	US	July–Aug '43	Fear of enemy weapons (combat returnees)	800
S-68	US	July '43	Classification and assignment	10,200
S-70	Persian Gulf	Oct–Nov '43	Attitudes toward allies, etc.	1800
S-71	US	Aug '43	Experimental study of training film on map reading	2400
S-72	US	July '43	Attitudes toward USO clubs	8400
S-74	US	Sept '43	Psychiatric patients and AWOL's	700

Survey designation	*Location*	*Date*	*Principal topics*	*Approximate sample size*
S-75	US	Sept '43	Study of film "Negro in World War II"	1000
S-76	US	Sept '43	Attitudes of noncoms toward discipline	600
S-77	US	Oct–Nov '43	Attitudes of hospital patients	5400
S-79	US	Oct '43	Attitudes of men in staging areas	1800
S-80	US	Oct '43	Utilization of transportation	1800
S-82	US	Nov '43	Tests on NP patients	200
S-83	US	Jan '44	Attitudes of ASF officers toward assignments	800
S-84	US	Nov '43	Word pronunciation	300
S-85, S-86, S-87	US	Nov–Dec '43	Officers and EM, attitudes compared	4200
S-88	ETO	Nov–Dec '43	Attitudes toward British	2500
S-90	US	Nov–Dec '43	Attitudes toward WACS	3400
S-91	ETO	Nov '43	Combat veteran attitudes	500
S-92	ETO	Nov '43	Attitudes toward Army life	3000
S-93	Southwest Pacific	Nov '43	Attitudes toward service in the tropics	3200
S-95	US	Jan–Feb '44	Attitudes toward Army, etc.	3600
S-96, S-97, S-98	US	Feb '44	Tests on map reading and first aid	4200
S-99	US	Jan–Feb '44	Problems relating to psychoneurosis	4800
S-100 A to G	Italy, ETO, So Pacific, IB	Jan–Apr '44	Attitudes of combat infantrymen	8300
S-101 B to F	ETO, So Pacific	Jan–Apr '44	Attitudes of combat Infantry officers	1300
S-102	Italy	July '44	Preferences in newspaper reading	2900
S-105	US	Apr–June '44	Attitudes of overseas returnees	400
S-106	US, ETO & Cent Pacific	June '44	Postwar job plans of white officers and EM	25,000
S-107	US	Mar '44	Attitudes of MP officers and EM	4500
S-108	US	Mar '44	Psychoneurotic screening	500
S-109, S-111, S-123	US	Mar–Apr '44	Experimental study of effects of Expert Infantrymen badge	3200
S-112	ETO	Dec '43	Attitudes in Field Forces	2400
S-113	ETO	Dec '43 Mar '44	Attitudes in Fighter Command	3000
S-115	Panama	Jan–Feb '44	Attitudes in Caribbean	4000

Survey designation	Location	Date	Principal topics	Approximate sample size
S-116	ETO	Jan '44	Attitudes toward assignment, etc.	2800
S-117	US	Apr '44	Psychiatric screening test	700
S-118	US	Apr–May '44	Film strips and graphic training aids	1100
S-119	US	Apr–May '44	Sociometric study	400
S-120	US	Apr '44	Attitudes of ASTP men	200
S-121, S-139	US	Apr–Aug '44	Study of effects of orientation program	15,100
S-122	ETO	Apr '44	Attitudes toward British, etc.	3300
S-124	So Pacif	Feb–Mar '44	Attitudes in the South Pacific	2500
S-125	Central Pacific	Feb–Apr '44	Attitudes in the Central Pacific	5800
S-126	ETO	Apr–May '44	Psychoneurotic study	500
S-127, S-131	IB	Feb–Mar '44	Attitudes in China-India-Burma	2400
S-128	ETO	Jan–Feb '44	Attitudes in Field Forces, 1st Army	12,200
S-129	ETO	Mar–May '44	Attitudes in Field Forces, 1st Army	23,400
S-130, S-149, S-152	US, ETO Italy, Central Pacific, IB	June–Nov '44	Readership preference in *Yank*, the Army magazine	8600
S-132	US	June–July '44	Troops on rotation from overseas	2800
S-133	Alaska	Apr–May '44	Attitudes of troops in Alaska	4000
S-134	ETO	May '44	Attitudes of Airborne troops	1000
S-135, S-136, S-142, S-150	ETO	May–June '44	Attitudes of officers and EM in 8th and 9th Air Force	7900
S-137	Italy, Panama, ETO, Central Pacific	May–June '44	Magazine reading preferences	8200
S-138	US	June–July '44	Desire for educational courses	700
S-140	US	July '44	Attitudes of Air Force returnees	1900
S-141	US, Iceland, Labrador	July '44	Attitudes in Air Transport Command	2400
S-144	US	Aug '44	Postwar plans of Negro soldiers	4700
S-145	US, ETO, Iceland	Aug '44	Attitudes toward demobilization	6600
S-146	IB	July '44	Attitudes toward venereal diseases	600

Survey designation	Location	Date	Principal topics	Approximate sample size
S-147	Italy, ETO, Central Pacific	July '44	Preferences in Christmas gifts	700
S-148	ETO	Aug '44	Radio and reading preferences	2200
S-151, S-154	ETO	Aug '44	Combat veterans in hospitals	500
S-155	Cent Pac IB	Nov '44 Jan '45	Quartermaster problems in the Pacific	6700
S-156	US	Sept '44	Attitudes toward insurance	1300
S-157	US	Nov '44	Attitudes of officers and enlisted returnees	7800
S-158	Italy	Aug–Sept '44	Interest in education	4300
S-159	US	Oct '44	Postwar plans of men leaving the Army	2100
S-160	ETO	Sept '44	Experience with equipment and supplies	800
S-161	ETO	Sept '44	Problems of replacements	300
S-162	ETO	Sept '44	Soldiers' savings	200
S-163	ETO	Sept '44	Fear of German weapons	1200
S-164	ETO	Oct '44	Attitudes of WAC officers and enlisted women	5000
S-165	ETO	Sept '44	Hospitalized combat men	300
S-166	Italy	July–Sept '44	Negro & white attitudes toward combat	4400
S-167	US	Oct–Nov '44	Experimental study of film "Opportunity Knocks Again"	900
S-168	US	Nov '44	Japanese ruses as reported by returnees from Pacific	600
S-170	IB	Oct–Nov '44	Trend study on attitudes in IB	1500
S-171	US	Nov '44	Infantry attitudes	400
S-172	US	Nov–Dec '44	Complaints of returnees	6200
S-174	Cent Pac	Sept–Oct '44	Attitudes of Negro quartermaster troops	1000
S-175	Cent Pac	Oct '44	Chemical warfare training	600
S-177	Italy	Nov–Dec '44	Psychoneurotic study	2500
S-178	Italy	Dec '44	Information and education problems	1900
S-179	Italy	Dec '44	Hospital survey	600
S-180, S-195	US	Dec '44 Jan '45	Methodological study of scaling	1200
S-181	US	Dec '44	Attitudes and objective indices of adjustment	4200
S-182	Italy	Oct '44	Problems in voting	2500
S-185	US	Nov–Dec '44	Reactions to a training film	1800

Survey designation	Location	Date	Principal topics	Approximate sample size
S-186	US	Mar '45	Experimental study of radio programs as propaganda	3600
S-188	US	Jan–Apr '45	Experimental study of audience participation as aid to learning	700
S-189	ETO	Jan '45	Reactions to radio and newspaper *Stars and Stripes*	1500
S-190	ETO	Dec '44	Army education program	1700
S-192	US, Cent Pacific IB	Jan '45	Attitudes of Army nurses	1400
S-193	Central Pacific	Jan '45	Hospital patients	1200
S-194	US	Feb '45	Attitudes of WACS	6700
S-196	ETO	Jan '45	White and Negro port battalions	4100
S-198	US	Feb '45	Attitudes of officers and enlisted men, compared	8500
S-199	ETO	Jan '45	Winter clothing preferences, among front line soldiers	1100
S-200	US	Feb–Mar '45	Postwar job plans	3000
S-201	US	Feb '45	Combat veterans convalescing in US	600
S-202	US	Feb–Mar '45	Branch preferences of recruits	1200
S-203	ETO	Feb '45	Attitudes toward I and E publications	2400
S-204	ETO	Feb '45	Attitudes of men in reinforcement depots	900
S-205	US, ETO, Italy, IB Pacific	May '45	Attitudes toward redeployment and demobilization	16,000
S-207	US	May '45	B-29 officers and EM	3400
S-208	US	Apr '45	Returnees' reports on trench foot	1400
S-210	IB	Mar–Apr '45	Trends in attitudes	900
S-211	US	June '45	Returnees' reactions to enemy and further duty	5100
S-212	US	May '45	Attitudes toward the war and further duty	2500
S-213, S-214	US	May '45	Omnibus attitude survey	5600
S-215	US	June '45	Methodological study	3600
S-216, S-217	US	June '45	Studies of paratroopers in training	6300
S-218	US, ETO, Pacific, IB	July '45	Attitudes toward redeployment and demobilization, EM	10,000
S-219	US, ETO, Pacific, IB	July '45	Attitudes toward redeployment and demobilization, officers	5700

Survey designation	Location	Date	Principal topics	Approximate sample size
S-220	US, ETO, Pacific, IB	July '45	Attitudes toward post V-J Day changes in point system	9000
S-221, S-226	US	July '45	Port of embarkation study	600
S-222	ETO	Apr '45	Length of time in combat	500
S-223	ETO	Apr–May '45	Attitudes toward post-hostilities problems	6000
S-224	ETO	June '45	Hospital patients	1300
S-225	US	Aug '45	Methodological study	600
S-227	ETO	July '45	Attitudes toward radio	800
S-228	US	Aug '45	Psychoneurotic study	1400
S-229	US	Oct '45	Attitudes toward the Army	5800
S-230	Pacific	Apr '45	Orientation problems	1000
S-231	Pacific	June '45	Attitudes at replacement stations	2700
S-232	Pacific	July–Aug '45	Savings, insurance, etc.	2400
S-233	Italy	Aug '45	Attitudes of white and Negro troops toward venereal diseases	2700
S-234	US	Nov '45	Attitudes of officers and EM toward the Army	2700
S-235	ETO	Aug '45	Attitudes toward post-hostilities problems	3000
S-236	ETO	Mar '45	Shipboard orientation	1600
S-237	ETO	Aug–Sept '45	Attitudes toward Germans and allies	2400
S-238	ETO	June–Sept '45	Attitudes toward Army, etc.	700
S-239	ETO	Oct '45	Attitudes toward newspaper *Stars and Stripes*	2300
S-240	US	Dec '45	Postwar plans of men leaving the Army	2000
S-242	Italy	July '45	Replacement depot survey	800
S-243	Philippines	Aug '45	Venereal disease study	1000

INDEX
TO VOLUMES I & II

INDEX

A

Abraham Lincoln Brigade, i. 484; ii. 234

Absent without leave, see "AWOL's"

Adjustment, attitudes reflecting: see "Criticism of Army," "Job satisfaction," "Personal commitment," "Personal esprit"; summary table for Army, i. 228

Adjutant General's Office, i. 26, 41, 230n, 291–292, 325

Adler, Leta M., i. 23

Advancement: and AGCT scores, i. 259–260; and age, i. 113–118, 121, 148–149, 241–243; ambivalence toward, i. 230–231; and attitudes reflecting adjustment, i. 147–154; and branch of service, i. 248–256, 271; and "bucking," i. 264–267, 273, 275; and conformity, i. 259–265; as criterion of adjustment, i. 82–84, 88–98; and criticism of Army, i. 148–152, 207–208; criticism of opportunities for, i. 250–258, 267–271, 275–283; desire for, i. 244–250; and educational level, i. 113–116, 121, 148–149, 245–250; and job satisfaction, i. 148, 207–208; and length of service, i. 115–121, 240–243, 248–250, 254–255, 259–260; and marital condition, i. 113–115, 117, 119–121, 148–149; among Negroes, i. 498–502, 583–586; opportunities for, i. 147–148, 150, 231–243, 245, 250, 421–422; and personal commitment, i. 123, 148–152, 207–208; and personal esprit, i. 148–152, 207–208; prediction of, i. 147–154; and stage in war, i. 231–243

AGCT scores: i. 21n, 149, 292; and advancement, i. 245, 259–260; of air combat men, ii. 341; and combat performance, ii. 36–38; of Negroes vs. whites, i. 492–493; and paratroop performance, ii. 217–218

Age: and advancement, i. 113–118, 121, 148–149, 150, 241–243; and assignment, i. 314, 318–319; and childhood experiences, i. 134–136; and combat anxiety, ii. 86; and combat performance, ii. 36–38; and criticism of Army, i. 107–109;

and demobilization credit, ii. 521–548; and educational level, i. 491; and health, i. 128–130, 138; and job satisfaction, i. 107–109, 320–321, 323, 324; and maladjustment, i. 113–118, 121; ii. 425–428; and marital condition, i. 106, 147; and paratroop training failures, ii. 217; and personal commitment, i. 107–109, 122, 124–126, 149–150, 456–457; and personal esprit, i. 107–109, 122; and postwar plans, i. 317–318; and psychoneurotic symptoms, ii. 420–428, 431ff; and recreation preferences, i. 180; and religion, i. 140; and status satisfaction, i. 107–109; and views of point system, ii. 533; and views of value of Army experience, ii. 611, 612–613; and willingness for combat, i. 524; ii. 342–343

Aggression: against Army, see "Criticism of Army"; in combat situation, ii. 96; "goldbricking" as, i. 420; in officer training, i. 390

Agriculture, soldiers' plans for, ii. 603–608

Air Corps: i. 16, 468; ii. 30n, 189, 475, 477, 618; advancement opportunities in, i. 248–250, 271–272, 292; ii. 344–346; criticism of Army in, i. 190–192, 366–367; criticism of advancement opportunities in, i. 250–258; demobilization in, ii. 529–530, 548; job satisfaction in, i. 190–192, 287–289, 290, 296–300, 305–309; personal commitment in, i. 190–192, 330n; personal esprit in, i. 92, 94, 190–192; preference for, i. 287–288, 300–303; ii. 312–314, 483, 488; prestige of, i. 299–300; ii. 342–344; psychiatric screening in, ii. 211–212; returnees' adjustment in, ii. 496–518; strength of, i. 494

Air Corps combat men: ii. 324–410; average work load of, ii. 363–366; background characteristics of, ii. 341–343; casualties among, ii. 363–364, 407–408; psychoneurotic symptoms among, ii. 449–451

Air Corps combat men, morale of: ii. 327–338; and advantages of flying job, ii. 350–352; and combat exposure, ii. 367–383; and medical care, ii. 357–358; and officer-men relations, ii. 348–350; and recruiting policy, ii. 340–343; and status and prestige, ii. 343–348; and time off, ii. 356–357, 393–397; and "tour of duty," ii. 359–361, 383–387; and type of aircraft flown, ii. 397–410; and work load, ii. 353–356, 366, 387–393

Air Corps vs. Infantry: *see also* "Air vs. ground combat"; branch preferences in, i. 306; casualty rates in, ii. 324; criticism of Army in, i. 190–194; job satisfaction in, i. 190–194, 288, 306; personal commitment in, i. 190–194; personal esprit in, i. 94, 190–194

Aircraft, type of and morale, ii. 397–410

Air Forces [AAF], *see* "Air Corps"

Air vs. Ground and Service Forces: advancement opportunities in, i. 238–243; branch satisfaction in, ii. 486–497; criticism of Army in, i. 159–160; criticism of promotion policy in, i. 275, 277, 278; front-rear antagonisms in, ii. 290–291; job satisfaction in, i. 290, 297–300, 307, 338–343; ii. 336–338, 486–497; learning of useful skills in, ii. 352; number of specialists in, ii. 351; overall adjustment in, i. 112, 159–160; personal esprit in, i. 159–160; status satisfaction in, i. 215; pride in outfit in, ii. 336–338; time off in, ii. 356–357; views of point system in, ii. 533, 535; willingness for combat in, i. 524; ii. 336–338

Air vs. ground combat: attitudes toward officers in, ii. 349; awards and decorations in, ii. 347; combat conditions in, ii. 324–327; morale attitudes in, ii. 327–338

Alaska: i. 16, 21, 166, 169n, 183, 336, 480, 549; ii. 456; criticism of officers in, i. 368; job satisfaction in, i. 341–342, 344–345; morale attitudes in, i. 162, 170–175; Research Branch personnel in, i. 25; views of point system in, ii. 523–524

Allies, attitudes toward: i. 475; ii. 39; before and after victory, ii. 554, 559, 573–578; of veterans, ii. 627–630; possible war with, i. 444–445

Alpha test, i. 4

American culture, individual aspiration in, ii. 550–551, 553

Amphibious operations, ii. 67–68

Anderson, Frances, i. 23

Anderson, Robert A., i. 25

Andrews, E. Wyllys, i. 23

Anxiety (about combat): *see also* "Fear (in combat)"; admission of, i. 331–332; ii. 200–204; and background factors, ii. 84–86; and combat performance, ii. 33; effects of precombat training on, ii. 222,

223; neurotic, ii. 207–213; among paratroop trainees, ii. 213–220; personal injury, i. 332–335; and psychoneurotic symptoms, ii. 445–455; in replacement depots, ii. 274–276; symptoms of, ii. 196–197, 203–204; and time in combat, ii. 362–363, 373–383; and time limit to combat, ii. 385–387; and willingness for combat, i. 330–337

Anxiety (about postwar): future wars, i. 443–446; jobs, ii. 553, 555, 560, 598–599, 608–609; personal adjustment, ii. 599

Anxiety Symptoms Index, ii. 415ff; *see also* "Psychoneurotic symptoms"

Anzio, i. 312; ii. 69, 299, 302

Appel, John W., i. 26

Appel, K. E., ii. 412n

Approval of Army, *see* "Criticism of Army"

Aptitudes: testing of, i. 4–5, 8, 35–36, 285, 291–292; utilization of, i. 293–296

Ardennes bulge, ii. 68

Armored Force: ii. 482; Negroes in, i. 494–495; preference for, i. 288, 299–300, 336; ii. 313–314; prestige of, i. 299–300; relative strength of, i. 494

Army: attitudes toward research in, *see* "Research, resistance of Army to"; criticism of, *see* "Criticism of Army"; differences in, between wars, i. 54–81, 289, 291; personnel problems in, i. 289–296; ratings of value of experience in, ii. 610–613, 631–633; size of, i. 54, 231–243

Army Air Forces: *see* "Air Corps"; "Air vs. Ground and Service Forces"

Army areas, definition of, ii. 61

Army General Classification Test, *see* "AGCT scores"

Army Ground Forces [AGF], *see* "Ground Forces"

Army Life, cited, ii. 196

Army Score Card Plan, *see* "Point system"

Army Services [ASF], *see* "Service Forces"

Army Specialized Training Program, i. 294

Arnold, Gen. Henry H., i. 55

Articles of War, ii. 112

Assignments, *see* "Job assignment"

Atlantic Charter, i. 433, 478

Atlantic City, ii. 353

Atrocities, sight of: as combat motivation, ii. 161–164; and fear, ii. 81–82

Attitude measurement: attitude profiles, i. 98–103; consistency of replications, i. 46–47, 263–264

controlled experiments, i. 47–51, 363, 386, 401; examples of, i. 309–311, 460–485; ii. 213–220

impact of Army needs on, i. 5–6, 38,

41–42; impact of intelligence testing on, i. 35–36, 98–99; impressionism vs. science, i. 38–41; intensity analysis, i. 43, 220–221; example of, i. 375–378; intervening variables, i. 131ff; limitations in, i. 42, 46–47, 48, 103–104, 220; matched comparisons, i. 92–93; of personal adjustment, i. 82–104; prediction, *which see;* problems of conceptualization, i. 33–37, 42; problems of dichotomization, i. 220–227; questionnaires, *which see;* relative deprivation, *see* "Deprivation, relative"; scalogram analysis, i. 43–44, 87–88, 220–221; example of, i. 375–378; standardization, i. 110–111, 117n, 120n

Attitude profiles: definition of, i. 98–103; summary table of, i. 228

Attu, i. 162; *see* "Alaska"

Australia: ii. 299; job satisfaction in, i. 338–340

Authoritarian methods: i. 55–56; attitudes toward, i. 65–71

Authority, institutional: *see also* "Status system"; abuses of, i. 413–414, 415; and combat motivation, ii. 108–111, 112–118; and social distance, i. 396–397

Aviation cadet training, i. 232–243; ii. 340, 344

AWOL's [Absent without leave]: ii. 6, 49, 112, 114; age of, i. 113–118, 121
attitudes toward: of combat replacements, ii. 280–281; of combat trainees, ii. 37–39; by length of time in combat, ii. 114–117
childhood experiences of, i. 132–146; educational level of, i. 113–116, 121; length of service of, i. 115–121; marital condition of, i. 113–115, 117, 119–121; overall adjustment of, i. 89; personal commitment of, i. 122–124

Axis, i. 448, 478

B

Babcock, James O., i. 27

Basic training: i. 292, 293–294; *see also* "Training program"; anxiety in, ii. 434; psychiatric screening during, ii. 210–211; of returnees, ii. 483–485; and social control, i. 411–415; at start of war, i. 75–80

Bastogne, ii. 171

Bataan, i. 312

"Battle inoculation," ii. 223–224, 228–231

Battle of the Bulge, i. 312; ii. 171

Battle, types of, ii. 66–68

B-Bag, i. 398

Becker, Ruben, i. 25

Beech, Gould M., i. 23, 25

Beecher, John, i. 595n

Behavior, control of, *see* "Social control"

Belden, Jack, ii. 80n; cited, ii. 83

A Bell for Adano, John Hersey, i. 40

Berg, Stanley, i. 25

Big Business, attitudes toward: before and after victory, ii. 554, 559, 583–585, 587–589; of Negroes, i. 508, 518; of veterans, ii. 614, 617; and views of war aims, i. 431, 432, 434

Big Three, i. 444–445

Bingham, Dr. Walter, i. 26, 284n

Blumer, Herbert, i. 435n

Boredom, as combat stress, ii. 87–88

Bradley, Gen. Omar, i. 55

Branch of service: changes in, returnees, ii. 481–483, 490–491; criticism of promotion opportunities, by, i. 255–256; inefficiency in assignments to, i. 293–296; and job satisfaction, *see separate branches;* per cent Negro vs. white, by, i. 494–495; personal commitment, by, i. 454; personal esprit, by, i. 92, 94; physical profiles, by, i. 496; ii. 496n; preferences for, i. 296–303; ii. 312–314; prestige of, i. 300–303, 309ff; ii. 305–312; relative strength of each, i. 494; satisfaction with camp location, by, ii. 497–503; satisfaction with, returnees, ii. 486–497

Brazil, i. 478

British, attitudes toward: before and after victory, ii. 554, 559, 573–576; of veterans, ii. 627–630; vs. other nationalities, ii. 564, 566, 574, 576, 627, 629

British Empire, i. 431, 432, 434; *see also* "England"

Brown, Arlein, i. 23

Bruner, Jerome S., cited, i. 435–437

"Bucking," i. 264–267, 273, 275, 414, 419–420

Buckner, Harriette, i. 24

Buna campaign, i. 340

Bureau of Agricultural Economics, i. 27; ii. 630

Bureau of the Budget, i. 27

Bureau of the Census, i. 27, 325, 490; ii. 608, 641

Bureau of Labor Statistics, i. 27

Butler, John M., i. 23

C

Camp Adair, ii. 30, 55n

Camp conditions, and job satisfaction, i. 349, 351–361

Camp, Daniel L., i. 25

Camp location, and adjustment, ii. 497–503

Camp preferences, of Negroes, i. 550–566
Campaign stars, *see* "Decorations"
Cantril, Hadley, i. 26, 33n
Capra, Frank, i. 50, 461
Captains: job satisfaction of, i. 308; number of, i. 233
Caribbean, *see* "Panama and the Caribbean"
Cassino, ii. 69
Casualties: in Europe vs. Pacific, ii. 69–70; in Infantry, i. 330; ii. 8, 9, 27, 101–104; nonbattle, *see* "Nonbattle casualty rate"; and prestige of outfit, ii. 307
    psychiatric: ii. 6–7, 205; attitudes toward, ii. 198–200; effects of on outfit, ii. 207–210; prediction of, ii. 213–220
    rate of and fear, ii. 81–82; sight of and vindictiveness, ii. 164
Catholic soldiers, i. 400
Cavalry: Negroes in, i. 494–495, 530–534; relative strength of, i. 494
CBI Talks, i. 470
Central Pacific theater, *see* "Pacific area" and individual localities
Chaplains, i. 400, 413
Chemical Warfare Service: Negroes in, i. 496; physical stamina in, i. 496; preference for, i. 288, 299–300; ii. 313–314; prestige of, i. 299–300
"Chicken," i. 390, 419; ii. 303, 508–510
Childhood experiences, and Army adjustment, i. 130–146
Children's Bureau, i. 27
China, i. 184; ii. 609f
China-Burma-India theater: *see also* "India-Burma theater"; criticism of officers in, i. 373n
Chinese, attitudes toward: vs. other nationalities, ii. 627, 629; veterans', ii. 627–630
Church attendance, and adjustment, i. 140, 144
Cisin, Ira, i. 25
Civil Service Commission, i. 27
Civil War, ii. 112
Civilians, attitudes toward: Army resistance to research in, ii. 613–614; before and after victory, ii. 554, 559, 582–586; of veterans, ii. 613–630
Class structure, U.S., i. 244
Classification, *see* "Job assignment"
Classification and Assignment Branch, i. 8
Clausen, John A., i. 23, 25, 28; ii. 456n, 520n, 596n
Closeness to fighting: *see also* "Front vs. rear," "Theater of operations"; and criticism of officers, i. 364, 365–368; ii. 128–129; and prestige of outfit, ii. 65; and psychoneurotic symptoms, ii. 447

CMTC [Civilian Military Training Camp], i. 232, 234
Coast Artillery and Anti-Aircraft: ii. 482; Negroes in, i. 494–495, 500; preference for, i. 288, 299–300; ii. 313–314; prestige of, i. 299–300; promotion rate in, i. 271; relative strength of, i. 494
Cobb, Virginia, i. 23, 24
Coffey, Joseph A., i. 25
Cohen, Reuben, i. 25
Coleman, A. Lee, i. 23, 25
Colonels, number of, i. 233
Combat: *see also* "Anxiety (in combat)," "Fear (in combat)," "Front vs. rear" aerial: ii. 324–410; *see* "Air Corps combat men," "Air vs. ground combat," "Fighter pilots," "Heavy bomber crews" definition of, i. 164; ii. 62–64; and demobilization credit, ii. 524–548; main variables in, ii. 64, 66; as situation of stress, ii. 76–96; social control in, ii. 96–104 (*see also* "Social control"); types of, ii. 66–69
Combat, attitudes toward: and individual performance, ii. 30–41; and nonbattle casualties, ii. 6–30, 42–44
Combat credit, evaluations of, ii. 62–64
Combat Infantryman's Badge: and morale attitudes, i. 309–311; and demobilization credit, ii. 542–543, 546
Combat, length of time in: and anxiety symptoms, ii. 362–363, 373–383, 451–453;
    and attitudes toward: AWOL's, ii. 116; combat evasion, ii. 141; officers, ii. 121–122; soldiers in U.S., ii. 319
    and combat efficiency, ii. 284–289; and personal commitment, ii. 152–155; and pride in outfit, ii. 140; and ratings of enemy weapons, ii. 236, 239–240; and willingness for combat, ii. 362–363, 367–373, 377–379
Combat motivations: ii. 105–191; in Air Corps, *see* "Air Corps combat men, morale of"; desire for home, ii. 108–111, 168–169; desire for status, i. 525–526; ending the task, ii. 108–110, 168–169, 170; fatalism, ii. 108–110, 188–190; idealistic reasons, ii. 108–111, 149–156; indifference, ii. 109–112, 189; institutional authority, ii. 108–118; leadership, ii. 108–110, 118–130; of Negroes, i. 525–535, 588; prayer, ii. 108–110, 136, 172–188; self-preservation, ii. 108–110, 169; sense of self-respect, ii. 108–110, 131–135; soldiers' ratings of, ii. 107–112, 175, 177, 179–185; solidarity with group, ii. 108–111, 130–149, 169, 349–350; victo-

ries, ii. 169–172; vindictiveness, ii. 108–111, 156–167

Combat performance: and attitudes toward combat, ii. 6–37; and background characteristics, ii. 36–37; of companies, ii. 5–30, 41–54; disturbance of by psychoneurotics, ii. 207–210; and general attitudes, ii. 37–40; of new replacements, ii. 282–284; peak of efficiency in, ii. 243, 284–289; views of factors in, ii. 73–76

Combat, readiness for further, and attitudes toward: leadership, ii. 125–126, 129–130; physical condition, ii. 93–95; and personal commitment, ii. 155–156; and pride in outfit, ii. 141–142; and vindictiveness, ii. 165

Combat replacements: i. 42n; ii. 242–289; assimilation of to veteran outfits, ii. 242–272, 277–289; assumption of vets' attitudes by, ii. 265–272; experience in replacement depots, ii. 272–276; psychoneurotic symptoms of, ii. 440–445

vs. veterans and men in fresh divisions: attitudes of toward: leaders, ii. 245, 246, 253–255; physical condition, ii. 245, 246, 261, 263–264

criticism of Army by, ii. 245, 246, 259–261; personal commitment of, ii. 245, 246, 262, 264–265; pride in outfit of, ii. 245, 246, 255–259, 261; self-confidence of, ii. 245, 246, 250–253; willingness for combat of, ii. 245, 246, 247–250

Combat skill, confidence in: definition of area, ii. 5; of combat veterans, ii. 22–23; measurement of, ii. 42–44, 47–48; and nonbattle casualties, ii. 11–30; and rank, ii. 23–27; of replacements, ii. 245, 246, 250–253, 266, 269–270

Combat soldiers, veteran vs. new: combat attitudes vs. performance of, ii. 11, 13n, 21–30; personal commitment of, ii. 151–152; pride in outfit of, ii. 138

Combat stamina, confidence in: definition of area, ii. 5; of combat veterans, ii. 22–23; measurement of, ii. 42–44, 46–47; and nonbattle casualties, ii. 11–30; and rank, ii. 23–27; of replacements, ii. 267, 271

Combat stresses: ii. 76–96; boredom, ii. 88; discomfort, ii. 78–79; effects of, ii. 91–95; factors resisting, ii. 96–104 (see also "Combat motivations"); fear of injury, ii. 77–78; grief, horror, rage, ii. 80–82, 208–209; impersonality, ii. 87; lack of privacy, ii. 87; lack of time limit, ii. 88–91; loss of mobility, ii. 82–83; psychiatric breakdowns, ii. 197–200, 207–210; sexual deprivation, ii. 79–80; uncertainty, ii. 83–84; value conflicts, ii. 84–87

Combat vs. noncombat soldiers: criticism of Army by, i. 159–161; overall adjustment of, i. 112; percentage of, i. 163–166, 312–313; ii. 61–62; personal commitment of, i. 159–161, 440, 455–456; personal esprit of, i. 159–161; views of point system of, ii. 526, 532–533

Combat, willingness for: air vs. ground, ii. 331–337; and combat exposure (Air), ii. 367–373, 377–379; of combat veterans, ii. 22–23; definition of area, ii. 5; measurement of, ii. 41–46; of Negroes, i. 522–535; and nonbattle casualties, ii. 6–30; and rank, i. 524; ii. 23–27; of replacements, ii. 245, 246, 247–250, 266, 269; summary table of, i. 524; and type of air combat, ii. 401–402; and work load (Air), ii. 391–393; and worry about injury, i. 330–337

Comfort, and job satisfaction, i. 337–361; see also "Discomfort"

Command Decision, W. W. Haines, i. 40

Command of Negro Troops, i. 597

Commanding Officers, attitudes toward, i. 383–384

Commissions: number of, i. 235; sources of, i. 232–243

Commitment, see "Personal commitment"

Committee on Human Resources, i. 3

Communications, opinions of, ii. 74

Communists, hostility toward, ii. 584–585

Complaints, see "Gripes," "Criticism of Army"

Compulsory military training, views of, i. 446, 480; ii. 621, 624

Conformity: and advancement, i. 259–265, 272–275; of combat replacements, ii. 281; of Negroes vs. whites, i. 526–527

Congress, ii. 530, 613

Conrad, Herbert S., i. 33n

Conrad, Joseph, i. 41

Conversion hysteria, ii. 206

Convictions about war, see "War aims"

Cooley, Charles H., i. 44

Coombs, Clyde, i. 26, 284n

Corporals: see also "Noncoms vs. privates"; educational level of, i. 248; job satisfaction of, i. 307; Negro, i. 499; number of, i. 233

Corps areas, ii. 61

Corzine, Esther M., i. 23

Cottrell, Leonard S., Jr., i. 3n, 22, 24, 25, 28, 486n; ii. 549n, 596n

Court martial, ii. 113

Crespi, Leo P., i. 33n

The Crisis, on Jim Crow Army, i. 598

Criticism of Army: see also "Officers, attitudes toward," "Status system, criticism of"; and advancement, i. 148, 150, 152, 207–208, 259–265; and age, i. 107–109, 150; before and after victory, ii. 553, 557–559, 581; and branch of service, i. 159–160, 190–194; and combat, i. 159–161; of combat replacements, ii. 245, 246, 259–261, 267, 271; definition of area, i. 87, 97–98, 99n; and educational level, i. 66–67, 107–109, 150, 153–154; extent of, at war's end, i. 219–228; free comments, cited, i. 211–219; and length of service, i. 112, 159–160, 199–210; and maladjustment, ii. 413–415; and marital condition, i. 107–110, 112; of Negroes, i. 504–506, 540–542; and overall adjustment, i. 87–93; and overseas service, i. 156–157, 159–161, 166–168, 170–173; and rank, i. 166–168, 170–171, 394; and stage in war, i. 195–197, 205–206; at start of war, i. 65–80; and theater of operations, i. 170–171

Cross section, Army: method for making comparisons, i. 110–111; representativeness of, i. 130

Crossley poll, i. 38

Crow, Jane B., i. 23

Currying favor, *see* "Bucking"

D

Danger, and job satisfaction, i. 329–337

Dating, pre-Army, and adjustment, i. 132–133, 143–144

Daugherty, Wayne F., i. 22

David, Virginia, i. 23

D Day, ii. 6ff, 152, 237n, 429, 430

Death: fear of, ii. 77–78; sight of, ii. 80–82

Debarkation centers, ii. 475–479

Decorations: i. 164; ii. 6, 346–347; and demobilization credit, ii. 347–348, 524, 529, 539, 542, 543

Deferment, attitudes toward, i. 122–124, 128–130

"Definitions of the situation," i. 125; *see also* "Deprivation, relative"; in combat, ii. 96–97; in racial terms, i. 502–507

DeGaulle, Gen. Charles, i. 478

Deming, W. Edwards, i. 46n

Demobilization: predicted morale problems in, ii. 555; suggestions for easing of, ii. 560; priority in, *see* "Point system"

Department of Agriculture, ii. 596, 600

Department of Commerce, ii. 600

Department of Labor, ii. 600

Dependents: and demobilization credit, ii. 521–548; and maladjustment, i. 122–124; and personal commitment, i. 122–124, 126

Depression postwar, ii. 597

Deprivation, relative: and advancement, i. 190; and criticism of advancement opportunities, i. 250–254, 279–280; and criticism of officers, i. 369; definition of, i. 124–130; and length of service, i. 208–211; of Negroes vs. whites, i. 542–543, 525–527; of Northern vs. Southern Negroes, i. 562–564; and personal commitment, i. 125–130; in recreation, i. 178–182; and theater of operations, i. 172–173

Desert Army, i. 16

Desertion, ii. 112–113

Deterioration of attitudes, *see* "Length of service" and "Stage in war"

DeVinney, Leland C., i. 3n, 20, 22, 25, 28, 54n, 82n, 230n, 362n

DeVinney, Margaret, i. 29

Dictatorship, i. 436

Disabled veterans, ii. 560

Discharge: *see also* "Point system"; desire for, i. 453–458; free comments about, i. 216–217; of returnees, ii. 473–474

Discipline, *see* "Punishment," "Social control"

Discomfort, as combat stress, ii. 78–79

Discrimination, *see* "Racial discrimination"

Distinguished Service Cross, ii. 4

Dive bombers, relative fear of, ii. 232–241

Division of Program Surveys, Agriculture Dep't., ii. 596n, 630

Division of Welfare and Recreation, i. 16

Dollard, Charles, i. 19, 20, 22, 25, 487n

Dollard, John, i. 26; ii. 192n; cited, i. 484; ii. 157, 195, 234–235

"Done my share" attitude: i. 451–454; in post-armistice period, ii. 552–553; among returnees, ii. 469–472

Doolittle Committee: i. 367; ii. 582; on officer-enlisted men relations, i. 379–381; on revision of promotion system, i. 283

Doolittle, Lt. Gen. James H., i. 75, 367, 379; ii. 384

Dorn, Harold F., i. 27

Draft, *see* "Induction," "Selective Service"

Dubin, Robert, i. 23

Dunkirk, ii. 559

Duration of war, soldiers' estimates of, i. 448–449

Durkheim, Emile, i. 31

E

Education, postwar plans for, ii. 601, 639–641

Education Branch, I & E Division, i. 9

Educational level: and advancement, i. 113–116, 121, 148–151, 245–250; and age, i. 491; and assignment, i. 314, 318–319, 500; by branch of service, i. 190, 192, 500; and branch preference, i. 335; and childhood experiences, i. 132–146; and combat performance, ii. 36–37; and combat self-confidence, ii. 252; and criticism of Army, i. 66–67, 70–77, 107–109, 153–154, 269–271; ii. 259–260; and criticism of officers, i. 364, 368; differences, World Wars I & II, i. 57–65; and fear of future war, i. 443–444; and health, i. 126–130, 137; and interpretation of war, i. 434; and job satisfaction, i. 107–109, 153–154, 185, 320–324, 326–327, 328; and leadership preferences, i. 406–407; and maladjustment, i. 113–116, 121; ii. 425–428; of Negro soldiers, i. 488–494, 499–500; northern vs. southern, i. 488n, 490–491; and overall adjustment, i. 99–103; and personal commitment, i. 107–109, 122, 123–127, 149–150, 185, 456–458; ii. 262; and personal esprit, i. 107–109, 123; and postwar plans, i. 317–318; and prayer in combat, ii. 180–181; and pride in outfit, ii. 256; and psychoneurotic symptoms, ii. 420–428, 431ff; and rank, i. 60–65, 113, 245, 247, 500; and recreation preferences, i. 180; and religion, i. 140; and socio-economic status, i. 58–60, 126–127, 137; and status satisfaction, i. 107–109, 153–154, 244–245; and willingness for combat, i. 335, 524; ii. 248; and worry about battle injury, i. 335

Educational program, see "Orientation"

Edwards, Allen, i. 13

Efficiency ratings, and advancement, i. 271–272

Egypt, i. 25

Eighth Air Force, i. 8, 42; ii. 4; criticism of training in, i. 79–80

88 mm. gun, relative fear of, ii. 232–241

Eisenhower, Dwight D., i. 19, 55

Elder, Genevieve, i. 23

Elinson, Jack, i. 23, 28, 284n

Elliott, Charles N., i. 25

Engineers, Corps of: job satisfaction in, i. 289, 291, 324–326; Negroes in, i. 494–497, 500; personal esprit in, i. 162; physical stamina in, i. 496–497; preference for, i. 288, 299–300; ii. 313–314; prestige of, i. 299–300; ii. 306–308; promotion rate in, i. 271; relative strength of, i. 494; returnees' adjustment in, ii. 496–518

England: i. 336, 442; ii. 237, 243; see also "British, attitudes toward"; job satisfaction in, i. 341–342, 356–361; Negro attitudes in, i. 544

Enlisted men: see also "Noncoms vs. privates," "Officers vs. enlisted men"; attitudes of toward WAC, i. 44–46; criticism of Army by, i. 75–80; number of, i. 54; outfit preferences of, i. 330–331; personal commitment of, i. 81

Equipment, attitudes toward, ii. 74–75, 145–146

Esprit, see "Personal esprit"

Esprit de corps, see "Solidarity with group"

Europe vs. Mediterranean: attitudes toward home front in, ii. 321–322

Europe vs. Pacific: combat motivations in, ii. 174–175; combat situation in, ii. 69–76; job satisfaction in, ii. 329; personal esprit in, i. 162–163; pride in outfit in, ii. 329; proportion of combat men in, i. 165–166; psychoneurotic symptoms in, ii. 443–444, 463, 466; vindictiveness toward enemy in, ii. 157–167

Europe vs. Pacific, attitudes in, toward: combat, ii. 70–71, 73–76; extreme fear reactions, ii. 198–199; further service, i. 454; physical condition, ii. 72–73; promotion policy, i. 279; service forces, ii. 293–295, 299–300, 304–305; strength of enemy, ii. 146–149

European Theater of Operations [ETO]: i. 18, 19, 39, 42, 169n, 215, 302, 315–316, 449; ii. 6ff, 113, 170f, 201f, 286ff, 292ff, 331n, 335ff, 359ff, 363ff, 430, 441ff, 461ff, 609f, 616f; see also "Europe vs. Pacific," "Normandy" etc.; American strength in, ii. 61–62; criticism of Army in, i. 171, 212–219; criticism of officers in, i. 368; job satisfaction in, i. 170–171, 214; morale problems after victory in, ii. 549–595; Negroes in, i. 509, 521, 538ff; personal esprit in, i. 169, 170; Research Branch personnel in, i. 24, 25; views of point system in, ii. 523, 531, 542, 546

Exhaustion cases, combat, ii. 136–137

Expectation, patterns of, i. 125; see also "Deprivation, relative"; and Negro adjustment, i. 542–544

"Expendable" attitude, ii. 87

Expert Infantryman's Badge, i. 309–311

F

Factor analysis, i. 35–37

Fair Employment Practices Commission, i. 513

Fascism, ending of as war aim, i. 436; ii. 587–589

Fatalism: ii. 88–89; and combat motivation, ii. 108–110, 188–190

Fear in Battle, J. Dollard, cited, i. 484; ii. 157, 195, 234–235

Fear (in combat): *see also* "Anxiety (in combat)"; admission of, ii. 200–204; and casualty rate, ii. 80–82; of enemy weapons, by type, ii. 231–241; in Europe vs. Pacific, ii. 70–71, 75; and group solidarity, ii. 179–185; and palliative thoughts, ii. 179–185; and prayer, ii. 179–185; and self-confidence, ii. 224–228; and sight of atrocities, ii. 80–82; and sight of breakdowns, ii. 208–209; and sight of death, ii. 80–82; symptoms of, reported, ii. 201–204

Fear, control of: ii. 192–241; by permissive attitude, ii. 196–207; by psychiatric screening, ii. 207–220; by training methods, ii. 220–231

Fears, childhood, and Army adjustment, i. 138–139, 144

Field Artillery: ii. 65, 482; casualty rate in, ii. 103; job satisfaction in, i. 306; Negroes in, i. 494–495, 500; personal esprit in, i. 162; preference for, i. 288, 299–300, 336; ii. 313–314; prestige of, i. 299–300; ii. 306–308; promotion rate in, i. 271; relative strength of, i. 494

Fifth Army, i. 42n

Fighter pilots: anxiety among, ii. 381; vs. bomber crews, ii. 397–410; casualties among, ii. 407–408; combat willingness of, ii. 333–334, 372–373; tour of duty of, ii. 359; work load of, ii. 354

Fighting, childhood, and Army adjustment, i. 132–133, 141–142, 144

Films, orientation: i. 597; effects of, i. 461–468

Finan, John L., i. 23, 25, 28; ii. 192n, 213n

First Army, i. 39

First Division (Infantry), ii. 3, 4, 5ff

First Lieutenants: job satisfaction of, i. 305–309; number of, i. 233

Flanagan, John C., i. 26

Flight officers, number of, i. 233

Florant, Lyonel C., i. 23, 486n

Food: adequacy of in combat, ii. 79; and job satisfaction, i. 353–357

Ford, Robert N., i. 23, 25, 486n; ii. 456n

Form 20 card, i. 259; ii. 31

Fort Belvoir, i. 17

Fort Benning, ii. 212ff

Fort Meade, i. 15, 16, 17

43d Division, ii. 4

Fosdick, Raymond B., cited, i. 381–382

Four Freedoms, i. 433–435, 439, 478

4th Division, ii. 5ff

France, i. 442–447; ii. 236ff

French, attitudes toward: before and after victory, ii. 576–578; of veterans, ii. 627–630; vs. other nationalities, ii. 564, 566, 576, 627, 629

Freud, Sigmund, i. 30; ii. 83n

Front vs. rear soldiers: ii. 134–135, 290–316; attitudes of toward headquarters, ii. 314–316; definition of combat by, ii. 62–64; informal status hierarchy, ii. 305–312; preference for noncombat jobs, ii. 312–314; resentment and envy among, ii. 299–305; views of adequacy of supply, ii. 293–299

Furloughs: free comments about, i. 216; for returnees, ii. 475–479

G

Galapagos, i. 179; *see also* "Panama and the Caribbean"

Gallup poll, i. 38

"Gangplank fever," ii. 440–441

Garrison, Katherine Jones, i. 23

Generals, number of, i. 233

Geographical location: and health attitudes, i. 174–175; and job satisfaction, i. 338–350; and recreation attitudes, i. 179–181

Germans: i. 164, 166, 485; ii. 56–57, 138, 155–156; attitudes toward, ii. 553, 557, 564–573

Germans vs. Japanese, attitudes toward: ease of victory over, ii. 146–149; killing, ii. 34; vindictiveness, ii. 157–167

Germany, i. 189, 442, 447, 448, 474, 480; nonfraternization in, i. 472; ii. 553, 567–572

Gibeaux, Celia L., i. 23, 28

GI Bill of Rights, i. 480; ii. 597, 598, 609, 639–641

Gilbert Islands, i. 162, 166

Gillem report, i. 586n; cited, i. 586–587, 597–598

Glick, Clarence, i. 23; ii. 456n

Glick, Paul C., i. 23, 25, 28, 39

Glueck, B. C., ii. 332n, 379n; cited, 212, 374–375

God Is My Co-Pilot, Scott, ii. 351

"Goldbricking," i. 420–421

Goldhamer, Herbert, i. 25

Goodenough, Ruth, i. 23

Goodenough, Ward H., i. 23, 25
Government officials, hostility toward, ii. 554
Grant, David A., i. 23
Greenberg, Alfred, i. 25
Grief, as combat stress, ii. 80
Grinker, Roy R., ii. 137n, 349n, 412n, 465n; cited, ii. 205, 206, 351, 409
Gripes: see also "Criticism of Army"; of Negroes vs. whites, i. 541–542; opportunities for expression of, i. 398–401, 413; ii. 4, 609; views on justice of, i. 395–396
Ground crews (Air Corps), job satisfaction of, i. 356–361
Ground Forces [AGF]: i. 468; ii. 475, 477; see also "Air vs. Ground and Service Forces"; advancement opportunities in, i. 248–250; assignments to, i. 293–294; criticism of advancement opportunities in, 254–258; job satisfaction in, i. 287–289, 290, 296–303, 307; Negroes in, i. 494–495; official opposition to point system of, ii. 520, 548; preferences for, i. 300–303; relative strength of, i. 494
Group identification: see also "Solidarity with group"; of enlisted men, i. 418; of officers, i. 389–390
Group sanctions, formal, see "Rewards, group," "Punishment, group"
Group sanctions, informal: against "bucking," i. 266–267, 414; and combat behavior, ii. 130–149; against excessive effort, i. 414; against "goldbricking," i. 420
Guadalcanal: i. 448; criticism of Army in, i. 427; malaria control in, i. 176; personal esprit in, i. 162
Guam: criticism of Army in, i. 212, 216, 218; job satisfaction in, i. 214; status satisfaction in, i. 215
Guernsey, Paul D., i. 20, 25, 28
Guthe, Lucy, i. 29
Guthrie, Edwin H., i. 13
Guttman, Louis, i. 26, 28, 43; ii. 411n, 520n, 528n

H

Hand, Harold C., i. 25
Hardesty, Beatrice N., i. 23, 28
Harrell, Margaret S., i. 23
Harrell, Thomas W., i. 26
Harvard Laboratory of Social Relations, i. 29
Hastings, D. W., ii. 332n, 379n; cited, ii. 212, 374–375
Hauser, Philip M., i. 26

Hausknecht, George, i. 23
Hausknecht, Rita, i. 23
Hawaii: ii. 299, 445; criticism of Army in, i. 212, 213, 216, 219; job satisfaction in, i. 214, 341–342, 344–345
Headquarters, attitudes toward: of combat men, ii. 314–316; and work load, ii. 391–393
Health, childhood, and Army adjustment, i. 132–133, 137–138, 144
Heavy bomber crews: anxiety among, ii. 373–383; casualties among, ii. 407–408; combat willingness of, ii. 333–334, 367–373; distribution of grades in, ii. 326; vs. light and medium, ii. 397–410; tour of duty of, ii. 359; work load of, ii. 355
Heavy weapons companies: ii. 64; casualty rates in, ii. 8, 9; combat attitudes vs. performance in, ii. 11–12, 16–18
Henderson, L. J., cited, i. 33–34
Hiroshima, ii. 580
Hitler, Adolph, i. 462, 467, 470; ii. 571
Home, desire for: i. 176, 185–189, 450; as combat motivation, ii. 108–111, 168–169
Home front, attitudes toward: before and after victory, ii. 582–586; and combat performance, ii. 39; of front-line vs. rear echelons, ii. 297, 320–323
Homes, broken, and Army adjustment, i. 132–133, 144
Horney, Karen, ii. 83n
Horton, Donald, i. 23; ii. 192n
Hostilities, cessation of: and attitudes toward: allies, ii. 573–578; Army, ii. 578–583; Germans, ii. 564–573; home front, ii. 583–586; war aims, ii. 586–594 and overall morale, ii. 561–563, 594–595; prediction of morale problems arising from, ii. 549–560
Hould, Marie L., i. 23
Housing, and job satisfaction, i. 356–357
Hovland, Carl I., i. 3n, 22, 25, 28, 430n
Hull, Dorothy P., i. 24
Hull, Richard L., i. 24, 25
Humor, as combat incentive, ii. 190
Hurt, Marshall, i. 23
Hurtgen Forest, ii. 69

I

Identification with war, see "Personal commitment"
Ideology, see "War aims"
Illiterates, i. 21n, 313
India-Burma Theater of Operations: i. 153, 169n, 176, 183, 337, 449, 450; ii. 456, 609f; criticism of Army in, i. 170, 212–219; job satisfaction in, i. 170–171,

214; orientation program in, i. 469–470; Negroes in, i. 509, 521, 536ff; percentage of combat men in, i. 166; personal commitment in, i. 170; personal esprit in, i. 162, 169, 170; relative deprivation in, i. 173; Research Branch personnel in, i. 20, 25; status satisfaction in, i. 215; views of point system in, ii. 523–524, 546

Indifference, and combat motivation, ii. 109–112, 189

Induction, attitudes toward, i. 122–127

Infantry: i. 8, 292, 476ff; ii. 440, 445ff, 482; *see also* "Air Corps vs. Infantry"; assignment to, i. 293–294; casualty rate in, i. 330; ii. 102–104; combat in, ii. 3–323 (see also "Combat"); criticism of Army in, i. 192–194; job satisfaction in, i. 192–194, 296–300, 305–306ff; Negroes in, i. 494–495, 500, 587ff; personal commitment in, i. 192–194; personal esprit in, i. 92, 94, 162, 192–194; preference for, i. 287–288, 300–303, 330–337; ii. 312–314; prestige of, i. 299–300, 309–312; ii. 305–312; promotion rate in, i. 271; returnees' adjustment in, ii. 496–518; size of, i. 330, 494

Infiltration warfare, ii. 67, 70

Information and Education Division, i. 9–11, 20, 459ff; ii. 524ff, 549ff; *see also* "Research Branch"

Inspector General system, i. 398–400

International Brigade, ii. 157

Internationalism: soldiers' attitudes toward, ii. 590–594; veterans' attitudes toward, ii. 624–626, 639

IQ tests: in World War I, i. 4–5, 34–35; development of techniques and concepts, i. 34–36, 98–99

Iran, i. 25

Italy: i. 42n, 176–178, 183, 336, 480; ii. 69n, 85ff, 102, 114, 122, 173, 180ff, 199, 202, 230f, 275ff, 298, 429, 452f, 609f; *see also* "Mediterranean Theater of Operations"; criticism of Army in, i. 212–219; job satisfaction in, i. 214; personal esprit in, i. 162; Negroes in, 547ff, 586ff

Iwo Jima, ii. 70, 445

J

Jacobson, Eugene H., i. 23

Jaffe, A. J., i. 23, 24, 28, 284n; ii. 3n, 324n, 362n

Janis, Irving L., i. 23, 24, 28, 362n; ii. 3n, 192n, 324n, 362n, 411n

Japan, i. 158, 164, 166, 447, 448, 475, 479; ii. 580

Japanese, i. 164, 189, 340, 431, 448, 464; ii. 155–156; *see also* "Germans vs. Japanese"

Jews, hostility toward: before and after victory, ii. 554, 559, 583–585; of veterans, ii. 617, 619, 637–638

Jim Crow, *see* "Segregation"

Job assignment: by age and education, i. 314; importance of attitude studies for, i. 285–296; inefficiency in, i. 293–296; of Negroes, i. 495–496, 499; preferences in, i. 285–293, 303; reasons for preferences, i. 315–329; of returnees, ii. 468, 479–485

Job satisfaction: i. 284–361; and advancement, i. 148, 207–208; and age, i. 107–109, 150, 320–321, 323, 324; and branch of service, i. 190–194, 296–303, 309, 329–337; ii. 328–330, 336; and branch satisfaction, ii. 489–490; and camp location, ii. 501–503; and civilian skills, i. 312–329; ii. 488; and comfortable milieu, i. 337–361; and danger of assignment, i. 329–337; definition of area, i. 86–87, 96–97; and educational level, i. 107–109, 150, 153–154, 320–324, 326–327, 328; free comments cited, i. 213–214; and length of service, i. 199–208, 342–346; and maladjustment, ii. 413–415; and marital condition, i. 107–109, 321, 346; of Negroes, i. 536–538; and overall adjustment, i. 88–93; and overseas service, i. 156–157, 166–168, 170–171, 173, 182; and personal commitment, i. 460; and prestige of outfit, i. 309–312; and rank, i. 166–168, 170–171, 304–308, 326, 328, 338–339, 342–343, 345, 347, 348, 350, 351, 359–360, 394; of returnees, ii. 486–497ff; and stage in war, i. 195–197, 205; and theater of operations, i. 170–171, 173, 182–185, 338–350; and type of combat (Air Corps), ii. 399, 401–402

Jobs, postwar: anxiety about, ii. 553, 555, 560, 598–599, 608–609; opportunities for, ii. 598, 634–636, 639–640; plans for, ii. 600–613; and skills learned in Army, i. 312–329; ii. 352, 609

Judd, Merle, i. 23

Junkers, i. 478

K

Keppel, Francis, i. 26

Kinsey, Alfred C., ii. 79n

Kohler, Wolfgang, ii. 83n

Kolstad, Arthur, i. 24
Kuder, G. Frederic, i. 24

L

Labor unions, attitudes toward: before and after victory, ii. 554, 559, 583–585; of veterans, ii. 614–615, 617, 637, 642
Lacey, Myrtle P., i. 23
Lanham, Charles T., i. 28
Lazarsfeld, Paul F., i. 26, 28, 43
Leadership: *see also* "Officers, attitudes toward"; and combat motivation, ii. 108–110, 118–130; and job satisfaction, i. 354–355; Negro opinions as to, i. 580–586; qualities preferred in, i. 383–387, 404–408
Leadership and the Negro Soldier, i. 597
League of Nations, i. 436
Ledo Road, i. 183
Leffler, Robert W., i. 25
Leisure, *see* "Time off"
Length of service: and advancement, i. 115–121, 238, 240–243, 259–261; and conformity, ii. 114–117; and criticism of advancement opportunities, i. 254–255; and criticism of Army, i. 112, 159–160, 199–210, 268–269; and criticism of officers, i. 364, 368; and demobilization credit, ii. 521–548; and job satisfaction, i. 199–208, 342–346; and maladjustment, i. 115–121; and Negro attitudes, i. 582; and personal commitment, i. 112, 159–160, 199–208, 455, 457; and personal esprit, i. 94, 112, 159–160, 199–208; and psychoneurotic symptoms, ii. 433–439, 444; and rotation, ii. 457–458; and willingness for combat, i. 524
Length of time in grade: and attitude toward promotion, i. 280
Length of time overseas: and job satisfaction, i. 342–347
Leningrad, i. 442
Lieutenant Colonels, number of, i. 233
Light bomber crews: anxiety among, ii. 380, 381; vs. heavy and medium, ii. 397–410; tour of duty of, ii. 359; willingness for combat of, ii. 333–334, 370–371
Likert, Rensis, i. 13, 26
Limited service, i. 159–160, 193–194; ii. 421–422, 430–433
Longevity in Army, *see* "Length of service"
Loveland, Nathene, T., i. 23
Loyalty, group, as combat motivation, ii. 85, 136–137, 142–145; *see also* "Solidarity with group"

"Lucky Bastard" certificates, ii. 383
Luftwaffe, i. 464
Lumsdaine, Arthur A., i. 23, 24, 28; ii. 3n, 324n, 362n
Lumsdaine, Marion Harper, i. 23, 24, 28; ii. 3n, 324n, 362n
Luria, A. R., ii. 83n

M

MacArthur, Gen. Douglas, i. 55, 183
Maccoby, Eleanor, ii. 596n
Maccoby, Nathan, i. 23, 24
Magic, as combat incentive, ii. 188, 190
Mail service, ii. 273
Majors, number of, i. 233
Maladjustment, *see* "AWOL's," "Casualties, psychiatric," "Psychoneurotics"
Malaria: ii. 7, 69, 70, 94; attitudes toward control of, i. 174–175; and job satisfaction, i. 348
Malcolm, Erna L., i. 23
Malingering, ii. 419–420
Manheimer, Dean, i. 23, 24, 25, 28, 486n
Manila, i. 25
Marblestone, Ansel L., i. 25
Mariana Islands, i. 166; ii. 546
Marine Corps, i. 287; ii. 434, 436, 641; prestige of, i. 309
Marital condition: and advancement, i. 113–115, 117, 119–121, 148–149, 151–152; and age, i. 106, 147; and assignment, i. 318–319; and branch preference, i. 334–336; and childhood experience, i. 132–146; and combat performance, ii. 36–38; and combat self-confidence, ii. 252; and criticism of Army, i. 107–111, 112; ii. 259–260; and demobilization credit, i. 125; ii. 526–548; and health, i. 128–130, 138; and job satisfaction, i. 107–109, 321, 346; and maladjustment, i. 113–115, 117, 119–121; and personal commitment, i. 107–111, 112, 122, 124–125, 456–457; ii. 262; and personal esprit, i. 107–111, 112, 122; and postwar plans, i. 317–318; and pride in outfit, ii. 256; and recreation preferences, i. 180; and religion, i. 140; and status satisfaction, i. 107–109; and views of point system, ii. 533; and willingness for combat, i. 334–336, 524; ii. 248; and worry about battle injury, i. 334–336; ii. 84–86.
Marriage, before and after entering Army; and advancement, i. 115, 117, 119–122; and maladjustment, i. 117, 119–122; and personal commitment, i. 128–129

Marshall, Gen. George C., i. 13, 55; ii. 61n, 540
Marshall Islands, i. 162
Martin, Clyde E., ii. 79n
Marzoni, Petterson, Jr., i. 25
Masculinity: ii, 308–309; as combat motivation, ii. 131–135, 150–151
Mauldin, Bill, i. 40, 163, 219, 398; ii. 78n, 80n, 88n, 137n, 190; cited, ii. 159, 309, 310–311
Mauldin, Frances J., i. 24
Mauldin, W. Parker, i. 22, 24, 25
McClellan, Raymond F., i. 24
McNemar, Quinn, i. 13, 26, 33n
McPeak, William, i. 24, 25, 28, 54n, 486n; ii. 3n, 456n
Mead, George H., i. 33
Mechanical Aptitude scores: i. 149; and combat performance, ii. 36–38
Mechanized warfare, i. 289, 291
Medical care, opinions about: of air combat men, ii. 357–358; free comments cited, i. 218; of ground combat men, ii. 85, 144–145
Medical Department: Negroes in, i. 494–497; physical stamina in, i. 496–497; preference for, i. 288, 299–300; ii. 313–314; prestige of, i. 299–300; ii. 306–308; relative strength of, i. 494
Medics, combat: attitudes toward, ii. 144–145
Mediterranean Theater of Operations: i. 42n, 79; ii. 243, 286ff, 292ff; see also "Italy," "North Africa"; Negroes in, i. 509, 521, 530–534, 538ff; Research Branch personnel in, i. 20, 25; vs. Pacific, ii. 69–76
Medium bomber crews: anxiety among, ii. 373, 380; casualties among, ii. 407–408; vs. heavy and light, ii. 397–410; tour of duty of, ii. 359; willingness for combat of, ii. 333–334, 370
Mein Kampf, i. 478
Men Under Stress, Grinker & Spiegel, cited, ii. 205, 206, 351, 409
Menninger, William C., i. 26
Merton, Robert K., i. 26
Mess, see "Food"
Meyer, Trienah, i. 24
Miami Beach, ii. 353
Military Courtesy and Discipline, cited, i. 387–388
Military Police, Corps of: i. 8; assignments to, i. 295–296; attitudes toward, by race, i. 558, 560–561; criticism of promotion opportunities in, i. 250–254; educational level in, i. 310; job satisfaction in, i. 310–312; Negroes in, i. 494–495; preference for, i. 288, 299–300; ii.

313–314, 482, 488; prestige of, i. 295–296, 299–300, 310–312; ii. 313–314; relative strength of, i. 494
Miller, Gloria, i. 29
Minor, Betty J., i. 24
Minority groups, vets' attitudes toward, ii. 615–620
Mitchell, Alexander, i. 25
Mobility, loss of in combat, ii. 82–83
Monthly Progress Report, i. 11
Monthly Summary of Events and Trends in Race Relations, i. 572n, 587; cited, i. 558n
Moore, Felix E., i. 19, 22, 24, 25, 54n
Moral conflicts, in combat, ii. 85–87
Morale: group, see "Solidarity with group"; individual, see "Personal esprit"; vs. personal adjustment, i. 83–85
Morgenthau Plan, ii. 572
Mortars, relative fear of, ii. 232–241
Mosteller, Frederick, i. 26, 33n
Motivation: see also "Combat motivation," "War aims"; conflicts in, i. 463; effect of information on, i. 465–468
Munson, Brig. Gen. Edward L., Jr., i. 13, 14, 16, 22
Murder, ii. 112
Murray, John M., cited, i. 211
Myrdal, Gunnar, i. 487, 506n

N

National Association for the Advancement of Colored People, i. 598
National Guard: i. 232, 235, 501; opinions of promotion policy in, i. 269–271
National Opinion Research Center, ii. 632
Navy, i. 287; ii. 434, 436, 641
Nazis, i. 448, 464, 465
"Negro Soldier, The," film, i. 597
Negro soldiers: i. 16, 56, 175, 211n, 298, 313, 486–599; and advancement, i. 498–502
    attitudes of, toward: camp location, i. 550–566; leadership, i. 580–586; point system, ii. 534; segregation, i. 566–580
    by branch of service, i. 494–497; combat performance of, i. 586–595; educational level of, i. 488–494, 499–500; induction rate of, i. 493–494; job assignments of, i. 495–496, 499, 586; job satisfaction of, i. 536–538; in mixed companies, i. 587–595; overall adjustment of, i. 535–550, 562–566; in overseas service, i. 497–498, 521–525; per cent of Army, i. 489, 494–495; personal commitment of, i. 507–521, 529; physical stamina of, i. 490–497; postwar expectations of, i. 513–521; postwar plans of,

ii. 602, 604; problems of testing, i. 21n, 488, 492–493; racial orientation of, i. 502–507; willingness for combat of, i. 521–535

Negroes, attitudes toward: before and after victory, ii. 554, 559, 583–585; combat performance of, i. 588–595; postwar status of, i. 519–520; of veterans, ii. 617–619, 637–638

Negroes, Northern vs. Southern: AGCT scores of, i. 493
attitudes of, toward: bus service, i. 561–562; discrimination, i. 510, 512–513, 570ff; military police, i. 558, 560–561; town police, i. 557–559
camp preferences of, i. 550–557; combat attitudes of, i. 529; educational level of, i. 489–491; officer preferences of, i. 580–582; overall adjustment of, i. 562–566; per cent inducted, i. 494; postwar expectations of, i. 516; status aspirations of, i. 585

Negroes vs. whites: advancement opportunities of, i. 498–500; AGCT scores of, i. 492
attitudes of, toward: bus service, i. 561–562; military police, i. 558, 560–561; physical condition, i. 539–540; segregation, i. 568–580; town police, i. 557–559
by branch of service, i. 494–495; camp preferences of, i. 552–555; combat motivations of, i. 525–526; criticism of Army by, i. 540–542; desire for promotion among, i. 583–584; educational level of, i. 490–492; job satisfaction of, i. 536–538; in mixed companies, i. 589–595; officers, i. 500–502; overseas preferences among, i. 521–525; personal commitment of, i. 507–509, 521; personal esprit of, i. 538–539; physical stamina of, i. 496; postwar expectations of, i. 514, 519–520, 537; pride in outfit of, i. 535–536; by rank and education, i. 500; sense of contribution of, i. 510–511; venereal disease among, i. 545–546; volunteer enlistments among, i. 542; willingness for combat among, i. 521–526, 530, 532

Nervous breakdown, in family, and adjustment, i. 134, 144

Neuropsychiatric Division, SGO, i. 8, 41

Neuropsychiatric Screening Adjunct [NSA], ii. 210, 416ff; see also "NSA scores," "Psychoneurotic symptoms"

Neville, Robert, ii. 302n

Newfoundland, i. 16

New Georgia: personal esprit in, i. 162; malaria control in, i. 176

New Guinea, job satisfaction in, i. 338–342

Newsmap, i. 477

Nimitz, Adm. Chester, i. 183

Nimkoff, M. F., i. 244n

9th Division, ii. 5ff

92d Division, i. 586

99th Fighter Squadron, i. 586

Nonbattle casualty rate: and attitudes toward combat, ii. 8–30; vs. battle casualties, ii. 102–103; computation of, ii. 48–54; definition of, ii. 6–8

Noncoms [Noncommissioned officers]: as combat replacements, ii. 279; educational level of, i. 60–64, 247–250; intermediary status of, i. 401–410; Negro, i. 498; number of, i. 233; opportunities to become, i. 237–240

Noncoms, attitudes toward: and attitudes toward officers, ii. 128–129; by branch of service, i. 191–194; of combat replacements, ii. 245, 246, 253–255, 266–270; and length of service, i. 200–201; of privates vs. officers, i. 401–402

Noncoms vs. privates: i. 66–69, 73; adjustment, by length of service, i. 200–201, 203–206; age of, i. 113–114
attitudes of, toward: AWOL's, ii. 115–116; combat evasion, ii. 141; combat excellence, ii. 133–134; combat officers, ii. 120–122; importance of theater, i. 185; physical condition, ii. 91–92; rear echelons, ii. 300, 304
branch satisfaction of, ii. 486, 492; combat anxiety of, ii. 86; combat incentives of, ii. 177; combat self-confidence of, ii. 23–27, 252; criticism of advancement opportunities by, i. 252; criticism of Army by, i. 93, 166–168; ii. 259, 260; educational level of, i. 113–114; job satisfaction of, i. 93, 166–168, 170–171, 185, 297, 328, 338–339, 342–343, 345, 347, 348, 350, 351, 352; ii. 486, 492; marital condition of, i. 113–115; overall adjustment of, i. 92–95; peak of combat efficiency of, ii. 284–289; personal commitment of, i. 93, 166–168, 170; ii. 154, 262; personal esprit of, i. 93–95, 166–170; pride in outfit of, ii. 256; vindictiveness of, ii. 165–166; willingness for combat of, ii. 23–27, 248

Nonfraternization: attitudes toward, ii. 567–572; predicted failure of, ii. 553

Normandy, i. 166; ii. 4, 5–58 passim, 69, 95, 170, 243, 313, 549

North Africa, i. 162, 166, 183, 448, 530; ii. 3, 21, 69n, 73ff, 99, 132, 144, 229f, 232ff

Northerners vs. Southerners: attitudes of, toward: Military Police, i. 560; Negroes, i. 506, 512; ii. 618; segregation, i. 569ff

    camp preferences of, i. 553–554; differences in general attitudes of, i. 175; educational level of, i. 491; health of, by climate, i. 174–175; job satisfaction of, i. 349–350; Negro opinions of, i. 580–582; willingness for combat of, i. 524

NSA scores: of air combat vets, ii. 375–377; effects of anonymity on, ii. 435–436; of new recruits, ii. 433–439; of psychoneurotics vs. others, ii. 417–418

O

Oahu, *see* "Hawaii"

Occupation of Germany: ii. 564–573; predicted morale problems in, ii. 555; easing of, ii. 560

OCS, *see* "Officer Candidate School"

Office of Education, ii. 600

Office of War Information, ii. 27

Officer Candidate School: i. 198, 232, 234, 236, 240, 243, 245, 380; ii. 124, status indoctrination in, i. 389–391

Officers: *see also* "Commissions"; advancement opportunities among, i. 271–275; attitudes of, toward promotion policy, i. 275–283; casualty rate among, ii. 8, 9, 102; confidence in, ii. 117, 145; criticism of training program by, i. 79, 388–389; educational level of, i. 245–247; leadership of, and morale, i. 386–387; misunderstanding of men by, i. 391–393, 395, 419; Negro, i. 500–502, 572, 580–586; number of, i. 54, 232–234; opportunities to become, i. 231–237

Officers, attitudes toward: *see also* "Status system, criticism of"; and advancement, i. 259–261; of air combat men, ii. 348–350; by branch of service, i. 191–194; and closeness to fighting, i. 364, 365–368; in combat outfits, ii. 117–130; and combat performance, ii. 39–40; and educational level, i. 364, 368; extent of unfavorable, i. 375–379; free comments cited, i. 67–71, 213, 369–373; by length of service, i. 200–201, 204, 364, 368; of Negroes, i. 580–586; officers' misconceptions of, i. 391–393; overall, i. 227; and overseas service, i. 364, 367–368; and specific leadership practices, i. 384–389; ii. 124–125; by stage in war, i. 196–197, 364–365, 375; at start of war, i. 65–71; and theater of operations, i. 365, 368; ii. 75; unit-to-unit differences in, i. 382–384

Officers' clubs, i. 370

Officers, staff vs. line, i. 276–278

Officers vs. enlisted men: *see also* "Doolittle Committee"; age of, i. 113–114

    attitudes of, toward: combat excellence, ii. 133–134; ease of victory, ii. 147; fear reactions, ii. 198–200; importance of theater, i. 185; officers' privileges, i. 374–375; rear echelons, ii. 294–295

    attitudes of, relating to social control, i. 416–423; barriers to understanding between, i. 391–401; casualty rates among, ii. 8; combat incentives of, ii. 108–112; confidence in equipment of, ii. 145–146; criticism of promotion policy by, i. 277, 280–283, 421–422; educational level of, i. 113–114, 246; job satisfaction of, i. 185, 304–308, 394; marital condition of, i. 113–115; morale of (Air Corps), ii. 403–406; NSA scores of (Air Corps), ii. 375–377; per cent of in combat, i. 165–166; personal esprit of, i. 393–394; postwar plans of, ii. 602–604; proportion of, i. 233; recreation opportunities of, i. 181; solidarity of, in combat, ii. 119; vindictiveness of, ii. 158; willingness for combat of, ii. 344, 345

Ogburn, W. F., i. 32, 244n, 435n

Okinawa, i. 212, 216; ii. 70, 546

Opinion, vs. attitudes, i. 34, 42

Ordnance: Negroes in, i. 494–497; physical stamina in, i. 496–497; preference for, i. 288, 299–300; ii. 313–314; prestige of, i. 299–300; ii. 306–308; relative strength of, i. 494

Orientation, i. 430–485; see "War aims," "Personal commitment"

Orientation Branch, I & E Division, i. 9

Orientation, effectiveness of: with discussion groups, i. 468–484; with films, i. 461–468; by theater of operations, i. 182–185

Orientation program: i. 458–485; Army compliance with, i. 468–470, 472, 476; for post-armistice period, ii. 555–560; soldiers' attitudes toward, i. 438, 471–472, 480–484

Osborn, Maj. Gen. Frederick F., i. 13, 19, 28; ii. 521, 524; cited, i. 14–18

Overoptimism: about America's strength, i. 463–464; about war's duration, i. 448–449

Overprotection, and Army adjustment, i. 135, 144

Overseas service: resentment of US troops in, ii. 317–319; willingness for, i. 521–525

Overseas (vs. US) service: *see also* "Returnees"

    and criticism of: Army, i. 156–157, 159–161, 166–168, 170–173; officers, i. 364, 367–368; promotion policy, i. 277–278

    demobilization credit for, ii. 521–548; job satisfaction in, i. 156–157, 166–168, 170–171, 173, 182, 338–340ff; and marital condition, i. 108; of Negroes, i. 497–498, 509, 521–525; opinions of *Yank* in, ii. 609–610; personal commitment in, i. 155–157, 159–161, 166–168, 170, 440, 454–456, 509; personal esprit in, i. 155, 157, 159–163, 166–173; psychoneurotic symptoms in, ii. 439–445; by stage in war, i. 497; views of point system in, ii. 526, 532; views of postwar change in, ii. 622; vindictiveness toward enemy in, ii. 157–158

P

Pacific area: i. 169n, 183, 302, 336–337, 449, 480; ii. 4, 81, 90, 92ff, 173, 180ff, 200f, 224ff, 306f, 311f, 335, 358, 375, 430, 446, 450, 458, 609f; *see also* "Europe vs. Pacific," "Mediterranean vs. Pacific," and specific localities

    criticism of Army in, i. 170–171; criticism of officers in, i. 368; desire for home in, i. 186–189; job satisfaction in, i. 170–171; Negroes in, i. 509, 521, 538ff; personal commitment in, i. 170; personal esprit in, i. 169–170; Research Branch personnel in, i. 25; views of point system in, ii. 523, 546

Panama and the Caribbean: i. 169n, 183, 449; criticism of Army in, i. 171; criticism of officers in, i. 368; health attitudes in, i. 174–175; job satisfaction in, i. 170–171, 341–342, 344–346; personal commitment in, i. 170; personal esprit in, i. 169, 170; recreation attitudes in, i. 179–181; relative deprivation in, i. 173; Research Branch personnel in, i. 25

Paratroopers: job satisfaction of, i. 290; prestige of, i. 304; psychiatric screening of, ii. 212–220; status satisfaction of, i. 329–330

Parenthood, *see* "Dependents"

Pareto, Vilfredo, i. 33–34

Parker, Myrtle L., i. 23

Parsons, Talcott, i. 519n

Pass policy: in Air Corps, ii. 396–397; free comments about, i. 216; and job satisfaction, i. 353

Patriotism: as combat motivation, ii. 149–150, 169; of Negroes, i. 509–510; as soldier motivation, i. 431, 449

Patterson, Mervin, i. 26

Patterson, Robert P., ii. 534; cited, ii. 112

Pavlov, I. P., i. 30; ii. 83n

Pay, soldiers', i. 309

Pearl Harbor, i. 431, 435, 447, 448, 460, 484; ii. 157, 596

Persian Gulf Command: criticism of officers in, cited, i. 369–373, 388

Personal adjustment: and advancement, i. 82, 88–98, 111–122, 147–154; definition of, i. 82–104; and performance, i. 85–86; soldiers' evaluations of, i. 90–91; of veterans, ii. 630–644

Personal commitment: and advancement, i. 123, 148–152, 207–208; and age, i. 107–109, 122–127, 149–150, 456–458; attempts to improve, i. 460–483; by branch of service, i. 159–160, 190–194, 330n, 454; and combat, i. 159–161, 440, 455–456; ii. 149–150, 166–167, 391–393; and combat performance, ii. 39; conditions making for, ii. 549–551, 555–560; definition of area, i. 86–87, 96, 430–433; and educational level, i. 107–109, 122–127, 149–150, 456–458; effects of victory on, ii. 561–563, 578–582, 587; and fear of future war, i. 443–444; and length of service, i. 112, 159–160, 199–208, 455, 457; "limited," i. 451; and maladjustment, i. 122–124; ii. 413–414; and marital condition, i. 107–110, 112, 122, 124–126, 456–457; of Negroes, i. 505, 507–521, 529; and overall adjustment, i. 88–93, 459–460; and overseas service, i. 155–157, 159–161, 166–168, 170, 440, 454–456; and physical condition, i. 457; predictions about post-armistice, ii. 553; and rank, i. 166–168, 170; ii. 154, 262; of replacements, ii. 245, 246, 262, 264–265, 267, 271; of returnees, ii. 469–472; significance of, i. 484–485; and stage of war, i. 157–158, 186, 195–197, 205–206, 441, 447–450; suggestions for raising, ii. 557, 580–582; and theater of operations, i. 170, 183–185; ii. 75; and "total war," i. 450–451; and understanding of war needs, i. 451–452, 465–468, 474, 477–481; and vindictiveness, ii. 166–167

Personal esprit: and advancement, i. 148, 150, 152, 207–208; and age, i. 107–109, 122, 150; and branch of service, i. 159–160, 162, 190–194; and combat, i. 159–161; and combat performance, ii. 39; definition of area, i. 86–87, 95–96; and educational level, i. 107–109, 122, 150; and length of service, i. 112, 159–160.

199–208; and maladjustment, i. 123; ii. 413–414; and marital condition, i. 107–110, 112, 122; of Negroes, i. 538–539; and overall adjustment, i. 88–98, 130–131; and overseas service, i. 155, 157, 159–163, 166–173; and personal commitment, i. 460; and rank, i. 92, 94, 166–170, 393–394; and stage in war, i. 169, 195–197, 205–206; and theater of operations, i. 161–163, 169–170, 172, 538

Personnel assignment, *see* "Job assignment"

Philippine Islands, i. 166, 176, 447

Philips, Col. Thomas R., cited, i. 382

Physical condition: of air combat men, ii. 341; and branch of service, ii. 496n; and psychoneurotic symptoms, ii. 420–423, 431; of returnees, ii. 459–460; and rotation, ii. 457–458

Physical condition, attitudes toward: and combat experience, ii. 91–94; of combat replacements, ii. 245, 246, 261, 263–264, 267, 271; in Europe vs. Pacific, ii. 72–73, 74; and maladjustment, i. 122–124, 128, 132–133, 137–138; of Negroes, i. 539–540; overseas vs. US, i. 155–157, 172; and personal commitment, i. 122–124, 126, 128–129; ii. 155–156; of returnees, ii. 460–461; and theater of operations, i. 174–175; and time in combat, ii. 379–381; and type of air combat, ii. 404, 406; and work load (air), ii. 390–391

Pittsburgh Courier, i. 516n

Point system: i. 84, 94, 110, 164; ii. 347–348, 520–548; alternatives to, ii. 520–521, 545–546, 547–548; first reactions to, ii. 530–534; initial effectiveness of, ii. 534–539; origin of, i. 7; ii. 521–530; plans for post V J Day, ii. 539–546

Police, attitudes toward, i. 557–559

Pomeroy, Wardell B., ii. 79n

Post regulations: and hostility to status system, i. 370–372; and job satisfaction, i. 353–354

Postwar expectations, of Negroes, i. 513–521, 537

Postwar planning, soldiers' interest in, i. 438; ii. 610

Postwar plans of soldiers: by age, education and marital status, i. 317–318; for employment, ii. 600–613, 634–640

Power, *see* "Authority"

Prayer in combat, ii. 108–110, 136, 172–188

Prediction: of advancement, i. 147–154; of combat performance, ii. 6–58; of paratroop training success, ii. 213–220;

of postwar employment, ii. 601–608; of psychoneurosis, ii. 207–208, 412–433

"Prelude to War," film, i. 462, 464

Price, Rosabelle, i. 23

Pride in outfit: in air vs. ground combat, ii. 329–331, 336; as combat motivation, ii. 135, 137–142; and combat performance, ii. 40; of combat replacements, ii. 245–246, 255–259, 261, 266, 270; of Negroes, i. 535–536

Privacy, lack of, as combat stress, ii. 87

Privates: *see also* "Noncoms vs. privates," "Officers vs. enlisted men"; advancement opportunities among, i. 147–148, 237–240; attitudes of, toward noncoms vs. officers, i. 403; criticism of Army by, i. 65–71, 72–75; educational level of, i. 61–63, 248; Negro, i. 499; number of, i. 233

Privileges, officers', *see* "Officers, attitudes toward" and "Status system, criticism of"

Promotion, *for breakdown, see* "Advancement"; desire for, i. 244–258; factors determining, i. 258–283; variation in opportunities for, i. 231–243

Propaganda, i. 460, 472

Protestant soldiers, i. 400

Psychiatric breakdowns (combat), ii. 332; *see also* "Casualties, psychiatric"

Psychiatric screening, ii. 207–220

Psychoneurotic symptoms: and branch satisfaction, ii. 495; and combat, ii. 445–455; by education and age, ii. 420–428, 431ff; indices of, ii. 412–420; and job satisfaction, ii. 493–495; among new recruits, ii. 433–439; by physical condition, ii. 420–423, 431; and prospect of overseas service, ii. 433–439; among psychoneurotics vs. others, ii. 417–418, 425–428, 454; among returnees, ii. 461–466; by stage in war, ii. 429–433, 434n

Psychoneurotics: age of, i. 113–118, 121; ii. 423, 425–428; childhood experience of, i. 132–146; criticism of Army by, ii. 413–415; disruption of combat outfit by, ii. 207–210; educational level of, i. 113–116, 121; ii. 423, 425–428; health of, i. 122–124, 128, 132–133, 137; job satisfaction of, ii. 413–415; length of service of, i. 115–121; marital condition of, i. 113–115, 117, 119–121; overall adjustment of, i. 89; personal commitment of, i. 122–124; ii. 413–414; personal esprit of, ii. 413–414; psychoneurotic index scores of, ii. 417–418, 425–428, 454; screening of, ii. 210–220

Psychosomatic Symptoms Index, ii. 416ff; *see also* "Psychoneurotic symptoms"

Public opinion polls, i. 436

Punishment: i. 415; *see also* "Social control"; by death penalty, ii. 97, 112–113; fear of, as combat incentive, ii. 112–117; group, i. 423–426

Punishment, attitudes toward: for combat breakdown, ii. 196–199; by rank, i. 408–410, 416–417

Punishment, childhood, and Army adjustment, i. 135, 144

Purple Heart, *see* "Decorations"

Pyle, Ernie, i. 40, 163, 219, 309

PX's (Post Exchanges), i. 370, 371, 372; ii. 297; segregation in, i. 567–571

Q

Quartermaster Corps: Negroes in, i. 494–497, 500; physical stamina in, i. 496–497; preference for, i. 288, 299–300; ii. 312–314, 482, 488; prestige of, i. 299–300; ii. 306–308; promotion rate in, i. 271; relative strength of, i. 494; returnees' adjustment in, ii. 496–518; willingness for combat in, i. 336

Questionnaires: *see also* "Attitude measurement," "Surveys"; development of for Army, i. 12, 14–22; limitations of, i. 42–43, 322; methods of administration of, i. 21, 131–132, 151n, 488; soldiers' reactions to, i. 21–22

Quota system (classification), i. 293–294

R

Racial discrimination: *see also* "Negro soldiers," "Segregation"; and camp location, i. 550–562; and combat attitudes, i. 526–528; effects of combat on, i. 589–595; in England, i. 544; Negro imputation of, i. 502–507, 510, 534, 576; and personal commitment, i. 507–521; and venereal disease, i. 545–549

Radio, use of in orientation, i. 464–465

Rage: as anxiety defense, ii. 208–209; as combat incentive, ii. 159; as combat stress, ii. 80–82

Rangers: job satisfaction of, i. 290; prestige of, i. 304

Rank: *see also* "Advancement," "Noncoms vs. privates," "Officers vs. enlisted men," "Status"; and advancement opportunities, i. 147; and combat anxiety, ii. 86; and combat preference, i. 524; and criticism of promotion policy, i. 270, 278, 281; and educational level, i. 60–65, 113, 114, 500; and job

satisfaction, i. 304–308, 326, 328, 338–339, 342–343, 345, 347, 348, 350, 351, 359–360; of Negroes vs. whites, i. 500; and personal esprit, i. 92, 94

Rape, ii. 112

Rear-echelon troops: combat infantrymen's views of, ii. 293–316

Reassignment centers, ii. 475–479

Reconversion, *see* "Returnees"

Recreation: i. 26; *see also* "Time off"; by branch of service, ii. 352–353; and job satisfaction, i. 356–357; opportunities for and attitudes toward, i. 178–182; segregation of facilities for, i. 567–581, 592–593, 598

Redeployment: predicted morale problems in, ii. 554; suggestions for easing of, ii. 560, 580

Reeder, William W., i. 24; cited, i. 397

Reforms, Army: in Negro policy, i. 597–598; in promotion system, i. 283; in status satisfaction, i. 309–311; in status system, i. 379–382, 397–398, 400

Refresher training, ii. 483–485

Regular Army men: *see also* "Selectees vs. Regulars"; job satisfaction of, i. 346; Negro, i. 597

Religion: *see also* "Prayer," "Church attendance"; and Army experience, ii. 612; and combat experience, ii. 185–187

Replacement depots, ii. 272–276

Replacements, *see* "Combat replacements"

Research and Development Board, i. 3

Research Branch: development of point system by, ii. 520–548; list of surveys of, ii. 645–651; origin and history of, i. 12–20; personnel in, i. *xi–xii*, 22–27; purpose and nature of activities, i. 5–11, 36–37, 49–51; structure of, i. 20–27

Research, resistance of Army to, i. 12–19, 39, 293–296, 362–363, 468–470, 472, 476; ii. 613–614

Resentment against Army, *see* "Criticism of Army," "Status system, criticism of"

Returnees: anxiety symptoms of, ii. 461–466; assignment of, ii. 479–485; attitudes toward postwar change, ii. 622; branch and job satisfaction of, i. 307; ii. 486–497; criticism of Army by, i. 159–160, 224–227; desire of for camp near home, ii. 497–503; expectation of deference by, ii. 466–469; internationalism of, ii. 625–626; physical condition of, ii. 459–461; personal commitment of, i. 159–161; ii. 469–472; personal esprit of, i. 159–160; processing of, ii. 474–478; retention in Army of, ii. 473–474; vs. nonoverseas men, ii. 503–518

Rewards: i. 415; attitudes toward, by rank, i. 421–423; in combat, ii. 170–171; group, i. 423, 425–429
Richardson, Linwood B., i. 26
Richardson, Marion W., i. 26, 284n
Rifle companies: ii. 64; casualties in, ii. 8, 9, 27, 50–52; combat attitudes vs. performance in, ii. 10–11, 14–16, 18–30
Roosevelt, Franklin, i. 7, 13; ii. 525
Roper, Elmo, i. 19, 38
Roper poll, i. 38
Rose, Arnold M., i. 23, 25, 39, 486n; ii. 411n, 620n; cited, i. 413–414
Rosen, Sidney H., i. 26
Rosenthal, Bernard G., i. 24
Rotation: 184ff; *see also* "Returnees"; of air combat men vs. others, ii. 360; factors determining, ii. 456–466; free comments about, i. 216; ii. 89–90; of Negroes, i. 498; quotas for, ii. 458; reclassification problems, i. 295–296
ROTC [Reserve Officers' Training Corps], i. 232, 234, 235, 245, 380
Royal Air Force, ii. 398
Rural vs. urban soldiers: anti-Semitism among, ii. 619–620; combat preference of, i. 332–336
Russians, i. 448, 485; ii. 157
Russians, attitudes toward: before and after victory, ii. 554, 559, 573–576; of veterans, ii. 627–630; vs. other nationalities, ii. 574, 576, 627, 629

S

Sad Sack, ii. 610
Saipan, i. 213–214; ii. 70, 445
Salerno, ii. 136
Sanctions, *see* "Group sanctions"
Sanitation, i. 176, 177; and job satisfaction, i. 352, 356f
San Francisco Conference, i. 483
Schmid, Alice H., i. 23
Schwartz, Catherine T., i. 24
Scott, Robert, ii. 351
Seabees, i. 287
Second Cavalry Division, i. 530–534
Second Lieutenants: casualty rate among, ii. 102; job satisfaction of, i. 305–309; number of, i. 233
Sectors, defined, ii. 61
Secretary of War's Board on Officer-Enlisted Men's Relationships, *see* "Doolittle Committee"
Seeman, Stanley H., i. 24
Segregation of Negroes: i. 498, 566–580; on bus lines, i. 561–562; in England, i.

544–545; proposals for reform in, i. 597–599; resistance to, i. 566–580; and combat attitudes, i. 527–528, 532–533
Selectees vs. regulars: attitudes of, toward: Army status system, i. 71–75; Army tradition, i. 63–65; authoritarian controls, i. 65–71; training program, i. 75–80
  educational level of, i. 61–63; job satisfaction of, i. 346
Selective Service: i. 27, 54, 68, 147, 198, 208, 240, 247, 492, 493, 494; ii. 437, 439; *see also* "Induction, attitudes toward"; attitudes toward, i. 450; free comments about, i. 218
Self-preservation, as combat motivation, ii. 108–110, 169
Self-respect, as combat motivation, ii. 108–110, 131–135ff
Sergeants: *see also* "Noncoms vs. privates," "Top three graders"; educational level of, i. 248; job satisfaction of, i. 305–309; Negro, i. 499; number of, by grade, i. 233
Service clubs, segregation in, i. 567–571
Service Forces (ASF): i. 11, 468; ii. 475, 477; *see also* "Air vs. Ground and Service Forces," "Rear-echelon troops"; advancement opportunities in, i. 248–250, 272; criticism of, i. 254–258; job satisfaction in, i. 287–289, 290, 296–300, 307; Negroes in, i. 494–497; personal commitment in, i. 330n; preference for, i. 300–303; relative strength of, i. 494
Service, length of, *see* "Length of service"
Services of Supply: job satisfaction in, i. 336, 337; prestige of, i. 298
Setzer, Martha E., i. 23
7th Division, ii. 4
70th Division, ii. 31
Sex hygiene, i. 176–178, 470
Sexual deprivation, as combat stress, ii. 79–80
Shattuck, Johanna, i. 23
Sheffield, Frederick D., i. 23, 25, 28
Sherif, Muzafer, i. 33n; ii. 83n
Sibley, Elbridge, i. 27
Sicily, i. 166; ii. 3, 21, 69n, 73ff, 132, 136
Sick-call rate, and combat exposure, ii. 381–382
Sidran, Louis, i. 23
Siegfried Line, ii. 31, 69
Siepmann, Mrs. Charles, i. 23
Signal Corps: job satisfaction in, i. 289, 291, 306, 324–326; Negroes in, i. 494–496; physical stamina in, i. 496; preference for, i. 287–289, 299–300; ii. 313–314; prestige of, i. 299–300; relative strength of, i. 494

Significance, tests of, i. 151n, 156n

Silver Star, ii. 4

Skills, specialized: and advancement, i. 232, 235, 259; in Air Corps, ii. 350–352; utilization and acquisition of, i. 312–329

Sleep: and air combat, ii. 373–374, 389–390; and ground combat, ii. 78–79

Smith, M. Brewster, i. 23, 25, 28; ii. 59n, 105n, 242n, 290n; cited, i. 389–390

Sociability, and Army adjustment, i. 132–133, 141, 144

Social change, vets' attitudes toward, ii. 620–624, 637–639

Social control: i. 410–429; *see also* "Group sanctions," "Punishment"; of combat behavior, ii. 96–104, 107, 112–118, 130–149; definition of, i. 410–411; formal vs. informal, i. 411; ii. 100–104, 107; by group rewards and punishments, i. 424–429; internalization of, i. 411–415, 417–418; ii. 117–118, 131–132, 136–137; pattern of development of in Army, i. 411–415; post-armistice problems in, ii. 549–560; views of officers vs. men relating to, i. 416–423

Social distance, *see* "Status system"

"Social frame of reference," i. 125; *see* "Deprivation, relative"

Social mobility: *see* "Advancement"; in American society, i. 55–56, 244, 599; in the Army, i. 230–283

Social psychology: problems of conceptualization in, i. 30–37; streams of influence on this study, i. 30–32

Social Science Research Council, i. 28, 38, 43

Socio-economic status: and Army status aspiration, i. 244; and attitudes toward Negroes, ii. 619n; and education, i. 58–60, 126–127, 137; and health, i. 126–127; and overprotection, i. 137; and personal commitment, i. 126–127

Solidarity with group: *see also* "Loyalty, group," "Pride in outfit"; in air combat, ii. 348–349, 382–383; as combat motivation, ii. 96, 130–149, 169, 179–185; of combat replacements, ii. 280; and fear in combat, ii. 179–185; between officers and men, ii. 119

Solomon, H. C., ii. 211n

Solomon Islands, i. 166, 341–342, 348; ii. 73ff

SOS, *see* "Services of Supply"

South, the, definition of, i. 550 *and note*

South Pacific theater, *see* "Pacific area" and individual localities

Southern Regional Conference, i. 587

Southerners, *see* "Negroes, Northern vs. Southern," "Northerners vs. Southerners"

Southwest Pacific theater, *see* "Pacific area" and individual localities

Soviet Union: i. 475; distrust of, i. 442, 444–445, 479

Spanish Civil War, i. 484; ii. 157, 195, 234

Spearman, Charles, i. 35

Special Planning Division, War Dep't., ii. 524ff

Specialists' school, i. 292

Spencer, Lyle M., i. 18, 22, 25; ii. 520n, 521, 524

Spiegel, John P., ii. 137n, 349n, 412n, 465n; cited, ii. 205, 206, 351, 409

"Spit and Polish," attitudes toward: i. 264; of officers vs. enlisted men, i. 419; at start of war, i. 75–80

Sports, participation in, and Army adjustment, i. 142–144

Stability, emotional, *see* "Psychoneurotic symptoms"

Stage in war: *see also* "Hostilities, cessation of"; and advancement opportunities, i. 231–243; and Air Corps casualties, ii. 363–364; and criticism of Army, i. 195–197, 205–206; and criticism of officers, i. 364–365, 375; and estimated duration, i. 448–449; and job satisfaction, i. 183–185, 195–197, 205–206; and overseas service, i. 497; and personal commitment, i. 157–158, 183–185, 195–197, 205–206, 441, 447–450; and personal esprit, i. 161–162, 169, 195–197, 205–206; and psychoneurotic symptoms, ii. 429–433, 438; and views of point system, ii. 547; and work load (Air Corps), ii. 363–366

Stalingrad, i. 442

Stamina, physical: definition of, i. 496; of Negroes vs. whites, i. 496

Standardization of variables, i. 117n, 120n

Stanley, John B., i. 14, 22

Stanton, Frank, i. 26

Star, Shirley A., i. 23, 28, 430n, 486n; ii. 411n, 456n, 520n, 596n

Stars and Stripes, i. 9, 482; ii. 190n, 580, 586; gripes in, i. 398

Status, *see* "Rank," "Advancement"

Status, informal: of combat men vs. rear troops, ii. 305–312; and job satisfaction, i. 304–312; of returnees, ii. 503–505

Status, satisfaction with: *see also* "Job satisfaction"; definition of area, i. 86–87, 96–97, 304; free comments cited, i. 215; and overall adjustment, i. 88–93; and personal commitment, i. 460; and symbols as incentives, i. 309–311, 329–330; ii. 346

Status system: abuses of, i. 413; ambivalence toward, i. 72, 230; as barrier between officers and men, i. 389–391; and combat behavior, ii. 100–101
   criticism of: *see also* "Officers, attitudes toward"; at beginning of war, i. 71–74; by branch of service, i. 250–258; at end of war, i. 227; ii. 553; free comments cited, i. 369–373; by returnees, ii. 508–510
   effects of combat on, ii. 114, 119, 302–303, 305–312; indoctrination of officers in, i. 389–391; reforms proposed in, i. 379–382, 397–398, 400; role of noncoms in, i. 401–410
Stimson, Henry L., i. 13; cited, i. 12
Stouffer, Samuel A., i. 3n, 13, 22, 25, 28, 54n, 82n, 230n, 284n, 362n, 486n; ii. 3n, 520n, 596n
Strecker, E. A., ii. 412n
Stresses, combat, *see* "Combat stresses"
Suchman, Edward A., i. 23, 28, 54n, 284n, 230n, 362n
Supply, combat troops' views of, ii. 293–299
Surgeon General's Office, i. 26, 27, 41, 485; ii. 210, 412
Surveys: *see also* "Attitude measurement"; attitudes of soldiers toward, i. 21–22; list of Research Branch, ii. 645–651; methods for, i. 20–22; planning surveys, i. 16; spot studies, i. 17
Sutton, Milton, i. 23

T

Tactics, attitudes toward, ii. 74
Taft, Gordon W., i. 27
Theater of operations: *see also* "Closeness to fighting"; and criticism of Army, i. 170–172; and criticism of officers, i. 365; and health attitudes, i. 174–175; importance of, and attitudes, i. 173, 182–185; and job satisfaction, i. 170–171, 173, 182–184, 349–350; and Negro commitment, i. 509, 521; opinions of *Yank*, by, ii. 609–610; organization of, ii. 60–62; and personal commitment, i. 170; and personal esprit, i. 161–163, 169–170, 172, 183, 538; and relative deprivation, i. 172–173; and views of point system, ii. 522–524
Thomas, W. I., i. 33
Thompson, James P., i. 23
Thurstone, L. L., i. 36
Time limit: for air combat, ii. 359–361, 383–387; lack of, as combat stress, ii. 88–90; to overseas service, ii. 456–457

Time off, and morale (air), ii. 393–397
Tito, J. B., i. 478
Tokyo, i. 183
Tolstoy, Leo, i. 8; cited, i. 3
Top three graders: job satisfaction of, i. 307, 356–360; number of, i. 238, 239
"Total war," i. 450–451
"Tough peace," attitudes toward, ii. 566–567
Tour of combat duty, ii. 359–361, 383–387
Training program: *see also* "Basic Training"
   attitudes toward: in Europe vs. Pacific, ii. 74; of combat veterans, ii. 227–231; free comments cited, i. 217; of replacements, ii. 281–282; of returnees, ii. 480
   precombat, ii. 220–231; preinvasion, ii. 243–244
Transportation Corps: combat preference in, i. 336; Negroes in, i. 494–497; physical stamina in, i. 496–497; preference for, i. 299–300; ii. 313–314; prestige of, i. 299–300; relative strength of, i. 494
Tregaskis, Richard, i. 40; ii. 87n
Trench foot, ii. 7, 69
Trinidad, i. 16
Truancy, and Army adjustment, i. 132–133, 139, 144
Truman, Harry S., ii. 546
Tuohey, John, i. 26
Turetsky, Adeline, i. 23
25th Division, ii. 4
29th Division, ii. 5ff.
270th Engineer Battalion, ii. 31
274th Infantry Regiment, ii. 31, 35
275th Infantry Regiment, ii. 31
276th Infantry Regiment, ii. 31

U

Uncertainty: and anxiety of replacements, ii. 275–276; as combat stress, ii. 83–84
United Nations, i. 478, 483
U.S. Employment Service, i. 325

V

Value conflicts, as combat stress, ii. 84–87
Van Cleve, William L., i. 26
Variables, intervening, i. 131ff
V E Day, i. 440, 452ff, 498; ii. 31, 429, 430, 458, 472, 529ff; problems arising after, ii. 549–595
Venereal disease: attitudes toward control of, i. 176–178; and educational level, i. 126, 546; among Negro soldiers, i. 493, 545–549

Veterans: ii, 596–644; personal adjustment of, ii. 630–644
    views of: civilian society, ii. 613–630; personal future, ii. 598–610; value of Army experience, ii. 610–613, 631–633
Veterans' Administration, i. 27; ii. 600ff, 639ff
Veterans' organizations, ii. 622–624, 642
Veterans' program, attitudes toward, i. 475
Victories, as combat incentives, ii. 169–172
Victory, reactions to, see "Hostilities, cessation of"
Vindictiveness, ii. 108–111, 156–167
V J Day, i. 441; ii. 443, 539ff, 580
Volunteer enlistments: in Air Corps vs. others, ii. 341; of Negroes vs. whites, i. 542

W

WAC, see "Women's Army Corps"
Wall, Joseph, i. 26
Wallace, Robert B., i. 19, 24; ii. 3n
Waller, Willard, cited, ii. 170
Wallin, Paul, i. 23, 28; ii. 192n
War aims: see also "Personal commitment"; as combat motivation, ii. 108–111, 149–156; Negro conceptions of, i. 503–521, 529; soldiers' conceptions of, i. 431–447, 448–449; before and after victory, ii. 586–594; soldiers' concern for, i. 437–439
War Department: i. 5, 6, 27, 28; ii. 600, 613; attitude of toward point system, ii. 520–548
War Manpower Commission, i. 27
Warfare, types of, ii. 66–68
Warner, W. L., i. 56, 244n
Warrant officers, number of, i. 233
Watrous, Col. Livingston, i. 20
Weapons, enemy: ii. 66; combat vets' evaluations of, ii. 231–241
Weber, Max, i. 519n
Weeks, H. Ashley, i. 23, 25, 28; ii. 456
Wehrmacht, ii. 170, 549
Weimer, Arthur, i. 26
West Point, i. 232, 380, 389, 391
What the Soldier Thinks, i. 9, 10, 23, 397–398
Wheeler, John T., i. 26

"Why We Fight" film series, i. 9, 50, 461–468
Wilkins, Roy, i. 598
Williams, F. Douglas, i. 22, 24, 25, 29
Williams, Robin M., Jr., i. 23, 24, 29, 486n; ii. 3n, 59n, 105n, 242n, 290n, 324n, 362n, 411n, 620n
Wilson, Woodrow, i. 441
Wolfbein, Seymour, i. 23
Women's Army Corps, attitudes toward, i. 44–46
Woodworth, William, i. 25
Work details, and job satisfaction, i. 353
Work load (air combat): ii. 353–357; and amount of sleep, i. 389–390; definition of, ii. 363; and morale, ii. 353–357, 366, 387–393
World War I: as impetus to psychology, i. 4–5; personnel assignment in, i. 249; psychological testing in, i. 8, 35, 285; status system in, i. 381–382
World War I vs. World War II: community pressure for service in, ii. 131; educational level in, i. 57–60, 490; fear reactions in, ii. 206; Negroes in, i. 490; technology in, i. 289–291; views of worth-whileness of, i. 437, 441–442; ii. 551, 552, 587, 593–594, 596–597
World War II: attitudes toward, see "War aims"; contribution to history of, i 4; as impetus to social science, i. 5ff, 38, 41–51
Wounded, care of, ii. 85, 144–145
Wright, D. G., ii. 332n, 379n; cited, ii 212, 374–375

Y

Yakovlev, P. T., ii. 211n
Yale Institute of Human Relations, i. 28, 29
Yank: i. 9, 17; on "bucking," i. 275; gripes in, i. 398; opinions of, ii. 609–610
Yeatman, Trezevant P., i. 26
YMCA, i. 363
Yoswein, David J., i. 26
Young, Donald, i. 26, 28, 487n
Young, Kimball, i. 25, 26

Z

Zander, Eugene, i. 24

THE SOCIAL SCIENCE RESEARCH COUNCIL was organized in 1923 and formally incorporated in 1924, composed of representatives chosen from the seven constituent societies and from time to time from related disciplines such as law, geography, psychiatry, medicine, and others. It is the purpose of the Council to plan, foster, promote, and develop research in the social field.

CONSTITUENT ORGANIZATIONS

American Anthropological Association
American Economic Association
American Historical Association
American Political Science Association
American Psychological Association
American Sociological Society
American Statistical Association